Town & Count[illegible]

BRITAIN

CONTENTS

Published by Collins
An imprint of HarperCollins*Publishers*
77-85 Fulham Palace Road, Hammersmith, London W6 8JB

www.collins.co.uk

Mapping generated from Collins/Bartholomew digital databases

The grid on this map is the National Grid taken from the Ordnance Survey map with the permission of the Controller of Her Majesty's Stationery Office.

Printed in	PB	ISBN 0 00 716036 4	Imp. 001	QC11494 CDDU
Great Britain	Spiral	ISBN 0 00 716037 2	Imp. 001	QC11495 CDDU

e-mail: roadcheck@harpercollins.co.uk

Key to map symbols

Key to route planning maps

SCALE: 1: 440,000 approx. 7 miles to 1inch / 4.4 km to 1cm

0 10 20 miles
0 10 20 30 km

M1 under constr. — Motorway
Motorway tunnel
1 restricted access 2 — Junction number
restricted access — Motorway service area
dual A1 — Primary route
dual A634 under constr. — 'A' road
dual B1246 under constr. — 'B' road
Other road

Gradient
Toll
Railway line / tunnel
Car ferry
Airport
Built-up area
Settlement
18 — Distance in miles

National boundary
National / Regional park
Forest park
Woodland
Beach
Canal
Lake, dam and river
718 — Height in metres
Place of interest

land below	0	328	657	985	1640	2295	2950	feet
water	sea level 0	100	200	300	500	700	900	metres

Key to approach route maps

SCALE: 1: 160,000 approx. 2.5 miles to 1inch / 1.6 km to 1cm

0 1 2 3 4 5 miles
0 1 2 3 4 5 6 7 8 km

M5 — Motorway
full access 30 29 restricted access — Motorway junction
Maidstone, Birch, Sarn — Motorway service area with full / restricted / off road access
dual A48 single — Primary route
Primary route with passing places
dual A30 single — 'A' road
'A' road with passing places
dual B1403 single — 'B' road
'B' road with passing places
Minor road
Restricted access
Road projected or under construction
14 — Multi-level junction (occasionally with junction number)
Roundabout
10 — Road distance in miles

Road tunnel
Steep hill (arrows point downhill)
Toll — Level crossing / Toll
Car ferry route
Railway line / station / tunnel
Airport with scheduled services
Heliport
Park and Ride site*
Built up area
Town / Village / Other settlement
National boundary
National / Regional park
Forest park boundary
Danger Zone — Military range
Woodland
468 941 — Spot height / summit height in metres
Beach
Lake / Dam / River / Waterfall
Canal / Dry canal / Canal tunnel

A selection of tourist detail is shown on the mapping. It is advisable to check with the local tourist information centre regarding opening times and facilities available.

Tourist information centre (all year/seasonal)
Ancient monument
1738 — Battlefield
Castle
Country Park
Ecclesiastical building
Factory shop village
Garden
Golf course
Historic house (with or without garden)
Major sports venue
Motor racing circuit
Museum / Art gallery
Nature reserve
Preserved railway
Theme park
Racecourse
Wildlife park or zoo
Other interesting feature
(NT) (NTS) — National Trust / National Trust for Scotland

Key to town plan maps

Motorway
dual — Primary route
dual — 'A' road
dual — 'B' road
dual — Through route
dual — Other road / One way street

Restricted access / Pedestrian street
Path / Footbridge
P — Car park / Park and Ride site*
Railway line / Station
U M — Underground / Metro / Light rail station
Tourist information centre / Ecclesiastical building

Tourist building
Important building
Higher education building
Hospital
Cemetery
Recreational area / Open space

*Park and Ride sites shown in this atlas operate a minimum of five days a week

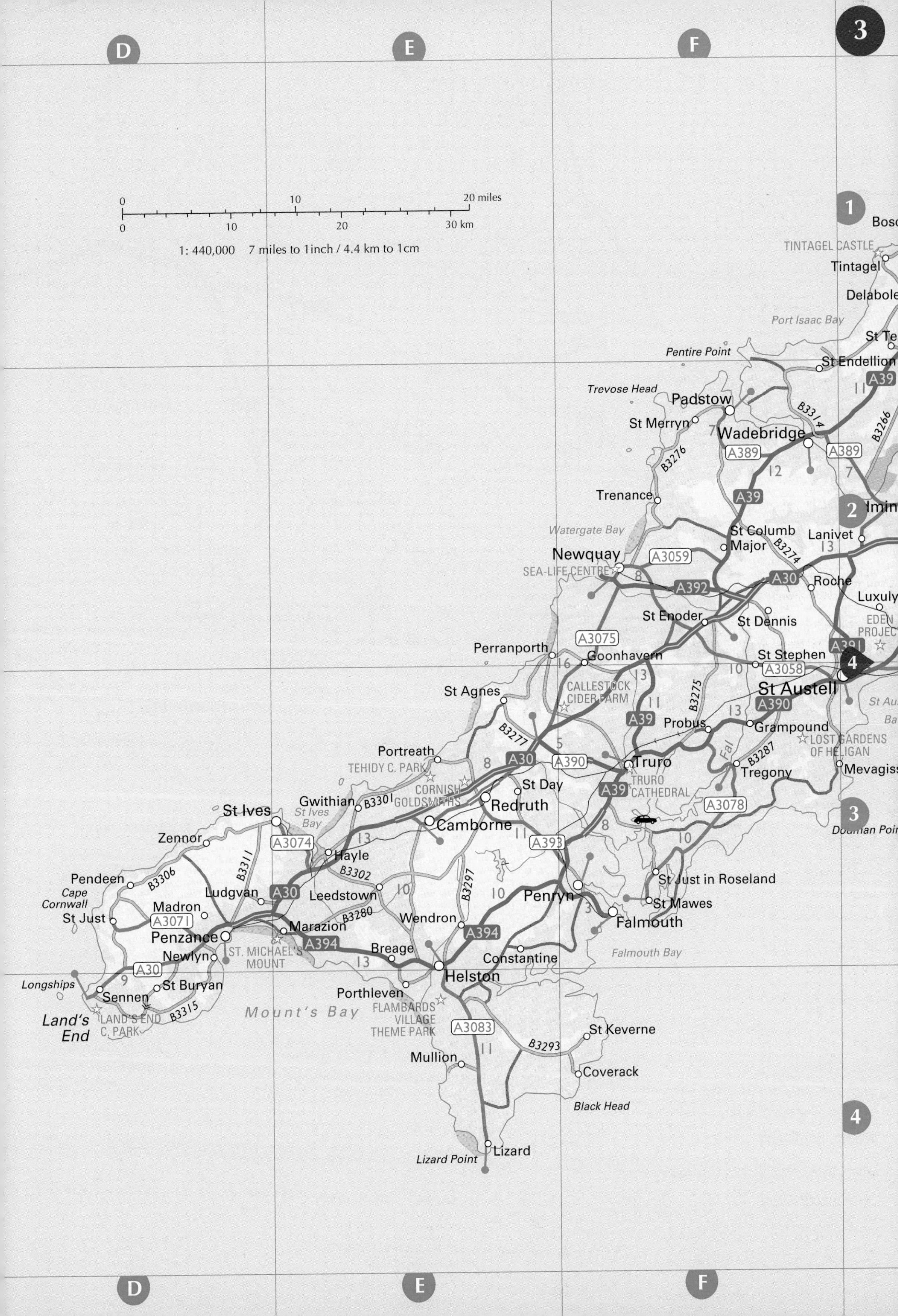
D
E
F
0
10
20 miles
0
10
20
30 km
1: 440,000 7 miles to 1inch / 4.4 km to 1cm
1
2
3
4
Bosc
TINTAGEL CASTLE
Tintagel
Delabole
Port Isaac Bay
St Te
Pentire Point
St Endellion
A39
Trevose Head
Padstow
St Merryn
Wadebridge
B3314
B3266
A389
A389
B3276
12
Trenance
A39
Watergate Bay
St Columb Major
Lanivet
B3274
Newquay
A3059
SEA-LIFE CENTRE
A30
Roche
A392
Luxuly
St Enoder
St Dennis
EDEN PROJEC
A3075
Perranporth
A391
Goonhavern
St Stephen
A3058
CALLESTOCK CIDER FARM
St Agnes
St Austell
B3275
A390
St Au
Ba
A39
Probus
Grampound
LOST GARDENS OF HELIGAN
B3277
Fal
Portreath
B3287
TEHIDY C. PARK
A30
A390
Truro
Mevagis
Tregony
St Day
TRURO CATHEDRAL
CORNISH GOLDSMITHS
A39
A3078
Gwithian
B3301
Redruth
St Ives
St Ives Bay
Camborne
Dodman Poir
A393
Zennor
A3074
Hayle
B3311
B3302
St Just in Roseland
Pendeen
B3306
Cape Cornwall
Ludgvan
A30
Leedstown
B3297
Penryn
St Mawes
Madron
St Just
A3071
B3280
Wendron
Falmouth
Marazion
Penzance
A394
A394
ST. MICHAEL'S MOUNT
Breage
Constantine
Falmouth Bay
Newlyn
A30
Helston
Longships
St Buryan
Porthleven
Sennen
Land's End
LAND'S END C. PARK
B3315
Mount's Bay
FLAMBARDS VILLAGE THEME PARK
A3083
St Keverne
B3293
Mullion
Coverack
Black Head
Lizard Point
Lizard

A
B
C
1
2
3
4
Stibb Cross
Kilkhampton
Stratton
Bude
Bude Bay
Holsworthy
Highampton
Hatherleigh
Winkleigh
Monkokehampton
Folly Gate
Okehampton
Whiddon Down
Chagford
Wainhouse Corner
Boscastle
BOSCASTLE POTTERY
TINTAGEL CASTLE
Tintagel
Delabole
Hallworthy
Launceston
Roadford Reservoir
Yes Tor 619
Lydford
Port Isaac Bay
Camelford
St Teath
St Endellion
Dartmoor
Dartmoor National Park
Congdon's Shop
Bolventor
Bodmin Moor
Widecombe in the Moor
Tavistock
Princetown
Dartmeet
Ashburton
BUCKFAST ABBEY
Buckfastleigh
Wadebridge
Colliford Reservoir
Pensilva
Gunnislake
Callington
Horrabridge
Bodmin
Lanivet
St Columb Major
Dobwalls
Liskeard
St Ive
Bere Alston
Bere Ferrers
Bickleigh
Lee Moor
South Brent
Roche
Luxulyan
Lostwithiel
St Dennis
EDEN PROJECT
Tywardreath
Sandplace
St Germans
Saltash
Plymouth City
Plympton
Ivybridge
St Stephen
St Austell
Par
Fowey
Pelynt
Looe
Polperro
Torpoint
Plymouth
NATIONAL MARINE AQUARIUM
Plymstock
Millbrook
Whitsand Bay
MOUNT EDGCUMBE COUNTRY PARK
Yealmpton
Modbury
St Austell Bay
Grampound
LOST GARDENS OF HELIGAN
Mevagissey
Rame Head
Newton Ferrers
Bigbury-on-Sea
The Sound
Bigbury Bay
Dodman Point
Salcombe
Bolt Head
Santander
Roscoff
Fowey
Tamar
Torridge
Ottery
Tavy
Plym
Avon
Okement
Taw
A39
A388
A386
A377
A3072
A3079
A395
A30
A389
A38
A390
A391
A3058
A387
A374
A3121
A379
A381
B3263
B3266
B3254
B3314
B3274
B3268
B3359
B3257
B3362
B3357
B3212
B3217
B3219
B3215
B3147
B3196
B3392
B3287

5
Witheridge
Tiverton
Culmstock
Hemyock
Uffculm
Black Down Hills
Ilminster
Combe St Nicholas
Crewkerne
Chard
South Chard
Chardstock
Broadwindsor
Beaminster
Bickleigh
Cullompton
Bradninch
Silverton
Copplestone
Crediton
Newton St Cyres
Honiton
Feniton
Whimple
KILLERTON HOUSE
Broadclyst
ROYAL ALBERT MUSEUM
Pinhoe
Ottery St Mary
West Hill
Sidbury
Axminster
Kilmington
Colyton
Colyford
Musbury
Uplyme
Charmouth
Bridport
Bradpole
Bothenhampton
Lyme Regis
Seaton
Beer
Sidford
Sidmouth
Newton Poppleford
Burton Bradstock
Exeter
EXETER CATHEDRAL
CREALY PARK
Topsham
Exminster
Moretonhampstead
Kenton
Lympstone
Starcross
Budleigh Salterton
Exmouth
Lyme Bay
Bovey Tracey
Chudleigh
Dawlish
TRAGO MILLS
Kingsteignton
Teignmouth
Babbacombe Bay
Newton Abbot
Kingskerswell
BABBACOMBE MODEL VILLAGE
Ipplepen
Marldon
COCKINGTON COURT C. PARK
Torquay
DARTINGTON CRYSTAL & CIDER PRESS CENTRE
ENGLISH RIVIERA CENTRE
Paignton
Totnes
PAIGNTON ZOO
Tor Bay
Berry Head
Brixham
Halwell
PAIGNTON & DARTMOUTH STEAM RLY
Dartmouth
Kingswear
WOODLANDS LEISURE PARK
Stokenham
Start Bay
Start Point
Prawle Point
Exe
Otter
Axe
Brit
Dart
M5
A30
A303
A356
A358
A373
A375
A35
A3066
A3052
A396
A3072
A377
A376
A38
A379
A380
A381
A383
A3022
A3122
B3137
B3180
B3178
B3193
B3192
B3165
B3162
0 10 20 miles
0 10 20 30 km
1: 440,000 7 miles to 1inch / 4.4 km to 1cm
D
E
F
1
2
3
4

Meidrim
Carmarthen
Clynderwen
A40
Llangunnor
National Botanic Garden of Wales
Gelli Aur C. Park
A48
A483
A4069
Black Mountain
Narberth
Whitland
St Clears
12
Llanddarog
Llandybie
Brynamman
Oakwood Leisure Park
Canaston Centre
B4328
A477
Llanddowror
Cywyn
Tywi
Llangendeirne
Drefach
Ammanford
A476
Glanaman
Cwmllynfell
Templeton
Red Roses
B4312
A484
B4309
Llyn Llech Owain C. Park
A474
Gwaun-Cae-Gurwen
A4608
A478
Laugharne
Llansteffan
Pontyberem
A483
Gurnos
Folly Farm
A4075
A4066
Pendine
St Ishmael
B4317
Llannon
Ystalyfera
Kilgetty
Kidwelly (Cydweli)
49
Saundersfoot
Trimsaran
A476
M4
Crynant
Carmarthen Bay
B4308
48
Pontarddulais
Pontardawe
Rhos
Pembroke
B4318
Pembrey
Burry Port
Clydach
Great Wedlock Dinosaur Experience
Tenby
Pembrey C. Park
Llanelli
Gorseinon
47
46
45
A4139
Penally
Llanelli Coastal Park
Llansamlet
Birchgrove
Freshwater East
Manorbier
Burry Inlet
Loughor
Morriston
44
Whitford Point
Crofty
A483
43
Plantasia
Landore
Caldey Island
Briton Ferry
St Govan's Head
Llanrhidian
B4295
Dunvant
Cockett
A483
42
Killay
Swansea
Baglan
Port Talbot
41
Gower
Swansea Museum
A4118
Rhossili
Bishopston
Worms Head
The Mumbles
Swansea Bay
Port Eynon
Swansea Maritime & Industrial Museum
Mumbles Head
Cork
0
10
20 miles
0
10
20
30 km
1: 440,000 7 miles to 1inch / 4.4 km to 1cm
A
B
C
1
2
3
4
Lynton
Lynmouth
Lynton & Lynmouth Cliff Rly
Ilfracombe
A399
Combe Martin
Lundy Island
Mortehoe
Combe Martin Wildlife & Dinosaur Park
B3223
Woolacombe
A3123
Blackmoor Gate
Morte Bay
A361
B3358
Baggy Point
Georgeham
B3230
A39
Croyde
Simonsbath
Span Head
439
Braunton
A399
Barnstaple or Bideford Bay
Fremington
Barnstaple
Bray
Northam Burrows C. Park
Appledore
A361
Westward Ho!
Northam
B3232
Bishop's Tawton
North Molton
Hartland Point
A377
Bideford
Taw
Hartland
Clovelly
Clovelly Village
A386
B3227
South Molton
Atherington
Umberleigh
B3226
A39
Torridge
B3227
B3217
Mole
Frithelstock Stone
Dartington Crystal
Great Torrington
A39
B3227
B3220
18
Stibb Cross
Chulmleigh
Little Dart
Kilkhampton
Waldon
A388
Torridge
A386
B3217
A377
Winkleigh
Stratton
4

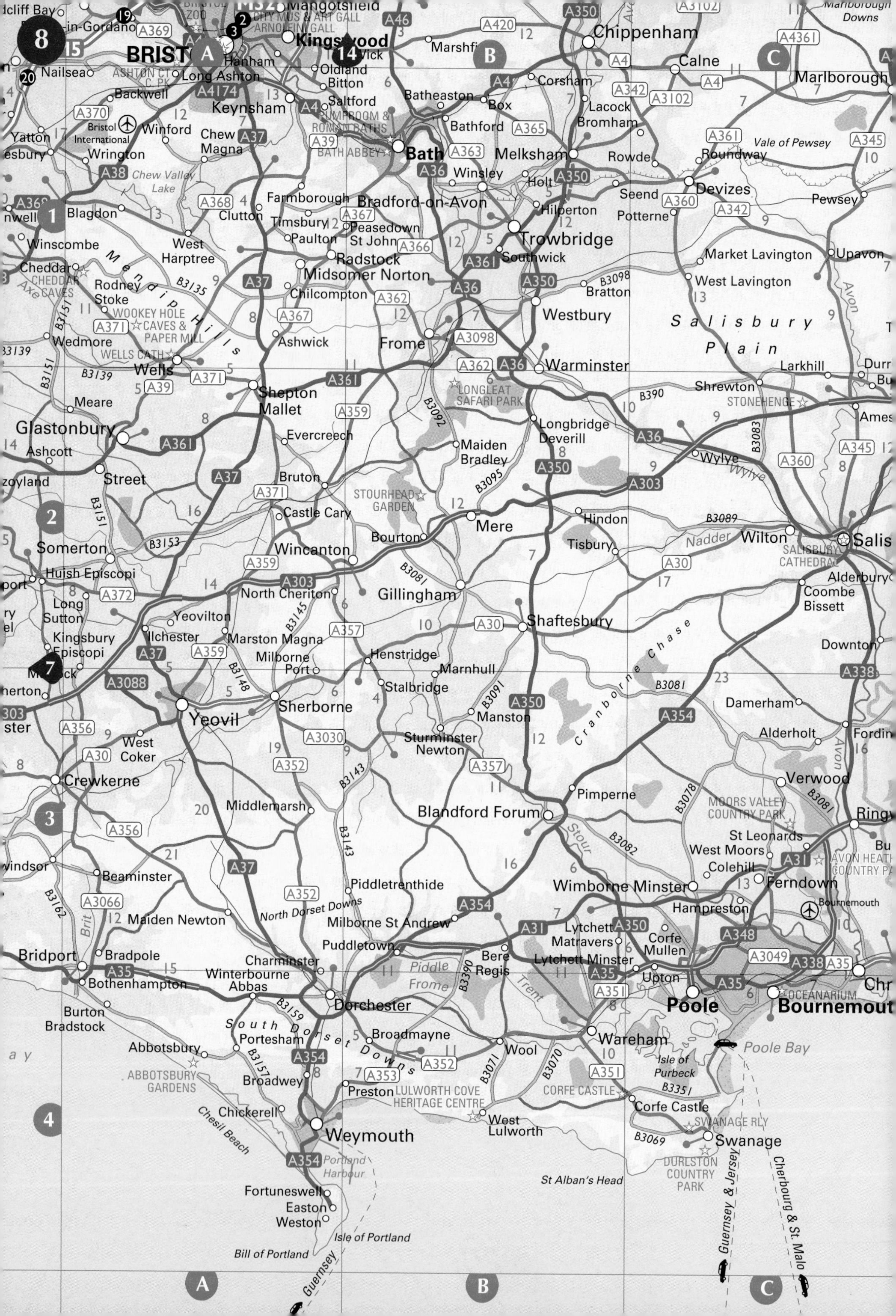

Bristol
Chippenham
Bath
Melksham
Devizes
Trowbridge
Bradford-on-Avon
Frome
Westbury
Warminster
Wells
Shepton Mallet
Glastonbury
Street
Somerton
Salisbury Plain
Mendip Hills
Wincanton
Gillingham
Shaftesbury
Mere
Yeovil
Sherborne
Crewkerne
Blandford Forum
Wimborne Minster
Ferndown
Poole
Bournemouth
Dorchester
Weymouth
Bridport
Wareham
Swanage
Poole Bay
Isle of Purbeck
Isle of Portland
Bill of Portland
Chesil Beach
Cranborne Chase
South Dorset Downs
North Dorset Downs
St Alban's Head
Guernsey & Jersey
Cherbourg & St. Malo
A
B
C
1
2
3
4

9
Reading
Newbury
Basingstoke
Andover
Winchester
Southampton
Eastleigh
Portsmouth
Fareham
Havant
Chichester
Petersfield
Midhurst
Alton
Farnham
Aldershot
Farnborough
Camberley
Bracknell
Wokingham
Egham
Romsey
Totton
Lymington
Gosport
Cowes
Ryde
Newport
Sandown
Shanklin
Ventnor
Isle of Wight
The Solent
The New Forest
Hampshire Downs
Southampton Water
Bognor Regis
Selsey
Selsey Bill
St. Catherine's Point
The Needles
St Malo & Bilbao
Cherbourg
Caen & Le Havre
1: 440,000 7 miles to 1inch / 4.4 km to 1cm
20 miles
30 km
D
E
F

10
Amersham
Chorleywood
Watford
Radlett
Aldenham
Borehamwood
Barnet
Enfield
Waltham Abbey
Loughton
Hatch
HOBBS CROSS OPEN FARM
Pilgrims Hatch
Chalfont St Giles
High Wycombe
Bushey
Rickmansworth
Harrow
South Oxhey
Harefield
Southgate
Chingford
Chigwell
HAINAULT FOREST C. PARK
Brentwood
Beaconsfield
Gerrards Cross
Wooburn
Bourne End
Stoke Poges
Denham
Cookham
Haringey
Hendon
Waltham Forest
Redbridge
Romford
Brent
Ilford
Havering
Burnham
Farnham Royal
Uxbridge
Hillingdon
MADAME TUSSAUD'S
BRITISH MUSEUM
Barking and Dagenham
South Ockendon
Slough
Iver
Ealing
Camden
Newham
London City
Aveley
Bray
Eton
Colnbrook
London Heathrow
NAT. GALL.
TOWER OF LONDON
LONDON
Greenwich
Purfleet
Grays
Windsor
WINDSOR CASTLE
LEGOLAND
Winkfield
KEW GARDENS
Richmond Upon Thames
Fulham
WESTMINSTER ABBEY
Lewisham
Northfleet
Bexley
Dartford
Stone
Wilmington
Bracknell
Egham
Ashford
Staines
THORPE PARK
Sunbury
Kingston Upon Thames
HAMPTON COURT
Wandsworth
Sidcup
Hextable
Ascot
Virginia Water
Sunninghill
Chertsey
Shepperton
Walton-on-Thames
Merton
Bromley
Swanley
Hartley
Crowthorne
Bagshot
Addlestone
Esher
Weybridge
CHESSINGTON WORLD OF ADVENTURES
Croydon
Orpington
Eynsford
New Ash Green
Lightwater
Byfleet
Ewell
Epsom
Sutton
Purley
New Addington
Shoreham
Camberley
Frimley
WISLEY RHS GARDENS
Oxshott
Cobham
Banstead
Warlingham
Biggin Hill
Otford
North Downs
West Malling
Woking
Farnborough
Send
Leatherhead
Kingswood
Caterham
Borough Green
Worplesdon
East Horsley
DENBIES WINE CENTRE
Westerham
Sevenoaks
Ash
POLESDEN LACEY
Oxted
Godstone
GODSTONE FARM
Guildford
Westcott
Reigate
Redhill
Dorking
Four Elms
Hildenborough
Tonbridge
Medway
Farnham
Shalford
Shere
Salfords
Edenbridge
Lingfield
HEVER CASTLE
Leith Hill
294
Godalming
Horley
Elstead
Milford
GATWICK SKYVIEW
Charlwood
London Gatwick
Capel
Southborough
Witley
Ewhurst
Cranleigh
Ashurst
Royal Tunbridge Wells
East Grinstead
Worth
Turners Hill
Forest Row
Hartfield
The Weald
Hindhead
Chiddingfold
Rudgwick
Crawley
TILGATE FOREST C. PARK
Haslemere
Crowborough
WAKEHURST PLACE GARDEN
Wadhurst
Liphook
Slinfold
Horsham
Lower Beeding
Balcombe
Rotherfield
Fernhurst
Billingshurst
Danehill
Ashdown Forest
SHEFFIELD PARK GARDEN
Cuckfield
Lindfield
Maresfield
Easebourne
Petworth
Cowfold
Haywards Heath
BLUEBELL RLY
Buxted
Framfield
Heathfield
Rother
West Grinstead
Chailey
Newick
Uckfield
Pulborough
Burgess Hill
Hurstpierpoint
Keymer
Horam
Henfield
Halland
Storrington
Clayton
Herstmonceux
South Downs
Steyning
Ringmer
Lewes
Hailsham
Arundel
Findon
Beddingham
Shoreham-by-Sea
Moulsecoomb
Woodingdean
Pevensey Levels
Chichester
Westergate
Yapton
Angmering
East Preston
Sompting
Lancing
Hove
SEA-LIFE CENTRE
ROYAL PAVILION
PARADISE PARK GARDENS
DRUSILLAS WILDLIFE PARK
Polegate
Wick
Rustington
Littlehampton
Worthing
Brighton
Rottingdean
Saltdean
Newhaven
Willingdon
Cuckmere
Ouse
Middleton-on-Sea
Bognor Regis
Peacehaven
Seaford
Eastbourne
Dieppe (summer only)
Beachy Head
Selsey
A
B
C

Southminster
Burnham-on-Crouch
Rayleigh
Southend-on-Sea
Shoeburyness
Canvey Island
River Thames
1: 440,000 7 miles to 1inch / 4.4 km to 1cm
Isle of Grain
Sheerness
Isle of Sheppey
Leysdown-on-Sea
Gillingham
Chatham
Sittingbourne
Whitstable
Herne Bay
Margate
Broadstairs
Ramsgate
North Foreland
Isle of Thanet
Faversham
Canterbury
Sandwich
Deal
Maidstone
Ashford
Dover
Folkestone
Hythe
Romney Marsh
New Romney
Lydd
Dungeness
Tenterden
Rye
Winchelsea
Rye Bay
Hastings
Bexhill
Strait of Dover
Calais & Oostende
Channel Tunnel
DREAMLAND THEME PARK
CANTERBURY CATHEDRAL
LEEDS CASTLE & GARDENS
SISSINGHURST GARDENS
DOVER CASTLE
CHURCH OF ST. MARY-IN-CASTRO
ROTUNDA AMUSEMENT PARK
ROMNEY HYTHE & DYMCHURCH RAILWAY
KENT AND E. SUSSEX STEAM RLY
BODIAM CASTLE
STADE FAMILY FUN PARK

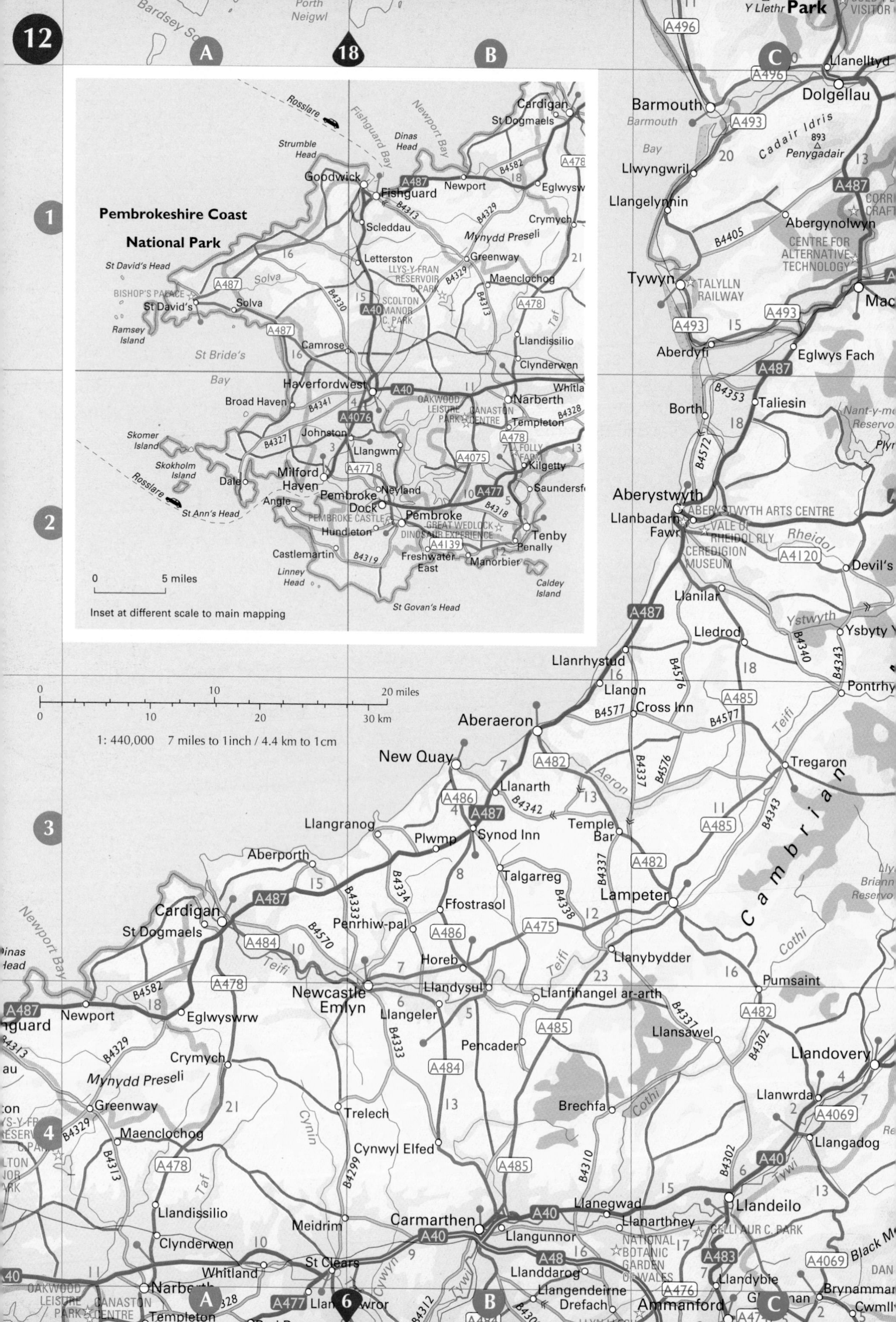

Pembrokeshire Coast National Park
Inset at different scale to main mapping
0 5 miles
Goodwick
Fishguard
Newport
Cardigan
St Dogmaels
Eglwyswrw
Crymych
Mynydd Preseli
Greenway
Maenclochog
Letterston
Scleddau
St David's Head
Bishop's Palace
St David's
Solva
Ramsey Island
Camrose
St Bride's Bay
Haverfordwest
Broad Haven
Llandissilio
Clynderwen
Narberth
Templeton
Oakwood Leisure Park
Canaston Centre
Whitland
Skomer Island
Skokholm Island
Johnston
Llangwm
Milford Haven
Dale
Neyland
Pembroke Dock
Pembroke
Angle
Pembroke Castle
Hundleton
Castlemartin
Linney Head
Freshwater East
Manorbier
Tenby
Penally
Kilgetty
Saundersfoot
Caldey Island
St Govan's Head
St Ann's Head
Rosslare
Strumble Head
Dinas Head
Fishguard Bay
Newport Bay
Llys-y-Fran Reservoir C. Park
Scolton Manor C. Park
Folly Farm
Great Wedlock Dinosaur Experience
0 10 20 miles
0 10 20 30 km
1: 440,000 7 miles to 1inch / 4.4 km to 1cm
Bardsey Sound
Porth Neigwl
Y Llethr
Park
Barmouth
Barmouth Bay
Llanelltyd
Dolgellau
Cadair Idris
893 Penygadair
Llwyngwril
Llangelynnin
Abergynolwyn
Centre for Alternative Technology
Tywyn
Talyllyn Railway
Aberdyfi
Eglwys Fach
Borth
Taliesin
Nant-y-moch Reservoir
Aberystwyth
Aberystwyth Arts Centre
Llanbadarn Fawr
Vale of Rheidol Rly
Ceredigion Museum
Rheidol
Devil's Bridge
Llanilar
Ystwyth
Lledrod
Ysbyty Ystwyth
Llanrhystud
Llanon
Pontrhydfendigaid
Cross Inn
Aberaeron
New Quay
Llanarth
Aeron
Tregaron
Cambrian
Temple Bar
Llangranog
Plwmp
Synod Inn
Aberporth
Talgarreg
Lampeter
Ffostrasol
Penrhiw-pal
Horeb
Cardigan
St Dogmaels
Newport Bay
Dinas Head
Teifi
Newcastle Emlyn
Llandysul
Llangeler
Llanybydder
Llanfihangel ar-arth
Pumsaint
Cothi
Newport
Eglwyswrw
Fishguard
Pencader
Llansawel
Llandovery
Crymych
Mynydd Preseli
Greenway
Maenclochog
Trelech
Cynin
Brechfa
Llanwrda
Llangadog
Cynwyl Elfed
Llandissilio
Clynderwen
Meidrim
Carmarthen
Llanegwad
Llanarthney
Llandeilo
Gelli Aur C. Park
Llangunnor
National Botanic Garden of Wales
Whitland
St Clears
Narberth
Templeton
Llanddarog
Llangendeirne
Drefach
Llandybie
Ammanford
Brynamman
Black Mountain
Tywi
Taf
Cywyn
Red Roses
A
B
C
18
6
1
2
3
4
A487
A493
A496
A470
A4120
A485
A482
A486
A484
A475
A478
A40
A48
A476
A483
A4069
A477
A4076
A4075
A4139
B4582
B4329
B4313
B4330
B4341
B4327
B4319
B4318
B4328
B4405
B4353
B4572
B4576
B4577
B4340
B4343
B4337
B4342
B4334
B4333
B4570
B4338
B4302
B4310
B4299
B4312
B4309

13
D
E
F
19
Lake Vyrnwy
Tanat
Llanwddyn
B4393
B4393
A490
A490
A495
A470
Mallwyd
A458
Llangadfan
B4395
B4382
Dolanog
Dyfi
A470
A458
Llanfair Caereinion
B4389
B4390
WELSHPOOL & LLANFAIR LIGHT RLY
POWIS CASTLE
Welshpool
A483
Severn
XI-Towns
Baschurch
A5
A49
A53
A528
B5062
A5112
Shrewsbury
A5
B4393
A458
Hanwood
Bayston Hill
Pontesbury
Minsterley
B4386
B4380
1
A488
A49
Much Wenlock
B4378
Church Stretton
516
The Long Mynd
B4371
Shipton
Wenlock Edge
B4368
Corve Dale
Burwarton
B4518
A470
Carno
Tregynon
Garthmyl
B4389
A483
Montgomery (Trefaldwyn)
Chirbury
A490
Llanllwchaiarn
Llanwnog
A489
Newtown (Y Drenewydd)
A489
Bishop's Castle
A489
Wistanstow
Craven Arms
Stokesay
Llyn Clywedog Reservoir
Trefeglwys
B4569
Llandinam
Severn
Dolfor
A483
B4368
Newcastle
A488
Clun
Clun
B4385
Clungunford
B4365
2
Llanidloes
A470
Llangurig
B4518
Felindre
B4355
Teme
Pant-y-dwr
A470
B4356
Llanbister
Knucklas
B4367
A4113
A49
Ludlow
Cleehill
A4113
Knighton
Wigmore
B4214
B4361
Craig Goch Reservoir
Rhayader
A44
Lugg
A488
B4355
A4110
14
Wells
A49
ELAN VALLEY VISITOR CENTRE
Claerwen Reservoir
Caban Coch Reservoir
Crossgates
Penybont
Great Rhos 660
Presteigne
B4356
B4362
Mortimer's Cross
A4112
Drygarn Fawr 645
A4081
Llandrindod Wells
A44
New Radnor
B4355
Arrow
Pembridge
Leominster
Crossway
A481
A44
Kington
A480
A4112
A4111
3
B4358
A483
Weobley
Bodenham
QUEENSWOOD C. PARK
A483
Builth Wells
Garth
Eardisley
A4110
A49
A417
A465
B4594
A470
A438
Clyro
B4352
Credenhill
Burghill
A4103
Llanwrtyd Wells
B4519
Hay-on-Wye
A438
Wye
HEREFORD CATHEDRAL
Hereford
Hagley
A483
475
Mynydd Eppynt
Golden Valley
B4348
Madley
Clehonger
Cynghordy
Glasbury
Kingstone
A465
A49
Fownhope
B4520
Nant Bran
Talgarth
A470
B4560
Black Mountains
800
B4347
B4348
Kingsthorne
A40
Usk
Trecastle
Sennybridge
Brecon
WELSH WHISKY VISITOR CENTRE
Usk
Llanthony
Pontrilas
4
Wye
A4215
BRECON BEACONS MOUNTAIN CENTRE
Brecon Beacons
A40
A479
Monnow
A466
A49
A4137
Gaer
Tretower
Pandy
Brecon Beacons
886
802
A470
National Park
A4067
A465
Skenfrith
A40
Llangynidr
B4560
Crickhowell
B4521
B4347
Ruardean
A40
Llantilio Pertholey
Mellte
Neath
Pontsticill Reservoir
FESTIVAL PARK VISITOR CENTRE
BRYN BACH C. PARK
Llanelly
Gilwern
B4233
7
Abergavenny
Monmouth (Trefynwy)
A4136
Brynmawr
A465
BRECON MOUNTAIN
RAGLAN

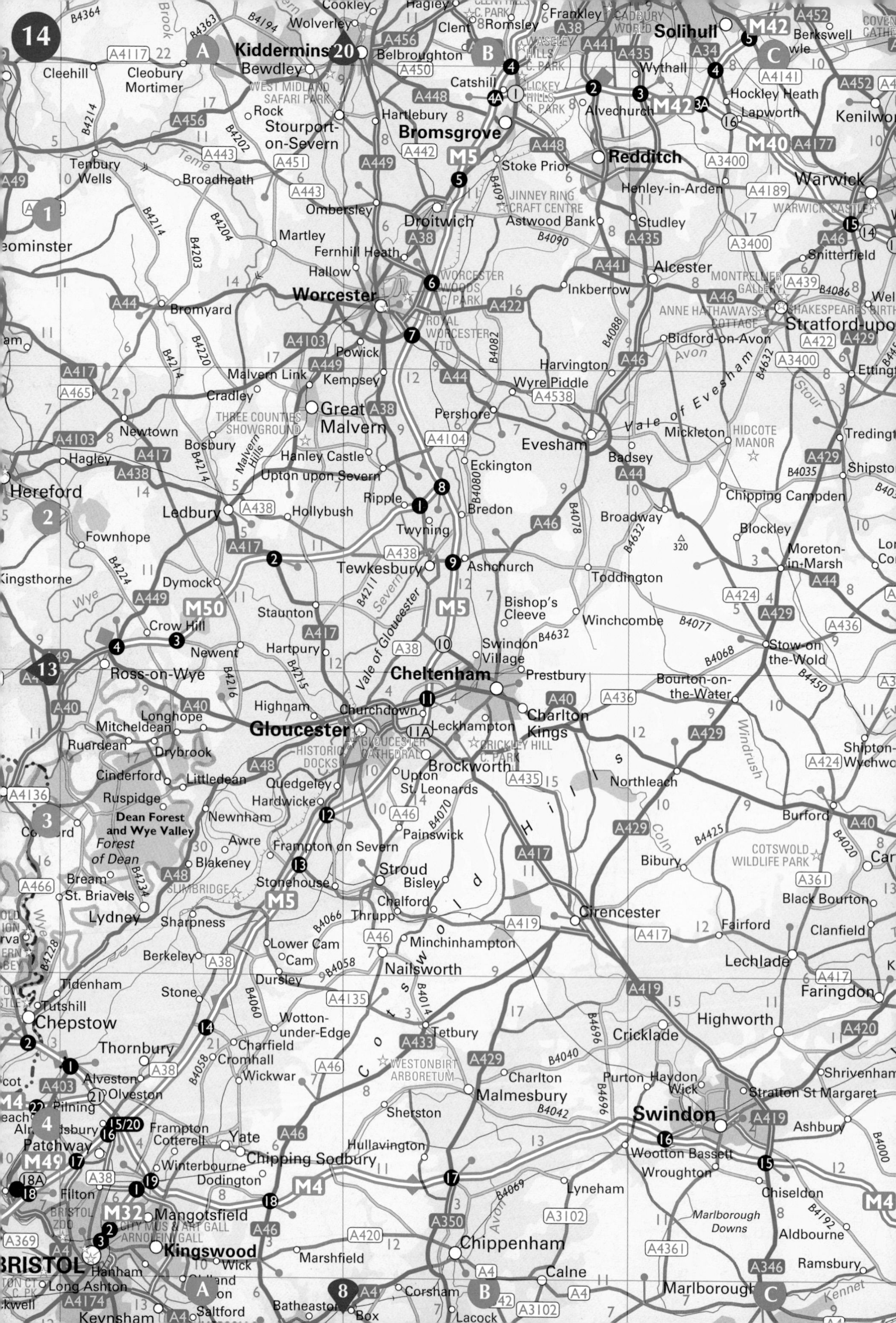
Cookley
Hagley
Frankley
Cadbury World
Solihull
M42
A452
Coventry Cathedral
B4364
Brook
B4363
B4194
Wolverley
Clent
Romsley
A38
Berkswell
A4117
22
Kidderminster
20
Belbroughton
A456
Waseley Hills C. Park
A441
A435
A34
Cleehill
Cleobury Mortimer
Bewdley
A450
Catshill
Lickey Hills C. Park
Wythall
A4141
West Midland Safari Park
A448
Alvechurch
Hockley Heath
A452
B4214
A456
Rock
Stourport-on-Severn
Hartlebury
Bromsgrove
Lapworth
Kenilworth
Teme
A443
B4202
A451
A442
M5
A448
Redditch
M40
A4177
Tenbury Wells
Broadheath
A449
Stoke Prior
A3400
A49
A443
B4091
Jinney Ring Craft Centre
Henley-in-Arden
A4189
Warwick
Ombersley
Droitwich
Astwood Bank
Studley
Warwick Castle
Leominster
B4214
B4204
B4203
Martley
A38
B4090
A435
A46
Snitterfield
Fernhill Heath
A3400
Hallow
A441
Alcester
Montpellier Gallery
A439
Worcester
Worcester Woods C. Park
Inkberrow
B4086
Wellesbourne
A44
Bromyard
A422
A46
Anne Hathaway's Cottage
Shakespeare's Birthplace
Stratford-upon-Avon
Royal Worcester Ltd
B4088
A422
A429
A4103
B4220
B4082
Bidford-on-Avon
Avon
A3400
B4214
Powick
Harvington
Ettington
A417
Malvern Link
A449
Kempsey
A44
A465
Wyre Piddle
A4538
Vale of Evesham
B4632
Stour
Cradley
Great Malvern
A38
Pershore
Three Counties Showground
Newtown
Bosbury
Malvern Hills
Evesham
Mickleton
Hidcote Manor
Tredington
A4103
A417
A4104
Hagley
B4214
Hanley Castle
Eckington
Badsey
A429
A438
Upton upon Severn
B4080
B4035
Shipston-on-Stour
Hereford
A44
Ripple
Bredon
B4078
Chipping Campden
Ledbury
A438
Hollybush
Twyning
Broadway
Fownhope
A46
Blockley
A417
B4632
320
Moreton-in-Marsh
B4224
A438
Ashchurch
Tewkesbury
Kingsthorne
Dymock
Toddington
A44
Wye
A449
M50
Staunton
B4211
Severn
Vale of Gloucester
M5
Bishop's Cleeve
A424
A429
Crow Hill
Winchcombe
B4077
A436
A417
Newent
Hartpury
A38
Swindon Village
B4632
Stow-on-the-Wold
B4215
B4068
B4216
Ross-on-Wye
Cheltenham
Prestbury
Bourton-on-the-Water
B4450
A40
A40
Highnam
Churchdown
A436
Longhope
Charlton Kings
Mitcheldean
Gloucester
Leckhampton
A429
Windrush
Ruardean
Drybrook
Historic Docks
Gloucester Cathedral
Crickley Hill C. Park
Shipton-under-Wychwood
Cinderford
Littledean
A48
Brockworth
A424
Quedgeley
A435
Northleach
A4136
Upton St. Leonards
Ruspidge
Hardwicke
Dean Forest and Wye Valley
Newnham
A46
B4070
A429
Coleford
Forest of Dean
Awre
Painswick
Colne
B4425
Burford
A40
Frampton on Severn
Cotswold Wildlife Park
B4020
Bream
Blakeney
A417
Bibury
Carterton
A48
Stroud
A466
St. Briavels
B4234
Slimbridge
Stonehouse
Bisley
A361
Wye
Lydney
M5
Chalford
Black Bourton
Sharpness
B4066
Thrupp
A419
Cirencester
Fairford
B4228
A46
Minchinhampton
A417
Clanfield
Lower Cam
Berkeley
A38
Cam
B4058
Nailsworth
Lechlade
Tidenham
Dursley
A417
Faringdon
A4135
B4014
A419
Stone
Tutshill
B4060
Cotswold Hills
B4696
Highworth
Chepstow
Wotton-under-Edge
Tetbury
Cricklade
A420
Thornbury
Charfield
A433
B4040
Cromhall
A38
B4058
A46
Westonbirt Arboretum
A429
Charlton
Purton
Haydon Wick
Shrivenham
Alveston
Wickwar
A403
Olveston
Malmesbury
B4696
Stratton St Margaret
M4
Pilning
Sherston
B4042
Swindon
A419
Ashbury
Almondsbury
Frampton Cotterell
B4000
Patchway
Yate
Hullavington
Wootton Bassett
M49
Winterbourne
Chipping Sodbury
Wroughton
A38
Dodington
Filton
M4
B4069
Lyneham
Chiseldon
M4
Bristol Zoo
M32
Mangotsfield
A350
Avon
A3102
Marlborough Downs
City Mus & Art Gall
Arnolfini Gall
A46
A420
B4192
Aldbourne
A369
A4
Chippenham
A4361
Bristol
Kingswood
Marshfield
Hanham
Wick
A4
Calne
A346
Ramsbury
Long Ashton
Oldland
Kennet
A4174
Corsham
A4
Marlborough
Keynsham
Saltford
Batheaston
Box
A4
Lacock
A3102

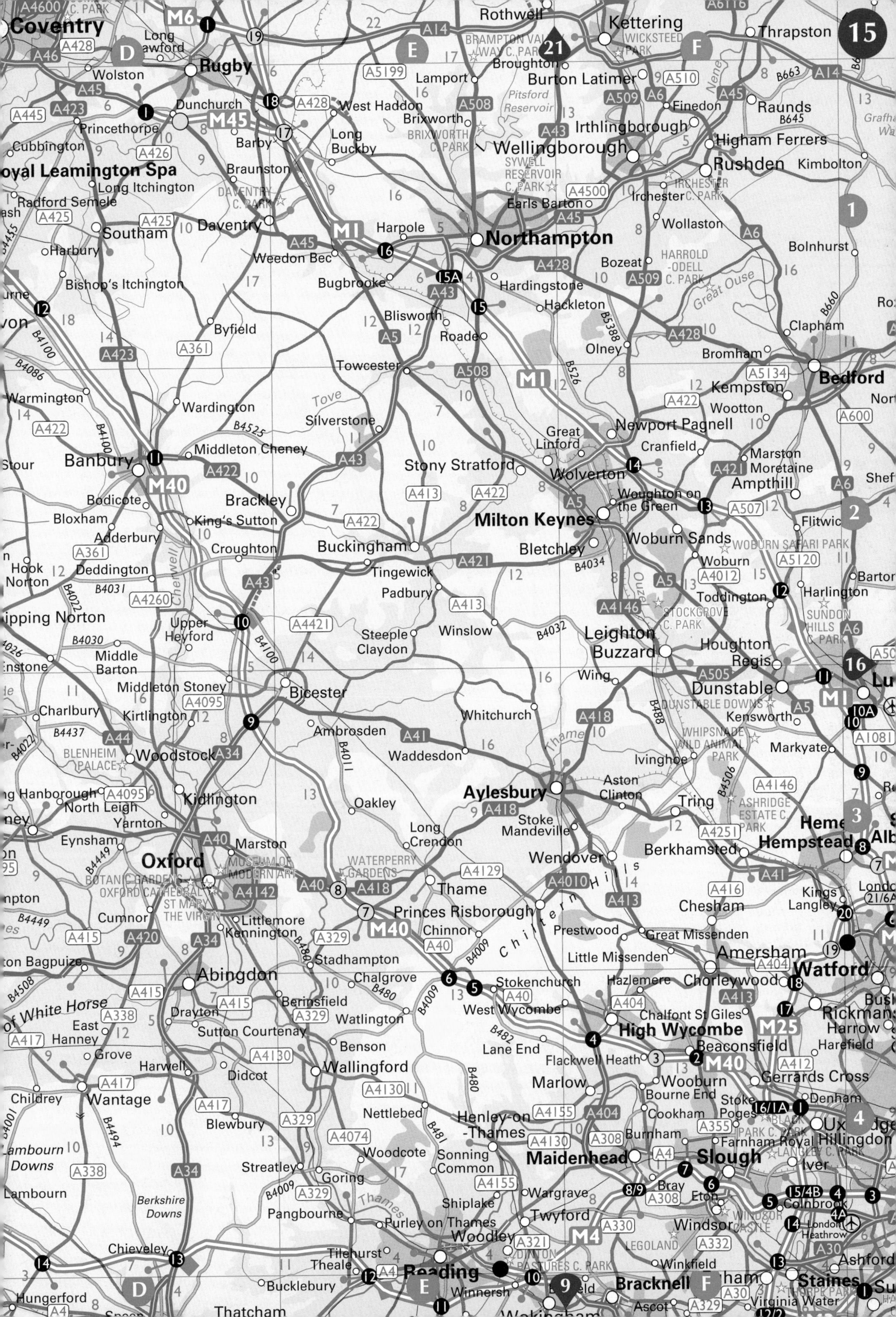
Coventry
Rugby
Long Lawford
Wolston
Dunchurch
Princethorpe
Cubbington
Royal Leamington Spa
Long Itchington
Radford Semele
Southam
Harbury
Bishop's Itchington
Barby
Braunston
Daventry
Daventry C. Park
West Haddon
Long Buckby
Brixworth
Brixworth C. Park
Lamport
Rothwell
Kettering
Brampton Valley Way C. Park
Wicksteed Park
Broughton
Pitsford Reservoir
Burton Latimer
Thrapston
Finedon
Raunds
Irthlingborough
Higham Ferrers
Wellingborough
Rushden
Kimbolton
Sywell Reservoir C. Park
Irchester
Irchester C. Park
Earls Barton
Wollaston
Harpole
Northampton
Weedon Bec
Bugbrooke
Hardingstone
Hackleton
Bozeat
Harrold-Odell C. Park
Great Ouse
Bolnhurst
Blisworth
Roade
Towcester
Byfield
Olney
Clapham
Bromham
Bedford
Kempston
Wootton
Warmington
Wardington
Tove
Silverstone
Newport Pagnell
Great Linford
Cranfield
Marston Moretaine
Ampthill
Banbury
Middleton Cheney
Stony Stratford
Wolverton
Woughton on the Green
Milton Keynes
Bodicote
Bloxham
Adderbury
Brackley
King's Sutton
Croughton
Buckingham
Bletchley
Woburn Sands
Woburn Safari Park
Woburn
Flitwick
Hook Norton
Deddington
Tingewick
Padbury
Toddington
Harlington
Cherwell
Chipping Norton
Upper Heyford
Steeple Claydon
Winslow
Leighton Buzzard
Stockgrove C. Park
Sundon Hills C. Park
Houghton Regis
Middle Barton
Middleton Stoney
Bicester
Wing
Dunstable
Dunstable Downs
Luton
Charlbury
Kirtlington
Whitchurch
Kensworth
Ambrosden
Waddesdon
Whipsnade Wild Animal Park
Markyate
Blenheim Palace
Woodstock
Thame
Ivinghoe
Long Hanborough
North Leigh
Kidlington
Oakley
Aylesbury
Aston Clinton
Tring
Ashridge Estate C. Park
Yarnton
Eynsham
Long Crendon
Stoke Mandeville
Hemel Hempstead
St Albans
Oxford
Marston
Museum of Modern Art
Botanic Gardens
Oxford Cathedral
St Mary the Virgin
Waterperry Gardens
Wendover
Berkhamsted
Chiltern Hills
Kings Langley
Cumnor
Littlemore
Kennington
Princes Risborough
Chinnor
Prestwood
Great Missenden
Chesham
Little Missenden
Amersham
Watford
Kingston Bagpuize
Stadhampton
Abingdon
Chalgrove
Stokenchurch
Hazlemere
Chorleywood
Vale of White Horse
Berinsfield
Drayton
Sutton Courtenay
Watlington
West Wycombe
Chalfont St Giles
Rickmansworth
East Hanney
Benson
Lane End
High Wycombe
Beaconsfield
Harrow
Harefield
Grove
Harwell
Didcot
Wallingford
Flackwell Heath
Gerrards Cross
Wantage
Childrey
Marlow
Wooburn
Bourne End
Denham
Nettlebed
Henley-on-Thames
Cookham
Stoke Poges
Blewbury
Burnham
Farnham Royal
Uxbridge
Hillingdon
Black Park C. Park
Langley C. Park
Lambourn Downs
Woodcote
Sonning Common
Maidenhead
Slough
Iver
Streatley
Goring
Wargrave
Bray
Eton
Colnbrook
Lambourn
Berkshire Downs
Shiplake
Pangbourne
Thames
Purley on Thames
Twyford
Windsor
Windsor Castle
London Heathrow
Woodley
Legoland
Chieveley
Tilehurst
Theale
Reading
Dinton Pastures C. Park
Winkfield
Ashford
Staines
Bucklebury
Winnersh
Bracknell
Ascot
Virginia Water
Thorpe Park
Hungerford
Thatcham
Wokingham
M1
M4
M6
M25
M40
M45
A34
A41
A43
A45
A421
A418
A508
A428
B4100
B526

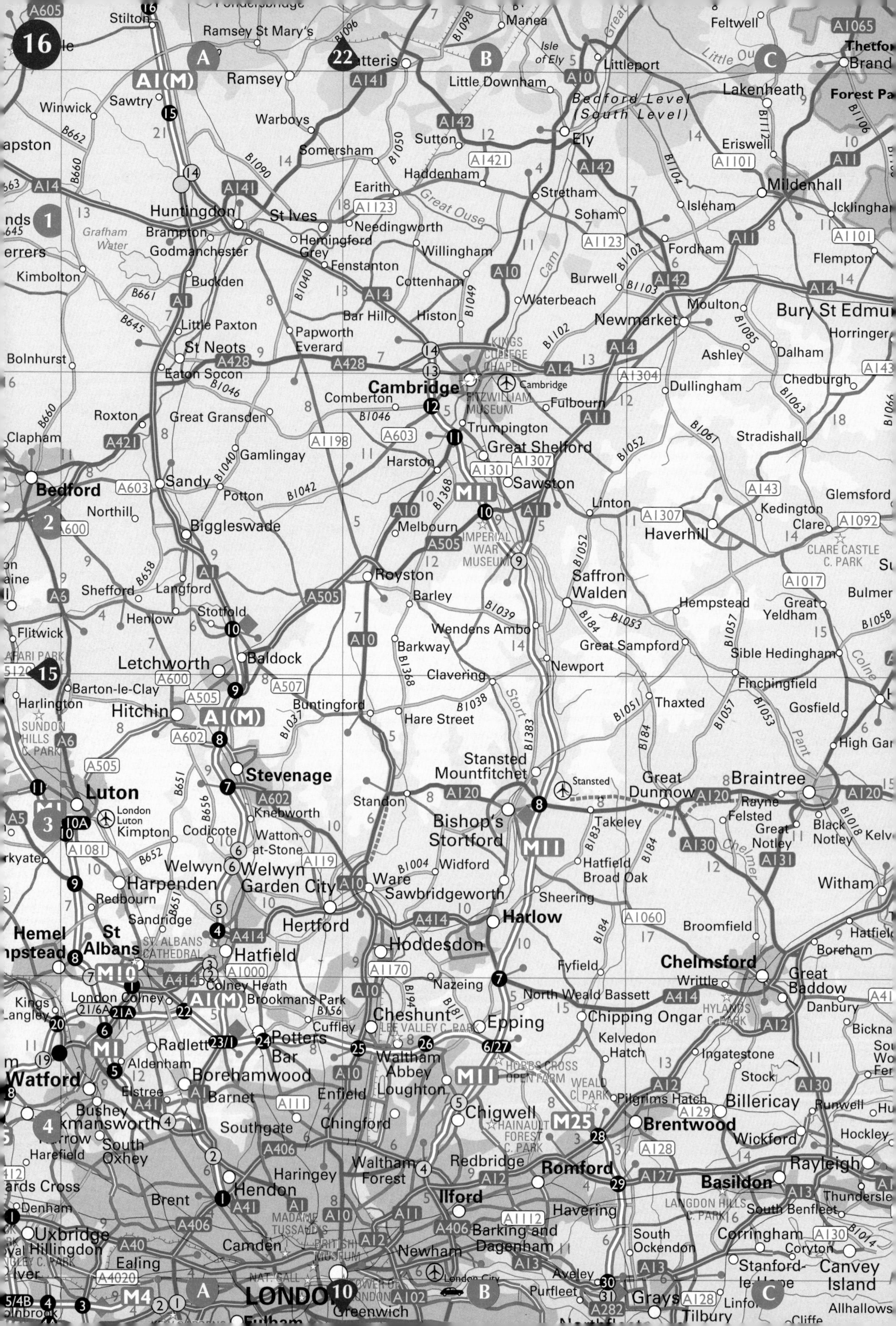

16
A605
Stilton
Ramsey St Mary's
B1096
22
Manea
Isle of Ely
Feltwell
A1065
Thetford
Brandon
A
B
C
A1(M)
Ramsey
A141
Little Downham
Littleport
Little Ouse
Lakenheath
Forest Park
Winwick
Sawtry
15
Warboys
A142
Bedford Level (South Level)
Ely
B1112
B1106
Eriswell
apston
B662
B660
Somersham
B1050
Sutton
A1421
A1101
A11
B1090
14
Haddenham
A142
Mildenhall
A14
Earith
A1123
Great Ouse
Stretham
Isleham
Icklingham
1
Huntingdon
St Ives
Needingworth
Soham
A1123
A1101
Grafham Water
Brampton
Hemingford Grey
Willingham
Fordham
Flempton
errers
Godmanchester
Fenstanton
Cam
B1102
A10
Burwell
B1103
A142
Kimbolton
Buckden
B1040
Cottenham
B1049
Waterbeach
A14
A14
Bury St Edmunds
B661
A1
Bar Hill
Histon
Moulton
B1085
Horringer
B645
Little Paxton
Papworth Everard
Newmarket
B1102
Dalham
St Neots
Ashley
Bolnhurst
A428
A428
KINGS COLLEGE CHAPEL
A14
A143
Eaton Socon
Cambridge
A1304
Chedburgh
B1046
Comberton
FITZWILLIAM MUSEUM
Cambridge
Dullingham
B1063
B660
Roxton
B1046
Fulbourn
Great Gransden
Trumpington
A11
Stradishall
Clapham
A421
A1198
A603
Great Shelford
B1061
B1052
Gamlingay
B1040
Harston
A1307
A1301
Bedford
A603
Sandy
Potton
B1042
B1368
M11
Sawston
Glemsford
Northill
A10
A11
Linton
A143
Kedington
2
A600
Biggleswade
Melbourn
A1307
Haverhill
Clare
A1092
A505
IMPERIAL WAR MUSEUM
CLARE CASTLE C. PARK
B658
A1
Royston
Saffron Walden
A1017
A6
Shefford
Langford
A505
Barley
B1052
Hempstead
Great Yeldham
Bulmer
B1058
Henlow
Stotfold
B1039
B1053
B184
B1057
Flitwick
A10
Wendens Ambo
Barkway
Great Sampford
Sible Hedingham
Colne
AFARI PARK
15
Letchworth
Baldock
B1368
Clavering
Newport
A600
A507
Finchingfield
Barton-le-Clay
A505
Buntingford
B1038
Stort
Thaxted
Gosfield
Harlington
Hitchin
A1(M)
B1037
Hare Street
B1051
B1057
B1053
SUNDON HILLS C. PARK
A6
A602
B184
B1383
Pant
High Garrett
A505
Stansted Mountfitchet
Great Dunmow
Braintree
B651
Stevenage
Stansted
Luton
A602
Standon
A120
A120
Rayne
A120
M1
London Luton
B656
Knebworth
Bishop's Stortford
Takeley
Felsted
B1018
A5
3
Kimpton
Codicote
Watton-at-Stone
B183
B184
Great Notley
Black Notley
Kelvedon
A1081
B652
A119
A130
Chelmer
rkyate
Welwyn
Welwyn Garden City
B1004
Widford
M11
Hatfield Broad Oak
A131
Harpenden
Ware
Witham
Redbourn
A10
Sawbridgeworth
Sheering
B651
Hertford
A414
Harlow
A1060
Sandridge
Broomfield
Hatfield
Hemel Hempstead
St Albans
ST. ALBANS CATHEDRAL
A414
Hoddesdon
B184
Boreham
Hatfield
M10
Hatfield
Chelmsford
A1000
A1170
Fyfield
Great Baddow
A414
Colney Heath
Nazeing
Writtle
Kings Langley
London Colney
A1(M)
Brookmans Park
A10
B194
B181
North Weald Bassett
A414
HYLANDS C. PARK
Danbury
A414
B156
Cheshunt
Epping
Chipping Ongar
M1
Radlett
Cuffley
LEE VALLEY C. PARK
Potters Bar
Kelvedon Hatch
A12
Bicknacre
Waltham Abbey
Ingatestone
Aldenham
HOBBS CROSS OPEN FARM
Watford
Borehamwood
A10
M11
Stock
WEALD C. PARK
A130
Elstree
A1
Barnet
Abbey
Loughton
A12
Pilgrims Hatch
Billericay
Runwell
Bushey
A41
Enfield
A111
Chigwell
A129
Rickmansworth
Southgate
Chingford
HAINAULT FOREST C. PARK
M25
Brentwood
Wickford
Hockley
Harrow
South Oxhey
A406
A128
Harefield
Waltham Forest
Redbridge
Rayleigh
Haringey
A12
Romford
A127
Basildon
Thundersley
Denham
Hendon
Ilford
Havering
LANGDON HILLS C. PARK
A13
Brent
A41
A1
A10
A11
South Benfleet
A406
MADAME TUSSAUD'S
A1112
Uxbridge
Hillingdon
A40
A406
Barking and Dagenham
South Ockendon
Corringham
A130
B1014
Camden
BRITISH MUSEUM
A12
Coryton
Ealing
Newham
A13
Stanford-le-Hope
Canvey Island
A4020
NAT. GALL.
London City
Aveley
A13
M4
A
LONDON
TOWER OF LONDON
A102
B
Purfleet
Grays
A128
Tilbury
C
Allhallows
Greenwich
A282
Fulham

Thetford
Larling
Banham
East Harling
South Lopham
Roydon
Diss
Scole
Harleston
Bungay
Homersfield
Metfield
Carlton Colville
Kessingland
Brampton
Reydon
Southwold
Walberswick
Halesworth
Fressingfield
Stradbroke
Eye
Hopton
Barningham
Rickinghall
Botesdale
Stanton
Ixworth
Finningham
Great Barton
Norton
Elmswell
Stoke Ash
Brundish
Dennington
Westleton
Yoxford
Saxmundham
Leiston
Thorpeness
Aldeburgh
Framlingham
Debenham
Stowmarket
Earl Stonham
Needham Market
Coddenham
Otley
Wickham Market
Tunstall
Melton
Woodbridge
Orford
Orford Ness
Lavenham
Monks Eleigh
Claydon
Rushmere St Andrew
Martlesham
Long Melford
Bramford
Kesgrave
Ipswich
Hollesley Bay
Hadleigh
Great Cornard
Capel St Mary
Kirton
Bawdsey
Stoke-by-Nayland
Holbrook
Old Felixstowe
Bures
East Bergholt
Shotley Gate
Manning's Amusement Park
Felixstowe
Dedham
Brantham
Manningtree
Great Horkesley
Lawford
New Mistley
Landguard Point
Harwich
Earls Colne
Ardleigh
Little Oakley
West Bergholt
Mile End
Colchester
Stanway
Colchester Zoo
Wivenhoe
Thorpe-le-Soken
The Naze
Walton on the Naze
Frinton-on-Sea
Coggeshall
Layer de la Haye
Alresford
Abberton Resr
Brightlingsea
Little Clacton
Tiptree
Mersea Island
St Osyth
Holland-on-Sea
Clacton-on-Sea
Jaywick
West Mersea
Tollesbury
Heybridge
Sales Point
Bradwell Waterside
Maldon
Latchingdon
Southminster
Burnham-on-Crouch
Foulness Point
Rochford
Great Wakering
Kids Kingdom
Peter Pans Playground
Southend-on-Sea
Shoeburyness
Thames
Blackwater
Stour
Deben
Orwell
Alde
Blyth
Waveney
Little Ouse
Dove
Esbjerg
Hamburg
Hoek van Holland
A140
A143
A144
A145
A12
A1066
A1088
A14
A1120
A1094
A1152
A134
A1141
A1071
A137
A120
A1124
A133
A1159
B1134
B1123
B1124
B1118
B1117
B1116
B1113
B1111
B1077
B1119
B1122
B1125
B1387
B1078
B1079
B1084
B1083
B1115
B1508
B1414
B1035
B1027
B1032
B1025
B1022
B1026
B1021
B1018
B1010
D
E
F
1
2
3
4
23
11

A
B
C
1
2
3
4
Llanbadrig
Amlwch
Carmel Head
A5025
Llyn Alaw
B5111
Holyhead Bay
Moelfre
Dublin & Dún Laoghaire
Llannerch-y-medd
Benllech
Red Wharf Bay
Holyhead
Anglesey
Valley
Llanynghenedl
B5110
Holy Island
B5109
ANGLESEY HERITAGE GALLERY
Pentraeth
Beaumaris
BEAUMARIS CASTLE
Llangoed
A5
A55
A4080
Llangefni
B5420
Llanfaelog
B4422
Llanfairpwllgwyngyll
Menai Bridge
Bangor
PENRHYN CASTLE
Aberffraw
B4419
PLAS NEWYDD
ANGLESEY SEA ZOO
Pentir
Bethesda
ROYAL WELSH FUSILIERS REG'T MUSEUM
Malltraeth Bay
B4366
Llanddeiniolen
Llanrug
WELSH SLATE MUS.
PADARN C. PARK
LLANBERIS LAKE RLY
Carnedd Llywelyn
1064
Llyn Cowlyd
Caernarfon
CAERNARFON CASTLE
Menai Strait
Llanberis
Glyder Fawr
999
Llanwnda
SNOWDON MOUNTAIN RLY
A4086
Caernarfon Bay
Llandwrog
WELSH HIGHLAND RLY
1085
Snowdon (Yr Wyddfa)
A498
Penygroes
Llanllyfni
A4085
A487
A499
Beddgelert
Snowdonia
Llanaelhaearn
B4417
Dolbenmaen
B4411
Morfa Nefyn
Nefyn
Llyn Peninsula
B4354
Llanystumdwy
Tremadog
Porthmadog
Criccieth
PORTMEIRION VILLAGE
Maentwrog
Penrhyndeudraeth
Tudweiliog
A497
Pwllheli
Tremadoc Bay
B4413
Llanbedrog
St Tudwal's Road
Aberdaron
Abersoch
Porth Neigwl
Bardsey Sound
Bardsey
Great Ormes Head
LLANDUDNO CABLE CAR
NORTH WALES THEATRE
GREAT ORME TRAMWAY
Llandudno
Penrhyn
Rhôs
Deganwy
Conwy
Conwy Bay
Penmaenmawr
CONWY CASTLE
Llansanffraid Glan Conwy
BODNANT GARDENS
Llanfairfechan
B5106
Caerhun
B5113
Dolgarrog
A470
Trefriw
TREFRIW WOOLEN MILLS
Llanrwst
Capel Curig
SWALLOW FALLS
Betws-y-coed
CONWY VALLEY RAILWAY MUSEUM
Conwy
LLECHWEDD SLATE CAVERNS
FFESTINIOG RAILWAY
Blaenau Ffestiniog
B4407
Ffestiniog
A4212
Arenig Fawr
854
National
Llyn Trawsfynydd
Trawsfynydd
HARLECH CASTLE
Harlech
Bronaber
Llanuwchllyn
Llanbedr
754
Y Llethr
Park
COED Y BRENIN VISITOR CENTRE
A494
905
A496
Llanelltyd
Dolgellau
Barmouth
Barmouth Bay
A493
Cadair Idris
893
Penygadair
Mallwyd
Llwyngwril
Llangelynnin
CORRIS CRAFT CENTRE
Abergynolwyn
B4405
CENTRE FOR ALTERNATIVE TECHNOLOGY
Dyfi
A489
Tywyn
TALYLLN RAILWAY
Machynlleth
Cardigan Bay
Aberdyfi
Eglwys Fach
B4353
Taliesin
Borth
Llyn Clywedog Reservoir
0
10
20 miles
0
10
20
30 km
1: 440,000 7 miles to 1inch / 4.4 km to 1cm
12

Belfast & Dublin
Dublin
D
E
F
Crosby
Bootle
Wallasey
NEW PALACE & ADVENTURELAND
Moreton
Hoylake
Birkenhead
West Kirby
Greasby
Wirral
Bebington
LIVERPOOL
ALBERT DOCK
LIVERPOOL CATHEDRALS
Kirkby
St Helens
KNOWSLEY SAFARI PARK
Prescot
Huyton
Rainhill
CROXTETH HALL
Aintree
Thornton
Billinge
Ashton-in-Makerfield
Golborne
Culcheth
Newton-le-Willows
Fearnhead
Great Sankey
Woolston
Warrington
WALTON HALL GARDENS
Stockton Heath
Widnes
Runcorn
Halewood
Liverpool John Lennon
Mersey
Ellesmere Port
Elton
Helsby
Frodsham
Kingsley
Barnton
Weaverham
MARBURY C. PARK
Cheshire Plain
Northwich
Cuddington
Davenham
Delamere
Winsford
Ashton
Tarvin
Tarporley
Willaston
Neston
Heswall
Point of Ayr
Dee
GREENFIELD VALLEY HERITAGE PARK
Holywell
Bagillt
Flint
Connah's Quay
Halkyn
WEPRE C. PARK
Shotton
Queensferry
CHESTER ZOO
Upton
CHESTER VISITORS CENTRE
Chester
CHESTER CATHEDRAL
Saltney
Hawarden
Buckley
Broughton
Bretton
Mold
LOGGERHEADS C. PARK
Cilcain
Moel Famau
554
Hope
Caergwrle
Llanfynydd
Rossett
Gresford
Holt
Tilston
Burwardsley
Gowy
OCEAN BEACH AMUSEMENT PARK
SEA-LIFE CENTRE
Rhyl
Prestatyn
Kinmel Bay
Towyn
Bay
Abergele
Bodelwyddan
Rhuddlan
Dyserth
St Asaph (Llanelwy)
Brynford
AFONWEN CRAFT & ANTIQUE CEN
Llanfair Talhaiarn
Llansannan
Denbigh
Clwydian Range
Ystrad
Bylchau
Mynydd Hiraethog
RUTHIN CRAFT CENTRE
Ruthin
Llyn Brenig
519
LLYN BRENIG VISITOR CENTRE
Alwen Reservoir
Cerrigydrudion
Minera
Wrexham
Bersham
ERDDIG HALL
Marchwiel
Rhosllanerchrugog
LOWER DEE EXHIB. CENT
Cefn-mawr
Ruabon
Overton
Penley
Malpas
Nantwich
Wistaston
STAPELEY WATER GARDEN
Audlem
Whitchurch
Corwen
Druid
EUROPEAN CENTRE FOR TRADITIONAL & REGIONAL CULTURE
LLANGOLLEN RAILWAY
Llangollen
CHIRK CASTLE
Chirk
Glyn Ceiriog
Llandderfel
Llandrillo
Berwyn
Bala
Llyn Tegid (Bala Lake)
BALA LAKE RAILWAY
St Martin's
Ellesmere
Gobowen
Selattyn
Whittington
Oswestry
Prees
Wem
Hodnet
Moel Sych
827
Llanrhaeadr-ym-Mochnant
Pen-y-bont-fawr
Lake Vyrnwy
Tanat
Ruyton-XI-Towns
Baschurch
Roden
Llanwddyn
Llanfyllin
Dolanog
Severn
Shrewsbury
Donnington
Wellington
Telford
Llangadfan
WELSHPOOL & LLANFAIR LIGHT RLY
Welshpool
POWIS CASTLE
Llanfair Caereinion
Hanwood
Bayston Hill
Pontesbury
Minsterley
IRONBRIDGE GORGE MUSEUM
Much Wenlock
Garthmyl
Chirbury
Tregynon
Montgomery (Trefaldwyn)
Carno
Llanllwchaiarn
Llanwnog
Newtown (Y Drenewydd)
Trefeglwys
Bishop's Castle
The Long Mynd
516
Church Stretton
Shipton
Bridgnorth
SEVERN VALLEY RAILWAY
Wenlock Edge
M53
M56
M62
A5036
A59
A58
A57
A552
A540
A41
A561
A562
A56
A559
A49
A550
A548
A547
A525
A5151
A55
A541
A5119
A494
A483
A5104
A534
A54
A51
A530
A500
A529
A542
A5
A539
A528
A495
A53
A442
A490
A458
A5112
A488
A470
A489
B5381
B5382
B5429
B5435
B4501
B5401
B5105
B5431
B5130
B5153
B5393
B5069
B5395
B5476
B5063
B5065
B4397
B5067
B5062
B4500
B4579
B4580
B4396
B4398
B4393
B4391
B4401
B4403
B4395
B4382
B4386
B4389
B4390
B4380
B4378
B4368
B4371
13
20
24

20
Stockton Heath
Appleton Thorn
High Legh
Hale
Manchester
Bramhall
Hazel Grove
Hayfield
New Mills
Whaley Bridge
Chapel-en-le-Frith
Hathersage
Frodsham
Tatton C. Park
Mobberley
Wilmslow
Poynton
Lyme Park
Bollington
Bradwell
Marbury C. Park
Knutsford
Alderley Edge
Prestbury
Rainow
Shining Tor
Peak District National Park
Kingsley
Barnton
Weaverham
Northwich
Macclesfield
Tegg's Nose C. Park
Pavilion Gardens
Tideswell
Calver
Baslow
Buxton
Chatsworth House
Cuddington
Davenham
Chelmorton
Delamere
Cranage
Holmes Chapel
Winsford
Middlewich
Youlgreave
Congleton
Sandbach
Biddulph
Warslow
Matlock Bath
Cromford
Wirksworth
Crewe
Alsager
Rode Heath
Church Lawton
Leek
Burwardsley
Wistaston
Kidsgrove
Endon
Cheddleton
Nantwich
Shavington
Audley
Stapeley Water Gardens
Potteries Museum & Art Gallery
Ipstones
Carsington Water
Newcastle-under-Lyme
Stoke-on-Trent
Kingsley
Mayfield
Ashbourne
Audlem
Madeley
Keele
Caverswall
Cheadle
Alton Towers
Alton
Whitchurch
Forsbrook
Brailsford
Barlaston
Upper Tean
Rocester
Checkley
Fulford
Loggerheads
Prees
Market Drayton
Stone
Uttoxeter
Doveridge
Sudbury
Hilton
Hatton
Tutbury
Hodnet
Eccleshall
Weston
Abbots Bromley
Stretton
Seighford
Stafford
Shugborough Estate
Burton upon Trent
Gnosall
Colwich
Haughton
Rugeley
Yoxall
Swadlincote
Barton-under-Needwood
Newport
Cannock Chase
Armitage
Handsacre
Church Aston
Lilleshall
Penkridge
Longdon
Alrewas
Overseal
Donnington
Wheaton Aston
Wellington
Hadley
Sheriffhales
Oakengates
Cannock
Burntwood Green
Lichfield
Appleby Magna
Telford
Shifnal
Brewood
Great Wyrley
Norton Canes
Heart of the Country Centre
Featherstone
Brownhills
Tamworth
Ironbridge
Albrighton
Pelsall
Shenstone
Fazeley
Polesworth
Ironbridge Gorge Museum
Codsall
Rushall
Aldridge
Drayton Manor Theme Park
Dordon
Broseley
Much Wenlock
Wolverhampton
Walsall
Sandwell Valley C. Park
Sutton Coldfield
Kingsbury
Worfield
Wednesbury
Black Country Museum
Morville
Sedgley
Cliff Railway
Bridgnorth
Dudley Zoo & Castle
West Bromwich
Water Orton
Shipton
Wombourne
Dudley
Oldbury
National Indoor Arena
Castle Bromwich
Coleshill
Severn Valley Railway
Sea-Life Centre
City Mus & Art Gall
Airport Visitors Centre
Smethwick
Amblecote
BIRMINGHAM
N.E.C.
Burwarton
Alveley
Stourbridge
Kingsford C. Park
Kinver
Cannon Hill Park
Halesowen
Birmingham International
Highley
Meriden
Cookley
Hagley
Clent Hills C. Park
Frankley
Cadbury World
Wolverley
Clent
Romsley
Solihull
Berkswell
Kidderminster
Belbroughton
Waseley Hills C. Park
Knowle
Cleehill
Cleobury Mortimer
Bewdley
West Midland Safari Park
Lickey Hills C. Park
Wythall
Hockley Heath

Aughton
Dinnington
Blyth
Carlton in Lindrick
Clarborough
Sturton le Steeple
Beighton
South Anston
Wales
Mosborough
Killamarsh
Eckington
Worksop
Babworth
Retford (East Retford)
South Leverton
SUNDOWN KIDDIES ADVENTURELAND
Scampton
Welton
Dunholme
Nettleham
Saxilby
Barlborough
Clowne
Staveley
Brimington
Elmton
Creswell
CLUMBER C. PARK
East Markham
Bolsover
Nether Langwith
Tuxford
Lincoln
LINCOLN CATHEDRAL
Washingborough
Bracebridge Heath
Heighington
Branston
HARTSHOLME C. PARK
Hasland
Scarcliffe
Market Warsop
SHERWOOD FOREST C. PARK
Boughton
Ollerton
Sutton on Trent
North Hykeham
Heath
Shirebrook
Edwinstowe
RUFFORD C. PARK
Old Clipstone
Carlton-on-Trent
Thorpe on the Hill
Waddington
North Wingfield
Pleasley
Mansfield
Mansfield Woodhouse
Sherwood
Collingham
Harmston
Metheringham
Tibshelf
Sutton in Ashfield
Rainworth
Forest
Bassingham
South Normanton
Shirland
Alfreton
Kirkby in Ashfield
Farnsfield
WHITE POST MODERN FARM
Newark-on-Trent
Coddington
Leadenham
Billinghay
Ravenshead
Somercotes
Selston
Southwell
Farndon
Balderton
Cranwell
Ruskington
Ripley
Hucknall
Calverton
Leasingham
Brinsley
BESTWOOD LODGE C. PARK
Woodborough
Claypole
Caythorpe
Codnor
Loscoe
Eastwood
Vale of Belvoir
Trent
Sleaford
SHIPLEY C. PARK
Heanor
Kimberley
Arnold
Lowdham
Long Bennington
Devon
Heckington
Kilburn
Smalley
AMERICAN ADVENTURE THEME PARK
Awsworth
Ilkeston
TALES OF ROBIN HOOD
Burton Joyce
East Bridgford
Ancaster
Barkston
Carlton
Colwick
Bingham
Bottesford
Great Gonerby
NOTTINGHAM
Sandiacre
Stapleford
Radcliffe on Trent
Sedgebrook
Ockbrook
West Bridgford
Beeston
Grantham
Ropsley
Horbling
Borrowash
Risley
NOTTINGHAM CASTLE MUSEUM
Cotgrave
Folkingham
Breaston
Long Eaton
Ruddington
Great Ponton
Aston on Trent
East Midlands International
Gotham
Keyworth
Dowsby
Kegworth
Castle Donington
East Leake
Waltham on the Wolds
Colsterworth
Ticknall
Hathern
Shepshed
Loughborough
Asfordby
Melton Mowbray
Wymondham
Bourne
Barrow upon Soar
Wreake
GREAT CENTRAL RAILWAY
Ashby de la Zouch
BEACON HILL C. PARK
Mountsorrel
Sileby
East Goscote
Cottesmore
Coalville
Rothley
Queniborough
Syston
Langham
Ryhall
Market Deeping
BRADGATE C. PARK
Ibstock
Markfield
Birstall
Thurmaston
Oakham
Stamford
Rutland Water
RUTLAND WATER
Anstey
Glenfield
Scraptoft
Ketton
Easton on the Hill
Kirby Muxloe
Newbold Verdon
LEICESTER
Market Bosworth
Braunstone
Wittering
Enderby
Oadby
Uppingham
Wigston
Narborough
Blaby
Great Glen
Welland
NENE VALLEY RLY
Earl Shilton
BURBAGE COMMON C. PARK
Cosby
Kibworth Harcourt
Caldecott
Elton
Hinckley
Sapcote
Broughton Astley
Rockingham
Rockingham Forest
FOXTON CANAL LOCKS
Cottingham
EAST CARLTON C. PARK
Bulkington
Market Harborough
Stoke Albany
Corby
Weldon
Oundle
BARNWELL C. PARK
Lutterworth
Brigstock
Husbands Bosworth
Desborough
Geddington
Winwick
COMBE ABBEY C. PARK
Rothwell
Coventry
Long Lawford
Kettering
WICKSTEED PARK
Thrapston
BRAMPTON VALLEY WAY C. PARK
Rugby
Broughton
Burton Latimer
Pitsford
Nene
M1
M6
M69
A1
A6
A14
A15
A17
A38
A42
A43
A45
A46
A47
A50
A52
A57
A60
A61
A444
A447
A453
A511
A607
A610
A614
A617
A619
A6003
A6006
A6075
A6121

Binbrook
Fotherby
27
Market Rasen
Lincolnshire Wolds
A631
A157
Louth
Grimoldby
Manby
B1200
Mablethorpe
A153
A157
A1104
A52
Maltby le Marsh
A16
A1111
Wragby
B1202
B1399
B1225
A46
A158
Alford
B1449
Huttoft
Tetford
Hogsthorpe
Chapel St Leonards
Willoughby
A1028
A52
Ingoldmells
MAGICAL WORLD OF FANTASY ISLAND
Bain
Washingborough
Bardney
B1190
B1191
Horncastle
A158
Partney
B1195
B1196
Heighington
Hundleby
Spilsby
A158
Burgh le Marsh
Woodhall Spa
A153
East Keal
B1195
Skegness
A52
Metheringham
B1191
B1192
A155
Mareham le Fen
Steeping
A16
Wainfleet All Saints
Tattershall
Coningsby
GIBRALTAR POINT NATURE RESERVE
Stickney
B1188
B1189
Billinghay
Dogdyke
B1183
East Fen
Boston Deeps
Witham
B1192
West Fen
A52
Ruskington
A153
Sibsey
Wrangle
Old Leake
Sleaford
B1395
Holland Fen
A17
A1121
Boston
Lynn Deeps
Heckington
B1394
A52
A16
Brancaster
A149
A15
Helpringham
Wyberton
The Wash
Hunstanton
B1153
B1155
Kirton
Heacham
Docking
A52
21
Donington
Sutterton
B1454
B1177
A152
Snettisham
Great Bircham
Gosberton
B1397
Welland
The Marsh
Holbeach Marsh
Dowsby
Surfleet
B1153
Dersingham
SANDRINGHAM
A149
A17
B1440
Pinchbeck
Holbeach
Whaplode
Morton
A151
B1515
Gedney
Terrington Marsh
South Wootton
Moulton
A148
Long Sutton
Spalding
B1165
A1078
Clenchwarton
Grimston
Bourne
A151
B1165
Sutton Bridge
Terrington St Clement
A17
King's Lynn
B1145
Gayton
A16
Cowbit
B1168
B1454
A6121
Thurlby
A1101
West Winch
Deeping St Nicholas
Middleton
A15
A47
A10
The Fens
Narborough
A1073
B1166
Great Ouse
Market Deeping
Deeping St James
Wisbech
A47
Crowland
B1169
Marham
B1166
B1167
A134
Swaffham
A16
Glinton
Elm
A1122
Newborough
A1101
B1443
Thorney
A47
Bedford Level (North Level)
A47
Downham Market
Stradsett
Easton on the Hill
A15
Outwell
A1122
Wittering
Eye
B1040
B1101
Nene
Denver
Wereham
A605
A141
A47
Peterborough
A10
B1160
Whittlesey
West Fen
March
A1
A605
B1093
B1099
Hilgay
Orton Longueville
A1101
Elton
B671
A15
B1040
Southery
A134
Welney
Methwold
Yaxley
Bedford Level (Middle Level)
Wimblington
Great Ouse
B1386
A605
Pondersbridge
B1093
B1106
Stilton
B1098
Manea
Feltwell
A1065
B1096
Oundle
Ramsey St Mary's
B660
Isle of Ely
Littleport
Little Ouse
Thetford
Brandon
Chatteris
A10
Ramsey
A141
A1(M)
Little Downham
Lakenheath
Forest Park
Winwick
Sawtry
Bedford Level (South Level)
Warboys
A
B
C
1
2
3
4
16

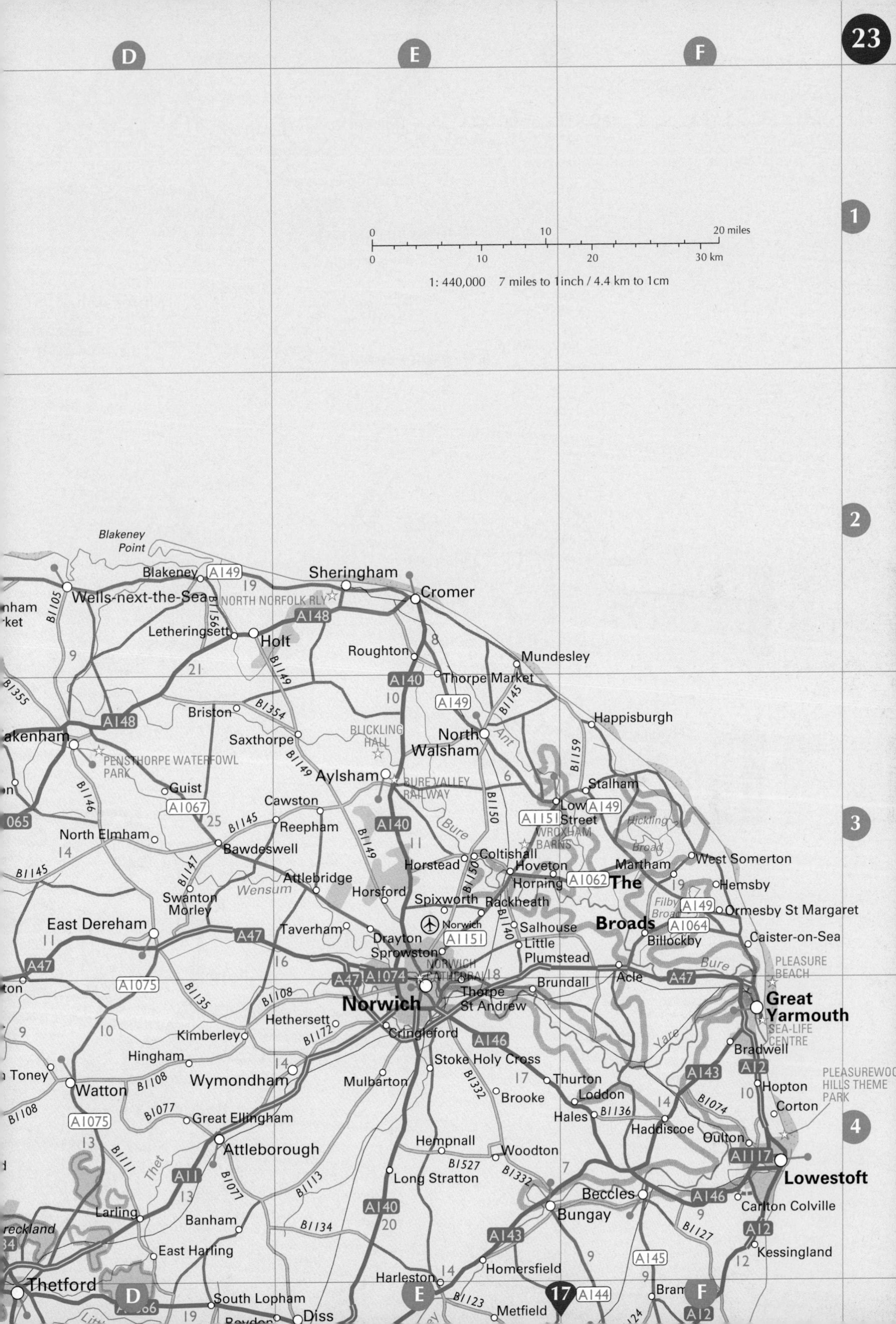
D
E
F
1
2
3
4
0
10
20 miles
0
10
20
30 km
1: 440,000 7 miles to 1inch / 4.4 km to 1cm
Blakeney Point
Blakeney
Sheringham
Cromer
Wells-next-the-Sea
NORTH NORFOLK RLY
Letheringsett
Holt
Roughton
Mundesley
Thorpe Market
Briston
Saxthorpe
BLICKLING HALL
North Walsham
Happisburgh
PENSTHORPE WATERFOWL PARK
Aylsham
BURE VALLEY RAILWAY
Guist
Stalham
Cawston
Reepham
Low Street
WROXHAM BARNS
Hickling Broad
North Elmham
Bawdeswell
Coltishall
Horstead
West Somerton
Martham
Hoveton
Horning
The Broads
Hemsby
Attlebridge
Horsford
Wensum
Swanton Morley
Spixworth
Rackheath
Filby Broad
Ormesby St Margaret
East Dereham
Taverham
Norwich
Salhouse
Billockby
Caister-on-Sea
Drayton
Sprowston
Little Plumstead
PLEASURE BEACH
NORWICH CATHEDRAL
Brundall
Acle
Bure
Thorpe St Andrew
Great Yarmouth
SEA-LIFE CENTRE
Hethersett
Kimberley
Cringleford
Yare
Bradwell
Hingham
Stoke Holy Cross
Wymondham
Mulbarton
Thurton
Hopton
PLEASUREWOOD HILLS THEME PARK
Watton
Brooke
Loddon
Corton
Great Ellingham
Hales
Haddiscoe
Oulton
Attleborough
Hempnall
Woodton
Lowestoft
Long Stratton
Beccles
Bungay
Carlton Colville
Larling
Banham
Kessingland
Thet
East Harling
Homersfield
Harleston
Thetford
South Lopham
Metfield
Diss
17
A149
A148
A140
A1067
A47
A1075
A1074
A1151
A1062
A1064
A146
A143
A12
A11
A1117
A145
A144
B1105
B1156
B1149
B1354
B1145
B1146
B1147
B1150
B1159
B1140
B1135
B1108
B1172
B1332
B1077
B1111
B1113
B1527
B1134
B1136
B1074
B1127
B1123

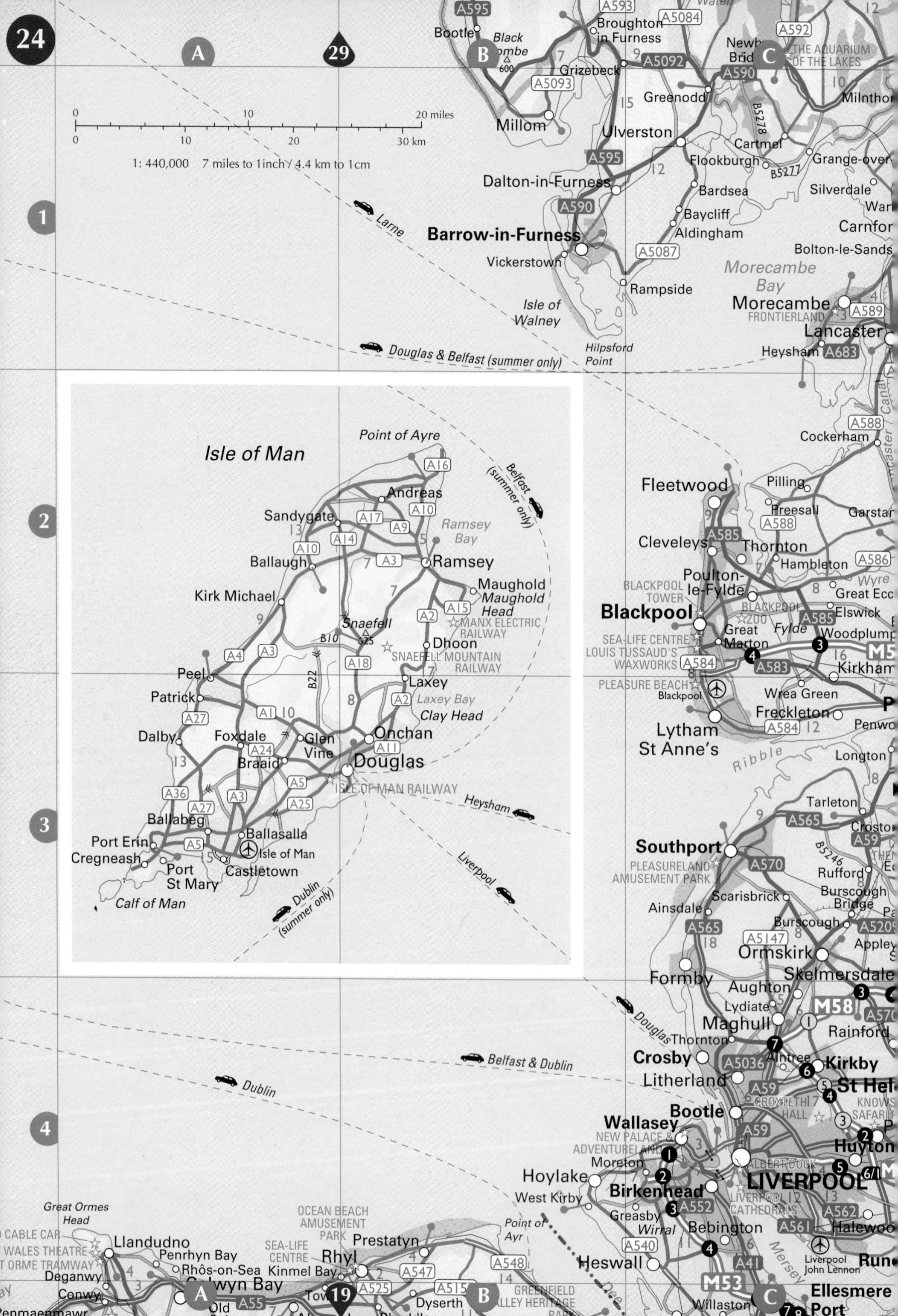

24
A
29
B
C
1
2
3
4
0 10 20 miles
0 10 20 30 km
1: 440,000 7 miles to 1inch / 4.4 km to 1cm
Bootle
Black Combe
600
Broughton in Furness
Grizebeck
Millom
Greenodd
Ulverston
Cartmel
Flookburgh
Grange-over-
Dalton-in-Furness
Bardsea
Silverdale
Baycliff
Aldingham
Barrow-in-Furness
Vickerstown
Rampside
Bolton-le-Sands
Morecambe Bay
Morecambe
FRONTIERLAND
Lancaster
Heysham
Isle of Walney
Hilpsford Point
THE AQUARIUM OF THE LAKES
Larne
Douglas & Belfast (summer only)
A593
A5084
A595
A592
A5092
A590
A5093
B5278
B5277
A5087
A589
A683
A588
Cockerham
Isle of Man
Point of Ayre
Andreas
Sandygate
Ramsey Bay
Ramsey
Ballaugh
Kirk Michael
Maughold
Maughold Head
MANX ELECTRIC RAILWAY
Snaefell
625
Dhoon
SNAEFELL MOUNTAIN RAILWAY
Peel
Laxey
Laxey Bay
Clay Head
Patrick
Dalby
Foxdale
Glen Vine
Onchan
Braaid
Douglas
ISLE OF MAN RAILWAY
Ballabeg
Ballasalla
Port Erin
Cregneash
Isle of Man
Port St Mary
Castletown
Calf of Man
A16
A17
A10
A9
A14
A3
A2
A15
A4
B10
A18
B22
A27
A1
A24
A11
A36
A5
A25
Belfast (summer only)
Heysham
Liverpool
Dublin (summer only)
Fleetwood
Pilling
Preesall
A588
Cleveleys
A585
Thornton
Hambleton
A586
Poulton-le-Fylde
BLACKPOOL TOWER
Wyre
Great Eccleston
Blackpool
BLACKPOOL ZOO
Elswick
SEA-LIFE CENTRE
LOUIS TUSSAUD'S WAXWORKS
Great Marton
Fylde
A585
A584
A583
Kirkham
PLEASURE BEACH
Blackpool
Wrea Green
Freckleton
Lytham St Anne's
A584
Ribble
Longton
Tarleton
A565
Southport
PLEASURELAND AMUSEMENT PARK
A570
B5246
Rufford
Scarisbrick
Burscough Bridge
Ainsdale
Burscough
A565
A5147
Ormskirk
Skelmersdale
Formby
Aughton
Lydiate
M58
Maghull
Rainford
Douglas
Thornton
Crosby
Belfast & Dublin
A5036
Aintree
Kirkby
Dublin
Litherland
A59
CROXTETH HALL
Bootle
KNOWSLEY SAFARI PARK
Wallasey
NEW PALACE & ADVENTURELAND
Huyton
Moreton
Hoylake
LIVERPOOL
ALBERT DOCK
West Kirby
Birkenhead
LIVERPOOL CATHEDRALS
Greasby
A552
A562
Wirral
Bebington
A561
Halewood
A540
Heswall
Liverpool John Lennon
Mersey
A41
M53
Willaston
Ellesmere Port
Dee
Great Ormes Head
CABLE CAR
WALES THEATRE
GT ORME TRAMWAY
Llandudno
Penrhyn Bay
Rhôs-on-Sea
Deganwy
Conwy
Colwyn Bay
Old Colwyn
A55
OCEAN BEACH AMUSEMENT PARK
SEA-LIFE CENTRE
Prestatyn
Rhyl
Kinmel Bay
A547
A525
A5151
Dyserth
Rhuddlan
Point of Ayr
A548
GREENFIELD VALLEY HERITAGE PARK
19

25
Yorkshire Dales
National Park
Pennines
Bainbridge
Aysgarth
Wensley
Bedale
Middleham
Gawthrop
Old Town
Barbon
Kirkby Lonsdale
Whernside
736
Langstrothdale Chase
Horsehouse
Masham
Buckden
Halton Gill
Burton-in-Kendal
Ingleton
Ingleborough
Pen-y-Ghent
694
Great Whernside
703
Middlesmoor
Kirkby Malzeard
LIGHTWATER VALLEY PARK
High Bentham
Horton in Ribblesdale
Arncliffe
Kettlewell
Nidderdale
Hornby
Clapham
MALHAM TARN NATURE RESERVE
Wharfe
FOUNTAINS ABBEY
Pateley Bridge
Greta
Wenning
Lune
Stainforth
Caton
Grassington
Settle
Threshfield
Summer Bridge
Quernmore
Ribblesdale
Wharfedale
Ward's Stone
560
Long Preston
Airton
Hetton
Killinghall
Forest of Bowland
Stocks Reservoir
Tosside
Hellifield
Gargrave
BOLTON ABBEY ESTATE C. PARK
Blubberhouses
Harrogate
Lee
Wyre
Slaidburn
HARLOW CARR GARDENS
Skipton
Newton
Holden
Gisburn
Addingham
Hodder
Earby
Burley in Wharfdale
Ilkley
Rombalds Moor
Barnoldswick
Glusburn
Silsden
Otley
BEACON FELL C. PARK
Brock
Clitheroe
Pendle Hill
557
Cowling
Steeton
Foulridge
Airedale
Keighley
Menston
Guiseley
Yeadon
Leeds Bradford International
Inglewhite
1853 GALLERY
Barrowford
Colne
Bingley
Baildon
Longridge
Nelson
KEIGHLEY WORTH RLY
Shipley
Horsforth
Haworth
Cullingworth
Ribchester
Boulsworth Hill
518
NATIONAL MUSEUM OF PHOTOGRAPHY, FILM & TV
Ribble
Padiham
Brierfield
Oxenhope
Great Harwood
Burnley
Denholme
Bradford
Pudsey
Rishton
Clayton-le-Moors
OGDEN WATER C. PARK
Walton-le-Dale
Queensbury
Blackburn
Accrington
Hebden Bridge
Shelf
Morley
Higher Walton
Oswaldtwistle
Cornholme
WALKEY CLOGS
EUREKA! MUSEUM FOR CHILDREN
Cleckheaton
Mytholmroyd
Halifax
Batley
Clayton-le-Woods
Haslingden
Bacup
Todmorden
Liversedge
Darwen
Rawtenstall
Sowerby Bridge
Brighouse
Dewsbury
EAST LANCASHIRE RLY
Euxton
Edenfield
Ripponden
Elland
Mirfield
Ossett
HOLLINGWORTH LAKE C. PARK
Ramsbottom
Whitworth
NEWMILLERDAM C. PARK
Horbury
Chorley
Edgworth
Littleborough
Huddersfield
Coppull
MUSEUM & ART GALLERY
Tottington
Rochdale
Milnrow
Slaithwaite
Kirkburton
Adlington
Bradshaw
Horwich
Marsden
Clayton West
Heywood
Standish
Bury
Shaw
Meltham
Honley
Shepley
Denby Dale
HAIGH HALL C. PARK
Bolton
Radcliffe
Royton
Holmfirth
CANNON HALL OPEN FARM
Wigan
Farnworth
Chadderton
Orrell
Kearsley
Middleton
HEATON PARK
Oldham
Black Hill
582
Dodworth
Atherton
Abram
Hindley
Prestwich
Penistone
PENNINGTON FLASH C. PARK
Swinton
Pendlebury
Failsworth
Mossley
Ashton-in-Makerfield
Leigh
G-MEX
Salford
BRIDGEWATER HALL
Ashton-under-Lyne
Stocksbridge
Stalybridge
Golborne
MANCHESTER
Droylsden
Howden Moors
Margery Hill
546
Culcheth
Urmston
Stretford
Hollingworth
Newton-le-Willows
WYTHENSHAWE HALL & PARK
Denton
Hyde
Glossop
Irlam
Derwent Reservoir
Sale
Bredbury
Charlesworth
High Peak
High Bradfield
Great Sankey
Fearnhead
Partington
Stockport
ETHEROW C. PARK
Kinder Scout
636
Altrincham
Woolston
Warrington
Lymm
Cheadle
Marple
WALTON HALL GARDENS
DUNHAM MASSEY
Gatley
Hayfield
Ladybower Reservoir
SHEFFIELD
Stockton Heath
Hale
Manchester
Hazel Grove
New Mills
Widnes
Appleton Thorn
High Legh
Bramhall
Poynton
Whaley Bridge
Chapel-en-le-Frith
Hathersage
TATTON C. PARK
STYAL C. PARK
LYME PARK
Mobberley
Wilmslow
Bradwell
Frodsham
Bollington
Peak
Knutsford
Alderley
Holmesfield

North Riding Forest Park
North Yorkshire Moors Rwy
Kirkbymoorside
Wrelton
Pickering
Vale of Pickering
Thornton-le-Dale
Snainton
Knayton
Boltby
Thirsk
Sowerby
Sproxton
Helmsley
Wass
Oswaldkirk
Coxwold
Topcliffe
Hovingham
Flamingo Land
Eden Camp Museum
West Knapton
Lightwater Valley Park
Ripon
Vale of York
Howardian Hills
Terrington
Malton
Norton
Butterwick
Easingwold
Castle Howard
Fountains Abbey
Boroughbridge
Stillington
Jorvik Glass
North Grimston
Sutton Park
Sheriff Hutton
Sutton-on-the-Forest
Sledmere
Yorkshire Wolds
Summer Bridge
Burton Leonard
Leavening
Ripley
Strensall
Fimber
Killinghall
Knaresborough
Shipton
Haxby
Fridaythorpe
Harrogate
Rawcliffe
York Minster
Castle Museum
National Railway Museum
York
Jorvik
Stamford Bridge
Huggate
Harlow Carr Gardens
Spofforth
Bainton
Wetherby
Fulford
Elvington
Pocklington
Middleton on-the-Wolds
Wharfe
Boston Spa
Harewood
Harewood House
Hayton
Golden Acre Park Gardens
Tadcaster
Yeadon
Leeds Bradford International
Ulleskelf
Market Weighton
Holme-on-Spalding-Moor
Tropical World
City Art Gall. & Mus.
Horsforth
Cawood
North Duffield
Lotherton Hall C. Park
Bubwith
Royal Armouries
Sherburn in Elmet
North Cave
South Cave
Leeds
Garforth
Selby
Temple Newsam C. Park
Brayton
Rothwell
Kippax
Gilberdyke
Howden
Elloughton
Brough
Morley
Castleford
Hook
North Ferriby
Batley
Lofthouse
Knottingley
Rawcliffe
Goole
Stanley
Snaith
Normanton
Swinefleet
Wakefield
Pontefract
Featherstone
Burton upon Stather
Winterton
Horbury
Crofton
Went
Eastoft
Normanby Hall
Crigglestone
Ackworth Moor Top
Moorends
Yorkshire Sculpture Park
Hemsworth
Askern
Thorne
Crowle
Clayton West
Royston
Stainforth
Crosby
Scunthorpe
Gunness
Denby Dale
Darton
South Kirkby
Carcroft
Hatfield
Cudworth
Adwick le Street
Kirk Sandall
Cannon Hall Open Farm
Barnsley
Thurnscoe
Bentley
Armthorpe
Bottesford
Dodworth
Darfield
Messingham
Penistone
Wombwell
Wath upon Dearne
Doncaster
Epworth
Scotter
Hoyland
Mexborough
Bessacarr
Finningly
Haxey
Kirton in Lindsey
Wentworth
Swinton
Rossington
New Rossington
Chapeltown
Rawmarsh
Conisbrough
Thrybergh
Misterton
Ecclesfield
Dalton
Braithwell
Blyton
Bramley
Tickhill
Bawtry
Rotherham
Brinsworth
Wickersley
Birtcotes
Morton
High Bradfield
Whiston
Maltby
Harworth
Gringley on the Hill
Beckingham
Gainsborough
Sheffield City
Thurcroft
Treeton
Ulley Reservoir C. Park
Langold
Ranskill
SHEFFIELD
Aughton
Dinnington
Blyth
Carlton in Lindrick
Clarborough
Sturton le Steeple
Beighton
Rother Valley C. Park
South Anston
Hathersage
Mosborough
Wales
South Leverton
Sundown Kiddies Adventureland
Scampton
Killamarsh
Dronfield
Eckington
Babworth
Retford (East Retford)
Barlborough
Worksop
Holmesfield
Unstone
Swale
Ure
Nidd
Ouse
Kyle
Riccal
Rye
Seven
Derwent
Dearne
Torne
Idle
Trent
A1
A1(M)
M1
M18
M62
M180
M181
M621
A19
A64
A59
A61
A168
A170
A169
A166
A1079
A614
A63
A645
A18
A614
A630
A631
A159
A15
A57

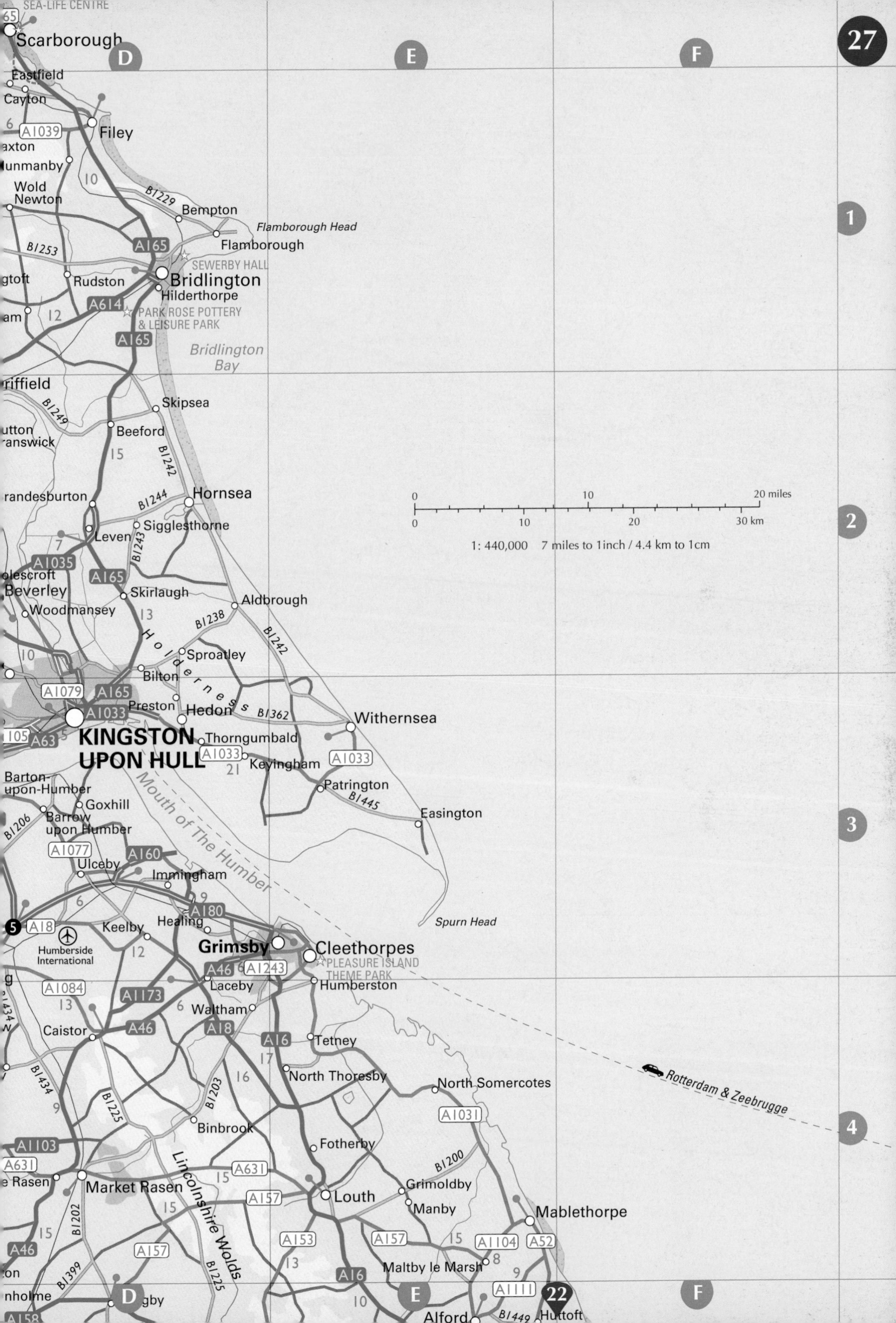
SEA-LIFE CENTRE
Scarborough
Eastfield
Cayton
Filey
Wold Newton
Bempton
Flamborough Head
Flamborough
SEWERBY HALL
Rudston
Bridlington
Hilderthorpe
PARK ROSE POTTERY & LEISURE PARK
Bridlington Bay
Skipsea
Beeford
Hornsea
Sigglesthorne
Leven
Beverley
Woodmansey
Skirlaugh
Aldbrough
Holderness
Sproatley
Bilton
Preston
Hedon
Withernsea
KINGSTON UPON HULL
Thorngumbald
Keyingham
Patrington
Easington
Barton-upon-Humber
Goxhill
Barrow upon Humber
Mouth of The Humber
Ulceby
Immingham
Spurn Head
Keelby
Healing
Humberside International
Grimsby
Cleethorpes
PLEASURE ISLAND THEME PARK
Laceby
Humberston
Waltham
Caistor
Tetney
North Thoresby
North Somercotes
Rotterdam & Zeebrugge
Binbrook
Fotherby
Lincolnshire Wolds
Market Rasen
Louth
Grimoldby
Manby
Mablethorpe
Maltby le Marsh
Alford
Huttoft
A1039
A165
A614
B1229
B1253
B1249
B1242
B1244
B1243
A1035
B1238
B1362
A1079
A1033
A63
B1445
B1206
A1077
A160
A180
A18
A46
A1243
A1084
A1173
A16
B1434
B1203
B1225
A1103
A631
A157
A1031
B1200
A153
A1104
A52
A1111
B1202
B1399
B1449
D
E
F
1
2
3
4
22
0 10 20 miles
0 10 20 30 km
1: 440,000 7 miles to 1inch / 4.4 km to 1cm

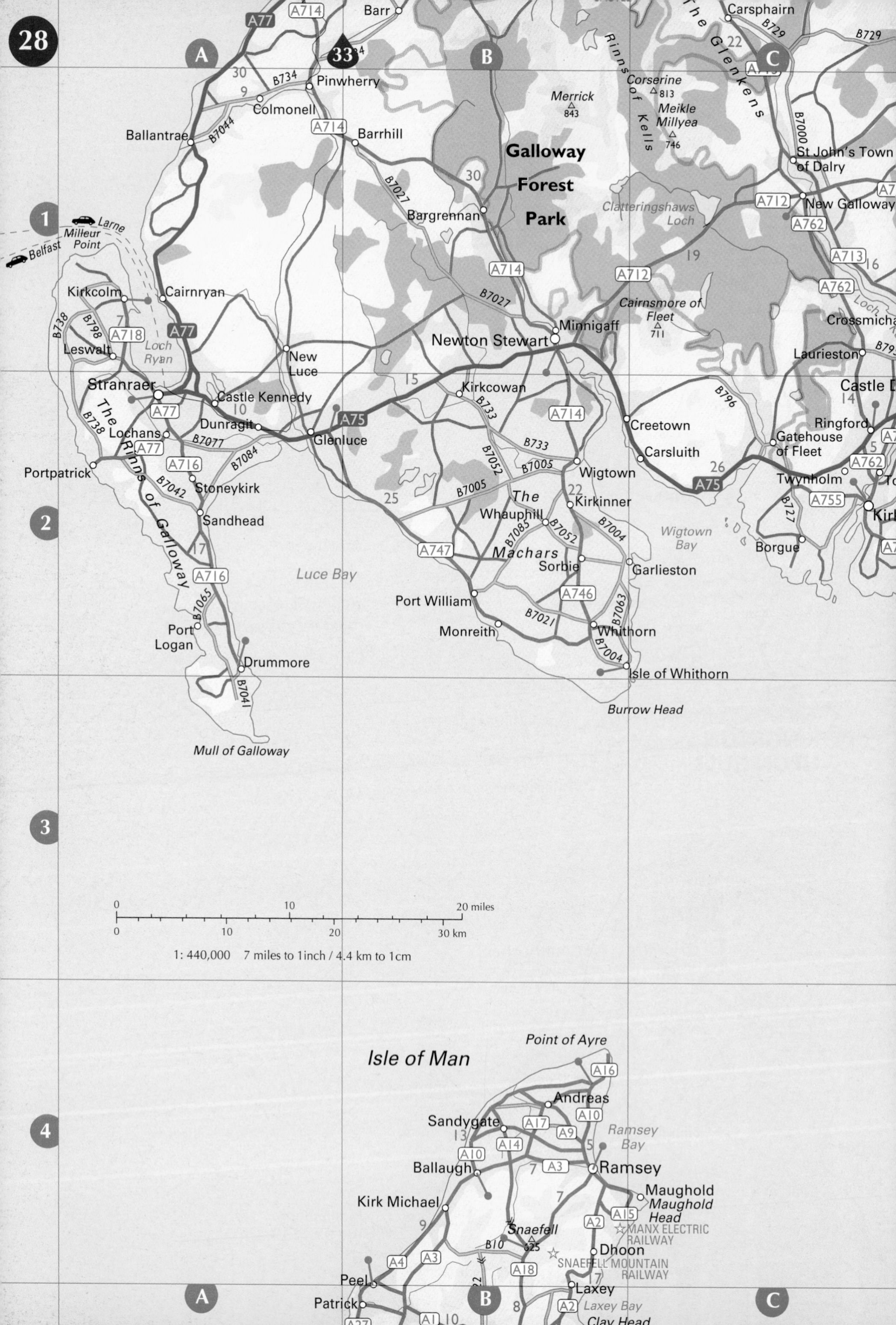
A
B
C
1
2
3
4
33
Barr
Carsphairn
The Glenkens
Pinwherry
Colmonell
Ballantrae
Barrhill
Rinns of Kells
Corserine
813
Merrick
843
Meikle Millyea
746
Galloway Forest Park
St John's Town of Dalry
New Galloway
Clatteringshaws Loch
Bargrennan
Larne
Milleur Point
Belfast
Kirkcolm
Cairnryan
Loch Ryan
Leswalt
Stranraer
Cairnsmore of Fleet
711
Minnigaff
Newton Stewart
New Luce
Crossmichael
Laurieston
Castle Kennedy
Kirkcowan
Creetown
Carsluith
Gatehouse of Fleet
Ringford
Twynholm
The Rinns of Galloway
Lochans
Dunragit
Glenluce
Portpatrick
Stoneykirk
Sandhead
Wigtown
Kirkinner
The Whauphill
Machars
Sorbie
Garlieston
Wigtown Bay
Borgue
Luce Bay
Port William
Monreith
Whithorn
Isle of Whithorn
Burrow Head
Port Logan
Drummore
Mull of Galloway
A77
A714
B734
B7044
B7027
A712
A762
A713
B729
B7000
A718
B738
B798
A75
A716
B7077
B7084
B7042
B733
B7052
B7005
B796
A747
B7085
B7004
A746
B7063
B7021
B7065
B7041
A755
B727
0
10
20 miles
0
10
20
30 km
1: 440,000 7 miles to 1inch / 4.4 km to 1cm
Isle of Man
Point of Ayre
Andreas
Sandygate
Ramsey Bay
Ballaugh
Ramsey
Maughold
Maughold Head
Kirk Michael
Snaefell
625
MANX ELECTRIC RAILWAY
Dhoon
SNAEFELL MOUNTAIN RAILWAY
Peel
Laxey
Patrick
Laxey Bay
Clay Head
A16
A10
A17
A9
A14
A3
A15
A2
B10
A4
A18
A1
A27

29
Dumfries
Lockerbie
Lochmaben
Langholm
Annan
Gretna
Carlisle
Wigton
Maryport
Workington
Cockermouth
Keswick
Whitehaven
Cleator Moor
Egremont
Ambleside
Windermere
Kendal
Solway Firth
Lake District National Park
Cumbrian Mountains
Scafell Pike 977
Helvellyn 949
Skiddaw 931

Kielder Forest Park
Northumberland National
Yorkshire Dales
National Park
Kielder Water (Reservoir)
Newcastleton
Falstone
Otterburn
Elsdon
Bellingham
Wark
Morpeth
Whalton
Belsay
Stamfordham
Ponteland
Newcastle International
Gosforth
Newburn
Newcastle upon Tyne
Blaydon
Whickham
Prudhoe
Stocksfield
Chopwell
Riding Mill
Corbridge
Acomb
Hexham
Haydon Bridge
Haltwhistle
Greenhead
Gilsland
HOUSESTEADS FORT (HADRIAN'S WALL)
Brampton
Warwick Bridge
Wetheral
Castle Carrock
Allendale Town
Derwent Reservoir
DERWENT WALK C.PARK
Burnopfield
Stanley
Leadgate
Consett
Castleside
Lanchester
Healeyfield
Edmundbyers
Alston
Nenthead
Allenheads
Cowshill
St John's Chapel
Westgate
Eastgate
Stanhope
Wolsingham
Tow Law
Crook
Bishop Auckland
High Etherley
West Auckland
Woodland
Copley
Cockfield
Staindrop
Barnard Castle
BOWES MUSEUM
Startforth
Winston
Gainford
Ingleton
High Hesket
Kirkoswald
Lazonby
Great Salkeld
Melmerby
Langwathby
Penrith
Temple Sowerby
Cross Fell 893
Chapelfell Top 699
Cow Green Reservoir
Teesdale
Middleton-in-Teesdale
Mickleton
Selset Reservoir
Balderhead Reservoir
Appleby-in-Westmorland
Shap
Crosby Ravensworth
Warcop
Brough
Bowes
Winton
Kirkby Stephen
Nateby
Orton
Tebay
Haweswater Reservoir
ULLSWATER STEAMERS
Caldwell
Melsonby
Gilling West
Richmond
Brompton on Swale
Catterick Camp
Scotton
High Seat 710
Thwaite
The Calf 676
Watchgate
Grayrigg
Kendal
Sedbergh
Garsdale Head
Hawes
Wensleydale
Bainbridge
Aysgarth
Leyburn
Wensley
Middleham
Gawthrop
Stalling Busk
Horsehouse
Masham
Old Town
Barbon
Milnthorpe
Ashington
Pegswood
Bedlington
Stannington
Rowlands Gill
Annfield Plain
Sacriston
Witton Gilbert
Satley
Esh Winning
Brandon
Billy Row
Beamish Museum
Darlington

D
E
F
1
2
3
4
0
10
20 miles
0
10
20
30 km
1: 440,000 7 miles to 1inch / 4.4 km to 1cm
Stavanger, Haugesund & Bergen
Göteborg & Kristiansand
Amsterdam
Ellington
Lynemouth
Newbiggin-by-the-Sea
Blyth
Cramlington
Seaton Sluice
Seaton Delaval
Seghill
Whitley Bay
Shiremoor
Tynemouth
North Shields
Wallsend
South Shields
SOUTH SHIELDS MUSEUM & ART GALLERY
Jarrow
Hebburn
Cleadon
Boldon
Sunderland
Washington
Chester-le-Street
Bournmoor
Hetton-le-Hole
Seaham
Murton
South Hetton
Easington Colliery
Easington
Haswell
Sherburn
DURHAM CATHEDRAL
Thornley
Peterlee
Horden
Wheatley Hill
Blackhall Colliery
Wingate
Trimdon
Fishburn
Ferryhill
Hartlepool
Tees Bay
Sedgefield
Newton Aycliffe
Billingham
Redcar
Marske-by-the-Sea
Saltburn-by-the-Sea
South Bank
Middlesbrough
ALBERT PARK
Stockton-on-Tees
Eston
Brotton
Skelton
Loftus
Hinderwell
Thornaby-on-Tees
STEWART PARK C. PARK
Guisborough
Roseberry Topping
320
Eaglescliffe
Teesside International
Egglescliffe
Yarm
Sandsend
Whitby
ST MARY'S
Great Ayton
Hutton Rudby
Stokesley
Great Broughton
Danby
Castleton
Sleights
Egton
High Hawsker
Robin Hood's Bay
NORTH YORKSHIRE MOORS RAILWAY
North Cowton
Cleveland Hills
Round Hill
454
North York Moors
Staintondale
Brompton
Northallerton
Rosedale Abbey
North York Moors National Park
Hambleton Hills
Cloughton
Burniston
Leeming
Gillamoor
Lockton
Hackness
North Riding Forest Park
Scalby
Knayton
NORTH YORKSHIRE MOORS RWY
Kirkbymoorside
Wrelton
Boltby
Helmsley
Thirsk
Sproxton
Pickering
Vale of Pickering
Thornton-le-Dale
Snainton
Seamer
Sowerby
Wass
26
A189
A196
A19
A1058
A183
A194
A1018
A1231
A182
A690
A181
A1086
A179
A1(M)
A177
A689
A178
A1085
A66
A67
A171
A172
A174
B1269
B1366
B1416
A167
B1264
B1257
A684
A169
A168
A170
A165
A1
A61
Tees
Wiske
Swale
Cod Beck
Rye
Dove

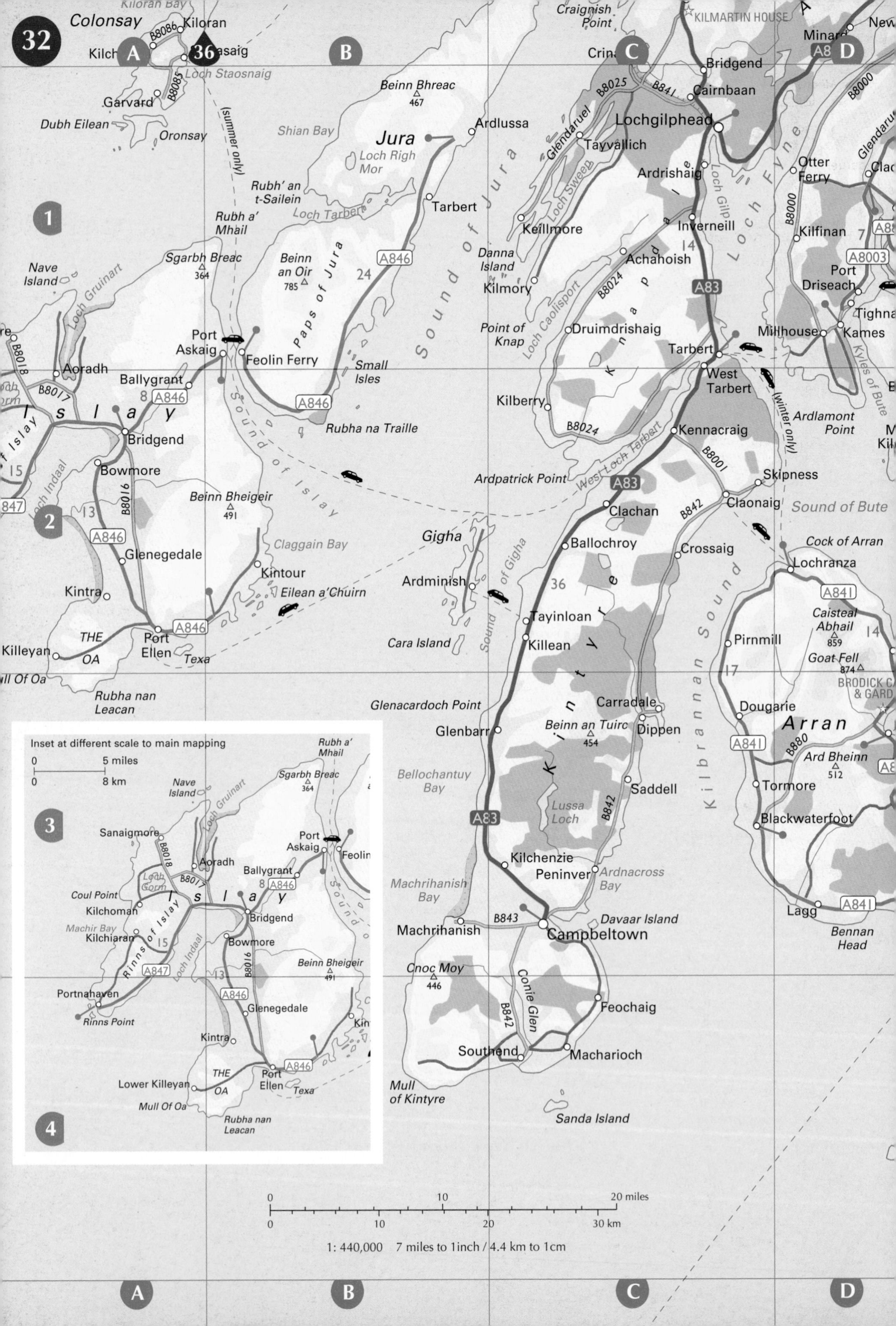

A
B
C
D
1
2
3
4
Colonsay
Kiloran Bay
Kiloran
B8086
36
Loch Staosnaig
B8085
Garvard
Dubh Eilean
Oronsay
(summer only)
Craignish Point
KILMARTIN HOUSE
Minard
A83
B8000
Bridgend
Cairnbaan
B841
B8025
Lochgilphead
Glendaruel
Tayvallich
Loch Sween
Ardrishaig
Loch Gilp
Loch Fyne
Otter Ferry
Kilfinan
A8003
Port Driseach
Tighnabruaich
Kames
Millhouse
Kyles of Bute
Beinn Bhreac
467
Ardlussa
Shian Bay
Jura
Loch Righ Mor
Rubh' an t-Sailein
Tarbert
Loch Tarbert
Rubh a' Mhail
Sound of Jura
Keillmore
Inverneill
14
Danna Island
Achahoish
Kilmory
B8024
Knapdale
Nave Island
Loch Gruinart
Sgarbh Breac
364
Beinn an Oir
785
Paps of Jura
A846
24
Port Askaig
Feolin Ferry
Small Isles
Point of Knap
Loch Caolisport
Druimdrishaig
Tarbert
West Tarbert
(winter only)
Ardlamont Point
B8018
Aoradh
B8017
Ballygrant
8
Islay
Bridgend
Rinns of Islay
15
Bowmore
Loch Indaal
B8016
A847
13
2
A846
Sound of Islay
Rubha na Traille
Kilberry
Kennacraig
West Loch Tarbert
Skipness
B8001
Ardpatrick Point
A83
Clachan
Claonaig
B842
Sound of Bute
Beinn Bheigeir
491
Claggain Bay
Gigha
Ballochroy
Crossaig
Cock of Arran
Lochranza
Glenegedale
Kintour
Eilean a'Chuirn
Ardminish
Sound of Gigha
36
Kintyre
Kilbrannan Sound
A841
Kintra
Caisteal Abhail
859
14
Tayinloan
Killean
Pirnmill
THE OA
Port Ellen
Killeyan
Texa
Cara Island
Goat Fell
874
17
BRODICK CASTLE & GARDENS
Mull Of Oa
Rubha nan Leacan
Glenacardoch Point
Carradale
Dougarie
Arran
Glenbarr
Beinn an Tuirc
454
Dippen
A841
B880
Ard Bheinn
512
Bellochantuy Bay
Saddell
Tormore
Lussa Loch
B842
A83
Blackwaterfoot
Kilchenzie
Machrihanish Bay
Peninver
Ardnacross Bay
A841
Lagg
B843
Machrihanish
Davaar Island
Campbeltown
Bennan Head
Cnoc Moy
446
Conie Glen
B842
Feochaig
Southend
Macharioch
Mull of Kintyre
Sanda Island
Inset at different scale to main mapping
0 5 miles
0 8 km
Rubh a' Mhail
Nave Island
Sgarbh Breac
364
Loch Gruinart
Port Askaig
Feolin
Sanaigmore
B8018
Aoradh
Loch Gorm
B8017
Ballygrant
A846
Coul Point
Kilchoman
Islay
Machir Bay
Kilchiaran
Rinns of Islay
15
Bridgend
Bowmore
B8016
Loch Indaal
A847
13
Beinn Bheigeir
491
Sound of Islay
Portnahaven
A846
Glenegedale
Rinns Point
Kintra
Lower Killeyan
THE OA
Port Ellen
A846
Texa
Mull Of Oa
Rubha nan Leacan
0 10 20 miles
0 10 20 30 km
1: 440,000 7 miles to 1inch / 4.4 km to 1cm

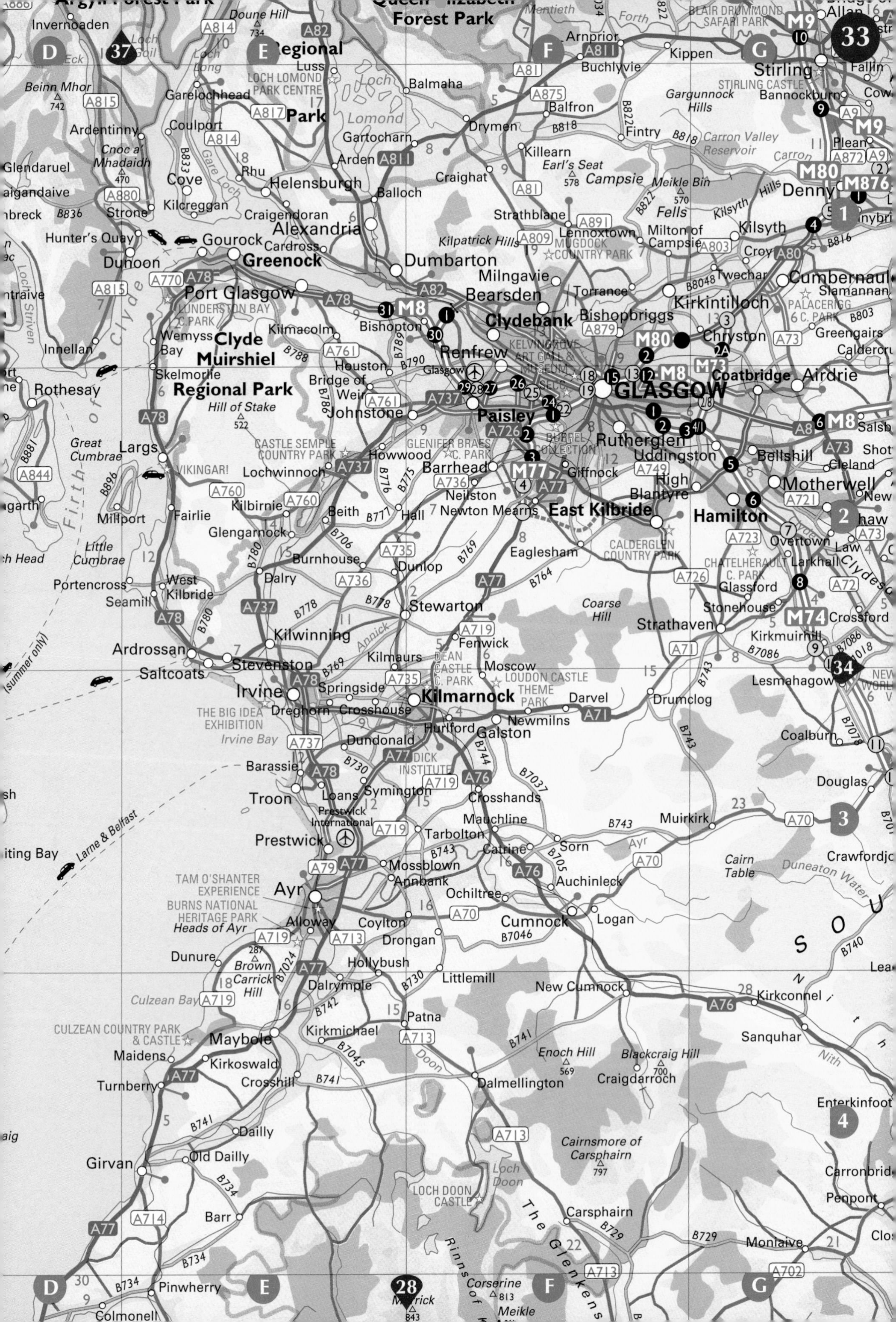

33
Forest Park
Invernoaden
Doune Hill
734
Regional
Park
Luss
LOCH LOMOND
PARK CENTRE
Loch
Lomond
Mentieth
Forth
BLAIR DRUMMOND
SAFARI PARK
Allan
Arnprior
Buchlyvie
Kippen
Stirling
STIRLING CASTLE
Fallin
Bannockburn
Beinn Mhor
742
Garelochhead
Balmaha
Balfron
Gargunnock
Hills
Ardentinny
Cnoc a'
Mhadaidh
470
Coulport
Gartocharn
Drymen
Fintry
Carron Valley
Reservoir
Plean
Glendaruel
Cove
Rhu
Arden
Killearn
Earl's Seat
578
Campsie
Meikle Bin
570
Denny
Kilcreggan
Helensburgh
Craighat
Balloch
Strone
Craigendoran
Fells
Strathblane
Kilsyth
Hills
Kilsyth
Hunter's Quay
Gourock
Alexandria
Kilpatrick Hills
Lennoxtown
Milton of
Campsie
Cardross
MUGDOCK
COUNTRY PARK
Croy
Dunoon
Greenock
Dumbarton
Milngavie
Twechar
Cumbernauld
Port Glasgow
Bearsden
Torrance
Kirkintilloch
Slamannan
Clydebank
Bishopbriggs
PALACERIGG
C. PARK
Greengairs
Innellan
Clyde
Muirshiel
Regional Park
Kilmacolm
Wemyss
Bay
Bishopton
Chryston
Renfrew
KELVINGROVE
ART GALL &
MUSEUM
Houston
Glasgow
Bridge of
Weir
Coatbridge
Airdrie
Skelmorlie
Rothesay
GLASGOW
Hill of Stake
522
Johnstone
Paisley
Rutherglen
Great
Cumbrae
Largs
CASTLE SEMPLE
COUNTRY PARK
GLENIFER BRAES
C. PARK
BURRELL
COLLECTION
Howwood
Barrhead
Uddingston
Bellshill
Cleland
VIKINGAR!
Lochwinnoch
Giffnock
High
Blantyre
Motherwell
Neilston
Newton Mearns
East Kilbride
Hamilton
Kilbirnie
Beith
Hall
Millport
Fairlie
Glengarnock
Eaglesham
CALDERGLEN
COUNTRY PARK
Overtown
Little
Cumbrae
Burnhouse
Dunlop
CHATELHERAULT
C. PARK
Larkhall
Glassford
Portencross
West
Kilbride
Dalry
Seamill
Stewarton
Coarse
Hill
Stonehouse
Crossford
Strathaven
Kilwinning
Annick
Fenwick
Kirkmuirhill
Ardrossan
Stevenston
Kilmaurs
DEAN
CASTLE
C. PARK
Moscow
LOUDON CASTLE
THEME
PARK
Saltcoats
(summer only)
Irvine
Springside
Kilmarnock
Darvel
Drumclog
Lesmahagow
THE BIG IDEA
EXHIBITION
Dreghorn
Crosshouse
Hurlford
Newmilns
Galston
Irvine Bay
Dundonald
Coalburn
DICK
INSTITUTE
Barassie
Troon
Loans
Symington
Crosshands
Douglas
Prestwick
International
Mauchline
Muirkirk
Larne & Belfast
Prestwick
Tarbolton
Sorn
Ayr
Catrine
Mossblown
Annbank
Auchinleck
Cairn
Table
Duneaton Water
Crawfordjo
TAM O'SHANTER
EXPERIENCE
Ayr
Ochiltree
BURNS NATIONAL
HERITAGE PARK
Heads of Ayr
Alloway
Coylton
Cumnock
Logan
Drongan
Dunure
287
Brown
Carrick
Hill
Hollybush
Littlemill
Culzean Bay
Dalrymple
New Cumnock
Kirkconnel
Patna
CULZEAN COUNTRY PARK
& CASTLE
Maybole
Kirkmichael
Sanquhar
Maidens
Kirkoswald
Doon
Enoch Hill
569
Blackcraig Hill
700
Nith
Turnberry
Crosshill
Dalmellington
Craigdarroch
Enterkinfoot
Dailly
Cairnsmore of
Carsphairn
797
Girvan
Old Daily
Loch
Doon
Carronbridge
LOCH DOON
CASTLE
Penpont
Barr
The Glenkens
Carsphairn
Moniaive
Rinns of Kells
Pinwherry
Corserine
813
Merrick
843
Meikle
Colmonell

Allan
Alva
Dollar
Powmill
Ballingry
Kinglassie
Thornton
Buckhaven
Menstrie
Tillicoultry
Lochore Meadows Country Park
Cardenden
East Wemyss
A
B
C
38
Hill End
Saline
Lochgelly
Stirling
Fallin
Alloa
Clackmannan
Cowdenbeath
Auchtertool
Kirkcaldy
Bannockburn
Cowie
Oakley
M90
Firth of
Airth
Dunfermline
Crossgates
Kinghorn
Kincardine
Plean
Culross
Cairneyhill
Crossford
Burntisland
Carron
Aberdour
Dirleton
M80
M876
Stenhousemuir
Limekilns
Dalgety Bay
Gullane
Denny
Grangemouth
Larbert
Inverkeithing
Inchkeith
Deep Sea World
North Queensferry
Aberlady
1
Bonnybridge
Bo'ness
Royal Botanic Gardens
Edinburgh Castle
National Gallery
Royal Museum of Scotland
Cockenzie and Port Seton
Falkirk
Polmont
Champany
South Queensferry
Cramond
M9
Lauriston Castle
Leith
Longniddry
Linlithgow
Winchburgh
Kirkliston
Musselburgh
Prestonpans
Cumbernauld
Beecraigs Country Park
Edinburgh
Slamannan
Torphichen
Palacerigg C. Park
Avonbridge
Dechmont
Broxburn
M8
EDINBURGH
Tranent
Macmerry
Bolton
Greengairs
Armadale
Livingston
East Calder
Ratho
Whitecraig
Ormiston
Caldercruix
Bathgate
Kirknewton
Pencaitland
Blackridge
Loanhead
Dalkeith
Airdrie
Whitburn
Pentland Hills Regional Park
Bonnyrigg
Blackburn
Harthill
Polbeth
West Calder
Bilston
Roslin
Vogrie C. Park
Humbie
Salsburgh
Polkemmet C. Park
Rosewell
Penicuik
Gorebridge
Bellshill
Shotts
Stane
Fauldhouse
Scald Law
Edinburgh Crystal Visitor Centre
Cleland
North Middleton
Motherwell
Allanton
Carlops
Gilston
Newmains
Leadburn
Pentland Hills
Wishaw
Heriot
Oxton
Hare Hill
Forth
West Linton
Moorfoot Hills
Overtown
Law
Carluke
Larkhall
Clydesdale
Kilcadzow
Blackhope Scar
Lauder
Carstairs
Carnwath
Dolphinton
Romannobridge
Eddleston
Gala Water
Crossford
Newbigging
Blyth Bridge
Windlestraw Law
Stow
Kirkmuirhill
Libberton
Elsrickle
Lanark
Peebles
Colquhar
Lesmahagow
33
New Lanark World Heritage Village
Biggar
Stobo
Tweeddale
Galashiels
Innerleithen
Broughton
Traquair House
Clovenfords
Abbotsford House
Coalburn
Rigside
Tinto
Symington
Minch Moor
Uddington
Douglas
Dun Rig
Culter Fell
Selkirk
Roberton
Yarrow
M74
3
Southern Uplands
Tweedsmuir
Mountbenger
Crawfordjohn
Broad Law
Duneaton Water
Abington
Glenbreck
Cappercleuch
Ettrickbridge
Black Knowe Head
Ashkirk
Ettrick Forest
Elvanfoot
Lowther Hills
White Coomb
Leadhills
Ettrick Water
Hawick
Kirkconnel
Hart Fell
Ettrick
Roberton
Green Lowther
Sanquhar
Capplegill
Teviotdale
Nith
Loch Fell
Moffat
Ballencleuch Law
Enterkinfoot
Teviothead
4
Beattock
Hermitage Castle
Eskdalemuir
Carronbridge
Thornhill
Penpont
Roan Fell
Moniaive
Closeburn
Johnstonebridge
Annandale
Eskdale
Boreland
Parkgate
29
Newcastleton

D
E
39
F
0
10
20 miles
0
10
20
30 km
1: 440,000 7 miles to 1inch / 4.4 km to 1cm
Zeebrugge
Bass Rock
SCOTTISH SEABIRD CENTRE
JOHN MUIR COUNTRY PARK
Dunbar
Stenton
Garvald
Cockburnspath
Meikle Black Law
St Abb's Head
St Abbs
Coldingham
Ecclaw
Grantshouse
Eyemouth
Burnmouth
Meikle Says Law
535
Cranshaws
Whiteadder Water
Auchencrow
Reston
Chirnside
Preston
Berwick-upon-Tweed
Foulden
Paxton
Dirrington Great Law
Duns
Tweedmouth
Blackadder Water
Westruther
Polwarth
Scremerston
Houndslow
Ladykirk
Norham
Tweed
Swinton
Greenlaw
Ancroft
Holy Island or Lindisfarne
Gordon
Eccles
Duddo
Coldstream
Cornhill-on-Tweed
Fenwick
Burrows Hole
Farne Islands
Earlston
Stichill
Lowick
Crookham
Ford
Smailholm
Flodden
Cockenheugh
211
Bamburgh
BAMBURGH CASTLE
FLOORS CASTLE
Kelso
KELSO ABBEY
Milfield
Belford
Seahouses
Kilham
Doddington
North Sunderland
DRYBURGH ABBEY
Kirknewton
Beadnell
Town Yetholm
Kirk Yetholm
Akeld
Chatton
Beadnell Bay
Wooler
Eckford
Ellingham
Nisbet
Ancrum
Morebattle
Cateran Hill
Christon Bank
Embleton
Bonjedward
JEDBURGH ABBEY
Jedburgh
Bowmont Water
The Cheviot
815
Craster
Eglingham
Rennington
Denholm
Oxnam
Kale Water
Powburn
Windy Gyle
619
Breamish
Glanton
Longhoughton
Alnwick
Camptown
Cheviot Hills
Whittingham
Lesbury
Alnmouth
Chesters
Southdean
Netherton
Edlingham
Shilbottle
Warkworth
Carter Bar
Coquet Island
Amble
Thropton
Rothbury
Longframlington
Rothbury Forest
Togston
Felton
DRUIDGE BAY COUNTRY PARK
Rochester
Redesdale
National Park
Kielder
Otterburn
Elsdon
Longhorsley
Ellington
Ulgham
Lynemouth
Kielder Forest Park
Ashington
Kielder Water (Reservoir)
Newbigg
Morpeth
Guide Post
WANSBECK C. PARK
30
1
2
3
4

A
40
B
C
1
2
3
4
INNER HEBRIDES
Rum (Rhum)
Kinloch
Askival
812
Aird of Sleat
Sound of Rum
Rubha nam Meirleach
Cleadale
Eigg
An Sgurr
393
Galmisdale
Sound of Eigg
Eilean nan Each
Muck
Lochboisdale
Castlebay
Sound of Arisaig
Eilean Shona
Ockle
Ardtoe
Achosnich
Point of Ardnamurchan
Ardnamurchan
Ben Hiant
528
Kilchoan
B8007
Glenbeg
Glenborrodale
Eilean Mor
Sorisdale
B8072
Coll
Clabhach
B8071
Arinagour
12
B8070
Loch Eatharna
Ardmore Point
Caliach Point
Tobermory
Drimnin
B8073
Calgary
Dervaig
Loch Frisa
Sound of Mull
Killundine
B849
Fiunar
A848
Calgary Bay
Gunna
Crossapol Bay
Hough Bay
B8068
B8069
Caolas
Tiree
Scarinish
B8065
Hynish Bay
Barrapoll
Balemartine
Balephuil
Kilninian
Loch Tuath
Salen
A849
Treshnish Isles
Gometra
Lagganulva
Ulva
B8073
B8035
23
Knock
Little Colonsay
Loch Na Keal
Loch Ba
Staffa
Balnahard
Mull
Ben More
966
B8035
Glen More
Ben Buie
717
IONA ABBEY
Baile Mòr
Iona
Sound of Iona
Fionnphort
Loch Scridain
Pennyghael
35
A849
Bunessan
Carsaig
Loch Buie
Ross of Mull
Soa Island
Ardchiavaig
Malcolm's Point
Garvellachs
0
10
20 miles
0
10
20
30 km
1: 440,000 7 miles to 1inch / 4.4 km to 1cm
Scarba
Kiloran Bay
Rubh' a'Geodha
Colonsay
B8086
Kiloran
Kilchattan
Scalasaig
Loch Staosnaig
B8085
Garvard
32
467

Knoydart
Loch Quoich
Loch Garry
Loch Oich
Invergarry
Meall Buidhe 946
Glen Garry
41
Sron a'Choire Ghairbh 935
Laggan
Carn Dearg 816
Spey
Sgurr na Ciche 1040
Loch Nevis
Bracora
Garvan
Roy
Loch Morar
Morar
Loch Arkaig
Loch Lochy
Glen
Lochaber
Gulvain 987
Clunes
Creag Meagaidh 1130
A86
Loch Beoraid
A82
B8005
Spean Bridge
Roybridge
Lochailort
Glenfinnan
B8004
Glen Spean
A861
Kinlocheil
A830
Loch Eil
Corpach
AONACH MOR MOUNTAIN GONDOLA & NEVIS RANGE SKI CENTRE
Beinn a'Chlachair 1087
Rois-Bheinn 882
Blaich
Loch Shiel
Stob Choire Claurigh 1177
Loch Treig
Moidart
Fort William
Glen Nevis
Ben Nevis 1344
Ardmolich
Beinn na Lap 937
Sgurr Dhomhnuill 888
Polloch
Beinn Resipol 845
Binnein Mor 1128
Loch Ossian
Clovullin
B863
Kinlochleven
Strontian
North Ballachulish
Onich
Loch Leven
Blackwater Reservoir
Fuar Bheinn 765
Kentallen
Glencoe
Ballachulish
GLENCOE VISITOR CENTRE
Altnafeadh
Kilmalieu
Sgorr Dhearg 1024
Bidean Nam Bian 1150
Glen Coe
Loch Laidon
A884
B8043
A828
GLENCOE SKI CENTRE
Rannoch Moor
Camasnacroise
Meall a'Bhuiridh 1108
Loch Linnhe
Invercharnan
Water of Tulla
Portnacroish
Beinn Sgulaird 932
Stob Ghabhar 1087
Stuchd an Lochain 960
38
Port Appin
Ben Starav 1078
Loch Tulla
Loch Lyon
Lismore
L. Creran
SEA LIFE CENTRE
Achnacroish
B8045
Bridge of Orchy
Beinn Dorain 1074
Beinn Heasgarnich 1076
Ledaig
B845
Loch Etive
Craignure
Glen Orchy
B8074
Lochay
Connel
Bonawe Quarries
Lochdon
A85
Bonawe
Ben Cruachan 1126
Glen Lochy
Tyndrum
Oban
Taynuilt
Kerrera
A816
Lochawe
B8077
Dalmally
Ben Lui 1130
Dochart
Loch Nant
A819
Crianlarich
Ben More 1174
Firth of Lorn
Kilchrenan
Kilninver
Cladich
Balquhidder
Beinn Chapull 515
B844
Beinn Bhuidhe 948
Inverarnan
Seil
Inverinan
B840
Shira
Easdale
Balvicar
B8003
Ardlui
Fyne
Clachan
Ben Vorlich 943
Cullipool
Loch Avich
Kilmelford
Loch Melfort
Luing
Sound of Luing
Beinn Bhreac 526
INVERARAY JAIL
INVERARAY CASTLE
A83
Cairndow
Stronachlachar
Loch Katrine
Toberonochy
Inveraray
Beinn Ime 1011
Loch Awe
Loch Fyne
Loch Tarbet
B828
B829
Ardfern
A815
Ben Lomond 974
The Trossachs
B8002
Argyll
Auchindrain
B839
Arrochar
Ford
Strachur
Lochgoilhead
Kinlochard
Kirkton
Furnace
Lomond
Aberfoyle
Kilmartin
Argyll Forest Park
SCOTTISH WOOL CENTRE
Queen Elizabeth Forest Park
Craignish Point
KILMARTIN HOUSE
A886
Invernoaden
Doune Hill 734
Newton
A814
Minard
Loch Goil
Loch Long
Regional
Crinan
Bridgend
Loch Eck
Luss
B8025
Cairnbaan
B8000
Beinn Mhor 742
33
Garelochhead
LOCH LOMOND PARK CENTRE
Balmaha
D
E
F
1
2
3
4

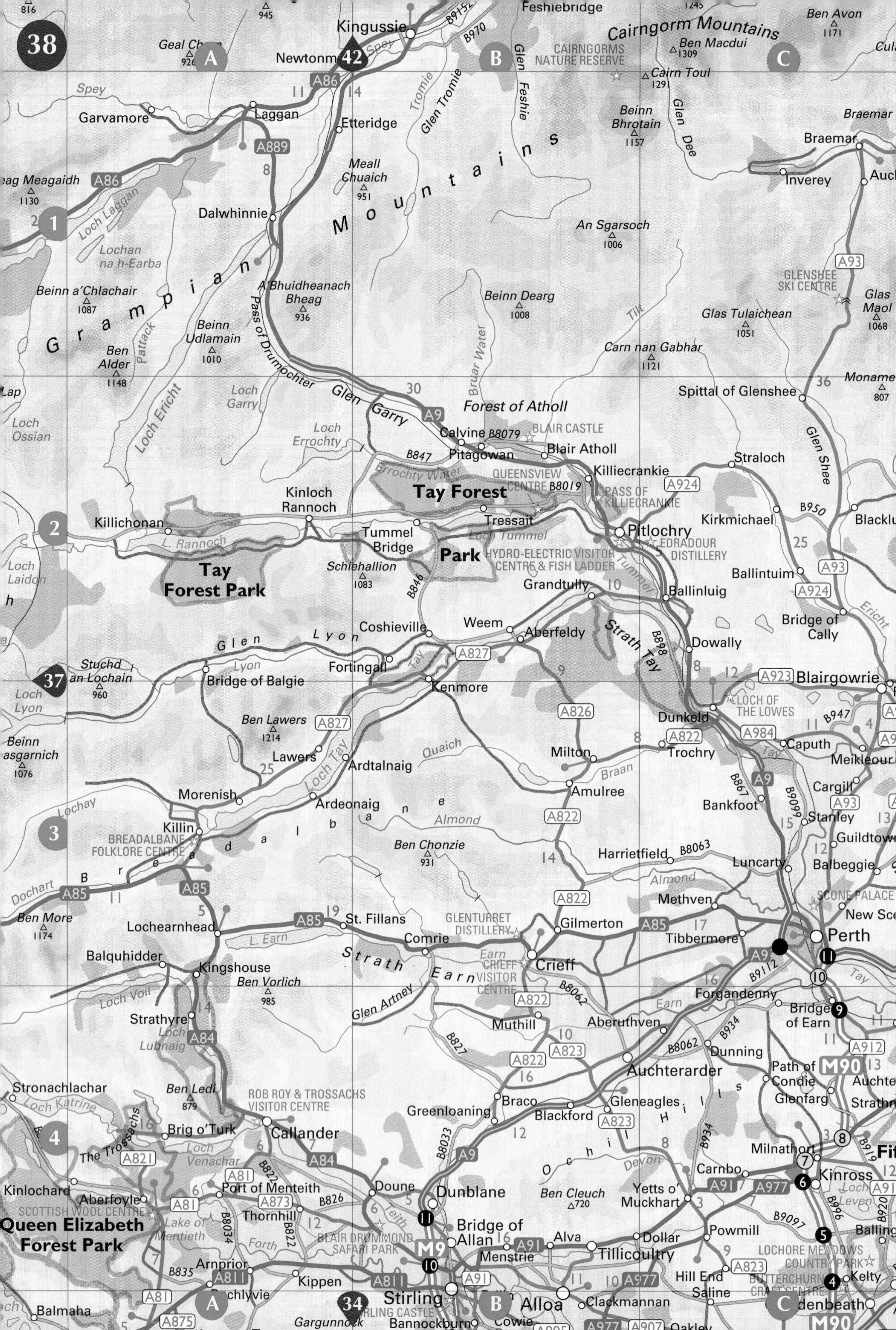

Kingussie
Newtonmore
Cairngorm Mountains
CAIRNGORMS NATURE RESERVE
Ben Macdui
Cairn Toul
Ben Avon
Feshiebridge
Geal Charn
Laggan
Garvamore
Etteridge
Dalwhinnie
Grampian Mountains
Loch Laggan
Lochan na h-Earba
Beinn a'Chlachair
Ben Alder
Beinn Udlamain
A'Bhuidheanach Bheag
Pass of Drumochter
Meall Chuaich
Beinn Bhrotain
Glen Dee
Glen Feshie
Glen Tromie
Braemar
Inverey
An Sgarsoch
GLENSHEE SKI CENTRE
Glas Maol
Glas Tulaichean
Beinn Dearg
Carn nan Gabhar
Bruar Water
Spittal of Glenshee
Loch Ericht
Loch Ossian
Loch Garry
Glen Garry
Forest of Atholl
Calvine
BLAIR CASTLE
Blair Atholl
Pitagowan
Loch Errochty
Errochty Water
QUEENSVIEW CENTRE
Tay Forest Park
Killiecrankie
PASS OF KILLIECRANKIE
Straloch
Glen Shee
Kinloch Rannoch
Killichonan
L. Rannoch
Loch Laidon
Tummel Bridge
Tressait
Loch Tummel
Pitlochry
EDRADOUR DISTILLERY
HYDRO-ELECTRIC VISITOR CENTRE & FISH LADDER
Kirkmichael
Schiehallion
Grandtully
Ballinluig
Ballintuim
Bridge of Cally
Coshieville
Weem
Aberfeldy
Strath Tay
Glen Lyon
Fortingall
Kenmore
Dowally
Blairgowrie
Stuchd an Lochain
Bridge of Balgie
Loch Lyon
LOCH OF THE LOWES
Dunkeld
Caputh
Ben Lawers
Beinn Heasgarnich
Lawers
Ardtalnaig
Loch Tay
Quaich
Milton
Trochry
Meikleour
Amulree
Braan
Cargill
Bankfoot
Stanley
Morenish
Ardeonaig
Breadalbane
Almond
Killin
BREADALBANE FOLKLORE CENTRE
Ben Chonzie
Harrietfield
Guildtown
Balbeggie
Luncarty
Dochart
Ben More
Methven
SCONE PALACE
New Scone
Lochearnhead
St. Fillans
GLENTURRET DISTILLERY
Gilmerton
Tibbermore
Perth
L. Earn
Comrie
Strath Earn
Crieff
CRIEFF VISITOR CENTRE
Balquhidder
Kingshouse
Ben Vorlich
Loch Voil
Forgandenny
Bridge of Earn
Glen Artney
Strathyre
Loch Lubnaig
Muthill
Aberuthven
Dunning
Auchterarder
Path of Condie
Glenfarg
Stronachlachar
Loch Katrine
Ben Ledi
ROB ROY & TROSSACHS VISITOR CENTRE
Braco
Greenloaning
Blackford
Gleneagles
Ochil Hills
Brig o'Turk
Callander
The Trossachs
Loch Venachar
Devon
Milnathort
Carnbo
Kinross
Kinlochard
Aberfoyle
SCOTTISH WOOL CENTRE
Port of Menteith
Doune
Dunblane
Ben Cleuch
Yetts o' Muckhart
Loch Leven
Queen Elizabeth Forest Park
Lake of Menteith
Thornhill
Forth
Teith
BLAIR DRUMMOND SAFARI PARK
Bridge of Allan
Alva
Dollar
Tillicoultry
Powmill
Menstrie
LOCHORE MEADOWS COUNTRY PARK
Arnprior
Kippen
Hill End
Saline
BUTTERCHURN CRAFT CENTRE
Kelty
Buchlyvie
Balmaha
Gargunnock
Stirling
STIRLING CASTLE
Bannockburn
Cowie
Alloa
Clackmannan
Oakley
Cowdenbeath
A86
A889
A9
A93
A924
A827
A826
A822
A984
A923
A85
A84
A821
A81
A873
A811
A91
A977
A823
A912
M90
M9
A875
A905
A907
B8079
B847
B8019
B846
B898
B950
B947
B867
B9099
B8063
B9112
B8062
B934
B827
B8033
B8034
B822
B826
B835
B9097
B996
B970

39
Torphins
Kincardine O'Neil
Dinnet
Aboyne
Peterculter
Charlestown
Ballater
Crathie
BALMORAL CASTLE
Glen Tanar
Carnferg
525
Marywell
Dee
Banchory
Kirkton of Durris
STORYBOOK GLEN
Portlethen
Newtonhill
Netherley
Muchalls
Strachan
Aucholzie
Glen Muick
Mount Keen
939
Mongour
376
Rickarton
Bridge of Dye
Stonehaven
Loch Muick
South Esk
Tarfside
Glen Esk
North Esk
Drumlithie
Auchenblae
Ben Tirran
896
Water of Saughs
Auchmull
Fettercairn
Fordoun
Roadside of Kinneff
Bervie Water
Inverbervie
Glen Clova
Clova
Laurencekirk
Gourdon
Prosen Water
Bridgend
Edzell
Inchbare
Marykirk
Kirkton of Menmuir
St Cyrus
Easter Lednathie
Fern
Trinity
Hillside
Dykehead
Brechin
Backwater Reservoir
Tannadice
Bridge of Dun
Montrose
Finavon
Kirkton of Kingoldrum
Ferryden
Aberlemno
Strathmore
Kirriemuir
Rescobie
Lunan Bay
Friockheim
Forfar
Inverkeilor
GLAMIS CASTLE
Douglastown
Craichie
Glamis
Inverarity
CROMBIE COUNTRY PARK
Redford
Meigle
Newtyle
Carmyllie
Arbirlot
Arbroath
Balgray
MONIKIE COUNTRY PARK
Muirdrum
Kellas
East Haven
Muirhead
Monifieth
Carnoustie
CAMPERDOWN WILDLIFE CENTRE
Broughty Ferry
Longforgan
DUNDEE
Tayport
Buddon Ness
Inchture
MC MANUS GALLERIES
Newport-on-Tay
Firth of Tay
Wormit
Errol
Leuchars
Rathillet
Newburgh
St Andrews
SEA-LIFE CENTRE
Lindores
Dairsie
Monimail
Cupar
CRAIGTOUN COUNTRY PARK
Pitscottie
Ceres
Kingsbarns
Ladybank
FALKLAND PALACE
Fife Ness
Largoward
Crail
Freuchie
Carnbee
Kilrenny
Lundin Links
Anstruther
Kennoway
Kilconquhar
Pittenweem
Markinch
St Monans
Windygates
Leven
Elie
Isle of May
Largo Bay
Thornton
Buckhaven
East Wemyss
Firth of Forth
Kirkcaldy
0 10 20 miles
0 10 20 30 km
1: 440,000 7 miles to 1inch / 4.4 km to 1cm
A90
A92
A93
A980
A97
B976
B9119
B977
B974
B979
B9077
A957
B966
B967
B9120
A937
A935
A933
A934
B9134
B9113
B957
B951
B955
B954
A926
A928
A932
B9128
B965
B961
A94
B9127
B978
A923
A930
A85
B946
B945
A914
A919
A91
A913
B939
B940
A917
A915
B9131
A916
A912
B941
B9171
B921
A955
B925
43
35
D
E
F
1
2
3
4

40
47
36
46
A
B
C
1
2
3
4
Tarbert (An Tairbeart)
Caolas Scalpaigh
Scalpay (Eilean Scalpaigh)
East Loch Tarbert
Loch Claidh
Loch Bhrollum
Shiant Islands
Greenstone Point
Rubha Reidh
Cove
Melvaig
Poolewe
Gairloch
Gair Loch
Port Henderson
Redpoint
0 10 20 miles
0 10 20 30 km
1: 440,000 7 miles to 1inch / 4.4 km to 1cm
Rubha Hunish
Kilmaluag
Staffin Bay
Balgown
Staffin
Lochmaddy
Vaternish Point
Little Minch
Idrigil
Uig
Trotternish
Culnaknock
Ben Geary
284
Loch Snizort
Lusta
Dunvegan Head
Loch Dunvegan
Boreraig
Milovaig
DUNVEGAN CASTLE
Dunvegan
Roskhill
Healabhal Bheag
488
The Storr
719
Kensaleyre
Bernisdale
Carbost
Borve
Portree
Skye
Sound of Raasay
Rona
Brochel
Raasay
Oskaig
Clachan
Inner Sound
Fearnmore
Loch Torridon
Lower Diabaig
Inveralligan
Shieldaig
Applecross
Beinn Bhan
896
Toscaig
Loch Kishorn
Crowlin Islands
Loch Bracadale
Bracadale
Portnalong
Talisker
Carbost
Sligachan
Peinchorran
Sconser
Scalpay
Beinn Bhreac
445
Cuillin Hills
Luib
Broadford
Torrin
Bla Bheinn (Blaven)
928
Glenbrittle
Sgurr Alasdair
993
Loch Brittle
Duirinish
Kyle of Lochalsh
Balmacara
Kyleakin
Loch Alsh
Breakish
Kylerhea
Beinn na Seamraig
561
Glenelg
Soay
Loch Scavaig
Elgol
Loch Eishort
Sleat
Teangue
Sound of Sleat
Loch Hourn
Beinn Sgr
981
Sea of the Hebrides
Cuillin Sound
Canna
Sound of Canna
Kilmory
Rum (Rhum)
Kinloch
Askival
812
CLAN DONALD CENTRE
Ardvasar
Aird of Sleat
Point of Sleat
Mallaig
Ladhar Bhe
1020
Knoyd
A859
A855
A87
A850
A863
A851
B886
B884
B885
B883
B8009
B8083
B8021
B8057
B8056

41
D
E
F
44
42
37
Isles
Culnacraig
Isle Martin
Stornoway
Loch Broom
Ardmair
Ullapool
Beinn Ghobhlach
635
Gruinard Bay
Little Loch Broom
Coast
Badcaul
Leckmelm
Inverlael
A835
A832
An Teallach
1062
Loch na Sealga
Fionn Loch
Meall Liath Choire
548
Einig
Glen Einig
Oykel Bridge
Oykel
Invercassley
Lairg
A839
A836
SHIN FALLS
Linsidemore
Strathcarron
Bonar Bridge
Ardgay
Carron
Carn Chuinneag
898
Beinn Dearg
1084
CORRIESHALLOCH GORGE
EASTER ROSS
Beinn Tharsuinn
692
Braeantra
Beinn nan Eun
742
Loch Morie
Averon
Boath
Dalnav
Alness
Loch Glass
Ben Wyvis
1046
Evanton
B817
B9176
Cromarty Firth
Mullach Coire Mhic Fhearchair
1019
Loch Maree
Sgurr Mor
1110
Loch Glascarnoch
Aultguish Inn
Black Water
20
Slioch
980
WESTER ROSS
A832
BEINN EIGHE NATURE RESERVE
Kinlochewe
A896
Loch Fannich
Grudie
Garve
Loch Luichart
Loch Garve
Dingwall
A862
A834
Strathpeffer
Contin
Culbokie
Black Isle
B9163
B9169
Achnasheen
Liathach
1054
Sgurr a'Mhuilinn
879
A835
Conon Bridge
Marybank
Strathconon
Tore
A9
Orrin Reservoir
Orrin
A832
Muir of Ord
Redcastle
Munlochy
North Kessock
Beauly Firth
Sgorr Ruadh
960
A890
Craig
Balnacra
Sgurr a'Chaorachain
1053
Sgurr a'Choire Ghlais
1083
Beauly
A831
A862
A833
Achintee
Loch Monar
Farrar
Beauly
Dochgarroch
Ness
Attadale
Carron
Lochend
B862
Strathglass
Ling
Glen Cannich
Aonach Buidhe
899
Loch Mullardoch
Cannich
LOCH NESS MONSTER EXHIBITION CENTRE
Milton
Drumnadrochit
URQUHART CASTLE
Dores
Loch Ashie
Loch Duntelchaig
Loch Long
Dornie
EILEAN DONAN CASTLE
Carn Eighe
1183
Loch Affric
Glen Affric
A82
B852
B862
B851
Loch Ness
Meal Fuar-mhonaidh
696
Errogie
Foyers
Loch Mhor
Carn Odhar
802
Bridge
Sgurr Fhuaran
1068
Invermoriston
Glen Shiel
A'Chralaig
1120
Dundreggan
Feehlin
A87
A887
Moriston
Glen Moriston
Glen Mòr
Fort Augustus
Aonach air Chrith
1021
Loch Cluanie
Meall Dubh
788
FORT AUGUSTUS ABBEY VISITOR CENTRE
Monadhliath Mountains
Kinloch Hourn
Oich
Carn a'Chuilinn
816
Carn Dearg
945
Loch Loyne
Loch Quoich
Garry
Loch Garry
Invergarry
Loch Oich
Glen Garry
Geal Charn
926
Kingie
Laggan
Carn Dearg
816
Sron a'Choire Ghairbh
Spey
Newton
Garvamore
Laggan
1040

A
B
C
1
2
3
4
45
41
38
Lairg
Strath Fleet
Rogart
Pittentrail
A839
Brora
Golspie
A9
Loch Fleet
Bonar Bridge
A949
Clashmore
Dornoch
Spinningdale
A836
Dornoch Firth
Edderton
Tain
Tarbat Ness
Kirkwall
Portmahomack
Tarrel
B9165
B9166
Hill of Fearn
B9175
Balintore
Beinn Tharsuinn
692
Cnoc an t-Sabhail
379
B9176
Dalnavie
Tomich
Barbaraville
Nigg Bay
Balnapaling
Alness
Invergordon
B817
Moray Firth
Lossiemouth
Hopeman
B9040
Burghead
Burghead Bay
B9013
B9012
A941
Kingston
Spey Bay
Cromarty Firth
Balblair
Cromarty
B9163
Cullicudden
Jemimaville
A832
B9160
Findhorn
B9011
B9089
Alves
Elgin
Lhanbryde
B9103
B9104
Kinloss
A96
Johnstons Cashmere Visitor Centre
Pluscarden Priory
Mosstodloch
Baxters Visitor Centre
Black Isle
Culbokie
B9169
Rosemarkie
Fortrose
Dyke
Forres
Nairn
Rafford
Longmorn
Auldearn
B9006
Ardersier
B9010
Kellas
Avoch
A832
B9092
B9091
B9101
A940
Lossie
Munlochy
Inverness
A939
Cawdor
Littlemill
Mill Buie
371
Dallas
B9015
Ben Aigan
471
North Kessock
Moray Firth
A96
Croy
Cawdor Castle
Beauly Firth
Inverness Museum & Art Gallery
A862
Rothes
B9007
Ferness
Craigellachie
B9102
Culloden Visitor Centre
A82
A9
B851
Upper Knockando
A941
Aberlour
B9014
Spey
Dufftown
Glenfiddich Distillery
Ness
B861
Daviot
Findhorn
Lochindorb
A939
Dava
Carne na Loine
549
Strathspey
Marypark
A95
Ben Rinnes
840
Loch Ashie
Nairn
B9154
B851
Moy
Dores
Farr
B9008
B9009
Fiddich
Loch Duntelchaig
Tomatin
Carn Glas-choire
659
B9007
Grantown-on-Spey
Bridgend
Cook's Cairn
755
Hills of Cromdale
B9136
Tomnavoulin
Glenlivet
A938
Dulnain Bridge
Lynemore
Knockandhu
Strath Dearn
Carrbridge
Nethy Bridge
Carn Odhar
802
Dulnain
Loch Garten Nature Reserve
Carn Mor
804
Ladder Hills
Boat of Garten
Tomintoul
Findhorn
Abernethy Forest
Cnoc Fraing
745
B970
Strathspey Railway
Lecht Ski Centre
Monadhliath Mountains
Aviemore
Glenmore Forest Park
Geal Charn
821
Carn Ealasaid
792
Strathdon
A944
Coylumbridge
Alvie
Loch an Eilein Visitor Centre
Cock Bridge
Colnabaichin
Don
Highland Wildlife Park
Kincraig
Cairngorm Ski Centre
Cairn Gorm
1245
Glen Avon
Avon
Carn Dearg
945
Feshiebridge
B9152
Ben Avon
1171
Kingussie
Cairngorm Mountains
B970
Ben Macdui
1309
Culardoch
900
B976
Newtonmore
Spey
Glen Feshie
Cairngorms Nature Reserve
Cairn Toul
1291
A86
Laggan
Glen Tromie
Braemar
Beinn
Balmoral

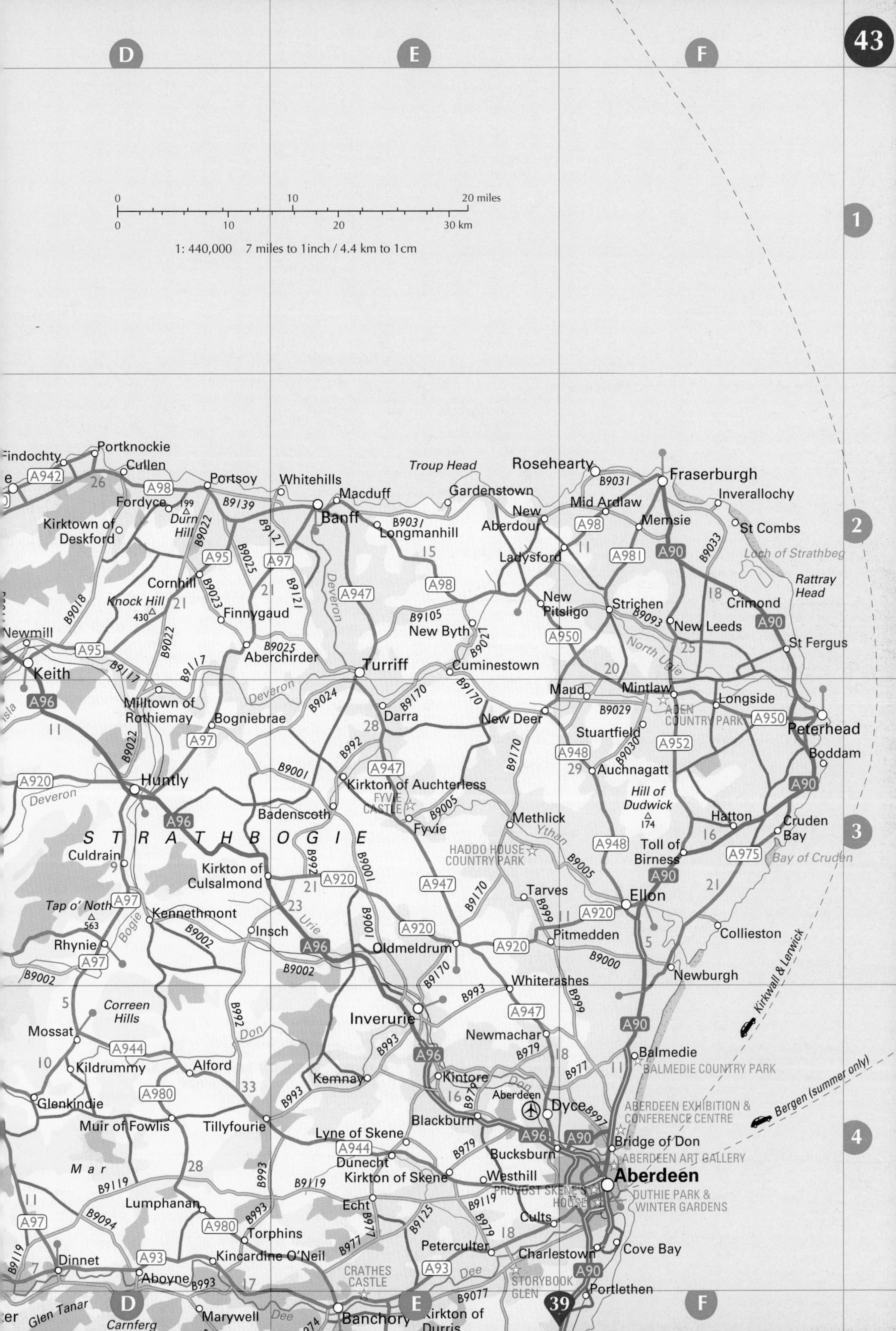
D
E
F
1
2
3
4
0
10
20 miles
0
10
20
30 km
1: 440,000 7 miles to 1inch / 4.4 km to 1cm
Findochty
Portknockie
Cullen
A942
26
A98
Portsoy
Whitehills
Macduff
Troup Head
Gardenstown
Rosehearty
B9031
Fraserburgh
Inverallochy
Mid Ardlaw
Memsie
St Combs
Fordyce
199
Durn Hill
B9139
Banff
B9031
Longmanhill
New Aberdour
A98
Kirktown of Deskford
B9022
B9121
15
Ladysford
11
A981
A90
B9033
Loch of Strathbeg
A95
B9025
A97
Rattray Head
Cornhill
B9023
21
B9121
Deveron
A947
A98
18
Crimond
B9018
Knock Hill
430
21
Finnygaud
New Pitsligo
Strichen
B9093
New Leeds
B9105
New Byth
A90
Newmill
B9022
B9025
Aberchirder
B9021
A950
North Ugie
25
St Fergus
A95
Keith
B9117
B9117
Turriff
Cuminestown
20
A96
Milltown of Rothiemay
Deveron
B9024
B9170
B9170
Maud
Mintlaw
Longside
11
Bogniebrae
Darra
B9029
ADEN COUNTRY PARK
A950
Peterhead
B9022
A97
28
New Deer
Stuartfield
A952
B9030
Boddam
B992
B9170
A948
A920
B9001
A947
29
Auchnagatt
A90
Deveron
Huntly
Kirkton of Auchterless
Hill of Dudwick
174
FYVIE CASTLE
B9005
A96
Badenscoth
Methlick
Hatton
Cruden Bay
Fyvie
Ythan
16
STRATHBOGIE
B992
B9001
HADDO HOUSE COUNTRY PARK
A948
Toll of Birness
A975
Bay of Cruden
Culdrain
9
Kirkton of Culsalmond
A920
B9005
A90
21
A947
Tarves
Ellon
Tap o' Noth
563
A97
23
B9170
B999
A920
Kennethmont
Urie
Bogie
B9002
Insch
B9001
A920
Pitmedden
5
Collieston
Rhynie
A96
Oldmeldrum
A920
B9000
A97
B9002
B9002
B9170
Whiterashes
Newburgh
Kirkwall & Lerwick
5
Correen Hills
B992
B993
B999
Mossat
Don
Inverurie
A947
A90
A944
B993
Newmachar
10
Kildrummy
Alford
A96
B979
18
Balmedie
BALMEDIE COUNTRY PARK
33
Kemnay
Kintore
B977
11
Glenkindie
A980
B993
16
Don
Aberdeen
Dyce
B997
ABERDEEN EXHIBITION & CONFERENCE CENTRE
Bergen (summer only)
Muir of Fowlis
Tillyfourie
Blackburn
A96
A90
Lyne of Skene
B979
Bridge of Don
A944
Bucksburn
ABERDEEN ART GALLERY
Mar
28
Dunecht
B9119
B9119
Kirkton of Skene
Westhill
Aberdeen
11
B993
PROVOST SKENE'S HOUSE
DUTHIE PARK & WINTER GARDENS
Lumphanan
Echt
B9119
B9094
B993
B977
B9125
B979
Cults
A97
A980
Torphins
18
Peterculter
Charlestown
Cove Bay
Kincardine O'Neil
B977
Dinnet
A93
CRATHES CASTLE
A93
Dee
STORYBOOK GLEN
A90
B9119
7
Aboyne
B993
17
B9077
Portlethen
Glen Tanar
Marywell
Dee
Banchory
Kirkton of Durris
Carnferg
39

44
A
B
C
1
2
3
4
Cape Wrath
Kyle of Durness
Durness
Whiten Head
Tongue Bay
Skerra
A838
Portnacon
Loch Eriboll
37
A838
A836
Kyle of Tongue
12
Borgie
Tongue
Kinlochbervie
B801
Loch Inchard
Achriesgill
A838
19
Cranstackie
802
Eriboll
Loch Hope
Loch Laxford
Rhiconich
Foinaven
915
Ben Hope
927
Ben Loyal
764
Beinn Stumanadh
527
17
Laxford Bridge
Arkle
787
Handa Island
Loch Loyal
Scourie
Ben Stack
721
Loch Stack
Strathmore
Allnabad
Syre
A894
B873
Loch Meadie
Achfary
A836
25
A838
Loch More
Ben Hee
873
Altnaharra
Loch Naver
Point of Stoer
Eddrachillis Bay
Kylestrome
Drumbeg
B869
Unapool
S U T H E R L A
Clashnessie
Beinn Leoid
792
Quinag
808
961
Ben Klibreck
Strath Vagastie
Stoer
Clachtoll
Glas Bheinn
776
Loch Choire
B869
10
A837
A894
Loch Assynt
37
Crask Inn
Lochinver
Inchnadamph
A838
Ben More Assynt
998
Rubha Coigeach
Inverkirkaig
Suilven
731
Canisp
846
9
A837
21
Enard Bay
Loch Shin
A836
Loch Sionascaig
Cul Mor
849
Ledmore
Shinness Lodge
Stac Pollaidh
613
Elphin
Cassley
Achiltibuie
INVEREWE GARDENS
Summer Isles
Loch Lurgainn
A835
A837
Glen Oykel
Lairg
17
18
8
Strath Fleet
Culnacraig
A839
Invercassley
Pitter
Isle Martin
Stornoway
Oykel Bridge
Oykel
SHIN FALLS
A836
Loch Broom
Glen Einig
Einig
11
Ardmair
Meall Liath Choire
548
Linsidemore
Gruinard Bay
Beinn Ghobhlach
635
12
A836
Ullapool
Strathcarron
42
Bonar Bridge
Coast
Badcaul
Little Loch Broom
Leckmelm
Ardgay
8
A9
Spinningdale
Carron
12
A836
Inverlael
15
Edderton
An Teallach
1062
Carn Chuinneag
898
B9176
Loch na Sealga
A835
Beinn Dearg
1084
Beinn Tharsuinn
692
A832
E A S T E R R
Fionn Loch
41
CORRIESHALLOCH GORGE
Beinn nan Eun
Braeantra
Cnoc t-Sab
379

45
48
42
D
E
F
1
2
3
4
Longhope
Pentland Firth
Stromness
(Summer only)
Swona
Burwick
Brough Ness
Island of Stroma
Dunnet Head
John o' Groats
Duncansby Head
Brough
Mey
Barrock
Dunnet
Dunnet Bay
Thurso Bay
Scrabster
Thurso
Castletown
Strathy Point
Strathy
Melvich
Dounreay
Buldoo
Reay
Freswick
Loch Heilen
Keiss
Sinclair's Bay
Noss Head
Reiss
Loch Calder
Halkirk
Roadside
Loch Watten
Watten
Olgrinmore
Spittal
Mybster
Bilbster
Westerdale
Wick
Badlipster
Strath Halladale
CAITHNESS
Forsinard
Loch More
Thurso
Thrumster
Achavanich
Ulbster
Halladale
Lybster
Latheron
Latheronwheel
Kinbrace
Helmsdale
Morven 706
Scaraben 626
Dunbeath
Borgue
Newport
Berriedale
Strath of Kildonan
Kildonan Lodge
Helmsdale
Lothmore
Loch Brora
Ben Horn 521
Rogart
Brora
Golspie
Loch Fleet
Dornoch
Dornoch Firth
Tarbat Ness
Portmahomack
Tain
Tarrel
of Fearn
A836
A9
A99
A882
A897
A839
A961
B870
B874
B876
B871
B9165
B9166
0 10 20 miles
0 10 20 30 km
1: 440,000 7 miles to 1inch / 4.4 km to 1cm

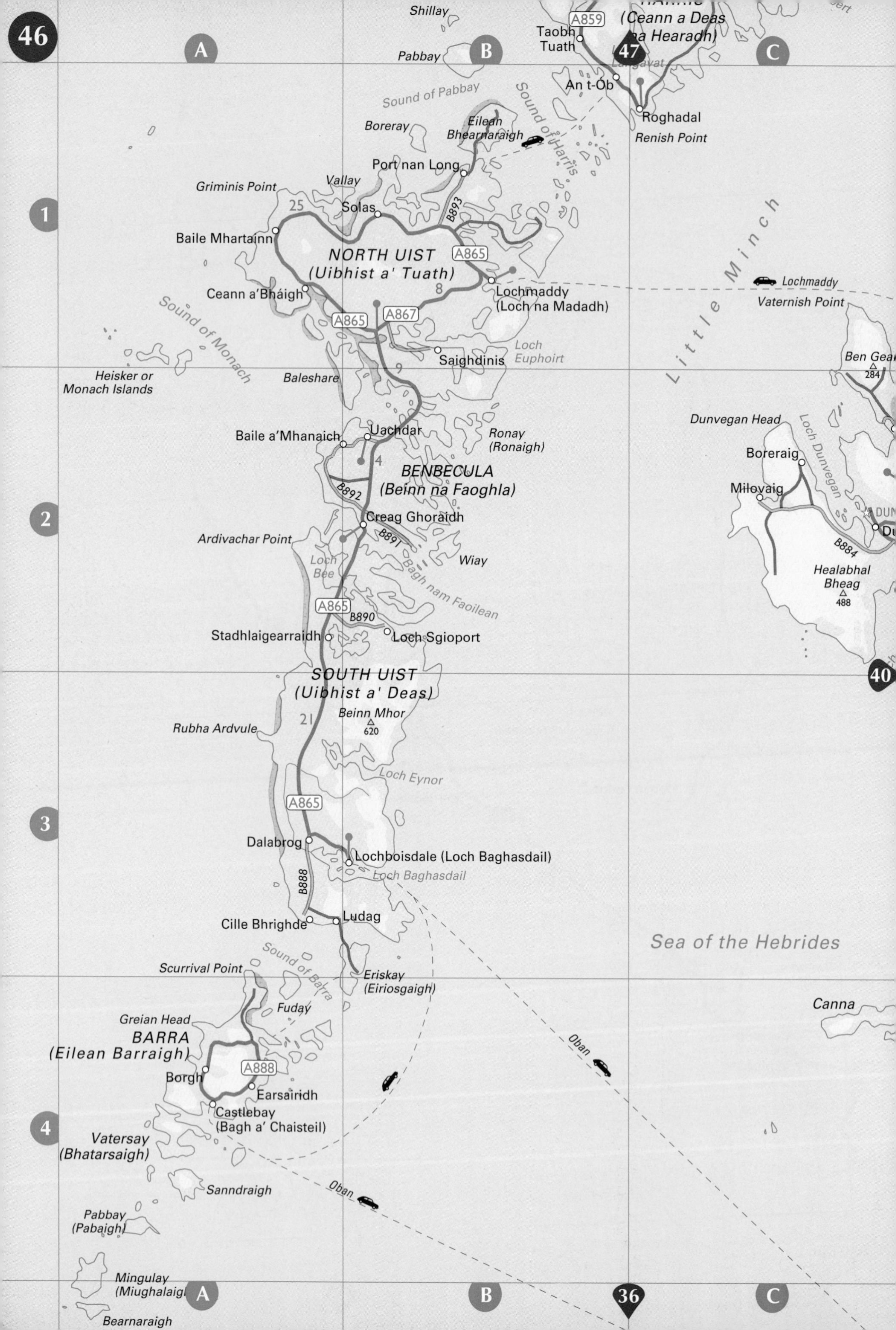

A
B
C
1
2
3
4
47
40
36
Shillay
Pabbay
A859
Taobh Tuath
(Ceann a Deas na Hearadh)
An t-Òb
Roghadal
Renish Point
Sound of Pabbay
Sound of Harris
Boreray
Eilean Bhearnaraigh
Port nan Long
Vallay
Griminis Point
Solas
Baile Mhartainn
B893
NORTH UIST
(Uibhist a' Tuath)
A865
Lochmaddy
(Loch na Madadh)
Ceann a'Bháigh
A867
Sound of Monach
Saighdinis
Loch Euphoirt
Little Minch
Lochmaddy
Vaternish Point
Ben Geary
284
Heisker or
Monach Islands
Baleshare
Dunvegan Head
Loch Dunvegan
Baile a'Mhanaich
Uachdar
Ronay
(Ronaigh)
Boreraig
BENBECULA
(Beinn na Faoghla)
B892
Milovaig
Creag Ghoraidh
B891
Ardivachar Point
Loch Bee
Wiay
Bagh nam Faoilean
B884
Healabhal Bheag
488
A865
B890
Stadhlaigearraidh
Loch Sgioport
SOUTH UIST
(Uibhist a' Deas)
Beinn Mhor
620
Rubha Ardvule
Loch Eynor
A865
Dalabrog
Lochboisdale (Loch Baghasdail)
Loch Baghasdail
B888
Cille Bhrighde
Ludag
Sea of the Hebrides
Sound of Barra
Scurrival Point
Eriskay
(Eiriosgaigh)
Fuday
Canna
Greian Head
BARRA
(Eilean Barraigh)
A888
Oban
Borgh
Earsairidh
Castlebay
(Bagh a' Chaisteil)
Vatersay
(Bhatarsaigh)
Sanndraigh
Oban
Pabbay
(Pabaigh)
Mingulay
(Miughalaigh
Bearnaraigh

0 10 20 miles
0 10 20 30 km
1: 440,000 7 miles to 1inch / 4.4 km to 1cm
Rubha Robhanais
Eoropaidh
Port Nis
Tabost
Sgiogarstaigh
Dail Bho Thuath
A857
Muirneag 248
Tolastadh Úr
Tolsta Head
Barabhas
Arnol
Bragar
Siabost
A858
ISLE OF LEWIS
(Eilean Leodhais)
Griais
Carlabhagh
East Loch Roag
West Loch Roag
Beinn Mholach 292
B895
Rubha an t-Siumpain
Port nan Giúran
Loch a' Tuath
Tunga
Tolastadh a'Chaolais
Great Bernera
Breascleit
Stornoway (Steornabhagh)
Newmarket
Siulaisiadar
Miabhig
Timsgearraidh
Calanais
Crulabhig
A866
An Rubha
Gearraidh na h-Aibhne
B8059
Loch Suainaval
B8011
Achadh Mór
A859
B897
Mealisval 574
Breanais
Einacleit
Crosbost
Loch Erisort
Mealasta Island
NORTH HARRIS
(Ceann a Tuath na Hearadh)
Baile Ailein
Ullapool
Cearsiadar
B8060
Loch Langavat
Airidh a'Bhruaich
Scarp
Loch Resort
Grabhair
Kebock Head
B8060
Huisinis
Tirga Mor 679
Leumrabhagh
Beinn Mhór 572
Loch Shell
Abhainnsuidhe
B887
Clishham 799
Loch Seaforth
Loch Claidh
Aird Asaig
Taransay (Taransaigh)
Tarbert (An Tairbeart)
Loch Bhrollum
Sound of Taransay
Caolas Scalpaigh
Shiant Islands
East Loch Tarbert
SOUTH HARRIS
(Ceann a Deas na Hearadh)
Scalpay (Eilean Scalpaigh)
Taobh Tuath
Loch Langavat
An t-Òb
Roghadal
Renish Point
Sound of Harris
Rubha Hunish
Kilmaluag
Staffin Bay
A855
Balgown
Staffin
Lochmaddy (Loch na Madadh)
Vaternish Point
Little Minch
Idrigil
Uig
Trotternish
Culnaknock
Loch Euphoirt
Ben Geary 284
Loch Snizort
A87
Rona
Fearnmore
Redpoint

46
40

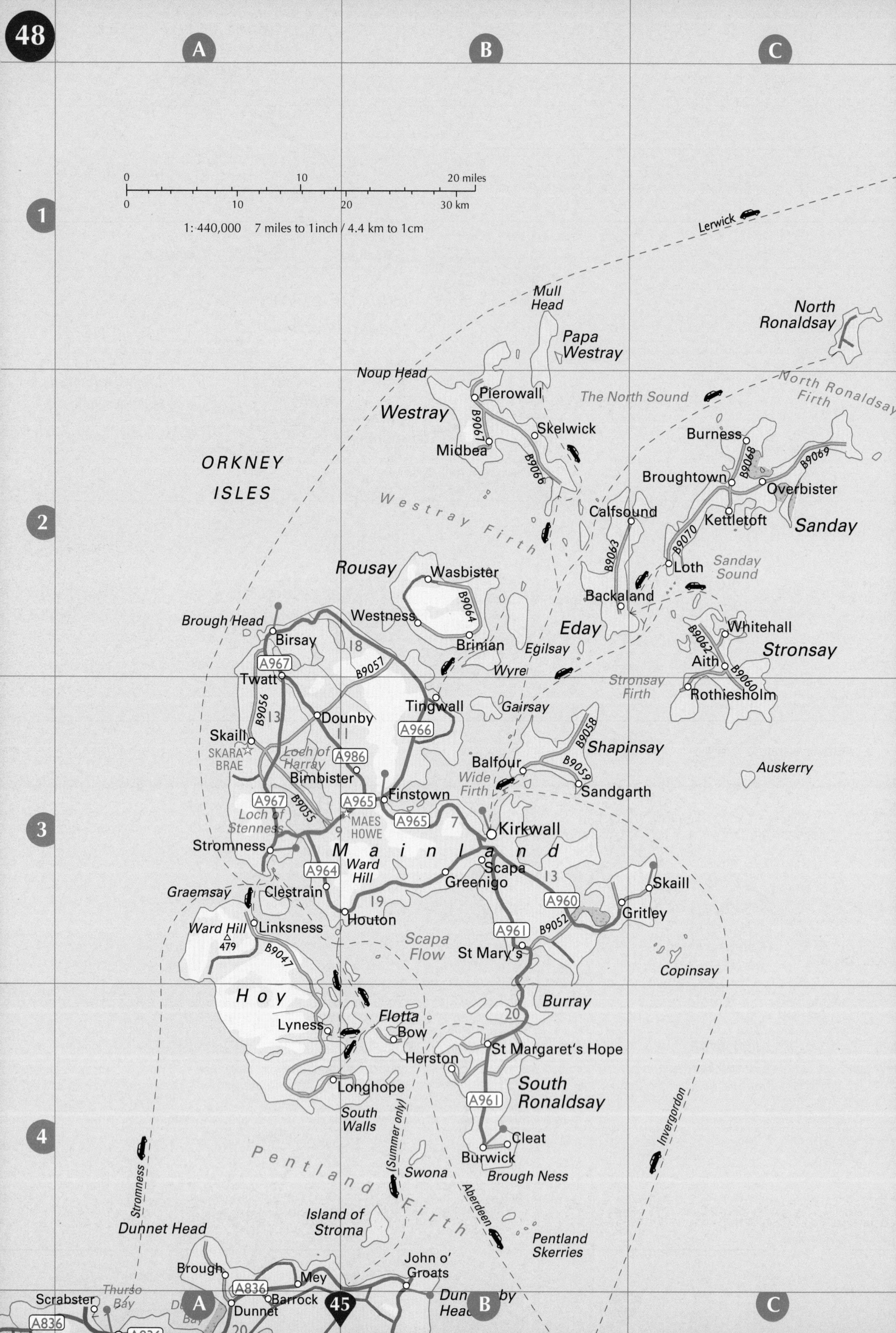
A
B
C
1
2
3
4
0
10
20 miles
0
10
20
30 km
1: 440,000 7 miles to 1inch / 4.4 km to 1cm
ORKNEY ISLES
Lerwick
Mull Head
Papa Westray
North Ronaldsay
Noup Head
Pierowall
Westray
The North Sound
North Ronaldsay Firth
Skelwick
Midbea
B9067
B9066
Burness
B9068
B9069
Broughtown
Overbister
Kettletoft
Sanday
Calfsound
B9070
Westray Firth
B9063
Loth
Sanday Sound
Rousay
Wasbister
Backaland
B9064
Westness
Eday
Whitehall
Brough Head
Birsay
Brinian
Egilsay
B9062
Stronsay
A967
18
Aith
B9057
Wyre
Twatt
Stronsay Firth
B9060
Rothiesholm
B9056
Tingwall
Gairsay
13
Dounby
A966
B9058
Skaill
11
Shapinsay
SKARA BRAE
Loch of Harray
A986
B9059
Auskerry
Bimbister
Balfour
Wide Firth
Sandgarth
A967
B9055
A965
Finstown
Loch of Stenness
MAES HOWE
A965
7
Kirkwall
9
Stromness
Mainland
Ward Hill
Scapa
A964
13
Skaill
Greenigo
Graemsay
Clestrain
A960
Gritley
19
Houton
Ward Hill
Linksness
479
A961
B9052
Scapa Flow
St Mary's
B9047
Copinsay
Hoy
Burray
20
Flotta
Lyness
Bow
St Margaret's Hope
Herston
Longhope
South Ronaldsay
A961
South Walls
Cleat
(Summer only)
Burwick
Invergordon
Stromness
Pentland Firth
Swona
Brough Ness
Aberdeen
Island of Stroma
Dunnet Head
Pentland Skerries
Brough
John o' Groats
Mey
A836
Thurso Bay
Barrock
Scrabster
Dunnet
45
A836
A836
20

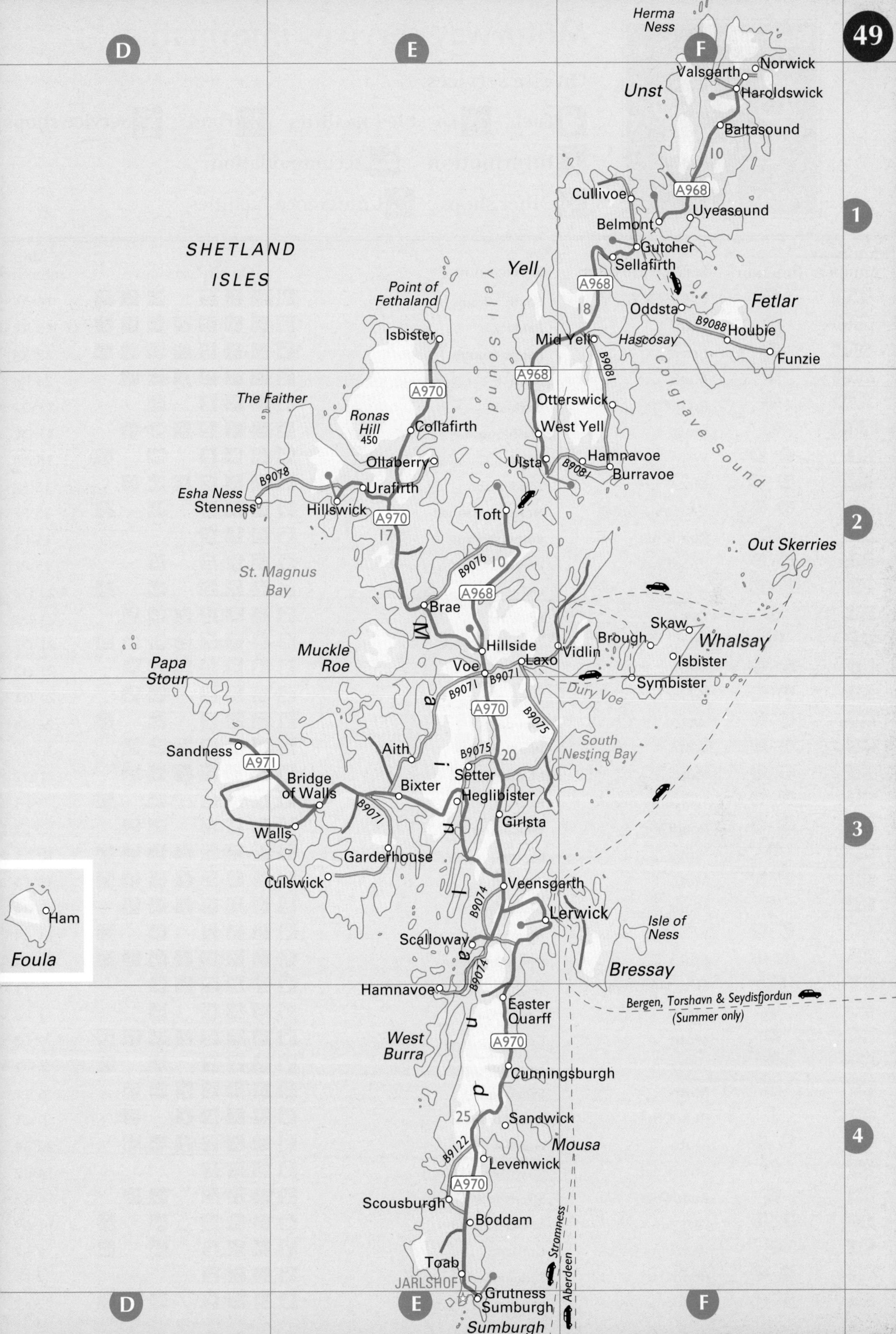

SHETLAND ISLES
Herma Ness
Norwick
Valsgarth
Unst
Haroldswick
Baltasound
A968
Cullivoe
Uyeasound
Belmont
Gutcher
Sellafirth
Yell
Yell Sound
Point of Fethaland
Oddsta
Fetlar
B9088
Houbie
Isbister
Mid Yell
Hascosay
Funzie
B9081
Colgrave Sound
A970
The Faither
Ronas Hill 450
Collafirth
Otterswick
West Yell
Ollaberry
Ulsta
Hamnavoe
Burravoe
B9078
Urafirth
Esha Ness
Stenness
Hillswick
Toft
Out Skerries
St. Magnus Bay
B9076
Brae
Mainland
Skaw
Whalsay
Brough
Muckle Roe
Hillside
Vidlin
Isbister
Papa Stour
Voe
Laxo
Symbister
B9071
Dury Voe
B9075
South Nesting Bay
Sandness
A971
Aith
Setter
Bridge of Walls
Bixter
Heglibister
Girlsta
Walls
Garderhouse
Culswick
Veensgarth
Ham
B9074
Lerwick
Isle of Ness
Foula
Scalloway
Bressay
Hamnavoe
Easter Quarff
Bergen, Torshavn & Seydisfjordun (Summer only)
West Burra
Cunningsburgh
Sandwick
Mousa
B9122
Levenwick
Scousburgh
Boddam
Stromness
Toab
Aberdeen
JARLSHOF
Grutness
Sumburgh
Sumburgh
D
E
F
1
2
3
4

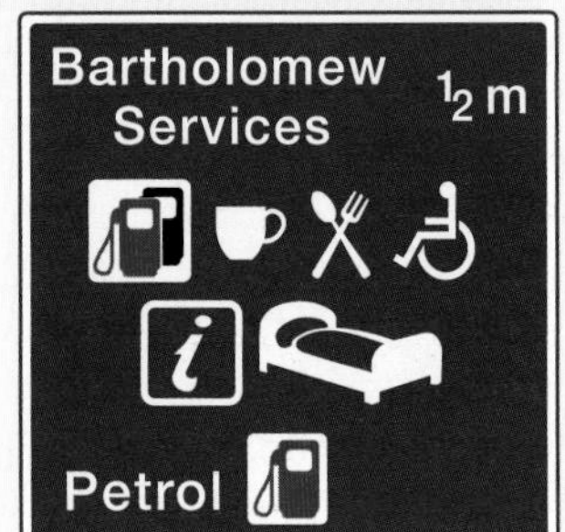

Motorway services information

On-site services:

Fuel · Disabled facilities · Food · Service shops · Information · Accommodation · Other shops · Conference facilities

Motorway number	Junction	Service provider	Service name	Fuel	Disabled facilities	Food	Service shops	Information	Accommodation	Other shops	Conference facilities	Map reference
A1(M)	1	Welcome Break	South Mimms	✓	✓	✓	✓		✓	✓	✓	16 A4
A1(M)	10	Extra	Baldock	✓	✓	✓	✓	✓	✓	✓	✓	16 A2
A1(M)	17	Extra	Peterborough	✓	✓	✓	✓	✓	✓	✓	✓	22 A4
A1(M)	34	Moto	Blyth	✓	✓	✓	✓	✓	✓	✓		26 B4
A1(M)	61	RoadChef	Durham	✓	✓	✓	✓		✓			31 D2
A1(M)	64	Moto	Washington	✓	✓	✓	✓	✓	✓	✓		31 D2
M1	2–4	Welcome Break	London Gateway	✓	✓	✓	✓		✓		✓	16 A4
M1	11–12	Moto	Toddington	✓	✓	✓	✓	✓	✓	✓		15 F2
M1	14–15	Welcome Break	Newport Pagnell	✓	✓	✓	✓		✓		✓	15 F2
M1	15A	RoadChef	Rothersthorpe	✓	✓	✓	✓					15 E1
M1	16–17	RoadChef	Watford Gap	✓	✓	✓	✓		✓			15 E1
M1	21–21A	Welcome Break	Leicester Forest East	✓	✓	✓	✓		✓		✓	21 D3
M1	22	Moto	Leicester	✓	✓	✓	✓	✓	✓	✓		21 D3
M1	23A	Moto	Donington Park	✓	✓	✓	✓	✓	✓	✓	✓	21 D3
M1	25–26	Moto	Trowell	✓	✓	✓	✓	✓	✓	✓		21 D2
M1	28–29	RoadChef	Tibshelf	✓	✓	✓	✓		✓	✓		21 D1
M1	30–31	Welcome Break	Woodall	✓	✓	✓	✓		✓		✓	26 A4
M1	38–39	Moto	Woolley Edge	✓	✓	✓	✓	✓	✓	✓		26 A3
M2	4–5	Moto	Medway	✓	✓	✓	✓	✓	✓	✓		11 D2
M3	4A–5	Welcome Break	Fleet	✓	✓	✓	✓		✓		✓	9 F1
M3	8–9	RoadChef	Winchester	✓	✓	✓	✓		✓	✓		9 E2
M4	3	Moto	Heston	✓	✓	✓	✓	✓	✓	✓	✓	10 A1
M4	11–12	Moto	Reading	✓	✓	✓	✓	✓	✓	✓	✓	9 E1
M4	13	Moto	Chieveley	✓	✓	✓	✓	✓	✓	✓		15 D4
M4	14–15	Welcome Break	Membury	✓	✓	✓	✓		✓		✓	14 C4
M4	17–18	Moto	Leigh Delamere	✓	✓	✓	✓	✓	✓	✓	✓	14 B4
M4	23A	First Motorway	Magor	✓	✓	✓	✓	✓	✓			7 F1
M4	30	Moto	Cardiff Gate	✓	✓	✓	✓		✓			7 E2
M4	33	Moto	Cardiff	✓	✓	✓	✓	✓	✓	✓	✓	7 E2
M4	36	Welcome Break	Sarn Park	✓	✓	✓	✓		✓		✓	7 D2
M4	47	Moto	Swansea	✓	✓	✓	✓	✓	✓	✓		6 C1
M4	49	RoadChef	Pont Abraham	✓	✓	✓	✓	✓		✓		6 C1
M5	3–4	Moto	Frankley	✓	✓	✓	✓	✓	✓	✓		20 B4
M5	8	RoadChef	Strensham (South)	✓	✓	✓	✓					14 B2
M5	8	RoadChef	Strensham (North)	✓	✓	✓	✓		✓	✓		14 B2
M5	13–14	Welcome Break	Michael Wood	✓	✓	✓	✓		✓		✓	14 A4
M5	19	Welcome Break	Gordano	✓	✓	✓	✓		✓		✓	7 F2
M5	21–22	RoadChef	Sedgemoor (South)	✓	✓	✓	✓					7 F3
M5	21–22	Welcome Break	Sedgemoor (North)	✓	✓	✓	✓		✓		✓	7 F3

Motorway number	Junction	Service provider	Service name	On-site services	
M5	24	Moto	Bridgwater		7 F4
M5	25–26	RoadChef	Taunton Deane		7 E4
M5	28	Margram	Cullompton		5 E1
M5	29–30	Moto	Exeter		5 D1
M6	3–4	Welcome Break	Corley		20 C4
M6	10–11	Moto	Hilton Park		20 B3
M6	14–15	RoadChef	Stafford (South)		20 B2
M6	14–15	Moto	Stafford (North)		20 B2
M6	15–16	Welcome Break	Keele		20 A2
M6	16–17	RoadChef	Sandbach		20 A1
M6	18–19	Moto	Knutsford		20 A1
M6	27–28	Welcome Break	Charnock Richard		25 D3
M6	32–33	Moto	Lancaster		25 D2
M6	35A–36	Moto	Burton-in-Kendal (North)		25 D1
M6	36–37	RoadChef	Killington Lake (South)		30 A4
M6	38–39	Westmorland	Tebay		30 A4
M6	41–42	Moto	Southwaite		29 F2
M8	4–5	RoadChef	Harthill		34 A2
M9	9	Moto	Stirling		34 A1
M11	8	Welcome Break	Birchanger Green		16 B3
M18	5	Moto	Doncaster North		26 B3
M20	8	RoadChef	Maidstone		11 D2
M23	11	Moto	Pease Pottage		10 B3
M25	5–6	RoadChef	Clacket Lane		10 C2
M25	23	Welcome Break	South Mimms		16 A4
M25	30	Moto	Thurrock		10 C1
M27	3–4	RoadChef	Rownhams		9 D3
M40	8	Welcome Break	Oxford		15 E3
M40	10	Moto	Cherwell Valley		15 D2
M40	12–13	Welcome Break	Warwick		15 D1
M42	2	Welcome Break	Hopwood Park		14 B1
M42	10	Moto	Tamworth		20 C3
M48	1	Moto	Severn View		14 A4
M50	4	Welcome Break	Ross Spur		14 A2
M56	14	RoadChef	Chester		19 F1
M61	6–7	First Motorway	Bolton West		25 D3
M62	7–9	Welcome Break	Burtonwood		25 D4
M62	18–19	Moto	Birch		25 E3
M62	25–26	Welcome Break	Hartshead Moor		25 F3
M62	33	Moto	Ferrybridge		26 A3
M65	4	Supermart	Blackburn Interchange		19 F1
M74	4–5	RoadChef	Bothwell (South)		33 F2
M74	5–6	RoadChef	Hamilton (North)		33 F2
M74	11–12	Cairn Lodge	Happendon		34 A3
M74	12–13	Welcome Break	Abington		34 A3
A74(M)	16	RoadChef	Annandale Water		34 B4
A74(M)	22	Welcome Break	Gretna Green		29 F1
M90	6	Moto	Kinross		38 C4

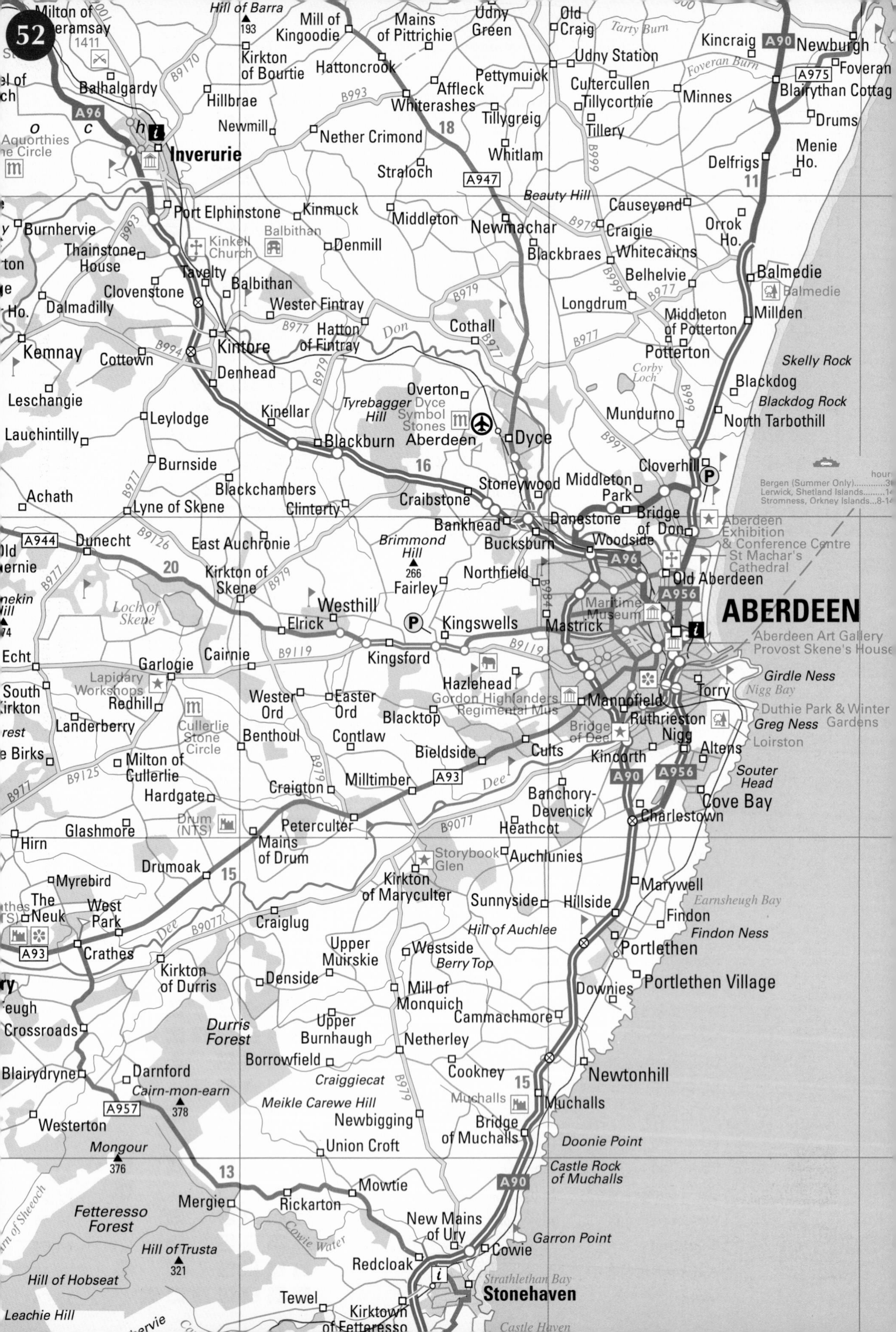
Inverurie
Kintore
Kemnay
Dyce
Aberdeen
ABERDEEN
Westhill
Newmachar
Balmedie
Newburgh
Portlethen
Newtonhill
Stonehaven
Cove Bay
Peterculter
Cults
Bieldside
Milltimber
Blackburn
Kingswells
Bucksburn
Danestone
Bridge of Don
Old Aberdeen
Mastrick
Mannofield
Torry
Nigg
Altens
Kincorth
Charlestown
Muchalls
Cowie
Drumoak
Crathes
Echt
Dunecht
Udny Station
Potterton
Hatton of Fintray
Aberdeen Exhibition & Conference Centre
St Machar's Cathedral
Maritime Museum
Aberdeen Art Gallery
Provost Skene's House
Gordon Highlanders Regimental Mus
Duthie Park & Winter Gardens
Storybook Glen
Drum (NTS)
Cullerlie Stone Circle
Dyce Symbol Stones
Kinkell Church
Bergen (Summer Only)
Lerwick, Shetland Islands
Stromness, Orkney Islands
Girdle Ness
Greg Ness
Souter Head
Findon Ness
Doonie Point
Garron Point
Skelly Rock
Blackdog Rock
Durris Forest
Fetteresso Forest
A90
A96
A93
A944
A947
A956
A957
A975
B979
B977
B9119
B9077

Area Code 01224

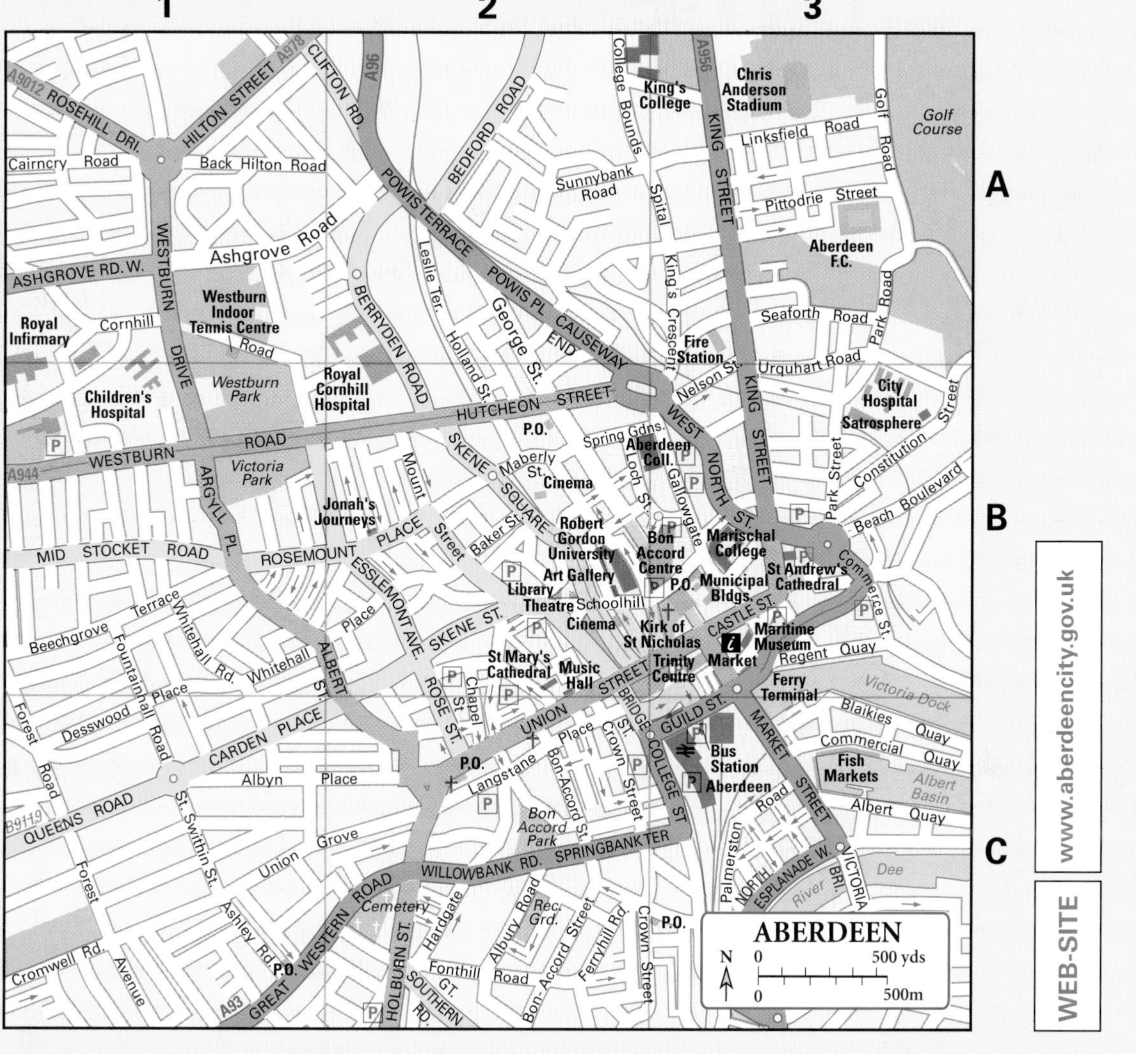

ABERDEEN

WEB-SITE www.aberdeencity.gov.uk

LOCAL RADIO BBC RADIO SCOTLAND 93.9 FM & 810 AM NORTHSOUND 1 96.9 FM, NORTHSOUND 2 1035 AM

INDEX TO STREET NAMES

Street	Grid
Albert Quay	C3
Albert Street	B2
Albury Road	C2
Albyn Place	C1
Argyll Place	B1
Ashgrove Road	A1
Ashgrove Road West	A1
Ashley Road	C1
Back Hilton Road	A1
Baker Street	B2
Beach Boulevard	B3
Bedford Road	A2
Beechgrove Terrace	B1
Berryden Road	A2
Blaikie's Quay	C3
Bon-Accord Street	C2
Bridge Street	B2
Cairncry Road	A1
Carden Place	C1
Castle Street	B3
Causewayend	A2
Chapel Street	B2
Clifton Road	A1
College Bounds	A2
College Street	C3
Commerce Street	B3
Commercial Quay	C3
Constitution Street	B3
Cornhill Road	A1
Cromwell Road	C1
Crown Street	C2
Desswood Place	C1
Esslemont Avenue	B2
Ferryhill Road	C2
Fonthill Road	C2
Forest Road	C1
Forest Avenue	C1
Fountainhall Road	B1
Gallowgate	B3
George Street	A2
Golf Road	A3
Great Southern Road	C2
Great Western Road	C1
Guild Street	C3
Hardgate	C2
Hilton Street	A1
Holburn Street	C2
Holland Street	A2
Hutcheon Street	B2
King's Crescent	A3
King Street	A3
Langstane Place	C2
Leslie Terrace	A2
Linksfield Road	A3
Loch Street	B2
Maberly Street	B2
Market Street	C3
Mid Stocket Road	B1
Mount Street	B2
Nelson Street	B3
North Esplanade West	C3
Palmerston Road	C3
Park Road	A3
Park Street	B3
Pittodrie Street	A3
Powis Place	A2
Powis Terrace	A2
Queens Road	C1
Regent Quay	B3
Rosehill Drive	A1
Rosemount Place	B1
Rose Street	B2
St. Swithin Street	C1
Schoolhill	B2
Seaforth Road	A3
Skene Square	B2
Skene Street	B2
Spital	A3
Springbank Terrace	C2
Spring Gardens	B2
Sunnybank Road	A2
Union Grove	C1
Union Street	C2
Urquhart Road	B3
Victoria Bridge	C3
Westburn Drive	A1
Westburn Road	B1
West North Street	B3
Whitehall Place	B1
Whitehall Road	B1
Willowbank Road	C2

TOURIST INFORMATION ☎ 01224 288828
23 UNION STREET,
ABERDEEN, AB10 1YL

HOSPITAL A & E ☎ 01224 681818
ABERDEEN ROYAL INFIRMARY, FORESTERHILL,
ABERDEEN, AB25 2ZN

COUNCIL OFFICE ☎ 01224 522000
TOWN HOUSE, BROAD STREET,
ABERDEEN, AB10 1FY

Aberdeen Population: 189,707. City, cathedral and university city and commercial centre on E coast 57m/92km NE of Dundee. Known as 'The Granite City', local stone having been used in many of its buildings. By 13c, Aberdeen had become an important centre for trade and fishing and remains a major port and commercial base. In 19c shipbuilding brought great prosperity to the city. These industries had receded by mid 20c but the city's prospects were transformed when North Sea oil was discovered in 1970, turning it into a city of great wealth. St. Machar's Cathedral at Old Aberdeen. Many museums and art galleries. Extensive flower gardens. Airport at Dyce, 6m/9km NW of Aberdeen.

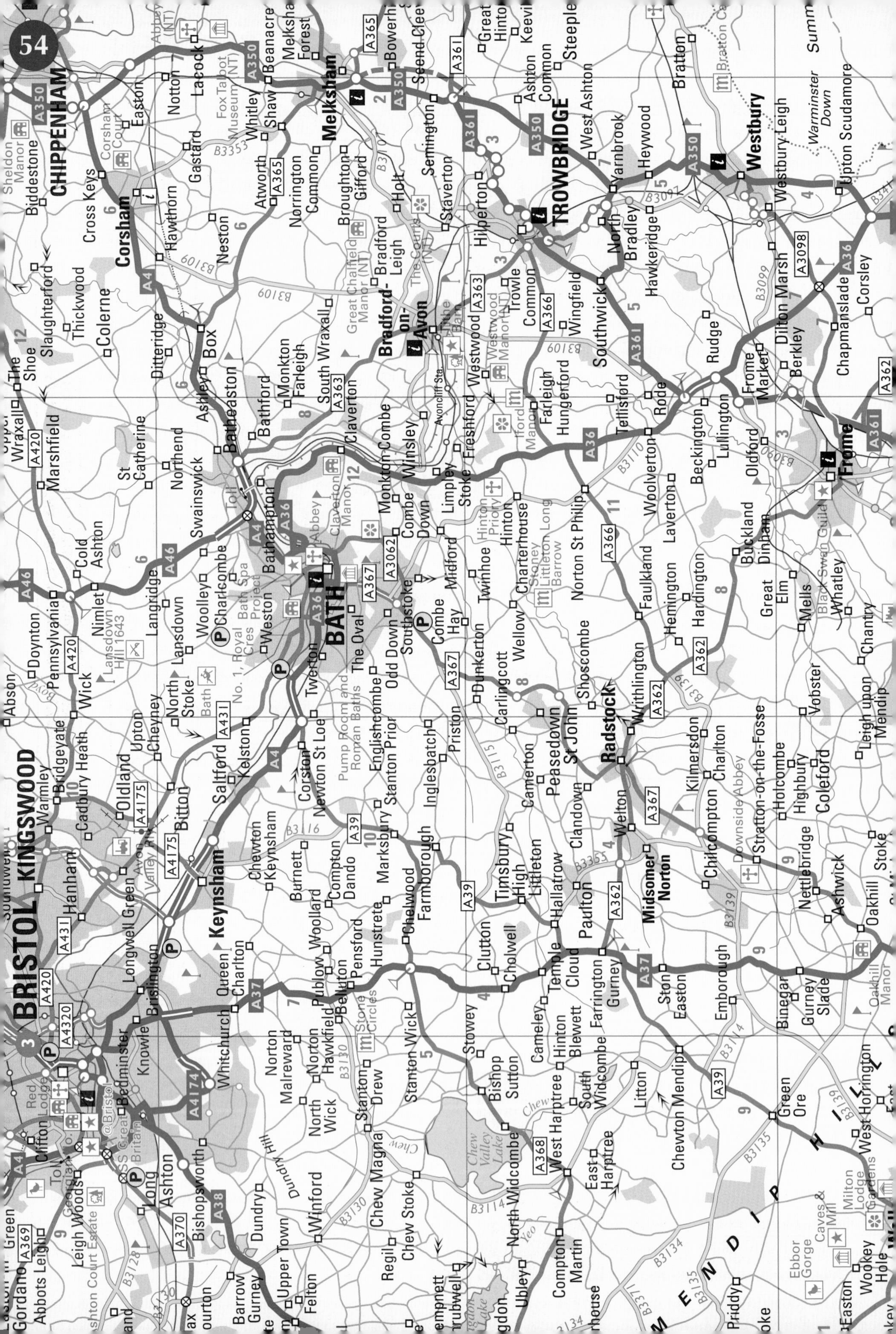

BRISTOL
KINGSWOOD
CHIPPENHAM
Corsham
Melksham
TROWBRIDGE
Westbury
Bradford-on-Avon
BATH
Keynsham
Radstock
Midsomer Norton
Frome

Gordano
Abbots Leigh
Green
Clifton
Red Lodge
Leigh Woods
Ashton Court Estate
Georgian Ho.
@Bristol
SS Great Britain
Bedminster
Knowle
Long Ashton
Bishopsworth
Whitchurch
Barrow Gurney
Dundry
Dundry Hill
Upper Town
Felton
Winford
North Wick
Norton Malreward
Norton Hawkfield
Queen Charlton
Brislington
Hanham
Warmley
Bridgeyate
Cadbury Heath
Longwell Green
Oldland
Avon Valley Rly
Upton Cheyney
Bitton
Abson
Doynton
Pennsylvania
Wick
Nimlet
Cold Ashton
Lansdown Hill 1643
Marshfield
Upper Wraxall
The Shoe
Slaughterford
Thickwood
Colerne
Biddestone
Sheldon Manor
Cross Keys
Corsham Court
Easton
Notton
Lacock
Abbey (NT)
Fox Talbot Museum (NT)
Hawthorn
Gastard
Neston
Whitley
Shaw
Beanacre
Melksham Forest
Atworth
Norrington Common
Broughton Gifford
Holt
Bowerhill
Seend Cleeve
Semington
Staverton
Hilperton
Great Hinton
Keevil
Ashton Common
Steeple Ashton
West Ashton
Yarnbrook
North Bradley
Heywood
Hawkeridge
Bratton
Bratton Camp
Westbury Leigh
Warminster Down
Upton Scudamore
Dilton Marsh
Chapmanslade
Corsley
Berkley
Frome Market
Rudge
Southwick
Wingfield
Trowle Common
Westwood
Westwood Manor (NT)
Iford Manor
Farleigh Hungerford
Tellisford
Rode
Woolverton
Laverton
Beckington
Lullington
Oldford
Buckland Dinham
Great Elm
Mells
Black Swan Guild
Whatley
Chantry
Leigh upon Mendip
Vobster
Coleford
Highbury
Holcombe
Stratton-on-the-Fosse
Downside Abbey
Chilcompton
Kilmersdon
Charlton
Emborough
Binegar
Gurney Slade
Nettlebridge
Ashwick
Oakhill
Oakhill Manor
Stoke
Ston Easton
Chewton Mendip
Litton
Green Ore
West Horrington
Priddy
Ebbor Gorge
Caves & Mill
Milton Lodge Gardens
Wookey Hole
Easton
MENDIP HILLS
Ditteridge
Box
Ashley
Batheaston
Bathford
Monkton Farleigh
South Wraxall
Great Chalfield Manor (NT)
Bradford Leigh
The Courts (NT)
Tithe Barn
Avoncliff Sta.
Claverton
Claverton Manor
Monkton Combe
Winsley
Limpley Stoke
Freshford
Combe Down
Midford
Hinton Priory
Hinton Charterhouse
Twinhoe
Wellow
Stoney Littleton Long Barrow
Norton St Philip
Faulkland
Hemington
Hardington
Writhlington
Shoscombe
Peasedown St John
Camerton
Carlingcott
Dunkerton
Combe Hay
Southstoke
Odd Down
The Oval
Englishcombe
Stanton Prior
Priston
Inglesbatch
Pump Room and Roman Baths
Abbey
Twerton
Weston
No. 1, Royal Cres
Bath Spa Project
Charlcombe
Woolley
Swainswick
Bathampton
Toll
Lansdown
North Stoke
Bath
Langridge
St Catherine
Northend
Saltford
Kelston
Corston
Newton St Loe
Chewton Keynsham
Burnett
Compton Dando
Woollard
Pensford
Publow
Belluton
Hunstrete
Marksbury
Farmborough
Chelwood
Stanton Wick
Stanton Drew
Stone Circles
Chew Magna
Chew Stoke
Regil
Stowey
Bishop Sutton
Chew Valley Lake
North Widcombe
Ubley
Compton Martin
West Harptree
East Harptree
Hinton Blewett
South Widcombe
Cameley
Temple Cloud
Clutton
Cholwell
Timsbury
High Littleton
Hallatrow
Paulton
Farrington Gurney
Clandown
Welton
Blagdon
Blagdon Lake
Nempnett Thrubwell

INDEX TO STREET NAMES

Street	Grid	Street	Grid	Street	Grid
Ambury	C1	Henrietta Street	A2	Quiet Street	A1
Argyle Street	B2	Henry Street	B2	Rossiter Road	C2
Avon Street	B1	High Street	B2	St. James's Parade	B1
Barton Street	B1	James Street West	B1	St. John's Road	A2
Bath Street	B2	John Street	A1	Sawclose	B1
Beau Street	B2	Kingsmead East	B1	Southgate Street	C2
Bridge Street	B2	Laura Place	A2	Stall Street	B2
Broad Quay	C1	Lower Borough Walls	B2	Sydney Place	A3
Broad Street	A2	Lower Bristol Road	C1	The Circus	A1
Brock Street	A1	Manvers Street	C2	Union Street	B2
Chapel Row	B1	Milk Street	B1	Upper Borough Walls	B1
Charles Street	B1	Milsom Street	A2	Walcot Street	A2
Charlotte Street	A1	Monmouth Place	A1	Wells Road	C1
Cheap Street	B2	Monmouth Street	B1	Westgate Buildings	B1
Claverton Street	C2	Newark Street	C2	Westgate Street	B1
Corn Street	C1	New Bond Street	B2	Wood Street	A1
Darlington Street	A3	New King Street	B1	York Street	B2
Dorchester Street	C2	New Orchard Street	B2		
Gay Street	A1	New Street	B1		
George Street	A1	North Parade	B2		
Grand Parade	B2	North Parade Road	B3		
Great Pulteney Street	A3	Old King Street	A1		
Green Park Road	B1	Orange Grove	B2		
Green Street	A2	Paragon	A2		
Grove Street	A2	Pierrepont Street	B2		
Henrietta Mews	A3	Pulteney Road	B3		
Henrietta Road	A2	Queen Street	B1		

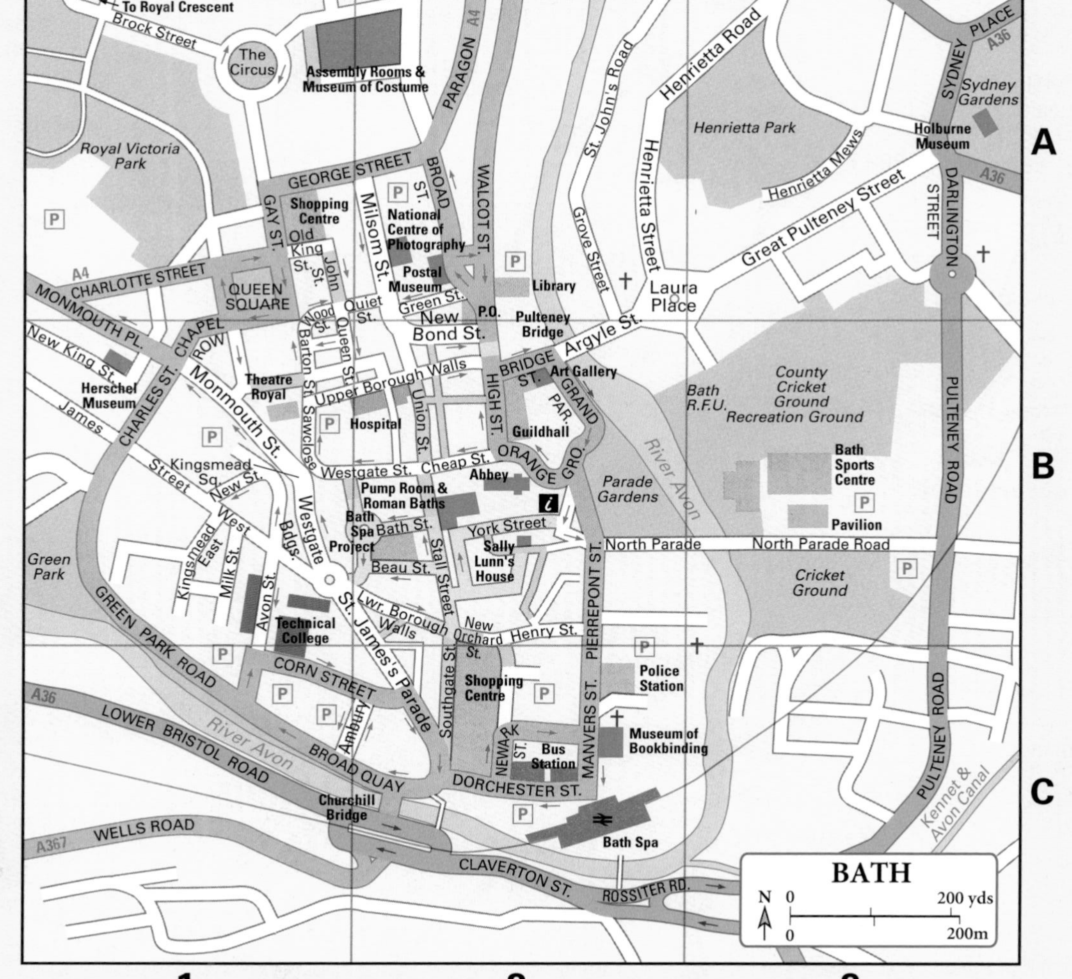

Bath *B. & N.E.Som.* Population: 85,202. City, spa on River Avon, 11m/18km SE of Bristol. Abbey church rebuilt 1501. Natural hot springs unique in Britain drew Romans to Bath, which they named 'Aquae Sulis'. Roman baths and 18c Pump Room are open to visitors. In 18c, it was most fashionable resort in country. Many Georgian buildings and elegant crescents remain, including The Circus and Royal Crescent. Museum of Costume in restored Assembly Rooms. Holds annual summer music festival. American Museum housed in Claverton Manor and University 3m/4km SE.

TOURIST INFORMATION ☎ 01225 477101
AVVEY CAMBERS, ABBEY CHURCHYARD,
BATH, BA1 1LY

HOSPITAL A & E ☎ 01225 428331
ROYAL UNITED HOSPITAL, COMBE PARK,
BATH, BA1 3NG

COUNCIL OFFICE ☎ 01225 477000
THE GUILDHALL, HIGH STREET,
BATH, BA1 5AW

WEB-SITE	www.bathnes.gov.uk

LOCAL RADIO	BBC RADIO BRISTOL 1548 AM & 104.6 FM CLASSIC GOLD 1260 AM, 103 GWR FM 103 FM

WOLVERHAMPTON
WALSALL
WEDNESFIELD
ALDRIDGE
SUTTON COLDFIELD
WEST BROMWICH
DUDLEY
OLDBURY
SMETHWICK
BIRMINGHAM
Castle Bromwich
SOLIHULL
HALESOWEN
STOURBRIDGE
KIDDERMINSTER
Wombourne
Sedgley
Knowle
Wergs
Tettenhall Wood
Tettenhall
Heath Town
Willenhall
Wightwick Manor (NT)
Perton
Trescott
Bradmore
Blakenhall
Monmore Green
Bilston
Darlaston
King's Hill
Moxley
Wednesbury
Maw Green
Rushall
Little Aston
Roughley
Streetly
Four Oaks
Mere Green
Middleton
Drayton Bassett
Dosthill
Gates
Wood End
Kingsbury
Children's Farm
The Belfry
Wishaw
Marston
Lea Marston
Nether Whitacre
Shustoke
Coleshill
Maxstoke
Priory (ruins)
Penn
Lower Penn
Ettingshall
Bradley
Coseley
Princes End
Upper Gornal
Tipton
Trysull
The Bratch
Gospel End
Baggeridge
Nature Cen
Shri Venkataswara (Balaji) Temple of the UK
Dudley Zoo & Castle
Dudley Port
Bird End
Great Barr
Hamstead
Queslett
Kingstanding
Sandwell Valley
Ashbury Cott.
Priory
Perry Barr
Short Heath
Walmley
Wylde Green
Sutton Park
Erdington
Tyburn
Minworth
Curdworth
Water Orton
Gravelly Hill
Aston Hall
Aston
Handsworth
Saltley
Ward End
Himley
Swindon
Gornalwood
Wall Heath
Pensnett
Kingswinford
Woodside
Brierley Hill
Merry Hill
Netherton
Rowley Regis
Quarry Bank
Old Hill
Blackheath
Wordsley
Amblecote
Cradley
Warley
Sea Life Centre
N.I.A.
Millennium Point
Digbeth
Chad Valley
Edgbaston
Harborne
Quinton
Stourton
Wollaston
Lye
Hasbury
Norton
Old Swinford
Pedmore
Whittington
Woodgate
Selly Oak
Bournbrook
Stirchley
King's Heath
Moseley
Nature Cen
Bournville
Cadbury World
Cotteridge
Blakesley Hall
Yardley
Tile Cross
Marston Green
Hay Mills
South Yardley
Acock's Green
Olton
Springfield
Hall Green
Kineton Green
Sheldon
Visitors Cen
Birmingham International
N.E.C.
Birmingham Int. Sta.
Elmdon
Bickenhill
Elmdon Heath
Stonebridge
Meriden
National Motorcycle Museum
Hampton in Arden
Four Oaks
Upper Eastcote
Berkswell
Eastcote
Barston
Balsall Common
Balsall
Temple Balsall
Fen End
Meer End
Chadwick End
Packwood (NT)
Hockley Heath
Dorridge
Bentley Heath
Copt Heath
Blossomfield
Shirley
Solihull Lodge
Whitlock's End
Earlswood
The Lakes Sta.
Drakes Cross
Wythall
Weatheroak Hill
Hopwood Park
Hopwood
King's Norton
Northfield
West Heath
Longbridge
Rednal
Rubery
Cofton Hackett
Barnt Green
Blackwell
Alvechurch
Lickey Hills
Lickey
Catshill
Upper Catshill
Bournheath
Fairfield
Dodford
Bell End
Waseley Hills (NT)
315 Clent Hills
Clent Hills (NT)
Clent
Romsley
Frankley
Illey
Hagley
Hagley Hall
West Hagley
Holy Cross
Broome
Blakedown
Churchill
Caunsall
Cookley
Belbroughton
Drayton
Stone House Cottage
Harvington
Harvington Hall
Chaddesley Corbett
Stone
Mustow Green
Kidderminster
M6
M5
M42
A38(M)
A41
A449
A454
A462
A463
A4123
A459
A4196
A461
A4031
A34
A4041
A452
A453
A5127
A51
A4091
A446
A38
A4097
A4040
A47
A45
A4034
A4100
A4101
A491
A458
A4036
A456
A441
A435
A451
A4141
A4177
A450
A448
B4464
B4151
B4154
B4148
B4138
B4114
B4117
B4118
B4098
B4128
B4182
B4121
B4217
B4025
B4425
B4438
B4102
B4101
B4105
B4176
B4175
B4187
B4188
B4551
B4096
B4120
B4091
B4409
Tame
Cole
Blythe

INDEX TO STREET NAMES

Street	Grid
Albert Street	B3
Aston Road	A3
Aston Street	A3
Bagot Street	A3
Bordesley Street	C3
Bridge Street	C1
Broad Street	C1
Bull Street	B2
Cambridge Street	B1
Charlotte Street	B1
Colmore Circus	B2
Colmore Row	B2
Constitution Hill	A1
Cornwall Street	B2
Corporation Street	B2/A3
Cox Street	A1
Curzon Street	B3
Dale End	B2
Dartmouth Street	A3
Digbeth	C3
Edgbaston Street	C2
Edmund Street	B1
Fazeley Street	B3
George Street	B1
Great Charles Street Queensway	B1
Great Hampton Street	A1
Hall Street	A1
High Street	C2
Hill Street	C2
Holliday Street	C1
James Watt Queensway	A3
Jennens Road	B3
John Bright Street	C2
Lister Street	A3
Livery Street	A1
Lower Loveday Street	A2
Ludgate Hill	B1
Masshouse Circus	B3
Meriden Street	C3
Moat Lane	C3
Moor Street Queensway	C3
Navigation Street	C1
New Canal Street	C3
New Street	C2
New Town Row	A2
Newhall Street	B1
Paradise Circus	B1
Paradise Street	C1
Park Street	C3
Princip Street	A2
Priory Queensway	B2
Queensway	B2
St. Chad's Circus	A2
St. Chad's Queensway	A2
St. Martin's Circus	C2
St. Paul's Square	A1
Shadwell Street	A2
Smallbrook Queensway	C2
Snow Hill	B2
Steelhouse Lane	B2
Suffolk Street Queensway	C1
Summer Lane	A2
Summer Row	B1
Temple Row	B2
Upper Dean Street	C2
Victoria Square	B2
Warstone Lane	A1
Waterloo Street	B2
Woodcock Street	A3

TOURIST INFORMATION ☎ 0121 643 2514
2 CITY ARCADE, BIRMINGHAM, WEST MIDLANDS, B2 4TX

HOSPITAL A & E ☎ 0121 554 3801
CITY HOSPITAL, DUDLEY ROAD, BIRMINGHAM, B18 7QH

COUNCIL OFFICE ☎ 0121 303 9944
COUNCIL HOUSE, VICTORIA SQUARE, BIRMINGHAM, B1 1BB

Birmingham *W.Mid.* City, England's second city and manufacturing, commercial and communications centre, 100m/160km NW of London. Birmingham was home to many pioneers of industrial revolution. Current economic trend is towards post-industrial activities, concentrating on convention and exhibition trades and tourism. To S of city is planned village of Bournville, established by Quaker chocolate magnates George and Richard Cadbury in 1879, influenced by utopian ideas of William Morris. Universities. City has many galleries and museums, particularly around 19c Victoria and Chamberlain Squares. Anglican and Catholic cathedrals. Birmingham International Airport 7m/11km E of city centre.

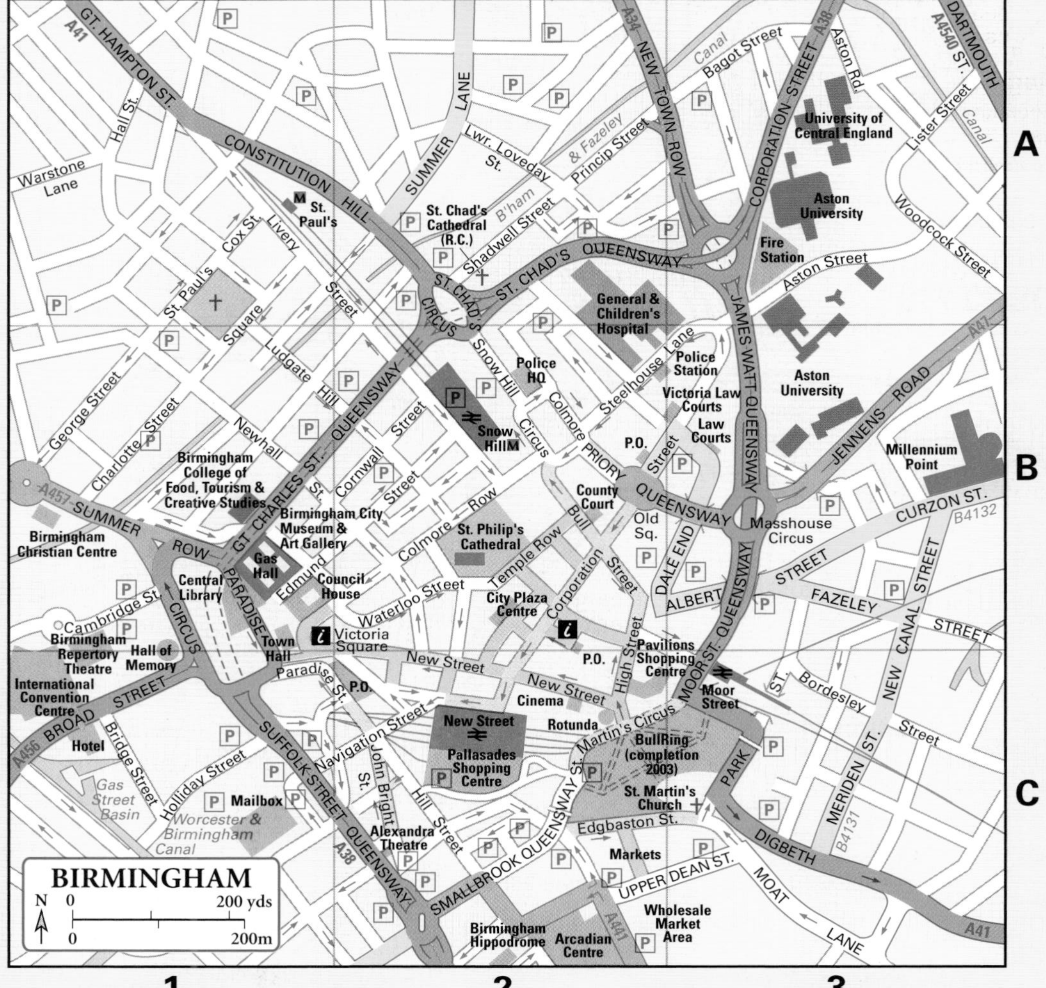

WEB-SITE www.birmingham.gov.uk

LOCAL RADIO BBC RADIO WM 95.6 FM
RADIO XL 1296 AM, BRMB 96.4 FM, HEART FM 100.7 FM, GALAXY 102.2 FM

FLEETWOOD
Rossall Point
Cleveleys
Thornton
Little Bispham
Norbreck
Bispham
North Shore
BLACKPOOL
Blackpool Tower
Sea Life Centre
South Shore
South Pier
Pleasure Beach
Squires Gate
Blackpool
LYTHAM ST ANNE'S
St Anne's
Salter's Bank
Ansdell
Lytham
Horse Bank
Banks Sands
Banks
Burn Naze
Trunnah
Carleton
Freeport
Wyre
Knott End-on-Sea
Preesall
Pilling
Stalmine
Staynall
Hambleton
Hambleton Moss Side
Out Rawcliffe
Toll
Fisher's Row
Stake Pool
Winmarleigh
Eagland Hill
Ratten Row
Great Eccleston
Whin Lane End
Poulton-le-Fylde
Normoss
Staining
Blackpool Zoo
Great Marton
Common Edge
Singleton
Thistleton
Elswick
Roseacre
Wharles
Esprick
Greenhalgh
Weeton
Great Plumpton
Westby
Moss Side
Higher Ballam
Saltcotes
Wesham
Kirkham
Treales
Wrea Green
Warton
Freckleton
Clifton
Salwick Sta.
Lea Town
Crossmoor
Inskip
Catforth
Woodplumpton
Swillbrook
Cottam
Cuddy Hill
St Michael's on Wyre
Churchtown
Catterall
Garstang
Nateby
Bowgreave
Bilsborrow
Lancaster Canal
Scorton
Calder Vale
Oakenclough
Calder Fell
Brock
Claughton
Whitechapel
Inglewhite
Barton
Newsham
Broughton
Goosnargh
Haighton Green
Chingle Hall
Beacon Fell
Parlick
Fair Snape Fell
520
Chipping
Hesketh Lane
Priest Hill
Longridge
Longridge Fell
Knowle Green
New Row
Moor Nook
Roman Road
Ribchester
Roman Fort & Museum
Copster Green
Salesbury
Whitewell
Totridge Fell
Bashall
Grimsargh
Elston
Samlesbury
Balderstone
Osbaldeston
Mellor
Mellor Brook
Samlesbury Hall
Samlesbury Bottoms
Darwen
BLACKBURN
Witton Park
Pleasington
Mill Hill Sta.
Cherry Tree Sta.
Feniscowles
Hoghton
Hoghton Tower
Higher Walton
Walton-le-Dale
Bamber Bridge
Preston Guildhall
Fishwick
Ribbleton
Fulwood
1648
Harris Mus & Art Gallery
PRESTON
Penwortham
Ribble Link
Ribble
Hutton
Longton
New Longton
Tardy Gate
Lostock Hall Sta.
Midge Hall
Farington
Leyland
Much Hoole
Walmer Bridge
Hesketh Bank
Becconsall
Tarleton
Hundred End
Clayton-le-Woods
Whittle-le-Woods
Cuerden Valley
Brindle
Wheelton
Withnell
Brinscall
Abbey Village
Tockholes
Ryal Fold
M6
M55
M65
M61
A6
A59
A583
A584
A585
A586
A587
A588
A5073
A5230
A5085
A6119
A677
A674
A675
A6062
B5269
B5260
B5266
B5259
B5261
B5262
B5411
B6241
B6243
B6245
B6430
B6230
B5256
B5248

INDEX TO STREET NAMES

Street	Grid	Street	Grid	Street	Grid
Abingdon Street	B1	Devonshire Road	A2	Mere Road	B3
Adelaide Street	B1	Devonshire Square	B3	Newton Drive	B3
Albert Road	C1	Dickson Road	A1	Palatine Road	C2
Ascot Road	A3	Egerton Road	A1	Park Road	C2
Bank Hey Street	B1	Elizabeth Street	A2	Peter Street	B2
Beech Avenue West	B3	Exchange Street	A1	Pleasant Street	A1
Birchway Avenue	A3	Forest Gate	B3	Portland Road	C3
Bonny Street	C1	George Street	B2/A2	Princess Parade	B1
Boothley Road	A2	Gloucester Avenue	C3	Promenade	A1/C1
Breck Road	C3	Gorse Road	C3	Queens Square	B1
Bryan Road	B3	Gorton Street	A2	Queen Street	B1
Buchanan Street	B2	Granville Road	B2	Rathlyn Avenue	A3
Caunce Street	B2/A3	Grosvenor Street	B2	Reads Avenue	C2
Central Drive	C1	High Street	A1	Regent Road	B2
Chapel Street	C1	Hornby Road	C1	Ribble Road	C2
Charles Street	B2	Hounds Hill	C1	Ripon Road	C2
Charnley Road	C1	King Street	B1	St. Albans Road	C3
Church Street	B2	Laycock Gate	A3	Seaside Way	C1
Clifton Street	B1	Layton Road	A3	South King Street	B2
Clinton Avenue	C2	Leamington Road	B2	Talbot Road	B1/A2
Cocker Square	A1	Leicester Road	B2	Topping Street	B1
Cocker Street	A1	Lincoln Road	B2	Victory Road	A2
Collingwood Avenue	A3	Liverpool Road	B2	Wayman Road	B3
Cookson Street	B2	London Road	A3	Whitegate Drive	B3/C3
Coronation Street	C1	Lord Street	A1	Woodland Grove	C3
Corporation Street	B1	Market Street	B1	Woolman Road	C2
Deansgate	B1	Mather Street	A3		

TOURIST INFORMATION ☎ 01253 478222
1 CLIFTON STREET,
BLACKPOOL, FY1 1LY

HOSPITAL A & E ☎ 01253 300000
VICTORIA HOSPITAL, WHINNEY HEYS ROAD,
BLACKPOOL, FY3 8NR

COUNCIL OFFICE ☎ 01253 477477
TOWN HALL, TALBOT SQUARE,
BLACKPOOL, FY1 1NA

Blackpool *B'pool* Population: 146,262. Town, large coastal resort and conference centre on Irish Sea, 15m/24km W of Preston. 19c fashionable resort, still very popular today. 7m/11km long 'Golden Mile' of tram route, beach, piers and amusement arcades. Blackpool Pleasure Beach funfair park, 518ft/158m high Tower entertainment complex, annual autumn Illuminations along 5m/8km of Promenade, Zoo, Sea Life Centre, The Sandcastle indoor pool complex and Winter Gardens. Airport 3m/5km S.

WEB-SITE www.blackpool.gov.uk

LOCAL RADIO BBC RADIO LANCASHIRE 104.5 FM
MAGIC 999 AM, RADIO WAVE 96.5 FM, ROCK FM 97.4 FM

THE NEW FOREST
BOURNEMOUTH
POOLE
CHRISTCHURCH
LYMINGTON
Ringwood
Ferndown
Wimborne Minster
Wareham
Swanage
New Milton
Isle of Purbeck
Poole Bay
Poole Harbour
Christchurch Bay
Studland Bay
Swanage Bay
Hengistbury Head
The Needles
The Foreland or Handfast Point
Peveril Point
Ballard Point
Brownsea Island
Bournemouth International
Russell-Cotes Art Gallery & Museum
Needles Pleasure Park
Totland Bay
Alum Bay
Brockenhurst
Sway
Milford on Sea
Barton on Sea
Highcliffe
Mudeford
Burton
Bransgore
Sopley
Winkton
St Leonards
St Ives
West Moors
West Parley
Kinson
Broadstone
Canford Heath
Corfe Mullen
Lytchett Minster
Lytchett Matravers
Hamworthy
Sandbanks
Studland
Corfe Castle
Kimmeridge
Langton Matravers
A31
A35
A338
A337
A348
A349
A350
A351
A3049
A3060
A347
A341
B3073
B3058
B3055
B3351
B3069
B3075
B3068
B3347
B3078
B3082
Cherbourg 2¼-4¼ (5¼)
Guernsey 2½
Jersey 3¾
St Malo (Summer Only) 4½

INDEX TO STREET NAMES

TOURIST INFORMATION ☎ 0906 802 0234
WESTOVER ROAD,
BOURNEMOUTH, BH1 2BU

HOSPITAL A & E ☎ 01202 303626
ROYAL BOURNEMOUTH HOSPITAL,
CASTLE LANE EAST, BOURNEMOUTH, BH7 7DW

COUNCIL OFFICE ☎ 01202 451451
TOWN HALL, BOURNE AVENUE,
BOURNEMOUTH, BH2 6DY

Bournemouth *Bourne.* Population: 155,488. Town, large seaside resort with mild climate, 24m/39km SW of Southampton. Town developed from a few cottages in 1810 to present conurbation. Sandy beach and pier. Extensive parks and gardens including Compton Acres, a display of international garden styles. Russell-Cotes Art Gallery and Museum houses Victorian and oriental collection. University. Conference, business and shopping centre. Bournemouth International Airport, 5m/8km NE of town centre.

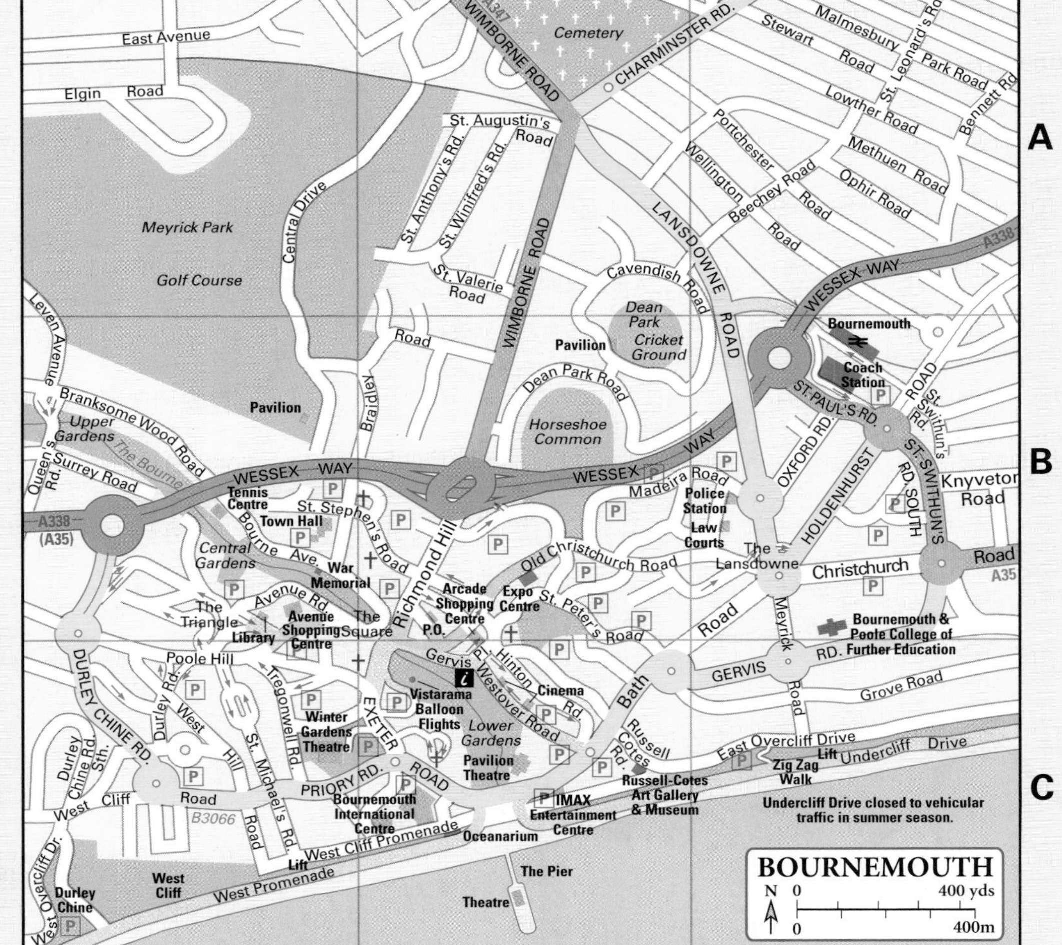

WEB-SITE www.bournemouth.gov.uk

LOCAL RADIO
BBC RADIO SOLENT FOR DORSET 103.8 FM
CLASSIC GOLD 828 AM, 2CR FM 102.3 FM, FIRE 107.6 FM

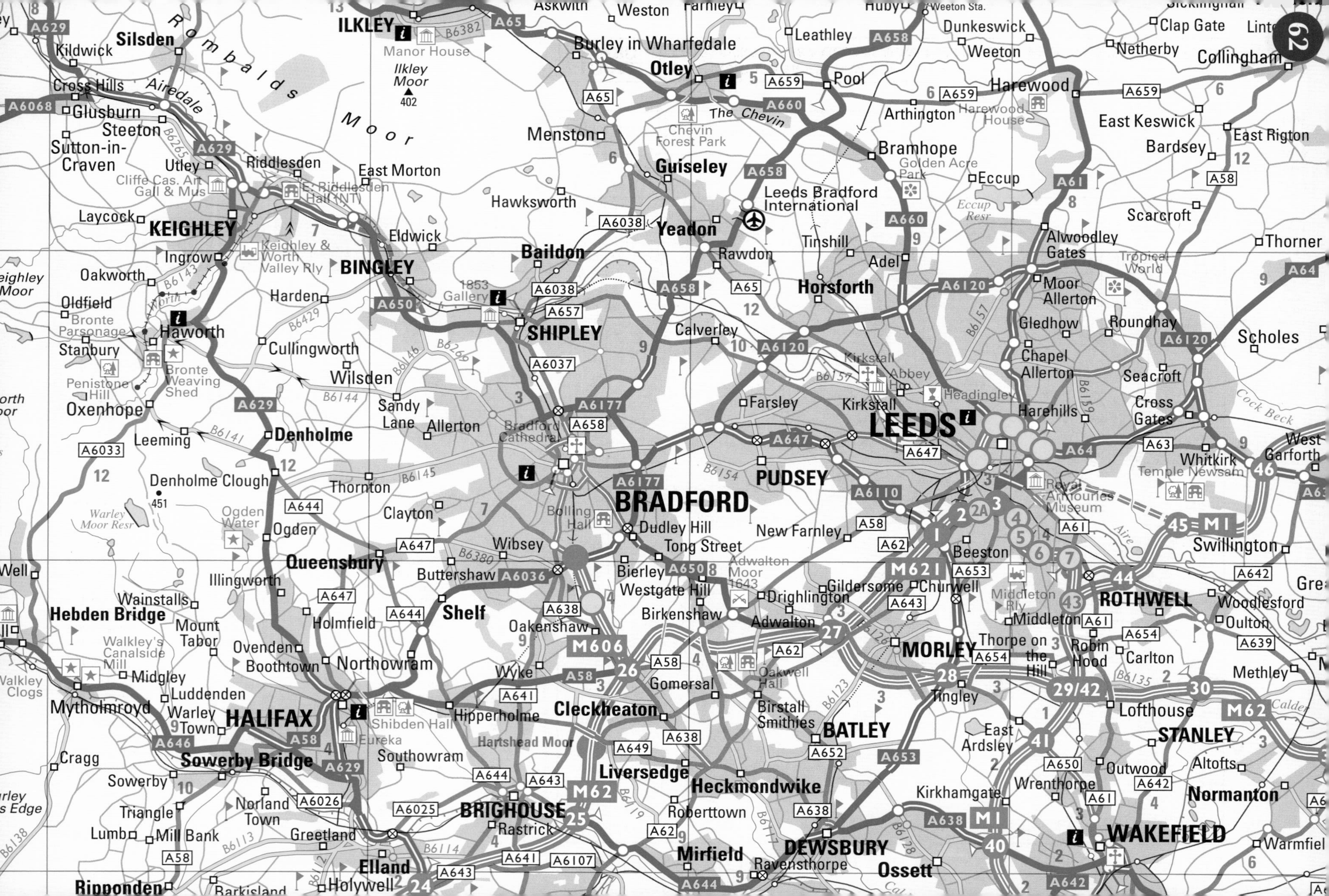

ILKLEY
Silsden
Kildwick
Cross Hills
Glusburn
Steeton
Sutton-in-Craven
KEIGHLEY
Laycock
Ingrow
Oakworth
Oldfield
Haworth
Stanbury
Oxenhope
Leeming
Denholme
Denholme Clough
Rombalds Moor
Ilkley Moor
Manor House
Airedale
Utley
Riddlesden
East Morton
Eldwick
BINGLEY
Harden
Cullingworth
Wilsden
Sandy Lane
Allerton
Thornton
Clayton
Queensbury
Ogden
Illingworth
Wainstalls
Hebden Bridge
Mount Tabor
Ovenden
Boothtown
Northowram
Midgley
Luddenden
Mytholmroyd
Warley Town
HALIFAX
Sowerby Bridge
Sowerby
Cragg
Triangle
Mill Bank
Lumb
Norland Town
Greetland
Elland
Holywell
Ripponden
Barkisland
Southowram
Shibden Hall
Eureka
Hipperholme
BRIGHOUSE
Rastrick
Shelf
Buttershaw
Wibsey
Wyke
Oakenshaw
Cleckheaton
Hartshead Moor
Liversedge
Roberttown
Mirfield
Ravensthorpe
DEWSBURY
Ossett
Heckmondwike
BATLEY
Birstall
Smithies
Gomersal
Birkenshaw
Westgate Hill
Bierley
Dudley Hill
Tong Street
BRADFORD
Bolling Hall
Bradford Cathedral
SHIPLEY
Baildon
1853 Gallery
Hawksworth
Menston
Guiseley
Yeadon
Rawdon
Leeds Bradford International
Otley
Burley in Wharfedale
Weston
Chevin Forest Park
The Chevin
Pool
Leathley
Bramhope
Golden Acre Park
Arthington
Dunkeswick
Weeton
Harewood
Harewood House
Eccup
Eccup Resr
Tinshill
Adel
Horsforth
Calverley
Farsley
PUDSEY
Kirkstall
Kirkstall Abbey
Headingley
LEEDS
New Farnley
Adwalton
Adwalton Moor 1643
Drighlington
Gildersome
Churwell
MORLEY
Tingley
Beeston
Middleton
Middleton Rly
Thorpe on the Hill
Robin Hood
Carlton
Lofthouse
East Ardsley
Kirkhamgate
Wrenthorpe
Outwood
WAKEFIELD
STANLEY
Altofts
Normanton
Warmfield
ROTHWELL
Woodlesford
Oulton
Methley
Swillington
Royal Armouries Museum
Temple Newsam
Whitkirk
West Garforth
Cross Gates
Seacroft
Harehills
Chapel Allerton
Gledhow
Moor Allerton
Roundhay
Alwoodley Gates
Tropical World
Scholes
Scarcroft
Thorner
Bardsey
East Rigton
East Keswick
Collingham
Netherby
Clap Gate
Cock Beck
Aire
Calder
Keighley & Worth Valley Rly
Bronte Parsonage
Bronte Weaving Shed
Penistone Hill
Cliffe Cas. Art Gall & Mus
E. Riddlesden Hall (NT)
Ogden Water
Warley Moor Resr
Walkley's Canalside Mill
Walkley Clogs
M1
M62
M606
M621
A629
A6068
A65
A658
A659
A660
A61
A58
A64
A6120
A6038
A657
A6037
A6177
A650
A647
A6110
A62
A653
A643
A654
A639
A642
A650
A638
A652
A649
A644
A641
A6107
A6025
A6026
A646
A6036
A6033
A63
B6382
B6265
B6143
B6429
B6146
B6144
B6141
B6269
B6145
B6154
B6157
B6159
B6380
B6123
B6126
B6135
B6117
B6119
B6114
B6113
B6128
B6138
402
451

INDEX TO STREET NAMES

Street	Grid
Ann Place	C1
Balme Street	A2
Bank Street	B2
Barkerend Road	A3
Barry Street	B1
Bolton Road	A3
Bridge Street	B2
Broadway	B2
Canal Road	A2
Carlton Street	B1
Charles Street	B2
Cheapside	B2
Chester Street	C1
Churchbank	B3
Claremont	C1
Croft Street	C2
Darley Street	A2
Drake Street	B2
Drewton Road	A1
Dryden Street	C3
Duke Street	A2
East Parade	B3
Fountain Street	A1
George Street	B3
Godwin Street	B2
Grattan Road	B1
Great Horton Road	C1
Grove Terrace	C1
Hall Ings	B2
Hamm Strasse	A2
Harris Street	B3
Hustlergate	B2
Ivegate	B2
James Street	B2
John Street	B1
Kirkgate	B2
Leeds Road	B3
Little Horton Lane	C1
Lumb Lane	A1
Manchester Road	C2
Manningham Lane	A1
Manor Row	A2
Market Street	B2
Morley Street	C1
Neal Street	C1
Nelson Street	C2
North Parade	A2
Otley Road	A3
Peel Street	B3
Prince's Way	B2
Sawrey Place	C1
Sharpe Street	C2
Shipley Airedale Road	A3
Simes Street	A1
Sunbridge Road	A1
Tetley Street	B1
Thornton Road	B1
Valley Road	A2
Vicar Lane	B3
Wakefield Road	C3
Westgate	A1

TOURIST INFORMATION ☎ 01274 753678
CENTRAL LIBRARY, PRINCES WAY,
BRADFORD, W.YORKS, BD1 1NN

HOSPITAL A & E ☎ 01274 542200
BRADFORD ROYAL INFIRMARY, DUCKWORTH LANE,
BRADFORD, BD9 6RJ

COUNCIL OFFICE ☎ 01274 752111
CITY HALL, CHANNING WAY,
BRADFORD, BD1 1HY

Bradford *W.Yorks.* Population: 289,376. City, industrial city, 8m/13km W of Leeds. Cathedral is former parish church. Previously known as wool capital of the world, Bradford is now less dependent upon the textile industry. Colour Museum documents history of dyeing and textile printing. University. Home to National Museum of Photography, Film and Television with IMAX cinema screen. Titus Salt built Saltaire 3m/5km N, which is now considered a model industrial village. Salt's Mill, originally for textiles, now houses David Hockney art in the 1853 gallery. Leeds Bradford International Airport at Yeadon, 6m/10km NE.

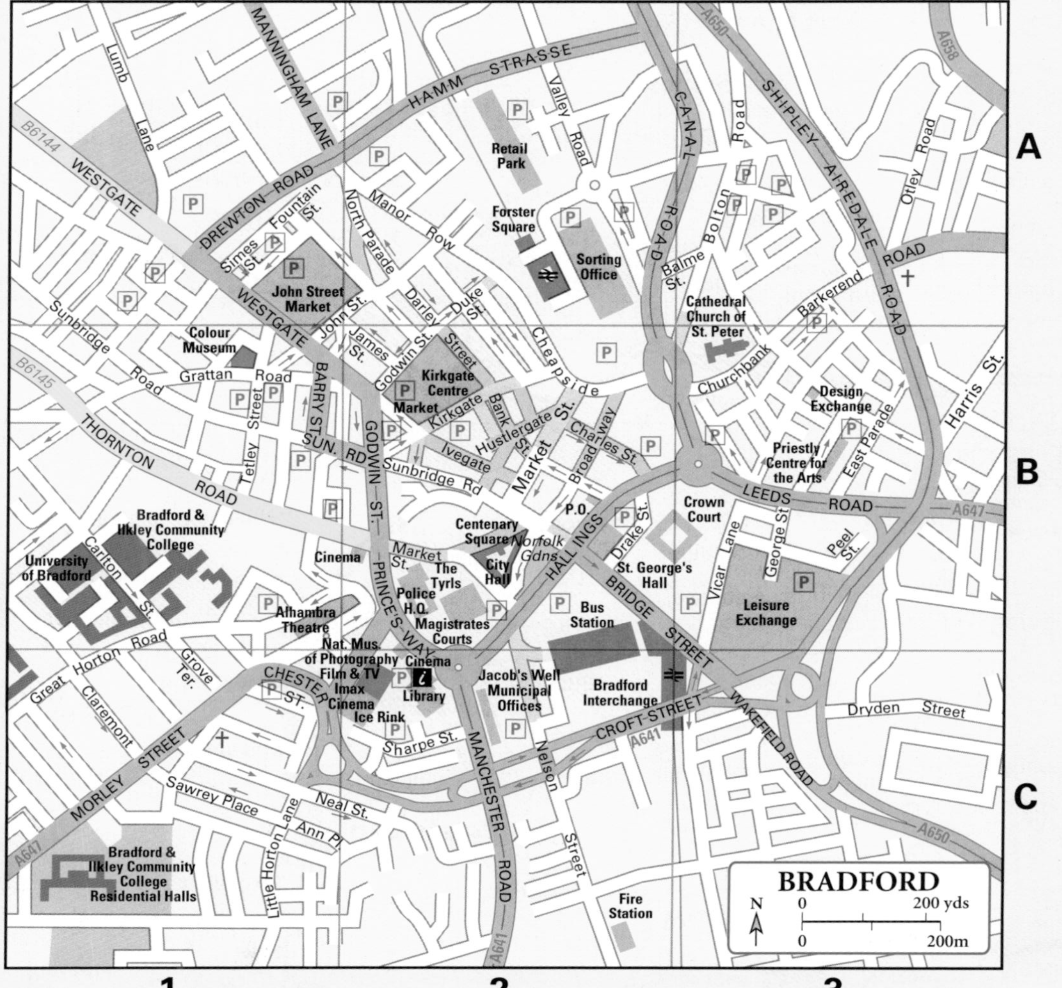

WEB-SITE www.bradford.gov.uk

LOCAL RADIO
BBC RADIO LEEDS 102.7 FM
WEST YORKS CLASSIC GOLD 1278 AM, THE PULSE 97.5 FM, SUNRISE RADIO 103.2 FM

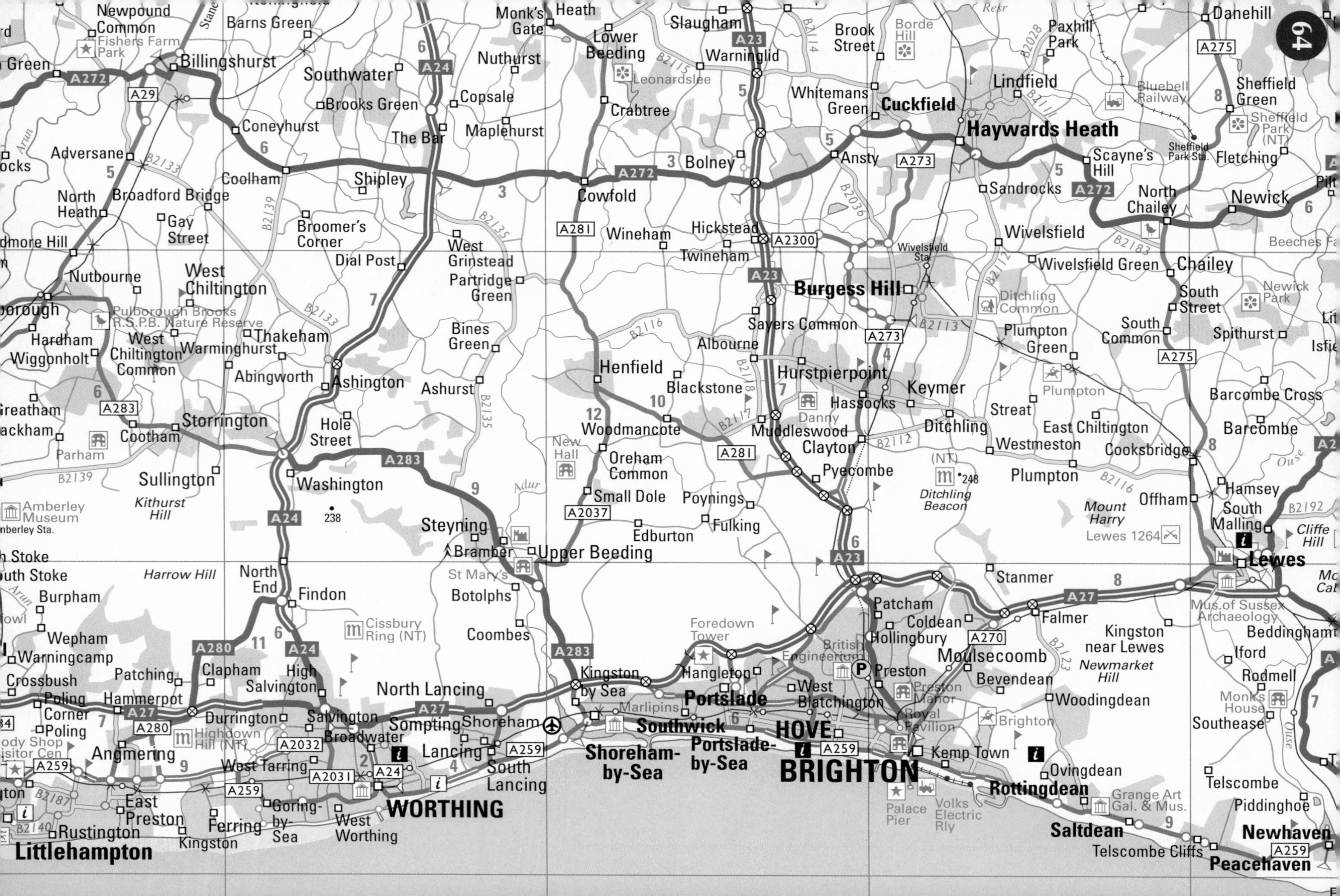
Newpound Common
Fishers Farm Park
Barns Green
Billingshurst
Southwater
Brooks Green
Copsale
Maplehurst
The Bar
Nuthurst
Monk's Gate
Heath
Lower Beeding
Leonardslee
Crabtree
Slaugham
Warninglid
Brook Street
Borde Hill
Whitemans Green
Cuckfield
Haywards Heath
Lindfield
Paxhill Park
Bluebell Railway
Sheffield Park Sta.
Danehill
Sheffield Green
Sheffield Park (NT)
Fletching
Scayne's Hill
Sandrocks
North Chailey
Newick
Beeches Fa
Coneyhurst
Adversane
Coolham
Shipley
Cowfold
Bolney
Ansty
North Heath
Broadford Bridge
Gay Street
Broomer's Corner
West Grinstead
Partridge Green
Wineham
Hickstead
Twineham
Wivelsfield
Wivelsfield Sta.
Wivelsfield Green
Chailey
South Street
Newick Park
Ditchling Common
Burgess Hill
Nutbourne
West Chiltington
Dial Post
Pulborough Brooks R.S.P.B. Nature Reserve
Hardham
West Chiltington Common
Wiggonholt
Thakeham
Warminghurst
Abingworth
Ashington
Bines Green
Ashurst
Henfield
Albourne
Sayers Common
Blackstone
Hurstpierpoint
Hassocks
Keymer
Plumpton Green
South Common
Spithurst
Plumpton
Barcombe Cross
Barcombe
Danny
Streat
East Chiltington
Ditchling
Westmeston
Cooksbridge
Storrington
Cootham
Parham
Hole Street
Woodmancote
Muddleswood
Clayton
Pyecombe
Oreham Common
New Hall
Small Dole
Poynings
Fulking
Edburton
Washington
Sullington
Kithurst Hill
Amberley Museum
Steyning
Bramber
Upper Beeding
Ditchling Beacon
Plumpton
Offham
Hamsey
South Malling
Mount Harry
Lewes 1264
Cliffe Hill
Lewes
Harrow Hill
North End
Findon
Burpham
Wepham
Warningcamp
Crossbush
Patching
Clapham
High Salvington
Cissbury Ring (NT)
St Mary's
Botolphs
Coombes
Foredown Tower
Stanmer
Patcham
Coldean
Hollingbury
Falmer
Kingston near Lewes
Newmarket Hill
Mus. of Sussex Archaeology
Beddingham
Iford
Rodmell
Monks House
Southease
Moulsecoomb
Bevendean
Woodingdean
Preston
Preston Manor
British Engineerium
Hangleton
Kingston by Sea
North Lancing
Hammerpot
Poling
Poling Corner
Durrington
Salvington
Sompting
Shoreham
Portslade
West Blatchington
Royal Pavilion
Brighton
Highdown Hill (NT)
Broadwater
Marlipins
Southwick
HOVE
Angmering
West Tarring
Lancing
South Lancing
Shoreham-by-Sea
Portslade-by-Sea
BRIGHTON
Kemp Town
Ovingdean
Rottingdean
Telscombe
Piddinghoe
East Preston
Goring-by-Sea
West Worthing
WORTHING
Palace Pier
Volks Electric Rly
Grange Art Gal. & Mus.
Saltdean
Telscombe Cliffs
Newhaven
Peacehaven
Rustington
Ferring
Kingston
Littlehampton
A272
A29
A24
A23
A273
A275
A281
A2300
A283
A2037
A280
A27
A2032
A2031
A259
A270
B2133
B2139
B2135
B2115
B2114
B2028
B2111
B2036
B2183
B2112
B2113
B2116
B2117
B2118
B2123
B2192
B2187
B2140
Adur
Arun
Ouse
248
238

BRIGHTON

Brighton & Hove

Area Code 01273

INDEX TO STREET NAMES

Street	Grid	Street	Grid	Street	Grid
Buckingham Road	B2	John Street	B3	Richmond Terrace	B3
Cheapside	B2	King's Road	C1	St. James's Street	C3
Church Street	B2	Lansdowne Road	B1	Southover Street	B3
Churchill Square	C2	Lewes Road	A3	Stanford Road	A2
Clifton Hill	B1	London Road	A2	The Lanes	C2
Davigdor Road	A1	Madeira Drive	C3	The Upper Drive	A1
Ditchling Rise	A2	Marine Parade	C3	Union Road	A3
Dyke Road	B2	Montefiore Road	A1	Upper Lewes Road	A3
Edward Street	C3	Montpelier Road	B1	Upper North Street	B1
Elm Grove	A3	North Street	B2	Viaduct Road	A2
Florence Road	A2	Old Shoreham Road	A1	West Street	C2
Freshfield Road	C3	Old Steine	C3	Western Road	B1
Gloucester Road	B2	Preston Circus	A2	York Avenue	B1
Grand Junction Road	C2	Preston Road	A2	York Place	B3
Holland Road	B1	Queen's Park Road	B3		
Hollingdean Road	A3	Queen's Road	B2		
Islingword Road	A3	Richmond Place	B3		

TOURIST INFORMATION ☎ 0906 711 2255
10 BARTHOLOMEW SQUARE,
BRIGHTON, BN1 1JS

HOSPITAL A & E ☎ 01273 696955
ROYAL SUSSEX COUNTY HOSPITAL, EASTERN ROAD,
BRIGHTON, BN2 5BE

COUNCIL OFFICE ☎ 01273 290000
TOWN HALL, BARTHOLOMEWS,
BRIGHTON, BN1 1JA

WEB-SITE	www.brighton-hove.gov.uk

LOCAL RADIO	BBC SOUTHERN COUNTIES RADIO 95.3 FM CAPITAL GOLD 1323 AM, SOUTHERN FM 103.5

Brighton *B. & H.* Population: 124,851. Town, seaside resort, sailing and conference centre, 48m/77km S of London. Previously a fishing village known as Brighthelmstone, centred on current Lanes area. Brighton became fashionable as a sea-bathing resort in the 18c. Patronized by the Prince Regent in 1780s who built the Royal Pavilion in Oriental style as a summer palace. Regency squares at Kemp Town. Amusement arcades on 1899 Palace Pier. Annual festivals. Language schools. Universities.

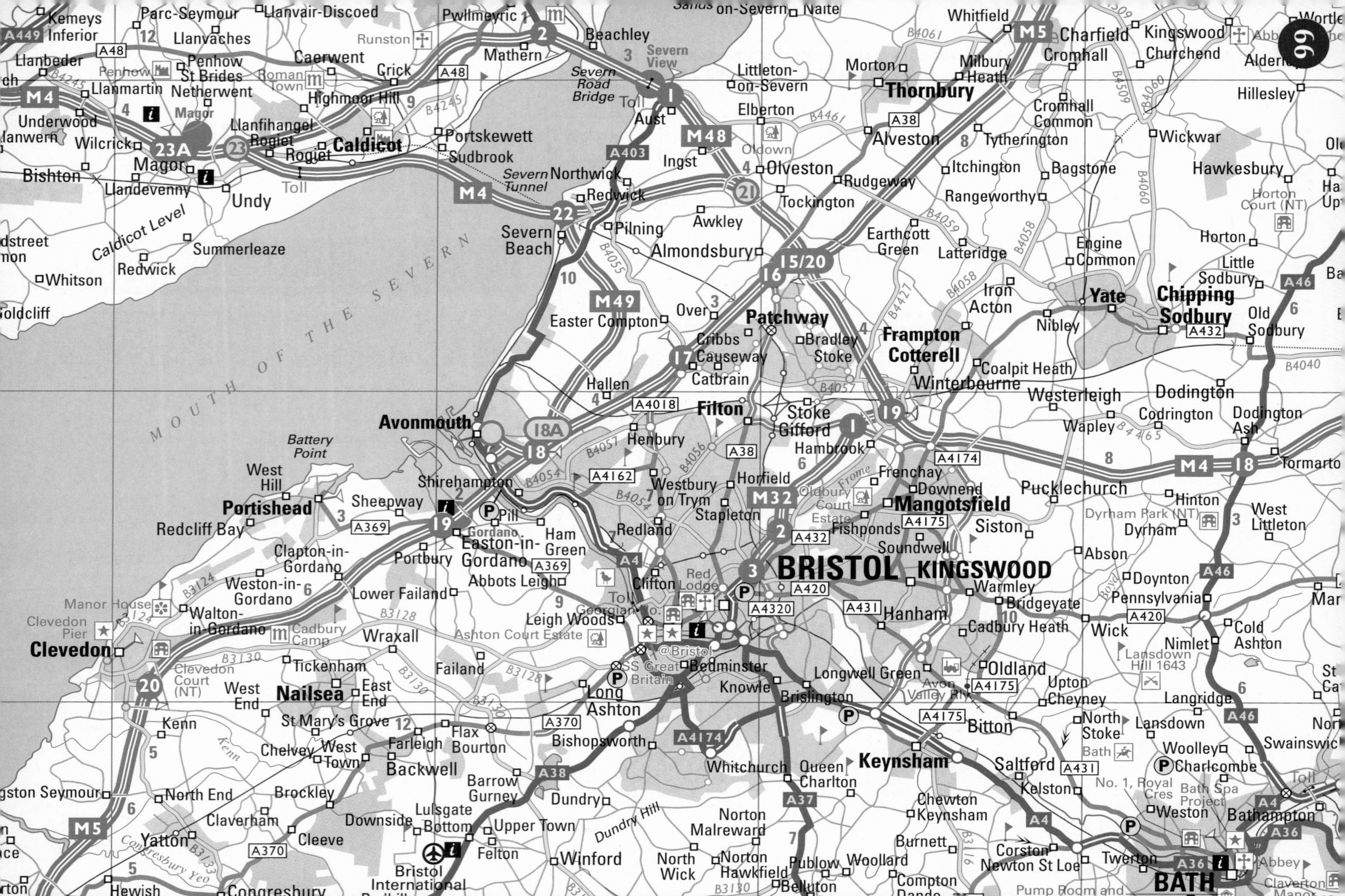

BRISTOL
KINGSWOOD
BATH
Chipping Sodbury
Yate
Thornbury
Frampton Cotterell
Mangotsfield
Patchway
Filton
Keynsham
Avonmouth
Portishead
Clevedon
Nailsea
Caldicot
Magor
Severn Beach
Pill
Long Ashton
Bradley Stoke
Stoke Gifford
Winterbourne
Westerleigh
Pucklechurch
Hanham
Fishponds
Downend
Warmley
Oldland
Bitton
Saltford
Whitchurch
Bishopsworth
Brislington
Bedminster
Clifton
Redland
Henbury
Westbury on Trym
Horfield
Hambrook
Almondsbury
Olveston
Alveston
Aust
Pilning
Easter Compton
Hallen
Shirehampton
Portbury
Easton-in-Gordano
Abbots Leigh
Leigh Woods
Failand
Wraxall
Backwell
Flax Bourton
Winford
Dundry
Barrow Gurney
Felton
Yatton
Congresbury
Cleeve
Claverham
Brockley
Chelvey
Kenn
Weston-in-Gordano
Walton-in-Gordano
Clapton-in-Gordano
Redcliff Bay
Battery Point
Sheepway
Caerwent
Undy
Rogiet
Portskewett
Sudbrook
Mathern
Beachley
Severn Road Bridge
Severn Tunnel
Severn View
MOUTH OF THE SEVERN
Bristol International
Hawkesbury
Hillesley
Wickwar
Charfield
Cromhall
Tytherington
Iron Acton
Rangeworthy
Engine Common
Dodington
Codrington
Wapley
Dyrham
Doynton
Pennsylvania
Cold Ashton
Lansdown
Weston
Twerton
Bathampton
Swainswick
Kelston
Corston
Newton St Loe
Chewton Keynsham
Burnett
Compton Dando
Queen Charlton
Woollard
Publow
Norton Malreward
Norton Hawkfield
North Wick
Dundry Hill
Upper Town
Lulsgate Bottom
Downside
Farleigh
West Town
St Mary's Grove
Tickenham
East End
Clevedon Pier
Clevedon Court (NT)
Manor House
Cadbury Camp
Ashton Court Estate
Dyrham Park (NT)
Horton Court (NT)
Oldbury Court Estate
Lansdown Hill 1643
SS Great Britain
@Bristol
Red Lodge
Georgian Ho.
Avon Valley Rly
Bath Spa Project
No. 1, Royal Cres
M4
M5
M32
M48
M49
A38
A46
A4
A36
A37
A370
A369
A403
A420
A431
A432
A4174
A4175
A4018
A4162
A4320
A48

INDEX TO STREET NAMES

Street	Grid	Street	Grid	Street	Grid
Anchor Road	C1	Lewins Mead	A1	Redcliff Street	B2
Approach Road	C3	Lower Castle Street	A3	Rupert Street	A1
Avon Street	B3	Lower Maudlin Street	A2	St. Michael's Hill	A1
Baldwin Street	B1	Malborough Street	A2	St. Thomas Street	B2
Bond Street	A2	Marsh Street	B1	Small Street	B1
Bridge Street	B2	Merchant Street	A2	Straight Street	B3
Bristol Bridge	B2	Nelson Street	A2	Temple Back	B3
Broadmead	A2	Newfoundland Street	A3	Temple Gate	C3
Broad Quay	B1	Newgate	B2	Temple Way	C3
Broad Weir	A3	North Street	A2	The Grove	C1
Canon's Road	C1	Old Market Street	B3	The Haymarket	A2
Canon's Way	C1	Park Row	B1	The Horsefair	A2
Castle Street	B3	Park Street	B1	Trenchard Street	B1
Christmas Steps	A1	Passage Street	B3	Tyndall Avenue	A1
College Green	B1	Penn Street	A3	Union Street	A2
Colston Avenue	B1	Perry Road	B1	Unity Street	B3
Colston Street	B1	Prince Street	C1	Upper Maudlin Street	A1
Corn Street	B1	Prince Street Bridge	C1	Victoria Street	B2
Counterslip	B2	Queen Charlotte Street	B2	Wapping Road	C1
Frogmore Street	B1	Redcliffe Bridge	C2	Wellington Road	A3
Harbour Way	C1	Redcliff Hill	C2	Welsh Back	B2
High Street	B2	Redcliffe Parade	C2	Wine Street	B2
Horfield Road	A1				
Houlton Street	A3				
King Street	B1				

TOURIST INFORMATION ☎ 0117 926 0767
THE ANNEXE, WILDSCREEN WALK, HARBOURSIDE, BRISTOL, BS1 5UD

HOSPITAL A & E ☎ 0117 923 0000
BRISTOL ROYAL INFIRMARY, MARLBOROUGH STREET, BRISTOL, BS2 8HW

COUNCIL OFFICE ☎ 0117 922 2000
THE COUNCIL HOUSE, COLLEGE GREEN, BRISTOL, BS1 5TR

Bristol Population: 407,992. City, 106m/171km W of London. Port on River Avon dates from medieval times. Bristol grew from transatlantic trade in rum, tobacco and slaves. In Georgian times, Bristol's population was second only to London and many Georgian buildings still stand, including the Theatre Royal, the oldest working theatre in the country. Bristol is now a commercial and industrial centre. Cathedral dates from 12c and was originally an abbey. 15c Temple Church tower and walls (English Heritage). Restored iron ship SS Great Britain and Industrial Museum in city docks area. Universities. 245ft/75m high Clifton Suspension Bridge completed in 1864 across the Avon Gorge NW of the city. Bristol International Airport at Lulsgate 7m/11km SW.

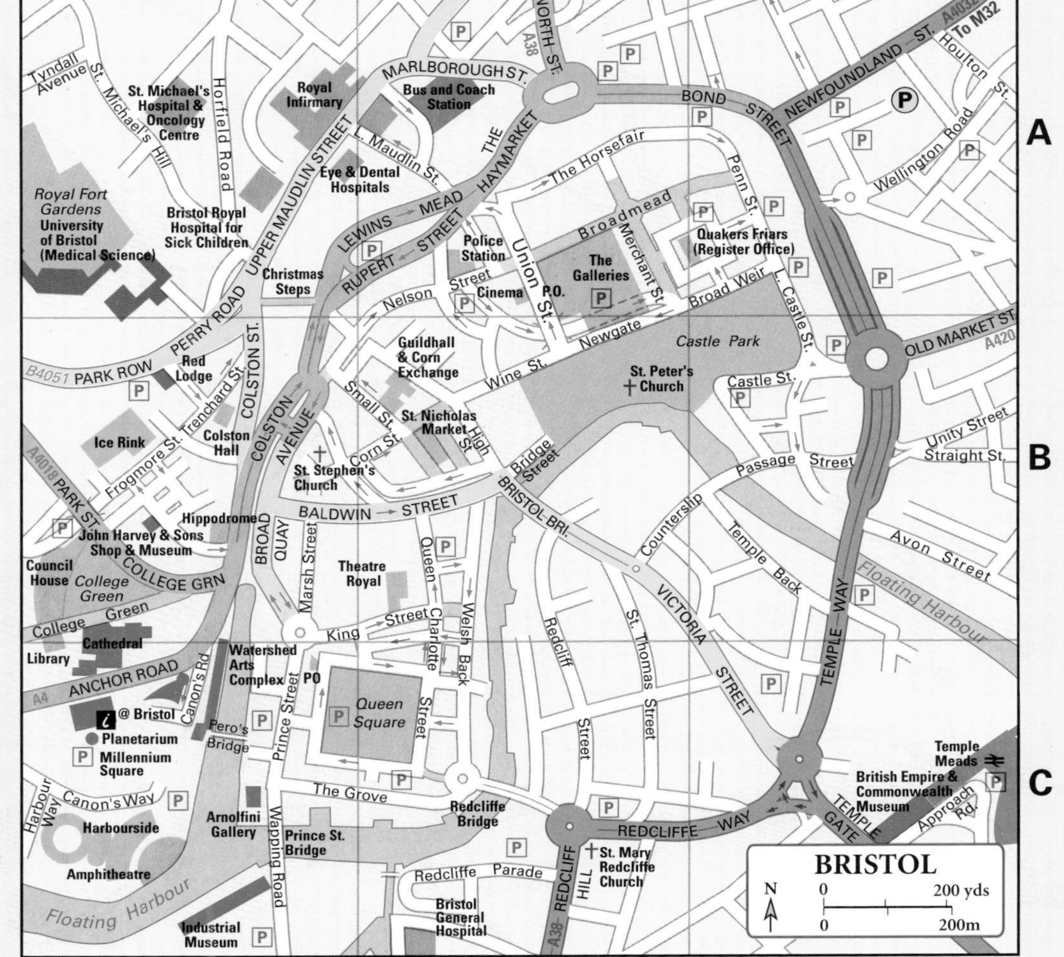

WEB-SITE	www.bristol-city.gov.uk

LOCAL RADIO	BBC RADIO BRISTOL 94.9 FM BRUNEL CLASSIC GOLD 1260 AM, GWR FM 96.3 FM, GALAXY 101 & 97.2FM, STAR 107.3 FM

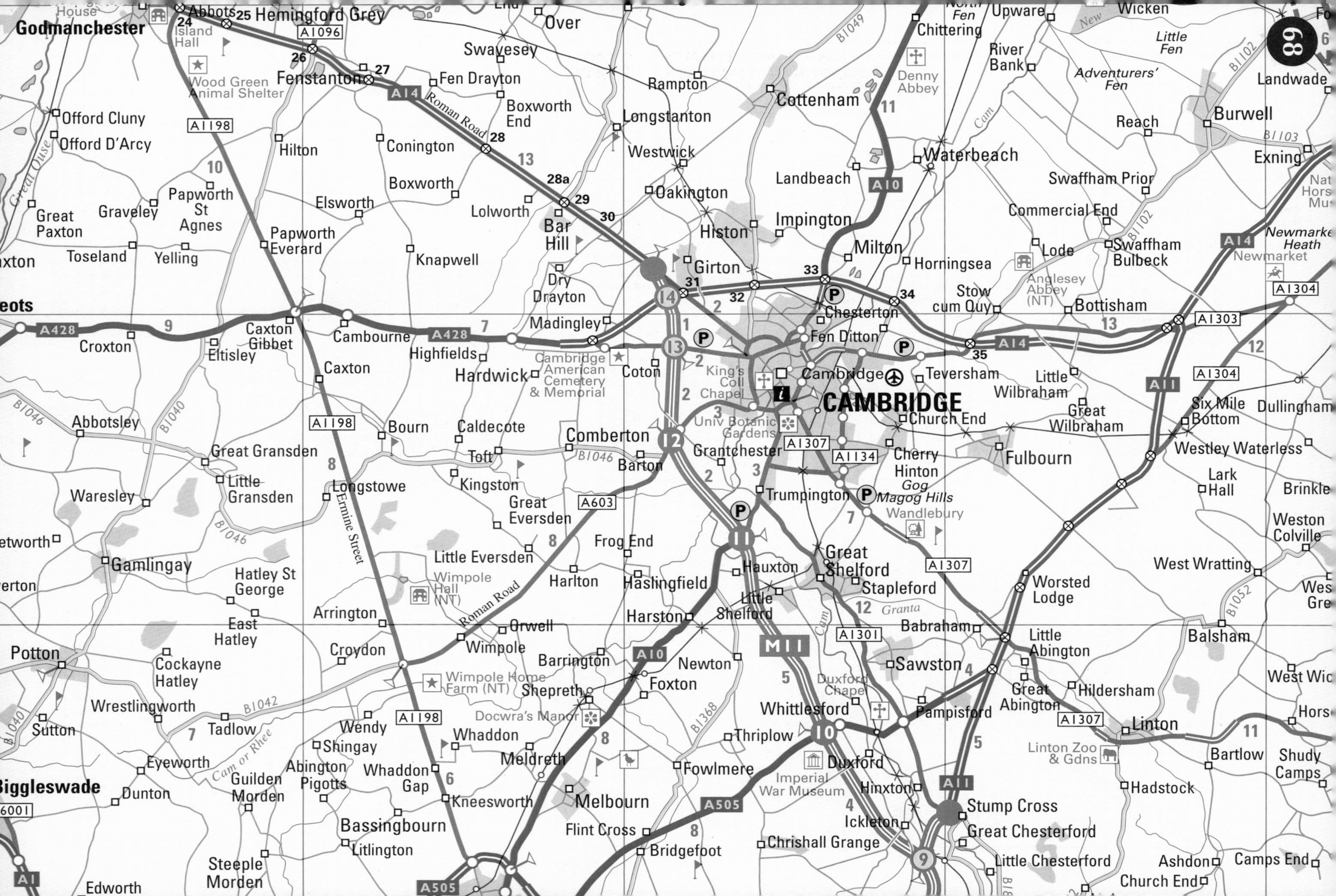
CAMBRIDGE
Godmanchester
Hemingford Grey
Abbots
Island Hall
Over
Swavesey
Fenstanton
Fen Drayton
Rampton
Cottenham
Chittering
Upware
River Bank
Wicken
Little Fen
Adventurers' Fen
Landwade
Burwell
Reach
Exning
Newmarket Heath
Newmarket
Wood Green Animal Shelter
Offord Cluny
Offord D'Arcy
Hilton
Conington
Boxworth End
Longstanton
Westwick
Denny Abbey
Waterbeach
Landbeach
Swaffham Prior
Commercial End
Swaffham Bulbeck
Lode
Anglesey Abbey (NT)
Bottisham
Great Paxton
Graveley
Papworth St Agnes
Papworth Everard
Toseland
Yelling
Elsworth
Boxworth
Lolworth
Knapwell
Bar Hill
Dry Drayton
Oakington
Histon
Impington
Milton
Horningsea
Girton
Chesterton
Fen Ditton
Stow cum Quy
Croxton
Eltisley
Caxton Gibbet
Cambourne
Caxton
Highfields
Hardwick
Madingley
Cambridge American Cemetery & Memorial
Coton
King's Coll Chapel
Cambridge
Teversham
Little Wilbraham
Great Wilbraham
Six Mile Bottom
Dullingham
Westley Waterless
Church End
Univ Botanic Gardens
Grantchester
Cherry Hinton
Fulbourn
Lark Hall
Brinkley
Abbotsley
Bourn
Caldecote
Comberton
Toft
Barton
Great Gransden
Little Gransden
Longstowe
Kingston
Great Eversden
Trumpington
Gog Magog Hills
Wandlebury
Waresley
Gamlingay
Little Eversden
Frog End
Great Shelford
Stapleford
Worsted Lodge
West Wratting
Weston Colville
Hatley St George
East Hatley
Wimpole Hall (NT)
Harlton
Haslingfield
Hauxton
Little Shelford
Harston
Arrington
Croydon
Orwell
Wimpole
Barrington
Newton
Babraham
Little Abington
Balsham
Potton
Cockayne Hatley
Wimpole Home Farm (NT)
Shepreth
Foxton
Sawston
Great Abington
Hildersham
Wrestlingworth
Tadlow
Wendy
Shingay
Docwra's Manor
Whaddon
Whittlesford
Duxford Chapel
Pampisford
Linton
Sutton
Eyeworth
Guilden Morden
Abington Pigotts
Whaddon Gap
Meldreth
Thriplow
Fowlmere
Duxford
Imperial War Museum
Linton Zoo & Gdns
Hadstock
Bartlow
Shudy Camps
Biggleswade
Dunton
Kneesworth
Melbourn
Hinxton
Stump Cross
Bassingbourn
Litlington
Flint Cross
Ickleton
Great Chesterford
Chrishall Grange
Bridgefoot
Steeple Morden
Edworth
Little Chesterford
Ashdon
Camps End
Church End
Roman Road
Ermine Street
Great Ouse
Cam
Granta
Cam or Rhee
New
A14
A1096
A1198
A10
A428
A1303
A1304
A11
A1307
A1134
A603
A1301
M11
A505
A1
B1049
B1102
B1103
B1046
B1040
B1042
B1368
B1052
B1040

CAMBRIDGE Cambridgeshire Area Code 01223

INDEX TO STREET NAMES

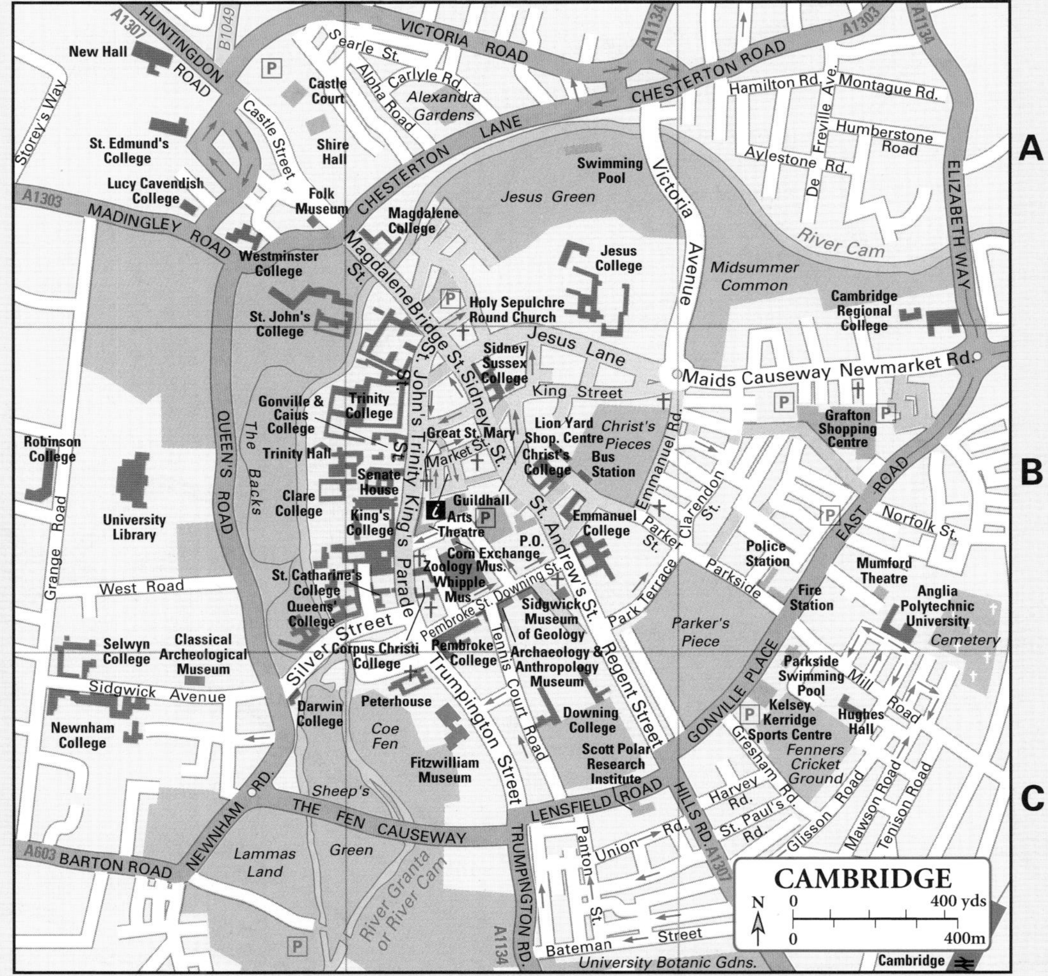

WEB-SITE	www.cambridge.gov.uk

LOCAL RADIO	BBC RADIO CAMBRIDGESHIRE 96 FM Q 103 FM, STAR 107.9 FM

TOURIST INFORMATION ☎ 01223 322640
WHEELER STREET, CAMBRIDGE, CAMBRIDGESHIRE, CB2 3QB

HOSPITAL A & E ☎ 01223 245151
ADDENBROOKE'S HOSPITAL, HILLS ROAD, CAMBRIDGE, CB2 2QQ

COUNCIL OFFICE ☎ 01223 457000
THE GUILDHALL, MARKET SQUARE, CAMBRIDGE, CB2 3QJ

Cambridge *Cambs.* Population: 95,682. City, university city on River Cam 49m/79km N of London. First college founded here in 1271. Historic tensions existed between students and townspeople since 14c, and came to a head during Peasants' Revolt of 1381 in which five townsfolk were hanged. Oliver Cromwell was a graduate of Sidney Sussex College and local MP at a time when the University was chiefly Royalist. 1870's saw foundation of first women's colleges, but women were not awarded degrees until after 1947. University's notable graduates include prime ministers, foreign heads of state, literary giants, philosophers and spies. Cambridge Footlights regularly provide a platform for future stars of stage, screen and television. Cambridge boasts many fine museums, art galleries and buildings of interest, including King's College Chapel and Fitzwilliam Museum. Airport at Teversham 3m/4km E.

Eastchurch
Warden
Leysdown-on-Sea
B2231
ISLE OF SHEPPEY
Eastchurch Marshes
Isle of Harty
Shell Ness
WHITSTABLE
Swalecliffe
B2205
A2090
HERNE BAY
Reculver
Towers & Roman Fort
Hillborough
Beltinge
Broomfield
Hunters Forstal
Highstead
A299
St Nicholas at Wade
Birchington
Westgate on Sea
MARGATE
Tudor House
Salmeston Grange
Quex House & Gdns
RAF Manston Spitfire & Hurricane Memorial Bldg
Acol
Isle of Thanet
B2050
A254
A256
Manston
Minster
Monkton
Cliffs End
Abbey
A253
St Augustine
Pegwell Bay
Sandwich Flats
Seasalter
Chestfield
West End
Herne
Herne Common
Maypole
Hoath
Chislet
Boyden Gate
Sarre
Gore Street
A28
Conyer
Uplees
Oare
Teynham Sta.
Luddenham Court
Graveney
Yorkletts
Clapham Hill
A290
Wealden Woodlands
Calcott
A291
Upstreet
West Stourmouth
East Stourmouth
Westmarsh
Stour
Richborough Castle
Stonar Cut
Faversham
Preston
Goodnestone
Dargate
Hernhill
Pean Hill
Tyler Hill
Honey Hill
Blean
Broadoak
Sturry
Roman Road
Hersden
Westbere
Grove
Stodmarsh
Preston
Ware
Elmstone
Cop Street
Great Stonar
Maison Dieu
Ospringe
Lynsted
A2
M2
Whitehill
North Street
Boughton Street
Dunkirk
Rough Common
Hales Place
Fordwich
Great Stour
Hoaden
Bird Park
Roman Amphitheatre
Sandwich
Salutation Gdn
Toll
Cath
St Augustine's Abbey
Littlebourne
Wickhambreaux
Ickham
A257
Wingham
Ash
Marshborough
Woodnesborough
Brogdale Horticultural Trust
Oversland
Harbledown
Thanington
CANTERBURY
A2050
Howletts Wild Animal Park
Bramling
Staple
Worth
Sheldwich
Eastling
Chartham Hatch
Selling
Old Wives Lees
Bekesbourne
Patrixbourne
B2046
Goodnestone Park
Goodnestone
Eastry
Ham
Hacklinge
Frith
Throwley
Badlesmere
Leaveland
Shottenden
Chilham
Chilham Castle
Shalmsford Street
Chartham
Street End
Nackington
Lower Hardres
Bridge
Adisham
Chillenden
Knowlton
Finglesham
A258
Bishopsbourne
Aylesham
Nonington
Easole Street
Tilmanstone
Betteshanger
Sholden
Northbourne
Stalisfield Green
A251
A252
Molash
Godmersham
Petham
Upper Hardres Court
Kingston
Womenswold
Elvington
East Studdal
Great Mongeham
Charing
Challock
Bilting
Crundale
Sole Street
Waltham
Bossingham
Derringstone
Barham
Barfrestone
Eythorne
Woollage Green
Ripple
Sutton
Ashley
Westwell Leacon
Westwell
Eastwell Park
Boughton Aluph
Boughton Lees
Wye
Hassell Street
Bodsham Green
B2068
Stone Street
Stelling Minnis
Lyminge Forest
Breach
Bladbean
Wingmore
Denton
Lydden
Shepherdswell (Sibertswold)
Coldred
West Langdon
Martin Mill Sta.
East Langdon
Ram Lane
Hothfield
A20
Kennington
ASHFORD
Brook
National Nature Trails
Hastingleigh
Lymbridge Green
Sixmile Cottages
Elham
Wootton
Selstead
A260
Lydden
Temple Ewell
Whitfield
Guston
West Cliffe

INDEX TO STREET NAMES

Street	Grid	Street	Grid	Street	Grid
Best Lane	B2	North Holmes Road	A3	St. Margarets Street	B2
Borough Northgate	A2	North Lane	A1	St. Peter's Lane	A2
Broad Street	A3	Nunnery Fields	C3	St. Peter's Place	B1
Burgate	B2	Oaten Hill	C3	St. Peter's Street	A1
Castle Street	C1	Old Dover Road	C2	St. Radigund's Street	A2
Dover Street	B3	Orchard Street	A1	St. Stephen's Road	A2
Gravel Walk	B2	Oxford Road	C2	Station Road East	C1
Hawk's Lane	B2	Palace Street	B2	Station Road West	A1
High Street	B2	Pin Hill	C1	Stour Street	B1
Ivy Lane	B3	Pound Lane	A1	The Friar's	B2
King Street	A2	Rheims Way	B1	Tourtel Road	A3
Lansdown Road	C2	Rhodaus Town	C2	Union Street	A3
Longport	B3	Roper Road	A1	Upper Bridge Street	C2
Lower Bridge Street	B3	Rose Lane	B2	Watling Street	B2
Lower Chantry Lane	B3	St. Dunstan's Street	A1	Whitehall Road	B1
Marlowe Avenue	C2	St. George's Lane	B2	Wincheap	C1
Military Road	A3	St. George's Place	B3	York Road	C1
Monastery Street	B3	St. George's Street	B2		
New Dover Road	C3				

TOURIST INFORMATION ☎ 01227 766567
34 ST. MARGARET'S STREET, CANTERBURY, KENT, CT1 2TG

HOSPITAL A & E ☎ 01227 766877
KENT & CANTERBURY HOSPITAL, ETHELBERT ROAD, CANTERBURY, CT1 3NG

COUNCIL OFFICE ☎ 01227 862000
COUNCIL OFFICES, MILITARY ROAD, CANTERBURY, CT1 1YW

Canterbury *Kent* Population: 36,464. City, premier cathedral city and seat of Primate of Church of England on Great Stour River, 54m/88km E of London. Site of Roman settlement Durovernum. After Romans left, Saxons renamed town Cantwarabyrig. First cathedral in England built on site of current Christ Church Cathedral in AD 602. Thomas à Becket assassinated in Canterbury in 1170, turning Cathedral into great Christian shrine and destination of many pilgrimages, such as those detailed in Geoffrey Chaucer's Canterbury Tales. Becket's tomb destroyed on orders of Henry VIII. Cathedral was backdrop for premiere of T.S. Eliot's play 'Murder in the Cathedral' in 1935. City suffered extensive damage during World War II. Many museums and galleries explaining city's rich heritage. Roman and medieval remains, including city walls. Modern shopping centre; industrial development on outskirts. University of Kent on hill to N.

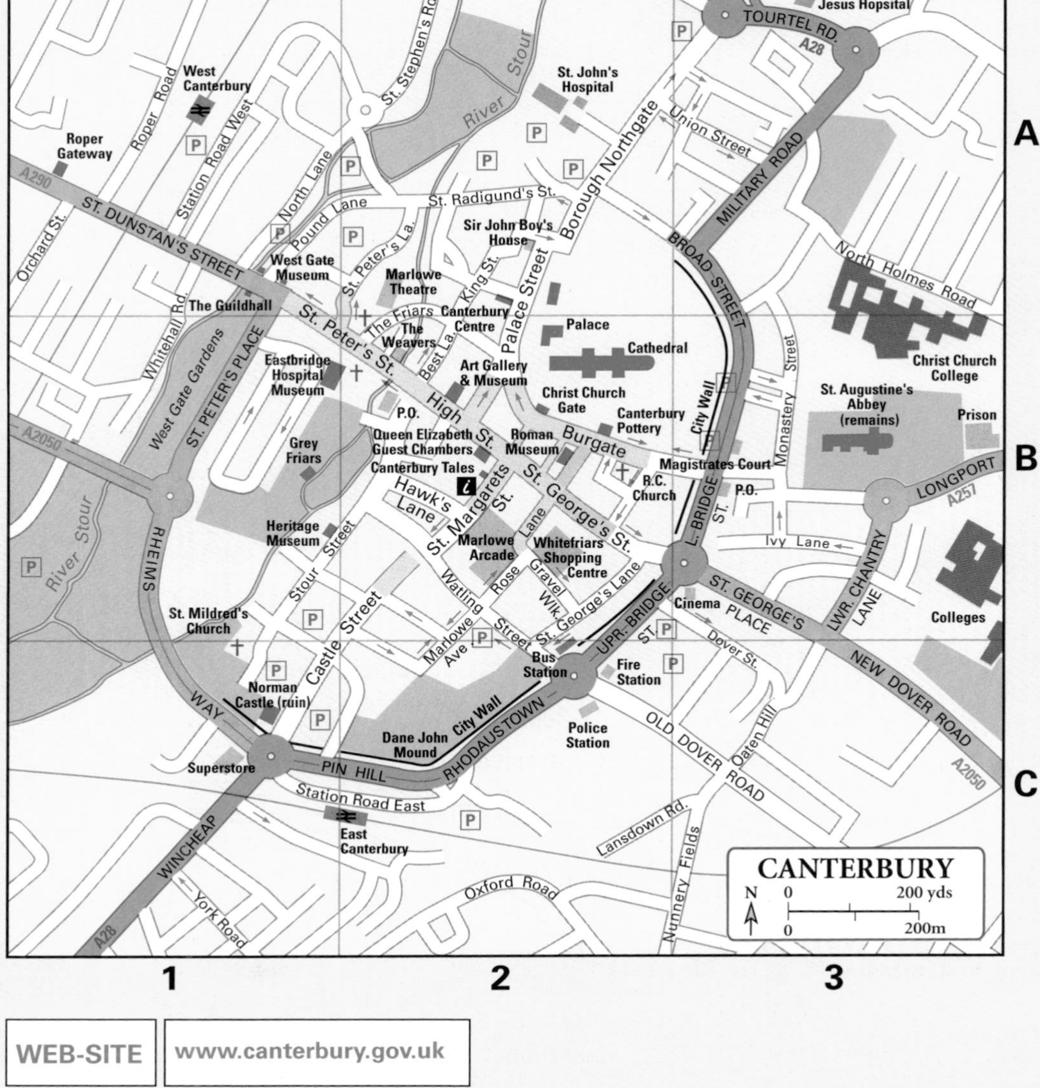

WEB-SITE	www.canterbury.gov.uk

LOCAL RADIO	BBC RADIO KENT 97.6 FM INVICTA FM 103.1 FM, 106 CTFM 106 FM

Trealaw
Ynyshir
Cilfynydd
Glyncoch
Senghenydd
Ynysddu
Cwmfelinfach
Pontywaun
Crosskeys
Castell-y-bwch
Risca
Croes-y-mwyalch
Caerleon
Porth
Trehafod
Cymmer
Hopkinstown
PONTYPRIDD
Llanbradach
Wattsville
Sirhowy Valley
Pontymister
Malpas
Bettws
Roman Fort
Christchurch
Llanbeder
Trebanog
Treforest
Abertridwr
Bedwas
Machen
Rogerstone
Milton
Underwood
Llanwern
Wilcrick
Tonyrefail
Pen-y-coedcae
Glyntaff
Rhydyfelin
Upper Boat
Rhymney Valley
CAERPHILLY
Caerphilly
Lower Machen
Rhiwderin
Draethen
Gaer
Liswerry
Bishton
NEWPORT
(Casnewydd)
Castellau
Ton-teg
Treforest Ind. Est.
Llantwit Fardre
Church Village
Coedely
Beddau
Nantgarw
Glan-y-llyn
Rudry
Parc Cefn Onn
Pentre-Poeth
Bassaleg
Michaelston-y-Fedw
Maesglas
Tredegar
Pye Corner
Broadstreet Common
Efail Isaf
Thornhill
Began
Coedkernew
Nash
Whitson
Llanharan
Talbot Green
Llantrisant
Gwaelod-y-garth
Taff's Well
(Ffynnon Taf)
Castell Coch
Lisvane
Castleton
Marshfield
St Brides Wentlooge
Goldcliff
Bryncae
Tyle-garw
Cross Inn
Pentyrch
Creigiau
Tongwynlais
Llanishen
Pentwyn
Cardiff Gate
Llanedeyrn
Blacktown
Llanharry
Pontyclun
Miskin
Groes-faen
Radyr
Birchgrove
St Mellons
Llanrumney
Rumney
Brynsadler
Whitchurch
Peterstone Wentlooge
Ely Valley
St Bride's-super-Ely
Llandaff North
Roath
Ystradowen
St Fagans
Llandaff
Mus. of Welsh Life
Maendy
Pendoylan
St George's
Ely
Canton
CARDIFF
(Caerdydd)
Peterston-super-Ely
Culverhouse Cross
Caerau
Cardiff Millennium Stadium
Welsh St Donats
Cowbridge
Grangetown
Wales Millennium Centre
Bonvilston
Twyn-yr-odyn
Leckwith
St Nicholas
Wenvoe
Llandough
St Hilary
Llantrithyd
Tinkinswood Burial Chamber
St Lythans
Michaelston-le-Pit
Dinas Powys
Cogan
Old Beaupre
Treguff
Dyffryn
St. Lythans Burial Chamber
PENARTH
Pleasure Steamers Waverley and Balmoral
St Mary Church
Llancarfan
St Andrews Major
Lower Penarth
Llanbethery
Flemingston
Palmerstown
Eglwys-Brewis
Penmark
Merthyr Dyfan
Colcot
Cadoxton
Cosmeston
St Athan
Lavernock
Cardiff International
Rhoose
Porthkerry Park
Barry Island Pleasure Park
Sully
Swanbridge
Lavenock Point
Gileston
East Aberthaw
Porthkerry
BARRY
Barry Island
Sully Island
Breaksea Pt
Whitmore Bay
Flat Holm
MOUTH OF THE SEVERN
Manor House
Clevedon Pier
Clevedon
Kingston Seymour
Middle Hope (NT)
Sand Point
Woodspring Priory
Icelton
Wick St Lawrence
Sand Bay
M4
M5
A48(M)
A4054
A469
A4233
A473
A470
A468
A4119
A4222
A4232
A4226
A4050
A4231
A4160
A4055
A4161
A467
A4051
A4042
A449
A455
A48
B4263
B4623
B4595
B4262
B4562
B4487
B4239
B4267
B4265
B4591
B4596
B4245
B4236
B4278
B4273
Ebbw
Rhymney
Taff
Ely

INDEX TO STREET NAMES

Street	Grid	Street	Grid	Street	Grid
Adam Street	C3	Cornwall Street	C1	Park Street	C2
Albany Road	A3	Cowbridge Road East	B1	Penarth Road	C2
Arran Place	A3	Crwys Road	A2	Queen Street	B2
Arran Street	A3	Duke Street	B2	Richmond Road	A3
Boulevard de Nantes	B2	Dumfries Place	B3	St. Mary Street	C2
Bridge Street	C2	Ellen Street	C3	Salisbury Road	A2
Bute Street	C2	Glossop Road	B3	Senghennydd Road	A2
Bute Terrace	C2	Hamilton Street	B1	Stuttgarter Strasse	B2
Castle Street	B1	High Street	B2	Talbot Street	B1
Cathays Terrace	A2	Kingsway	B2	Tudor Street	C1
Cathedral Road	B1	Maindy Road	A1	Tyndall Street	C3
Central Link	C3	Merches Gardens	C1	Wells Street	C1
Charles Street	B2	Meteor Street	B3	West Grove	B3
Churchill Way	B3	Mill Lane	C2	Westgate Street	B2
City Road	A3	Moira Place	B3	Windsor Place	B2
Clare Road	C1	Moira Terrace	B3	Windsor Road	B3
Clare Street	B1	Museum Avenue	A2	Wood Street	C2
Claude Road	A3	Neville Street	B1	Woodville Road	A2
Coburn Street	A2	Newport Road	B3	Working Street	B2
College Road	B2	Ninian Park Road	C1		
Colum Road	A1	North Road	A1		
Corbett Road	A2	Park Place	A2		

TOURIST INFORMATION ☎ 029 2022 7281
CARDIFF VISITOR CENTRE, 16 WOOD STREET, CARDIFF, CF10 1ES

HOSPITAL A & E ☎ 029 2074 7747
CARDIFF UNIVERSITY OF WALES HOSPITAL, HEATH PARK, CARDIFF, CF14 4XW

COUNCIL OFFICE ☎ 029 2087 2087
THE HELP CENTRE, MARLAND HOUSE, CENTRAL SQUARE, CARDIFF, CF10 1EP

Cardiff (Caerdydd). Population: 272,129. City, capital of Wales since 1955. Romans founded military fort and small settlement on site of present day Cardiff. Uninhabited between departure of Romans and Norman conquest centuries later. Fishing village until development of coal mining in 19c. Population rose from 1000 in 1801 to 170,000 a century later, with city becoming one of busiest ports in the world. Dock trade collapsed in 1930's. Since establishment as Welsh capital, many governmental, administrative and media organisations have moved to city. Major refurbishment and development programme still under way. Cardiff Bay area now major tourist centre and includes Techniquest, a science discovery centre, and has been selected as the location of the new Welsh Assembly building. Millennium Stadium Cardiff Arms Park is the home of the Welsh Rugby Union and also hosts other sporting and entertainment events. Many museums including National Museum of Wales. Universities.

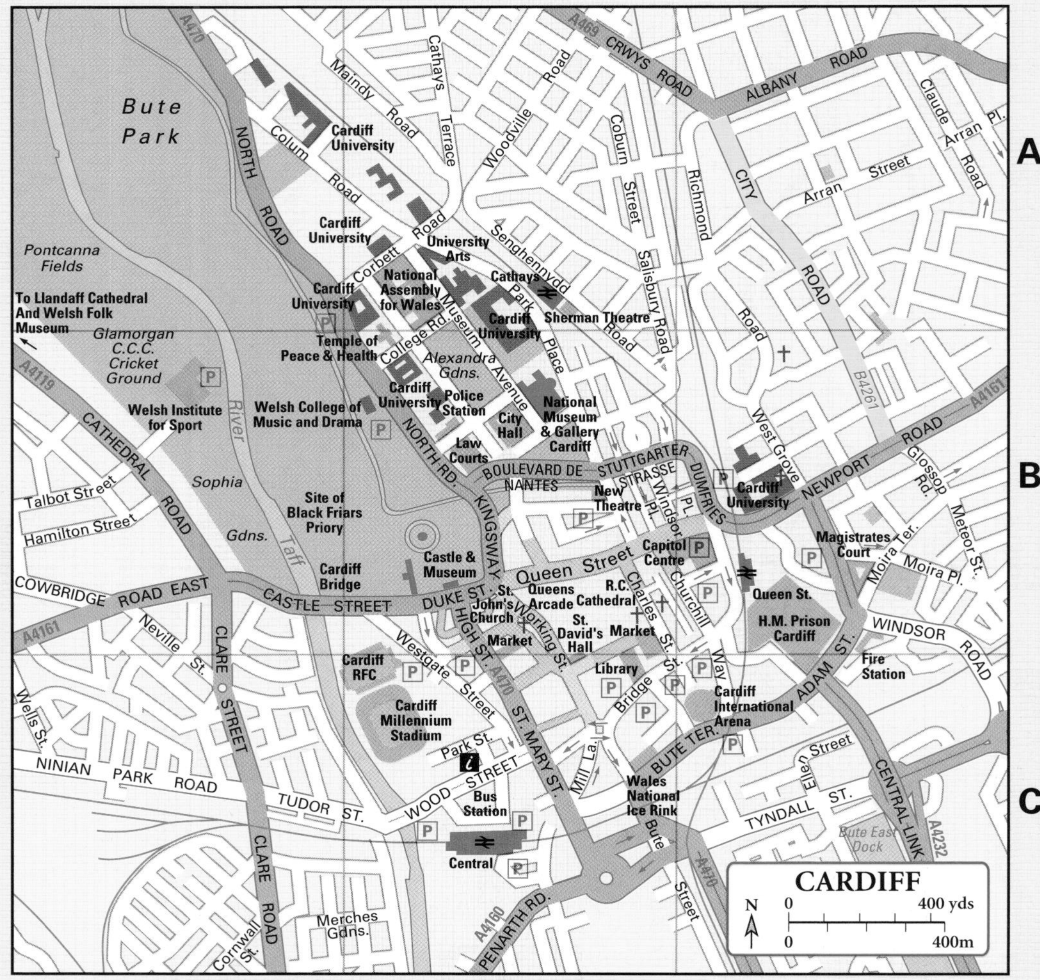

WEB-SITE www.cardiff.gov.uk

LOCAL RADIO
BBC RADIO WALES 96.8 FM
CAPITAL GOLD 1305 & 1359 AM, RED DRAGON FM 103.2 FM

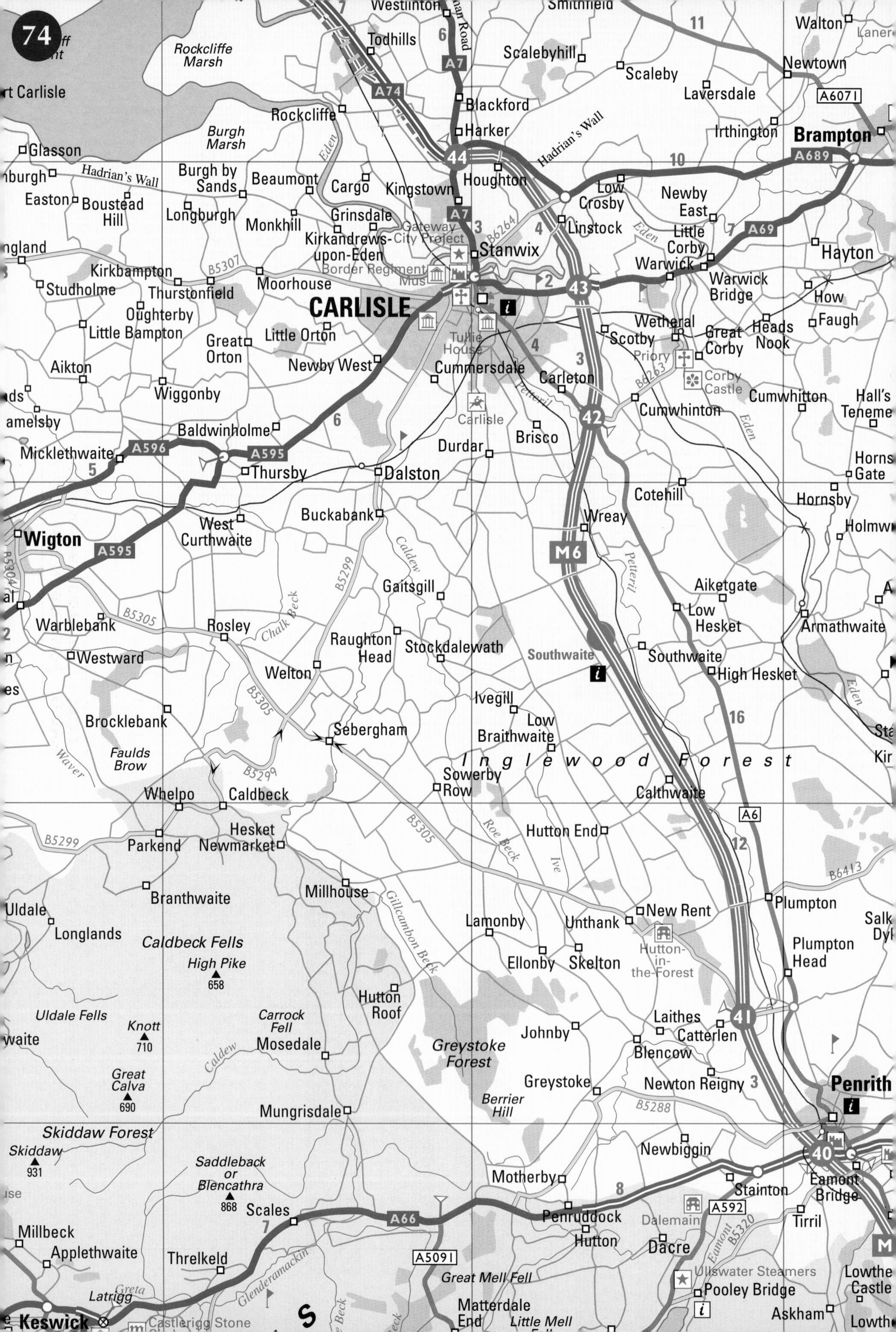
Westlinton
Smithfield
Walton
Todhills
Scalebyhill
Scaleby
Newtown
Rockcliffe Marsh
Laversdale
A6071
A7
A74
Blackford
Rockcliffe
Irthington
Brampton
Burgh Marsh
Harker
Hadrian's Wall
Glasson
44
A689
Burgh by Sands
Beaumont
Cargo
Kingstown
Houghton
Low Crosby
Newby East
Easton
Boustead Hill
Longburgh
Monkhill
Grinsdale
Linstock
Little Corby
A69
Kirkandrews-upon-Eden
Gateway City Project
Stanwix
Hayton
Kirkbampton
B5307
Border Regiment Mus
Warwick
Studholme
Thurstonfield
Moorhouse
43
Warwick Bridge
How
CARLISLE
Oughterby
Little Bampton
Wetheral
Faugh
Great Orton
Little Orton
Scotby
Great Corby
Heads Nook
Tullie House
Priory
Aikton
Newby West
Cummersdale
Carleton
Corby Castle
Cumwhitton
Hall's Tenement
Wiggonby
B6263
Cumwhinton
Petteril
Carlisle
42
Baldwinholme
Brisco
Durdar
Micklethwaite
A596
A595
Thursby
Dalston
Horns Gate
Cotehill
Hornsby
Buckabank
Wreay
Holmwrangle
West Curthwaite
Wigton
A595
M6
Caldew
B5299
Gaitsgill
Aiketgate
Low Hesket
Armathwaite
Warblebank
B5305
Rosley
Chalk Beck
Raughton Head
Stockdalewath
Southwaite
Westward
Welton
High Hesket
Eden
Ivegill
Brocklebank
Low Braithwaite
Sebergham
16
Faulds Brow
Waver
Inglewood Forest
Sowerby Row
Calthwaite
Whelpo
Caldbeck
A6
Roe Beck
Hutton End
Hesket Newmarket
Parkend
12
B6413
Branthwaite
Millhouse
Uldale
New Rent
Plumpton
Longlands
Lamonby
Unthank
Gillcambon Beck
Hutton-in-the-Forest
Caldbeck Fells
Plumpton Head
Ellonby
Skelton
High Pike
658
Hutton Roof
Uldale Fells
Carrock Fell
Laithes
Knott
710
Johnby
Catterlen
41
Mosedale
Greystoke Forest
Blencow
Great Calva
690
Greystoke
Newton Reigny
Penrith
Berrier Hill
B5288
Mungrisdale
Skiddaw Forest
Skiddaw
931
Newbiggin
40
Saddleback or Blencathra
868
Motherby
Stainton
Eamont Bridge
Scales
A66
Penruddock
Millbeck
A592
Dalemain
Tirril
Applethwaite
Hutton
Dacre
Threlkeld
A5091
Eamont
B5320
Great Mell Fell
Ullswater Steamers
Lowther Castle
Glenderamackin
Greta
Latrigg
Pooley Bridge
Matterdale End
Keswick
Castlerigg Stone
Little Mell Fell
Askham

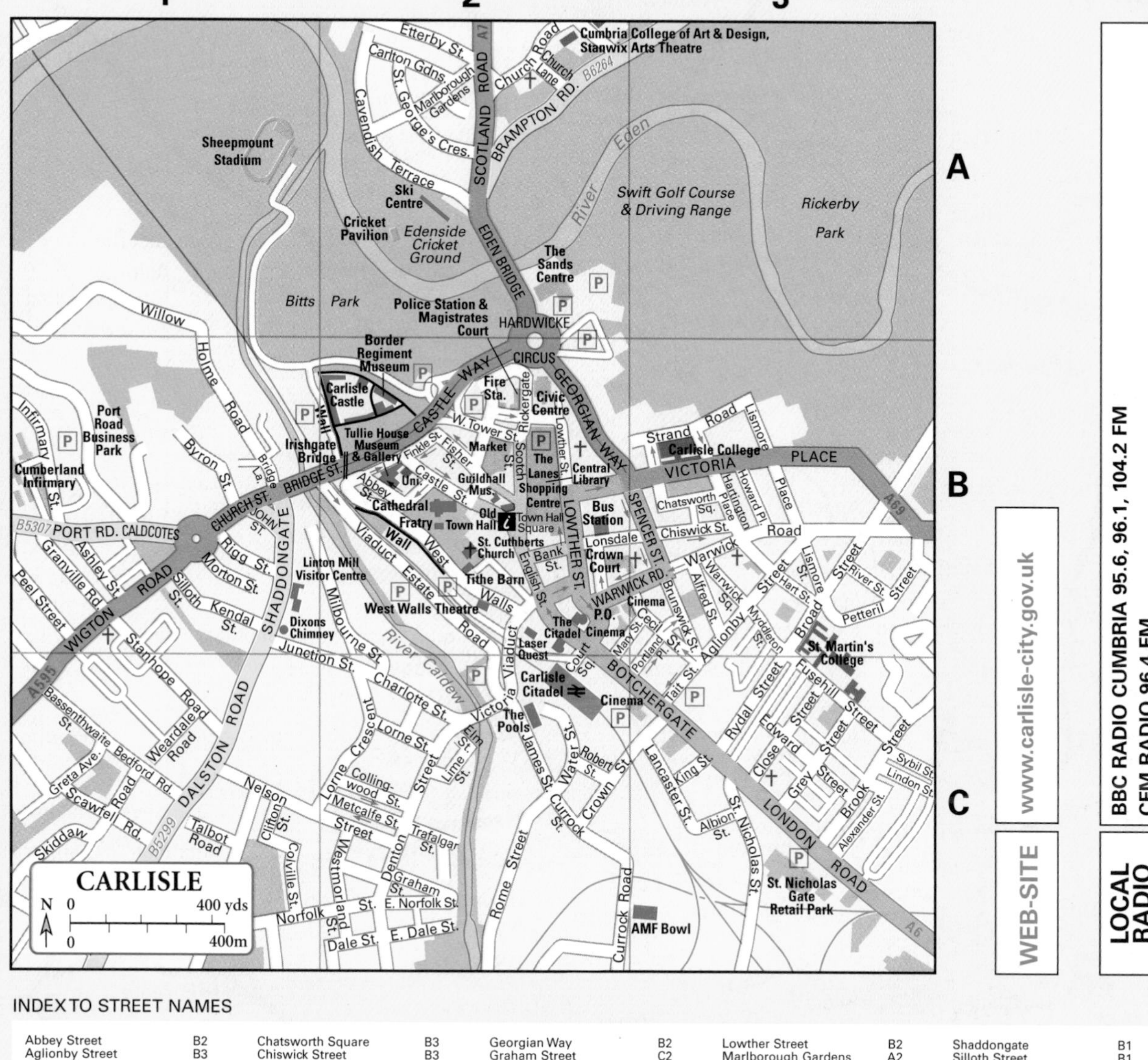

WEB-SITE

www.carlisle-city.gov.uk

LOCAL RADIO

BBC RADIO CUMBRIA 95.6, 96.1, 104.2 FM
CFM RADIO 96.4 FM

INDEX TO STREET NAMES

TOURIST INFORMATION ☎ 01228 625600
OLD TOWN HALL, GREEN MARKET,
CARLISLE, CA3 8JH

HOSPITAL A & E ☎ 01228 523444
CUMBERLAND INFIRMARY, NEWTOWN ROAD,
CARLISLE, CA2 7HY

COUNCIL OFFICE ☎ 01228 817000
CARLISLE CITY COUNCIL, THE CIVIC CENTRE,
CARLISLE, CA3 8QG

Carlisle *Cumb.* Population: 72,439. Cathedral city at confluence of River Eden and River Caldew, 54m/87km W of Newcastle upon Tyne. Once a Roman military base and later fought over by Scots and English, line of Hadrian's wall runs through the northern suburbs. Castle above the River Eden, completed in 12c, houses a military museum. Cathedral partially destroyed by fire in 17c has two surviving bays of 12c and a magnificent East window. Tullie House Museum imaginatively tells of the city's turbulent past. University of Northumbria. Racecourse 2m/4km S. Airport 6m/9km NE.

Three Counties Showground
Hanley Castle
Baughton
Eckington
Great Comberton
Bricklehampton (ruins)
A46
Malvern Wells
Welland
A4104
Upton upon Severn
Holly Green
Strensham
Bredon Hill 293
Elmley Castle
Netherton
Hinton on the Green
A38
Strensham
Naunton
8
Bredon's Norton
Little Welland
Uckinghall
Stratford
Ashton under Hill
Sedgeberrow
Childswickham
Ashton
B4208
Ripple
Twyning Green
Tithe Barn (NT)
Overbury
Kemerton
Conderton
Hollybush
Castlemorton
M50
Twyning
Bredon's Hardwick
Bredon
Elaine Rippon Hand Painted Silk
A438
Birts Street
Longdon
Shuthonger
A38
B4079
Dumbleton
Beckford
B4078
Isbourne
Camer's Green
Sledge Green
B4211
The Mythe
Great Washbourne
Bushley
B4080
Northway
Aston Cross
Alderton
A438
Pamington
B4077
New Town
Toddington
10
Forthampton
Tewkesbury
9
Ashchurch
Teddington
Pendock
Walton Cardiff
Alstone
Eldersfield
Abbey
Oxenton
Chaceley
Tewkesbury 1471
M5
Fiddington
A435
223
Dixton
Greet
B4632
B4208
B4211
Corse Lawn
Deerhurst
Gotherington
Gretton
Staunton
Tredington
GLOUCESTER
Langley Hill
Glos. Rly Farm
Apperley
Odda's Chapel
Stoke Orchard
Bishop's Cleeve
Winchcombe
Corse
Tirley
B4213
A38
Hardwicke
Cleeve Hill
Sudeley
Hasfield
Lower Apperley
Elmstone Hardwicke
Woodmancote
Roman Villa
Isbourne
12
A417
Nup End
White End
Coombe Hill
The Leigh
Southam
Ashleworth
Gorsley
Hartpury
Ashleworth Tithe Barn (NT)
Boddington
10
Uckington
Swindon Village
Cheltenham
330
Belas Knap Long Barrow
A38
A4019
B4632
Highleadon
Sandhurst
Norton
Staverton
B4634
Prestbury
Charlton Abbots
Down Hatherley
Staverton Bridge
A4013
A4019
Nature in Art
Twigworth
Golden Valley
CHELTENHAM
Brockhampton
Leadon
Maisemore
Gloucestershire
Sevenhampton
Innsworth
Up Hatherley
Whittington
Syreford
Rudford
Lassington
Longford
A40
A40
Dowdeswell
A436
Highnam
Churchdown
Leckhampton
Charlton Kings
Andoversford
A40
A38
Cath
Badgeworth
Pilley
Kilkenny
Shipton
B4063
Shurdington
A435
Nat Waterways Mus
A48
Barnwood
IIA
A46
Crickley Hill
295
A436
Foxcote
A40
GLOUCESTER
Hucclecote
A417
Blackfriars
Bentham
Brockworth
Hempsted
Seven Springs
Ullenwood
Severn
A430
A38
Matson
Upton St Leonards
Roman Villa
Little Witcombe
Coberley
Upper Coberley
Withington
Elmore Back
B4008
Cowley
Withington Woods
Elmore
Tuffley
Robinswood Hill
Great Witcombe
Birdlip
Prinknash Abbey
Chedworth Roman Villa (NT)
297
15
Quedgeley
Pottery
Prinknash Park
Colesbourne
Whaddon
Chedworth
A417
Hardwicke
B4073
A46
Cranham
Elkstone
Chedworth
Brookthorpe
Roman Road
Brimpsfield
10
M5
A435
A38
A4173
Rococo Gardens
Churn
12
B4070
Moreton Valence
Harescombe
Whiteway
Syde
Rendcomb
Haresfield
Sheepscombe
Painswick
11
Putloe
Edge
The Camp
Miserden
Winstone
Woodmancote
Calmsden
Misarden Park Gardens
Ermin Way
North Cerney
Pitchcombe
Slad
Sudgrove
Duntisbourne Abbots
Duntisbourne Leer
Stroud Green
Edgeworth
Bagendon
Whiteshill
13
Randwick
STROUD
Bisley
Duntisbourne Rouse
A419
B4008
Stonehouse
Daglingworth
A429
Eastington
Eastcombe
Bournes Green
COTSWOLD HILLS
Baunton
Oakridge Lynch
Rodborough
Leonard Stanley
King's Stanley
Bussage
Stratton
Sapperton
A46
Frocester
Woodchester
Thrupp
Chalford
Corinium
St John's Church
Cirencester
Frampton Mansell
Coaley
St. Leonards Priory
Brimscombe
12
B4066
A419
Hyde
Amberley

Area Code 01242

Gloucestershire

CHELTENHAM

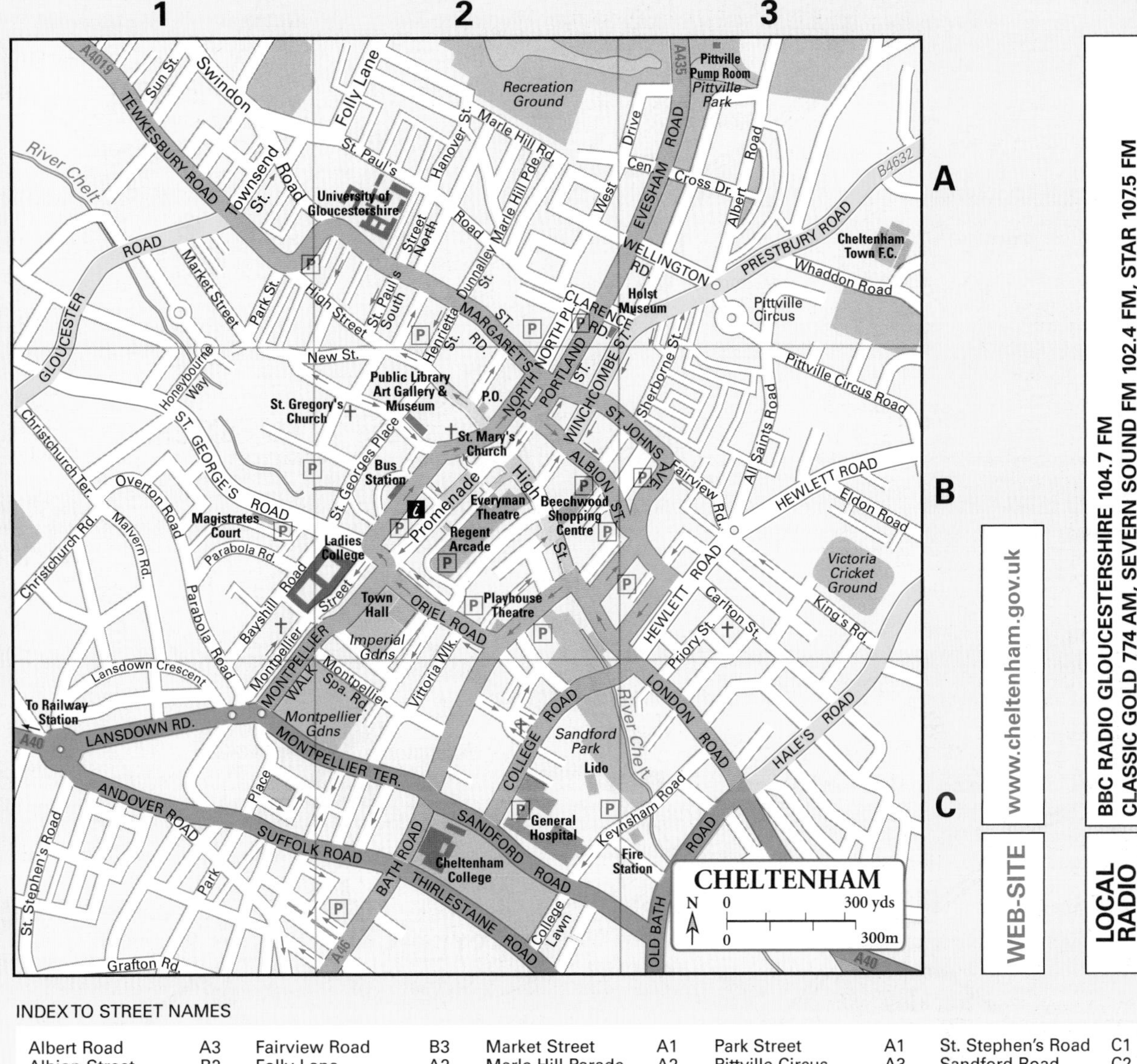

WEB-SITE www.cheltenham.gov.uk

LOCAL RADIO BBC RADIO GLOUCESTERSHIRE 104.7 FM CLASSIC GOLD 774 AM, SEVERN SOUND FM 102.4 FM, STAR 107.5 FM

INDEX TO STREET NAMES

TOURIST INFORMATION ☎ 01242 522878
77 THE PROMENADE, CHELTENHAM, GLOUCESTERSHIRE, GL50 1PP

HOSPITAL A & E ☎ 01242 222222
CHELTENHAM GENERAL HOSPITAL, SANDFORD ROAD, CHELTENHAM, GL53 7AN

COUNCIL OFFICE ☎ 01242 262626
MUNICIPAL OFFICES, THE PROMENADE, CHELTENHAM, GL50 1PP

Cheltenham *Glos.* Population: 91,301. Town, largest town in The Cotswolds, 8m/12km NE of Gloucester. Shopping and tourist centre, with some light industry. Mainly residential, with many Regency and Victorian buildings and public gardens. Formerly a spa town, Pittville Pump Room built between 1825 and 1830 overlooks Pittville Park and is now used for concerts. Art Gallery and Museum. Ladies' College founded 1853. Racecourse to the N hosts Cheltenham Gold Cup race meeting, Cheltenham International Music Festival and Festival of Literature, among other events. Birthplace of composer Gustav Holst. University of Gloucestershire.

Moreton
BIRKENHEAD
West Kirby
Frankby
Greasby
Woodchurch
Oxton
Prenton
Rock Ferry
New Ferry
Lady Lever Art Gallery
Port Sunlight
Caldy
Thurstaston
Irby
Storeton
Barnston
BEBINGTON
The Wirral (NT)
Pensby
Brimstage
Heswall
Dawpool Bank
Voirrey Embroidery
Bromborough
Eastham Woods
Gayton
Thornton Hough
Eastham
Raby
WIRRAL
MERSEY
DEE
Mossley Hill
Childwall
National Wildflower Centre
Gateacre
Halewood
Hough
Woolton
Sudley Art Gal & Mus
Aigburth
Allerton
Grassendale
Garston
Hunt's Cross
Speke
Speke Hall (NT)
Liverpool John Lennon
Cathedral
HM Customs National Museum
Mount Manisty
Ince Banks
ELLESMERE PORT
Manchester Ship Canal
Hooton
Childer Thornton
Overpool
Little Sutton
Willaston
Parkgate
Neston
Little Neston
Ness
Botanic Gardens
Greenfield Valley
Greenfield (Maes-Glas)
Holywell Bank
Ince
Elton
McArthurGlen Cheshire Oaks
Great Sutton
Whitby
Blue Planet Aquarium
Ledsham
Burton
Capenhurst
Little Stanney
Stoak
Thornton-le-Moors
Hapsford
Dunham-on-the-Hill
Puddington
Shotwick
Backford
Wervin
Picton
Bridge Trafford
Flint (ruins)
Flint (Y Fflint)
White Sands
Bagillt
Bedol
Flint Mountain
Connah's Quay
Saughall
Mollington
Zoo
Mickle Trafford
Northop
Northop Hall
Wepre
Garden City
Sealand
Upton
Guilden Sutton
Great Barrow
Rhosesmor
Shotton
Queensferry
Blacon
Hoole
Ewloe (ruins)
Mancot Royal
Sandycroft
Soughton
Aston
CHESTER
Cathedral
Littleton
Christleton
Roman Road
Ewloe
Hawarden
Saltney
Handbridge
Mold (Yr Wyddgrug)
Buckley (Bwcle)
Drury
Prenbrigog
Broughton
Bretton
Rowton
Waverton
Rowton Heath 1645
Llong
Padeswood
Penyffordd
Lower Kinnerton
Eccleston
Saighton
Hargrave
Moel Findeg
Maeshafn
Nercwys
Rhos-y-brwyner
Dodleston
Eaton Hall
Hatton Heath
Pontblyddyn
Plas Teg
Cuckoo's Nest
Bruera
Leeswood
Pontybodkin
Gatesheath
Aldford
Hope
Burton Green
Pulford
Milton Green
Tattenhall
Eryrys
Treuddyn
Waun-y-Llyn
Caergwrle
Lavister
Handley
Pantyffordd
Rossett
Trevalyn
Aldersey Green
Llanfynydd
Cefn-y-bedd
Churton
Chowley
Ffrith
Llay
Marford
Coddington
Rhydtalog
Llyn Cyfynwy
Gresford
Farndon
Bridge
Barton
Clutton
Summerhill
Brymbo
Gwersyllt
Holt
Fuller's Moor
Bwlchgwyn
Moss
Borras Head
Crewe
Moel Garegog
Brynteg
Stretton
Minera
Southsea
Rhosddu
Llan-y-pwll
Hugmore
Ridleywood
Duckington
Coedpoeth
New Broughton
Rhosnesni
Tilston
Esclusham Mountain
Rhos-berse
WREXHAM (Wrecsam)
Wrexham Industrial Estate
Bersham
Shocklach
Horton Green
Hampton Heath
World's End
Rhostyllen
Wrexham Arts Centre
Pentre
M53
M56
A41
A55
A483
A550
A5117
A540
A548
A5119
A494
A5104
A541
A549
A5118
A525
A5152
A534
A51
A56
A5032
A5116
A5268
A552
A553
A5027
A562
A561
A5300
A5137
A5058

Area Code 01244

Cheshire

CHESTER

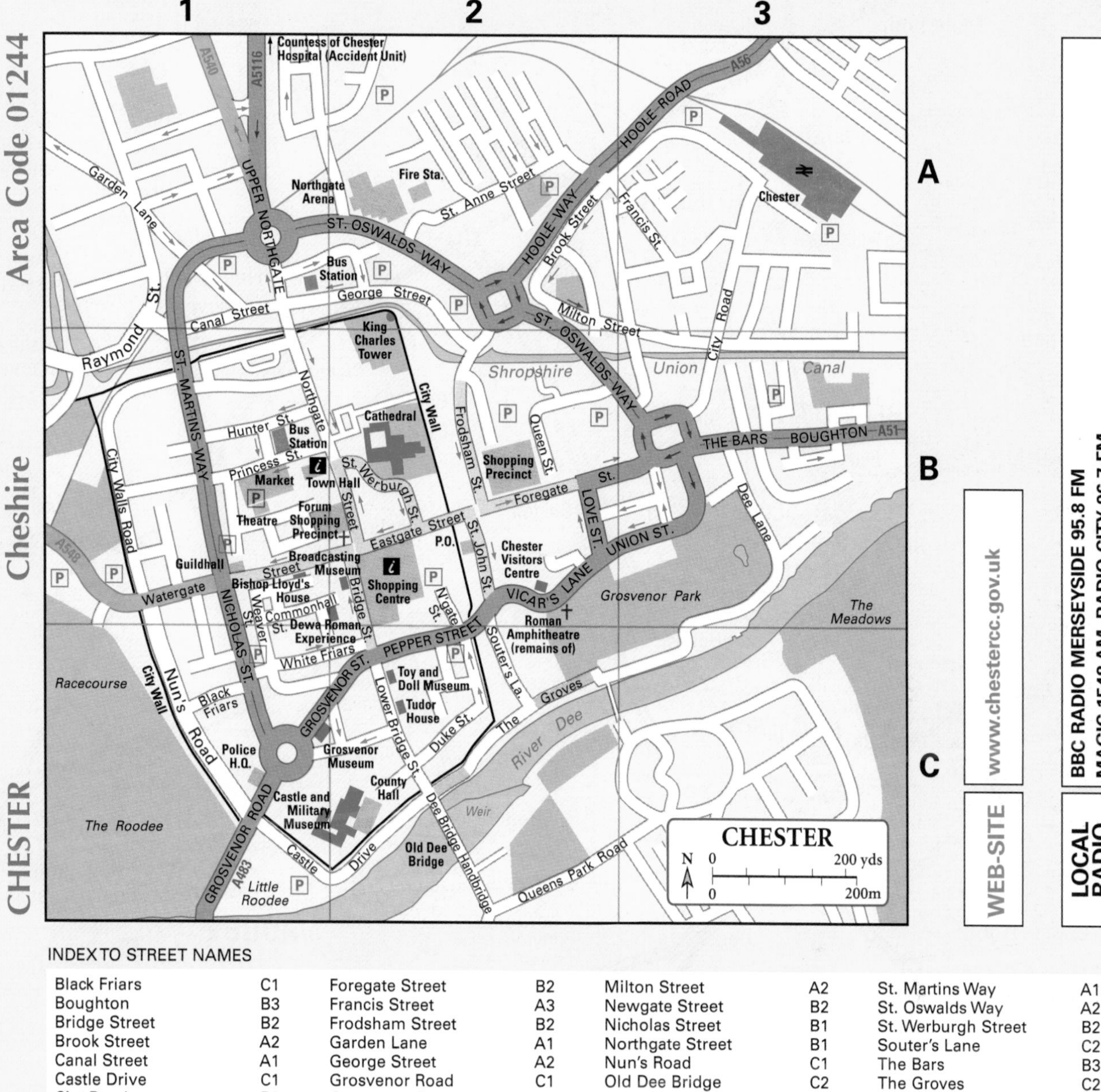

WEB-SITE

www.chestercc.gov.uk

LOCAL RADIO

BBC RADIO MERSEYSIDE 95.8 FM
MAGIC 1548 AM, RADIO CITY 96.7 FM

INDEX TO STREET NAMES

Black Friars	C1	Foregate Street	B2	Milton Street	A2	St. Martins Way	A1
Boughton	B3	Francis Street	A3	Newgate Street	B2	St. Oswalds Way	A2
Bridge Street	B2	Frodsham Street	B2	Nicholas Street	B1	St. Werburgh Street	B2
Brook Street	A2	Garden Lane	A1	Northgate Street	B1	Souter's Lane	C2
Canal Street	A1	George Street	A2	Nun's Road	C1	The Bars	B3
Castle Drive	C1	Grosvenor Road	C1	Old Dee Bridge	C2	The Groves	C2
City Road	B3	Grosvenor Street	C1	Pepper Street	C2	Union Street	B2
City Walls Road	B1	Handbridge	C2	Princess Street	B1	Upper Northgate	A1
Commonhall Street	B1	Hoole Road	A2	Queens Park Road	C2	Vicar's Lane	B2
Dee Bridge	C2	Hoole Way	A2	Queen Street	B2	Watergate Street	B1
Dee Lane	B3	Hunter Street	B1	Raymond Street	A1	Weaver Street	B1
Duke Street	C2	Love Street	B2	St. Anne Street	A2	White Friars	C1
Eastgate Street	B2	Lower Bridge Street	C2	St. John Street	B2		

TOURIST INFORMATION ☎ 01244 402111
TOWN HALL, NORTHGATE STREET,
CHESTER, CHESHIRE, CH1 2HJ

HOSPITAL A & E ☎ 01244 365000
COUNTESS OF CHESTER HOSPITAL, HEALTH PK,
LIVERPOOL ROAD, CHESTER, CH2 1UL

COUNCIL OFFICE ☎ 01244 324324
THE FORUM,
CHESTER, CH1 2HS

Chester *Ches.* Population: 80110. City, county town and cathedral city on River Dee, 34m/54km SW of Manchester and 15m/24km SE of Birkenhead. Commercial, financial and tourist centre built on Roman town of Deva. Includes biggest Roman amphitheatre in Britain (English Heritage) and well preserved medieval walls (English Heritage). Castle, now county hall, includes 12c Agricola Tower (English Heritage). Cathedral with remains of original Norman abbey. Famed for Tudor timber-framed buildings which include Chester Rows, two-tier galleried shops and Bishop Lloyd's House, with ornate 16c carved façade. Eastgate clock built to commemorate Queen Victoria's diamond jubilee in 1897. Racecourse 1m/2km SW of city centre; zoo 3m/4km N of city centre.

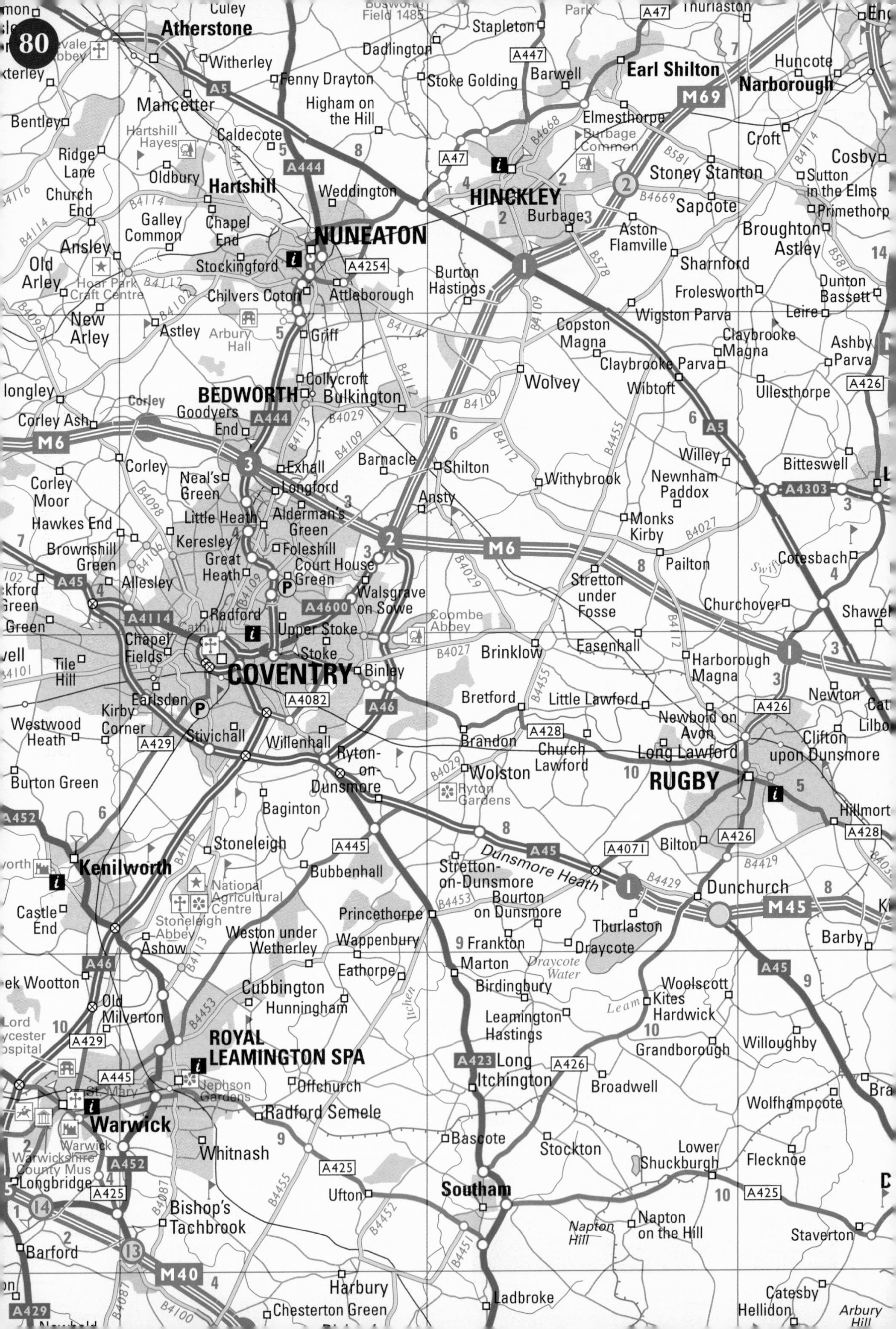

Culey
Atherstone
Bosworth Field 1485
Park
A47
Thurlaston
Stapleton
Witherley
Dadlington
A447
Earl Shilton
Huncote
Fenny Drayton
Stoke Golding
Barwell
Narborough
A5
M69
Mancetter
Higham on the Hill
Elmesthorpe
Bentley
Hartshill Hayes
Caldecote
B4668
Burbage Common
Croft
Ridge Lane
A444
A47
B581
Cosby
Oldbury
Stoney Stanton
Sutton in the Elms
Church End
Hartshill
Weddington
HINCKLEY
B4114
B4669
Sapcote
Primethorpe
Galley Common
Chapel End
Burbage
Broughton Astley
Aston Flamville
Ansley
NUNEATON
B578
Old Arley
Stockingford
A4254
Burton Hastings
Sharnford
B581
Hoar Park Craft Centre
B4112
Chilvers Coton
Attleborough
Frolesworth
Dunton Bassett
B4098
New Arley
B4102
Astley
Arbury Hall
Griff
B4114
B4109
Wigston Parva
Leire
Copston Magna
Claybrooke Magna
Ashby Parva
Claybrooke Parva
Collycroft
Wolvey
Wibtoft
Ullesthorpe
A426
Longley
Corley
BEDWORTH
Bulkington
B4112
Goodyers End
B4109
Corley Ash
A444
B4113
B4029
M6
B4455
A5
B4109
B4112
Willey
Bitteswell
Corley
Exhall
Barnacle
Shilton
Withybrook
Corley Moor
Neal's Green
Longford
Newnham Paddox
A4303
B4098
Ansty
Little Heath
Alderman's Green
Monks Kirby
Hawkes End
Keresley
B4027
Brownshill Green
Foleshill
M6
Great Heath
Court House Green
B4029
Pailton
Cotesbach
Stretton under Fosse
Swift
A45
B4106
Allesley
B4109
Walsgrave on Sowe
A4600
Churchover
Shawell
A4114
Radford
Coombe Abbey
Chapel Fields
Cath.
Upper Stoke
Easenhall
Brinklow
B4112
Stoke
B4027
Harborough Magna
Tile Hill
B4101
COVENTRY
Binley
B4455
Newton
Earlsdon
Westwood Heath
A4082
A46
Bretford
Little Lawford
Newbold on Avon
A426
Kirby Corner
Stivichall
Willenhall
Brandon
A428
Clifton upon Dunsmore
A429
Ryton-on-Dunsmore
Church Lawford
Long Lawford
Burton Green
B4029
Wolston
RUGBY
Ryton Gardens
Baginton
A452
Hillmorton
A428
Stoneleigh
A445
A45
A4071
Bilton
A426
Dunsmore Heath
Kenilworth
B4115
Bubbenhall
Stretton-on-Dunsmore
B4429
Dunchurch
B4429
National Agricultural Centre
Bourton on Dunsmore
M45
Castle End
B4453
Princethorpe
Thurlaston
Stoneleigh Abbey
Weston under Wetherley
Wappenbury
Frankton
Draycote
Barby
Ashow
Draycote Water
B4113
A46
Eathorpe
Marton
A45
Leek Wootton
Cubbington
Birdingbury
Woolscott
Old Milverton
Hunningham
Kites Hardwick
Leam
Itchen
Leamington Hastings
Lord Leycester Hospital
A429
B4453
ROYAL LEAMINGTON SPA
Grandborough
Willoughby
A423
Long Itchington
A426
A445
St. Mary
Jephson Gardens
Offchurch
Broadwell
Wolfhampcote
Radford Semele
Warwick
Bascote
Stockton
Lower Shuckburgh
Flecknoe
Warwick
A452
Whitnash
Warwickshire County Mus
A425
Longbridge
A425
B4455
Ufton
Southam
A425
B4087
Bishop's Tachbrook
B4452
Napton Hill
Napton on the Hill
Staverton
B4451
Barford
M40
Harbury
Catesby
A429
B4100
Chesterton Green
Ladbroke
Hellidon
Arbury Hill

Area Code 024

West Midlands

COVENTRY

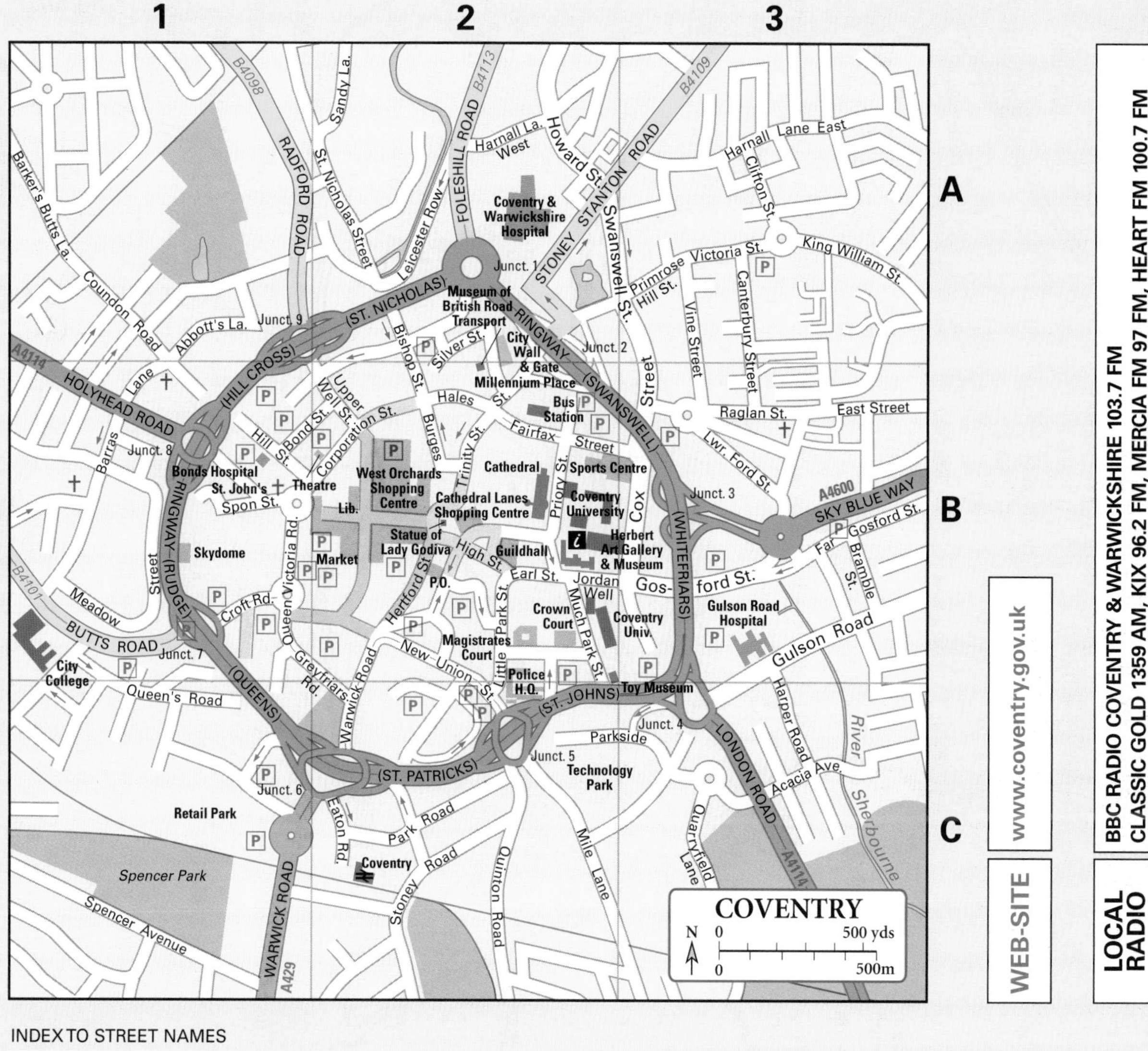

WEB-SITE

www.coventry.gov.uk

LOCAL RADIO

BBC RADIO COVENTRY & WARWICKSHIRE 103.7 FM
CLASSIC GOLD 1359 AM, KIX 96.2 FM, MERCIA FM 97 FM, HEART FM 100.7 FM

INDEX TO STREET NAMES

Street	Ref	Street	Ref	Street	Ref	Street	Ref	Street	Ref
Abbott's Lane	A1	East Street	B3	Howard Street	A2	Queen's Road	C1	Sky Blue Way	B3
Acacia Avenue	C3	Eaton Road	C2	Jordan Well	B2	Queen Victoria Road	B1	Spencer Avenue	C1
Barker's Butts Lane	A1	Fairfax Street	B2	King William Street	A3	Quinton Road	C2	Spon Street	B1
Barras Lane	B1	Far Gosford Street	B3	Leicester Row	A2	Radford Road	A1	Stoney Road	C2
Bishop Street	A2	Foleshill Road	A2	Little Park Street	C2	Raglan Street	B3	Stoney Stanton Road	A2
Bond Street	B1	Gosford Street	B3	London Road	C3	Ringway Hill Cross	B1	Swanswell Street	A2
Bramble Street	B3	Greyfriars Road	B1	Lower Ford Street	B3	Ringway St. Johns	C2	Trinity Street	B2
Burges	B2	Gulson Road	B3	Meadow Street	B1	Ringway St. Nicholas	A2	Upper Well Street	B2
Butts Road	B1	Hales Street	B2	Mile Lane	C2	Ringway St. Patricks	C2	Victoria Street	A3
Canterbury Street	A3	Harnall Lane East	A3	Much Park Street	B2	Ringway Queens	B1	Vine Street	A3
Clifton Street	A3	Harnall Lane West	A2	New Union Street	B2	Ringway Rudge	B1	Warwick Road	C1
Corporation Street	B2	Harper Road	C3	Park Road	C2	Ringway Swanswell	B2		
Coundon Road	A1	Hertford Street	B2	Parkside	C2	Ringway Whitefriars	B3		
Cox Street	B3	High Street	B2	Primrose Hill Street	A3	St. Nicholas Street	A2		
Croft Road	B1	Hill Street	B1	Priory Street	B2	Sandy Lane	A2		
Earl Street	B2	Holyhead Road	B1	Quarryfield Lane	C3	Silver Street	A2		

TOURIST INFORMATION ☎ 024 7622 7264
BAYLEY LANE, COVENTRY,
WEST MIDLANDS, CV1 5RN

HOSPITAL A & E ☎ 024 7622 4055
COVENTRY & WARWICKSHIRE HOSPITAL,
STONEY STANTON ROAD, COVENTRY, CV1 4FH

COUNCIL OFFICE ☎ 024 7683 3333
COUNCIL HOUSE, EARL STREET,
COVENTRY, CV1 5RR

Coventry *W.Mid.* Population: 299,316. City, 17m/27km E of Birmingham. St. Michael's cathedral built 1954-62 beside ruins of medieval cathedral destroyed in air raid in 1940. The centre of the city was rebuilt in the 1950s and 1960s following WW II bombing, but some old buildings remain, including Bonds Hospital and the medieval Guildhall. A town rich from textile industry in middle ages, Coventry is now known for its motor car industry; other important industries are manufacturing and engineering. Museum of British Road Transport. Herbert Art Gallery and Museum. Universities. Civil airport at Baginton to S. Coventry Canal runs N to Trent and Mersey Canal at Fradley Junction near Lichfield.

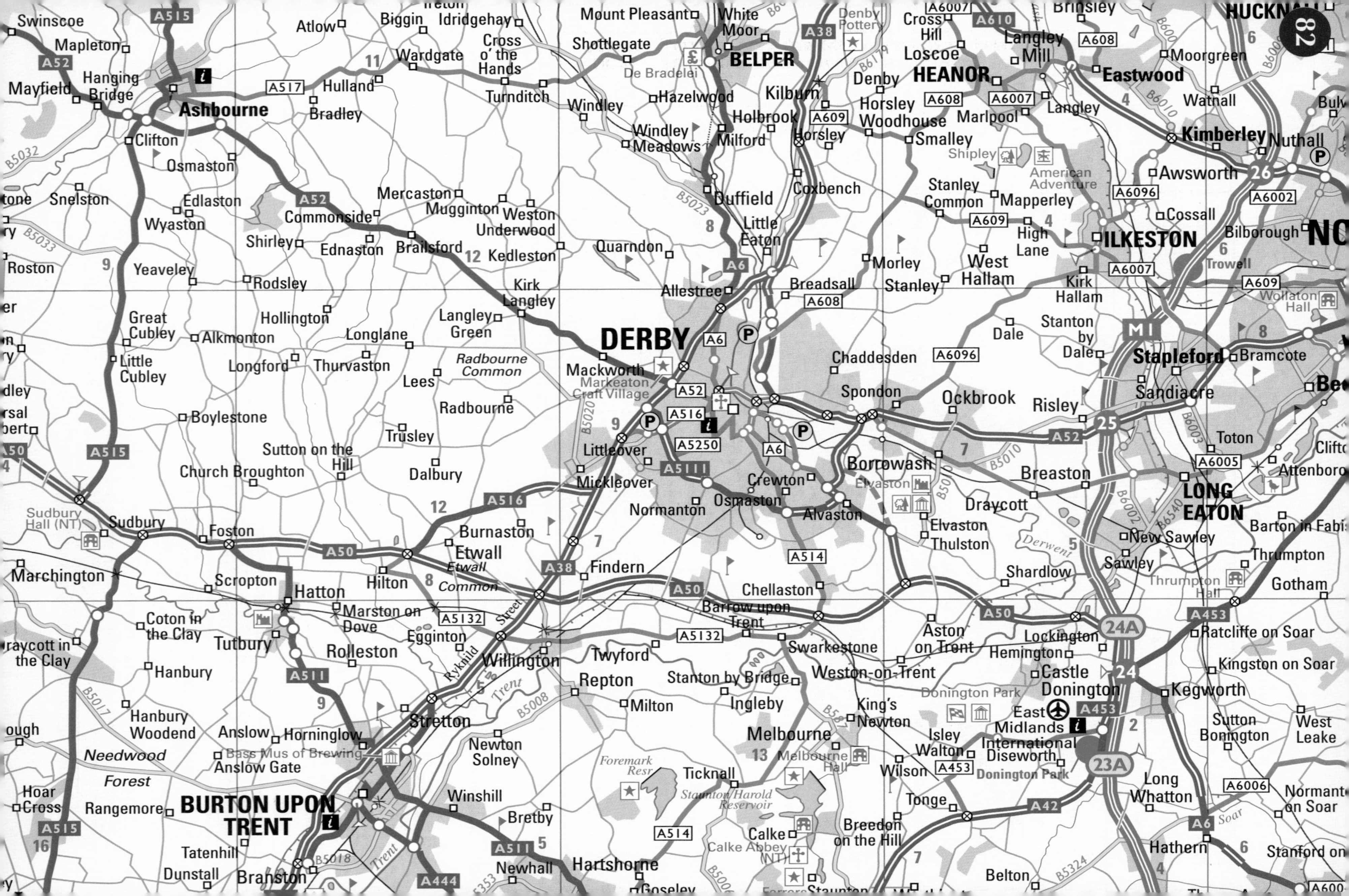

Swinscoe
Mapleton
Hanging Bridge
Mayfield
Ashbourne
Clifton
Osmaston
Snelston
Edlaston
Wyaston
Roston
Yeaveley
Great Cubley
Little Cubley
Boylestone
Church Broughton
Sudbury
Sudbury Hall (NT)
Marchington
Foston
Scropton
Hatton
Coton in the Clay
Tutbury
Draycott in the Clay
Hanbury
Hanbury Woodend
Needwood
Forest
Hoar Cross
Rangemore
BURTON UPON TRENT
Tatenhill
Dunstall
Branston
Anslow
Anslow Gate
Horninglow
Bass Mus of Brewing
Stretton
Rolleston
Marston on Dove
Egginton
Hilton
Etwall
Etwall Common
Burnaston
Findern
Willington
Rykneld Street
Newton Solney
Winshill
Bretby
Newhall
Hartshorne
Goseley
Repton
Milton
Twyford
Ingleby
Stanton by Bridge
Foremark Resr
Ticknall
Staunton Harold Reservoir
Calke
Calke Abbey (NT)
Staunton
Melbourne
Melbourne Hall
Breedon on the Hill
Tonge
Wilson
Isley Walton
King's Newton
Weston-on-Trent
Swarkestone
Barrow upon Trent
Chellaston
Aston on Trent
Shardlow
Derwent
Donington Park
East Midlands International
Diseworth
Castle Donington
Hemington
Lockington
Belton
Long Whatton
Hathern
Kegworth
Sutton Bonington
West Leake
Normanton on Soar
Stanford on Soar
Soar
Kingston on Soar
Ratcliffe on Soar
Gotham
Thrumpton
Thrumpton Hall
Barton in Fabis
Sawley
New Sawley
LONG EATON
Attenborough
Toton
Breaston
Draycott
Elvaston
Thulston
Alvaston
Borrowash
Ockbrook
Risley
Spondon
Chaddesden
Crewton
Osmaston
Normanton
Mickleover
Littleover
DERBY
Mackworth
Markeaton Craft Village
Radbourne
Radbourne Common
Dalbury
Trusley
Sutton on the Hill
Lees
Longford
Thurvaston
Longlane
Langley Green
Kirk Langley
Alkmonton
Rodsley
Hollington
Shirley
Ednaston
Brailsford
Commonside
Mercaston
Mugginton
Weston Underwood
Kedleston
Quarndon
Allestree
Breadsall
Duffield
Little Eaton
Coxbench
Morley
Stanley
West Hallam
Kirk Hallam
Dale
Stanton by Dale
Sandiacre
Stapleford
Bramcote
Beeston
Wollaton Hall
Trowell
ILKESTON
Bilborough
Cossall
Awsworth
Kimberley
Nuthall
Watnall
Moorgreen
Eastwood
HUCKNALL
Brinsley
Langley Mill
Langley
Marlpool
HEANOR
Loscoe
Cross Hill
Denby
Denby Pottery
Horsley Woodhouse
Smalley
Shipley
American Adventure
Mapperley
Stanley Common
High Lane
Horsley
Kilburn
Holbrook
Milford
BELPER
White Moor
Mount Pleasant
Shottlegate
De Bradelei
Hazelwood
Windley
Windley Meadows
Turnditch
Cross o' the Hands
Idridgehay
Biggin
Wardgate
Hulland
Bradley
Atlow

A52 A515 A517 A50 A516 A38 A5132 A511 A444 A514 A5111 A5250 A6 A608 A6096 A609 A6007 A610 A6096 A6002 A6005 A453 A42 A6006 M1 B5032 B5033 B5017 B5018 B5008 B5020 B5023 B5010 B6002 B6540 B6003 B6010 B600 B5324 B587 B6179

INDEX TO STREET NAMES

TOURIST INFORMATION ☎ 01332 255802
ASSEMBLY ROOMS, MARKET PLACE, DERBY, DE1 3AH

HOSPITAL A & E ☎ 01332 347141
DERBYSHIRE ROYAL INFIRMARY, LONDON ROAD, DERBY, DE1 2QY

COUNCIL OFFICE ☎ 01332 293111
THE COUNCIL HOUSE, CORPORATION STREET, DERBY, DE1 2FS

Derby Population: 223,836. City, industrial city and county town on River Derwent, 35m/56km NE of Birmingham. Shopping and entertainment centre. Cathedral mainly by James Gibbs, 1725. Both manufacturing and engineering are important to local economy. Derby Industrial Museum charts city's industrial history with emphasis on Rolls Royce aircraft engineering. Tours at Royal Crown Derby porcelain factory. University.

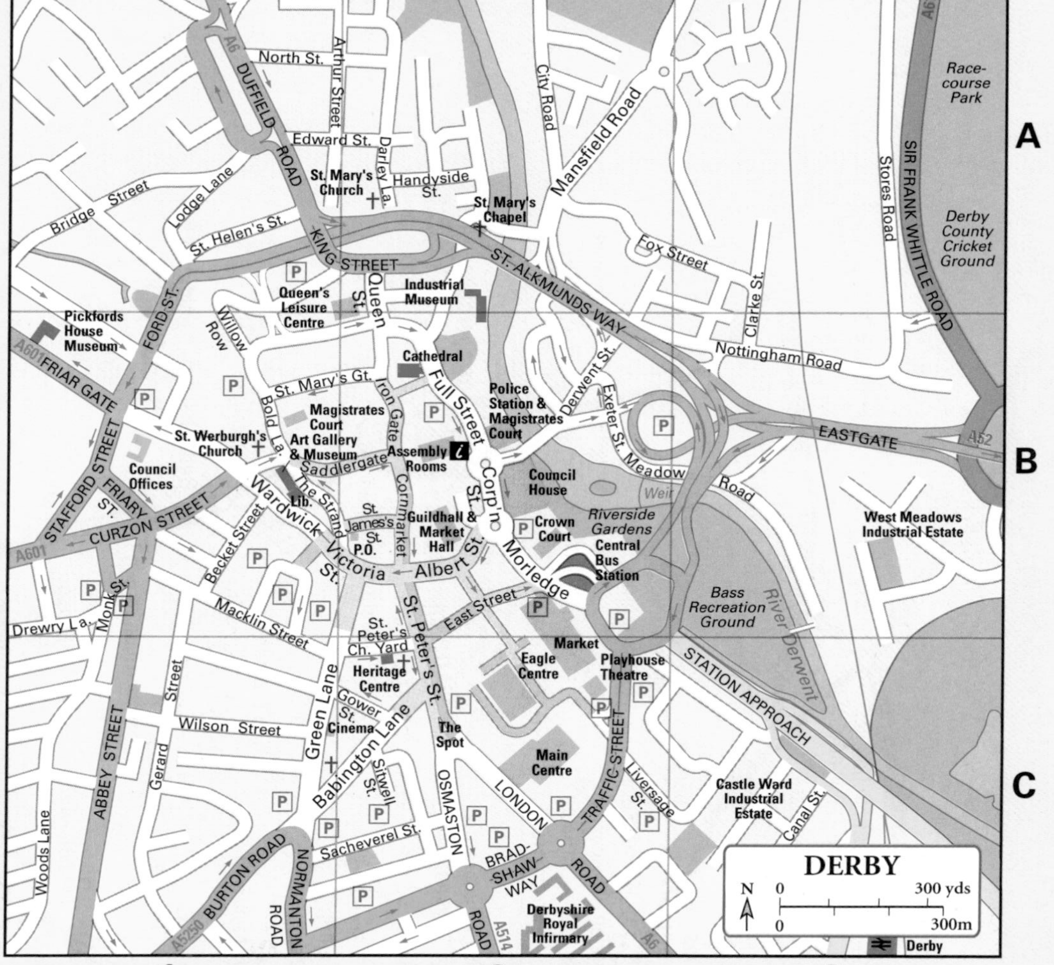

WEB-SITE	www.derby.gov.uk

LOCAL RADIO	BBC RADIO DERBY 104.5 FM CLASSIC GOLD GEM 945 AM, RAM FM 102.8 FM

Long Nose Spit
South Channel
Dreamland
Foreness Point
MARGATE
Tudor House
Cliftonville
White Ness
Westgate on Sea
Kingsgate
North Foreland
HERNE BAY
Reculver
Salmeston Grange
St Peter's
Towers & Roman Fort
Birchington
Quex House & Gdns
A255
A254
Bleak House
Hillborough
Beltinge
A299
A28
RAF Manston Spitfire & Hurricane Memorial Bldg
BROADSTAIRS
A2090
West End
Broomfield
St Nicholas at Wade
Acol
Isle of Thanet
A256
A255
A254
Dickens House
Herne
Hunters Forstal
Highstead
Boyden Gate
Sarre
Minster
Manston
A253
RAMSGATE
Herne Common
Maypole
Hoath
Chislet
Gore Street
Monkton
Abbey
Cliffs End
Vealden Woodlands
A28
West Stourmouth
Stour
St Augustine's Cross
Calcott
Upstreet
A256
Pegwell Bay
Roman Road
East Stourmouth
A291
Grove
Westmarsh
Broadoak
Hersden
Stodmarsh
Richborough Castle
Sandwich Flats
Sturry
Westbere
Preston
Ware
Stonar Cut
Fordwich
Great Stour
Stodmarsh
Elmstone
Cop Street
Great Stonar
Hoaden
Roman Amphitheatre
Sandwich
Bird Park
Sandwich Bay
Wickhambreaux
St Augustine's Abbey
Littlebourne
Ickham
A257
Ash
Salutation Gdn
A257
Toll
CANTERBURY
Howletts Wild Animal Park
Wingham
Marshborough
Bramling
Staple
Woodnesborough
A2050
Bekesbourne
Worth
Patrixbourne
Goodnestone Park
B2046
Eastry
Hacklinge
Ham
Goodnestone
A2
Bridge
Adisham
Knowlton
Finglesham
A258
Lower Hardres
Chillenden
DEAL
Betteshanger
Sholden
Bishopsbourne
Aylesham
Nonington
Northbourne
Deal
Roman Road
Easole Street
Tilmanstone
A256
Kingston
Great Mongeham
Womenswold
Elvington
East Studdal
Walmer
Barham
Barfrestone
Ripple
Walmer Castle & Garden
Derringstone
Woollage Green
Eythorne
Sutton
Ashley
Kingsdown
Shepherdswell (Sibertswold)
West Langdon
Ringwould
Lyminge Forest
Breach
Denton
Lydden
Martin Mill Sta.
A258
Bladbean
Coldred
Wingmore
Wootton
East Langdon
Lydden
A2
Whitfield
St Margaret's at Cliffe
Selstead
Guston
West Cliffe
St Margaret's Bay
Cottages
Elham
A260
Temple Ewell
A256
The Pines
Acrise Place
Ottinge
Ewell Minnis
Swingfield Minnis
Alkham
Buckland
South Foreland
St Radigund's Abbey
Dover
DOVER
Lyminge
Densole
De Bradelei Wharf
Drellingore
Maxton
Paddlesworth
Hawkinge
West Hougham
Farthingloe
Etchinghill
A20
Knights Templar Church
Capel le Ferne
Channel Tunnel
Channel Tunnel Terminal
Newington
B2011
A20
M20
11A
12
13
East Wear Bay
Cheriton
FOLKESTONE
A259
Sandgate
Rotunda Amusement Park
Hythe
STRAIT OF DOVER
hours
Calais ¾-1¼
Oostende 2
Zeebrugge 4½

Area Code 01304

Kent

DOVER

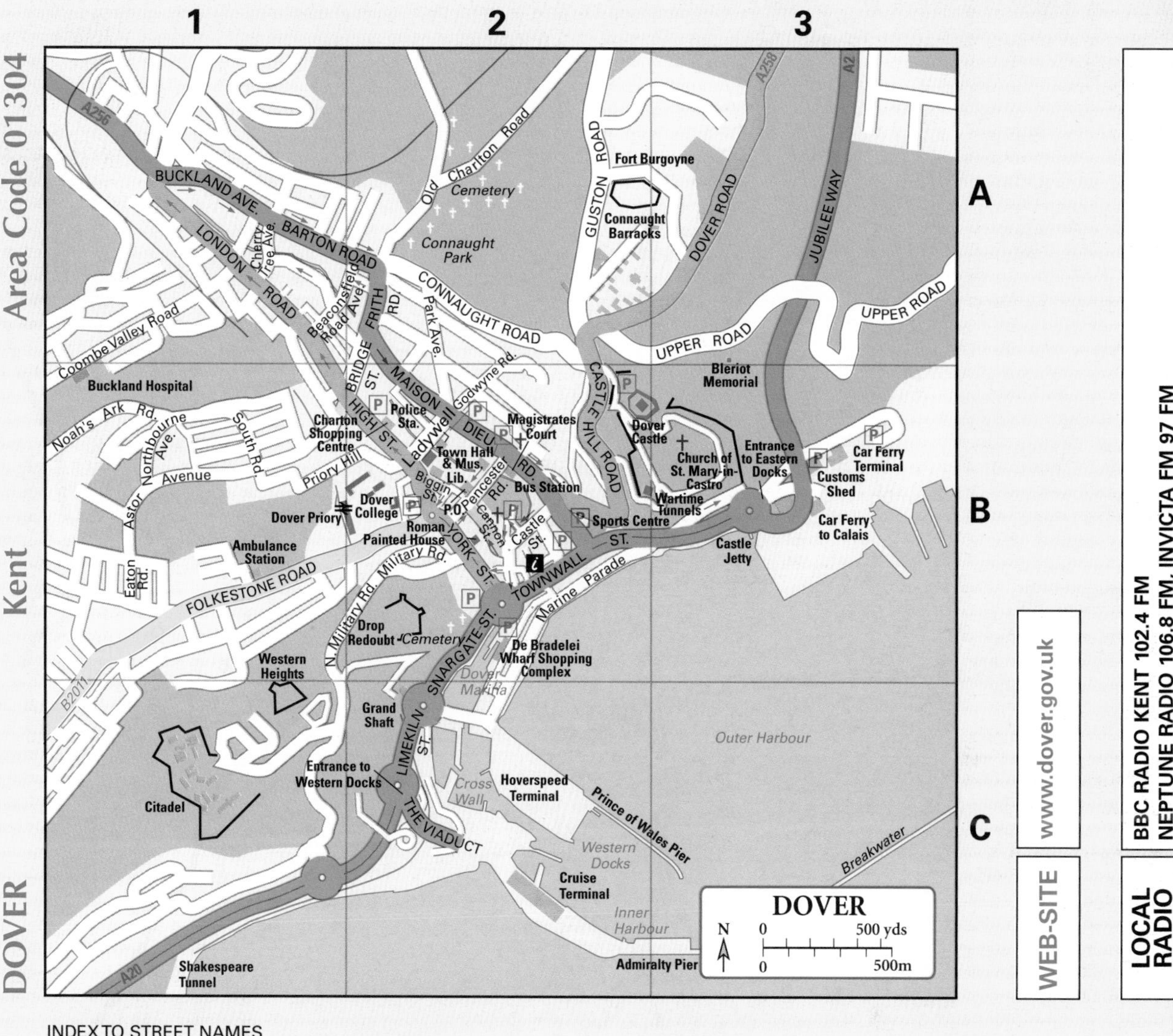

WEB-SITE www.dover.gov.uk

LOCAL RADIO BBC RADIO KENT 102.4 FM
NEPTUNE RADIO 106.8 FM, INVICTA FM 97 FM

INDEX TO STREET NAMES

TOURIST INFORMATION ☎ 01304 205108
TOWNWALL STREET,
DOVER, KENT, CT16 1JR

HOSPITAL A & E ☎ 01227 766877
KENT & CANTERBURY HOSPITAL,
ETHELBERT ROAD, CANTERBURY, CT1 3NG

COUNCIL OFFICE ☎ 01304 821199
WHITE CLIFFS BUSINESS PARK,
DOVER, CT16 3PJ

Dover *Kent* Population: 34,179. Town, cinque port, resort and Channel port on Strait of Dover, 15m/24km SE of Canterbury, with large modern docks for freight and passengers. Dominated by high white cliffs and medieval castle (English Heritage) enclosing the Pharos, 50AD remains of Roman lighthouse. Remains of 12c Knights Templar Church (English Heritage) across valley from castle. Sections of moat of 19c fort at Western Heights (English Heritage), above town on W side of harbour. White Cliffs Experience re-creates Roman and wartime Dover.

Rattray
Blairgowrie
Rosemount
A923
Stormont Loch
A984
Coupar Angus
Keithick
Woodside
Leitfie
Kinloch
Ericht
Arthurstone
Ardler
A94
Meigle
Newbigging
Auchtertyre
Newtyle
Keillor
Markethill
A923
Kettins
Campmuir
Burrelton
Leys
Pitcur
Balkeerie
Kirkinch
Eassie and Nevay
Ark Hill
Nether Handwick
Kinpurney Hill
Auchterhouse Hill
16
Milton
Glen Ogilvy
6
Gallow Hill
Craigowl Hill
455
Long Loch
Thriepley
Lundie
Bonnyton
Kirkton of Auchterhouse
Auchterhouse
Kirkton of Tealing
Dovecot & Earth House
Leoch
B954
Kirkton of Strathmartine
Dighty Water
Dronley
Muirhead
Clatto
Springfield
Hallyburton Forest
King's Seat
Littleton
Blacklaw Hill
A94
Saucher
Kinrossie
Collace
Kirkton of Collace
14
A923
Fowlis
Birkhill
Liff
Camperdown
Downfield
Abernyte
Knapp
Benvie
Lochee
Denhead
B953
Pitmiddle Wood
Rossie Priory
DUNDEE
Invergowrie
Longforgan
Ballindean
Balbeggie
Braes of the Carse
SIDLAW HILLS
Kinnaird
Craigdallie
Inchture
Kingoodie
A85
Dundee Contemporary Arts
Dundee
Discovery Point & R.R.S. Discovery
Tay Road Bridge
Toll
Rait
A90
Kilspindie
Pitroddie
Pole Hill
Megginch Castle
Grange
CARSE OF GOWRIE
Kinfauns
Glendoick
Forest
Errol
Glencarse
Chapelhill
Port Allen
Inchyra
Tay
FIRTH OF TAY
Tay Bridge
Dog Bank
Balmerino
Kirkton
Bottomcraig
Abbey (NTS)
Gauldry
Carthagena Bank
Coultra
Kilmany
13
Balhelvie
Hazelton Walls
Norman's Law
285
Brunton
Creich
Rathillet
Forret Hill
North Deep
South Deep
Mugdrum Island
Glenduckie Hill
Glenduckie
Newburgh
Lindores Abbey
6
A913
Dunbog
Lindores
A913
8
Ormiston Hill
Luthrie
Norman's Hill
A92
Moonzie
Lindifferon
Craigsanquhar
Cairney Lodge
Kincaldrum
Gateside
Gallowfauld
A928
A90
Carrot Hill
Todhills
Balgray
Newbigging
East March
Burnside of Duntrune
Kellas
6
Douglas and Angus
Baldovie
B961
Murroes
Drumsturdy
Wellbank
Bucklerheads
Inverarity
B9127
Hill
Carrot
Whigstreet
Kirkbuddo
Hayhillock
Crombie Resr
Crombie
Greenburn
B978
Affleck
Newton of Affleck
Monikie
Monikie
Craigton
Kirkton of Monikie
B9128
B961
Crombie Mill
Lochlair
12
Mosston
Greystone
Carmyllie
B9127
Guynd
Elliot Water
Bonnyton
Upper Victoria
Muirdrum
A92
Newbigging
Laws
11
Barry Mill (NTS)
2
Barry
Panbride
Carnoustie
Mains of Ardestie
A930
Buddon
Monifieth
A92
Claypotts
12
Broughty Ferry
Broughty
Barry Links
Buddon Ness
Tayport
B946
Newport-on-Tay
Woodhaven
Wormit
B946
A914
B945
Pickletillem
Tentsmuir Point
Tentsmuir
Forest
Cruivie
Carrick
Lucklawhill
Balmullo
Logie
Leuchars
RAF Memorial
Earlshall
Eden Mouth
A919
A914
Guardbridge
A91
Dairsie
Kincaple
Out Head
St Andrews Bay
British Golf Museum
St Andrews
St Andrews
Sea Life Centre
Strathkinness

Area Code 01382

INDEX TO STREET NAMES

Street	Grid
Albany Terrace	A1
Albert Street	B3
Alexander Street	A2
Ann Street	B2
Arbroath Road	B3
Arklay Street	A3
Arthurstone Terrace	B3
Barrack Road	B1
Blackness Road	B1
Blackscroft	B3
Blinshall Street	B1
Brook Street	B1
Broughty Ferry Road	B3
Brown Street	B1
Bruce Street	A1
Byron Street	A1
Canning Street	A2
City Square	C2
Constitution Road	B2
Constitution Street	A2
Court Street	A3
Cowgate Street	B2
Dens Road	A2
Douglas Street	B1
Dudhope Street	A1
Dudhope Terrace	A3
Dundonald Street	A3
Dura Street	B3
East Dock Street	B3
East Marketgait	B2
Guthrie Street	B1
Hawkhill	B1
High Street	C2
Hill Street	A2
Hilltown	A2
Kenmore Terrace	A1
Killin Avenue	A1
Kinghorne Road	A1
King Street	B2
Larch Street	B1
Law Crescent	A1
Lawside Avenue	A1
Leng Street	A2
Lochee Road	B1
Mains Road	A2
Main Street	A2
Meadowside	B2
Nelson Street	B2
Nethergate	C1
North Marketgait	B1
Perth Road	C1
Princes Street	B3
Roseangle	C1
Riverside Drive	C1
Seagate	B2
South Marketgait	C2
South Tay Street	C1
Strathmartine Road	A2
Tay Road Bridge	C2
Trades Lane	B2
Upper Constitution Street	A1
Victoria Road	B2
Victoria Street	B3
Ward Road	B1
West Marketgait	B1
West Port	B1

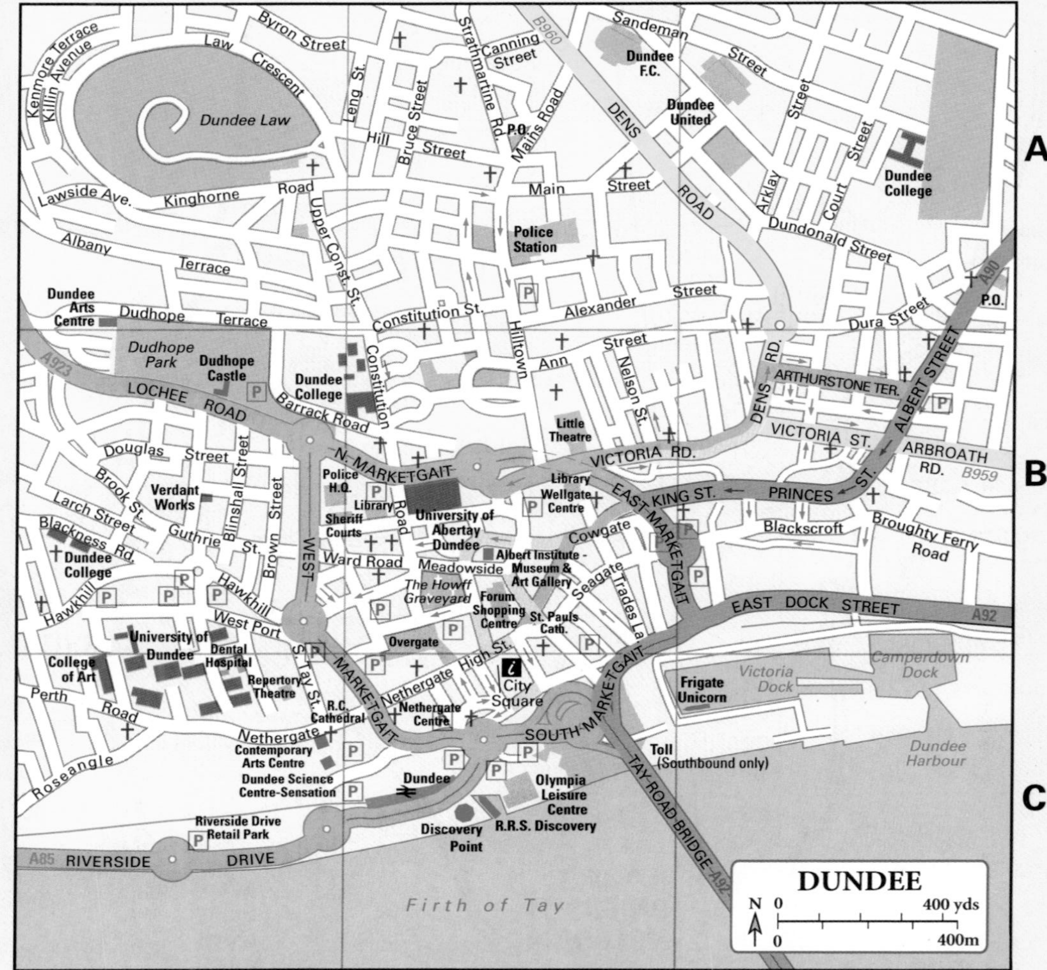

TOURIST INFORMATION ☎ 01382 527527
21 CASTLE STREET,
DUNDEE, DD1 3BA

HOSPITAL A & E ☎ 01382 660111
NINEWELLS HOSPITAL, NINEWELLS ROAD,
DUNDEE, DD1 9SY

COUNCIL OFFICE ☎ 01382 434000
CITY CHAMBERS, 21 CITY SQUARE,
DUNDEE, DD1 3BY

Dundee Population: 158,981. City, Scotland's fourth largest city, commercial and industrial centre and port, 18m/29km E of Perth on N side of Firth of Tay, crossed here by a 1m/2km road bridge and a 2m/3km railway bridge. Robert the Bruce declared King of the Scots in Dundee in 1309. Sustained severe damage during Civil War and again prior to Jacobite uprising. City recovered in early 19c and became Britain's main processor of jute. One of largest employers in Dundee today is D.C. Thomson, publisher of The Beano and The Dandy. Many museums and art galleries. Cultural centre, occasionally playing host to overflow from Edinburgh Festival. Episcopal cathedral on site of former castle. Universities. Ship 'Discovery' in which Captain Scott travelled to Antarctic has returned to Victoria dock, where she was built.

WEB-SITE	www.dundeecity.gov.uk

LOCAL RADIO	BBC RADIO SCOTLAND 810 AM/92.4-94.7 FM TAY AM 1161 AM, WAVE 102 FM, TAY FM 102.8 FM

SUNDERLAND
SEAHAM
WASHINGTON
STANLEY
CHESTER-LE-STREET
CONSETT
HOUGHTON LE SPRING
Hetton-le-Hole
DURHAM
Peterlee
Easington
Spennymoor
Ferryhill
Crook
Willington
Tow Law
Bishop Auckland
Annfield Plain

Newlands
Ebchester
Derwent Walk
Hobson
Tanfield
Beamish Open Air Museum
Ouston
Washington
Penshaw
New Silksworth
Hendon
Medomsley
Tantobie
Pelton
Fatfield
Herrington
Silksworth
Ryhope
Shotleyfield
Shotley Bridge
Dipton
Beamish
Shiney Row
Grange Villa
Newfield
Bournmoor
Leadgate
Iveston
South Moor
Waldridge Fell
Lumley
Fence Houses
Consett & Sunderland Rly Path
Craghead
Delves
Maiden Law
Waldridge
Great Lumley
Colliery Row
Seaton
Dalton-le-Dale
Nose's Point
Knitsley
Rowley
Greencroft
Burnhope
Holmside
Edmondsley
Plawsworth
Kimblesworth
West Rainton
East Rainton
Cold Hesledon
Lanchester
Lanchester Valley Walk
Sacriston
Witton Gilbert
Pity Me
Finchale
Easington Lane
Murton
South Hetton
Butsfield
Langley Park
Framwellgate Moor
Hawthorn
Esh
Browney
Pittington
Littletown
Easington Colliery
Satley
Cornsay
Cornsay Colliery
Quebec
Bearpark
Carrville
Haswell
Turning the Tide
Little Thorpe
Ushaw Moor
Neville's Cross 1346
Sherburn
Horden
Tunstall Resr
Waterhouses
Esh Winning
Cathedral
Shadforth
Ludworth
Deerness Valley Walk
Langley Moor
Shincliffe
Botanic Garden
Shotton Colliery
Shotton
Dene Mouth
East Hedleyhope
Brandon
Thornley
Blackhall
Cassop
Wheatley Hill
Sunniside
Brancepeth
Bowburn
Durham
Hesleden
Castle Eden
Thornley
Billy Row
Oakenshaw
Sunderland Bridge
Croxdale
Quarrington Hill
Wingate
Hett
Coxhoe
Trimdon Colliery
Station Town
Hutton Henry
Crimdon Park
Brandon to Bishop Auckland Walk
Tudhoe
Kelloe
Hart
Trimdon Grange
Sheraton
Knitsley Fell
Fir Tree
St Johns Hall
Howden-le-Wear
Byers Green
Cornforth
Trimdon
South Wingate
Newfield
Hurworth Burn Resr
Historic Quarter of Hartlepool
Dean Bank
Elwick
Toll
Bedburn
High Grange
Hunwick
Middlestone Moor
Hamsterley
Westerton
Bishop Middleham
Fishburn
Skerne
Dalton Piercy
Witton-le-Wear
Kirk Merrington
Bedburn Beck
Witton Park
Crookfoot Resr
Coundon
Hardwick Hall
High Etherley
Chilton
Sedgefield
Low Etherley
Morley
Toft
Coundon Grange
Rushyford
Great

INDEX TO STREET NAMES

Street	Grid	Street	Grid
Aykley Heads	A1	New Elvet	B2
Church Street	C2	North Bailey	B2
Clay Lane	C1	North End	A1
Claypath	B2	North Road	B2
Crossgate	B2	Old Elvet	B3
Crossgate Peth	C1	Pity Me Bypass	A1
Darlington Road	C1	Potters Bank	C1
Fieldhouse Lane	A1	Quarryheads Lane	C2
Framwelgate	B2	Providence Row	B2
Framwelgate Peth	A2	Redhills	B1
Framwelgate Waterside	B2	Sidegate	B2
Gilesgate	B3	Silver Street	B2
Great North Road	A1	South Bailey	C2
Green Lane	B3	South Road	C2
Grove Street	C2	South Street	C2
Hallgarth Street	C3	Southfield Way	A1
Hawthorn Terrace	B1	Stockton Road	C2
Leazes Road	B2	Sutton Street	B2
Margery Lane	C2	The Avenue	C1
Market Place	B2	Western Hill	B1
Millburngate Bridge	B2	Whinney Hill	C3
Newcastle Road	A1	Whitesmocks	A1

TOURIST INFORMATION ☎ 0191 384 3720
MARKET PLACE, DURHAM,
COUNTY DURHAM, DH1 3NJ

HOSPITAL A & E ☎ 0191 333 2333
DRYBURN HOSPITAL, NORTH ROAD,
DURHAM, DH1 5TW

COUNCIL OFFICE ☎ 0191 386 4411
COUNTY HALL,
DURHAM, DH1 5UB

Durham *Dur.* Population: 36,937. Cathedral city on narrow bend in River Wear, 14m/22km S of Newcastle upon Tyne. Norman-Romanesque cathedral founded in 1093 on site of shrine of St. Cuthbert is World Heritage Site. England's third oldest University founded in 1832. Motte-and-bailey castle dating from 1072 now part of the University. Collection in Fulling Mill Museum of Archaelogy illustrates history of city. Museum of Oriental Art. Light Infantry Museum. Art Gallery. Universtiy Botanic Garden S of city.

Area Code 0191

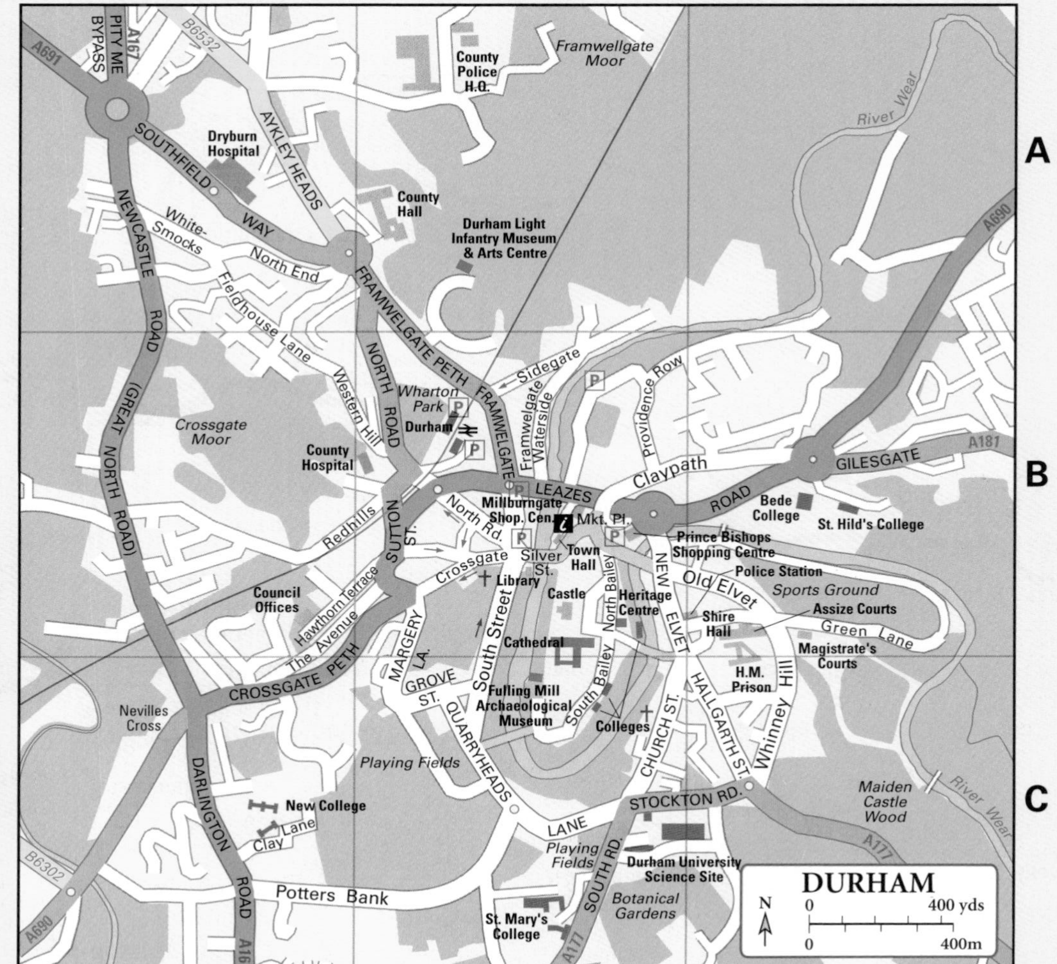

WEB-SITE	www.durhamcity.gov.uk

LOCAL RADIO	BBC RADIO NEWCASTLE 95.4 FM SUN FM 103.4 FM, GALAXY 105-106 105.3, 105.6, 105.8 & 106.4 FM

Sheffield Park Sta.
Fletching
Piltdown
Newick
Chailey
South Street
Newick Park
Spithurst
Isfield
Barcombe Cross
Barcombe
Hamsey
South Malling
Lewes
Mus. of Sussex Archaeology
Cliffe Hill
Glyndebourne
Ringmer
Mount Caburn
Glynde Place
Glynde
Beddingham
Iford
Rodmell
Monk's House
Southease
Telscombe
Piddinghoe
Art Mus.
Newhaven
Peacehaven
Denton
Paradise Family Leisure Park
South Heighton
Tarring Neville
Bishopstone
East Blatchington
Seaford
Dieppe (Summer Only)..........2 hours
Buxted
Ringles Cross
Uckfield
Beeches Farm
Ridgewood
Horsted Place
Little Horsted
New Town
Framfield
Blackboys
Pound Green
Hadlow Down
Possingworth Park
Stonebridge
Waldron
Little London
Cross in Hand
Broad Oak
Heathfield
Cade Street
Chapel Cross
Burwash Common
Burwash Weald
Punnett's Town
Three Cups Corner
Maynard's Green
Vine's Cross
Warbleton
Rushlake Green
Horam
Foxhunt Green
Halland
Bentley Motor Museum
Wildfowl Park
Shortgate
East Hoathly
Whitesmith
Laughton
Holme's Hill
Golden Cross
Chiddingly
Muddles Green
Burlow
Lealands
Hellingly
Lower Horsebridge
Lower Dicker
Upper Dicker
The Dicker
Ripe
Chalvington
Middle Farm & English Farm Cider Centre
West Firle
Firle Place
Charleston Farmhouse
Firle Beacon
Alciston
Selmeston
Berwick Sta.
Arlington Resr
Michelham Priory
Arlington
Berwick
Drusillas Park
Alfriston
Old Clergy House
Priory
Wilmington
Folkington
Filching Manor
Lullington Heath
Litlington
Charleston Manor
Jevington
Willingdon Hill
Westdean
Seven Sisters
Friston
East Dean
Birling Gap
Beachy Head
Holywell
EASTBOURNE
Eastbourne Pier & Glass Studio
Fort Fun
Sovereign Harbour
Langney Point
Pevensey Bay
Hampden Park
Langney
Willingdon
Wannock
Polegate
Stone Cross
Friday Street
Westham
Pevensey
Pevensey Bay
Hankham
Pevensey Levels
Hailsham
Upper Horsebridge
Magham Down
Herstmonceux
Herstmonceux Castle
Stunts Green
Cowbeech
Foul Mile
Bodle Street Green
Windmill Hill
Boreham Street
Wartling
Waller's Haven
Ashburnham Place
Ponts Green
Penhurst
Dallington
Brightling
Oxley's Green
Darvell
Darwell Resr
Dudwell
Mountfield
John's Cross
Netherfield
Whatlington
Robertsbridge
Vinehall Street
Cripp's Corner
Sedlescombe
Kent Street
Westfield
Battle
Buckleys Yesterday's World
Abbey
Hastings 1066
Telham
Beauport Park
Catsfield
Henley's Down
Crowhurst
Hollington
Stadium
Amusement Park
Silverhill
Lower Street
Ninfield
Lunsford's Cross
Hooe Common
Hooe
Sidley
Bulverhythe
St Leonards
Little Common
Cooden
BEXHILL
Norman's Bay
Brede
Ouse
Cuckmere
201
A272
A22
A275
A26
A27
A267
A265
A21
A2100
A271
A295
A269
A2036
A259
A2270
A2021
B2102
B2192
B2124
B2203
B2096
B2244
B2204
B2092
B2095
B2104
B2182
B2191
B2103

EASTBOURNE East Sussex Area Code 01323

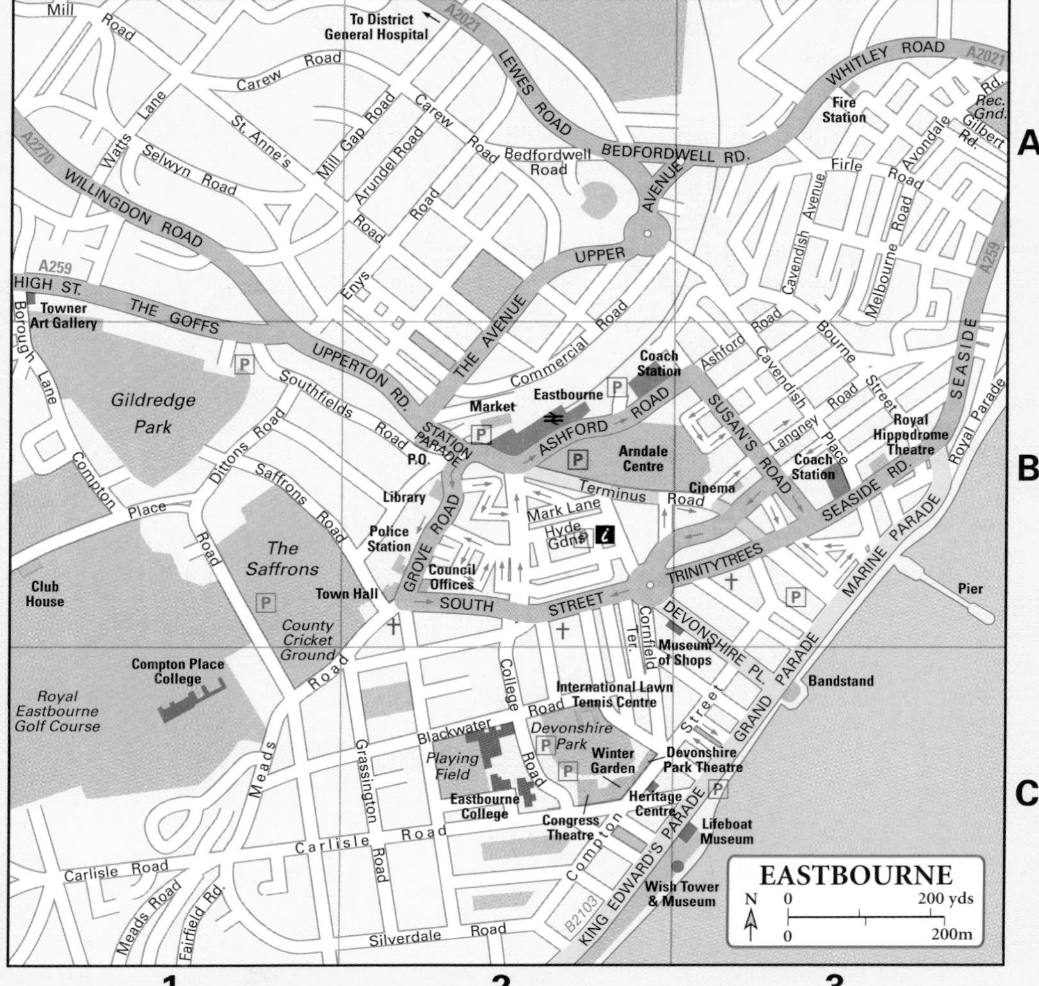

WEB-SITE	www.eastbourne.gov.uk

LOCAL RADIO	BBC SOUTHERN COUNTIES RADIO 104.5 FM, 1161 AM SOVEREIGN RADIO 107.5 FM

INDEX TO STREET NAMES

Street	Grid	Street	Grid
Arundel Road	A2	Langney Road	B3
Ashford Road	B2/B3	Lewes Road	A2
Avondale Road	A3	Marine Parade	B3
Bedfordwell Road	A2	Mark Lane	B2
Blackwater Road	C2	Meads Road	C1
Borough Lane	A1	Melbourne Road	A3
Bourne Street	B3	Mill Gap Road	A1
Carew Road	A1/A2	Mill Road	A1
Carlisle Road	C1	Royal Parade	B3
Cavendish Avenue	A3	Saffrons Road	B1
Cavendish Place	B3	St. Anne's Road	A1
College Road	C2	Seaside	B3
Commercial Road	B2	Seaside Road	B3
Compton Place Road	B1	Selwyn Road	A1
Compton Street	C2	Silverdale Road	C2
Cornfield Terrace	B2	South Street	B2
Devonshire Place	B2	Southfields Road	B1
Dittons Road	B1	Station Parade	B2
Enys Road	A2	Susan's Road	B3
Fairfield Road	C1	Terminus Road	B2
Firle Road	A3	The Avenue	B2
Gilbert Road	A3	The Goffs	A1
Grand Parade	C3	Trinity Trees	B3
Grassington Road	C2	Upper Avenue	A2
Grove Road	B2	Upperton Road	A1
High Street	A1	Watts Lane	A1
Hyde Gardens	B2	Whitley Road	A1
King Edward's Parade	C2	Willingdon Road	A1

TOURIST INFORMATION ☎ 01323 411400
3 CORNFIELD ROAD,
EASTBOURNE, BN21 4QL

HOSPITAL A & E ☎ 01323 417400
EASTBOURNE DISTRICT GENERAL HOSPITAL, KING'S DRIVE,
EASTBOURNE, BN21 2UD

COUNCIL OFFICE ☎ 01323 410000
EASTBOURNE BOROUGH COUNCIL, TOWN HALL,
GROVE ROAD, EASTBOURNE BN21 4UG,

Eastbourne *E.Suss.* Population: 94,793. Town, coastal resort and conference centre, 19m/31km E of Brighton. Towner Art Gallery in 18c manor house shows a contemporary collection of work. South Downs Way begins at Beachy Head, the 163m/536ft chalk cliff on the outskirts of the town. Eastbourne hosts an International Folk Festival and international tennis at Devonshire Park.

FIRTH OF FORTH
Firth of Forth
EDINBURGH
DUNFERMLINE
Kinghorn
Pettycur
Burntisland
Aberdour
Hawkcraig Point
Dalgety Bay
St Davids
Inverkeithing
Rosyth
Limekilns
Charlestown
Crossford
Cairneyhill
Torryburn
Low Torry
Valleyfield
Milesmark
Dunearn
The Binn
Kinghorn Loch
Cullaloe Hills
Fordell
Hillend
North Queensferry
Deep Sea World
Forth Bridge
Forth Road Bridge
Inch Garvie
Hound Point
Inchcolm
St Colm's Abbey
Inchmickery
Inchkeith
Cramond Island
Zeebrugge
hours
Bo'ness
Carriden
Muirhouses
Blackness
Champany
Hopetoun
Abercorn
Newton
South Queensferry
Dalmeny
Cramond
Eagle Rock
Lauriston Castle
Royal Botanic Gdns
Royal Yacht Britannia
Black Rocks
Leith
Portobello
Joppa
Musselburgh
Prestonpans
Cockenzie and Port Seton
Levenhall
Wallyford
Inveresk
Whitecraig
Elphinstone
Crossgatehall
Cousland
Dalkeith
Eskbank
Lasswade
Bonnyrigg
Loanhead
Polton
Newtongrange
Mayfield
Easthouses
Gorebridge
Rosewell
Roslin
Auchendinny
Penicuik
Carrington
Kirkliston
Winchburgh
Philpstoun
Kingscavil
Bridgend
Broxburn
Uphall
Ecclesmachan
Newbridge
Ratho
Ratho Station
Gogar
Corstorphine
Blackhall
Duddingston
Craigmillar
Niddrie
Newcraighall
Morningside
Liberton
Gilmerton
Danderhall
Millerhill
Craiglockhart
Colinton
Juniper Green
Currie
Balerno
Hermiston
Wilkieston
Kirknewton
East Calder
Mid Calder
Oakbank
Pumpherston
Livingston
Livingston Village
Dechmont
Seafield
Bellsquarry
Polbeth
West Calder
Addiewell
Harburn
PENTLAND HILLS
REGIONAL PARK
Threipmuir Reservoir
Water of Leith
A90
A720
M8
M9
M90
A1
A7
A68
A701
A702
A703

INDEX TO STREET NAMES

TOURIST INFORMATION ☎ 0131 473 3800
INFORMATION CENTRE, 3 PRINCES STREET, EDINBURGH, EH2 2QP

HOSPITAL A & E ☎ 0131 536 1000
ROYAL INFIRMARY OF EDINBURGH, 1 LAURISTON PLACE, EDINBURGH, EH3 9YW

COUNCIL OFFICE ☎ 0131 200 2000
COUNCIL HEADQUARTERS, 10 WATERLOO PLACE, EDINBURGH, EH1 3EG

Edinburgh *Edin.* Population: 401,910. City, historic city and capital of Scotland, built on a range of rocky crags and extinct volcanoes, on S side of Firth of Forth, 41m/66km E of Glasgow. Administrative, financial and legal centre of Scotland. Medieval castle (Historic Scotland) on rocky eminence overlooks central area and was one of main seats of Royal court, while Arthur's Seat (largest of the volcanoes) guards eastern approaches. Three universities. Port at Leith, where Royal Yacht Britannia is now docked and open to public. Important industries include brewing, distilling, food and electronics. Palace of Holyroodhouse (Historic Scotland) is chief royal residence of Scotland. Old Town typified by Gladstone's Land (Historic Scotland), 17c six-storey tenement with arcaded front, outside stair and stepped gables. Numerous literary associations including Sir Arthur Conan Doyle who was born here. Many galleries and museums including National Gallery of Scotland. Annual arts festival attracts over a million visitors each year and is largest such event in the world.

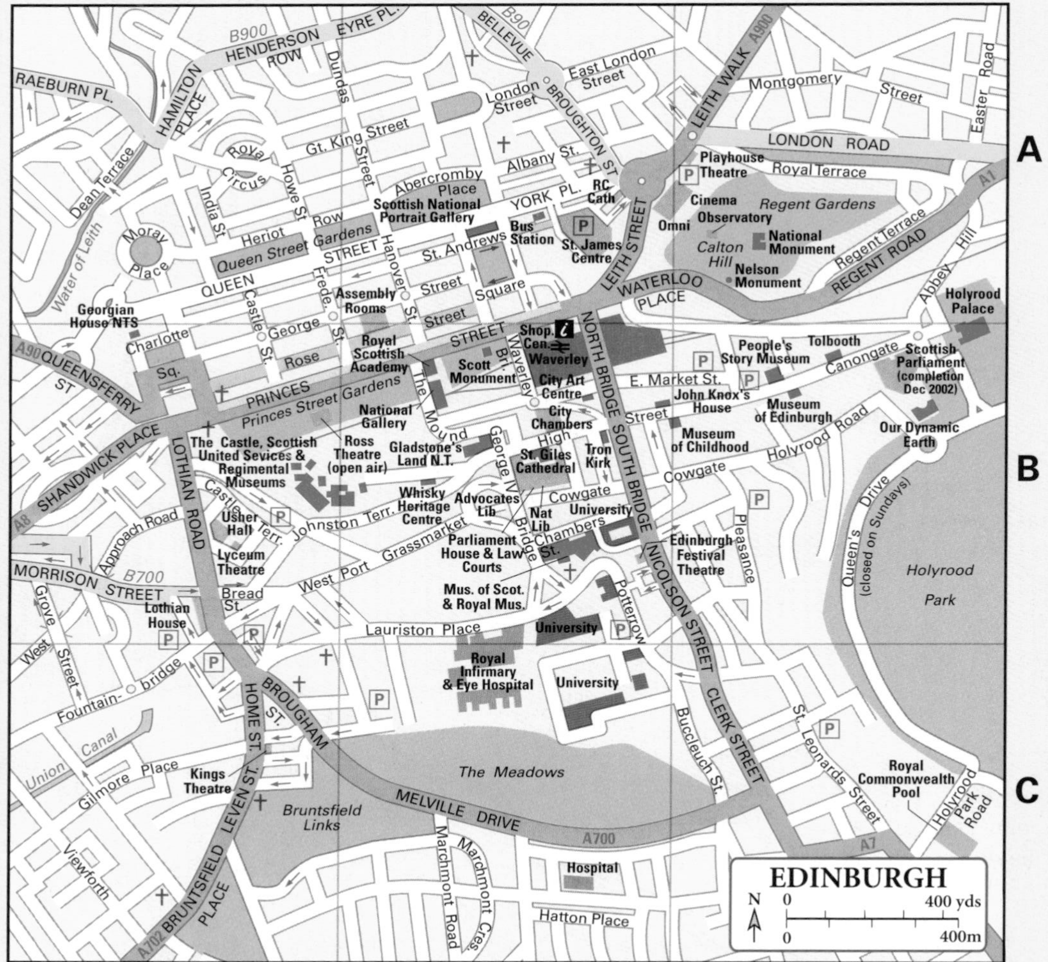

WEB-SITE www.edinburgh.gov.uk

LOCAL RADIO
BBC RADIO SCOTLAND 810 AM & 92.4-94.7 FM
FORTH 2 1548 AM, FORTH 1 97.3 FM, REAL RADIO 101.1 FM

Fursdon
Ravenshayes
Mutterton
Broadhembury
Beacon
A3072
Cadbury
A396
Bradninch
Westcott
Colliton
A373
11
Monkton
Upton
Hellions
Stockleigh
Pomeroy
Silverton
Norman's
Green
Combe
Raleigh
Sandford
13
Up Exe
Hele
Langford
Plymtree
Luton
Upton
A30
Creedy
Park
Thorverton
14
Clyst Hydon
Tale
Godford
Cross
Awliscombe
A377
Crediton
Efford
Killerton
(NT)
B3181
Higher
Tale
Payhembury
Shobrooke
Aunk
A35
Budlake
Colestocks
Buckerell
Honiton
Nether
Exe
Rewe
Clyst
St
Lawrence
Talaton
Higher
Cheriton
Newton
St
Cyres
Brampford
Speke
Hamlet
Offwell
Uton
Westwood
Feniton
Gittisham
10
Clyst
Hookway
M5
Fenny Bridges
Escot
Stoke
Canon
Alfington
8
Upton
Pyne
Broadclyst
A375
Church
Green
Coly
Court
Barton
Oldridge
A377
Whimple
Fairmile
Poltimore
B3174
Dog
Village
A396
Cadhay
Ottery
St Mary
Putts Corner
13
Farway
Cowley
Fernwood
Tedburn
St Mary
Pinhoe
Clyst
Honiton
Rockbeare
Wiggaton
8
Exwick
Exeter
A30
West
Hill
Otter
Farway
Bishop
Whipton
Marsh
Green
Broad
Down
15
Whitestone
Pathfinder
Village
B3212
EXETER
Cath.
B3183
29
Exeter
Sowton
Aylesbeare
Tipton St
John
A30
4
Sidbury
Sand
B3180
B3184
Longdown
Crealy Park
Half Way
Inn
30
Farringdon
B3182
Venn
Ottery
A3052
Pocombe
Bridge
Countess
Wear
Clyst
St Mary
Harpford
9
Sidford
Harcombe
B3212
Ide
A3052
Old Bakery
(NT)
11
White Cross
Alphington
12
Bowd
Dunsford
Westpoint
Exhibition
Centre
Woodbury
Salterton
Newton Poppleford
Weston
Shillingford
St George
Clyst
St George
3
B3176
2
Salcombe
Regis
Kenn
4
Hawkerland
Donkey
Sanctuary
Branscombe
A379
Topsham
B3175
Exeter Ship Canal
31
B3179
Colaton Raleigh
Sidmouth
Ebford
Woodbury
Pinn
Dunchideock
Exminster
James
Countryside
Collection
Bridford
Boddiscombsleigh
Kennford
Exe
Exton
B3178
Teign
Yettington
A38
Bicton Park
Higher
Ashton
Kenn
A376
Black Hill
Kennick
Resr
Christow
Bickham House
A379
Powderham
East
Budleigh
Otterton
5
Great Haldon
10
Coombe
Lower
Ashton
Powderham
Lympstone
A La
Ronde
Tottiford
Resr
Devon and
Exeter
Kenton
B3179
B3178
Withycombe Raleigh
B3178
Fairlynch Arts Centre
& Museum
Trenchford
Resr
Trusham
Canonteign Falls
Knowle
Starcross
5
Budleigh Salterton
A38
Littleham
Hennock
A380
Mamhead
Cockwood
EXMOUTH
A382
8
Chudleigh
Stuart
Line
Cruises
Ashcombe
Langdon
House
15
Bovey Tracey
11
Dawlish Water
Dawlish Warren
Devon Guild
of Craftsmen
Ugbrooke
A379
Dawlish Warren Sta.
B3344
Chudleigh
Knighton
Ideford
Haldon
Bovey
Luton
Dawlish

INDEX TO STREET NAMES

Street	Grid	Street	Grid
Alphington Street	C1	Mount Pleasant Road	A3
Barnfield Road	B2	New Bridge Street	C1
Bartholomew Street West	B1	New North Road	A1/A2
Bedford Street	B2	Okehampton Road	C1
Belmont Road	A3	Okehampton Street	C1
Blackboy Road	A3	Old Tiverton Road	A3
Blackall Road	A2	Paris Street	B2
Bonhay Road	B1	Paul Street	B2
Clifton Hill	A3	Pennsylvania Road	A2
College Road	B3	Prince of Wales Road	A1
Cowick Street	C1	Queen Street	B2
Fore Street	B2	Richmond Road	B1
Heavitree Road	B3	St. David's Hill	A1
Hele Road	A1	Sidwell Street	B2
High Street	B2	South Street	B2
Holloway Street	C2	The Quay	C2
Howell Road	A2	Topsham Road	C2
Longbrook Street	A2	Western Way	B2
Magdalen Road	B3	Wonford Road	C3
Magdalen Street	C2	York Road	A2
Matford Lane	C3		

TOURIST INFORMATION ☎ 01392 265700
CIVIC CENTRE, PARIS STREET,
EXETER, EX1 1RP

HOSPITAL A & E ☎ 01392 411611
ROYAL DEVON & EXETER HOSPITAL (WONFORD),
BARRACK ROAD, EXETER, EX2 5DW

COUNCIL OFFICE ☎ 01392 277888
CIVIC CENTRE, PARIS STREET,
EXETER, EX1 1JN

Exeter *Devon* Population: 94,717. City, county capital on River Exe, 64m/103km SW of Bristol. Major administrative, business and financial centre on site of Roman town Isca Dumnoniorum. Cathedral is Decorated, with Norman towers and façade with hundreds of stone statues. 15c guildhall. Modern buildings in centre built after extensive damage from World War II. Beneath the city lie remains of medieval water-supply system built in 14c to supply fresh water to city centre. Royal Albert Memorial Museum and Art Gallery. Early 16c mansion of Bowhill (English Heritage), with preserved Great Hall, 2m/3km SW. University 1m/2km N of city centre. Airport 5m/8km E at Clyst Honiton.

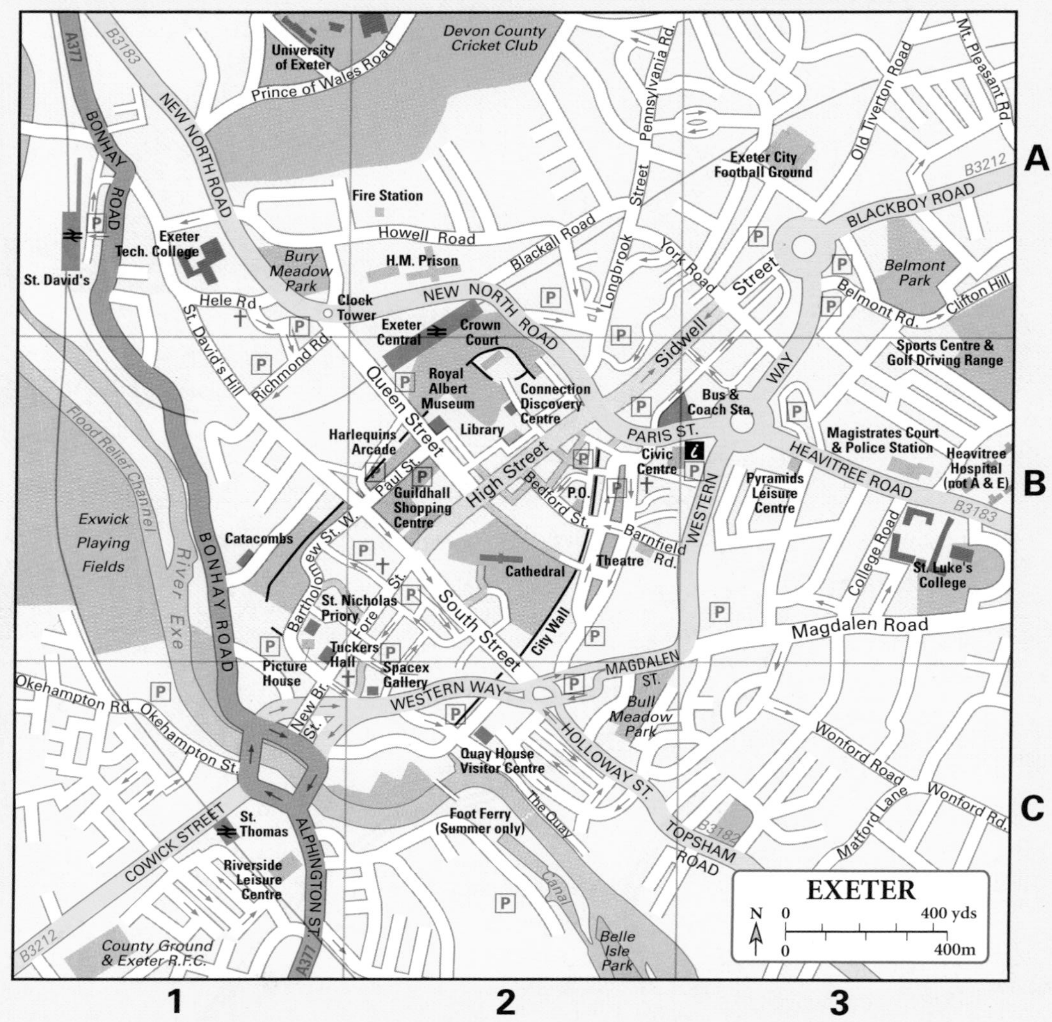

WEB-SITE	www.exeter.gov.uk

LOCAL RADIO	BBC RADIO DEVON 95.8 FM CLASSIC GOLD 666 AM, GEMINI FM 97 & 103 FM

Sheldwich
Selling
Old Wives Lees
Chartham
A2050
Bekesbourne
Patrixbourne
Goodnestone Park
Eastry
Worth
Ham
Hacklinge
A258
Badlesmere
Leaveland
Shottenden
Chilham
Shalmsford Street
Nackington
Bridge
A2
Adisham
Goodnestone
Knowlton
Finglesham
DEAL
Street End
Lower Hardres
Chillenden
Chilham Castle
A252
Aylesham
Nonington
Betteshanger
Sholden
Deal
Bishopsbourne
Roman Road
Easole Street
Tilmanstone
A256
Northbourne
A251
Molash
Petham
Kingston
Great Mongeham
Godmersham
Upper Hardres Court
Womenswold
Elvington
East Studdal
Walmer
A252
Challock
A28
Barham
Barfrestone
Ripple
Walmer Castle & Garden
Bilting
Bossingham
Derringstone
Woollage Green
Eythorne
Sutton
Eastwell Park
Boughton Aluph
Crundale
Sole Street
Waltham
Ashley
Kingsdown
Shepherdswell (Sibertswold)
West Langdon
Ringwould
Boughton Lees
Hassell Street
B2068
Lyminge Forest
Breach
Denton
Lydden
Martin Mill Sta.
A258
A251
Wye
Bodsham Green
Bladbean
Wingmore
Coldred
Stone Street
Stelling Minnis
Wootton
Lydden
East Langdon
National Nature Trails
Kennington
A2
Whitfield
St Margaret's at Cliffe
Brook
Hastingleigh
Sixmile Cottages
Elham
Selstead
Guston
ASHFORD
Lymbridge Green
A260
Temple Ewell
A256
West Cliffe
St Margaret's Bay
The Pines
Willesborough Lees
Hinxhill
Rhodes Minnis
Ottinge
Acrise Place
Swingfield Minnis
Ewell Minnis
Alkham
Buckland
South Foreland
Stowting
Dover
B2229
Willesborough
Brabourne
St Radigund's Abbey
DOVER
Sevington
Densole
Lyminge
Arthur Glen
Willesborough
Brabourne Lees
Hawkinge
Drellingore
Maxton
M20
A20
Newbarn
Paddlesworth
De Bradelei Wharf
Kingsnorth
Mersham
Smeeth
West Hougham
Farthingloe
Postling
Etchinghill
A20
Knights Templar Church
Sellindge
Capel le Ferne
Cheeseman's Green
Swanton Mill
East Stour
Beachborough
Newington
Channel Tunnel Terminal
B2011
Channel Tunnel
Stanford
A20
hours
Calais ¾-1¼
Oostende 2
Zeebrugge 4½
A2070
Stonestreet Green
Westenhanger Sta. Folkestone
M20
11A
East Wear Bay
Stone Cross
Aldington
Cheriton
Saltwood
FOLKESTONE
Bonnington
Court-at-Street
A261
Bilsington
B2067
Port Lympne
Lympne
West Hythe
A259
Sandgate
Rotunda Amusement Park
Hythe
Ruckinge
Hamstreet
Romney Marsh
Newchurch
Burmarsh
STRAIT OF DOVER
Romney, Hythe & Dymchurch Railway
Snave
A2070
Dymchurch
St Mary in the Marsh
Martello Tower
St Mary's

INDEX TO STREET NAMES

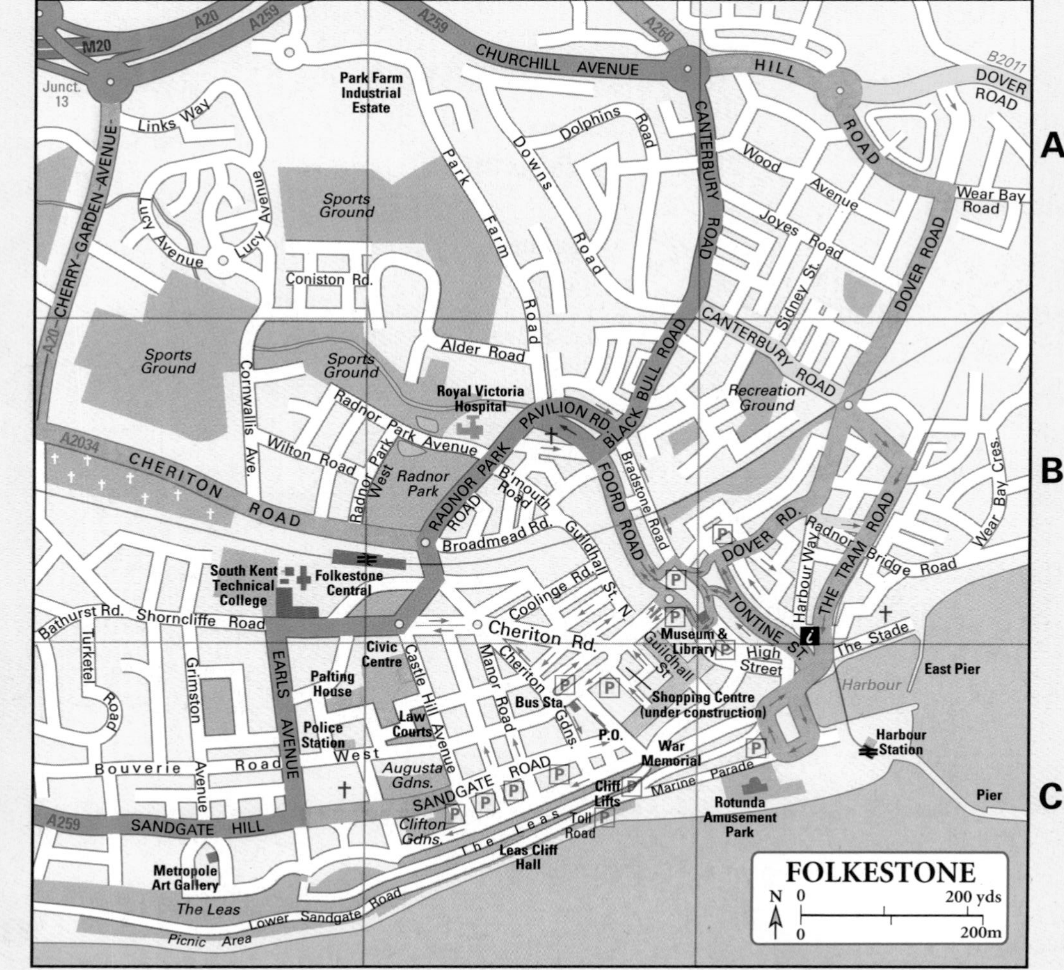

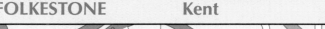

TOURIST INFORMATION ☎ 01303 258594
HARBOUR STREET, FOLKESTONE,
KENT, CT20 1QN

HOSPITAL A & E ☎ 01233 633331
WILLIAM HARVEY HOSPITAL, KENNINGTON RD,
WILLESBOROUGH, ASHFORD, TN24 OLZ

COUNCIL OFFICE ☎ 01303 850388
CIVIC CENTRE, CASTLE HILL AVENUE,
FOLKESTONE, CT20 2QY

Folkestone *Kent* Population: 45,587. Town, Channel port and resort, 14m/22km E of Ashford. Russian submarine docked in harbour is open to the public. The Lear marine promenade accessed by Victorian cliff lift. Ornate Victorian hotels. Martello tower on East Cliff. Kent Battle of Britain Museum at Hawkinge airfield 3m/5km N. Channel Tunnel terminal on N side.

WEB-SITE	www.shepway.gov.uk

LOCAL RADIO	BBC RADIO KENT 97.6 FM INVICTA FM 97 FM

Loch Lomond
Dumbarton Muir
Bonhill
Carbeth
Strathblane
Campsie
Haughhead
Lennoxtown
Lennox Forest
Kilsyth Hills
Milton of Campsie
Queenzieburn
Kilsyth
Colzium House
Townhead Resr
Banton
Banknock
Castlecary
Roman
Dullatur
Abronhill
Townend
Crosslet
Kilpatrick Hills
Loch Humphrey
DUMBARTON
Milton
Bowling
Cochno
Edinbarnet
Mugdock
Milngavie
Lillie Art Gallery
Baldernock
Dougalston
Torrance
Balmore
Kinkell
Twechar
Croy
Balloch
CUMBERNAULD
Palacerigg
Carbrain
Condorrat
Luggiebank
Old Kilpatrick
Duntocher
Faifley
BEARSDEN
KIRKINTILLOCH
Lenzie
Waterside
Luggie Water
Erskine
Toll
Drumchapel
Cadder
Moodiesburn
Mollinsburn
Bishopton
CLYDEBANK
Bishopbriggs
Auchinloch
Chryston
Riggend
Greengairs
Wattston
Southbar
Inchinnan
Maryhill
Muirhead
Glenboig
Stand
Yoker
Springburn
Stepps
Gartcosh
Georgetown
Glasgow
Renfrew
Botanic Gdns
Partick
Provan Hall
Bishop Loch
Woodend Loch
Glenmavis
Summerlee Heritage Trust
Drumpellier
Caldercruix
Plains
Crosslee
Gryfe
Govan
Glasgow Science Centre
GLASGOW
Peoples Palace Museum
COATBRIDGE
Rawyards
AIRDRIE
Linwood
PAISLEY
Johnstone
Milliken Park
Elderslie
Crookston
(NTS)
Museum of Education
Burrell
Pollok
Shettleston
Tollcross
Whifflet
Chapelhall
Calderbank
Johnstone Castle
Howwood
Gleniffer Braes
Pollokshaws
Hampden Park
RUTHERGLEN
Carmyle
Cambuslang
Tannochside
Viewpark
Mossend
Newhouse
Holytown
Nitshill
Castlemilk
Uddingston
Calderglen
Bothwell
Bellshill
Newarthill
Cleland
Caplaw
Barrhead
Thornliebank
Flemington
Giffnock
Balgray Resr
Neilston
Carmunnock
Dechmont Hill
Stonefield
Bothwell Bridge
Strathclyde
MOTHERWELL
Corkindale Law
Loch Libo
Clarkston
Nerston
High Blantyre
Hamilton
Cambusnethan
Hall
Uplawmoor
Neilston Pad
Malletsheugh
Newton Mearns
Busby
Waterfoot
Mearns
Lymekilns
Thorntonhall
EAST KILBRIDE
HAMILTON
Shieldmuir Sta.
Wishaw
Meikle Earnock
Low Waters
Chatelherault
Allanton
Caldwell
Lugton
Harelaw Dam
Long Loch
Earn Water
Jackton
Calder Glen
Eddlewood
Overtown
Gabroc Hill
Eaglesham
Polnoon
Torrance
Crutherland
Fairholm

INDEX TO STREET NAMES

Argyle Street	B1	Glassford Street	B2	Pitt Street	B1
Baird Street	A3	Gloucester Street	C1	Port Dundas Road	A2
Bath Street	A1/B1	Gordon Street	B2	Renfield Street	B2
Bell Street	B3	Great Western Road	A1	Renfrew Street	A1
Blythswood Street	B1	High Street	B3	Robertson Street	B1
Bothwell Street	B1	Holland Street	B1	Saltmarket	C2
Bridge Street	C2	Hope Street	B2	Sauchiehall Street	A1
Broomielaw	C1	Hunter Street	C3	Scotland Street	C1
Brown Street	B1	Ingram Street	B2	Scott Street	A1
Buccleuch Street	A1	Inner Ring Road	A3	Springburn Road	A3
Buchanan Street	B2	Jamaica Street	C2	St. George's Road	A1
Castle Street	B3	James Watt Street	B1	St. Mungo Avenue	B3
Cathedral Street	B2	Kennedy Street	A3	St. Vincent Street	B1
Clyde Street	C2	Kingston Bridge	C1	Stirling Road	B3
Cochrane Street	B2	Kingston Street	C1	Stockwell Street	C2
Commerce Street	C1	London Road	C3	Trongate	B2
Cowcaddens Road	A2	Maryhill Road	A1	Union Street	B2
Craighall Road	A2	McAlpine Street	B1	Victoria Bridge	C2
Dobbie's Loan	A2	Mitchell Street	B2	Washington Street	B1
Duke Street	B3	Montrose Street	B3	Wellington Street	B1
Eglington Street	C1	Morrison Street	C1	West Campbell Street	B1
Gallowgate	C3	Nelson Street	C1	West George Street	B1
Garnet Street	A1	Norfolk Street	C2	West Nile Street	B2
Garscube Road	A1	North Hanover Street	B2	West Regent Street	B1
George Square	B2	Oswald Street	C1	West Street	C1
George Street	B3	Paisley Road	C1	Wilson Street	B2
George V Bridge	C1			York Street	B1
Glasgow Bridge	C2				

TOURIST INFORMATION ☎ 0141 204 4400
11 GEORGE SQUARE,
GLASGOW, G2 1DY

HOSPITAL A & E ☎ 0141 211 2000
WESTERN INFIRMARY, DUMBARTON ROAD,
GLASGOW, G11 6NT

COUNCIL OFFICE ☎ 0141 287 2000
CITY CHAMBERS, GEORGE SQUARE,
GLASGOW, G2 1DU

Glasgow *Glas.* Population: 662,954. City, largest city in Scotland. Port and commercial, industrial, cultural and entertainment centre on River Clyde, 41m/66km W of Edinburgh and 346m/557km NW of London. Major industrial port and important trading point with America until War of Independence. During industrial revolution, nearby coal seams boosted Glasgow's importance and its population increased ten-fold between 1800 and 1900. By beginning of 20c shipbuilding dominated the city, although industry went into decline in 1930's. Glasgow is now seen to be a city of culture and progress. It has a strong performing arts tradition and many museums and galleries including Burrell Collection (set in Pollok Country Park). Cathedral is rare example of an almost complete 13c church. Early 19c Hutcheson's Hall (National Trust for Scotland) in Ingram Street is one of city's most elegant buildings; Tenement House (National Trust for Scotland) is late Victorian tenement flat retaining many original features. Three universities. Airport 7m/11km W.

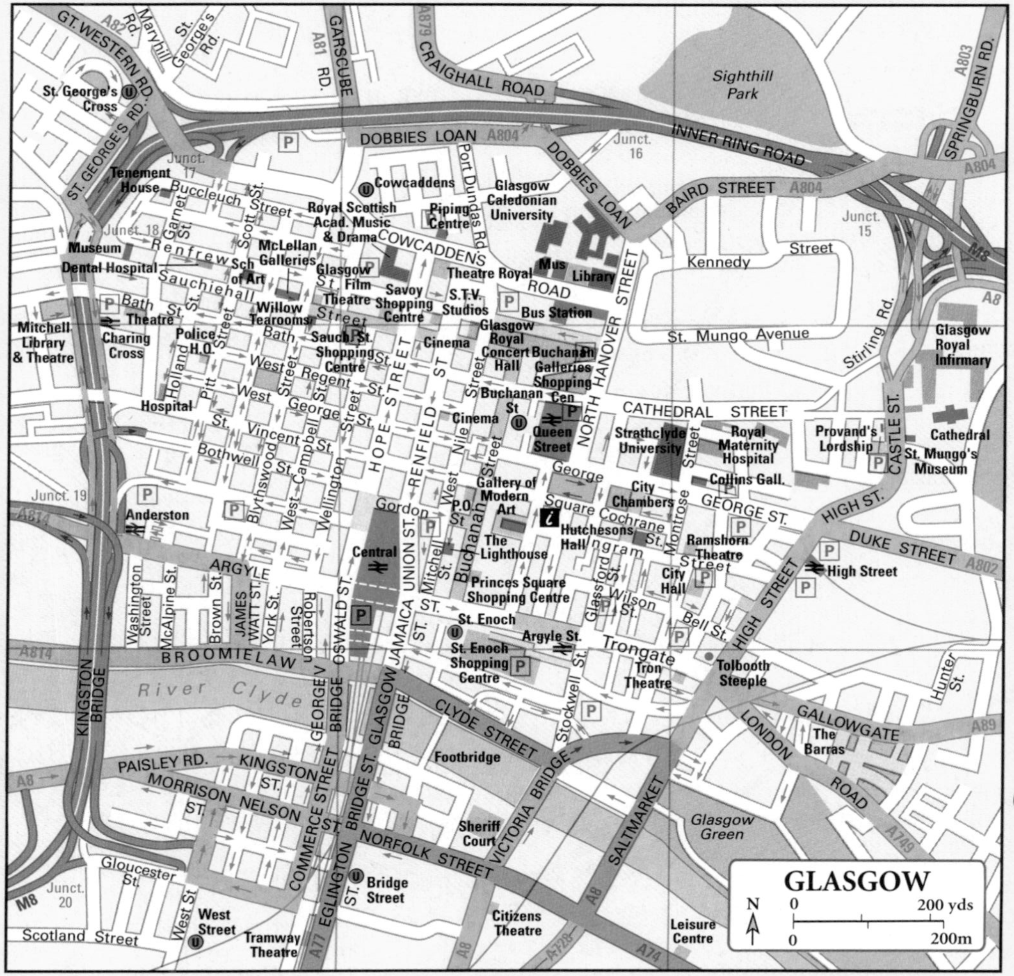

WEB-SITE www.glasgow.gov.uk

LOCAL RADIO
BBC RADIO SCOTLAND 810 AM & 92.4-94.7 FM
CLYDE 1 102.5 FM, CLYDE 2 1152 AM, REAL RADIO 100.3 FM

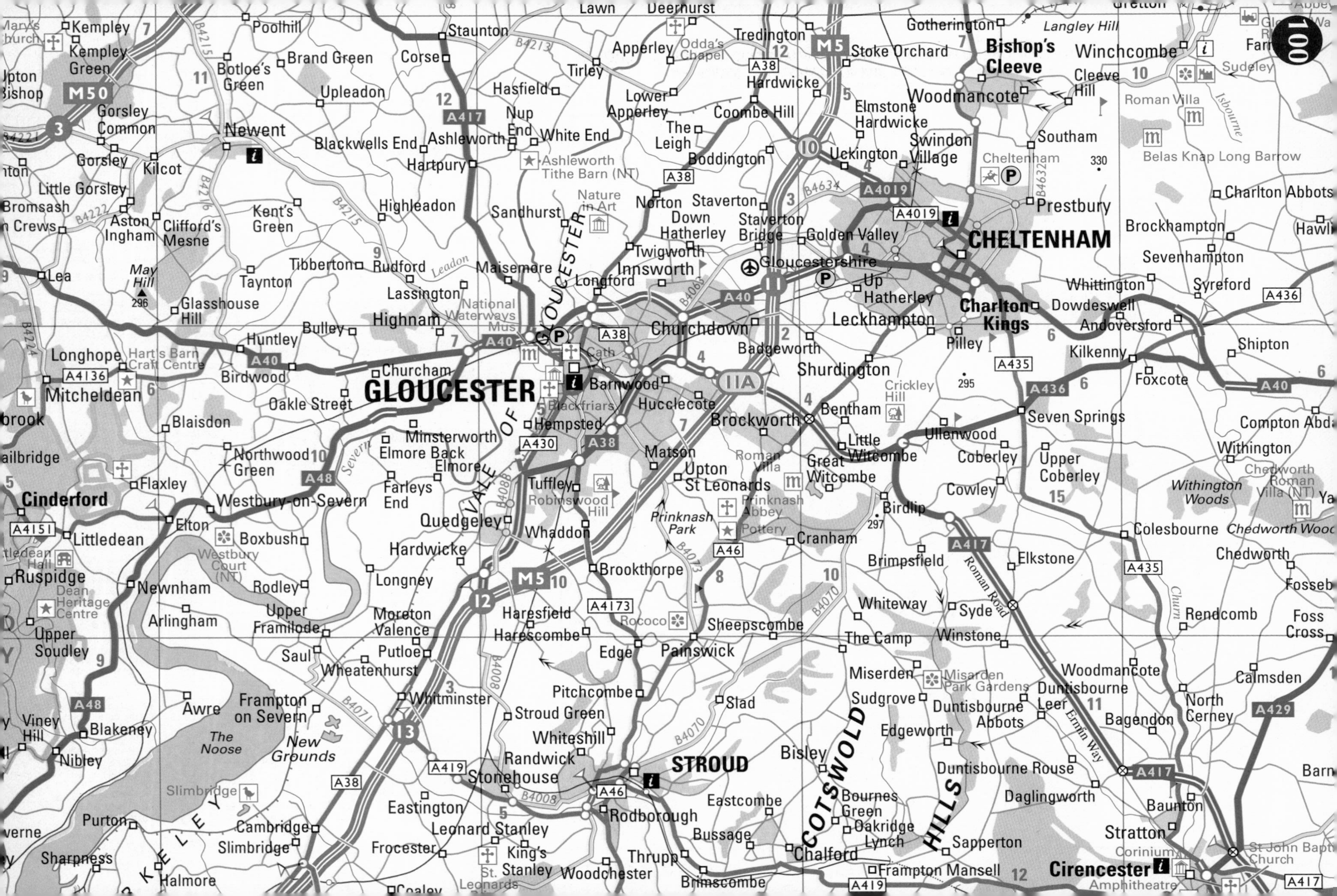

Kempley
Kempley Green
Upton Bishop
M50
3
Gorsley Common
Gorsley
Kilcot
Little Gorsley
Bromsash
Crews
Aston Ingham
Clifford's Mesne
Lea
May Hill
296
Glasshouse Hill
Longhope
Hart's Barn Craft Centre
A4136
Mitcheldean
Cinderford
A4151
Littledean
Dean Hall
Ruspidge
Dean Heritage Centre
Upper Soudley
Viney Hill
Blakeney
Nibley
A48
Sharpness
Purton
Halmore
Poolhill
Botloe's Green
Brand Green
Upleadon
Newent
Kent's Green
Taynton
Tibberton
Rudford
Blaisdon
Flaxley
Elton
Westbury-on-Severn
Boxbush
Westbury Court (NT)
Newnham
Arlingham
Rodley
Upper Framilode
Saul
Awre
The Noose
Frampton on Severn
New Grounds
Slimbridge
Cambridge
Berkeley
Staunton
Corse
A417
Hasfield
Tirley
Nup End
White End
Ashleworth
Blackwells End
Hartpury
Ashleworth Tithe Barn (NT)
Highleadon
Sandhurst
Nature in Art
Maisemore
Lassington
Highnam
Bulley
Huntley
Birdwood
Churcham
Oakle Street
Minsterworth
Elmore Back
Elmore
Northwood Green
Farleys End
Quedgeley
Hardwicke
Longney
Moreton Valence
Putloe
Wheatenhurst
Whitminster
A38
Eastington
Frocester
Leonard Stanley
King's Stanley
St. Leonards
Coaley
Deerhurst
Apperley
Odda's Chapel
Lower Apperley
The Leigh
Tredington
Hardwicke
Coombe Hill
Boddington
Norton
Down Hatherley
Staverton
Staverton Bridge
Twigworth
Innsworth
Longford
GLOUCESTER
National Waterways Mus
Cath
Blackfriars
Barnwood
Hempsted
Tuffley
Robinswood Hill
Vale of Gloucester
Churchdown
Hucclecote
Matson
Whaddon
Brookthorpe
Haresfield
Harescombe
Edge
Pitchcombe
Stroud Green
Whiteshill
Randwick
Stonehouse
STROUD
Rodborough
Woodchester
Thrupp
Brimscombe
Bussage
Eastcombe
Chalford
Gotherington
Stoke Orchard
Elmstone Hardwicke
Uckington
Swindon Village
Gloucestershire
Golden Valley
Up Hatherley
Leckhampton
Badgeworth
Shurdington
Brockworth
Bentham
Crickley Hill
Little Witcombe
Great Witcombe
Roman Villa
Upton St Leonards
Prinknash Abbey
Prinknash Park
Pottery
Cranham
Birdlip
297
Brimpsfield
Sheepscombe
Painswick
Rococo
Slad
The Camp
Whiteway
Miserden
Misarden Park Gardens
Sudgrove
Bisley
Edgeworth
Bournes Green
Oakridge Lynch
Cotswold Hills
Frampton Mansell
Sapperton
Langley Hill
Bishop's Cleeve
Woodmancote
Cleeve Hill
Winchcombe
Sudeley
Roman Villa
Belas Knap Long Barrow
Southam
330
Cheltenham
Prestbury
CHELTENHAM
Charlton Kings
Pilley
295
Ullenwood
Coberley
Cowley
Seven Springs
Upper Coberley
Elkstone
Roman Road
Syde
Winstone
Charlton Abbots
Brockhampton
Sevenhampton
Whittington
Dowdeswell
Andoversford
Syreford
Kilkenny
Shipton
Foxcote
Compton Abdale
Withington
Withington Woods
Chedworth Roman Villa (NT)
Colesbourne
Chedworth Woods
Chedworth
Fossebridge
Foss Cross
Rendcomb
Churn
Woodmancote
Calmsden
North Cerney
Duntisbourne Leer
Duntisbourne Abbots
Ermin Way
Bagendon
Duntisbourne Rouse
Daglingworth
Baunton
Stratton
Cirencester
Corinium Amphitheatre
St John Baptist Church
Barnsley
A40
A436
A435
A417
A4019
A46
A4173
A430
A419
A429
M5
B4632
B4634
B4063
B4073
B4070
B4008
B4071
B4088
B4213
B4215
B4216
B4221
B4222
B4224
Leadon
Severn
Isbourne

INDEX TO STREET NAMES

Street	Grid	Street	Grid	Street	Grid
Adelaide Street	C2	Greyfriars	B2	Ryecroft Street	C2
Alma Place	C1	Hatherley Road	C2	St. Ann Way	C1
Alvin Street	A2	High Street	C2	St. Oswald's Road	A1
Archdeacon Street	A1	Hopewell Street	C2	Secunda Way	C1
Barnwood Road	A3	Horton Road	B3	Severn Road	B1
Barton Street	B2	King Edward's Avenue	C2	Seymour Road	C1
Black Dog Way	A2	Kingsholm Road	A2	Southgate Street	B1
Bristol Road	C1	Linden Road	C1	Spa Road	B1
Brunswick Road	B2	London Road	A2	Station Road	B2
Bruton Way	B2	Lower Westgate Street	A1	Stroud Road	C1
Calton Road	C2	Merevale Road	A3	The Quay	B1
Cheltenham Road	A3	Metz Way	B2	Tredworth Road	C2
Churchill Road	C1	Millbrook Street	B2	Trier Way	C1
Conduit Street	C2	Northgate Street	B2	Upton Street	C2
Dean's Way	A2	Oxford Road	A2	Victoria Street	B2
Denmark Road	A2	Oxstalls Lane	A3	Wellington Street	B2
Derby Road	B2	Painswick Road	C3	Westgate Street	A1
Estcourt Road	A2	Park Road	B2	Weston Road	C1
Eastern Avenue	C3	Parkend Road	C2	Wheatstone Road	C2
Eastgate Street	B2	Pitt Street	A2	Worcester Street	A2
Gouda Way	A1	Quay Street	B1		
Great Western Road	B2				

TOURIST INFORMATION ☎ 01452 421188
28 SOUTHGATE STREET, GLOUCESTER,
GLOUCESTERSHIRE, GL1 2DP

HOSPITAL A & E ☎ 01452 528555
GLOUCESTER ROYAL HOSPITAL
GREAT WESTERN RD, GLOUCESTER, GL1 3NN

COUNCIL OFFICE ☎ 01452 522232
COUNCIL OFFICES, NORTH WAREHOUSE,
THE DOCKS, GLOUCESTER, GL1 2EP

Gloucester *Glos.* Population: 114,003. City, industrial city on River Severn, on site of Roman town of Glevum, 32m/52km NE of Bristol. Norman era saw Gloucester grow in political importance, from here William the Conqueror ordered survey of his Kingdom which resulted in Domesday Book of 1086. City became a religious centre during middle ages. Cathedral built in mixture of Norman and Perpendicular styles, has cloisters and England's largest stained glass window, dating from 14c. Remains of 15c-16c Franciscan friary, Greyfriars, (English Heritage). Historic docks, now largely redeveloped, on Gloucester and Sharpness Canal. Three Choirs Festival held every third year.

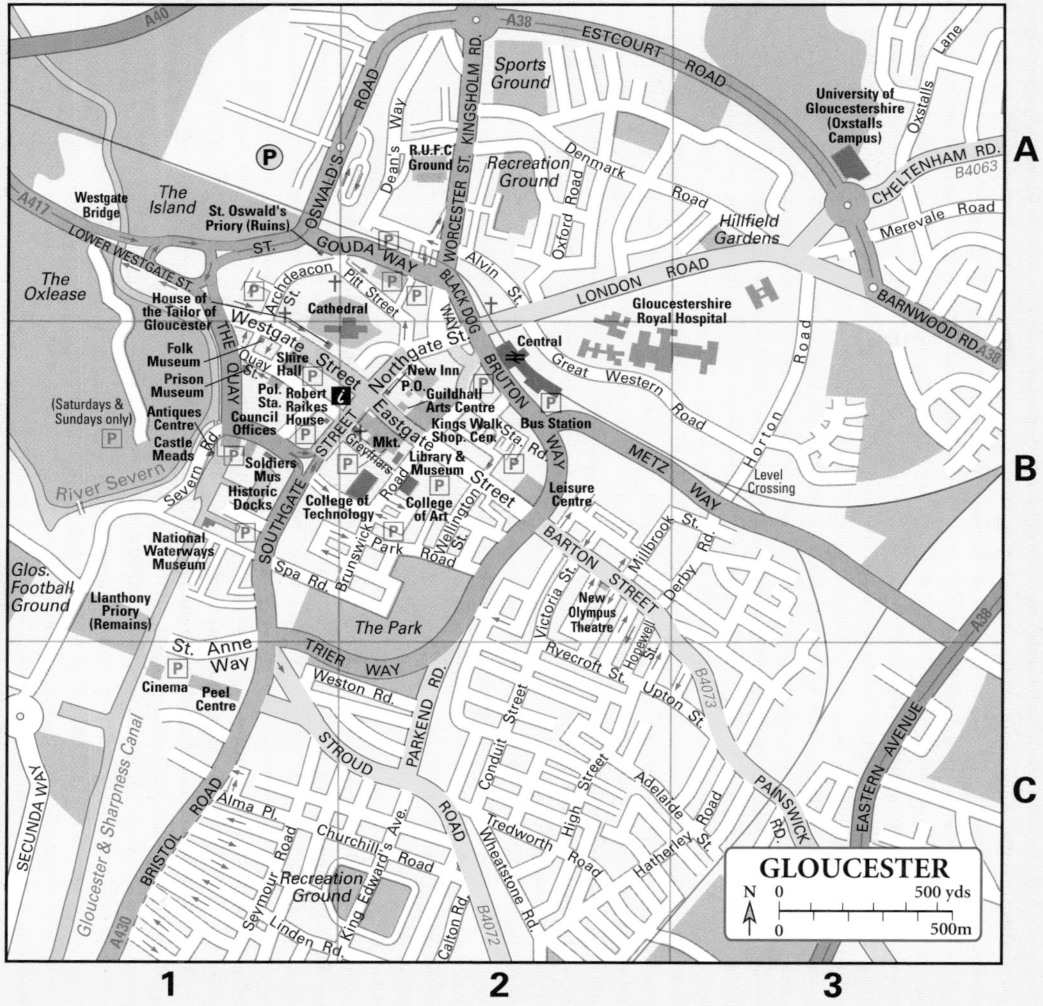

WEB-SITE www.glos-city.gov.uk

LOCAL RADIO
BBC RADIO GLOUCESTERSHIRE 104.7 FM
CLASSIC GOLD 774 AM, SEVERN SOUND FM 102.4 & 103 FM

Wokingham
BRACKNELL
Ascot
Sunninghill
Sunningdale
Virginia Water
Thorpe
Laleham
Littleton
Sunbury
West Molesey
Hampton
East Molesey
Thames Ditton
Long Ditton
Tolworth
Easthampstead
Eastheath
South Ascot
Shepperton
Upper Halliford
Weston Green
Chertsey
WALTON-ON-THAMES
Lyne
Longcross
Chobham Common
Look Out Discovery Park
Surrey Hill
Weybridge
ESHER
Claygate
Hook
Chessington
Hersham
West End
Addlestone
Ottershaw
Windlesham
Crowthorne
Bagshot
Wick Hill
Sandhurst
Yateley
CAMBERLEY
Lightwater
Burrowhill
Chobham
West End
Row Town
Woodham
New Haw
Brooklands
Whiteley Village
Malden Rushett
Oxshott
Darby Green
Blackwater
Frogmore
Donkey Town
Chobham Ridges
Bisley
Byfleet
West Byfleet
Cobham
Stoke D'Abernon
Danger Zone
Hawley
Knaphill
Horsell
Wisley
Downside
Ashtead
Minley Manor
Fox Lane
FRIMLEY
St John's
WOKING
Pyrford
Martyr's Green
Wintney
West Heath
Farnborough Green
Deepcut
Brookwood
Newark Priory
Ripley
LEATHERHEAD
Fleet
Cove
Frimley Green
Old Woking
Ockham
Effingham Junc. Sta.
Fetcham
Mytchett
Pirbright
Mayford
Send
Send Marsh
Little Bookham
Great Bookham
FARNBOROUGH
Worplesdon Sta.
Sutton Green
Bocketts Farm Park
Givons Grove
FLEET
Army Mus
North Camp
Henley Park
Worplesdon
Pitch Place
Sutton Place
Hatchlands (NT)
East Horsley
Effingham
Mickleham
Crookham Village
Ash Vale
Normandy
Stoughton
West Clandon
West Horsley
Chapel Farm Animal Trail
Box Hill (NT)
Church Crookham
Long Valley
North Town
Wanborough Sta.
Wood Street Village
Burpham
Merrow
Polesden Lacey (NT)
Westhumble
ALDERSHOT
Ash
Flexford
Clandon Park (NT)
East Clandon
Denbies Wine Centre
Ewshot
Heath End
Tongham
Wanborough
Onslow Village
Guildford House Gall
Newland's Corner
Dorking
Brockham
Hale
Badshot Lea
Hog's Back
GUILDFORD
Shere
Gomshall
Wotton
Westcott
Runfold
Seale
Puttenham
Loseley
Manor
Albury
Albury Park
Abinger Hammer
Dippenhall
FARNHAM
The Sands
Compton
Shalford
Chilworth
North Holmwood
Wrecclesham
The Bourne
Lower Bourne
Waverley Abbey
Shackleford
Hurtmore
Farncombe
Wonersh
Blackheath
Albury Heath
Sutton Abinger
Friday Street
South Holmwood
Charleshill
Bramley
Farley Green
Peaslake
Abinger Common
Tilford
Peper Harow
Eashing
Godalming
Shamley Green
Holmbury St Mary
Leith Hill
Coldharbour
Holmwood Sta.
Beare Green
Bentley
Rowledge
Birdworld
Elstead
Busbridge
Hurtwood Common
Spreakley
Millbridge
Milford
Thorncombe Street
Stroud Common
Rowly
Tower (NT)
Frensham
Milford Sta.
Witley Common (NT)
Winkworth Arboretum (NT)
Grafham
Forest Green
Newdigate
N O R T H   D O W N S

INDEX TO STREET NAMES

Street	Grid	Street	Grid	Street	Grid
Abbot Road	C3	Friary Street	B2	Park Road	A2
Artillery Road	A2	Genyn Road	B1	Park Street	B2
Artillery Terrace	A2	Guildford	A1	Pewley Hill	B3
Bedford Road	A2	Park Avenue		Portsmouth Road	C2
Bridge Street	B2	Guildford	B1	Quarry Street	B2
Bright Hill	B3	Park Road		Rookwood Court	C1
Bury Fields	C2	Harevy Road	B3	Sand Terrace	A2
Bury Street	C2	Haydon Place	A2	Semaphore Road	C3
Castle Hill	C3	High Street	B2/B3	South Hill	B3
Castle Square	B3	Laundry Road	A2	Springfield Road	A3
Castle Street	B2	Lawn Road	C2	Station Approach	A3
Chertsey Street	A3	Leap Lane	B2	Station View	A1
Cheselden Road	B3	Leas Road	A2	Stoke Road	A3
Commercial Road	B2	Ludlow Road	B1	Swan Lane	B2
Dapdune Road	A2	Market Street	B2	Sydenham Road	B3
Dapdune Wharf	A2	Martyr Road	B2	The Bars	B2
Dene Road	A3	Mary Road	A2	The Mount	C1
Denmark Road	A3	Millbrook	C2	Victoria Road	A3
Denzil Road	B1	Millmead	B2	Walnut Tree Close	A1
Drummond Road	A2	Millmead Terrace	C2	Warwicks	C3
Eagle Road	A3	Mount Pleasant	C1	Wharf Road	A2
Eastgate Gardens	A3	Nightingale Road	A3	Wherwell Road	B1
Farnham Road	B1	North Street	B2	Wodeland Avenue	C1
Flower Walk	C2	Onslow Road	A3	Woodbridge Road	A2
Fort Road	C3	Onslow Street	B2	York Road	A2
Friary Bridge	B2	Pannells Court	B3		

TOURIST INFORMATION ☎ 01483 444333
14 TUNSGATE,
GUILDFORD, GU1 3QT

HOSPITAL A & E ☎ 01483 571122
ROYAL SURREY COUNTY HOSPITAL, EGERTON ROAD,
GUILDFORD, GU2 5XX

COUNCIL OFFICE ☎ 01483 505050
GUILDFORD BOROUGH COUNCIL, MILLMEAD HOUSE,
MILLMEAD, GUILDFORD, GU2 4BB

Guildford *Surr.* Population: 65,998. County town and former weaving centre on River Wey, 27m/43km SW of London. High Street lined with Tudor buildings, the Guildhall the most impressive. Remains of Norman castle keep built c.1173, on an 11c motte, used as county gaol for 400 years. Cathedral consecrated in 1961 and built of red brick, the interior is designed in a modern gothic style. University of Surrey. Royal Grammar School noted for its chained library

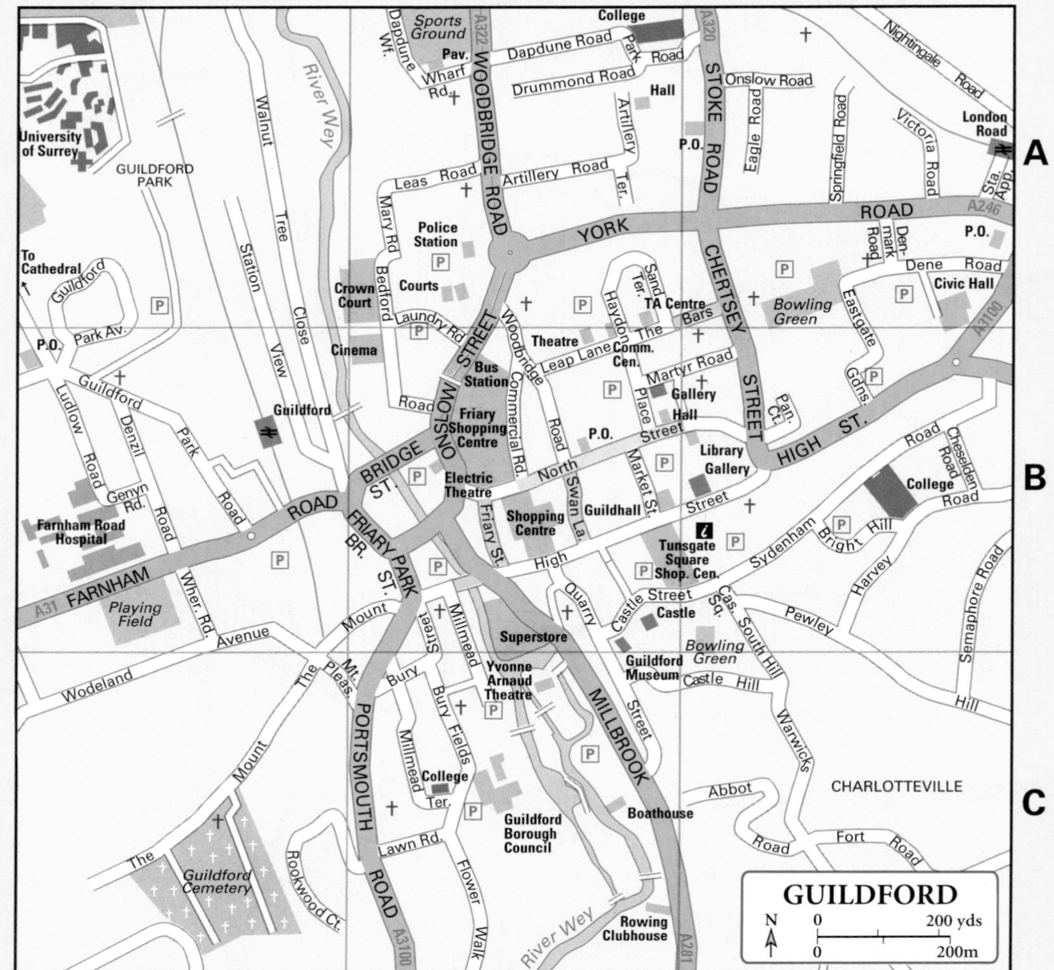

WEB-SITE	www.guildford.gov.uk

LOCAL RADIO	BBC SOUTHERN COUNTIES RADIO 104.6 FM THE EAGLE 96.4 FM, COUNTY SOUND 1566 AM

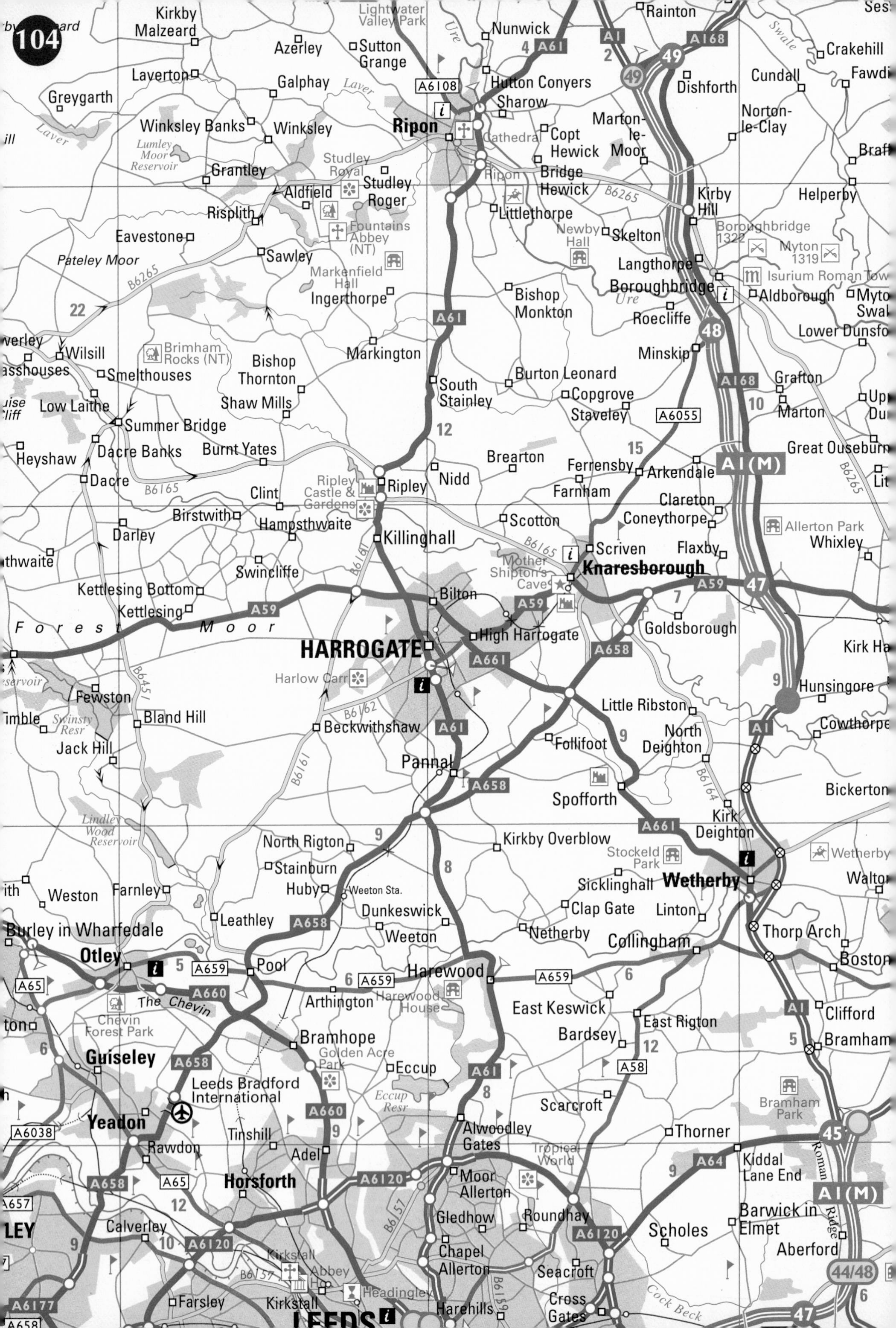

104
Kirkby Malzeard
Lightwater Valley Park
Azerley
Sutton Grange
Ure
Nunwick
Rainton
A61
A1
A168
Swale
Crakehill
Laverton
Galphay
Laver
A6108
Hutton Conyers
Sharow
Dishforth
Cundall
Greygarth
Ripon
Marton-le-Moor
Norton-le-Clay
Winksley Banks
Winksley
Cathedral
Copt Hewick
Lumley Moor Reservoir
Studley Royal
Studley Roger
Grantley
Bridge Hewick
B6265
Kirby Hill
Helperby
Aldfield
Risplith
Littlethorpe
Fountains Abbey (NT)
Eavestone
Newby Hall
Skelton
Boroughbridge 1322
Myton 1319
Sawley
Pateley Moor
Markenfield Hall
Langthorpe
Isurium Roman Town
Boroughbridge
Aldborough
Ingerthorpe
Bishop Monkton
Roecliffe
Lower Dunsforth
Wilsill
Brimham Rocks (NT)
Bishop Thornton
Markington
Minskip
Smelthouses
Burton Leonard
Grafton
South Stainley
Copgrove
Staveley
A6055
Marton
Low Laithe
Shaw Mills
Summer Bridge
Burnt Yates
Heyshaw
Dacre Banks
Brearton
Great Ouseburn
Ferrensby
Arkendale
A1(M)
Dacre
B6165
Ripley Castle & Gardens
Ripley
Nidd
Farnham
Clint
Clareton
Birstwith
Hampsthwaite
Scotton
Coneythorpe
Allerton Park
Darley
Killinghall
B6161
B6165
Scriven
Flaxby
Whixley
Swincliffe
Mother Shipton's Cave
Knaresborough
A59
Kettlesing Bottom
Bilton
Kettlesing
Forest Moor
High Harrogate
Goldsborough
HARROGATE
A661
A658
Kirk Hammerton
Harlow Carr
B6451
Fewston
Hunsingore
B6162
Little Ribston
Swinsty Resr
Bland Hill
Beckwithshaw
North Deighton
Cowthorpe
Jack Hill
Follifoot
Pannal
B6164
Spofforth
Bickerton
Kirk Deighton
Lindley Wood Reservoir
North Rigton
Kirkby Overblow
Stockeld Park
Wetherby
Stainburn
Huby
Weeton Sta.
Sicklinghall
Weston
Farnley
Dunkeswick
Clap Gate
Linton
Leathley
Netherby
Thorp Arch
Burley in Wharfedale
Weeton
Collingham
Otley
Pool
A659
Harewood
Boston Spa
A65
A660
The Chevin
Arthington
Harewood House
East Keswick
Clifford
Chevin Forest Park
Bramhope
East Rigton
Bardsey
Bramham
Golden Acre Park
Guiseley
Eccup
A58
Leeds Bradford International
Eccup Resr
Scarcroft
Bramham Park
Yeadon
A6038
Tinshill
Alwoodley Gates
Thorner
Rawdon
Adel
Tropical World
Kiddal Lane End
Horsforth
A6120
Moor Allerton
A64
Roman Ridge
Calverley
Gledhow
Roundhay
Scholes
Barwick in Elmet
Chapel Allerton
Aberford
Kirkstall Abbey
Seacroft
Headingley
B6157
B6159
Farsley
Kirkstall
Harehills
Cross Gates
Cock Beck
A6177
LEEDS

Area Code 01423

North Yorkshire

HARROGATE

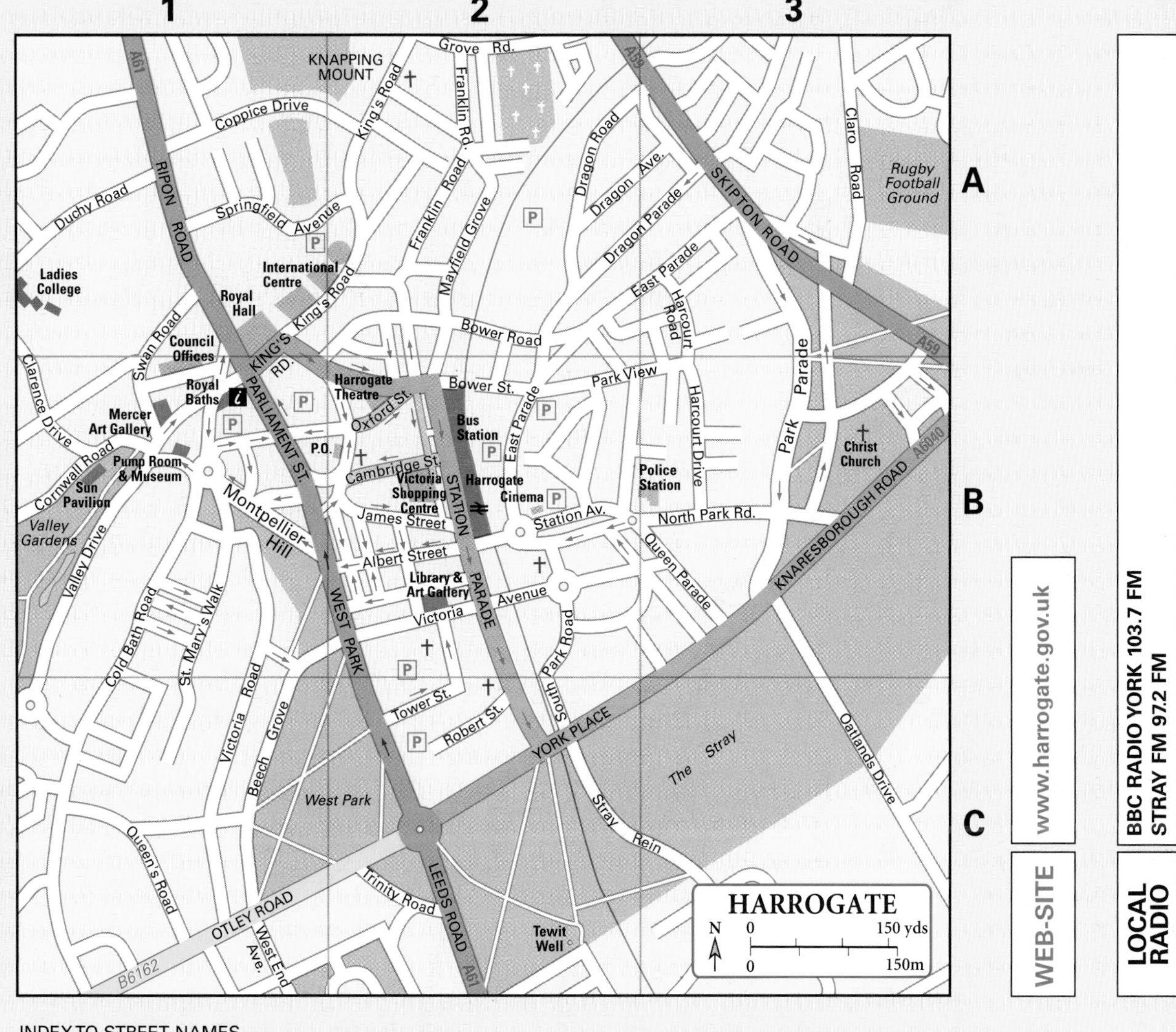

INDEX TO STREET NAMES

TOURIST INFORMATION ☎ 01423 537300
ROYAL BATHS ASSEMBLY ROOMS, CRESCENT RD, HARROGATE, NORTH YORKSHIRE, HG1 2RR

HOSPITAL A & E ☎ 01423 885959
HARROGATE DISTRICT HOSPITAL, LANCASTER PARK ROAD, HARROGATE, HG2 7SX

COUNCIL OFFICE ☎ 01423 500600
COUNCIL OFFICES, CRESCENT GARDENS HARROGATE, HG1 2SG

Harrogate *N.Yorks.* Population: 66,178. Town, spa town and conference centre, 12m/21km N of Leeds. Fashionable spa town of 19c with many distinguished Victorian buildings, extensive gardens and pleasant tree-lined streets. Royal Baths Assembly Rooms (1897) open for Turkish baths. Royal Pump Room (1842) now a museum. The Stray park and gardens are S of town centre. The Valley Gardens to the SW are the venue for band concerts and flower shows. Harlow Carr Botanical Gardens and Museum of Gardening 2m/3km SW. Mother Shipton's cave, reputed home to the 16c prophetess, near Knaresborough, 4m/6km NW.

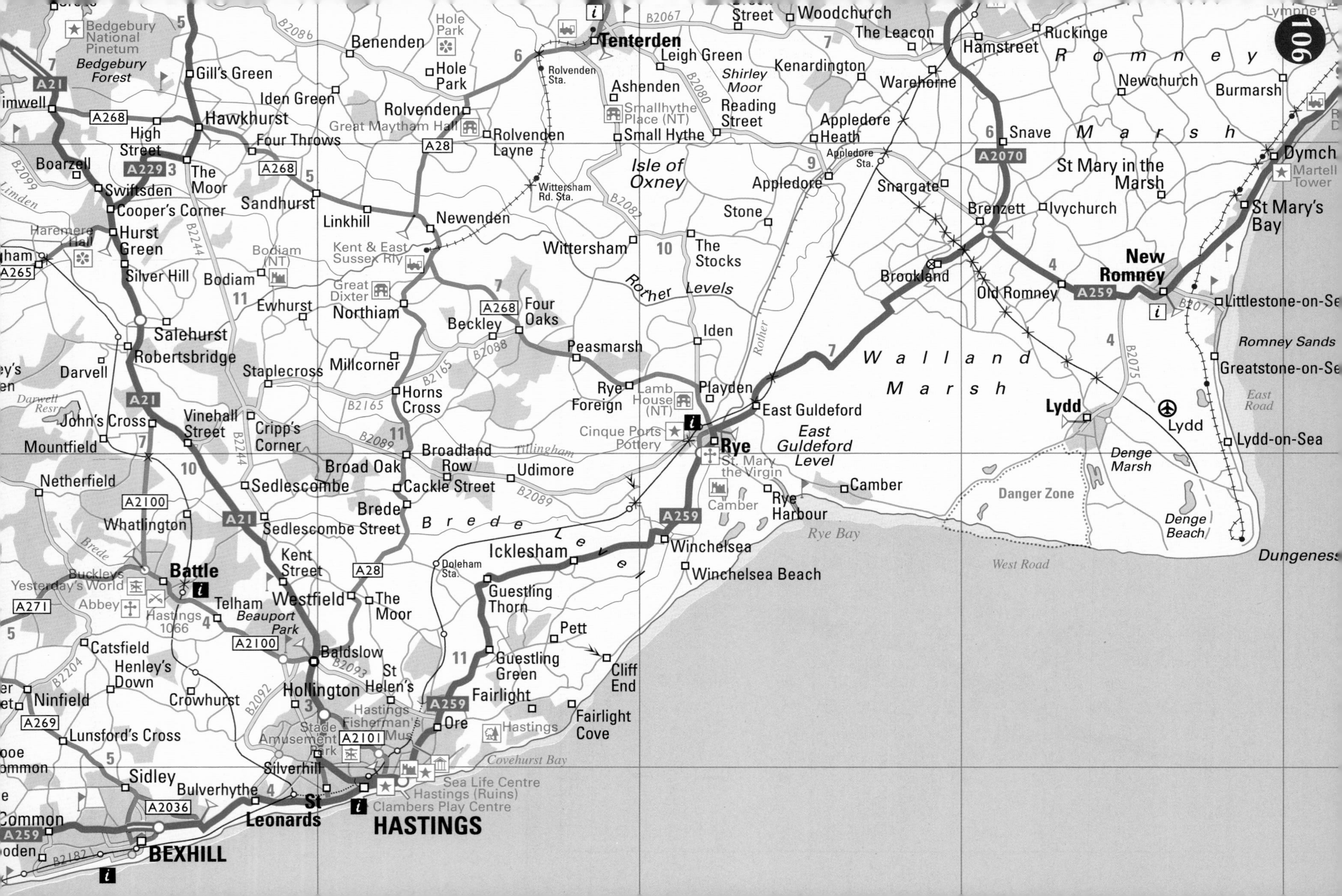

Bedgebury National Pinetum
Bedgebury Forest
Benenden
Hole Park
Tenterden
Rolvenden Sta.
Leigh Green
Woodchurch
The Leacon
Hamstreet
Ruckinge
Romney Marsh
Lympne
Dymchurch
Martello Tower
Gill's Green
Iden Green
Rolvenden
Great Maytham Hall
Rolvenden Layne
Ashenden
Smallhythe Place (NT)
Small Hythe
Shirley Moor
Reading Street
Kenardington
Warehorne
Appledore Heath
Appledore Sta.
Appledore
Newchurch
Burmarsh
Snave
St Mary in the Marsh
St Mary's Bay
Hawkhurst
High Street
Four Throws
Boarzell
The Moor
Swiftsden
Cooper's Corner
Sandhurst
Linkhill
Newenden
Wittersham Rd. Sta.
Isle of Oxney
Stone
Snargate
Brenzett
Ivychurch
Hurst Green
Haremere Hall
Bodiam (NT)
Bodiam
Kent & East Sussex Rly
Wittersham
The Stocks
Rother Levels
Brookland
Old Romney
New Romney
Littlestone-on-Sea
Silver Hill
Salehurst
Robertsbridge
Ewhurst
Great Dixter
Northiam
Beckley
Four Oaks
Peasmarsh
Iden
Walland Marsh
Romney Sands
Greatstone-on-Sea
Darvell
Darwell Resr
Staplecross
Millcorner
Rye Foreign
Lamb House (NT)
Playden
East Guldeford
Lydd
East Road
John's Cross
Mountfield
Vinehall Street
Cripp's Corner
Horns Cross
Cinque Ports Pottery
Rye
St. Mary the Virgin
East Guldeford Level
Lydd-on-Sea
Denge Marsh
Netherfield
Broad Oak
Broadland Row
Udimore
Tillingham
Sedlescombe
Cackle Street
Camber
Danger Zone
Brede
Rye Harbour
Denge Beach
Whatlington
Sedlescombe Street
Brede Level
Icklesham
Winchelsea
Rye Bay
Dungeness
Battle
Buckleys Yesterday's World
Abbey
Kent Street
Doleham Sta.
Winchelsea Beach
West Road
Telham
Hastings 1066
Beaufort Park
Westfield
The Moor
Guestling Thorn
Pett
Catsfield
Henley's Down
Baldslow
Guestling Green
Cliff End
Ninfield
Crowhurst
Hollington
St Helen's
Fairlight
Fairlight Cove
Hastings
Hastings Fisherman's Mus
Stade Amusement Park
Ore
Lunsford's Cross
Covehurst Bay
Silverhill
Sidley
Bulverhythe
Sea Life Centre
Hastings (Ruins)
Clambers Play Centre
St Leonards
HASTINGS
BEXHILL
A21
A268
A229
A28
A2070
A259
A265
A2100
A271
A269
A2036
A2101
B2086
B2067
B2080
B2082
B2244
B2099
B2088
B2165
B2089
B2093
B2092
B2204
B2182
B2075
B2071

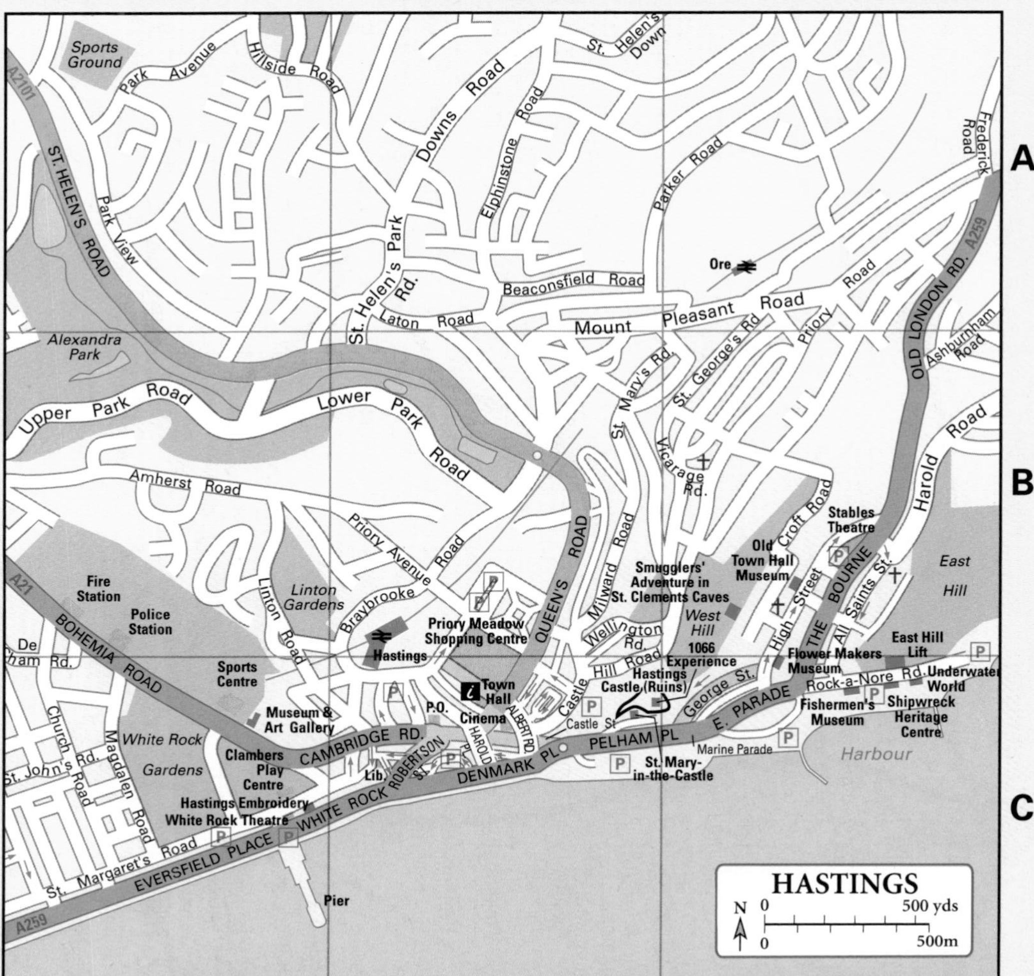

INDEX TO STREET NAMES					
Albert Road	C2	George Street	C3	Robertson Street	C2
All Saints Street	B3	Harold Place	C2	Rock-a-Nore Road	C3
Amherst Road	B1	Harold Road	B3	St. George's Road	B3
Ashburnham Road	B3	High Street	B3	St. Helen's Down	A2
Beaconsfield Road	A2	Hillside Road	A1	St. Helen's Park Road	B2
Bohemia Road	B1	Laton Road	A2	St. Helen's Road	A1
Braybrooke Road	B2	Linton Road	B1	St. John's Road	C1
Cambridge Road	C1	Lower Park Road	B1	St. Margaret's Road	C1
Castle Hill Road	C2	Magdalen Road	C1	St. Mary's Road	B2
Castle Street	C2	Marine Parade	C3	The Bourne	B3
Church Road	C1	Milward Road	B2	Upper Park Road	B1
Croft Road	B3	Mount Pleasant Road	A2	Vicarage Road	B2
De Cham Road	C1	Old London Road	B3	Wellington Road	B2
Denmark Place	C2	Park Avenue	A1	White Rock	C1
Downs Road	A2	Park View	A1		
East Parade	C3	Parker Road	A2		
Elphinstone Road	A2	Pelham Place	C2		
Eversfield Place	C1	Priory Avenue	B2		
Frederick Road	A3	Priory Road	B3		
		Queen's Road	B2		

TOURIST INFORMATION ☎ 01424 781111
QUEENS SQUARE, PRIORY MEADOW, HASTINGS, TN34 1TL

HOSPITAL A & E ☎ 01424 755255
CONQUEST HOSPITAL, THE RIDGE, ST. LEONARDS-ON-SEA, TN37 7RD

COUNCIL OFFICE ☎ 01424 781066
HASTINGS BOROUGH COUNCIL, TOWN HALL, QUEENS ROAD, HASTINGS, TN34 1QR

Hastings *E.Suss.* Population: 84,139. Town, Cinque port and seaside resort 32m/52km E of Brighton. Remains of Norman castle built 1068-1080 on hill in town centre, houses the 1066 exhibition which relates the history of castle and Norman invasion. Battle of 1066 fought at Battle, 6m/9km NW. Former smugglers caves have a display on smuggling, once a vital part of the towns economy.

WEB-SITE www.hastings.gov.uk

LOCAL RADIO BBC SOUTHERN COUNTIES RADIO 104.5 FM, 1161 AM
ARROW FM 107.8 FM

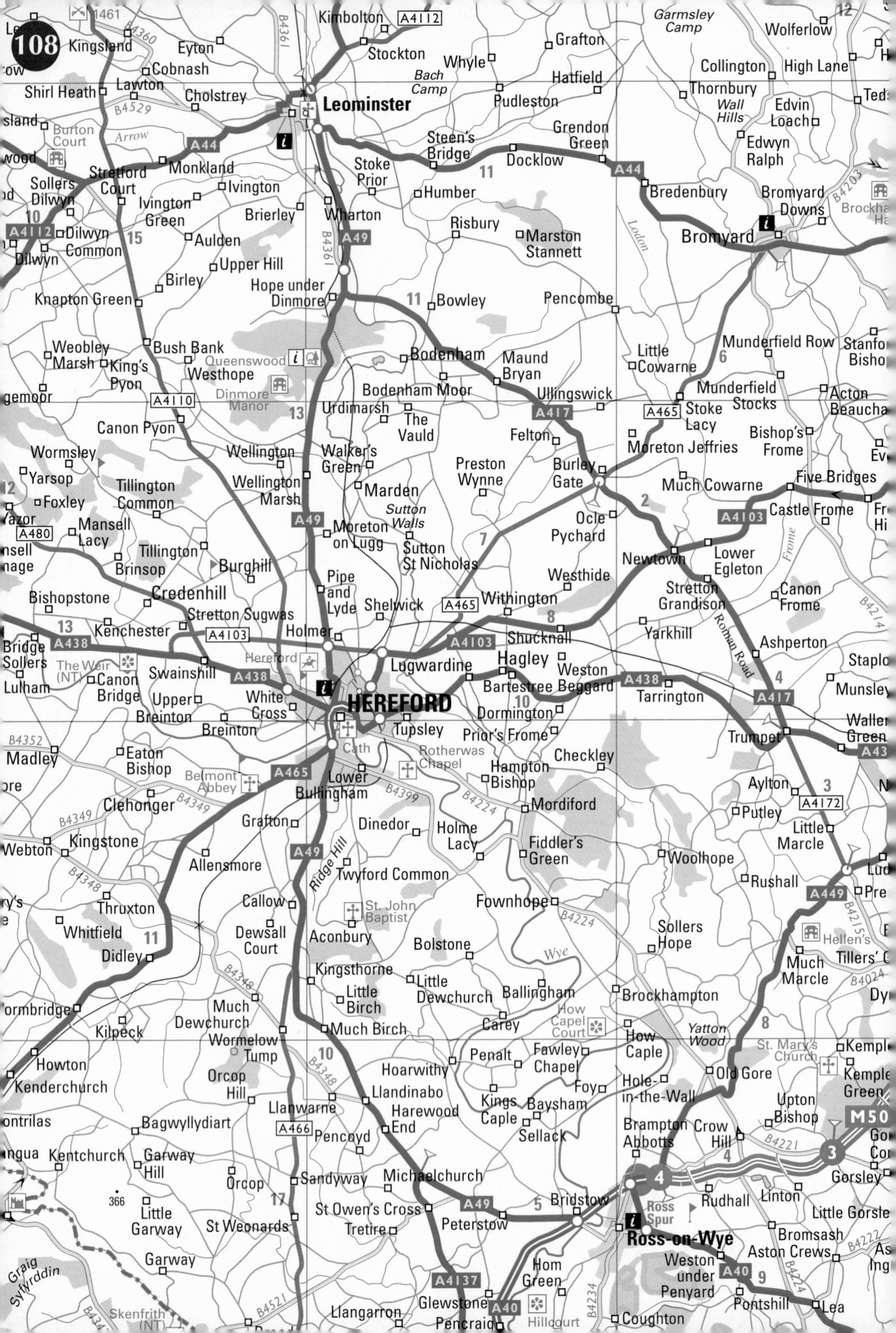

Kingsland
Eyton
Cobnash
Lawton
Shirl Heath
Cholstrey
Burton Court
Arrow
Leominster
Kimbolton
Stockton
Grafton
Whyle
Bach Camp
Hatfield
Pudleston
Grendon Green
Garmsley Camp
Wolferlow
Collington
High Lane
Thornbury
Wall Hills
Edvin Loach
Edwyn Ralph
Steen's Bridge
Docklow
Stoke Prior
Humber
Bredenbury
Bromyard Downs
Bromyard
Stretford Court
Monkland
Sollers Dilwyn
Ivington
Ivington Green
Brierley
Wharton
Dilwyn Common
Dilwyn
Aulden
Risbury
Marston Stannett
Upper Hill
Birley
Hope under Dinmore
Knapton Green
Bowley
Pencombe
Weobley Marsh
King's Pyon
Bush Bank
Queenswood
Westhope
Dinmore Manor
Bodenham
Maund Bryan
Little Cowarne
Munderfield Row
Stanford Bishop
Bodenham Moor
Munderfield Stocks
Ullingswick
Acton Beauchamp
Urdimarsh
The Vauld
Stoke Lacy
Canon Pyon
Felton
Moreton Jeffries
Bishop's Frome
Wormsley
Yarsop
Wellington
Walker's Green
Preston Wynne
Burley Gate
Tillington Common
Foxley
Wellington Marsh
Marden
Much Cowarne
Five Bridges
Castle Frome
Mansell Lacy
Sutton Walls
Moreton on Lugg
Ocle Pychard
Tillington
Sutton St Nicholas
Newtown
Lower Egleton
Brinsop
Burghill
Westhide
Stretton Grandison
Canon Frome
Bishopstone
Credenhill
Pipe and Lyde
Shelwick
Withington
Stretton Sugwas
Kenchester
Holmer
Shucknall
Yarkhill
Ashperton
Roman Road
Frome
Bridge Sollers
The Weir (NT)
Canon Bridge
Swainshill
Hereford
Lugwardine
Hagley
Weston Beggard
Bartestree
Tarrington
Staplow
Munsley
Lulham
Upper Breinton
White Cross
HEREFORD
Dormington
Breinton
Tupsley
Prior's Frome
Trumpet
Wallers Green
Madley
Eaton Bishop
Cath
Rotherwas Chapel
Hampton Bishop
Checkley
Belmont Abbey
Lower Bullingham
Aylton
Putley
Clehonger
Mordiford
Little Marcle
Grafton
Dinedor
Holme Lacy
Fiddler's Green
Webton
Kingstone
Ridge Hill
Woolhope
Allensmore
Twyford Common
Rushall
Thruxton
Callow
St. John Baptist
Fownhope
Whitfield
Dewsall Court
Aconbury
Sollers Hope
Didley
Bolstone
Wye
Hellen's
Much Marcle
Tillers' Green
Kingsthorne
Little Birch
Little Dewchurch
Ballingham
Brockhampton
Much Dewchurch
How Capel Court
Carey
Kilpeck
Much Birch
How Caple
Yatton Wood
St. Mary's Church
Kempley
Wormelow Tump
Penalt
Fawley Chapel
Howton
Orcop Hill
Hoarwithy
Old Gore
Kempley Green
Kenderchurch
Llandinabo
Foy
Hole-in-the-Wall
Kings Caple
Baysham
Upton Bishop
Llanwarne
Harewood End
Bagwyllydiart
Pencoyd
Sellack
Brampton Abbotts
Crow Hill
Kentchurch
Garway Hill
Orcop
Sandyway
Michaelchurch
Gorsley
Little Garway
St Weonards
St Owen's Cross
Tretire
Peterstow
Bridstow
Ross Spur
Rudhall
Linton
Little Gorsley
Ross-on-Wye
Bromsash
Aston Crews
Garway
Weston under Penyard
Hom Green
Graig Syfyrddin
Llangarron
Glewstone
Pontshill
Lea
Skenfrith (NT)
Pencraig
Hillcourt
Coughton
366
A4112
A44
A49
A417
A465
A4110
A480
A4103
A438
A466
A4137
A40
A449
A4172
M50
B4361
B4360
B4529
B4203
B4214
B4352
B4349
B4348
B4399
B4224
B4215
B4024
B4221
B4222
B4234
B4521

Area Code 01432

Herefordshire

HEREFORD

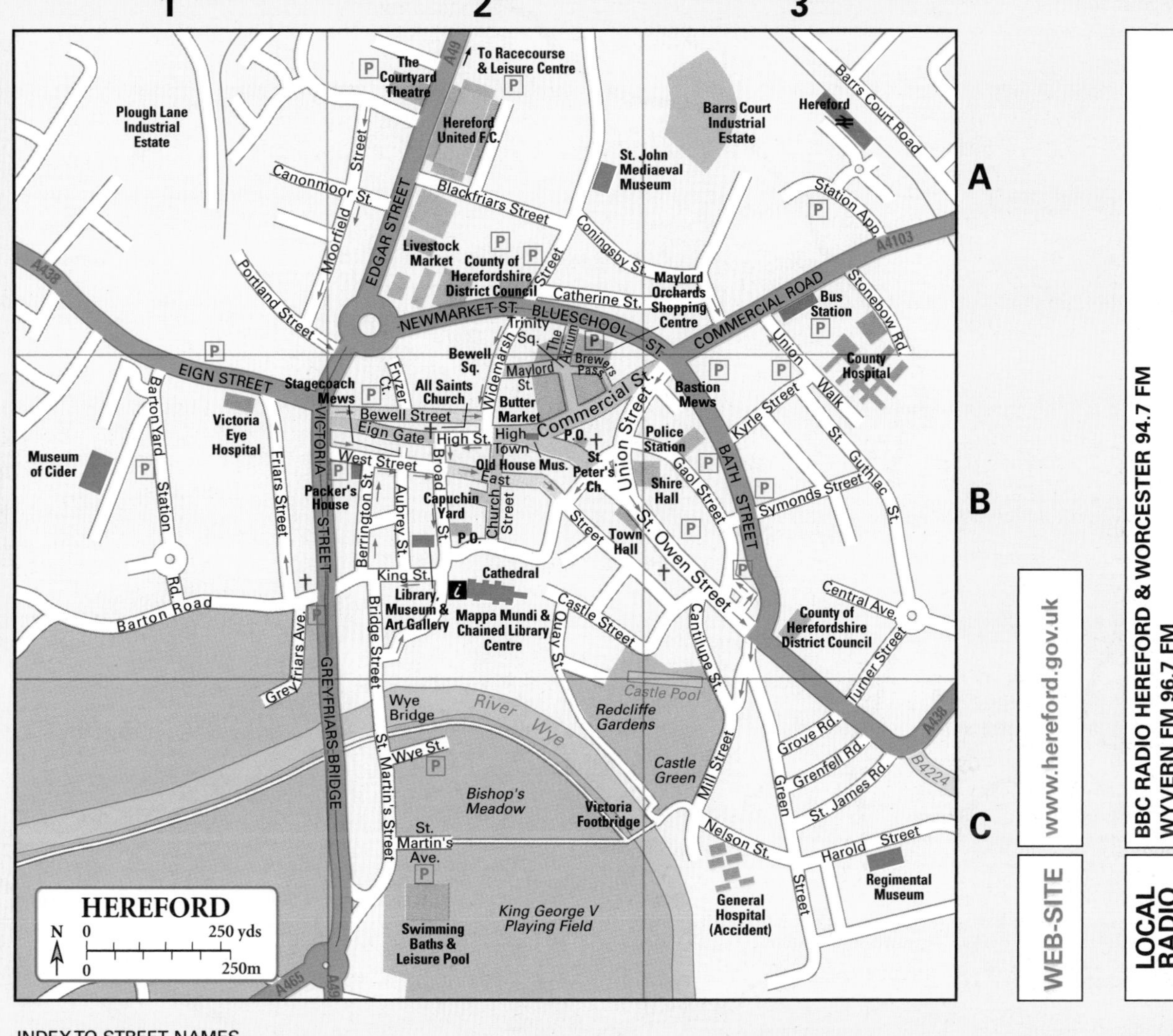

WEB-SITE

www.hereford.gov.uk

LOCAL RADIO

BBC RADIO HEREFORD & WORCESTER 94.7 FM
WYVERN FM 96.7 FM

INDEX TO STREET NAMES

Aubrey Street	B2	Cantilupe Street	B3	Fryzer Court	B2	Mill Street	C3	Stonebow Road	A3
Barrs Court Road	A3	Castle Street	B2	Gaol Street	B3	Moorfield Street	A1	Symonds Street	B3
Barton Road	B1	Catherine Street	A2	Green Street	C3	Nelson Street	C3	The Atrium	A2
Barton Yard	B1	Central Avenue	B3	Grenfell Road	C3	Newmarket Street	A2	Turner Street	C3
Bath Street	B3	Church Street	B2	Greyfriars Avenue	C1	Portland Street	A1	Union Street	B2
Berrington Street	B2	Commercial Road	A3	Greyfriars Bridge	B2	Quay Street	B2	Union Walk	A3
Bewell Street	B2	Commercial Street	B2	Grove Road	C3	St. Guthiac Street	B3	Victoria Street	B1
Blackfriars Street	A2	Coningsby Street	A2	Harold Street	C3	St. James Road	C3	West Street	B2
Blueschool Street	A2	East Street	B2	High Street	B2	St. Martin's Avenue	C2	Widemarsh Street	B2
Brewers Passage	B2	Edgar Street	A2	High Town	B2	St. Martin's Street	C2	Wye Street	C2
Bridge Street	B2	Eign Gate	B2	King Street	B2	St. Owen Street	B3		
Broad Street	B2	Eign Street	B1	Kyrle Street	B3	Station Approach	A3		
Canonmoor Street	A1	Friars Street	B1	Maylord Street	B2	Station Road	B1		

TOURIST INFORMATION ☎ 01432 268430
1 KING STREET,
HEREFORD, HR4 9BW

HOSPITAL A & E ☎ 01432 355444
HEREFORD GENERAL HOSPITAL,
NELSON STREET, HEREFORD, HR1 2PA

COUNCIL OFFICE ☎ 01432 260456
COUNCIL OFFICES, THE TOWN HALL,
HEREFORD, HR1 2PJ

Hereford *Here.* Population: 54,326. City, county town and cathedral city on River Wye, 45m/72km SW of Birmingham. Many old buildings and museums, including Waterworks museum and City Museum and Art Gallery. 1621 Old House is a museum of local history. Medieval Wye Bridge. Cathedral includes richly ornamented Early English style Lady chapel. New building houses Chained Library of 1500 volumes and 1289 Mappa Mundi Map of the world. Three Choirs Festival every third year. Cider Museum and King Offa Distillery W of city centre depicts history of cider making.

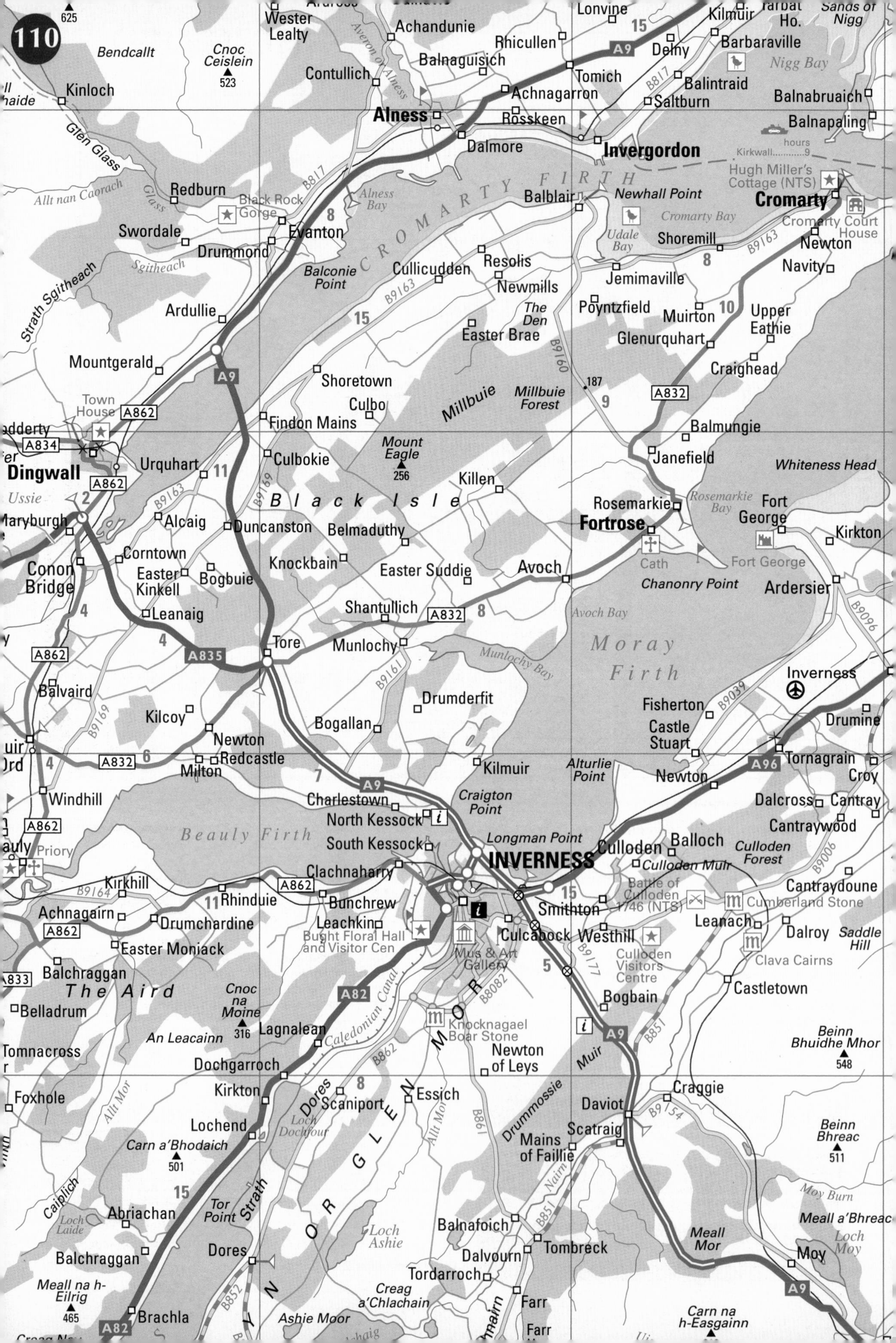

625
Bendcallt
Cnoc Ceislein
523
Kinloch
Glen Glass
Wester Lealty
Achandunie
Averon or Alness
Contullich
Balnaguisich
Rhicullen
Lonvine
Kilmuir
Tarbat Ho.
Sands of Nigg
Delny
Barbaraville
Nigg Bay
Tomich
Achnagarron
B817
Balintraid
Saltburn
Balnabruaich
Alness
Rosskeen
Dalmore
Invergordon
Balnapaling
hours
Kirkwall............9
Hugh Miller's Cottage (NTS)
Cromarty
Cromarty Court House
Redburn
Allt nan Caorach
Glass
Black Rock Gorge
Alness Bay
CROMARTY FIRTH
Balblair
Newhall Point
Cromarty Bay
Swordale
Evanton
Drummond
Udale Bay
Shoremill
B9163
Newton
Navity
Sgitheach
Strath Sgitheach
Balconie Point
Cullicudden
Resolis
Newmills
Jemimaville
Poyntzfield
Muirton
Upper Eathie
Ardullie
The Den
Easter Brae
B9160
Glenurquhart
Mountgerald
Shoretown
Craighead
187
A832
A9
Town House
A862
Culbo
Millbuie
Millbuie Forest
Findon Mains
Balmungie
A834
Mount Eagle
256
Janefield
Dingwall
Urquhart
Culbokie
Whiteness Head
Killen
Ussie
B9169
Black Isle
Rosemarkie
Rosemarkie Bay
Fort George
Maryburgh
Alcaig
Duncanston
Belmaduthy
Fortrose
Kirkton
Corntown
Knockbain
Cath
Fort George
Conon Bridge
Easter Kinkell
Bogbuie
Easter Suddie
Avoch
Chanonry Point
Ardersier
Leanaig
Shantullich
Avoch Bay
B9096
A835
Tore
Munlochy
Munlochy Bay
Moray Firth
Balvaird
B9161
Inverness
Kilcoy
Drumderfit
Fisherton
B9039
Drumine
Bogallan
Castle Stuart
Newton
Redcastle
Milton
Kilmuir
Alturlie Point
Tornagrain
Croy
A96
Windhill
Charlestown
Craigton Point
Dalcross
Cantray
North Kessock
Cantraywood
Beauly Firth
South Kessock
Longman Point
Culloden
Balloch
Culloden Forest
Priory
INVERNESS
Culloden Muir
B9006
Kirkhill
B9164
Clachnaharry
Battle of Culloden 1746 (NTS)
Cantraydoune
Rhinduie
Bunchrew
Smithton
Cumberland Stone
Achnagairn
Drumchardine
Leachkin
Leanach
Dalroy
Saddle Hill
Bught Floral Hall and Visitor Cen
Culcabock
Westhill
Easter Moniack
Mus & Art Gallery
Culloden Visitors Centre
B9177
Clava Cairns
Balchraggan
A833
The Aird
Cnoc na Moine
316
A82
Caledonian Canal
B8082
Castletown
Belladrum
Bogbain
Lagnalean
Knocknagael Boar Stone
An Leacainn
B851
Beinn Bhuidhe Mhor
548
Tomnacross
Newton of Leys
Dochgarroch
B862
Muir
Foxhole
Allt Mor
Kirkton
Dores
Scaniport
Essich
Craggie
Loch Dochfour
Drummossie
Daviot
B9154
Lochend
Mains of Faillie
Scatraig
Beinn Bhreac
511
Carn a'Bhodaich
501
B861
Nairn
Caiplich
Moy Burn
Loch Laide
Abriachan
Tor Point
Strath
Loch Ashie
Balnafoich
Meall a'Bhreac
Loch Moy
Meall Mor
Balchraggan
Dores
Tombreck
Dalvourn
Moy
Tordarroch
Meall na h-Eilrig
465
Creag a'Chlachain
Farr
B852
Brachla
Ashie Moor
Carn na h-Easgainn
STRATH NAIRN
GLEN MOR

Area Code 01463

Highland

INVERNESS

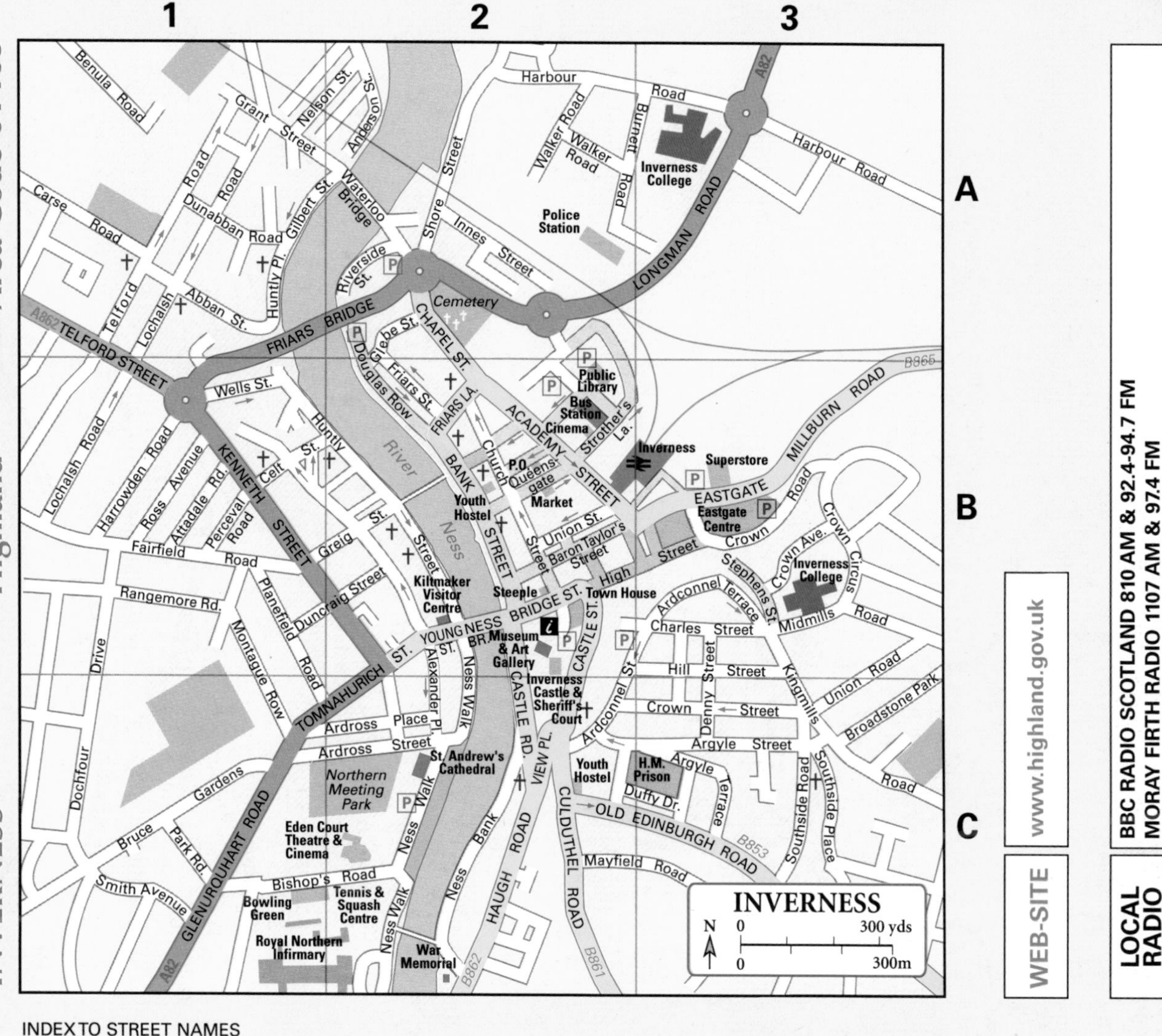

WEB-SITE

www.highland.gov.uk

LOCAL RADIO

BBC RADIO SCOTLAND 810 AM & 92.4-94.7 FM
MORAY FIRTH RADIO 1107 AM & 97.4 FM

INDEX TO STREET NAMES

Abban Street	A1	Burnett Road	A3	Eastgate	B3	Kenneth Street	B1	Riverside Street	A2
Academy Street	B2	Carse Road	A1	Fairfield Road	B1	Kingsmills Road	B3	Ross Avenue	B1
Alexander Place	B2	Castle Road	B2	Friars Bridge	A1	Lochalsh Road	A1	Shore Street	A2
Anderson Street	A2	Castle Street	B2	Friars Lane	B2	Longman Road	A2	Smith Avenue	C1
Ardconnel Street	C2	Celt Street	B1	Friars Street	B2	Mayfield Road	C2	Southside Place	C3
Ardconnel Terrace	B3	Chapel Street	A2	Gilbert Street	A1	Midmills Road	B3	Southside Road	C3
Ardross Place	B2	Charles Street	B3	Glebe Street	A2	Millburn Road	B3	Stephens Street	B3
Ardross Street	C1	Church Street	B2	Glen Urquhart Road	C1	Montague Row	B1	Strother's Lane	B2
Argyle Street	C3	Crown Avenue	B3	Grant Street	A1	Nelson Street	A1	Telford Road	A1
Argyle Terrace	C3	Crown Circus	B3	Greig Street	B1	Ness Bank	C2	Telford Street	A1
Attadale Road	B1	Crown Road	B3	Harbour Road	A2	Ness Bridge	B2	Tomnahurich Street	C1
Bank Street	B2	Crown Street	C3	Harrowden Road	A1	Ness Walk	C2	Union Road	C3
Baron Taylor's Street	B2	Culduthel Road	C2	Haugh Road	C2	Old Edinburgh Road	C2	Union Street	B2
Benula Road	A1	Denny Street	C3	High Street	B2	Park Road	C1	View Place	C2
Bishop's Road	C1	Dochfour Drive	C1	Hill Street	B3	Perceval Road	B1	Walker Road	A2
Bridge Street	B2	Douglas Row	A2	Hontly Place	A1	Planefield Road	B1	Waterloo Bridge	A2
Broadstone Park	C3	Duffy Drive	C2	Huntly Street	B1	Queensgate	B2	Wells Street	B1
Bruce Gardens	C1	Duncraig Street	B1	Innes Street	A2	Rancemore Road	B1	Young Street	B2

TOURIST INFORMATION ☎ 01463 234353
CASTLE WYND,
INVERNESS, IV2 3BJ

HOSPITAL A & E ☎ 01463 704000
RAIGMORE HOSPITAL, OLD PERTH ROAD,
INVERNESS, IV2 3UJ

COUNCIL OFFICE ☎ 01463 702000
COUNCIL OFFICES, GLENURQUHART ROAD,
INVERNESS, IV3 5NX

Inverness *High.* Population: 41,234. Town, at mouth of River Ness at entrance to Beauly Firth, 105m/169km NW of Aberdeen and 113m/181km NW of Edinburgh. Administrative, commercial and tourist centre. Caledonian Canal passes to W of town. Victorian castle in town centre used as law courts. Inverness Museum and Art Gallery depicts history of Highlands. Balnain House is a museum of Highland music and musical instruments. University of the Highlands and Islands. 1746 Culloden battle site 5m/8km E. Airport at locality of Dalcross, 7m/11km NE of town.

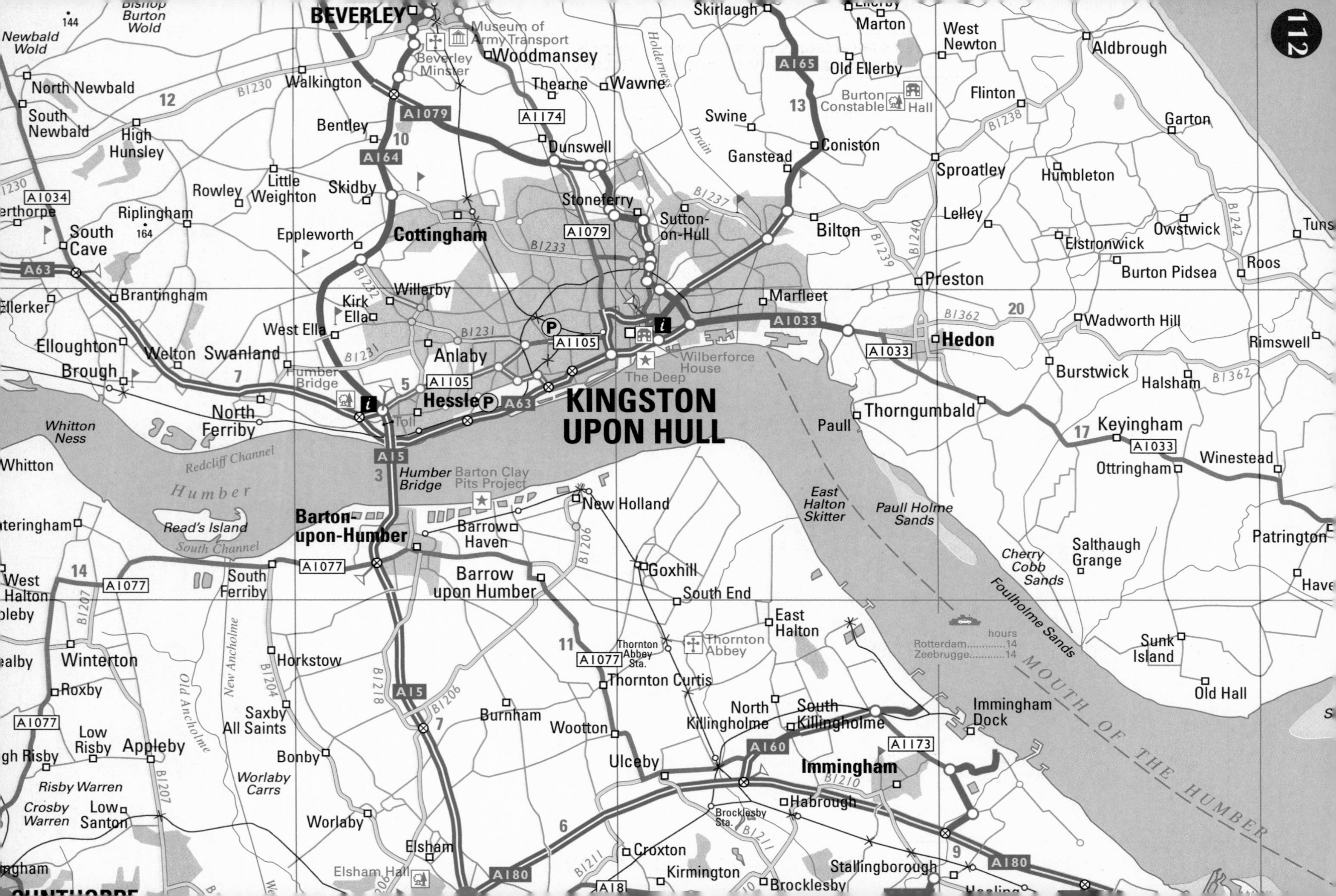
Newbald Wold
144
Bishop Burton Wold
BEVERLEY
Museum of Army Transport
Beverley Minster
Woodmansey
Skirlaugh
Marton
West Newton
Aldbrough
Old Ellerby
North Newbald
South Newbald
Walkington
Thearne
Wawne
Holderness
Burton Constable Hall
Flinton
Garton
High Hunsley
Bentley
Dunswell
Swine
Drain
Coniston
Ganstead
Sproatley
Humbleton
Rowley
Little Weighton
Skidby
Stoneferry
Sutton-on-Hull
Lelley
Owstwick
Elstronwick
Tuns
Riplingham
164
South Cave
Eppleworth
Cottingham
Bilton
Burton Pidsea
Roos
Preston
Brantingham
Ellerker
Kirk Ella
Willerby
Marfleet
Wadworth Hill
Hedon
Rimswell
West Ella
Elloughton
Welton
Swanland
Anlaby
Brough
Humber Bridge
Wilberforce House
The Deep
Burstwick
Halsham
Hessle
Toll
KINGSTON UPON HULL
Thorngumbald
Paull
Keyingham
Ottringham
Winestead
Whitton Ness
North Ferriby
Whitton
Redcliff Channel
Humber
Humber Bridge
Barton Clay Pits Project
New Holland
East Halton Skitter
Paull Holme Sands
Salthaugh Grange
Cherry Cobb Sands
Patrington
Read's Island
South Channel
Barton-upon-Humber
Barrow Haven
Goxhill
South End
Barrow upon Humber
West Halton
South Ferriby
Foulholme Sands
Have
East Halton
Thornton Abbey
Thornton Abbey Sta.
hours
Rotterdam 14
Zeebrugge 14
Sunk Island
Winterton
Horkstow
New Ancholme
Old Ancholme
Thornton Curtis
MOUTH OF THE HUMBER
Old Hall
Roxby
Saxby All Saints
Burnham
Wootton
North Killingholme
South Killingholme
Immingham Dock
Low Risby
Appleby
Bonby
Ulceby
Immingham
Risby Warren
Worlaby Carrs
Habrough
Brocklesby Sta.
Crosby Warren
Low Santon
Worlaby
Elsham
Croxton
Stallingborough
Elsham Hall
Kirmington
Brocklesby
A63
A1034
A1079
A164
A1174
A165
A1033
A1105
A15
A1077
A160
A1173
A180
A18
B1230
B1238
B1242
B1237
B1233
B1239
B1240
B1232
B1231
B1362
B1206
B1204
B1218
B1207
B1210
B1211
3
5
6
7
9
10
11
12
13
14
17
20

KINGSTON UPON HULL

INDEX TO STREET NAMES

Street	Grid	Street	Grid	Street	Grid
Albion Street	B1	Garrison Road	B3	New George Street	A2
Alfred Gelder Street	B2	George Street	B2	Norfolk Street	A1
Anlaby Road	B1	Great Union Street	A3	North Bridge	A2
Anne Street	B1	Green Lane	A2	Osborne Street	B1
Beverley Road	A1	Guildhall Road	B2	Porter Street	C1
Brunswick Avenue	A1	Hessle Road	C1	Prospect Street	A1
Caroline Street	A2	High Street	A3	Queen Street	C2
Carr Lane	B1	Jameson Street	B1	Reform Street	A2
Castle Street	B2	Jarratt Street	A2	St. Mark Street	A3
Charles Street	A2	Jenning Street	A2	Scale Lane	B2
Charterhouse Lane	A2	King Edward Street	B1	Scott Street	A2
Church Street	B3	Kingston Street	C1	Scott Street Bridge	A2
Clarence Street	B3	Liddell Street	A1	Southbridge Road	B3
Cleveland Street	A3	Lister Street	C1	Spring Bank	A1
Dansom Lane	A3	Lowgate	B2	Spyvee Street	A3
English Street	C1	Market Place	B2	Waterhouse Lane	B1
Ferensway	A1	Myton Street	B1	Wellington Street	C2
Francis Street	A2	New Cleveland Street	A3	Witham	A3
Freetown Way	A1			Worship Street	A2

TOURIST INFORMATION ☎ 01482 223559
1 PARAGON STREET,
KINGSTON UPON HULL, HU1 3NA

HOSPITAL A & E ☎ 01482 328541
HULL ROYAL INFIRMARY, ANLABY ROAD,
KINGSTON UPON HULL, HU3 2JZ

COUNCIL OFFICE ☎ 01482 300300
GUILDHALL, ALFRED GELDER STREET,
KINGSTON UPON HULL, HU1 2AA

Kingston upon Hull (Commonly known as Hull.) *Hull* Population: 310,636. City, port at confluence of Rivers Humber and Hull, 50m/80km E of Leeds. Much of town destroyed during bombing of World War II; town centre has been rebuilt. Formerly had a thriving fishing industry. Major industry nowadays is frozen food processing. Restored docks, cobble streeted Old Town and modern marina. Universities. Birthplace of William Wilberforce, slavery abolitionist, 1759. Wilberforce Museum covers history of slavery. Streetlife Transport Museum. Town Docks Museum explores city's maritime history. Famous for associations with poets Andrew Marvell, Stevie Smith and Philip Larkin.

WEB-SITE	www.hullcc.gov.uk

LOCAL RADIO	BBC RADIO HUMBERSIDE 95.9 FM MAGIC 1161 AM, VIKING FM 96.9 FM

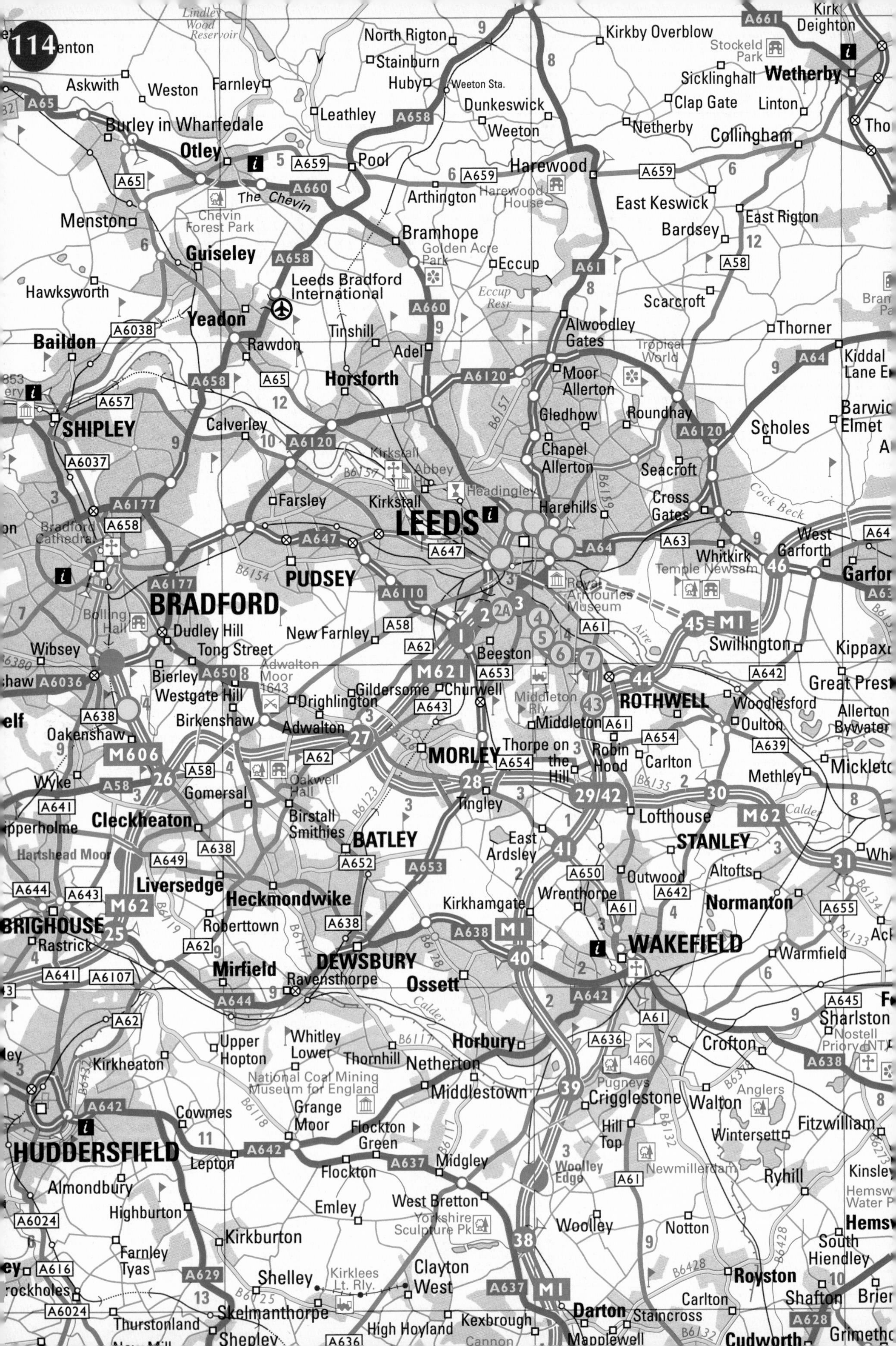
Otley
Guiseley
Yeadon
Baildon
SHIPLEY
Horsforth
LEEDS
PUDSEY
BRADFORD
MORLEY
ROTHWELL
BATLEY
Cleckheaton
Liversedge
Heckmondwike
BRIGHOUSE
Mirfield
DEWSBURY
Ossett
Horbury
WAKEFIELD
STANLEY
Normanton
HUDDERSFIELD
Wetherby
Harewood
Collingham
Leeds Bradford International
Royston
Darton
Cudworth

Area Code 0113

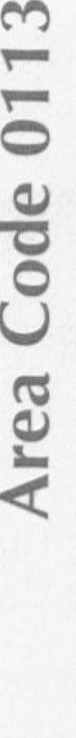

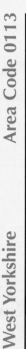

West Yorkshire

LEEDS

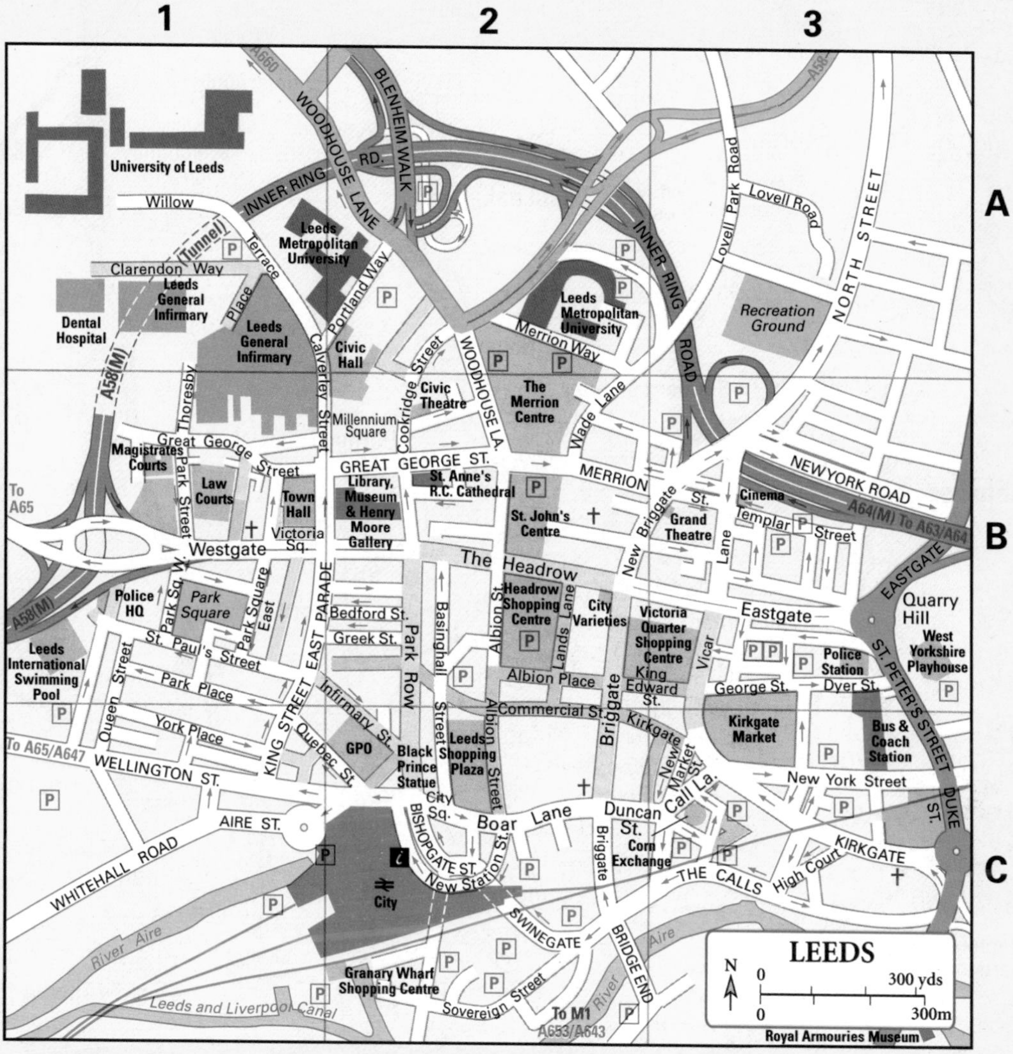

WEB-SITE

www.leeds.gov.uk

LOCAL RADIO

BBC RADIO LEEDS 92.4, 95.3 FM, 774 AM
MAGIC 828 AM, 96.3 AIRE FM

INDEX TO STREET NAMES

Aire Street	C1
Albion Place	B2
Albion Street	B2
Basinghall Street	B2
Bedford Street	B2
Bishopgate Street	C2
Blenheim Walk	A2
Boar Lane	C2
Bridge End	C2
Briggate	C2
Call Lane	C3
Calverley Street	A1
City Square	C2
Clarendon Way	A1
Commercial Street	B2
Cookridge Street	B2
Duke Street	C3
Duncan Street	C2
Dyer Street	B3
East Parade	B1
Eastgate	B3
George Street	B3
Great George Street	B1
Greek Street	B2
High Court	C3
Infirmary Street	B1
Inner Ring Road	A1/A2
King Edward Street	B2
King Street	C1
Kirkgate	C2/C3
Lands Lane	B2
Lovell Park Road	A3
Lovell Road	A3
Merrion Street	B2
Merrion Way	A2
New Briggate	B2
New Market Street	C3
New Station Street	C2
New York Road	B3
New York Street	C3
North Street	A3
Park Place	B1
Park Row	B2
Park Square East	B1
Park Square West	B1
Park Street	B1
Portland Way	A2
Quebec Street	C1
Queen Street	C1
Sovereign Street	C2
St. Paul's Street	B1
St. Peter's Street	B3
Swinegate	C2
Templar Street	B3
The Calls	C3
The Headrow	B2
Thoresby Place	B1
Vicar Lane	B3
Victoria Square	B1
Wade Lane	B2
Wellington Street	C1
Westgate	B1
Whitehall Road	C1
Willow Terrace	A1
Woodhouse Lane	A1/A2
York Place	C1

TOURIST INFORMATION ☎ 0113 242 5242
GATEWAY YORKSHIRE, THE ARCADE,
CITY STATION, LEEDS, LS1 1PL

HOSPITAL A & E ☎ 0113 243 2799
LEEDS GENERAL INFIRMARY,
GREAT GEORGE STREET, LEEDS, LS1 3EX

COUNCIL OFFICE ☎ 0113 234 8080
CIVIC HALL, CALVERLEY STREET,
LEEDS, LS1 1UR

Leeds *W.Yorks.* Population: 424,194. City, commercial and industrial city on River Aire and on Leeds and Liverpool Canal, 36m/58km NE of Manchester and 170m/274km NW of London. Previously important for textile industry. Prospered during Victorian period, the architecture of a series of ornate arcades containing some magnificent clocks reflecting the affluence of this time. City Art Gallery has a fine collection of 20c British Art. Edwardian Kirkgate Market is the largest in north of England. Royal Armouries Museum houses arms and armour collection from the Tower of London. Universities. Leeds Bradford International Airport at Yeadon, 7m/11km NW.

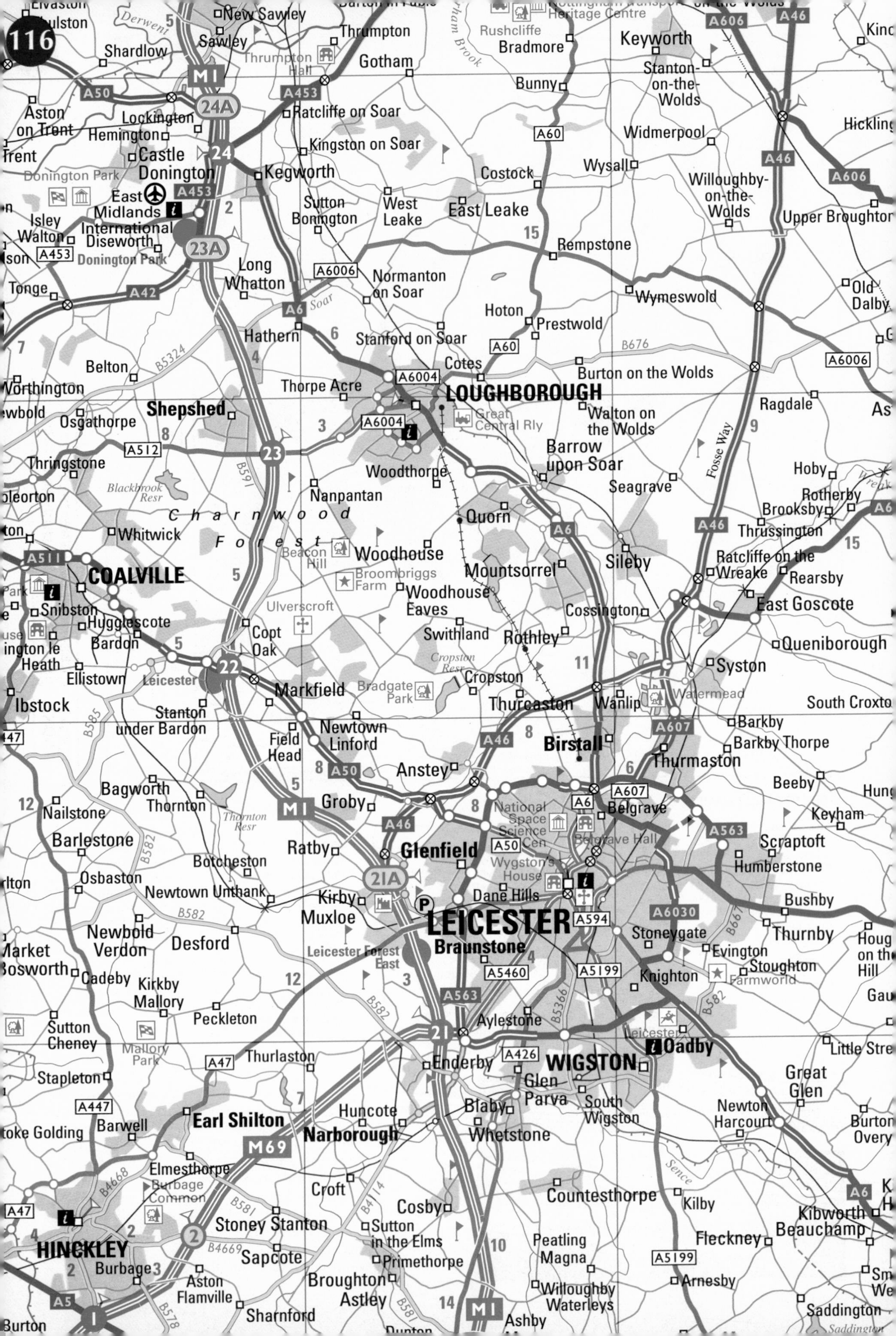

New Sawley
Sawley
Shardlow
Thrumpton
Thrumpton Hall
Gotham
Rushcliffe
Bradmore
Heritage Centre
Keyworth
Bunny
Stanton-on-the-Wolds
Widmerpool
Hickling
Aston on Trent
Lockington
Hemington
Castle Donington
Donington Park
Ratcliffe on Soar
Kingston on Soar
Kegworth
Costock
Wysall
Willoughby-on-the-Wolds
Upper Broughton
East Midlands International
Isley Walton
Diseworth
Sutton Bonington
West Leake
East Leake
Rempstone
Tonge
Long Whatton
Normanton on Soar
Hoton
Prestwold
Wymeswold
Old Dalby
Hathern
Stanford on Soar
Cotes
Burton on the Wolds
Belton
Worthington
Thorpe Acre
LOUGHBOROUGH
Ragdale
Osgathorpe
Shepshed
Walton on the Wolds
Great Central Rly
Barrow upon Soar
Fosse Way
Thringstone
Woodthorpe
Nanpantan
Seagrave
Hoby
Rotherby
Brooksby
Blackbrook Resr
Charnwood Forest
Quorn
Thrussington
Whitwick
Beacon Hill
Woodhouse
Sileby
Ratcliffe on the Wreake
Rearsby
COALVILLE
Broombriggs Farm
Mountsorrel
Woodhouse Eaves
Ulverscroft
Cossington
East Goscote
Snibston
Hugglescote
Bardon
Copt Oak
Swithland
Rothley
Queniborough
Ellistown
Cropston Resr
Syston
Ibstock
Leicester
Markfield
Bradgate Park
Cropston
Thurcaston
Wanlip
Watermead
South Croxton
Stanton under Bardon
Newtown Linford
Field Head
Birstall
Barkby
Barkby Thorpe
Thurmaston
Anstey
Beeby
Bagworth
Thornton
Groby
Nailstone
Thornton Resr
National Space Science Cen
Belgrave
Keyham
Barlestone
Ratby
Glenfield
Belgrave Hall
Scraptoft
Humberstone
Botcheston
Osbaston
Wygston's House
Newtown Unthank
Kirby Muxloe
Dane Hills
Bushby
LEICESTER
Stoneygate
Thurnby
Newbold Verdon
Desford
Market Bosworth
Braunstone
Evington
Cadeby
Leicester Forest East
Stoughton
Kirkby Mallory
Knighton
Farmworld
Sutton Cheney
Peckleton
Aylestone
Mallory Park
Oadby
Little Stretton
Stapleton
Thurlaston
Enderby
WIGSTON
Great Glen
Glen Parva
Barwell
Earl Shilton
Huncote
Blaby
South Wigston
Newton Harcourt
Narborough
Whetstone
Burton Overy
Stoke Golding
Elmesthorpe
Burbage Common
Croft
Countesthorpe
Kilby
Cosby
Kibworth Beauchamp
Stoney Stanton
Sutton in the Elms
Fleckney
HINCKLEY
Peatling Magna
Sapcote
Primethorpe
Burbage
Aston Flamville
Broughton Astley
Arnesby
Willoughby Waterleys
Sharnford
Saddington
Ashby
Burton
M1
M69
A50
A453
A42
A6
A6006
A60
A606
A46
A6004
A512
A511
A607
A563
A6030
A594
A5199
A5460
A426
A47
A447
A5
B5324
B676
B591
B585
B582
B5366
B667
B4114
B581
B4668
B4669
B578
B581
21A
23A
24A

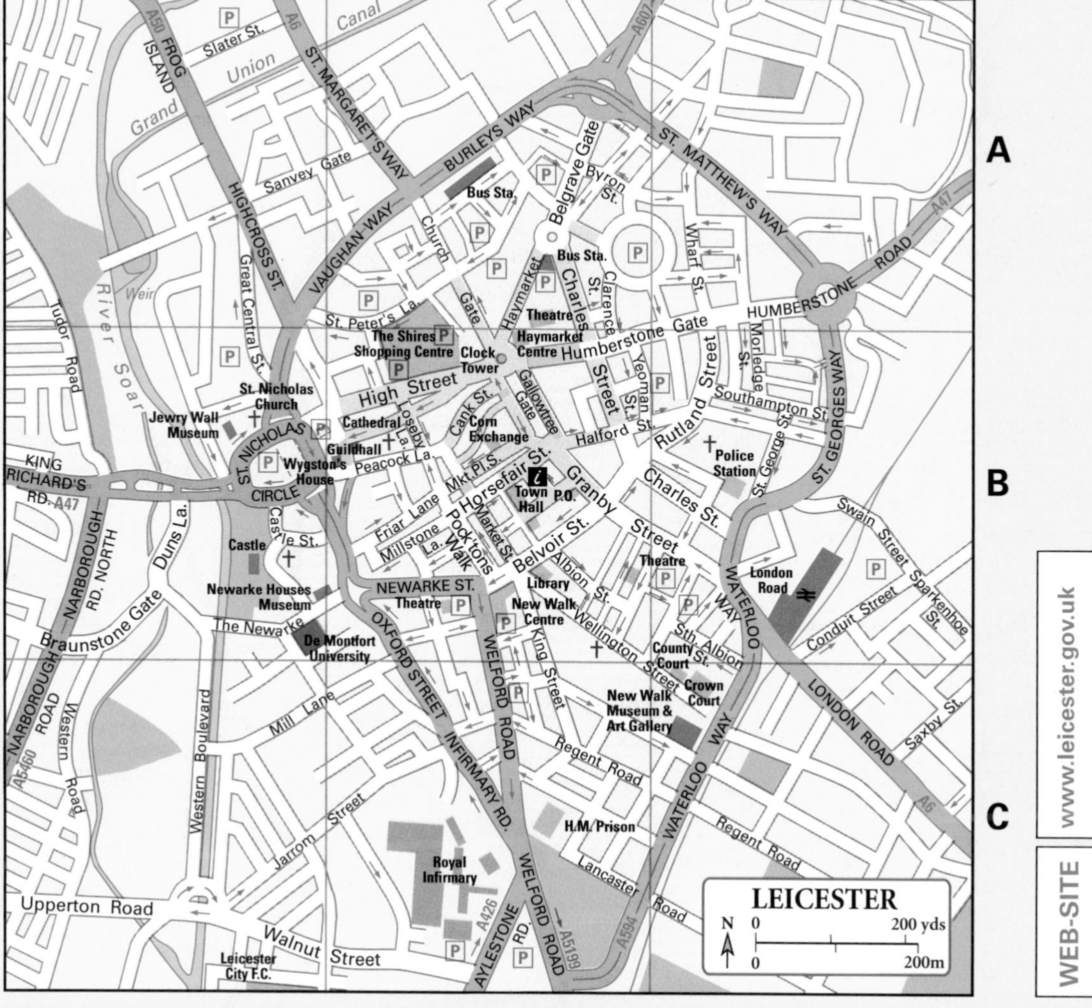

LOCAL RADIO	BBC RADIO LEICESTER 104.9 FM SABRAS 1260 AM, LEICESTER SOUND 105.4 FM
WEB-SITE	www.leicester.gov.uk

INDEX TO STREET NAMES

TOURIST INFORMATION ☎ 0116 299 8888
7-9 EVERY STREET, TOWN HALL SQUARE, LEICESTER, LE1 6AG

HOSPITAL A & E ☎ 0116 254 1414
LEICESTER ROYAL INFIRMARY, INFIRMARY SQUARE, LEICESTER, LE1 5WW

COUNCIL OFFICE ☎ 0116 252 6480
COUNCIL OFFICES, NEW WALK CENTRE, WELFORD PLACE, LEICESTER, LE1 6ZG

Leicester *Leic.* Population: 318,518. City, county town and commercial and industrial centre on River Soar, on site of Roman town of Ratae Coritanorum, 89m/143km NW of London. Industries include hosiery and footwear, alongside more modern industries. Universities. Many historic remains including Jewry Wall (English Heritage), one of largest surviving sections of Roman wall in the country, Roman baths and a medieval guildhall. Saxon Church of St. Nicholas. 11c St. Martin's Cathedral. Victorian clock tower. Newarke Houses Museum explores the city's social history. Home to England's second biggest street festival after Notting Hill Carnival. Joseph Merrick, the 'Elephant Man' born and lived here.

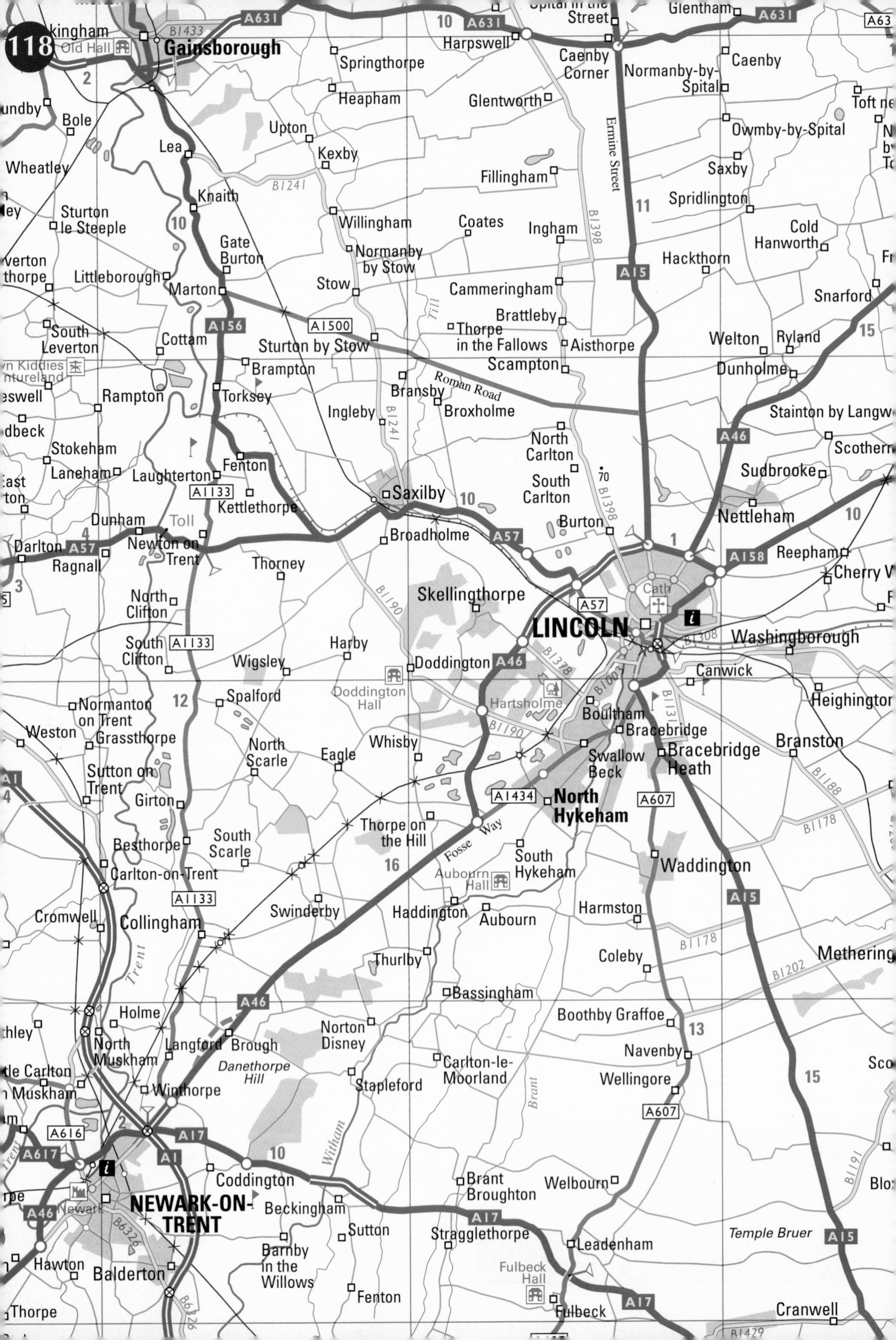

kingham
Old Hall
Gainsborough
B1433
A631
10
A631
Harpswell
Spital in the Street
Glentham
A631
A63
Caenby Corner
Caenby
Normanby-by-Spital
Springthorpe
Heapham
Glentworth
Toft ne
2
undby
Bole
Upton
Kexby
Owmby-by-Spital
Wheatley
Lea
Fillingham
Saxby
Ermine Street
B1241
Knaith
Spridlington
11
ley
Sturton le Steeple
10
Willingham
Coates
Ingham
Cold Hanworth
verton thorpe
Littleborough
Gate Burton
Normanby by Stow
B1398
Hackthorn
A15
Marton
Stow
Cammeringham
Snarford
A156
A1500
Till
Brattleby
Thorpe in the Fallows
South Leverton
Cottam
Sturton by Stow
Aisthorpe
Welton
Ryland
15
wn Kiddies ntureland
Brampton
Scampton
Dunholme
eswell
Rampton
Torksey
Roman Road
Bransby
dbeck
Ingleby
B1241
Broxholme
Stainton by Langw
A46
Stokeham
North Carlton
Scothern
Laneham
Laughterton
Fenton
South Carlton
70
Sudbrooke
East ton
A1133
Kettlethorpe
Saxilby
10
B1398
Nettleham
10
Dunham
Toll
Burton
4
Newton on Trent
Broadholme
A57
1
Darlton
A57
Ragnall
Thorney
A158
Reepham
Cherry W
3
North Clifton
Skellingthorpe
Cath
B1190
A57
LINCOLN
South Clifton
A1133
Harby
B1308
Washingborough
Wigsley
Doddington
A46
B1378
Canwick
Doddington Hall
Hartsholme
B1003
Heighington
Normanton on Trent
12
Spalford
Boultham
B1131
Weston
Grassthorpe
B1190
Bracebridge
Branston
North Scarle
Whisby
Swallow Beck
Bracebridge Heath
A1
Eagle
4
Sutton on Trent
B1188
Girton
A1434
North Hykeham
A607
Thorpe on the Hill
Fosse Way
B1178
South Scarle
Besthorpe
South Hykeham
Waddington
Carlton-on-Trent
16
Aubourn Hall
A15
A1133
Harmston
Cromwell
Collingham
Swinderby
Haddington
Aubourn
B1178
Coleby
Trent
Thurlby
B1202
Methering
Bassingham
A46
Holme
Boothby Graffoe
13
thley
Norton Disney
North Muskham
Langford
Brough
Navenby
Danethorpe Hill
Carlton-le-Moorland
Sco
tle Carlton
Muskham
Winthorpe
Stapleford
Wellingore
15
Brant
A607
A616
2
A17
Witham
A617
10
A1
Coddington
Brant Broughton
Welbourn
B1191
Blo
Newark
NEWARK-ON-TRENT
Beckingham
A17
B6326
Sutton
Stragglethorpe
Temple Bruer
A15
Leadenham
Barnby in the Willows
Hawton
Balderton
Fulbeck Hall
Fenton
A17
Thorpe
B6326
Fulbeck
Cranwell
B1429

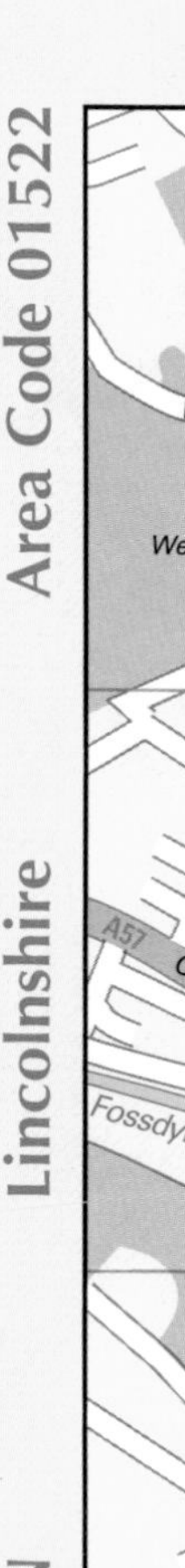

Area Code 01522

Lincolnshire

LINCOLN

1 2 3

A
B
C

www.lincoln-info.org.uk

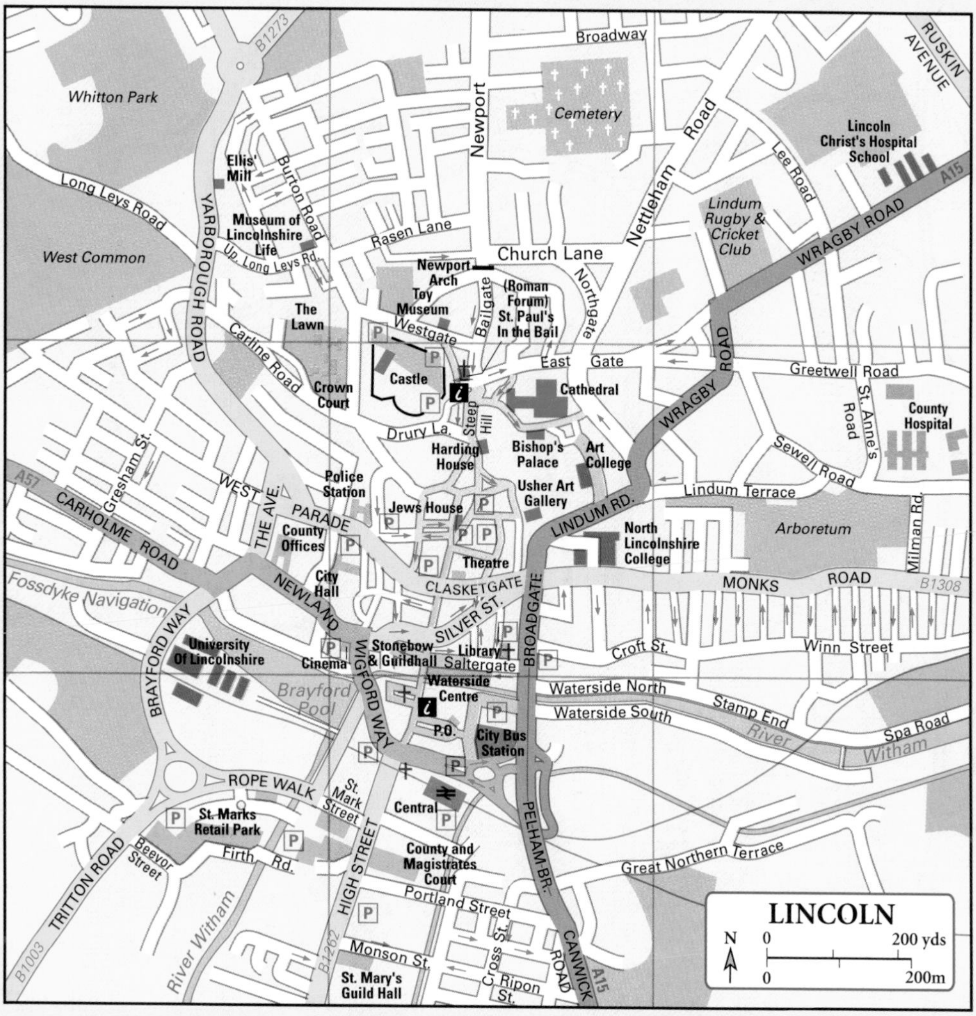

WEB-SITE

BBC RADIO LINCOLNSHIRE 94.9 FM
LINCS FM 102.2 FM

LOCAL RADIO

INDEX TO STREET NAMES

TOURIST INFORMATION ☎ 01522 873213
9 CASTLE HILL,
LINCOLN, LN1 3AA

HOSPITAL A & E ☎ 01522 512512
LINCOLN COUNTY HOSPITAL,
GREETWELL ROAD, LINCOLN, LN2 5QY

COUNCIL OFFICE ☎ 01522 552222
COUNTY OFFICES, NEWLAND,
LINCOLN, LN1 1YG

Lincoln *Lincs.* Population: 80,281. City, county town and cathedral city on River Witham, on site of Roman town of Lindum, 120m/193km N of London. City grew as a result of strategic importance in the wool trade. Many ancient monuments and archaeological features. Castle built by William I. 13c cathedral, is the third largest in Britain with its three towers on hilltop dominating the skyline. Carvings in the Angel Choir include the stone figure of the Lincoln Imp which is the city's emblem. Lincoln Bishop's Old Palace (English Heritage) is medieval building on S side of cathedral. 12c Jew's House. Museum of Lincolnshire Life. Universities.

LIVERPOOL
BOOTLE
WALLASEY
BIRKENHEAD
BEBINGTON
CROSBY
LITHERLAND
KIRKBY
ST HELENS
Prescot
Huyton
Roby
Halewood
Speke
Garston
WIDNES
RUNCORN
WARRINGTON
NEWTON-LE-WILLOWS
Haydock
Ashton-in-Makerfield
Golborne
LEIGH
Abram
Billinge
Rainford
Maghull
ELLESMERE PORT
Frodsham
Neston
Liverpool John Lennon
Manchester Ship Canal
MERSEY
Crosby Channel

INDEX TO STREET NAMES

Addison Street	A2	Gradwell Street	C2	Paradise Street	C2
Argyle Street	C2	Great Crosshall Street	A2	Park Lane	C2
Bath Street	A1	Great Howard Street	A1	Parker Street	B3
Berry Street	C3	Hanover Street	C2	Preston Street	B2
Bold Street	C3	Hartley Quay	C1	Princes Parade	B1
Brownlow Hill	B3	Hatton Garden	A2	Queens Square	B2
Brunswick Street	B1	Hawke Street	B3	Ranelagh Street	B3
Byrom Street	A3	Henry Street	C2	Renshaw Street	B3
Canning Place	C2	Hood Street	B2	Roe Street	B3
Castle Street	B2	Hunter Street	A3	Salthouse Quay	C1
Chapel Street	B1	James Street	B1	School Lane	B2
Cheapside	A2	King Edward Street	A1	Scotland Road	A3
Christian Street	A3	Leeds Street	A1	Seel Street	C3
Church Street	B2	Lime Street	B3	Sir Thomas Street	B2
Concert Street	C3	Liver Street	C2	Skelhorne Street	B3
Cook Street	B2	London Road	B3	Slater Street	C3
Copperas Hill	B3	Lord Nelson Street	B3	South John Street	B2
Crosshall Street	B2	Lord Street	B2	St. Anne Street	A3
Dale Street	B2	Marybone	A2	St. John's Lane	B3
Dawson Street	B2	Matthews Street	B2	The Strand	B1
Derby Square	B2	Midghall Street	A2	Tithebarn Street	B2
Duke Street	C2	Moorfields	B2	Vauxhall Road	A2
East Street	A1	Mount Pleasant	B3	Victoria Street	B2
Eaton Street	A1	Naylor Street	A2	Wapping	C2
Elliot Street	B3	New Quay	B1	Water Street	B1
Freemasons Row	A2	North John Street	B2	Waterloo Road	A1
Gascoyne Street	A1	Old Hall Street	A1	Whitechapel	B2
Gibraltar Row	A1	Old Haymarket	B2	William Brown Street	A3
Gilbert Street	C2	Paisley Street	A1		
Goree	B1	Pall Mall	A1		

TOURIST INFORMATION ☎ 09066 806886
MERSEYSIDE WELCOME CENTRE, CLAYTON SQ. SHOPPING CEN, LIVERPOOL, L1 1QR

HOSPITAL A & E ☎ 0151 525 5980
UNIVERSITY HOSPITAL OF AINTREE, LOWER LANE, FAZAKERLEY, LIVERPOOL, L9 7AL

COUNCIL OFFICE ☎ 0151 233 3000
MUNICIPAL BUILDINGS, DALE STREET, LIVERPOOL, L69 2DH

Liverpool *Mersey.* Population: 481,786. City, major port and industrial city on River Mersey estuary, 178m/286km NW of London. Originally a fishing village it experienced rapid expansion during early 18c due to transatlantic trade in sugar, spice and tobacco and was involved in slave trade. Docks declined during 20c, now Albert Dock is home to shops, museums and Tate Liverpool. In 19c a multicultural city developed as Liverpool docks were point of departure for Europeans emigrating to America and Australia. Also became home to refugees from Irish potato famine of 1845. Present day Liverpool is home to variety of industries and many museums and art galleries. Also home of the Beatles, who performed at Liverpool's Cavern Club. Universities. Modern Anglican and Roman Catholic cathedrals. On Pier Head the famous Royal Liver Building is situated, topped by Liver Birds. Railway tunnel and two road tunnels under River Mersey to Wirral peninsula. Airport at Speke, 6m/10km.

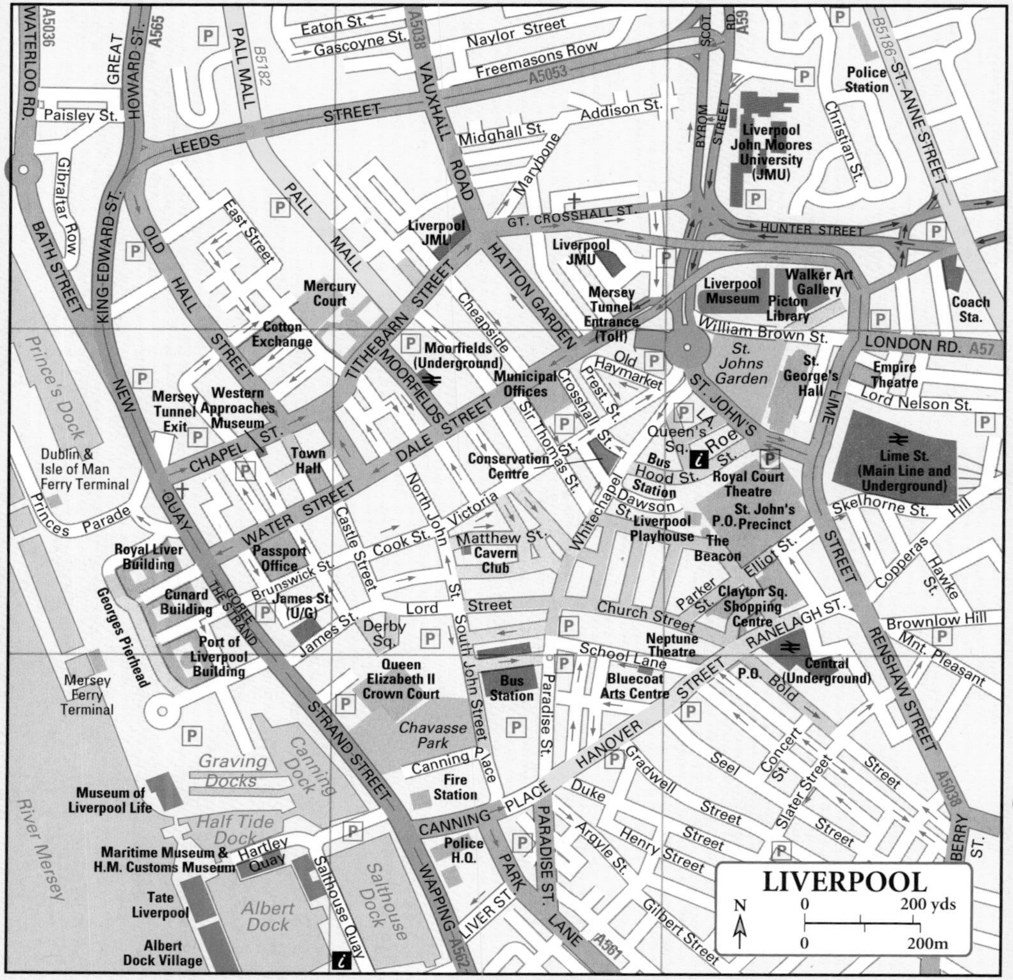

WEB-SITE www.liverpool.gov.uk

LOCAL RADIO	BBC RADIO MERSEYSIDE 95.8 FM MAGIC 1548 AM, RADIO CITY 96.7 FM, JUICE 107.6 FM

Edenfield
Whittle Hill
468
418
Stubbins
Edgworth
Ramsbottom
Shuttleworth
A680
Turton Tower
Turton Bottoms
Chapeltown
Jumbles Resr
Summerseat
Cheesden
Ashworth Moor Resr
Wolstenholme
A676
Greenmount
Walmersley
Toppings
Bromley Cross Sta.
Tottington
Bradshaw
Limefield
Hall i' th' Wood
Harwood
M66
B6222
Art Gallery & Museum
A666
BOLTON
Ainsworth
Fishpool
BURY
A58
HEYWOOD
Castleton
Mus & Art Gallery
Moses Gate
A665
RADCLIFFE
A6053
Hollins
Birch
Little Lever
Whitefield
A6045
MIDDLETON
FARNWORTH
Prestolee
A667
Kearsley
Heaton Park
M61
A666
M60
Little Hulton
A665
A576
Higher Blackley
A6104
Walkden
A6
Moorside Sta.
PRESTWICH
Bowker Vale Sta.
A575
A6044
A56
Worsley
Swinton
Pendlebury
Harpurhey
Boothstown
A572
A580
Lower Broughton
Cheetham Hill
Higher Green
M602
SALFORD
Art Galleries
A664
A62
ECCLES
A57
A6010
Lowry Centre
Trafford Centre
A5081
A5066
A662
MANCHESTER
Barton
Moss
A57
M62
URMSTON
Trafford Park
Old Trafford
A5103
Manchester Museum
Gorton
Rusholme
Levenshulme
Irlam
A5181
STRETFORD
Platt Hall
A34
Flixton
B5213
A6144(M)
Chorlton-cum-Hardy
A6010
Reddish
Carrington
Carrington Moss
A56
Ashton upon Mersey
SALE
A5103
Withington
A5145
Burnage
Heaton Moor
Partington
M60
Didsbury
A5145
A6144
Baguley
A560
Broadheath
Timperley
ALTRINCHAM
GATLEY
CHEADLE
STOCKPORT
Dunham Town
Dunham Massey (NT)
A56
Bowdon
Hale
A538
Cheadle Hulme
Little Bollington
Heald Green
Broomedge
Halebarns
Moss Nook
Manchester
M56
Styal
Ashley
A556
Rostherne
Aviation Viewing Park
A538
Quarry Bank Mill (NT)
Handforth
A5034
Tatton Park (NT)
Morley Green
A34
Mere
Tatton Park
A538
WILMSLOW
Over Tabley
A50
Knolls Green
Mobberley
Mottram St Andrew
A537
Alderley
Whitworth
A671
Calderbrook
Summit
Soyland Moor
Watergrove Resr
A6033
A58
Clough
Rishworth Moor
Spring Mill Resr
Wardle
Broadley
Healey
Naden Resrs
Littleborough
472
Smithy Bridge Sta.
Hollingworth Lake
Greenbooth Resr
B6377
Syke
Smallbridge
Visitor Centre
Shawclough
M62
Firgrove
ROCHDALE
Art Gall
Milnrow
A672
A640
Newhey
Denshaw
A6046
A671
Crompton Fold
Slattocks
Tandle Hill
A663
A6052
Shaw
A627(M)
Royton
A664
Heyside
A672
Moorside
Strinesdale Countryside Area
A669
B6195
Chadderton
A62
OLDHAM
A663
A669
Lees
A62
B6393
Failsworth
Bardsley
Daisy Nook
B6194
A627
M60
Hurst
A670
A635
ASHTON-UNDER-LYNE
Droylsden
A635
Dukinfield
STALYBRIDGE
Portland Basin Museum
A6018
Audenshaw
Newton
A57
Denton
HYDE
A57
M67
A627
Gee Cross
A6017
Haughton Green
Tame
A560
Werneth Low
A6
Bredbury
A626
Etherow
Romiley
Compstall
A627
Offerton
Heaviley
Marple
A6
A627
A5102
Bramall Hall
HAZEL GROVE
A5143
Bramhall
Middlewood
Disley
Newtown
B5094
Brookside Miniature Rly
A5149
Poynton
Lyme Park (NT)
Woodford
Lyme Hall (NT)
A5102
Black Hill
Dean
Dean Row
Whaley Bridge
A523
Adlington
Adlington Hall
Kettleshulme
Pott Shrigley
Bollington
Roman Road

MANCHESTER
Greater Manchester
Area Code 0161

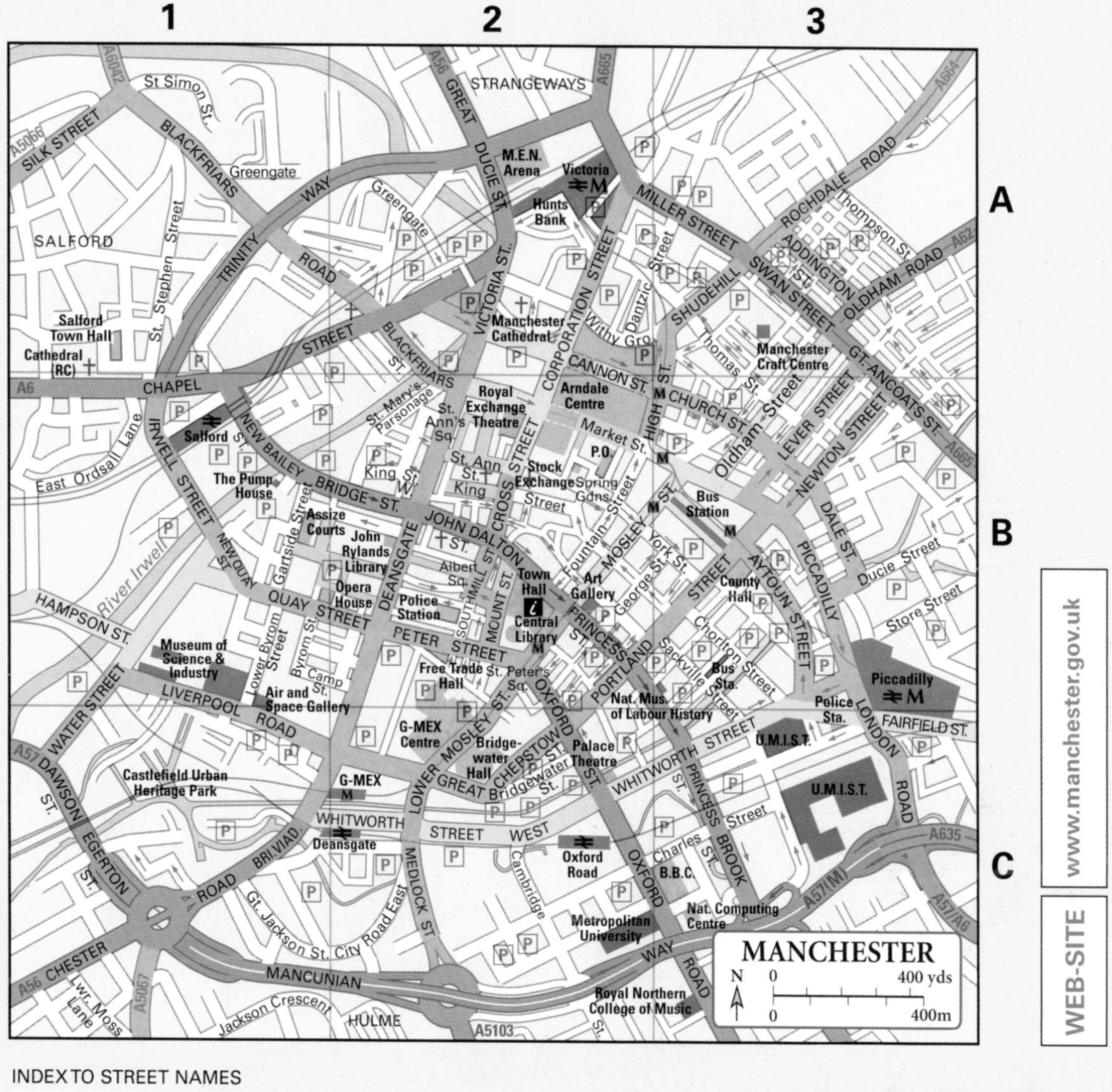

WEB-SITE
www.manchester.gov.uk

LOCAL RADIO
BBC RADIO GMR 95.1 FM
MANCHESTER'S MAGIC 1152 AM, CAPITAL GOLD 1458 AM, GALAXY 102 FM, KEY 103 FM

INDEX TO STREET NAMES

TOURIST INFORMATION ☎ 0161 234 3157/8
MANCHESTER VISITOR CENTRE, TOWN HALL EXTENSION, LLOYD ST, MANCHESTER, M60 2LA

HOSPITAL A & E ☎ 0161 276 1234
MANCHESTER ROYAL INFIRMARY, OXFORD ROAD, MANCHESTER, M13 9WL

COUNCIL OFFICE ☎ 0161 234 5000
TOWN HALL, ALBERT SQUARE, MANCHESTER, M60 2LA

Manchester *Gt.Man.* Population: 402,889. City, important industrial, business, cultural and commercial centre and port, 164m/264km NW of London. Access for ships by River Mersey and Manchester Ship Canal, opened in 1894. 15c cathedral, formerly parish church, has widest nave in England. Experienced rapid growth during industrial revolution. In 1750, Manchester was essentially still a village. During Victorian era, city was global cotton milling capital. Present day city is home to wide range of industries and is unofficial capital of nation's 'youth culture'. Major shopping centres include Arndale and Trafford Centres. Universities. International airport 9m/14km S of city centre.

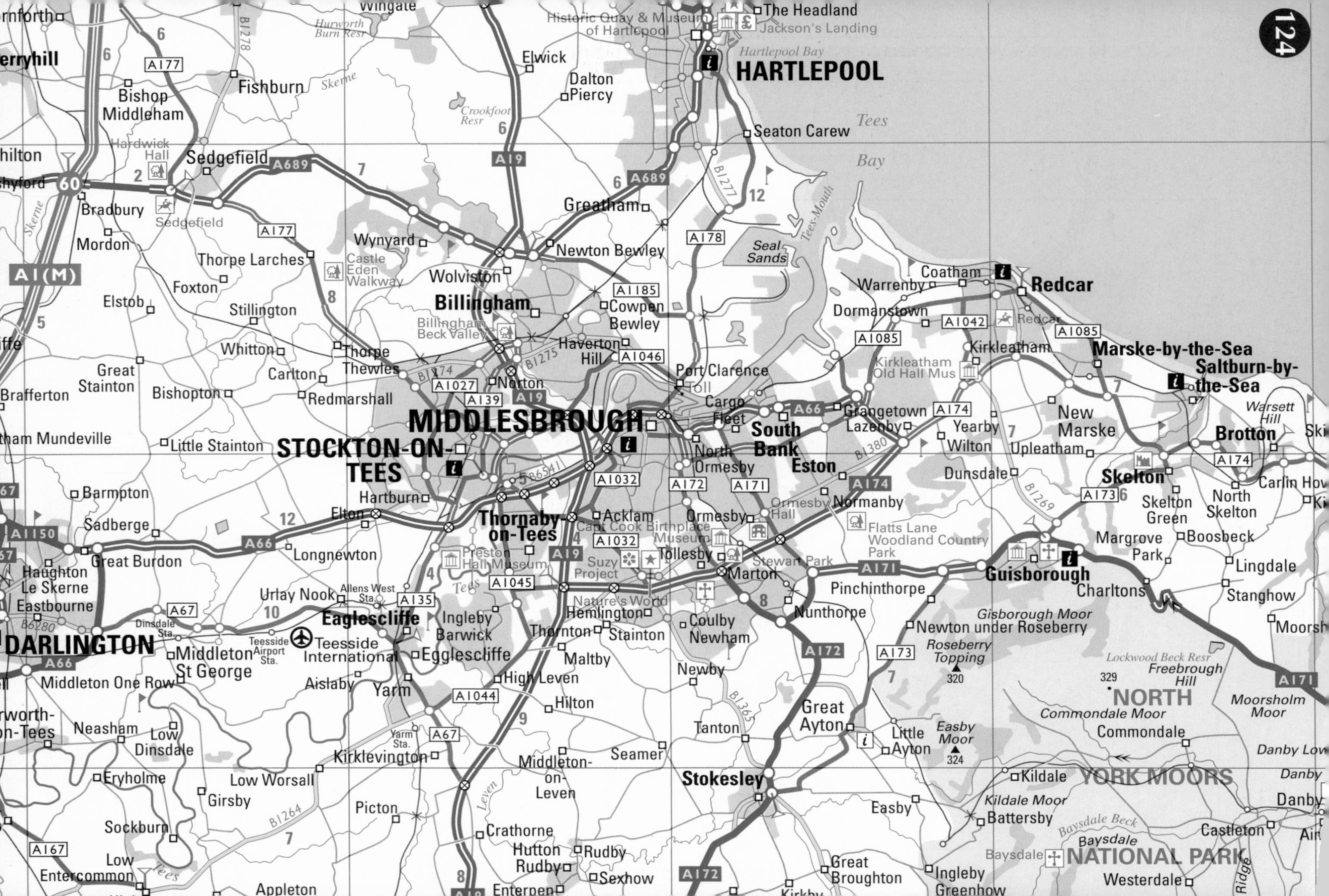
HARTLEPOOL
The Headland
Jackson's Landing
Hartlepool Bay
Historic Quay & Museum of Hartlepool
Seaton Carew
Tees Bay
Tees Mouth
Seal Sands
Redcar
Coatham
Warrenby
Dormanstown
Kirkleatham
Kirkleatham Old Hall Mus
Marske-by-the-Sea
Saltburn-by-the-Sea
New Marske
Brotton
Warsett Hill
Skelton
Skelton Green
North Skelton
Boosbeck
Lingdale
Stanghow
Moorsholm Moor
Carlin How
Margrove Park
Charltons
Upleatham
Yearby
Wilton
Grangetown
Lazenby
Dunsdale
Guisborough
Gisborough Moor
Newton under Roseberry
Roseberry Topping
320
Flatts Lane Woodland Country Park
Normanby
Eston
South Bank
Pinchinthorpe
Nunthorpe
Lockwood Beck Resr
Freebrough Hill
329
NORTH YORK MOORS NATIONAL PARK
Commondale Moor
Commondale
Castleton
Danby Low Moor
Danby
Ridge
Baysdale Beck
Baysdale
Kildale
Kildale Moor
Battersby
Westerdale
Easby Moor
324
Little Ayton
Great Ayton
Easby
Ingleby Greenhow
Great Broughton
Stokesley
Tanton
Newby
Seamer
Sexhow
Rudby
Hutton Rudby
Crathorne
Middleton-on-Leven
Enterpen
Leven
Hilton
High Leven
Maltby
Thornton
Stainton
Hemlington
Nature's World
Coulby Newham
Marton
Stewart Park
Tollesby
Ormesby
Ormesby Hall
North Ormesby
Acklam
Capt Cook Birthplace Museum
Suzy Project
Thornaby-on-Tees
Preston Hall Museum
Ingleby Barwick
Egglescliffe
Eaglescliffe
Yarm
Yarm Sta.
Kirklevington
Picton
Appleton
Low Worsall
Girsby
Aislaby
Teesside International
Teesside Airport Sta.
Allens West Sta.
Urlay Nook
Longnewton
Elton
Hartburn
MIDDLESBROUGH
STOCKTON-ON-TEES
Cargo Fleet
Port Clarence
Toll
Haverton Hill
Cowpen Bewley
Billingham
Billingham Beck Valley
Norton
Wolviston
Newton Bewley
Greatham
Dalton Piercy
Elwick
Crookfoot Resr
Wynyard
Castle Eden Walkway
Thorpe Thewles
Redmarshall
Carlton
Stillington
Whitton
Thorpe Larches
Foxton
Bishopton
Little Stainton
Great Stainton
Elstob
Sedgefield
Hardwick Hall
Bradbury
Mordon
Fishburn
Bishop Middleham
Hurworth Burn Resr
Skerne
Ferryhill
Chilton
Brafferton
Barmpton
Sadberge
Great Burdon
Haughton Le Skerne
Eastbourne
DARLINGTON
Dinsdale Sta.
Middleton St George
Middleton One Row
Low Dinsdale
Neasham
Eryholme
Sockburn
Low Entercommon
Tees
A1(M)
A1150
A66
A67
A167
A177
A689
A19
A139
A1027
A1032
A1045
A1044
A135
A171
A172
A173
A174
A1042
A1085
A178
A1185
A1046
B1277
B1269
B1380
B1365
B1264
B1278
B1275
B1274
B6280
B6541
60

INDEX TO STREET NAMES

Street	Grid	Street	Grid
Abingdon Road	B2	Marton Burn Road	C2
Albert Road	A2	Marton Road	B3/C3
Ayresome Green Lane	B1	Newport Road	A1/A2
Ayresome Street	B1	North Ormesby Road	A3
Belle Vue Grove	C3	Orchard Road	C1
Bishopton Road	C2	Park Road North	B2
Borough Road	A2/C3	Park Road South	B2
Bridge Street West	A2	Park Vale Road	B2
Burlam Road	C1	Parliament Road	B1
Cargo Fleet Road	A3	Riverside Park Road	A1
Clairville Road	B2	Roman Road	C1
Corporation Road	A2	St. Barnabas Road	B1
Crescent Road	B1	Scotts Road	A3
Cumberland Road	C2	Sheperdson Way	A3
Dockside Road	A2/A3	Snowdon Road	A2
Eastbourne Road	C2	Southfield Road	B2
Forty Foot Road	A1	The Avenue	C2
Grange Road	A2	The Crescent	C1
Gresham Road	B1	Union Street	B1
Hartington Road	A1	Valley Road	C2
Heywood Street	B1	Victoria Road	B2
Highfield Road	C3	Westbourne Grove	B3
Holwick Road	A1	Wilson Street	A2
Linthorpe Road	C2	Woodlands Road	B2
Longlands Road	B3		

TOURIST INFORMATION ☎ 01642 358086/243425
99-101 ALBERT ROAD,
MIDDLESBROUGH, TS1 2PA

HOSPITAL A & E ☎ 01642 617617
NORTH TEES GENERAL HOSPITAL, HARDWICK ROAD,
STOCKTON-ON-TEES, TS19 8PE

COUNCIL OFFICE ☎ 01642 245432
MUNICIPAL BUILDINGS, PO BOX 99A, RUSSELL STREET,
MIDDLESBROUGH, TS1 2QQ

Middlesbrough *Middbro.* Population: 147,430. Town, port, with extensive dock area, on S bank of River Tees, forming part of Teesside urban complex. A former iron and steel town, its chief industries now involve oil and petrochemicals. Unusual 1911 transporter bridge over River Tees. University of Teesside. Captian Cook Birthplace Museum in Stewart Park at Marton.

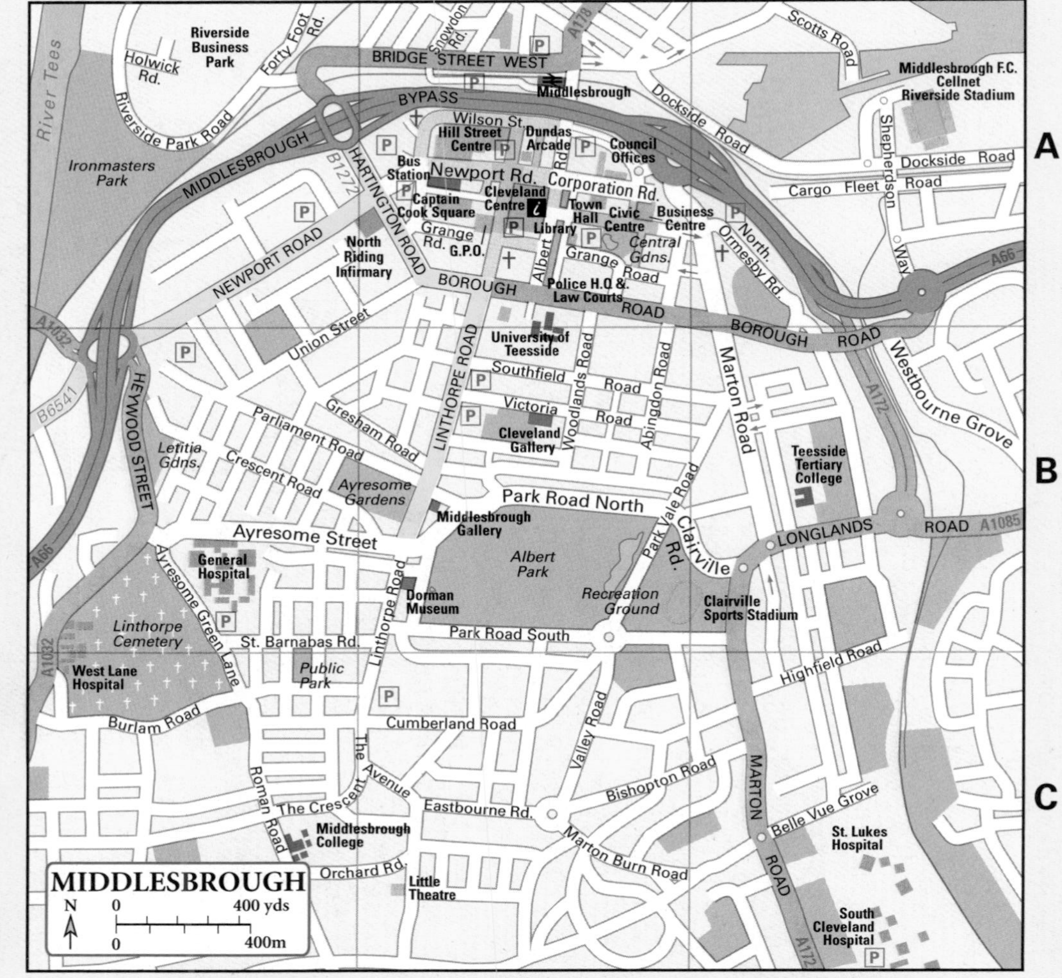

WEB-SITE
www.middlesbrough.gov.uk

LOCAL RADIO
BBC RADIO CLEVELAND 95 FM
MAGIC 1170 AM, TFM 96.6 FM, CENTURY FM 100.7 FM

Nedderton
Bedlington
Cowpen
BLYTH
Bebside
Saltwick
Plessey Woods
Bedlington
East Hartford
Newsham
Stannington
Nelson Village
Shankhouse
Cramlington
New Hartley
Seaton Sluice
Seaton
Hartley
Berwick Hill
Brenkley
Horton Grange
Seaton Delaval
St Mary's or Bait Island
Dudley
Seghill
Seaton Burn
Dinnington
Wide Open
Burradon
Backworth
Earsdon
Spanish City
WHITLEY BAY
Prestwick
Hazlerigg
Camperdown
Shiremoor
Monkseaton
Newcastle International
Killingworth
Marden
Cullercoats
New York
Amsterdam
Bergen
Göteborg
Haugesund
Kristiansand
Stavanger
Benton Square
Preston
TYNEMOUTH
Fawdon
Forest Hall
NORTH SHIELDS
Gosforth
Longbenton
Willington
North Tyneside Steam Rly
SOUTH SHIELDS
Kenton
Jesmond
Wallsend
Wallbottle
Blakelaw
Heaton
Royal Quays
Harton
NEWCASTLE UPON TYNE
Bede's World
Marsden Bay
Jarrow
Marsden
Byker
Walker
Hebburn
Monkton
Blaydon
Winlaton
Swalwell
Metrocentre
Pelaw
Whitburn
Cleadon
Dunston
FELLING
BOLDON
Metroland
GATESHEAD
WHICKHAM
West Boldon
East Boldon
Whitburn Bay
Team Valley
Roker
Southwick
Fulwell
Wrekenton
Hylton
Marley Hill
Sunniside
Lamesley
Springwell
Monkwearmouth
National Glass Cent
Gibside Chapel (NT)
Castletown
SUNDERLAND
Kibblesworth
Angel of the North
South Hylton
Tanfield Rly
Burnopfield
Birtley
WASHINGTON
Hendon
Tanfield
Beamish Open Air Museum
Washington
Ouston
Fatfield
Penshaw
Tantobie
New Silksworth
Beamish
Pelton
Herrington
Silksworth
Ryhope
STANLEY
Newfield
Shiney Row
Grange Villa
Plain
South Moor
CHESTER-LE-STREET
Bournmoor
Waldridge Fell
Lumley
Fence Houses
Craghead
SEAHAM
Waldridge
Great Lumley
Colliery Row
HOUGHTON LE SPRING
Seaton
Maiden Law
Hetton-le-Hole
Dalton-le-Dale
Edmondsley
Holmside
Burnhope
Plawsworth
West Rainton
Kimblesworth
East Rainton
Nose's
Cold Hesledon
Lanchester Valley Walk
Sacriston
Witton Gilbert
Pity Me
Finchale
Easington Lane
Murton
South Hetton
Langley Park
Framwellgate Moor
Hawthorn
Esh
Pittington
Easington
Bearpark
Littletown
Quebec
DURHAM
Carrville
Haswell
Easington
Little Thorpe
Ushaw Moor
Neville's Cross 1346
Sherburn
Esh Winning
Cathedral
Shadforth
Ludworth
Peterle
Deerness
Shincliffe
A1
A19
A69
A167
A1(M)
A194(M)
A690
A691
A693
A692
A6076
A1018
A1300
A1231
A184
A186
A185
A187
A188
A189
A191
A192
A193
A1061
A1068
A1056
A1171
A1058
A190
A194
A183
A182
A195
A1290
A1052
A181
A1086
A696
B1505
B1326
B1318
B1426
B1296
B1298
B1301
B1405
B1286
B1404
B1284
B1285
B1280
B1283
B1432
B1287
B6313
B6532
B6302
Browney
Wear
Team
Tyne
Derwent
Blyth

Area Code 0191

Tyne & Wear

NEWCASTLE

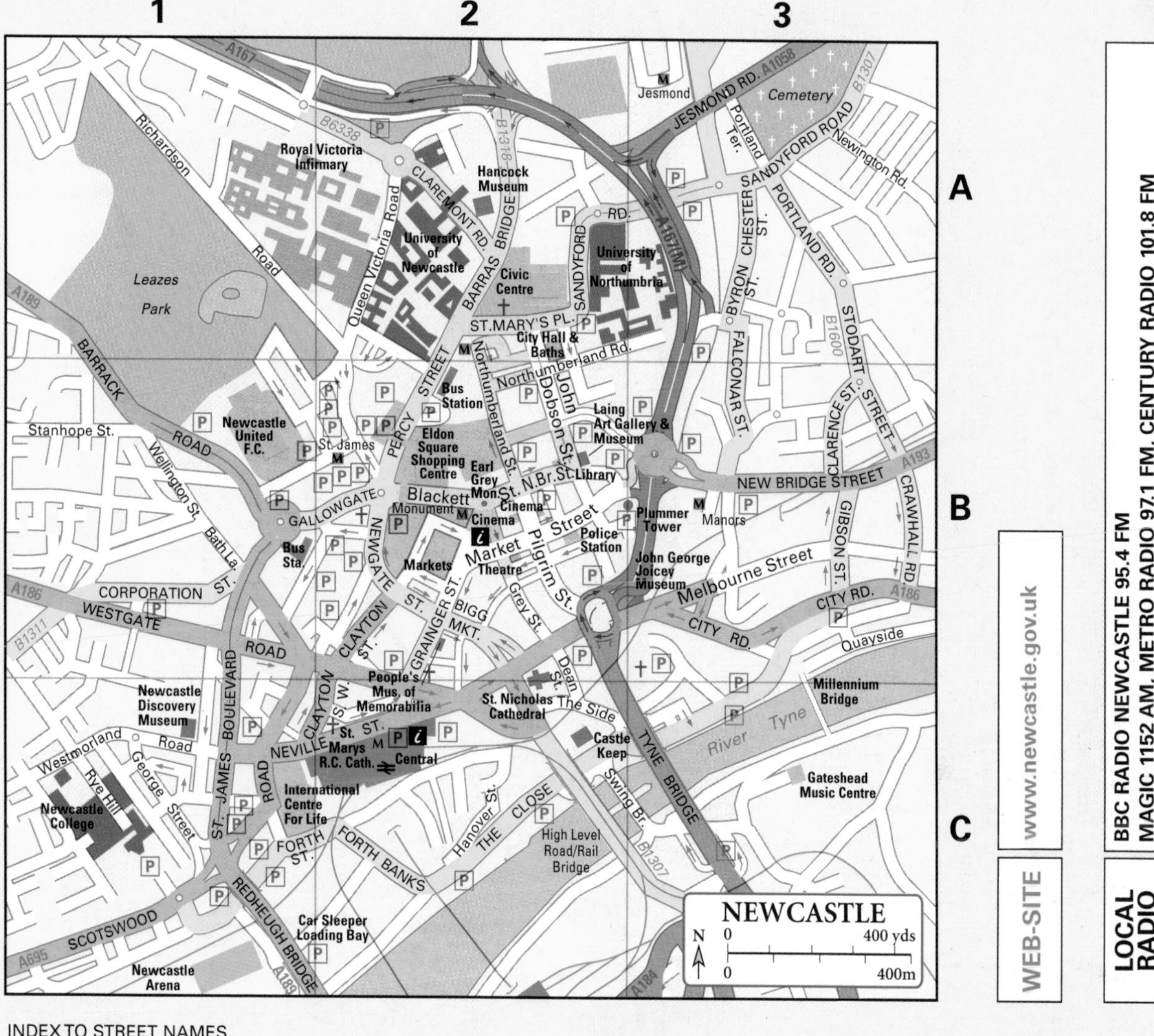

INDEX TO STREET NAMES

Street	Grid	Street	Grid	Street	Grid	Street	Grid
Barrack Road	A1	Dean Street	B2	Neville Street	C1	Rye Hill	C1
Barras Bridge	A2	Falconar Street	A3	New Bridge Street	B3	St. James Boulevard	C1
Bath Lane	B1	Forth Banks	C2	Newgate Street	B2	St. Mary's Place	A2
Bigg Market	B2	Forth Street	C1	Newington Road	A3	Sandyford Road	A2/A3
Blackett Street	B2	Gallowgate	B1	Northumberland Road	B2	Scotswood Road	C1
Byron Street	A3	George Street	C1	Northumberland Street	A2	Stanhope Street	B1
Chester Street	A3	Gibson Street	B3	Percy Street	B2	Stodart Street	A3
City Road	B3	Grainger Street	B2	Pilgrim Street	B2	Swing Bridge	C2
Claremont Road	A2	Grey Street	B2	Portland Road	A3	The Close	C2
Clarence Street	B3	Hanover Street	C2	Portland Terrace	A3	The Side	B2
Clayton Street	B2	Jesmond Road	A3	Quayside	B3	Tyne Bridge	C3
Clayton Street West	C1	John Dobson Street	B2	Queen Victoria Road	A2	Wellington Street	B1
Corporation Street	B1	Market Street	B2	Redheugh Bridge	C1	Westgate Road	B1
Crawhall Road	B3	Melbourne Street	B3	Richardson Road	A1	Westmorland Road	C1

TOURIST INFORMATION ☎ 0191 277 8000
128 GRAINGER STREET,
NEWCASTLE UPON TYNE, NE1 5AF

HOSPITAL A & E ☎ 0191 273 8811
NEWCASTLE GENERAL HOSPITAL, WESTGATE ROAD, NEWCASTLE UPON TYNE, NE64 6BE

COUNCIL OFFICE ☎ 0191 232 8520
CIVIC CENTRE, BARRAS BRIDGE,
NEWCASTLE UPON TYNE, NE99 1RD

Newcastle upon Tyne *T. & W.* Population: 189,150. City, port on River Tyne about 11m/17km upstream from river mouth and 80m/129km N of Leeds. The 'new castle' of city's name started in 1080 by Robert Curthose, eldest son of William the Conqueror. 13c castle gatehouse known as 'Black Gate'. Commercial and industrial centre, previously dependent upon coalmining and shipbuilding. In its heyday, 25 percent of world's shipping built here. Cathedral dates from 14 to 15c. Bessie Surtees House (English Heritage) comprises 16c and 17c merchants' houses. Tyne Bridge, opened in 1928 and longest of its type at the time. Venerable Bede (AD 672-735) born near Jarrow. Catherine Cookson, writer, also born in Jarrow, Universities. Newcastle International Airport 5m/8km NW.

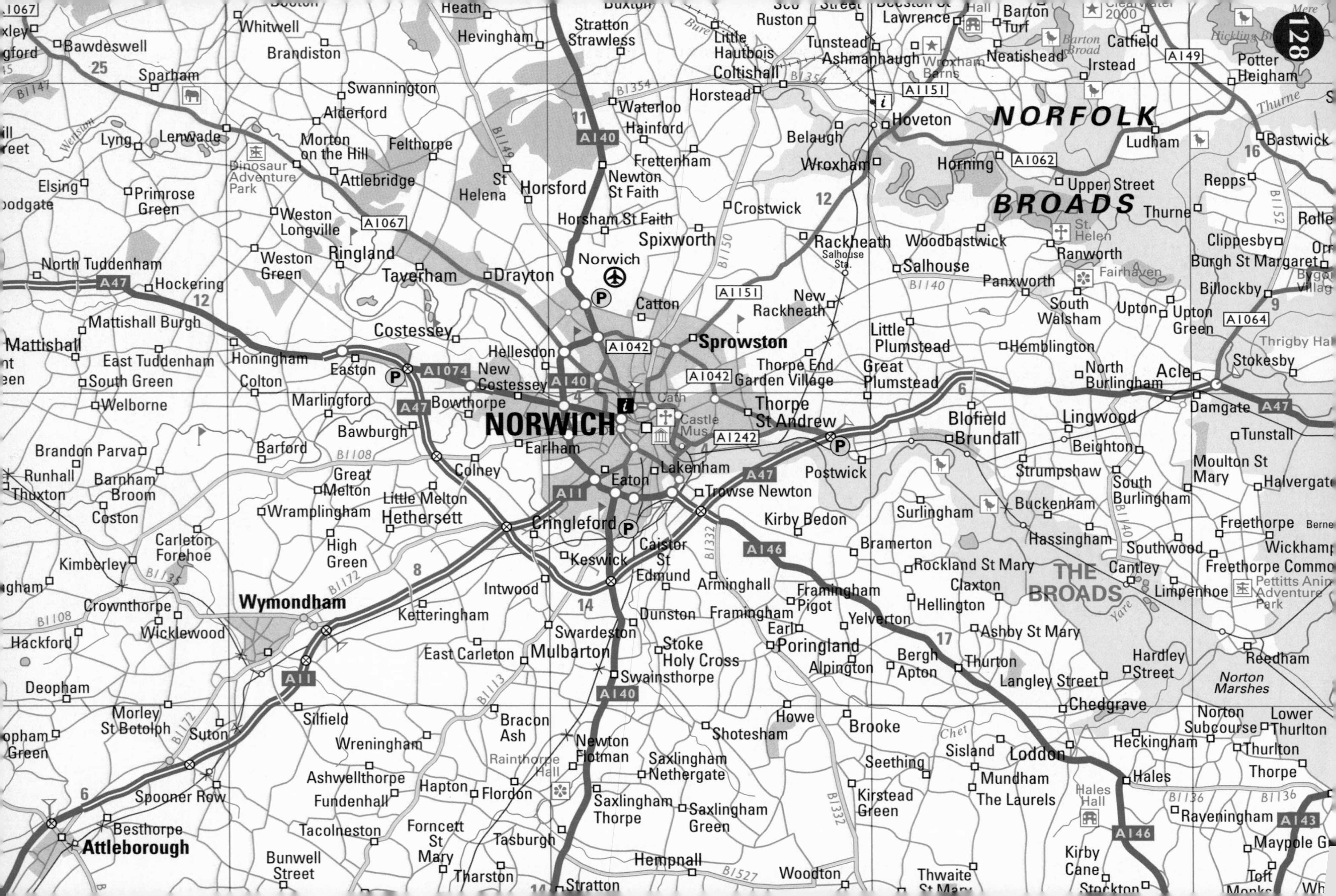

NORFOLK
BROADS
THE BROADS
NORWICH

Whitwell
Bawdeswell
Brandiston
Heath
Hevingham
Stratton Strawless
Little Hautbois
Coltishall
Ruston
Tunstead
Ashmanhaugh
Lawrence
Wroxham Barns
Barton Turf
Neatishead
Barton Broad
Catfield
Irstead
Potter Heigham
Hickling Broad
Thurne
Sparham
Swannington
Alderford
Waterloo
Hainford
Horstead
B1354
Hoveton
A1151
A149
Ludham
Bastwick
Lyng
Lenwade
Morton on the Hill
Felthorpe
Attlebridge
Dinosaur Adventure Park
A140
Frettenham
Newton St Faith
Belaugh
Wroxham
Horning
A1062
Upper Street
Repps
B1152
Elsing
Primrose Green
St Helena
Horsford
Crostwick
Thurne
St. Helen
Rollesby
Weston Longville
A1067
Horsham St Faith
Spixworth
Rackheath
Salhouse Sta.
Woodbastwick
Ranworth
Clippesby
Burgh St Margaret
North Tuddenham
Hockering
A47
Weston Green
Ringland
Taverham
Drayton
Norwich
B1150
Salhouse
Fairhaven
Panxworth
Billockby
Mattishall Burgh
Mattishall
East Tuddenham
South Green
Honingham
Costessey
Catton
A1151
New Rackheath
South Walsham
Upton
Upton Green
A1064
Thrigby Hall
Easton
Colton
Hellesdon
A1042
Sprowston
Little Plumstead
Hemblington
North Burlingham
Acle
Stokesby
A1074
New Costessey
A140
Thorpe End Garden Village
Great Plumstead
Welborne
Marlingford
Bowthorpe
A47
Cath
Castle Mus
Thorpe St Andrew
Blofield
Lingwood
Damgate
Tunstall
Bawburgh
Earlham
A1242
Brundall
Beighton
Brandon Parva
Barford
B1108
Colney
Lakenham
Postwick
Strumpshaw
Moulton St Mary
Halvergate
Runhall
Barnham Broom
Thuxton
Great Melton
Little Melton
Eaton
Trowse Newton
South Burlingham
Coston
Wramplingham
Hethersett
A11
Cringleford
Surlingham
Buckenham
B1140
Freethorpe
Carleton Forehoe
High Green
Caistor St Edmund
Kirby Bedon
Hassingham
Southwood
Wickhampton
Kimberley
B1135
Keswick
B1332
A146
Bramerton
Rockland St Mary
Cantley
Freethorpe Common
Pettitts Animal Adventure Park
Crownthorpe
Wymondham
B1172
Intwood
Arminghall
Claxton
Limpenhoe
Yare
Wicklewood
Ketteringham
Swardeston
Dunston
Framingham Pigot
Framingham Earl
Hellington
Yelverton
Ashby St Mary
Hackford
B1108
Mulbarton
East Carleton
Stoke Holy Cross
Poringland
Alpington
Bergh Apton
Thurton
Hardley Street
Reedham
Norton Marshes
Deopham
A11
Swainsthorpe
Langley Street
A140
B1113
Chedgrave
Morley St Botolph
Suton
Silfield
Bracon Ash
Howe
Brooke
Chet
Norton Subcourse
Lower Thurlton
Deopham Green
Wreningham
Newton Flotman
Shotesham
Rainthorpe Hall
Saxlingham Nethergate
Seething
Sisland
Loddon
Heckingham
Thurlton
Ashwellthorpe
Hapton
Flordon
Mundham
The Laurels
Hales
Thorpe
Spooner Row
Fundenhall
Saxlingham Thorpe
Saxlingham Green
Kirstead Green
Hales Hall
B1136
Ravenigham
A143
Besthorpe
Attleborough
Tacolneston
Forncett St Mary
Tasburgh
B1332
A146
Maypole Green
Bunwell Street
Tharston
Hempnall
B1527
Woodton
Thwaite St Mary
Kirby Cane
Toft Monks
Stockton
Stratton

INDEX TO STREET NAMES

Street	Grid	Street	Grid	Street	Grid
Albion Way	C3	Grapes Hill	B1	Rupert Street	C1
All Saints Green	C2	Grove Road	C1	St. Andrew's Street	B2
Bakers Road	A1	Grove Walk	C1	St. Augustine's Street	A1
Bank Plain	B2	Gurney Road	A3	St. Benedict's Street	B1
Barker Street	A1	Hall Road	C2	St. Crispin's Road	A1
Barn Road	B1	Heigham Street	A1	St. George's Street	A2
Barrack Street	A2	Ipswich Road	C1	St. Giles Street	B1
Bedford Street	B2	Ketts Hill	A3	St. Leonards Road	B3
Ber Street	C2	King Street	C2	St. Martin's Road	A1
Bethel Street	B1	Koblenz Avenue	C3	St. Stephen's Road	C1
Bishopbridge Road	B3	Lower Clarence Road	B3	St. Stephen's Street	C2
Bishopgate	B3	Magdalen Street	A2	Silver Road	A2
Brazen Gate	C2	Magpie Road	A2	Southwell Road	C2
Brunswick Road	C1	Market Avenue	B2	Surrey Street	C2
Bullclose Road	A2	Mountergate	B2	Sussex Street	A1
Canary Way	C3	Mousehold Street	A3	Theatre Street	B1
Carrow Road	C3	Newmarket Road	C1	Thorn Lane	C2
Castle Meadow	B2	Newmarket Street	C1	Thorpe Road	B3
Chapel Field Road	B1	Oak Street	A1	Tombland	B2
Chapelfield North	B1	Orchard Street	A1	Trinity Street	C1
City Road	C2	Palace Street	B2	Union Street	C1
Clarence Road	C3	Pitt Street	A2	Unthank Road	C1
Colegate	A2	Pottergate	B1	Vauxhall Street	C1
Coslany Street	B1	Prince of Wales Road	B2	Victoria Street	C1
Cowgate	A2	Queens Road	C2	Wensum Street	A2
Dereham Road	B1	Rampant Horse Street	B2	Wessex Street	C1
Duke Street	A2	Riverside	C3	Westwick Street	A1
Earlham Road	B1	Riverside Road	B3	Wherry Road	C3
Edward Street	A2	Rosary Road	B3	Whitefriars	A2
Elm Hill	B2	Rose Lane	B2		
Fishergate	A2	Rouen Road	C2		

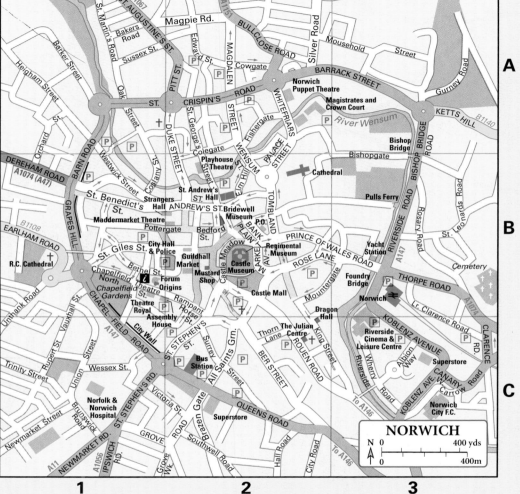

TOURIST INFORMATION ☎ 01603 666071
THE FORUM, MILLENNIUM PLAIN,
NORWICH, NR2 1TF

HOSPITAL A & E ☎ 01603 286286
NORFOLK & NORWICH HOSPITAL,
BRUNSWICK ROAD, NORWICH, NR1 3SR

COUNCIL OFFICE ☎ 01603 622233
CITY HALL, ST. PETER'S STREET,
NORWICH, NR2 1NH

Norwich *Norf.* Population: 171,304. City, county town and cathedral city at confluence of River Wensum and River Yare, 98m/158km NE of London. Middle ages saw Norwich become second richest city in country through exporting textiles. Medieval streets and buildings are well preserved. Sections of 14c flint city wall defences still exist, including Cow Tower (English Heritage). Current chief industries are high technology and computer based. Notable buildings include partly Norman cathedral with second highest spire in Britain, Norman castle with keep (now museum and art gallery), 15c guildhall, modern city hall, numerous medieval churches. University of East Anglia 2m/4km W of city centre. Airport 3m/5km N.

WEB-SITE	www.norwich.gov.uk

LOCAL RADIO	BBC RADIO NORFOLK 95.1 & 104.4 FM CLASSIC GOLD AMBER 1152 AM, BROADLAND 102 102.4 FM

Blackwell
Westhouses
South Normanton
Fourlane Ends
Alfreton
Pinxton
Somercotes
Swanwick
Pentrich
Riddings
Butterley
Ironville
Midland Rly
Ripley
Codnor
Selston
Bagthorpe
Underwood
New Brinsley
Brinsley
Denby Pottery
Cross Hill
Loscoe
Langley Mill
HEANOR
Denby
Eastwood
Moorgreen
Horsley Woodhouse
Langley
Marlpool
Smalley
Shipley
American Adventure
Horsley
Coxbench
Stanley Common
Mapperley
High Lane
West Hallam
Morley
Stanley
Breadsall
Kirk Hallam
ILKESTON
Awsworth
Cossall
Kimberley
Watnall
Nuthall
Trowell
Bilborough
McArthurGlen
Kirkby in Ashfield
Annesley Woodhouse
Annesley
Newstead Abbey
Newstead
Linby
HUCKNALL
Butler's Hill
Bestwood Lodge
Bulwell
Papplewick
Burntstump
Rainworth
Blidworth
Ravenshead
Haywood Oaks
Wonderland Pleasure Park
White Post Modern Farm Centre
SHERWOOD
Oxton
Patchings Farm Art Centre
Calverton
Dorket Head
Woodborough
Redhill
Arnold
Lambley
Highbury Vale
Old Basford
Burton Joyce
Gedling
Carlton
NOTTINGHAM
Netherfield
Royal Concert Hall & Theatre Royal
National Ice Centre
Colwick
Castle Mus
Wollaton Hall
Holme Pierrepont
Trent Bridge
West Bridgford
Wilford
Gamston
Bassingfield
Cotgrave Country Park
Cotgrave
Tollerton
Edwalton
Beeston
Bramcote
Stapleford
Sandiacre
Stanton by Dale
Dale
Chaddesden
Spondon
Ockbrook
Risley
Borrowash
Elvaston
Alvaston
Draycott
Breaston
Elvaston
Thulston
Toton
LONG EATON
Attenborough
Clifton
Ruddington
Barton in Fabis
Plumtree
Normanton-on-the-Wold
Nottingham Transport Heritage Centre
Rushcliffe
Bradmore
Keyworth
Stanton-on-the-Wolds
Bunny
New Sawley
Sawley
Thrumpton
Thrumpton Hall
Gotham
Shardlow
Aston on Trent
Lockington
Hemington
Swarkestone
Weston-on-Trent
Castle Donington
Donington Park
Ratcliffe on Soar
Kingston on Soar
Kegworth
Widmerpool
Wysall
Costock
Willoughby-on-the-Wolds
King's Newton
East Midlands International
Isley Walton
Diseworth
Sutton Bonington
West Leake
East Leake
Rempstone
Melbourne Hall
Wilson
Tonge
Long Whatton
Normanton on Soar
Wymeswold
Breedon on the Hill
Hathern
Hoton
Prestwold
Stanford on Soar
Belton
Worthington
Staunton Harold Hall
Newbold
Osgathorpe
Shepshed
Thorpe Acre
Cotes
Burton on the Wolds
LOUGHBOROUGH
Great Central Rly
Walton on the Wolds
Lount
Thringstone
Woodthorpe
Barrow upon Soar
Fosse Way
Trent
Derwent
Soar
Erewash
Leen
Amber
Fairham Brook
M1
A38
A611
A60
A617
A614
A6097
A610
A6007
A608
A609
A6096
A6002
A6514
A6211
A6011
A606
A52
A6005
A50
A453
A514
A42
A6006
A6
A6004
A512
B6019
B6020
B6021
B6018
B6139
B6025
B6013
B600
B6016
B6374
B6179
B6010
B6009
B6011
B683
B6004
B684
B686
B5010
B6003
B6002
B6540
B680
B676
B5324
28
27
26
25
24A
24
23A
23

Area Code 0115

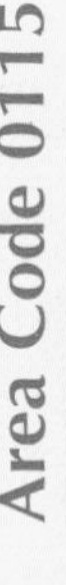

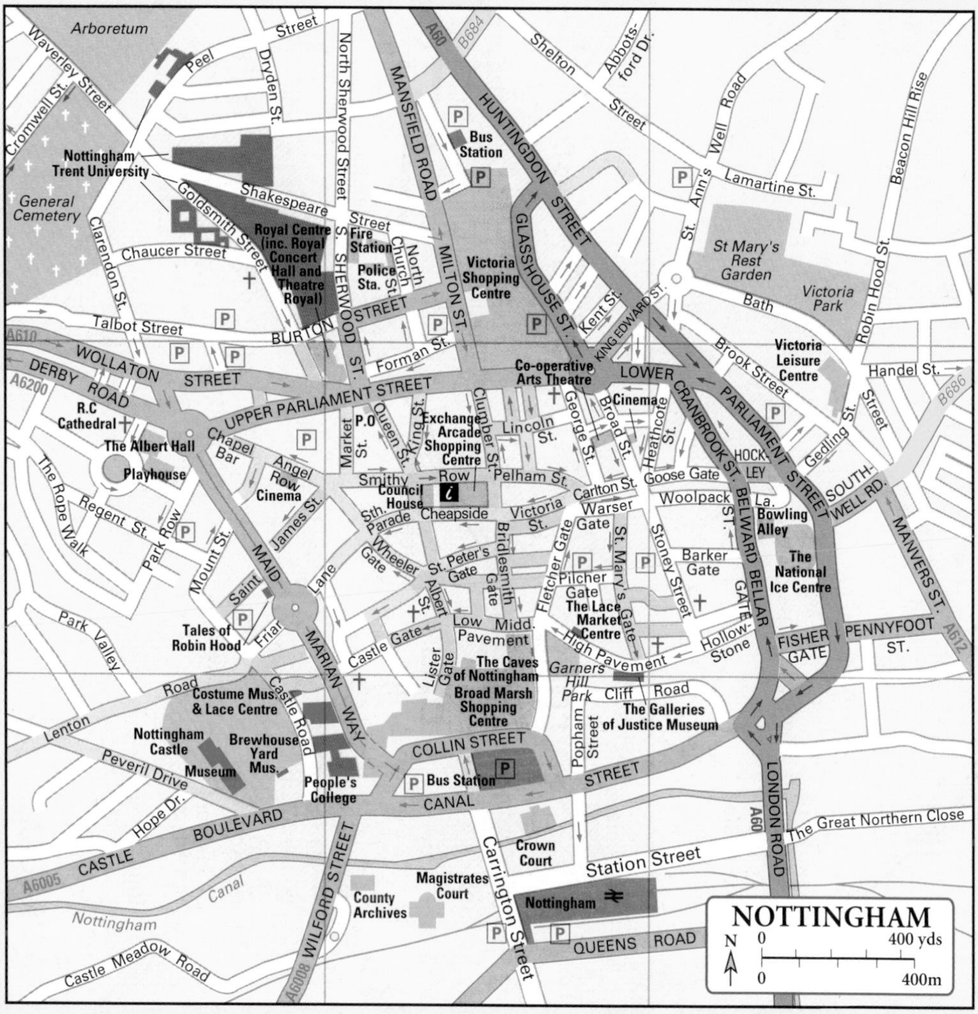

NOTTINGHAM

WEB-SITE

www.nottinghamcity.gov.uk

LOCAL RADIO

BBC RADIO NOTTINGHAM 103.8 FM
CENTURY FM 106 FM, CLASSIC GOLD GEM 999 AM, TRENT FM 96.2 FM

INDEX TO STREET NAMES

TOURIST INFORMATION ☎ 0115 915 5330
1-4 SMITHY ROW,
NOTTINGHAM, NG1 2BY

HOSPITAL A & E ☎ 0115 924 9924
QUEENS MEDICAL CENTRE, UNIVERSITY HOSP,
DERBY ROAD, NOTTINGHAM, NG7 2UH

COUNCIL OFFICE ☎ 0115 915 5555
THE GUILDHALL, SOUTH SHERWOOD STREET,
NOTTINGHAM, NG1 4BT

Nottingham *Nott.* Population: 270,222. City, on River Trent, 45m/72km NE of Birmingham. Originally Saxon town built on one of a pair of hills. In 1068, Normans built castle on other hill and both communities traded in valley between. Important commercial, industrial, entertainment and sports centre. Key industries include manufacture of lace, mechanical products, tobacco and pharmaceuticals. 17c castle, restored 19c, houses museum and art gallery. Two universities. Repertory theatre.

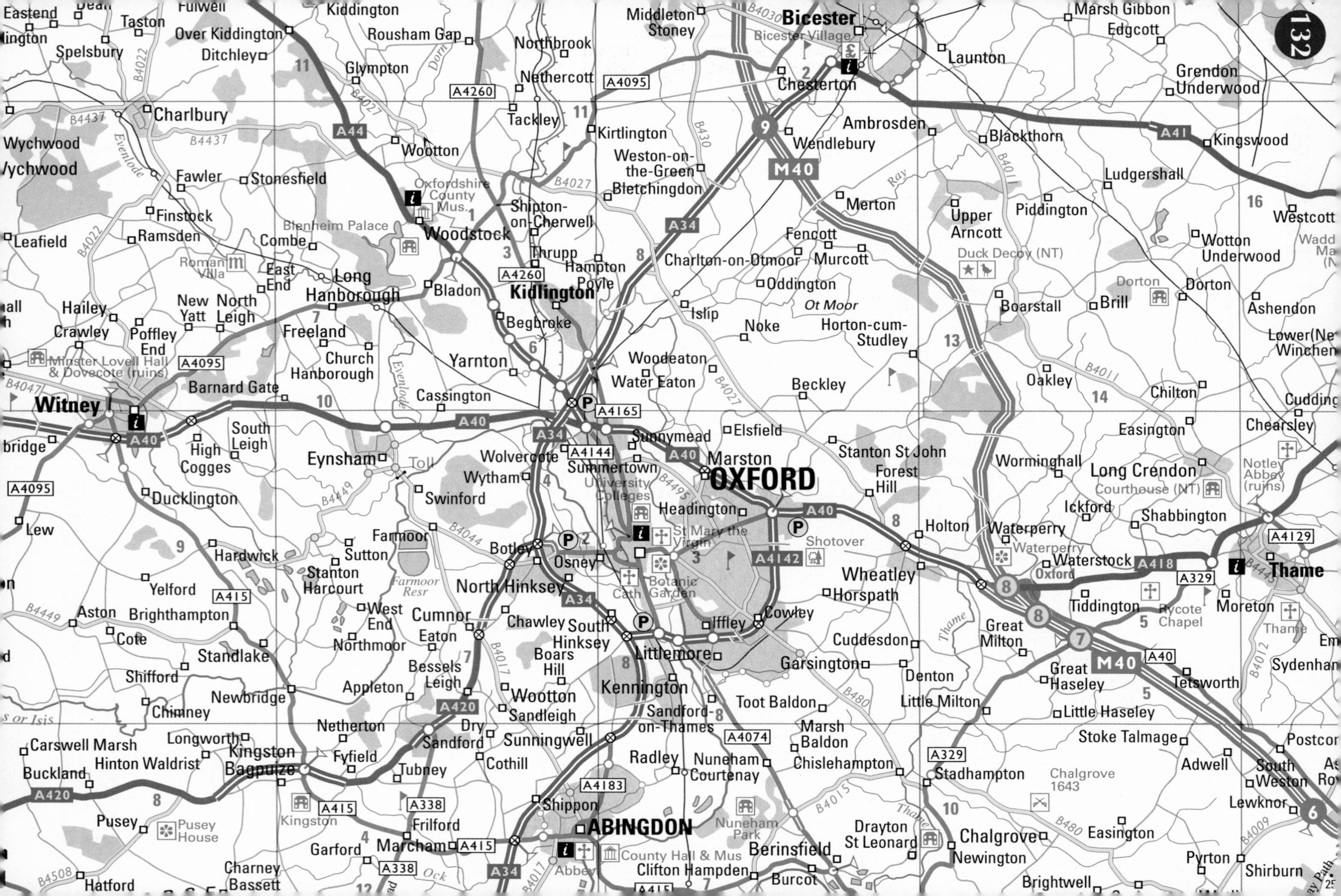

Eastend, Taston, Spelsbury, Over Kiddington, Ditchley, Kiddington, Rousham Gap, Glympton, Northbrook, Nethercott, Tackley, Middleton Stoney, Bicester, Bicester Village, Chesterton, Launton, Marsh Gibbon, Edgcott, Grendon Underwood

Charlbury, Wychwood, Fawler, Stonesfield, Wootton, Kirtlington, Weston-on-the-Green, Bletchingdon, Ambrosden, Wendlebury, Blackthorn, Kingswood, Ludgershall, Merton, Piddington, Upper Arncott, Westcott, Wotton Underwood

Leafield, Finstock, Ramsden, Combe, Oxfordshire County Mus., Woodstock, Blenheim Palace, Shipton-on-Cherwell, Thrupp, Hampton Poyle, Kidlington, Fencott, Murcott, Charlton-on-Otmoor, Oddington, Ot Moor, Duck Decoy (NT), Boarstall, Brill, Dorton, Ashendon

Hailey, Crawley, Poffley End, New Yatt, North Leigh, Roman Villa, East End, Long Hanborough, Bladon, Freeland, Church Hanborough, Begbroke, Islip, Noke, Horton-cum-Studley, Oakley, Chilton, Lower Winchendon, Cuddington

Minster Lovell Hall & Dovecote (ruins), Witney, Barnard Gate, Yarnton, Cassington, Woodeaton, Water Eaton, Beckley, Easington, Chearsley, Notley Abbey (ruins)

South Leigh, High Cogges, Ducklington, Eynsham, Toll, Wolvercote, Wytham, Swinford, Sunnymead, Summertown, University Colleges, Elsfield, Marston, OXFORD, Stanton St John, Forest Hill, Worminghall, Long Crendon, Courthouse (NT), Ickford, Shabbington, Thame

Lew, Hardwick, Yelford, Stanton Harcourt, Sutton, Farmoor, Farmoor Resr, Botley, Osney, Headington, St Mary the Virgin, Cath, Botanic Garden, Shotover, Holton, Waterperry, Waterstock, Oxford, Tiddington, Rycote Chapel, Moreton

Aston, Brighthampton, Cote, Standlake, Shifford, Chimney, Newbridge, West End, Northmoor, Cumnor, Eaton, North Hinksey, Chawley, South Hinksey, Boars Hill, Bessels Leigh, Appleton, Wootton, Sandleigh, Littlemore, Iffley, Cowley, Wheatley, Horspath, Cuddesdon, Garsington, Denton, Great Milton, Great Haseley, Little Milton, Little Haseley, Tetsworth, Sydenham

Carswell Marsh, Buckland, Longworth, Hinton Waldrist, Kingston Bagpuize, Netherton, Fyfield, Dry Sandford, Tubney, Cothill, Sunningwell, Kennington, Sandford-on-Thames, Toot Baldon, Marsh Baldon, Radley, Nuneham Courtenay, Chislehampton, Stadhampton, Chalgrove 1643, Stoke Talmage, Adwell, South Weston, Postcombe, Lewknor

Pusey, Pusey House, Kingston, Frilford, Garford, Marcham, Shippon, ABINGDON, County Hall & Mus, Abbey, Clifton Hampden, Nuneham Park, Berinsfield, Burcot, Drayton St Leonard, Chalgrove, Newington, Easington, Brightwell, Pyrton, Shirburn, Hatford, Charney Bassett, Ock, Thame, Evenlode, Dorn, Ray, Thames or Isis

A40, A34, A44, A41, A420, A415, A338, A4095, A4260, A4165, A4144, A4142, A4183, A4074, A418, A329, A4129, M40, B4022, B4437, B4027, B4030, B430, B4011, B4449, B4044, B4017, B4495, B480, B4015, B4012, B4009, B4047, B4508

INDEX TO STREET NAMES

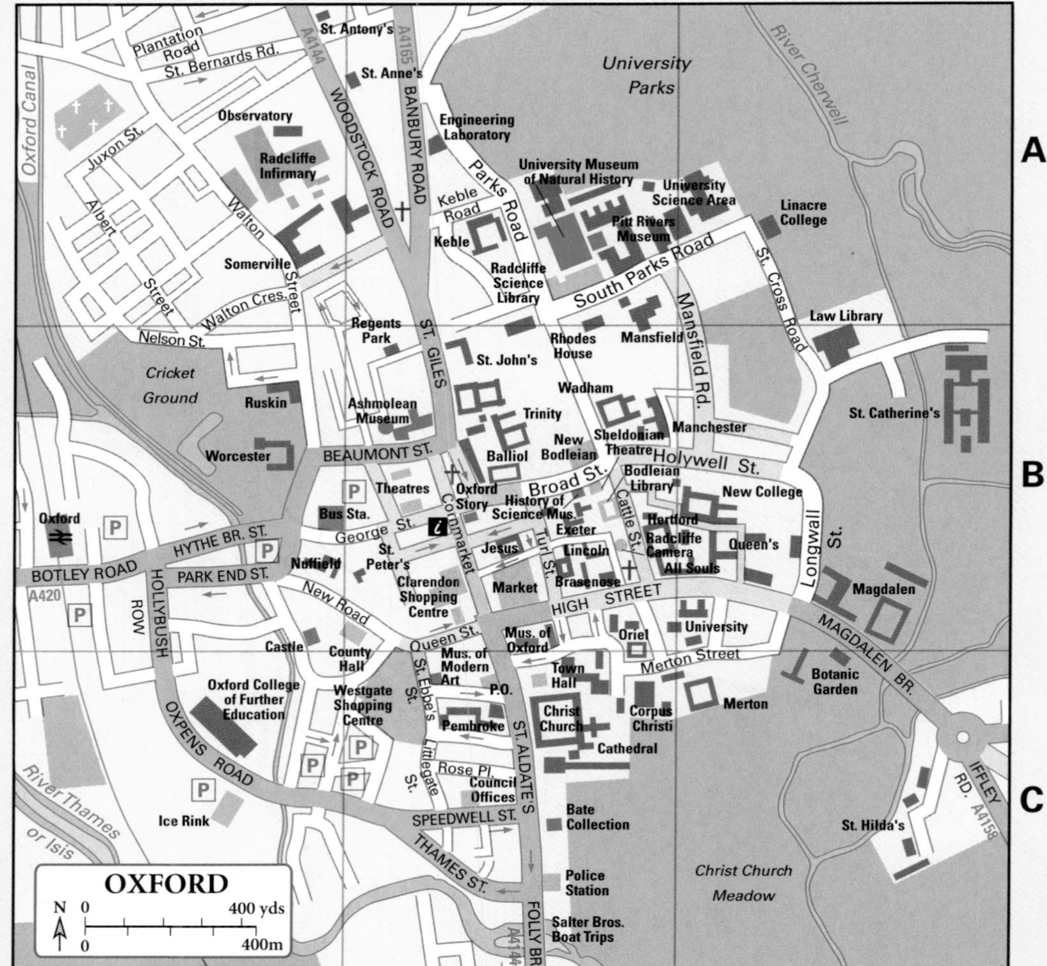

TOURIST INFORMATION ☎ 01865 726871
15-16 BROAD STREET,
OXFORD, OX1 3AS

HOSPITAL A & E ☎ 01865 741166
JOHN RADCLIFFE HOSPITAL, HEADLEY WAY, HEADINGTON,
OXFORD, OX3 9DU

COUNCIL OFFICE ☎ 01865 249811
PO BOX 10,
OXFORD, OX1 1EN

Oxford *Oxon.* Population: 118,795. City, at confluence of Rivers Thames and Cherwell, 52m/84km NW of London. Began as Saxon settlement, flourished under Normans when it was chosen as royal residence. University dating from 13c, recognised as being among best in the world. Many notable buildings create spectacular skyline. Cathedral. Bodleian Library, second largest in UK. Ashmolean museum, oldest public museum in country. Tourist and commercial centre. Ancient St. Giles Fair held every September. Oxford Brookes University at Headington, 2m/4km E of city centre. Airport at Kidlington.

WEB-SITE	www.oxford.gov.uk

LOCAL RADIO	BBC RADIO OXFORD 95.2 FM FOX FM 102.6 FM, FUSION 107.9 FM

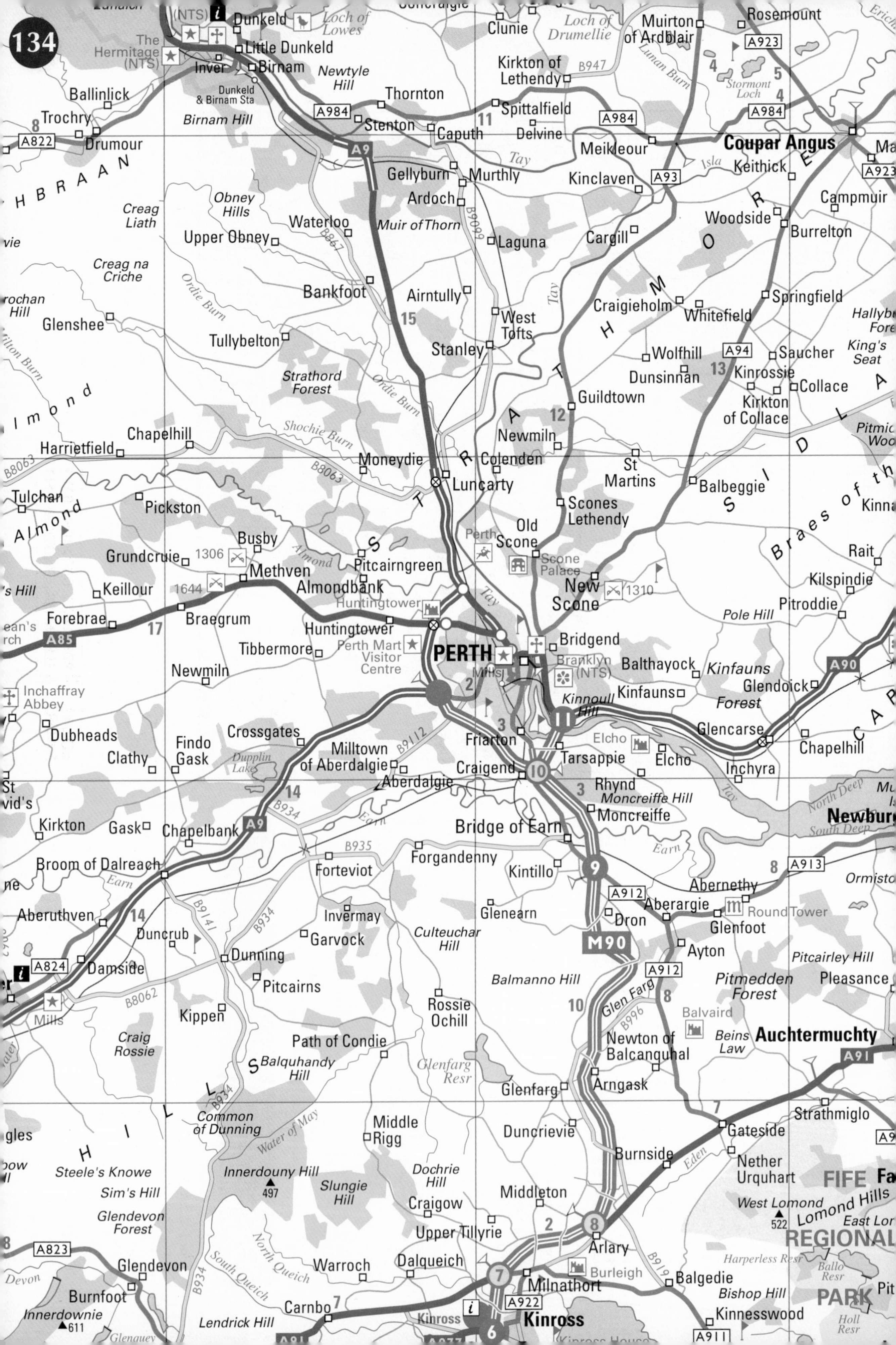
Dunkeld
Loch of Lowes
Little Dunkeld
The Hermitage (NTS)
Inver
Birnam
Newtyle Hill
Dunkeld & Birnam Sta
Birnam Hill
Ballinlick
Trochry
Drumour
A822
A984
A9
Thornton
Stenton
Caputh
Clunie
Loch of Drumellie
Kirkton of Lethendy
Spittalfield
Delvine
Muirton of Ardblair
Rosemount
A923
Stormont Loch
Coupar Angus
Meikleour
Kinclaven
A93
Keithick
Isla
Campmuir
Woodside
Burrelton
Gellyburn
Murthly
Ardoch
Muir of Thorn
Laguna
Cargill
Obney Hills
Creag Liath
Upper Obney
Waterloo
Creag na Criche
Bankfoot
Airntully
Craigieholm
Whitefield
Springfield
Glenshee
Tullybelton
West Tofts
Stanley
Wolfhill
Saucher
King's Seat
Dunsinnan
Kinrossie
Collace
Kirkton of Collace
Strathord Forest
Guildtown
Newmiln
Chapelhill
Harrietfield
Shochie Burn
Moneydie
Colenden
St Martins
Luncarty
Balbeggie
Tulchan
Pickston
Scones Lethendy
Old Scone
Busby
Grundcruie
Pitcairngreen
Methven
Almondbank
Scone Palace
New Scone
Rait
Kilspindie
Keillour
Huntingtower
Pole Hill
Pitroddie
Forebrae
Braegrum
A85
Tibbermore
Perth Mart Visitor Centre
PERTH
Bridgend
Branklyn (NTS)
Balthayock
Kinfauns Forest
Kinfauns
Glendoick
A90
Newmiln
Inchaffray Abbey
Kinnoull Hill
Dubheads
Crossgates
Clathy
Findo Gask
Dupplin Lake
Milltown of Aberdalgie
Friarton
Elcho
Glencarse
Chapelhill
Tarsappie
Craigend
Aberdalgie
Rhynd
Inchyra
Moncreiffe Hill
Moncreiffe
Newburgh
Kirkton
Gask
Chapelbank
Bridge of Earn
Broom of Dalreach
Forteviot
Forgandenny
Kintillo
Abernethy
A913
Aberargie
Round Tower
Glenfoot
Aberuthven
Invermay
Glenearn
Dron
Duncrub
Garvock
Culteuchar Hill
M90
Ayton
Pitcairley Hill
Dunning
A824
Damside
A912
Pitcairns
Balmanno Hill
Pitmedden Forest
Pleasance
Mills
Kippen
Rossie Ochill
Glen Farg
Balvaird
Craig Rossie
Path of Condie
Newton of Balcanquhal
Beins Law
Auchtermuchty
A91
Balquhandy Hill
Glenfarg Resr
Arngask
Glenfarg
Strathmiglo
Common of Dunning
Middle Rigg
Duncrievie
Gateside
Steele's Knowe
Innerdouny Hill
497
Slungie Hill
Dochrie Hill
Burnside
Nether Urquhart
FIFE
Sim's Hill
Craigow
Middleton
West Lomond
Lomond Hills
522
Glendevon Forest
Upper Tillyrie
REGIONAL
A823
Glendevon
Warroch
Dalqueich
Arlary
Harperless Resr
Burleigh
Milnathort
Balgedie
Bishop Hill
PARK
Burnfoot
Innerdownie
611
Carnbo
A922
Kinross
Kinnesswood
Lendrick Hill
A911
Holl Resr
Devon
North Queich
South Queich
Water of May
Ochil Hills
Tay
Earn
Almond

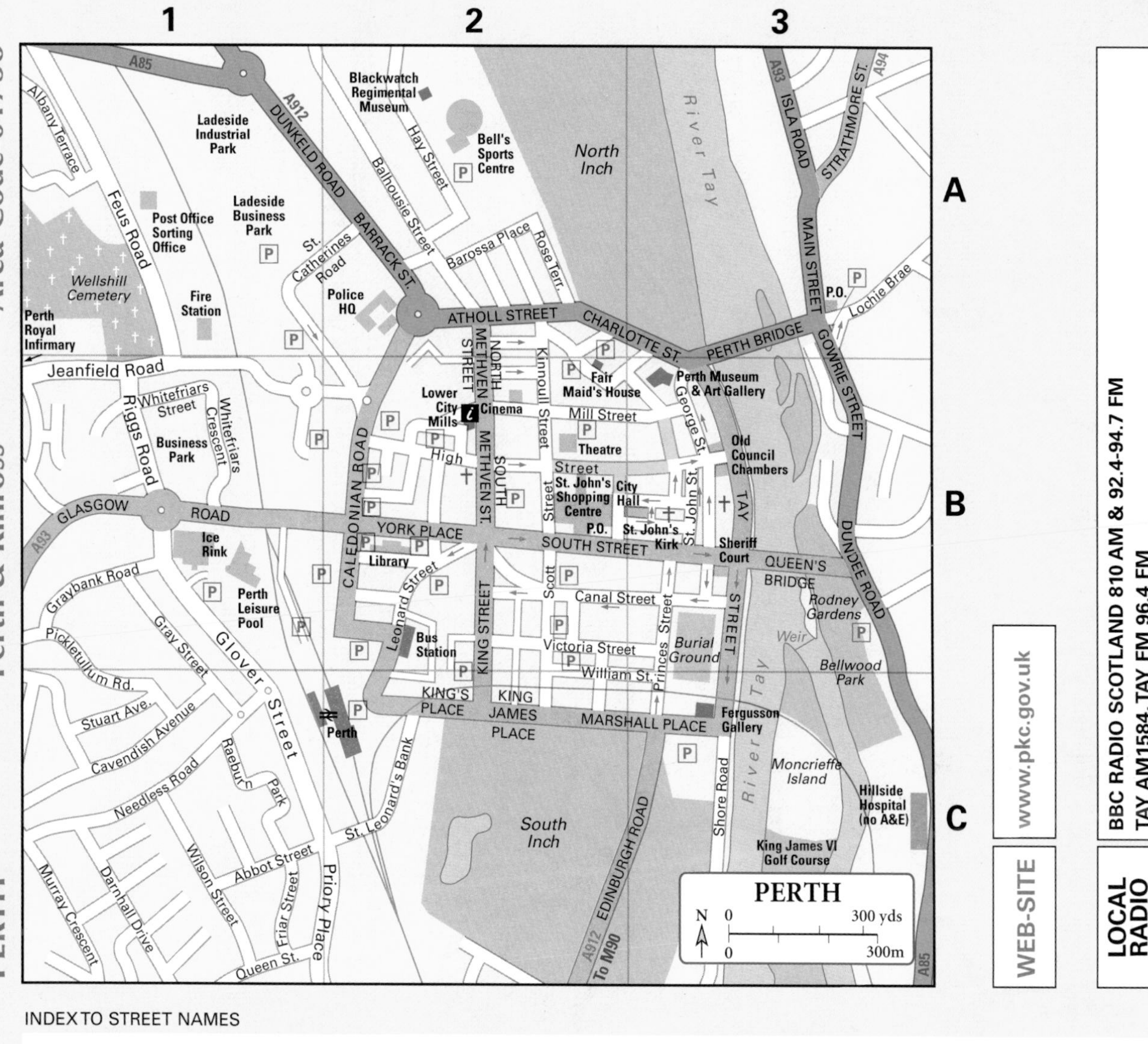

INDEX TO STREET NAMES

Street	Grid	Street	Grid	Street	Grid	Street	Grid	Street	Grid
Abbot Street	C1	Feus Road	A1	King Street	B2	Priory Place	C2	South Street	B2
Albany Terrace	A1	Friar Street	C1	Kinnoull Street	A2	Queen Street	C1	Strathmore Street	A3
Atholl Street	A2	George Street	B3	Leonard Street	B2	Queens Bridge	B3	Stuart Avenue	C1
Balhousie Street	A2	Glasgow Road	B1	Lochie Brae	A3	Raeburn Park	C1	Tay Street	B3
Barossa Place	A2	Glover Street	B1	Main Street	A3	Riggs Road	B1	Victoria Street	B2
Barrack Street	A2	Gowrie Street	A3	Marshall Place	C2	Rose Terrace	A2	Whitefriars Crescent	B1
Caledonian Road	B2	Gray Street	B1	Mill Street	B2	St. Catherines Road	A1	Whitefriars Street	B1
Canal Street	B2	Graybank Road	B1	Murray Crescent	C1	St. John Street	B3	William Street	B2
Cavendish Avenue	C1	Hay Street	A2	Needless Road	C1	St. Leonard's Bank	C2	Wilson Street	C1
Charlotte Street	A2	High Street	B2	North Methven Street	A2	Scott Street	B2	York Place	B2
Darnhall Drive	C1	Isla Road	A3	Perth Bridge	A3	Shore Road	C3		
Dundee Road	B3	Jeanfield Road	B1	Pickletullum Road	B1	South Methven Street	B2		
Dunkeld Road	A1	King's Place	C2	Princes Street	C3				
Edinburgh Road	C2	King James Place	C2						

TOURIST INFORMATION ☎ 01738 450600
LOWER CITY MILLS, WEST MILL STREET, PERTH, PH1 5QP

HOSPITAL A & E ☎ 01738 623311
PERTH ROYAL INFIRMARY, TAYMOUNT TERRACE, PERTH, PH1 1NX

COUNCIL OFFICE ☎ 01738 475000
PERTH & KINROSS COUNCIL, 2 HIGH STREET, PERTH, PH1 5PH

Perth *P. & K.* Population: 41,453. City, ancient cathedral city (Royal Charter granted 1210) on River Tay, 31m/50km N of Edinburgh. Once capital of Medieval Scotland. Centre of livestock trade. Previously cotton manufacturing centre; now important industries include whisky distilling. St. John's Kirk founded 1126. 15c Balhousie Castle houses regimental headquarters and Museum of the Black Watch. Art Gallery and Museum. 16c Fair Maid's House. Gothic mansion Scone Palace 2m/3km N contains collections of furniture, needlework and porcelain with site of Coronation Stone of Destiny in its grounds. Airfield (Scone) to NE.

DARTMOOR NATIONAL PARK
Princetown
Walkhampton Common
Prehistoric Settlement
Sampford Spiney
Walkhampton
Horrabridge
Dousland
Yelverton
Meavy
Sheepstor
Burrator Resr
Crapstone
The Garden House
Clearbrook
Shaugh Prior
Cadover Bridge
Lee Moor
Lutton
Shell Top
475
Penn Moor
445
342
Bickleigh
Roborough
Plymouth City
Plym Forest
Plym Bridge
Drakeland Corner
Sparkwell
Lee Mill Bridge
Yealmpton
Battisborough Cross
Brixton
Kitley
Torr
Newton Ferrers
Noss Mayo
Netton
Plympton
Elburton
PLYMOUTH
National Marine Aquarium
Saltram (NT)
Egg Buckland
Crabtree
Oreston
Plymstock
Goosewell
Staddiscombe
Hooe
Down Thomas
Wembury
Knighton
Worswell
Gara Pt
Wembury Bay
Heybrook Bay
Great Mew Stone
Plymouth Breakwater
The Sound
Turnchapel
Drake's Island
Mount Edgcumbe
Royal Citadel
Stonehouse
Devonport
Crownhill
St Budeaux
Tamerton Foliot
Milton Combe
Buckland Abbey (NT)
Maristow House
Bere Ferrers
Bere Alston
Buckland Monachorum
Morwellham
Morwellham Quay Mus.
Tavistock
Whitchurch
Higher Walreddon
Gulworthy
Latchley
Gunnislake
Albaston
Calstock
St Ann's Chapel
Cotehele (NT)
St Dominick
Chilsworthy
Harrowbarrow
Hingston Down
Kit Hill
Dupath Well
Luckett
Downgate
Kelly Bray
Callington
Golberdon
Haye
South Hill
Bray Shop
Linkinhorne
Bathpool
Rilla Mill
Upton Cross
Upton
Henwood
Minions
Caradon Hill
Hurlers Stone Circle
Common Moor
Siblyback Resr
Darite
Trethevy Quoit
Tremar
Middlehill
Pensilva
Trevigro
Newbridge
St Ive
Merrymeet
Pengover Green
Menheniot
St Cleer
King Doniert's Stone
Dobwalls
Dobwalls Family Adventure Park
Doublebois
Liskeard
Trevelmond
St Pinnock
Lamellion
Horningtops
St Keyne
Herodsfoot
Duloe
Trewidland
Bylane End
Widegates
Morval
Tredinnick
Sandplace
Muchlarnick
Pelynt
Looe
West Looe
East Looe
St George's or Looe Island
Looe Bay
St Martin
Polperro
Porthallow
Quethiock
Blunts
Pillaton
St Mellion
Ashton
Hatt
Landrake
Carkeel
Botusfleming
Cargreen
Landulph
Saltash
St Stephens
Trematon
Markwell
St Germans
Tideford
Trerulefoot
Hessenford
Polbathic
Seaton
Downderry
Portwrinkle
Whitsand Bay
Crafthole
Sheviock
Antony
Antony Ho. (NT)
Torpoint
St John
St John's Lake
Freathy
Danger Zone
Millbrook
Cremyll
Kingsand
Cawsand
Cawsand Bay
Penlee Point
Rame
Rame Head
Roscoff.................6-7½ hours
Santander
Tamar
Tavy
Lynher
St Germans or Lynher
Tiddy
Seaton
East Looe
West Looe
Plym
Meavy
Yealm
Toll
A38
A386
A388
A390
A374
A379
A387
A3064
B3257
B3254
B3212
B3147
B3416
B3432
B3373
B3413
B3247
B3249
B3253
B3251
B3359
B3186

INDEX TO STREET NAMES

Street	Grid
Alexandra Road	A3
Alma Road	A1
Armada Way	B2
Ashford Road	A3
Barbican Approach	C3
Beaumont Road	B3
Beechwood Avenue	A2
Bretonside	B2
Buckwell Street	C2
Camden Street	B2
Cattledown Road	C3
Cecil Street	B1
Central Park Avenue	A1
Charles Street	B2
Citadel Road	C1
Clarence Place	B1
Cliff Road	C1
Clifton Place	A2
Clovelly Road	C3
Cobourg Street	B2
Cornwall Street	B2
Dale Road	A2
Drake Circus	B2
East Street	C1
Eastlake Street	B2
Ebrington Street	B2
Elliot Street	C1
Embankment Road	B3
Exeter Street	B2
Ford Park Road	A2
Gdynia Way	C3
Grand Parade	C1
Greenbank Road	A3
Grenville Road	B3
Harwell Street	B1
Hoe Road	C2
Houndiscombe Road	A2
James Street	B2
King Street	B1
Lipson Hill	A3
Lipson Road	B3
Lisson Grove	A3
Lockyer Street	C2
Looe Street	B2
Madeira Road	C2
Manor Road	B1
Martin Street	C1
Mayflower Street	B2
Millbay Road	C1
Mount Gould Road	A3
Mutley Plain	A2
New George Street	B1
North Cross	B2
North Hill	B2
North Road East	B2
North Road West	B1
North Street	B2
Notte Street	C2
Oxford Street	B1
Pentillie Road	A2
Princess Street	C2
Queen's Road	A3
Royal Parade	B2
Salisbury Road	B3
Saltash Road	A1
Seaton Avenue	A2
Seymour Avenue	B3
Southside Street	C2
Stoke Road	B1
Stuart Road	A1
Sutton Road	B3
Sydney Street	B1
Teats Hill Road	C3
The Crescent	C1
Tothill Avenue	B3
Tothill Road	B3
Union Street	B1
Vauxhall Street	C2
West Hoe Road	C1
Western Approach	B1
Whittington Street	A1
Wilton Street	B1
Wyndham Street	B1

TOURIST INFORMATION ☎ 01752 264849
ISLAND HOUSE, 9 THE BARBICAN,
PLYMOUTH, PL1 2LS

HOSPITAL A & E ☎ 01752 777111
DERRIFORD HOSPITAL, DERRIFORD ROAD,
CROWNHILL, PLYMOUTH, PL6 8DH

COUNCIL OFFICE ☎ 01752 668000
CIVIC CENTRE, ARMADA WAY,
PLYMOUTH, PL1 2EW

Plymouth *Plym.* Population: 245,295. City, largest city in SW England, 100m/160km SW of Bristol. Port and naval base. Regional shopping centre. City centre rebuilt after bombing in World War II. Has strong commercial and naval tradition. In 1588 Sir Francis Drake sailed from Plymouth to defeat Spanish Armada. Captain Cook's voyages to Australia, South Seas and Antarctica all departed from here. University. Plymouth City Airport to N of city.

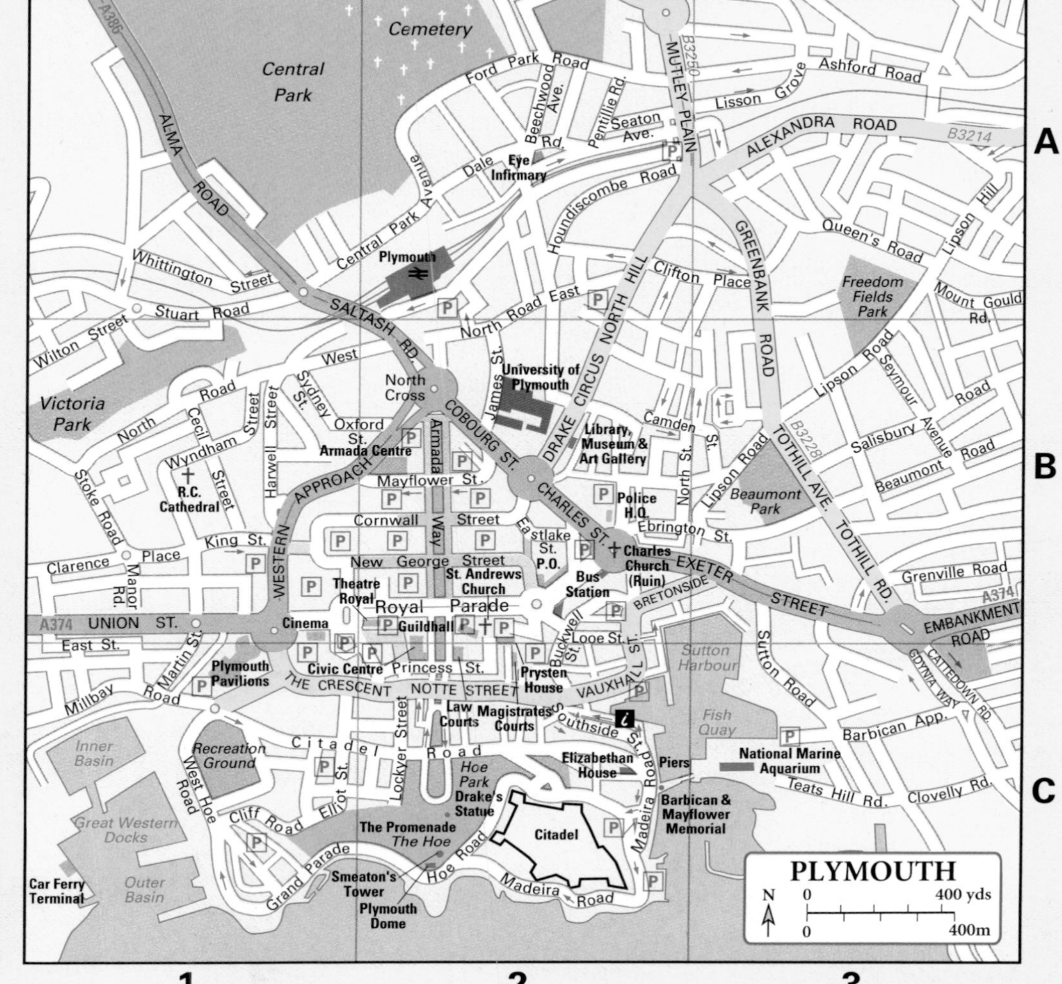

WEB-SITE www.plymouth.gov.uk

LOCAL RADIO
BBC RADIO DEVON 103.4 FM
CLASSIC GOLD 1152 AM, PLYMOUTH SOUND FM 97 FM

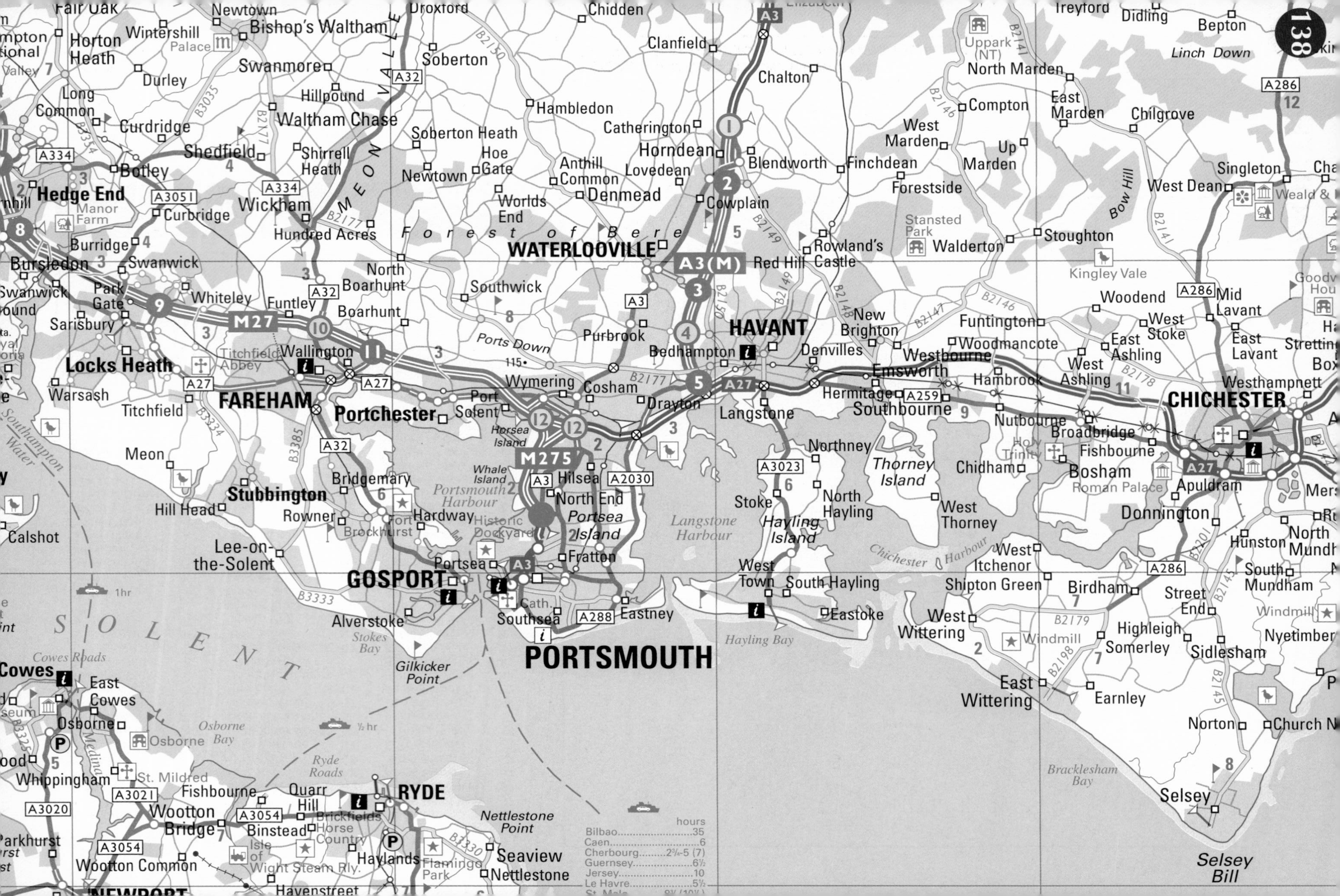

CHICHESTER
HAVANT
WATERLOOVILLE
PORTSMOUTH
GOSPORT
FAREHAM
Portchester
Stubbington
Locks Heath
Hedge End
RYDE
Cowes
Selsey
Selsey Bill
Bracklesham Bay
East Wittering
West Wittering
Chichester Harbour
Hayling Island
Hayling Bay
Langstone Harbour
Portsea Island
Portsmouth Harbour
Whale Island
Horsea Island
Thorney Island
SOLENT
Southampton Water
Stokes Bay
Gilkicker Point
Nettlestone Point
Osborne Bay
Ryde Roads
Cowes Roads
Forest of Bere
MEON VALE
Ports Down
Bow Hill
Linch Down
Kingley Vale
Stansted Park
Uppark (NT)
Singleton
West Dean
Chilgrove
East Marden
North Marden
Up Marden
West Marden
Compton
Stoughton
Walderton
Forestside
Finchdean
Rowland's Castle
Red Hill
Chalton
Clanfield
Blendworth
Horndean
Catherington
Lovedean
Cowplain
Denmead
Hambledon
Chidden
Soberton
Soberton Heath
Hoe Gate
Newtown
Worlds End
Anthill Common
Southwick
Wickham
Shirrell Heath
Waltham Chase
Hillpound
Swanmore
Bishop's Waltham
Wintershill
Horton Heath
Durley
Curdridge
Long Common
Shedfield
Botley
Swanwick
Burridge
Bursledon
Sarisbury
Park Gate
Whiteley
Funtley
North Boarhunt
Boarhunt
Hundred Acres
Titchfield
Titchfield Abbey
Wallington
Warsash
Hill Head
Lee-on-the-Solent
Calshot
Meon
Bridgemary
Rowner
Alverstoke
Brockhurst
Hardway
Historic Dockyard
Portsea
Southsea
Eastney
Fratton
North End
Hilsea
Cosham
Wymering
Port Solent
Drayton
Bedhampton
Purbrook
Langstone
Northney
North Hayling
Stoke
West Town
South Hayling
Eastoke
Emsworth
Southbourne
Westbourne
Hermitage
Denvilles
New Brighton
Woodmancote
Funtington
Hambrook
Nutbourne
Chidham
West Thorney
Bosham
Fishbourne
Broadbridge
Roman Palace
West Ashling
East Ashling
West Stoke
Woodend
Mid Lavant
East Lavant
Westhampnett
Apuldram
Donnington
Birdham
West Itchenor
Shipton Green
Earnley
Somerley
Highleigh
Sidlesham
Street End
Hunston
North Mundham
South Mundham
Norton
Church Norton
Nyetimber
Windmill
Bepton
Didling
Quarr Hill
Binstead
Haylands
Fishbourne
Wootton Bridge
Wootton Common
Whippingham
St. Mildred
East Cowes
Osborne
Isle of Wight Steam Rly.
Flamingo Park
Seaview
Nettlestone
Havenstreet
Horse Country
M27
M275
A3(M)
A3
A27
A32
A334
A3051
A286
A259
A3023
A2030
A288
A3054
A3021
A3020
B2141
B2146
B2147
B2148
B2149
B2150
B2177
B2178
B2179
B2198
B2145
B2201
B3035
B3334
B3385
B3333
B3354
B3330
B3325
½ hr
1hr
hours
Bilbao 35
Caen 6
Cherbourg 2¾-5 (7)
Guernsey 6½
Jersey 10
Le Havre 5½

INDEX TO STREET NAMES

Street	Grid	Street	Grid	Street	Grid
Alfred Road	B2	Green Road	C2	Park Road	B2
Anglesea Road	B2	Greetham Street	B3	Pembroke Road	C1
Arundel Street	B3	Grosvenor Street	C3	Penny Street	C1
Bailey's Road	C3	Gunwharf Road	C1	Playfair Road	C3
Bellevue Terrace	C2	Hampshire Terrace	C2	Queen Street	B1
Blackfriars Road	B3	High Street	C1	Raglan Street	B3
Bradford Road	B3	Holbrook Road	A3	St. Andrews Road	C3
Britain Street	B1	Hope Street	A2	St. Edward's Road	C2
Broad Street	C1	Hyde Park Road	B3	St. George's Road	B1
Burnaby Road	B2	Isambard Brunel Road	B2	St. James Road	C2
Cambridge Road	C2			St. James Street	B2
Canal Walk	B3	Kent Road	C2	St. Paul's Road	C2
Castle Road	C2	King Charles Street	C1	St. Thomas's Street	C1
Church Road	A3	King's Road	C2	Somers Road	B3
Church Street	A3	King's Terrace	C2	Southsea Terrace	C2
Clarendon Street	A3	King Street	C2	Station Street	B3
College Street	B1	Lake Road	A3	Sultan Road	A3
Commercial Road	B2	Landport Terrace	C2	The Hard	B1
Cottage Grove	C3	Lombard Street	C1	Turner Road	A3
Crasswell Street	A3	Margate Road	C3	Victoria Road North	C3
Cross Street	A1	Market Way	A2	Warblington Street	C1
Cumberland Street	A1	Millennium Boulevard	B1	White Hart Road	C1
Edinburgh Road	B2			Wingfield Street	A3
Eldon Street	C2	Museum Road	C2	Winston Churchill Avenue	B2
Elm Grove	C3	Nelson Road	A3		
Flathouse Road	A3	Norfolk Street	C2		

TOURIST INFORMATION ☎ 023 9282 6722
THE HARD,
PORTSMOUTH, PO1 3QJ

HOSPITAL A & E ☎ 023 9228 6000
QUEEN ALEXANDRA HOSPITAL, SOUTHWICK
HILL ROAD, COSHAM, PORTSMOUTH, PO6 3LY

COUNCIL OFFICE ☎ 023 9282 2251
CIVIC OFFICES, GUILDHALL SQUARE,
PORTSMOUTH, PO1 2BG

Portsmouth *Ports.* Population: 174,690. City, port and naval base (Portsmouth Harbour, on W side of city) 65m/105km SW of London, extending from S end of Portsea Island to S slopes of Ports Down. Various industries, including tourism, financial services and manufacturing. Partly bombed in World War II and now rebuilt; however, some 18c buildings remain. Boat and hovercraft ferries to Isle of Wight. University. Two cathedrals. Nelson's ship, HMS Victory, in harbour, alongside which are remains of Henry VIII's flagship, Mary Rose, which sank in 1545. King James's Gate and Landport Gate were part of 17c defences, and Fort Cumberland is 18c coastal defence at Eastney (all (English Heritage). Royal Garrison Church (English Heritage) was 16c chapel prior to Dissolution. Museums, many with nautical theme.

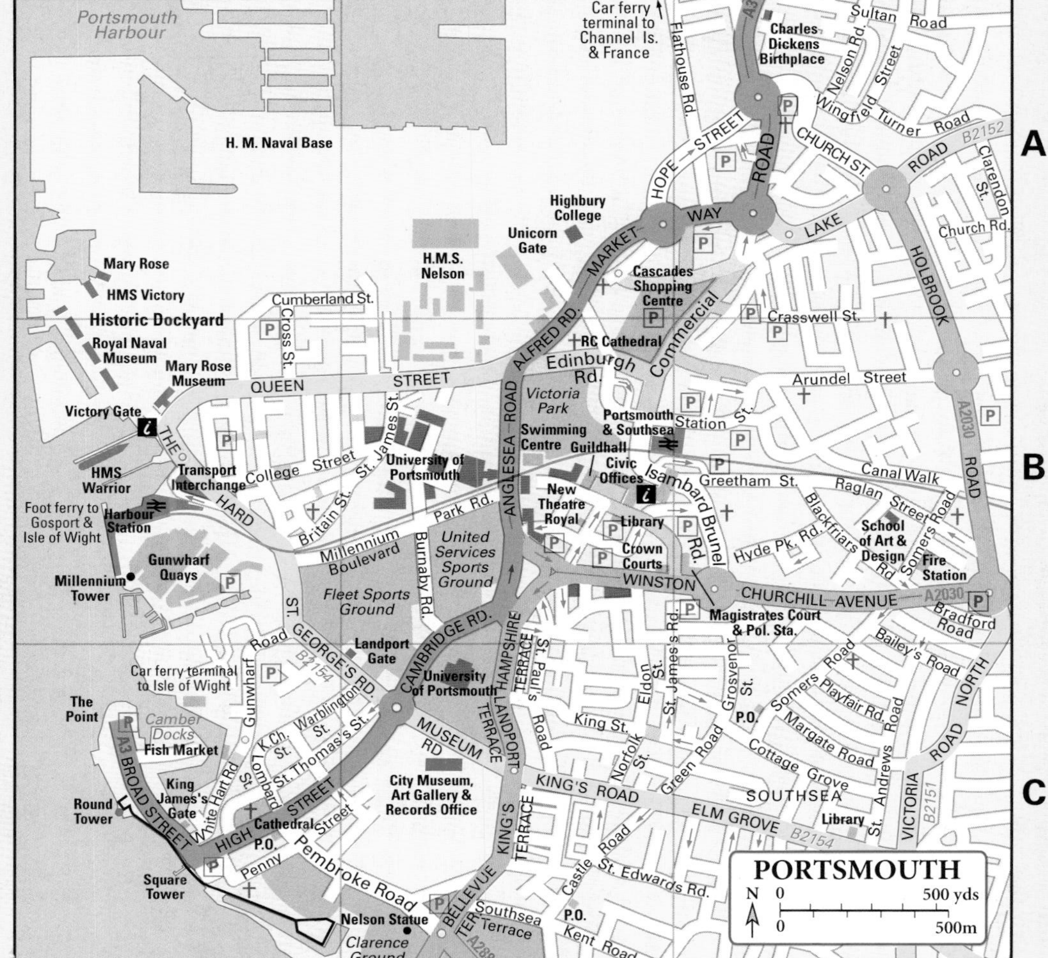

WEB-SITE www.portsmouth.gov.uk

LOCAL RADIO
BBC RADIO SOLENT 96.1 FM
CAPITAL GOLD 1170 AM, OCEAN FM 97.5 FM, THE QUAY 107.4 FM, WAVE 105.2 FM

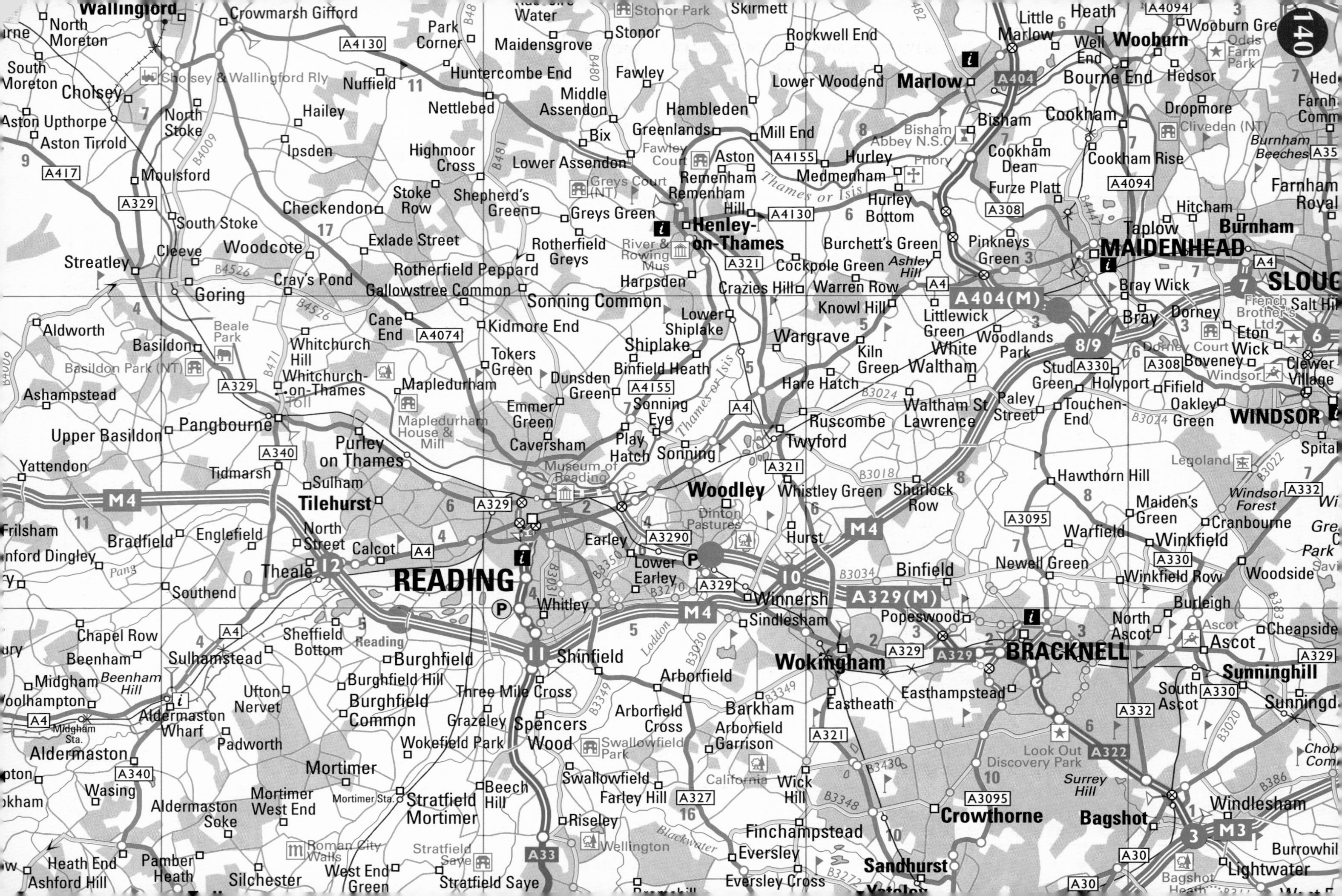

Wallingford
Crowmarsh Gifford
Park Corner
Water
Stonor Park
Skirmett
Little Marlow
Heath
A4094
Wooburn Green
North Moreton
Maidensgrove
Stonor
Rockwell End
Well End
Wooburn
Odds Farm Park
South Moreton
Cholsey
Chosey & Wallingford Rly
Nuffield
Huntercombe End
Fawley
Lower Woodend
Marlow
A404
Bourne End
Hedsor
A4130
B48
B480
Nettlebed
Middle Assendon
Hambleden
Bisham
Cookham
Dropmore
Aston Upthorpe
North Stoke
Hailey
Bix
Greenlands
Mill End
Bisham Abbey N.S.C.
Cliveden (NT)
Aston Tirrold
Ipsden
Highmoor Cross
Lower Assendon
Fawley Court
Aston
A4155
Hurley
Priory
Cookham Dean
Cookham Rise
Burnham Beeches
A35
A417
Moulsford
B4009
B481
Remenham
Medmenham
Thames or Isis
Furze Platt
A4094
Farnham Royal
A329
Stoke Row
Shepherd's Green
Greys Court (NT)
Remenham Hill
Hurley Bottom
A308
Hitcham
South Stoke
Checkendon
Greys Green
Henley-on-Thames
A4130
Pinkneys Green
Taplow
Burnham
Cleeve
Woodcote
Exlade Street
Rotherfield Greys
River & Rowing Mus
Burchett's Green
MAIDENHEAD
Streatley
B4526
Cray's Pond
Rotherfield Peppard
Harpsden
A321
Cockpole Green
Ashley Hill
A4
SLOUGH
Goring
Gallowstree Common
Sonning Common
Crazies Hill
Warren Row
A4
Bray Wick
Knowl Hill
A404(M)
French Brother's Ltd
Salt Hill
Aldworth
Beale Park
B4526
Cane End
A4074
Kidmore End
Lower Shiplake
Wargrave
Littlewick Green
Bray
Dorney
Eton
Basildon
Whitchurch Hill
Shiplake
Kiln Green
White Waltham
Woodlands Park
8/9
Dorney Court
Wick
Basildon Park (NT)
B471
Tokers Green
Binfield Heath
Stud Green
A330
A308
Boveney
Clewer Village
A329
Whitchurch-on-Thames
Toll
Mapledurham
Dunsden Green
A4155
Hare Hatch
Holyport
Fifield
Windsor
Ashampstead
Emmer Green
Sonning Eye
A4
B3024
Waltham St Lawrence
Paley Street
Touchen-End
Oakley Green
Pangbourne
Mapledurham House & Mill
Ruscombe
B3024
WINDSOR
Upper Basildon
A340
Purley on Thames
Caversham
Play Hatch
Sonning
Twyford
Spital
Yattendon
Tidmarsh
Museum of Reading
A321
B3018
Legoland
B3022
Sulham
Hawthorn Hill
M4
Tilehurst
A329
Woodley
Whistley Green
Shurlock Row
Windsor Forest
A332
Dinton Pastures
Maiden's Green
Frilsham
Bradfield
Englefield
North Street
A3290
Hurst
A3095
Warfield
Cranbourne
Calcot
Earley
M4
Winkfield
Bucklebury
Pang
A4
Lower Earley
B3350
B3031
Newell Green
Binfield
A330
Park
Theale
READING
A329
B3270
Winnersh
B3034
Winkfield Row
Woodside
Southend
A329(M)
Burleigh
Whitley
M4
Popeswood
North Ascot
Ascot
Chapel Row
A4
Sheffield Bottom
Reading
Sindlesham
BRACKNELL
Cheapside
Beenham
Sulhamstead
Burghfield
Shinfield
Loddon
B3030
Wokingham
A329
A329
Sunninghill
Midgham
Beenham Hill
Burghfield Hill
Arborfield
A329
Woolhampton
Ufton Nervet
Three Mile Cross
B3349
Easthampstead
South Ascot
A330
Sunningdale
A4
Midgham Sta.
Aldermaston Wharf
Burghfield Common
Grazeley
Spencers Wood
Arborfield Cross
Barkham
Eastheath
A332
B3020
Padworth
Wokefield Park
Swallowfield Park
Arborfield Garrison
A321
A322
Aldermaston
Mortimer
B3430
Look Out Discovery Park
Chobham Common
Brimpton
A340
Mortimer West End
Mortimer Sta.
Stratfield Mortimer
Beech Hill
Swallowfield
California
Wick Hill
Surrey Hill
Wasing
Farley Hill
A327
B3348
A3095
Windlesham
Aldermaston Soke
Riseley
Crowthorne
Bagshot
B386
Roman City Walls
Blackwater
Finchampstead
M3
Heath End
Pamber Heath
Stratfield Saye
Wellington
A33
Eversley
Sandhurst
A30
Burrowhill
Ashford Hill
Silchester
West End Green
Stratfield Saye
Eversley Cross
B3272
Bagshot Heath
Lightwater
A30

INDEX TO STREET NAMES

Street	Grid
Addington Road	C3
Addison Road	A1
Alexandra Road	B3
Allcroft Road	C3
Alpine Street	C2
Amersham Road	A3
Amity Road	B1
Ardler Road	A2
Audley Street	B1
Basingstoke Road	C2
Bath Road	C1
Bedford Road	B1
Berkeley Avenue	C1
Blagrave Street	B2
Blenheim Road	B3
Briant's Avenue	A3
Bridge Street	B2
Broad Street	B2
Cardiff Road	A1
Castle Hill	B1
Castle Street	B2
Catherine Street	B1
Caversham Road	B2
Chatham Street	B1
Cheapside	B2
Cholmeley Road	B3
Christchurch Road	C2
Church Road	A1
Church Street	A2
Coley Avenue	C1
Cow Lane	B1
Craven Road	B3
Crown Place	B3
Crown Street	C2
Cumberland Road	B3
Curzon Street	B1
De Beauvoir Road	B3
Donnington Road	B3
Duke Street	B2
East Street	B2
Eldon Road	B3
Eldon Terrace	B3
Elgar Road	C2
Elgar Road South	C2
Erleigh Road	B3
Fobney Street	B2
Forbury Road	B2
Friar Street	B2
Gas Works Road	B3
George Street *Caversham*	A2
George Street *Reading*	B1
Gosbrook Road	A2
Gower Street	B1
Great Knollys Street	B1
Greyfriars Road	B2
Hemdean Road	A2
Hill Street	C2
Holybrook Road	C1
Kenavon Drive	B3
Kendrick Road	C2
King's Road *Caversham*	A2
King's Road *Reading*	B2
London Road	B3
London Street	B2
Lower Henley Road	A3
Mill Road	A3
Millford Road	A1
Millman Road	C2
Minster Street	B2
Morgan Road	C3
Napier Road	B2
Orts Road	B3
Oxford Road	B1
Pell Street	C2
Portman Road	A1
Priest Hill	A2
Prospect Street *Caversham*	A2
Prospect Street *Reading*	B1
Queen's Road *Caversham*	A2
Queen's Road *Reading*	B2
Redlands Road	C3
Richfield Avenue	A1
Rose Kiln Lane	C2
Russell Street	B1
St. Ann's Road	A2
St. John's Road	A3
St. Mary's Butts	B2
St. Peters Avenue	A1
St. Saviour's Road	C1
Silver Street	C2
South Street	B2
Southampton Street	C2
South View Road	A2
Star Road	A3
Station Hill	B2
Station Road	B2
Swansea Road	A2
Tessa Road	A1
The Warren	A1
Tilehurst Road	B1
Upper Redlands Road	C3
Vastern Road	A2
Waldeck Street	C2
Waterloo Road	C2
Wensley Road	C1
Western Elms Avenue	B1
Westfield Road	A2
West Street	B2
Whitley Street	C2
Wolsey Road	A2
York Road	A2

TOURIST INFORMATION ☎ 0118 956 6226
TOWN HALL, BLAGRAVE STREET,
READING, RG1 1QH

HOSPITAL A & E ☎ 0118 987 5111
ROYAL BERKSHIRE HOSPITAL, LONDON ROAD,
READING, RG1 5AN

COUNCIL OFFICE ☎ 0118 939 0900
CIVIC CENTRE, CIVIC OFFICES, (OFF CASTLE ST.)
READING, RG1 7TD

Reading *Read.* Population: 213,474. Town, county and industrial town and railway centre on River Thames, 36m/58km W of London. During Victorian times Reading was an important manufacturing town, particularly for biscuit-making and brewing. University. Remains of Norman abbey, founded by Henry I who lies buried there.

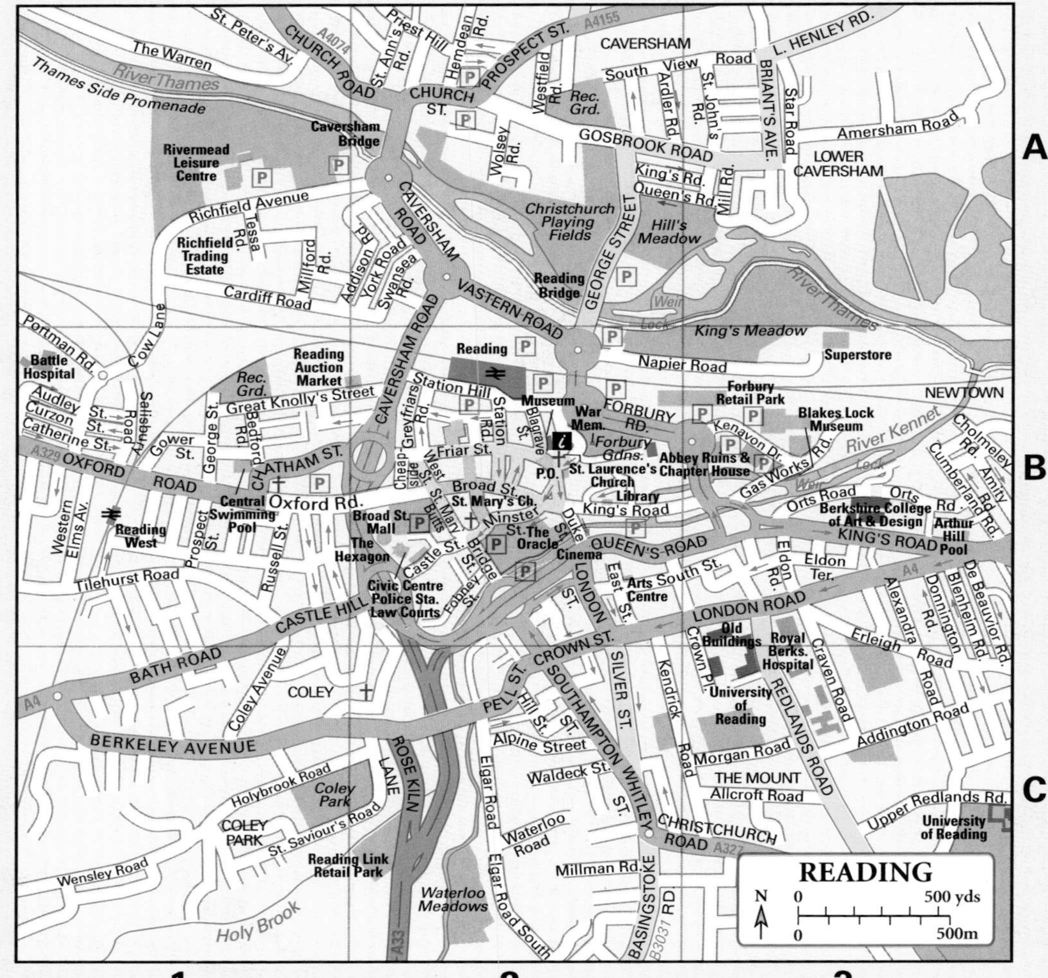

WEB-SITE www.reading.gov.uk

LOCAL RADIO: BBC RADIO BERKSHIRE 104.4 FM; CLASSIC GOLD 1431 AM, 2-TEN FM 97 FM

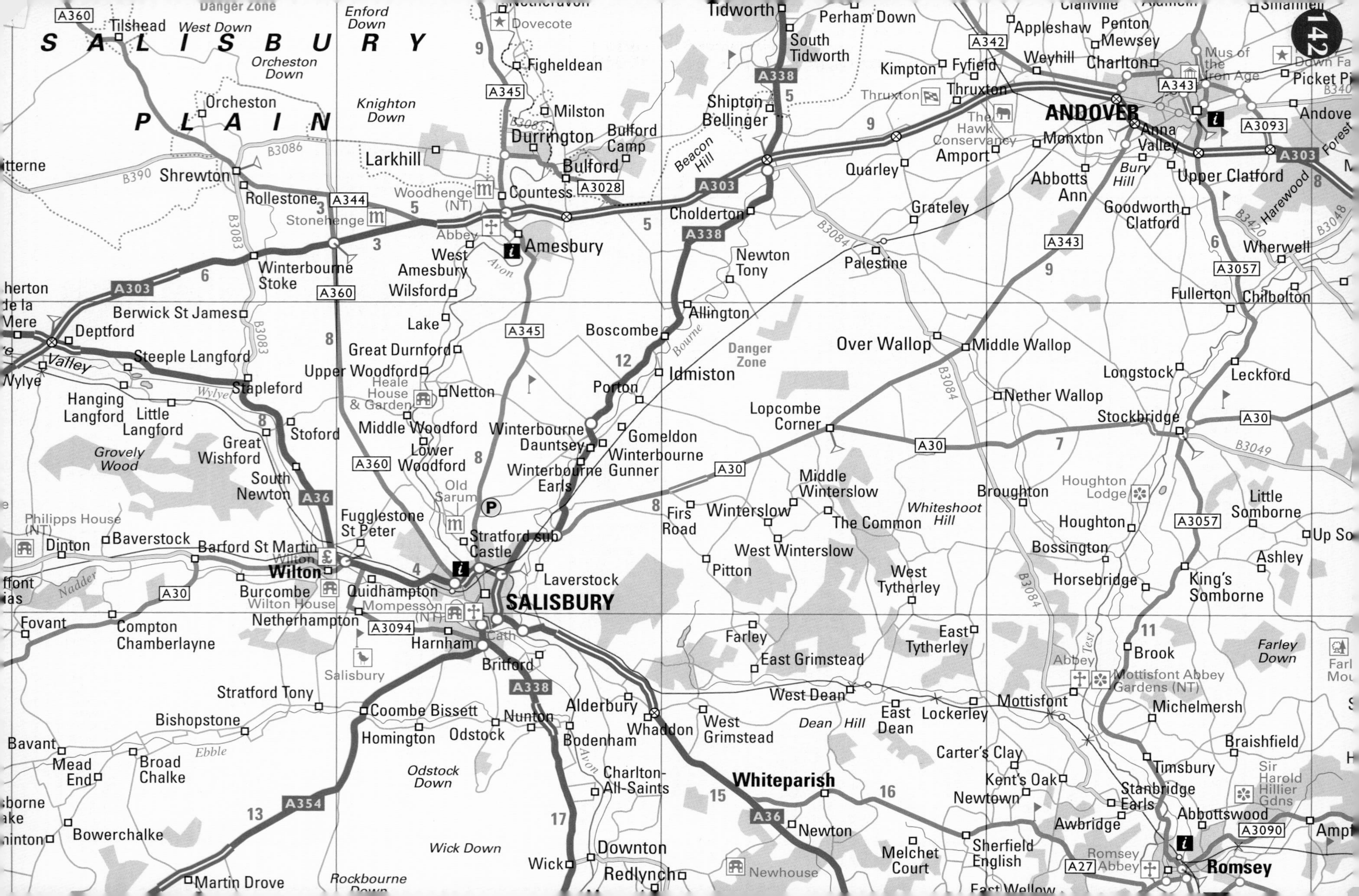

SALISBURY PLAIN

A360 Tilshead West Down Enford Down Orcheston Down Orcheston Knighton Down Dovecote Figheldean A345 Milston Durrington Bulford Camp Bulford Larkhill B3086 B390 Shrewton Rollestone A344 Stonehenge Woodhenge (NT) Countess A3028 Abbey Amesbury West Amesbury Avon Winterbourne Stoke A360 Wilsford A303 B3083 Berwick St James Deptford Steeple Langford Valley Wylye Stapleford Hanging Langford Little Langford Great Wishford Stoford Grovely Wood South Newton A36 Great Durnford Upper Woodford Heale House & Garden Netton Lake Middle Woodford Lower Woodford A360 Old Sarum Fugglestone St Peter Stratford sub Castle Philipps House (NT) Dinton Baverstock Barford St Martin Wilton Nadder Burcombe Wilton House Quidhampton Mompesson (NT) A30 Fovant Compton Chamberlayne Netherhampton A3094 Harnham Cath Salisbury Britford A338 Stratford Tony Bishopstone Coombe Bissett Homington Odstock Nunton Bodenham Alderbury Whaddon Bavant Mead End Broad Chalke Ebble Odstock Down Charlton-All-Saints Bowerchalke A354 Wick Down Wick Downton Redlynch Martin Drove Rockbourne Down

SALISBURY Laverstock Tidworth South Tidworth Perham Down A338 Shipton Bellinger Beacon Hill A303 Cholderton Newton Tony Allington Boscombe A345 Bourne Idmiston Porton Danger Zone Winterbourne Dauntsey Gomeldon Winterbourne Gunner Winterbourne Earls Firs Road Winterslow West Winterslow Pitton Middle Winterslow The Common Lopcombe Corner A30 Farley East Grimstead West Dean Dean Hill West Grimstead East Dean Whiteparish A36 Newton Newhouse Melchet Court

Kimpton Fyfield Thruxton The Hawk Conservancy Amport Quarley Grateley B3084 Palestine Over Wallop Middle Wallop Nether Wallop Appleshaw Weyhill A342 Penton Mewsey Charlton ANDOVER Monxton Abbotts Ann Anna Valley Bury Hill Upper Clatford Goodworth Clatford A343 Mus of the Iron Age A3093 Andover Picket Piece Down Farm Harewood Forest B3420 B3048 Wherwell A3057 Chilbolton Fullerton Longstock Leckford Stockbridge B3049 A30 Broughton Houghton Lodge Houghton Bossington Horsebridge Whiteshoot Hill West Tytherley East Tytherley Little Somborne Up Somborne Ashley King's Somborne A3057 Brook Farley Down Abbey Test Mottisfont Abbey Gardens (NT) Mottisfont Lockerley Michelmersh Braishfield Carter's Clay Kent's Oak Newtown Timsbury Stanbridge Earls Awbridge Sir Harold Hillier Gdns Abbotswood A3090 Sherfield English Romsey Abbey A27 Romsey East Wellow

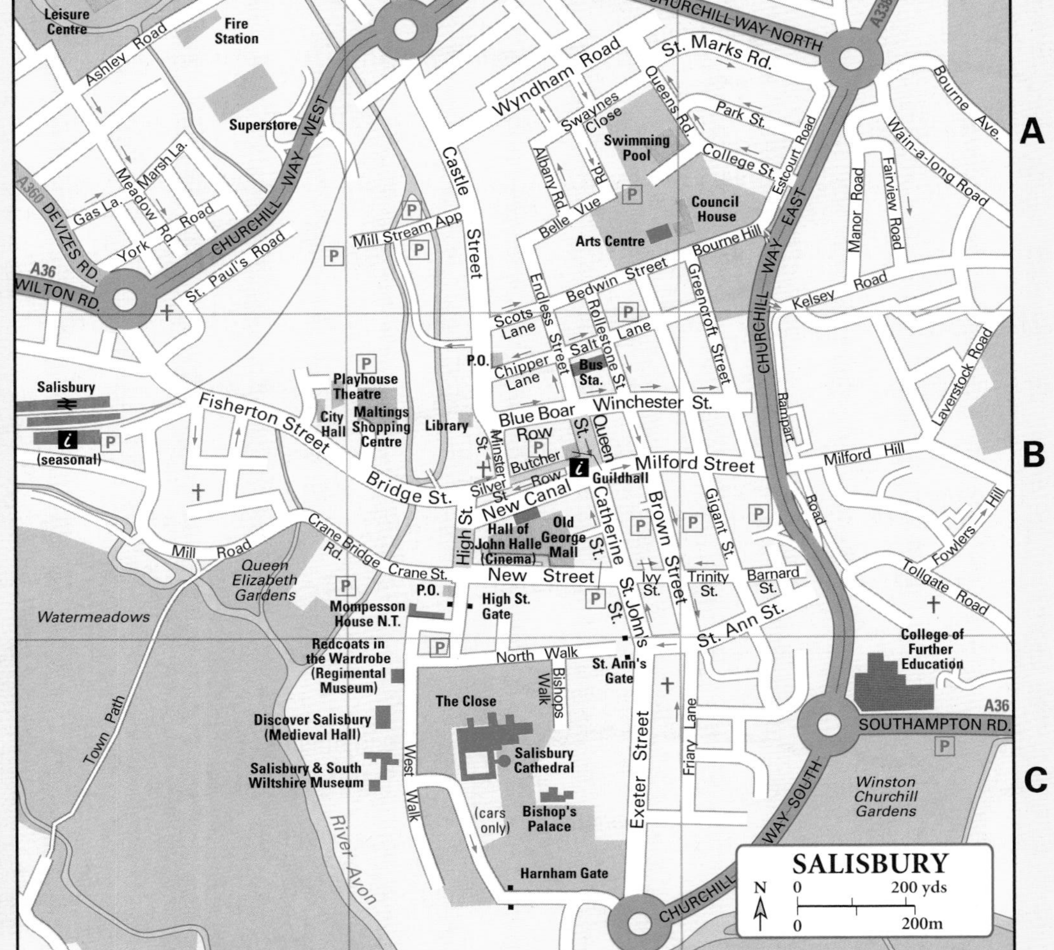

INDEX TO STREET NAMES

Street	Grid	Street	Grid	Street	Grid
Albany Road	A2	Crane Street	B2	New Street	B2
Ashley Road	A1	Devizes Road	A1	North Walk	C2
Barnard Street	B3	Endless Street	A2	Park Street	A3
Bedwin Street	A2	Estcourt Road	A3	Queen Street	B2
Belle Vue Road	A2	Exeter Street	C2	Queens Road	A2
Bishops Walk	C2	Fairview Road	A3	Rampart Road	B3
Blue Boar Row	B2	Fisherton Street	B1	Rollestone Street	B2
Bourne Avenue	A3	Fowlers Hill	B3	St. Ann Street	C3
Bourne Hill	A3	Friary Lane	C3	St. John's Street	B2
Bridge Street	B2	Gas Lane	A1	St. Marks Road	A2
Brown Street	B2	Gigant Street	B3	St. Paul's Road	A1
Butcher Row	B2	Greencroft Street	A3	Salt Lane	B2
Castle Street	A2	High Street	B2	Scots Lane	B2
Catherine Street	B2	Ivy Street	B2	Silver Street	B2
Chipper Lane	B2	Kelsey Road	A3	Southampton Road	C3
Churchill Way East	B3	Laverstock Road	B3	Swaynes Close	A2
Churchill Way North	A2	Manor Road	A3	Tollgate Road	B3
Churchill Way South	C2	Marsh Lane	A1	Trinity Street	B3
Churchill Way West	A1	Meadow Road	A1	Wain-a-long Road	A3
College Street	A3	Milford Hill	B3	West Walk	C2
Crane Bridge Road	B1	Milford Street	B2	Wilton Road	A1
		Mill Road	B1	Winchester Street	B2
		Millstream Approach	A2	Wyndham Road	A2
		Minster Street	B2	York Road	A1
		New Canal	B2		

TOURIST INFORMATION ☎ 01722 334956
FISH ROW,
SALISBURY, SP1 1EJ

HOSPITAL A & E ☎ 01722 336262
SALISBURY DISTRICT HOSPITAL, ODSTOCK ROAD,
SALISBURY, SP2 8BJ

COUNCIL OFFICE ☎ 01722 336272
THE COUNCIL HOUSE, BOURNE HILL,
SALISBURY, SP1 3UZ

Salisbury *(Former and official name New Sarum) Wilts.* Population: 39,268. Cathedral city at confluence of Rivers Avon and Nadder, 21m/34km NW of Southampton. Shopping centre and market town, with buildings ranging from medieval to Victorian; several medieval churches. Cathedral, in Early English style, built between 1220 and 1260, has the tallest spire in England at 123m/404ft.

WEB-SITE	www.salisbury.gov.uk

LOCAL RADIO	BBC WILTSHIRE SOUND 103.5 FM, 1368 AM SPIRE FM 102 FM

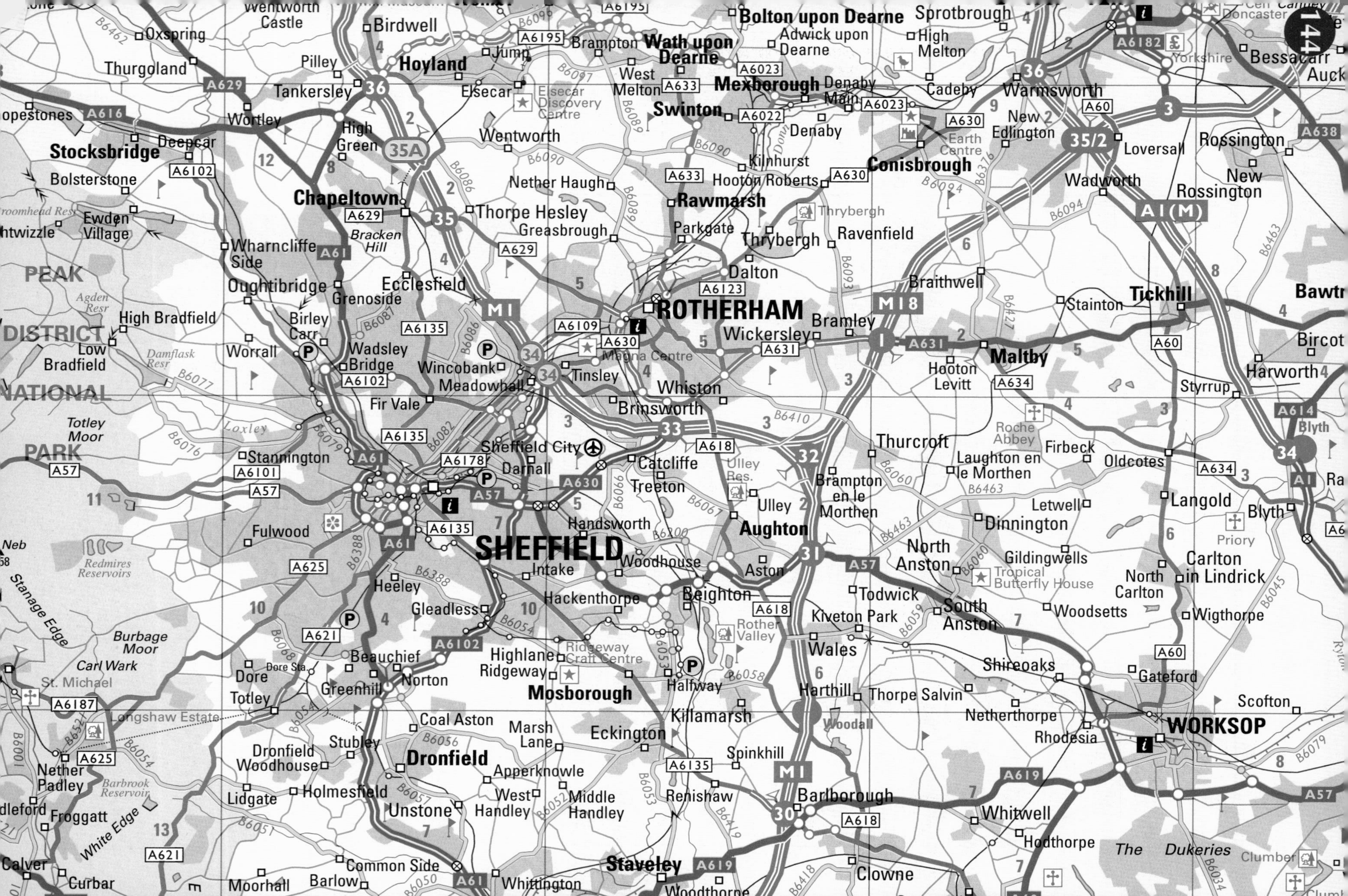
SHEFFIELD
ROTHERHAM
WORKSOP
Stocksbridge
Chapeltown
Hoyland
Wath upon Dearne
Bolton upon Dearne
Mexborough
Swinton
Conisbrough
Rawmarsh
Tickhill
Maltby
Bawtr
Dronfield
Mosborough
Aughton
Staveley
PEAK
DISTRICT
NATIONAL
PARK
Oxspring
Thurgoland
Pilley
Tankersley
Birdwell
Jump
Elsecar
Elsecar Discovery Centre
Wentworth
Wentworth Castle
Brampton
West Melton
Adwick upon Dearne
Sprotbrough
High Melton
Cadeby
Denaby Main
Denaby
Earth Centre
Warmsworth
New Edlington
Loversall
Rossington
New Rossington
Wadworth
Bessacarr
Auck
Yorkshire
Wortley
Deepcar
Bolsterstone
Ewden Village
High Green
Thorpe Hesley
Greasbrough
Nether Haugh
Kilnhurst
Hooton Roberts
Thrybergh
Ravenfield
Parkgate
Dalton
Braithwell
Stainton
Wharncliffe Side
Bracken Hill
Ecclesfield
Grenoside
Oughtibridge
Birley Carr
High Bradfield
Low Bradfield
Agden Resr
Damflask Resr
Worrall
Wadsley Bridge
Wincobank
Meadowhall
Tinsley
Magna Centre
Wickersley
Bramley
Hooton Levitt
Whiston
Brinsworth
Fir Vale
Totley Moor
Loxley
Stannington
Sheffield City
Darnall
Catcliffe
Treeton
Ulley Res.
Ulley
Thurcroft
Brampton en le Morthen
Laughton en le Morthen
Roche Abbey
Firbeck
Oldcotes
Styrrup
Harworth
Bircot
Blyth
Langold
Letwell
Dinnington
Gildingwells
Tropical Butterfly House
North Anston
South Anston
Todwick
Kiveton Park
Wales
Carlton in Lindrick
North Carlton
Woodsetts
Wigthorpe
Priory
Fulwood
Redmires Reservoirs
Handsworth
Woodhouse
Intake
Aston
Beighton
Hackenthorpe
Heeley
Gleadless
Rother Valley
Stanage Edge
Burbage Moor
Carl Wark
St. Michael
Dore
Dore Sta.
Totley
Beauchief
Greenhill
Norton
Highlane
Ridgeway
Ridgeway Craft Centre
Halfway
Killamarsh
Harthill
Woodall
Thorpe Salvin
Shireoaks
Netherthorpe
Rhodesia
Gateford
Scofton
Longshaw Estate
Nether Padley
Barbrook Reservoir
Froggatt
White Edge
Calver
Curbar
Coal Aston
Stubley
Dronfield Woodhouse
Holmesfield
Lidgate
Unstone
Apperknowle
Marsh Lane
West Handley
Middle Handley
Eckington
Spinkhill
Renishaw
Barlborough
Whitwell
Hodthorpe
The Dukeries
Clumber
Clowne
Woodthorpe
Whittington
Common Side
Barlow
Moorhall
M1
M18
A1(M)
A1
A57
A61
A60
A616
A629
A6102
A6135
A6109
A630
A631
A634
A618
A619
A621
A625
A6187
A6101
A6178
A6123
A633
A6022
A6023
A6195
A6182
A638
A614

INDEX TO STREET NAMES

Street	Grid	Street	Grid	Street	Grid
Allen Street	A2	Eyre Street	C2	Portobello Street	B1
Angel Street	A3	Fitzwilliam Street	B1	Queen Street	A2
Arundel Gate	B3	Flat Street	A3	Rockingham Street	B2
Arundel Street	C2	Furnace Hill	A2	St. Mary's Gate	C2
Bank Street	A3	Furnival Gate	B2	St. Mary's Road	C2
Barker's Pool	B2	Furnival Square	B2	St. Philip's Road	A1
Best Street	A1	Furnival Street	B2	Scotland Street	A2
Blonk Street	A3	Garden Street	A1	Sheaf Square	B3
Bridge Street	A3	Gell Street	B1	Sheaf Street	B3
Broad Lane	B1	Gibraltar Street	A2	Shepherd Street	A2
Broomhall Street	C1	Glossop Road	B1	Shoreham Street	C3
Brown Street	C3	Hanover Way	C1	Shrewsbury Road	C3
Brunswick Street	B1	Harmer Lane	B3	Sidney Street	C2
Campo Lane	A2	Haymarket	A3	Snig Hill	A3
Carver Street	B2	Headford Street	C1	Solly Street	A1
Castle Square	A3	High Street	A3	Spring Street	A2
Castlegate	A3	Hollis Croft	A2	Suffolk Road	C3
Cavendish Street	B1	Howard Street	B3	Surrey Street	B2
Charles Street	B2/B3	Hoyle Street	A1	Tenter Street	A2
Charter Row	C2	Leadmill Road	C3	The Moor	C2
Charter Square	B2	Leopold Street	B2	Thomas Street	C1
Church Street	A2	Mappin Street	B1	Townhead Street	A2
Commercial Street	A3	Matilda Street	C3	Trippet Lane	B2
Corporation Street	A2	Meadow Street	A1	Upper Allen Street	A1
Devonshire Street	B1	Moore Street	C1	Upper Hanover Street	B1
Division Street	B2	Netherthorpe Road	A1	Waingate	A3
Dover Street	A1	Norfolk Street	B3	Wellington Street	B2
Ecclesall Road	C1	Nursery Street	A3	West Bar	A2
Eldon Street	B2	Pinstone Street	B2	West Street	B2
Exchange Street	A3	Pond Hill	B3	Westbar Green	A2
Eyre Lane	C2	Pond Street	B3	Weston Street	A1

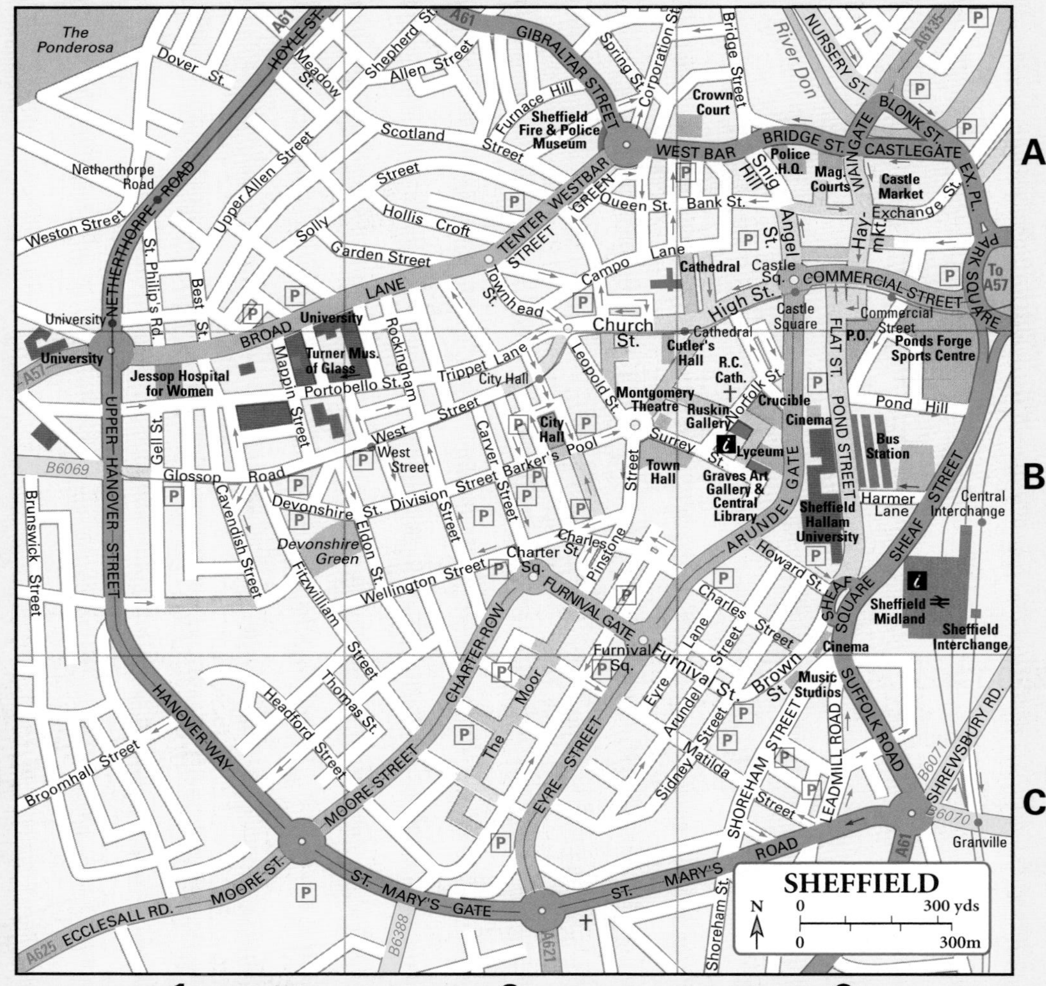

TOURIST INFORMATION ☎ 0114 221 1900
1 TUDOR SQUARE,
SHEFFIELD, S1 2LA

HOSPITAL A & E ☎ 0114 243 4343
NORTHERN GENERAL HOSPITAL, HERRIES ROAD,
SHEFFIELD, S5 7AU

COUNCIL OFFICE ☎ 0114 272 6444
FIRST POINT, 1 UNION STREET,
SHEFFIELD, S1 2LA

WEB-SITE	www.sheffield.gov.uk

LOCAL RADIO	BBC RADIO SHEFFIELD 88.6 FM MAGIC AM, SOUTH YORKSHIRE 1548 AM, HALLAM FM 97.4 FM

Sheffield *S.Yorks.* Population: 431,607. City, on River Don, 144m/232km NW of London. Former centre of heavy steel industry, now largely precision steel and cutlery industries. University of Sheffield and Sheffield Hallam University. Various museums dedicated to Sheffield's industrial past. National Centre for Popular Music in city centre. Meadowhall shopping centre and Sheffield City Airport, 3m/5km NE of city centre.

PORTSMOUTH
SOUTHAMPTON
EASTLEIGH
WATERLOOVILLE
FAREHAM
GOSPORT
LYMINGTON
Romsey
Totton
Hythe
Fawley
Lyndhurst
Cowes
Portchester
Stubbington
Locks Heath
Hedge End
Bishop's Waltham
Wickham
Eling
Beaulieu
East Meon
Horndean
Cosham
Southsea
Lee-on-the-Solent
Hamble-le-Rice
Netley Abbey
Marchwood
Dibden
Blackfield
Calshot
Exbury
Bucklers Hard
East Cowes
Gurnard
Chandler's Ford
Bishopstoke
Fair Oak
Botley
Titchfield
Swanwick
Sarisbury
Warsash
Whiteley
Southwick
Droxford
Meonstoke
Hambledon
Denmead
Purbrook
Bedhampton
Hilsea
Alverstoke
Rowner
Bridgemary
Southampton International
Portsea Island
Whale Island
Portsmouth Harbour
Southampton Water
Gilkicker Point
Stokes Bay
Osborne Bay
Cowes Roads
Stone Point
Forest of Bere
MEON VALLEY
THE SOLENT
Ports Down
M27
M3
M271
M275
A3(M)
A27
A32
A33
A35
A36
A326
A334
A335
A337
A3024
A3025
A3051
A3057
A3090
A2030
A288
hours
Bilbao 35
Caen 6
Cherbourg 2¾-5 (7)
Guernsey 6½
Jersey 10

INDEX TO STREET NAMES

Street	Grid
Above Bar Street	B2
Albert Road North	C3
Bedford Place	A1
Belvidere Road	B3
Bernard Street	C2
Brintons Road	A2
Britannia Road	A3
Briton Street	C2
Canute Road	C2
Castle Way	B2
Central Bridge	C2
Central Road	C2
Chapel Road	B2
Civic Centre Road	B1
Clovelly Road	A2
Commercial Road	A1
Cranbury Avenue	A2
Cumberland Place	A1
Derby Road	A3
Devonshire Road	A1
Dorset Street	A2
East Park Terrace	A2
East Street	B2
Harbour Parade	B1
Herbert Walker Avenue	B1
High Street	B2
Hill Lane	A1
Howard Road	A1
Kingsway	B2
Landguard Road	A1
London Road	A2
Marine Parade	B3
Marsh Lane	B2
Millbank Street	A3
Morris Road	A1
Mount Pleasant Road	A3
New Road	B2
Northam Road	A3
Ocean Way	C2
Onslow Road	A2
Oxford Street	C2
Palmerston Road	B2
Platform Road	C2
Portland Terrace	B1
Princes Street	A3
Queen's Way	C2
Radcliffe Road	A3
St. Andrews Road	A2
St. Mary's Road	A2
St. Mary Street	B2
Shirley Road	A1
Solent Road	B1
Southern Road	B1
Terminus Terrace	C2
Town Quay	C1
Trafalgar Road	C2
West Quay Road	B1
West Road	C2
Western Esplanade	B1
Wilton Avenue	A1

TOURIST INFORMATION ☎ 023 8022 1106
9 CIVIC CENTRE ROAD,
SOUTHAMPTON, SO14 7LP

HOSPITAL A & E ☎ 023 8077 7222
SOUTHAMPTON GENERAL HOSPITAL, TREMONA RD,
SHIRLEY, SOUTHAMPTON, SO16 6YD

COUNCIL OFFICE ☎ 023 8083 3333
CIVIC CENTRE, CIVIC CENTRE ROAD,
SOUTHAMPTON, SO14 7LY

Southampton *S'ham.* Population: 210,138. City, at confluence of Rivers Itchen and Test at head of Southampton Water, 70m/113km SW of London. Southern centre for business, culture and recreation. Container and transatlantic passenger port, dealing with 7 percent of UK's seaborne trade. Site of many famous departures: Henry V's army bound for Agincourt; the Pilgrim Fathers sailed to America on the Mayflower in 1620; maiden voyage of Queen Mary and only voyage of Titanic. Remains of medieval town walls. Medieval Merchant's House (English Heritage) has authentically recreated furnishings. Boat and helicopter ferries to Isle of Wight. Host to many international boating events including Southampton International Boat Show, Whitbread Round the World, and BT Global Challenge. University. Southampton International Airport 1m/2km S of Eastleigh.

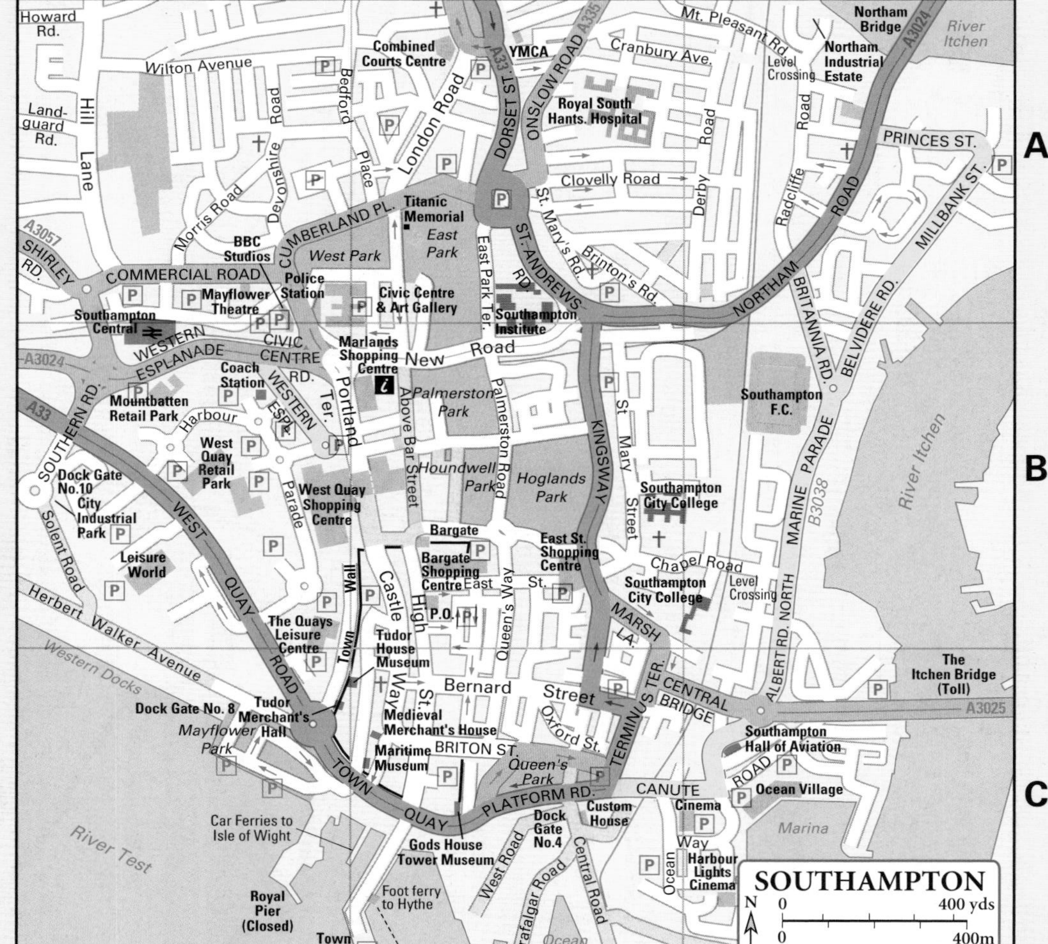

WEB-SITE	www.southampton.gov.uk

LOCAL RADIO	BBC RADIO SOLENT 96.1 FM CAPITAL GOLD 1557 AM, POWER FM 103.2 FM, SOUTH CITY 107.8 FM, WAVE 105.2 FM

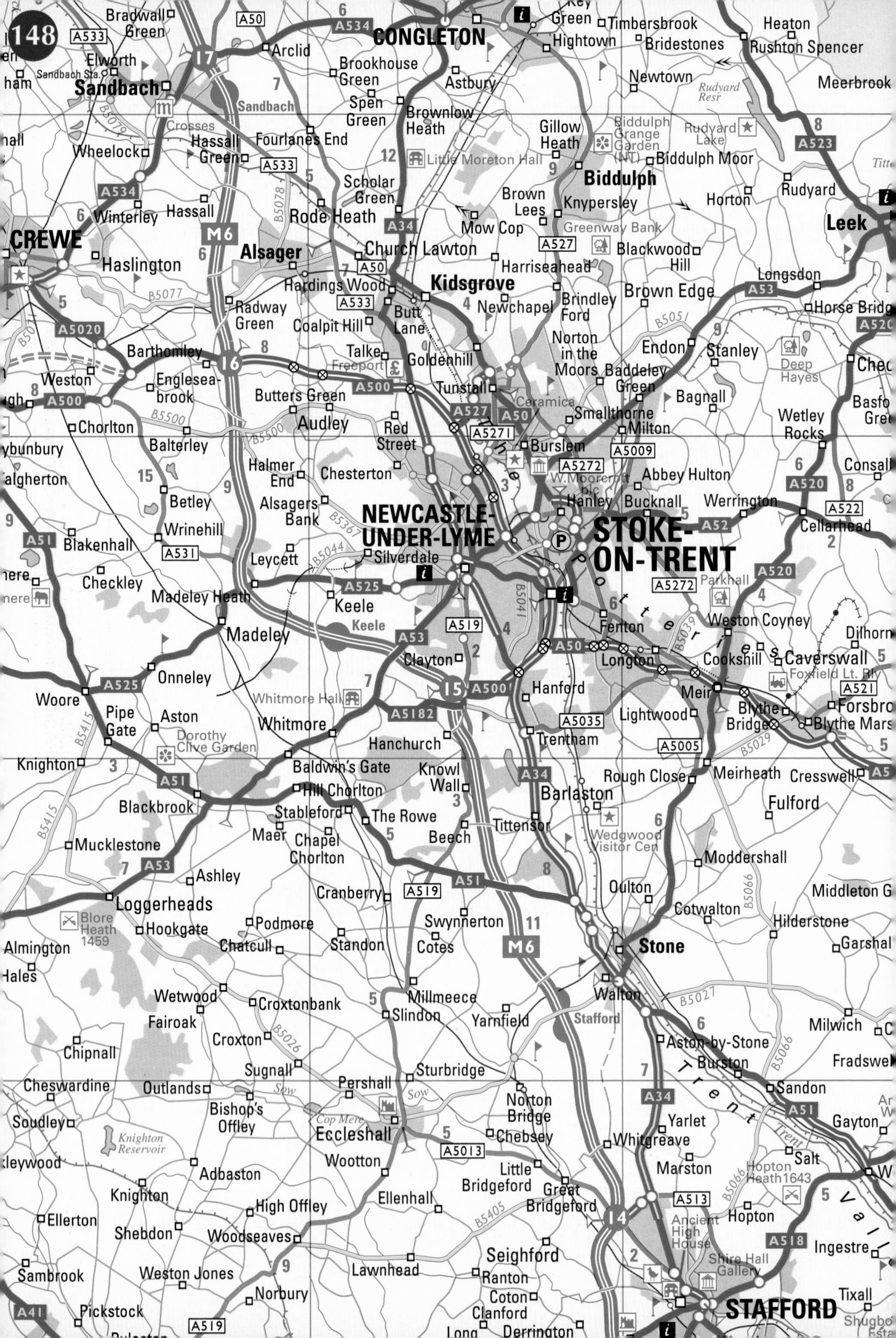
Bradwall Green
A533
A50
A534
CONGLETON
Key Green
Timbersbrook
Heaton
Rushton Spencer
Elworth
Sandbach Sta.
Arclid
Brookhouse Green
Hightown
Bridestones
Sandbach
Astbury
Newtown
Meerbrook
Spen Green
Brownlow Heath
Rudyard Resr
Sandbach
Crosses
Hassall Green
Fourlanes End
Gillow Heath
Biddulph Grange Garden (NT)
Rudyard Lake
Wheelock
A533
Little Moreton Hall
Biddulph Moor
A523
Biddulph
A534
Scholar Green
Brown Lees
Rudyard
Winterley
Hassall
Rode Heath
Knypersley
Horton
CREWE
M6
Alsager
A34
Mow Cop
Greenway Bank
Leek
Haslington
Church Lawton
A527
Blackwood Hill
A50
Harriseahead
Hardings Wood
Kidsgrove
Longsdon
B5077
A533
A53
Radway Green
Butt Lane
Newchapel
Brindley Ford
Brown Edge
Horse Bridge
A5020
Coalpit Hill
B5051
Barthomley
Norton in the Moors
Endon
Stanley
Deep Hayes
Talke
Freeport
Goldenhill
Weston
Englesea-brook
Baddeley Green
Cheddleton
A500
A500
Tunstall
Bagnall
Butters Green
Ceramica
Basford Green
Chorlton
B5500
Audley
Red Street
A527
A50
Smallthorne
Wetley Rocks
Milton
A5271
Burslem
Wybunbury
Balterley
B5500
A5009
Halmer End
Chesterton
A5272
Abbey Hulton
Consall
Walgherton
W. Moorcroft plc
A520
Betley
Hanley
Bucknall
Werrington
Alsagers Bank
NEWCASTLE-UNDER-LYME
A522
Wrinehill
A51
B5367
STOKE-ON-TRENT
A52
Cellarhead
Blakenhall
A531
Leycett
B5044
Silverdale
Checkley
A525
A5272
Parkhall
A520
Madeley Heath
Keele
B5041
Weston Coyney
Dilhorne
Madeley
Keele
A519
Fenton
B5039
Potteries
A53
A50
Longton
Cookshill
Caverswall
Clayton
Foxfield Lt. Rly
Onneley
A525
Whitmore Hall
A500
Hanford
Meir
A521
Woore
Pipe Gate
Aston
A5182
Whitmore
Lightwood
Blythe Bridge
Forsbrook
Blythe Marsh
B5415
Dorothy Clive Garden
A5035
Trentham
Hanchurch
A5005
B5029
Knighton
A51
Baldwin's Gate
Knowl Wall
Rough Close
Meirheath
Cresswell
Blackbrook
Hill Chorlton
A34
Barlaston
Fulford
B5415
Stableford
The Rowe
Tittensor
Maer
Chapel Chorlton
Beech
Wedgwood Visitor Cen
Mucklestone
Moddershall
A53
Ashley
A51
Oulton
Middleton Green
Cranberry
A519
Loggerheads
Cotwalton
B5066
Blore Heath 1459
Podmore
Swynnerton
Hilderstone
Hookgate
Almington
Chatcull
Standon
Cotes
M6
Stone
Garshall Green
Hales
Wetwood
Croxtonbank
Millmeece
Walton
B5027
Fairoak
Slindon
Yarnfield
Stafford
Milwich
Croxton
B5026
Aston-by-Stone
Chipnall
Sugnall
Sturbridge
Burston
B5066
Fradswell
Trent
Cheswardine
Outlands
Pershall
Sow
Sow
Sandon
Bishop's Offley
Norton Bridge
A34
A51
Soudley
Cop Mere
Eccleshall
Yarlet
Gayton
Knighton Reservoir
Chebsey
Whitgreave
Trent
A5013
Salt
Wootton
Little Bridgeford
Marston
Hopton Heath 1643
Adbaston
Knighton
Great Bridgeford
A513
Ellenhall
High Offley
B5066
Hopton
Ellerton
Ancient High House
B5405
Ingestre
Shebdon
Woodseaves
A518
Seighford
Shire Hall Gallery
Sambrook
Weston Jones
Lawnhead
Ranton
Tixall
Norbury
Coton
STAFFORD
Pickstock
A41
Clanford
A519
Long
Derrington
Shugborough Estate

Area Code 01782

STOKE-ON-TRENT

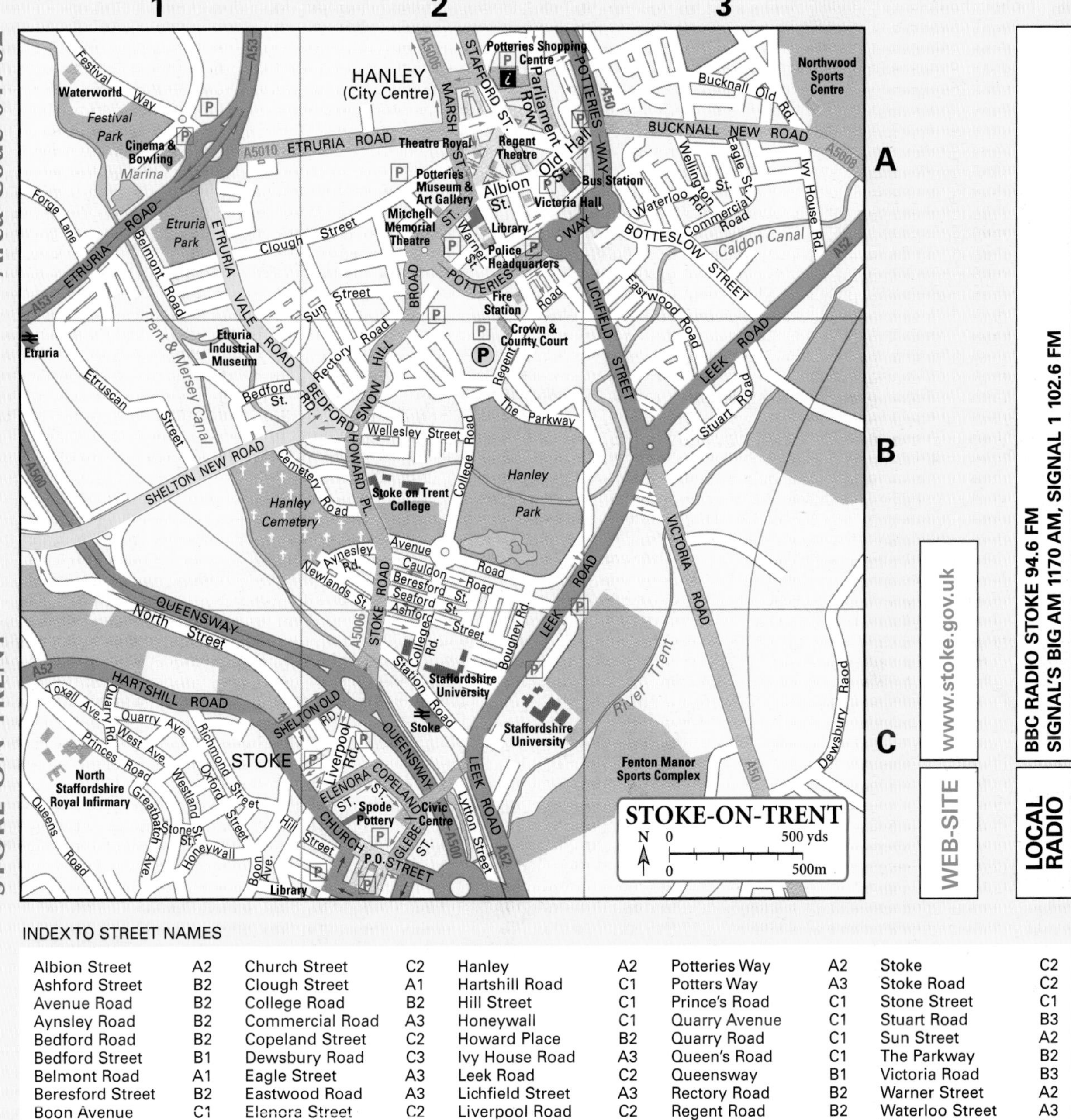

WEB-SITE

www.stoke.gov.uk

LOCAL RADIO

BBC RADIO STOKE 94.6 FM
SIGNAL'S BIG AM 1170 AM, SIGNAL 1 102.6 FM

INDEX TO STREET NAMES

Albion Street	A2	Church Street	C2	Hanley	A2	Potteries Way	A2	Stoke	C2
Ashford Street	B2	Clough Street	A1	Hartshill Road	C1	Potters Way	A3	Stoke Road	C2
Avenue Road	B2	College Road	B2	Hill Street	C1	Prince's Road	C1	Stone Street	C1
Aynsley Road	B2	Commercial Road	A3	Honeywall	C1	Quarry Avenue	C1	Stuart Road	B3
Bedford Road	B2	Copeland Street	C2	Howard Place	B2	Quarry Road	C1	Sun Street	A2
Bedford Street	B1	Dewsbury Road	C3	Ivy House Road	A3	Queen's Road	C1	The Parkway	B2
Belmont Road	A1	Eagle Street	A3	Leek Road	C2	Queensway	B1	Victoria Road	B3
Beresford Street	B2	Eastwood Road	A3	Lichfield Street	A3	Rectory Road	B2	Warner Street	A2
Boon Avenue	C1	Elenora Street	C2	Liverpool Road	C2	Regent Road	B2	Waterloo Street	A3
Botteslow Street	A3	Etruria Road	A1	Lytton Street	C2	Richmond Street	C1	Wellesley Street	B2
Boughey Road	C2	Etruria Vale Road	A1	Marsh Street	A2	Seaford Street	B2	Wellington Road	A3
Broad Street	A2	Etruscan Street	B1	Newlands Street	B2	Shelton New Road	B1	West Avenue	C1
Bucknall New Road	A3	Festival Way	A1	North Street	B1	Shelton Old Road	C1	Westland Street	C1
Bucknall Old Road	A3	Forge Lane	A1	Old Hall Street	A2	Snow Hill	B2	Yoxall Avenue	C1
Cauldon Road	B2	Glebe Street	C2	Oxford Street	C1	Stafford Street	A2		
Cemetery Road	B1	Greatbatch Avenue	C1	Parliament Row	A2	Station Road	C2		

TOURIST INFORMATION ☎ 01782 236000
POTTERIES SHOPPING CENTRE, QUADRANT RD,
STOKE-ON-TRENT, ST1 1RZ

HOSPITAL A & E ☎ 01782 715444
NORTH STAFFORDSHIRE ROYAL INFIRMARY,
PRINCE'S ROAD, STOKE-ON-TRENT, ST4 7LN

COUNCIL OFFICE ☎ 01782 234567
TOWN HALL, CIVIC CENTRE, GLEBE STREET,
STOKE-ON-TRENT, ST4 1RN

Stoke-on-Trent *Stoke* Population: 266,543. City, on River Trent, 135m/217km NW of London. Centre for employment, shopping and leisure. Created by an amalgamation of former Stoke-upon-Trent and the towns of Burslem, Fenton, Hanley, Longton and Tunstall in 1910. Capital of The Potteries (largest claywear producer in the world), now largely a finishing centre for imported pottery. Many pottery factories open to public including Wedgewood, Royal Doulton and Spode. Potteries Museum in Hanley charts history of the potteries. Gladstone Pottery Museum in Longton is centred around large bottle-kiln and demonstrates traditional skills of pottery production. Staffordshire University.

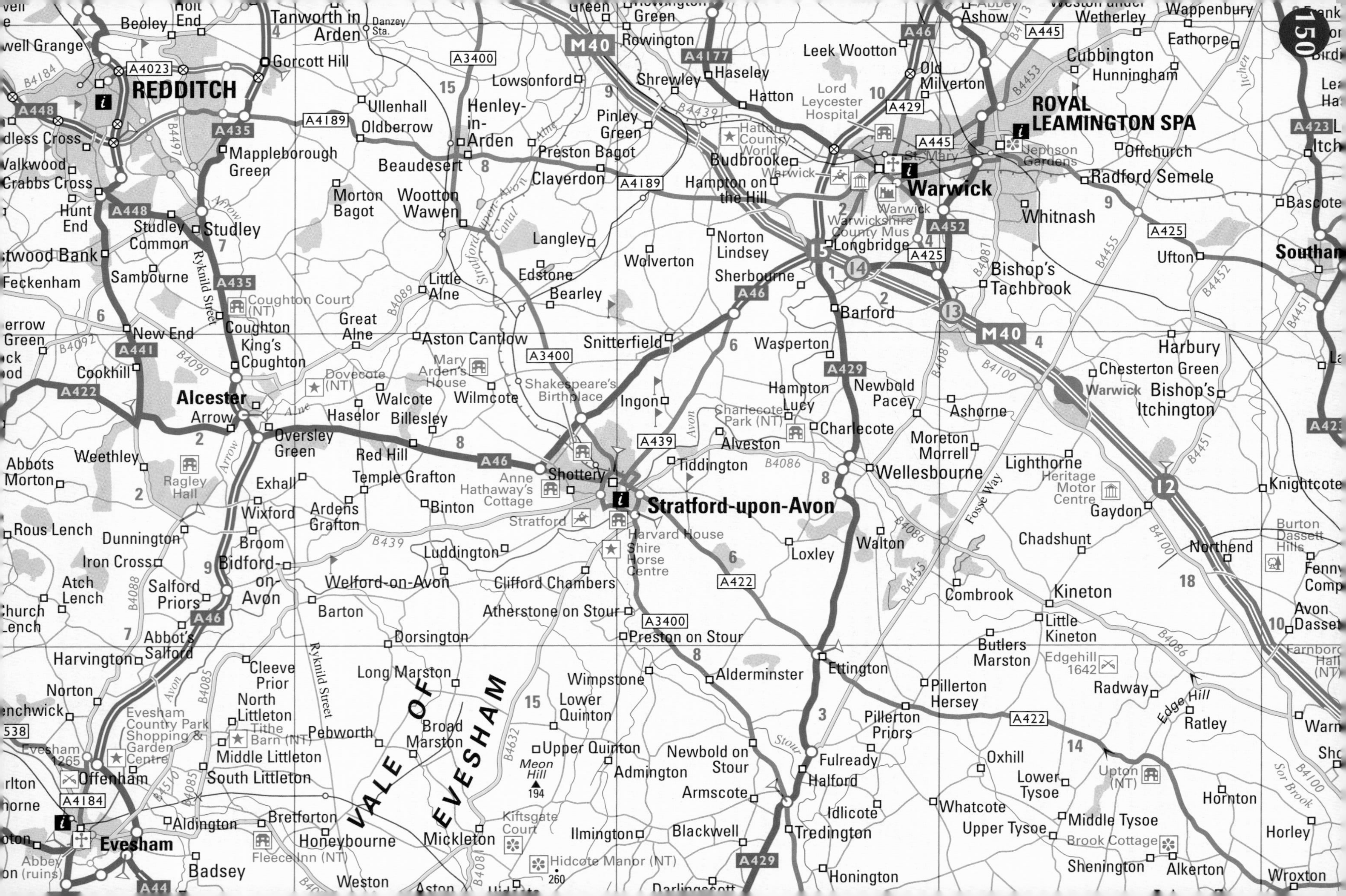

Tanworth in Arden
Danzey Sta.
Beoley
Holt End
Gorcott Hill
Redditch
Lowsonford
Rowington
Shrewley
Haseley
Leek Wootton
Old Milverton
Ashow
Wetherley
Wappenbury
Eathorpe
Cubbington
Hunningham
Royal Leamington Spa
Jephson Gardens
Offchurch
Radford Semele
Bascote
Southam
Ullenhall
Oldberrow
Henley-in-Arden
Pinley Green
Hatton
Lord Leycester Hospital
Hatton Country World
Budbrooke
St. Mary
Warwick
Whitnash
Mappleborough Green
Beaudesert
Preston Bagot
Claverdon
Hampton on the Hill
Warwickshire County Mus
Crabbs Cross
Hunt End
Studley Common
Studley
Morton Bagot
Wootton Wawen
Langley
Norton Lindsey
Longbridge
Bishop's Tachbrook
Ufton
Sambourne
Ryknild Street
Stratford-upon-Avon Canal
Wolverton
Sherbourne
Barford
Feckenham
Coughton Court (NT)
Coughton
Little Alne
Edstone
Bearley
Snitterfield
Wasperton
Harbury
New End
King's Coughton
Great Alne
Aston Cantlow
Chesterton Green
Cookhill
Dovecote (NT)
Mary Arden's House
Shakespeare's Birthplace
Hampton Lucy
Newbold Pacey
Bishop's Itchington
Alcester
Arrow
Walcote
Wilmcote
Ingon
Charlecote Park (NT)
Charlecote
Ashorne
Haselor
Billesley
Alveston
Moreton Morrell
Weethley
Oversley Green
Red Hill
Tiddington
Wellesbourne
Lighthorne
Heritage Motor Centre
Knightcote
Abbots Morton
Ragley Hall
Exhall
Temple Grafton
Anne Hathaway's Cottage
Shottery
Stratford-upon-Avon
Fosse Way
Gaydon
Wixford
Ardens Grafton
Binton
Stratford
Harvard House
Shire Horse Centre
Walton
Loxley
Chadshunt
Burton Dassett Hills
Northend
Rous Lench
Dunnington
Broom
Iron Cross
Bidford-on-Avon
Luddington
Welford-on-Avon
Clifford Chambers
Combrook
Kineton
Atch Lench
Salford Priors
Barton
Atherstone on Stour
Little Kineton
Avon Dassett
Abbot's Salford
Dorsington
Preston on Stour
Butlers Marston
Edgehill 1642
Harvington
Cleeve Prior
Long Marston
Wimpstone
Alderminster
Ettington
Pillerton Hersey
Radway
Norton
North Littleton
Tithe Barn (NT)
Lower Quinton
Pillerton Priors
Edge Hill
Ratley
Evesham Country Park Shopping & Garden Centre
Pebworth
Vale of Evesham
Broad Marston
Upper Quinton
Meon Hill 194
Newbold on Stour
Fulready
Oxhill
Lower Tysoe
Upton (NT)
Hornton
Offenham
Middle Littleton
South Littleton
Admington
Halford
Armscote
Idlicote
Whatcote
Upper Tysoe
Middle Tysoe
Brook Cottage
Horley
Evesham
Aldington
Bretforton
Honeybourne
Fleece Inn (NT)
Mickleton
Kiftsgate Court
Hidcote Manor (NT) 260
Ilmington
Blackwell
Tredington
Honington
Shenington
Alkerton
Wroxton
Abbey (ruins)
Badsey
Weston
Sor Brook
Itchen
Arrow
Alne
Avon
Stour

INDEX TO STREET NAMES

Street	Ref	Street	Ref	Street	Ref
Albany Road	B1	Great William Street	A2	Sanctus Street	C1
Alcester Road	A1	Greenhill Street	B1	Sandfield Road	C1
Arden Street	A1	Grove Road	B1	Scholar's Lane	B1
Avonside	C2	Guild Street	A2	Shakespeare Street	A2
Banbury Road	B3	Henley Street	A2	Sheep Street	B2
Bancroft Place	B3	High Street	B2	Shipston Road	C3
Birmingham Road	A1	John Street	A2	Shottery Road	B1
Bridgefoot	B3	Kendall Avenue	A2	Seven Meadow Road	C1
Bridge Street	B2	Maidenhead Road	A2	Southern Lane	C2
Bridgeway	B3	Mansell Street	A1	Station Road	A1
Bridgetown Road	C3	Meer Street	B2	Swans Nest Lane	B3
Broad Street	C1	Mill Lane	C2	Tiddington Road	B3
Broad Walk	C1	Mulberry Street	A2	Trinity Street	C2
Bull Street	C1	Narrow Lane	C1	Tyler Street	A2
Chapel Lane	B2	New Street	C2	Union Street	B2
Chapel Street	B2	Old Town	C2	Warwick Road	A3
Cherry Orchard	C1	Old Tramway Walk	C3	Waterside	B2
Chestnut Walk	B1	Orchard Way	C1	Welcombe Road	A3
Church Street	B2	Payton Street	A2	Westbourne Grove	B1
Clopton Bridge	B3	Rother Street	B1	Western Road	A1
Clopton Road	A2	Ryland Street	C2	West Street	C1
College Lane	C2	St. Andrews Crescent	B1	Windsor Street	B2
College Street	C2	St. Gregory's Road	A2	Wood Street	B2
Ely Street	B2	Sanctus Road	C1		
Evesham Place	C1				
Evesham Road	C1				

TOURIST INFORMATION ☎ 01789 293127
BRIDGEFOOT,
STRATFORD-UPON-AVON, CV37 6GW

HOSPITAL A & E ☎ 01926 495321
WARWICK HOSPITAL, WAKIN ROAD,
WARWICK, CV34 5BW

COUNCIL OFFICE ☎ 01789 267575
COUNCIL OFFICES, ELIZABETH HOUSE,
CHURCH ST, STRATFORD-UPON-AVON, CV37 6HX

Stratford-upon-Avon (Also called Stratford-on-Avon.) *Warks.* Population: 22,231. Town, on River Avon, 8m/13km SW of Warwick. Tourist centre. Many attractive 16c buildings. Reconstructed Shakespeare's Birthplace. Elizabethan garden at New Place. Hall's Croft Elizabethan town house and doctor's dispensary. Royal Shakespeare Theatre. Shakespeare's grave at Holy Trinity Church. Anne Hathaway's Cottage to W, at Shottery.

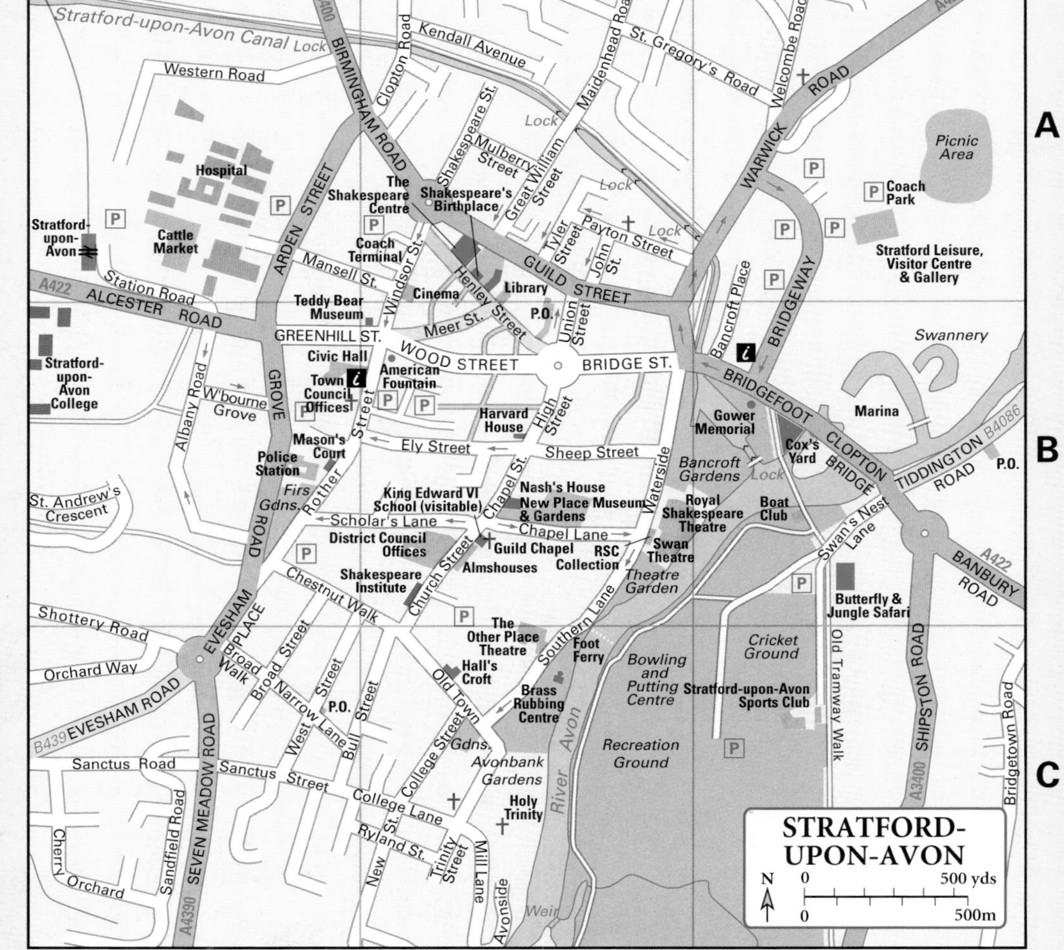

WEB-SITE www.stratford.gov.uk

LOCAL RADIO: BBC RADIO COVENTRY & WARWICKSHIRE 94.8 & 103.7 FM
102 FM - THE BEAR 102 FM

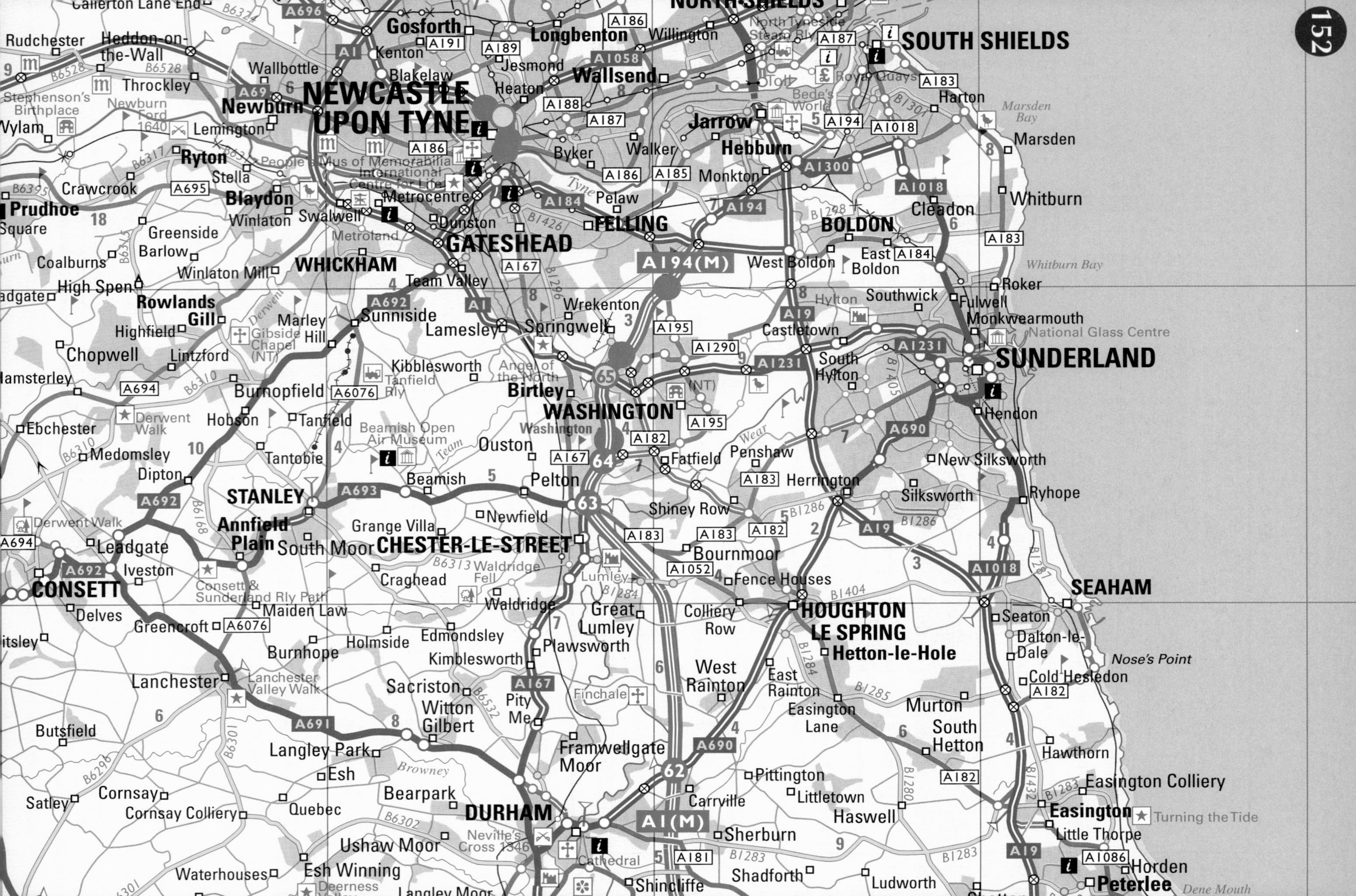
NEWCASTLE UPON TYNE
SOUTH SHIELDS
SUNDERLAND
GATESHEAD
WASHINGTON
CHESTER-LE-STREET
HOUGHTON LE SPRING
DURHAM
SEAHAM
CONSETT
STANLEY
WHICKHAM
FELLING
BOLDON
Gosforth
Longbenton
Willington
Wallsend
Kenton
Blakelaw
Jesmond
Heaton
Wallbottle
Newburn
Throckley
Heddon-on-the-Wall
Rudchester
Callerton Lane End
Stephenson's Birthplace
Wylam
Newburn Ford 1640
Lemington
Ryton
Stella
Crawcrook
Blaydon
Winlaton
Swalwell
Prudhoe
Greenside
Barlow
Coalburns
Winlaton Mill
High Spen
Rowlands Gill
Highfield
Chopwell
Lintzford
Gibside Chapel (NT)
Marley Hill
Sunniside
Lamesley
Team Valley
Metrocentre
Metroland
Dunston
Byker
Walker
Pelaw
Jarrow
Hebburn
Monkton
Bede's World
Royal Quays
North Tyneside Steam Rly
Harton
Marsden Bay
Marsden
Whitburn
Cleadon
East Boldon
West Boldon
Whitburn Bay
Roker
Fulwell
Monkwearmouth
National Glass Centre
Southwick
Hylton
Castletown
South Hylton
Hendon
New Silksworth
Silksworth
Ryhope
Herrington
Penshaw
Fatfield
Shiney Row
Bournmoor
Fence Houses
Wrekenton
Springwell
Angel of the North
Birtley
Kibblesworth
Tanfield Rly
Burnopfield
Hobson
Tanfield
Tantobie
Beamish Open Air Museum
Ouston
Beamish
Pelton
Newfield
Grange Villa
South Moor
Annfield Plain
Craghead
Waldridge Fell
Waldridge
Lumley
Great Lumley
Colliery Row
West Rainton
East Rainton
Hetton-le-Hole
Easington Lane
Murton
South Hetton
Seaton
Dalton-le-Dale
Nose's Point
Cold Hesledon
Hawthorn
Easington Colliery
Easington
Turning the Tide
Little Thorpe
Horden
Peterlee
Dene Mouth
Pittington
Littletown
Haswell
Carrville
Sherburn
Shadforth
Ludworth
Shincliffe
Cathedral
Neville's Cross 1346
Framwellgate Moor
Finchale
Pity Me
Plawsworth
Kimblesworth
Edmondsley
Sacriston
Witton Gilbert
Holmside
Maiden Law
Burnhope
Lanchester
Lanchester Valley Walk
Langley Park
Esh
Bearpark
Ushaw Moor
Esh Winning
Deerness Valley
Langley Moor
Quebec
Cornsay
Cornsay Colliery
Satley
Butsfield
Waterhouses
Greencroft
Delves
Consett & Sunderland Rly Path
Iveston
Leadgate
Derwent Walk
Dipton
Medomsley
Ebchester
Hamsterley
A1
A19
A1(M)
A194(M)
A692
A693
A690
A691
A694
A695
A696
A69
A167
A1231
A1290
A1300
A1018
A1058
A1052
A183
A184
A185
A186
A187
A188
A189
A191
A194
A195
A182
A181
A1086
A6076

INDEX TO STREET NAMES

TOURIST INFORMATION ☎ 0191 553 2000
50 FAWCETT STREET, SUNDERLAND, SR1 1RF

HOSPITAL A & E ☎ 0191 565 6256
SUNDERLAND DISTRICT GENERAL HOSPITAL,
KAYLL ROAD, SUNDERLAND, SR4 7TP

COUNCIL OFFICE ☎ 0191 553 1000
SUNDERLAND CITY COUNCIL, CIVIC CENTRE, BURDON ROAD
SUNDERLAND, SR2 7DN

Sunderland *T. & W.* Population 183,310. Industrial city and seaport at mouth of River Wear, 11m/17km SE of Newcastle upon Tyne. Previously largest ship-building town in the world; coal mining was also important. Several museums celebrate city's industrial past. Service sector and manufacturing account for largest contribution to local economy. National Glass Centre commemorates importance of stained glass to area. University. Airport 4m/6km W.

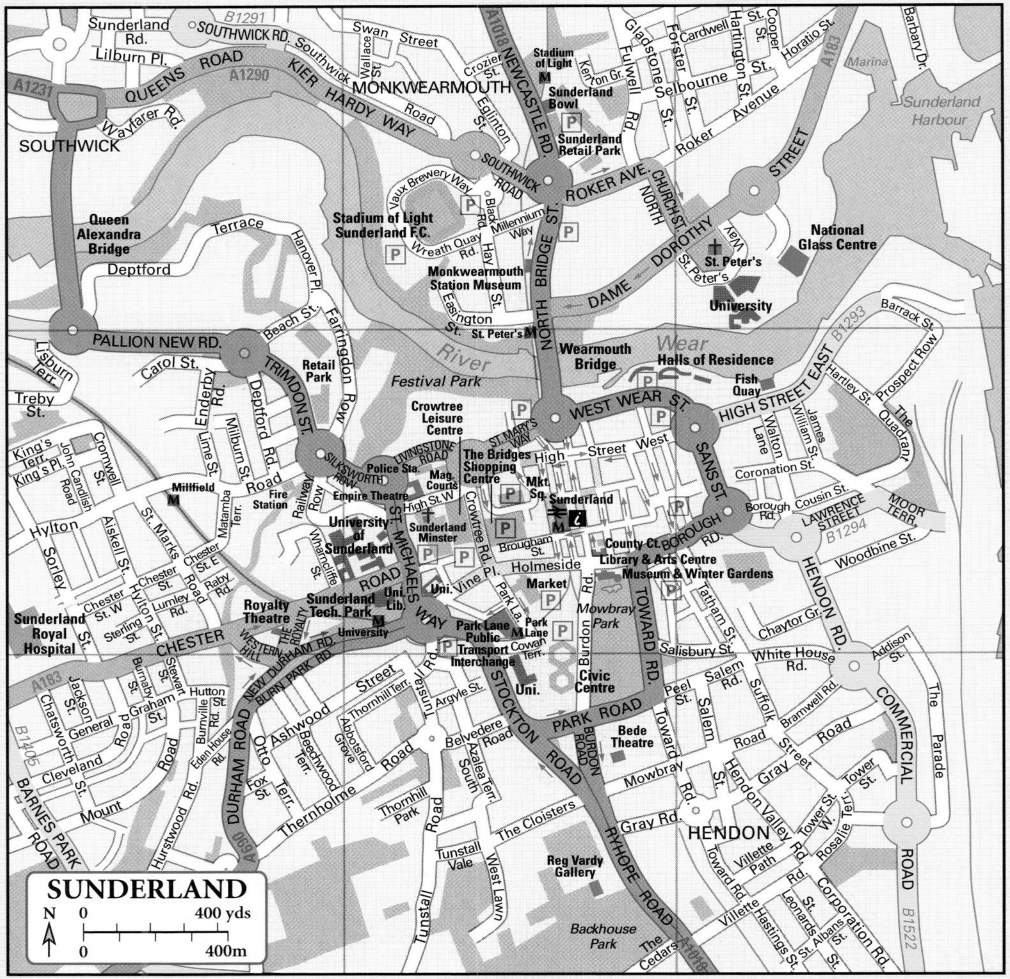

WEB-SITE	www.sunderland.gov.uk

LOCAL RADIO	BBC RADIO NEWCASTLE 95.4 FM, 1458 AM SUN FM 103.4 FM

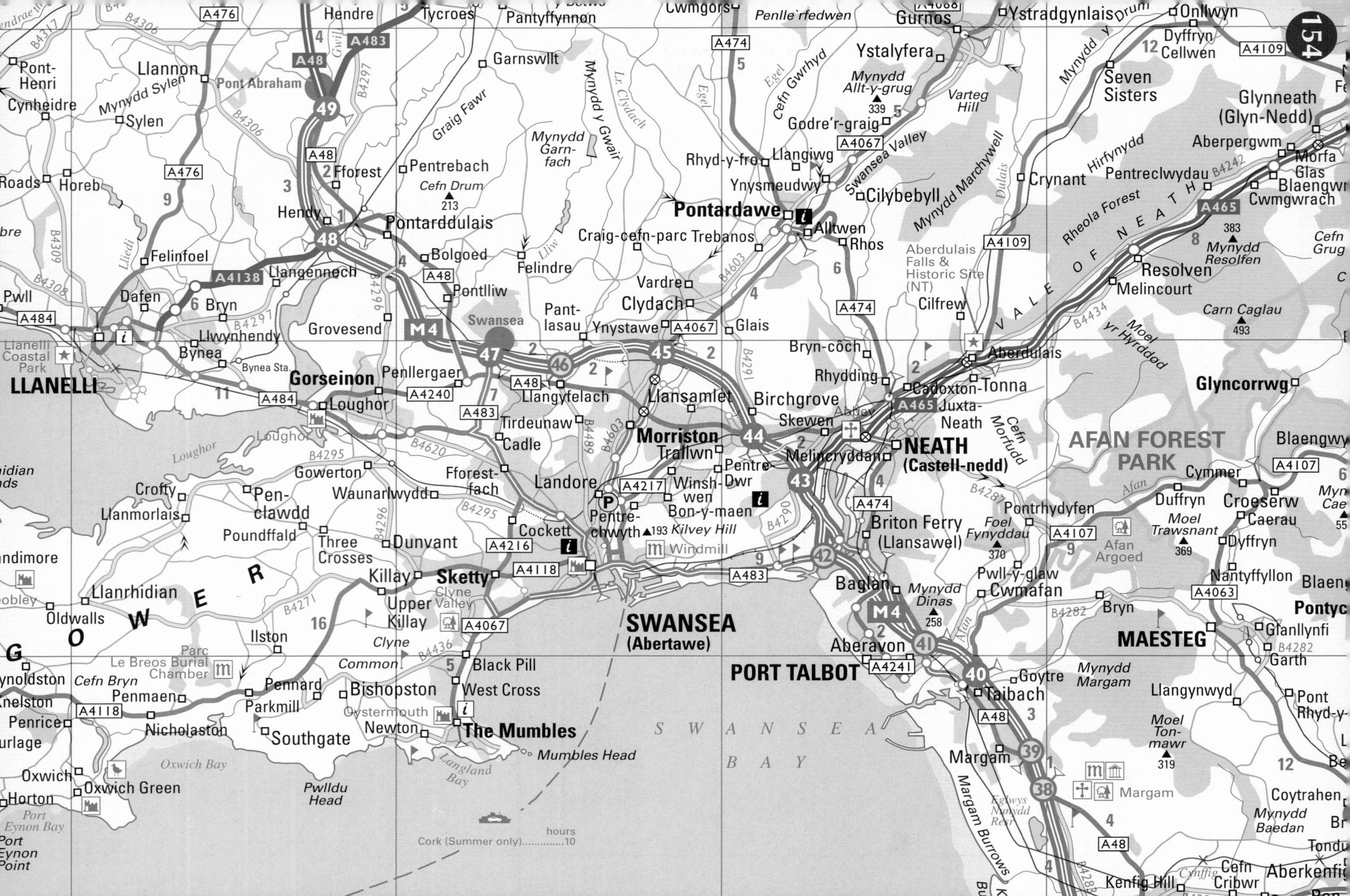

SWANSEA
(Abertawe)
NEATH
(Castell-nedd)
PORT TALBOT
MAESTEG
LLANELLI
AFAN FOREST PARK
VALE OF NEATH
GOWER
SWANSEA BAY
Glynneath
(Glyn-Nedd)
Seven Sisters
Ystradgynlais
Ystalyfera
Gurnos
Cilybebyll
Pontardawe
Glyncorrwg
Resolven
Melincourt
Aberdulais
Tonna
Cadoxton-Juxta-Neath
Cilfrew
Aberdulais Falls & Historic Site (NT)
Rhos
Alltwen
Godre'r-graig
Clydach
Ynystawe
Morriston
Llansamlet
Skewen
Birchgrove
Briton Ferry
(Llansawel)
Baglan
Aberavon
Margam
Taibach
Cymmer
Croeserw
Pontrhydyfen
Cwmafan
Gorseinon
Loughor
Gowerton
Pontarddulais
Pontlliw
Penllergaer
Llangyfelach
Fforest-fach
Sketty
Killay
Dunvant
Three Crosses
Black Pill
West Cross
The Mumbles
Mumbles Head
Bishopston
Southgate
Penmaen
Nicholaston
Oxwich
Oxwich Green
Llanrhidian
Llanmorlais
Crofty
Pen-clawdd
Bynea
Dafen
Felinfoel
Llannon
Hendy
Llangennech
Mynydd y Gwair
Margam Burrows
Kenfig Hill
M4
A48
A483
A465
A474
A4067
A4109
A4107
A4118
A476
A484
A4138
A4240
A4216
A4217
A4241
A4063
Cork (Summer only)..............10 hours

INDEX TO STREET NAMES

Street	Grid
Albert Row	C2
Alexandra Road	B2
Argyle Street	C1
Beach Street	C1
Belle Vue Way	B2
Bond Street	C1
Brooklands Terrace	B1
Brynymor Crescent	C1
Brynymor Road	C1
Burrows Place	C3
Cambrian Place	C3
Carmarthen Road	A2
Castle Street	B2
Clarence Terrace	C2
Constitution Hill	B1
Cromwell Street	B1
De La Beche Street	B2
Delhi Street	B3
Dyfatty Street	A2
Dyfed Avenue	B1
East Burrows Road	C3
Fabian Way	B3
Foxhole Road	A3
Glamorgan Street	C2
Gors Avenue	A1
Grove Place	B2
Gwent Road	A1
Hanover Street	B1
High Street	B2
Islwyn Road	A1
King Edward's Road	C1
Llangyfelach Road	A2
Lower Oxford Street	C1
Mackworth Street	B3
Mansel Street	B1
Mayhill Road	A1
Morris Lane	B3
Mount Pleasant	B2
Mumbles Road	C1
Neath Road	A3
New Cut Road	B3
New Orchard Street	A2
North Hill Road	A2
Orchard Street	B2
Oystermouth Road	C1
Page Street	B2
Pentre Guinea Road	A3
Pen-y-Craig Road	A1
Powys Avenue	A1
Princess Way	B2
Rose Hill	B1
St. Helen's Avenue	C1
St. Helen's Road	C1
St. Mary Street	B2
Singleton Street	C2
Somerset Place	C3
South Guildhall Road	C1
Strand	B3
Terrace Road	B1
The Kingsway	B2
Townhill Road	A1
Vincent Street	C1
Walter Road	C1
Waun-Wen Road	A2
Wellington Street	C2
Westbury Street	C1
Western Street	C1
West Way	C2

TOURIST INFORMATION ☎ 01792 468321
WESTWAY,
SWANSEA, SA1 3QG

HOSPITAL A & E ☎ 01792 702222
MORRISTON HOSPITAL, MORRISTON,
SWANSEA, SA6 6NL

COUNCIL OFFICE ☎ 01792 636000
COUNTY HALL, OYSTERMOUTH ROAD,
SWANSEA, SA1 3SN

Swansea (Abertawe). Population: 171,038. City, port on Swansea Bay at mouth of River Tawe, and Wales' second city, 35m/57km W of Cardiff. Settlement developed next to Norman castle built in 1099, but claims made that a Viking settlement existed before this date. Previously a port for local metal smelting industries. Bombed in World War II, and city centre rebuilt. Birthplace of Dylan Thomas, who described it as 'an ugly, lovely town'. Remains of 14c castle (Cadw) or fortified manor house. University of Wales. Tropical plant and wildlife leisure centre, Plantasia. Airport 5m/9km W at Fairwood Common.

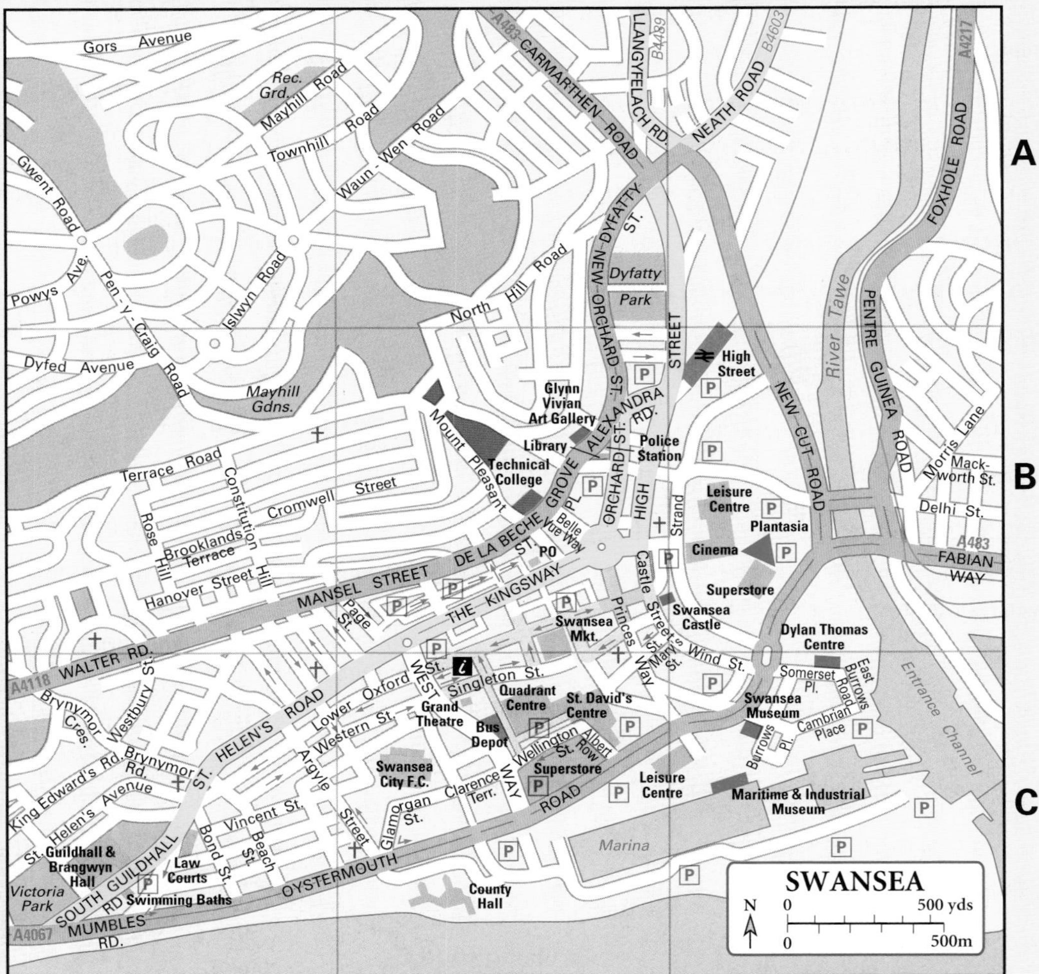

WEB-SITE www.swansea.gov.uk

LOCAL RADIO
BBC RADIO WALES 93.9 FM
SWANSEA SOUND 1170 AM

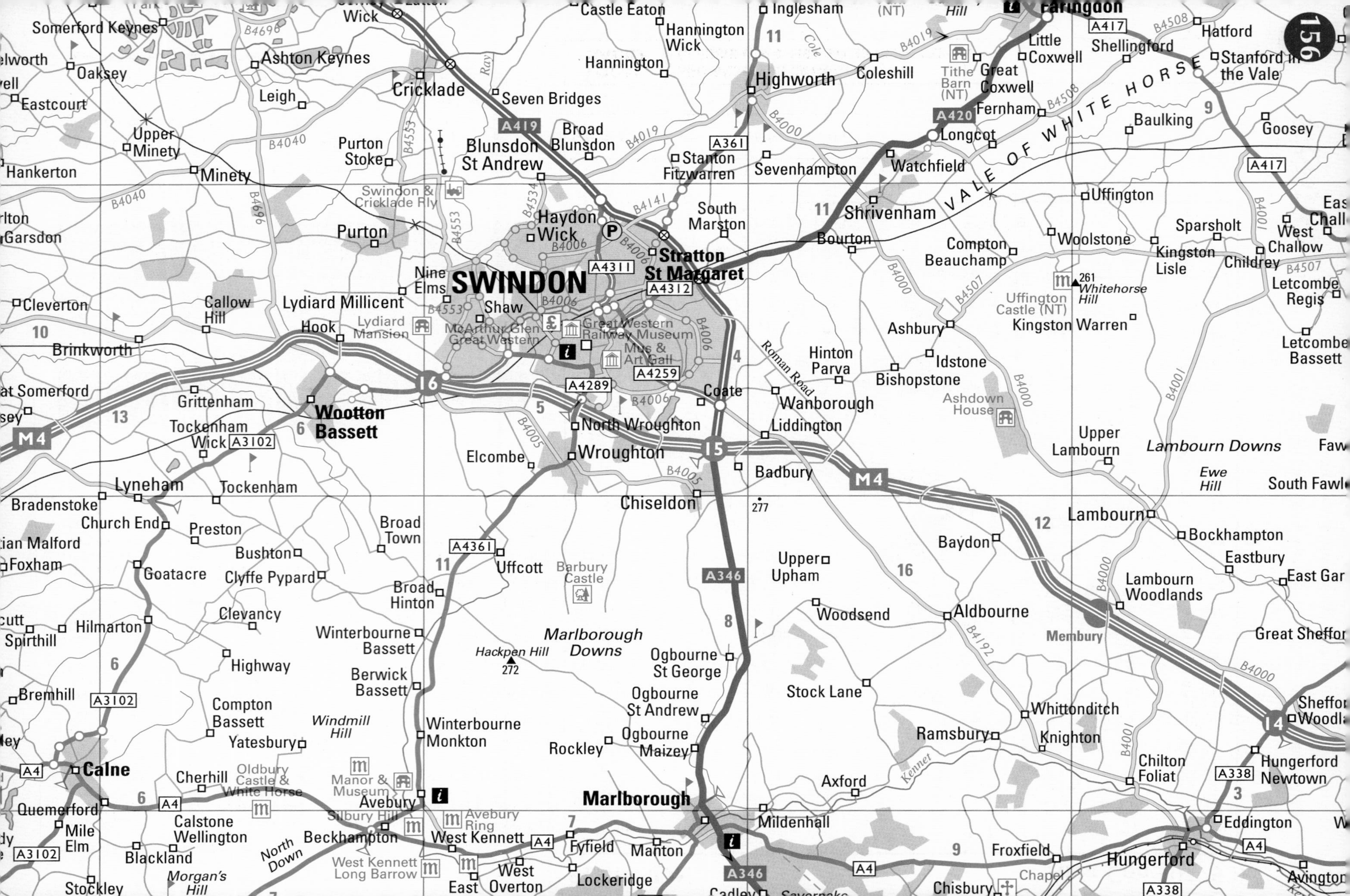
SWINDON
Stratton St Margaret
Highworth
Cricklade
Wootton Bassett
Marlborough
Calne
Faringdon
Hungerford
Somerford Keynes
Ashton Keynes
Oaksey
Eastcourt
Leigh
Upper Minety
Minety
Hankerton
Garsdon
Cleverton
Brinkworth
Callow Hill
Purton
Purton Stoke
Swindon & Cricklade Rly
Seven Bridges
Blunsdon St Andrew
Broad Blunsdon
Castle Eaton
Hannington Wick
Hannington
Inglesham
Coleshill
Stanton Fitzwarren
Sevenhampton
South Marston
Haydon Wick
Nine Elms
Shaw
Lydiard Millicent
Lydiard Mansion
Hook
McArthurGlen Great Western
Great Western Railway Museum
Mus & Art Gall
Grittenham
Tockenham Wick
Tockenham
Lyneham
Bradenstoke
Church End
Preston
Bushton
Goatacre
Clyffe Pypard
Broad Town
Elcombe
North Wroughton
Wroughton
Coate
Chiseldon
Badbury
Liddington
Wanborough
Hinton Parva
Roman Road
Bishopstone
Idstone
Ashbury
Ashdown House
Bourton
Shrivenham
Watchfield
Longcot
Fernham
Great Coxwell
Little Coxwell
Tithe Barn (NT)
VALE OF WHITE HORSE
Shellingford
Hatford
Stanford in the Vale
Baulking
Goosey
Uffington
Woolstone
Compton Beauchamp
Sparsholt
Kingston Lisle
Childrey
West Challow
Letcombe Regis
Letcombe Bassett
Uffington Castle (NT)
Whitehorse Hill
261
Kingston Warren
Upper Lambourn
Lambourn Downs
Ewe Hill
South Fawley
Lambourn
Bockhampton
Eastbury
Lambourn Woodlands
Membury
Great Shefford
Baydon
Aldbourne
Upper Upham
Woodsend
Stock Lane
Whittonditch
Ramsbury
Knighton
Chilton Foliat
Hungerford Newtown
Eddington
Froxfield
Chisbury
Chapel
Avington
Axford
Mildenhall
Kennet
Ogbourne St George
Ogbourne St Andrew
Ogbourne Maizey
Rockley
Marlborough Downs
Hackpen Hill
272
277
Barbury Castle
Uffcott
Broad Hinton
Winterbourne Bassett
Berwick Bassett
Winterbourne Monkton
Windmill Hill
Avebury
Manor & Museum
Avebury Ring
Silbury Hill
Beckhampton
West Kennett
West Kennett Long Barrow
East Overton
West Overton
Fyfield
Manton
Lockeridge
North Down
Oldbury Castle & White Horse
Cherhill
Yatesbury
Compton Bassett
Highway
Clevancy
Hilmarton
Spirthill
Bremhill
Quemerford
Calstone Wellington
Blackland
Mile Elm
Stockley
Morgan's Hill
Foxham
M4
A419
A420
A417
A361
A4311
A4312
A4259
A4289
A346
A4361
A3102
A4
A338
B4696
B4040
B4553
B4534
B4006
B4141
B4019
B4000
B4508
B4507
B4001
B4005
B4192

SWINDON

Area Code 01793

INDEX TO STREET NAMES

Street	Grid	Street	Grid	Street	Grid
Bath Road	C2	Fleet Street	B2	Okus Road	C1
Beatrice Street	A2	Fleming Way	B2	Park Lane	B1
Birch Street	B1	Folkstone Road	C2	Penzance Drive	B1
Bridge Street	B2	Great Western Way	A1	Princes Street	B3
Broad Street	A3	Groundwell Road	B3	Queen Street	B2
Canal Walk	B2	Hawksworth Way	A1	Redcliffe Street	B1
Cirencester Way	A3	High Street	C3	Regent Street	B2
Clifton Street	C2	Hythe Road	C2	Rodbourne Road	A1
Commercial Road	B2	Jennings Street	B1	Rosebery Way	A3
County Road	A3	Kemble Drive	A1	Spring Gardens	B3
Courtsknap Court	B1	Kent Road	C2	Stafford Street	C2
Cricklade Street	C3	Kingshill Street	C1	Station Road	A2
Curtis Street	B2	Manchester Road	A2	Swindon Road	C2
Dean Street	B1	Market Street	B2	The Parade	B2
Drove Road	C3	Milford Street	B2	Upham Road	C3
Eastcott Hill	C2	Milton Road	B2	Victoria Road	B3
Edmund Street	B2	Morris Street	A1	Westcott Place	C1
Euclid Street	B3	Newburn Crescent	B1	Western Street	C3
Faringdon Road	B1	North Star Avenue	A2	William Street	C1
Farnby Street	B2	Ocotal Way	A3		

TOURIST INFORMATION ☎ 01793 530328
37 REGENT STREET,
SWINDON, SN1 1JL

HOSPITAL A & E ☎ 01793 604105
THE GREAT WESTERN HOSPITAL, MARLBOROUGH ROAD,
SWINDON, SN3 6BB

COUNCIL OFFICE ☎ 01793 463000
CIVIC OFFICES, EUCLID STREET,
SWINDON, SN1 2JH

Swindon *Swin.* Population: 145,236. Town, industrial and commercial centre, 70m/113km W of London. Large, modern shopping centre. Town expanded considerably in 19c with arrival of the railway. The Museum of the Great Western Railway exhibits Swindon built locomotives and documents the history of the railway works.

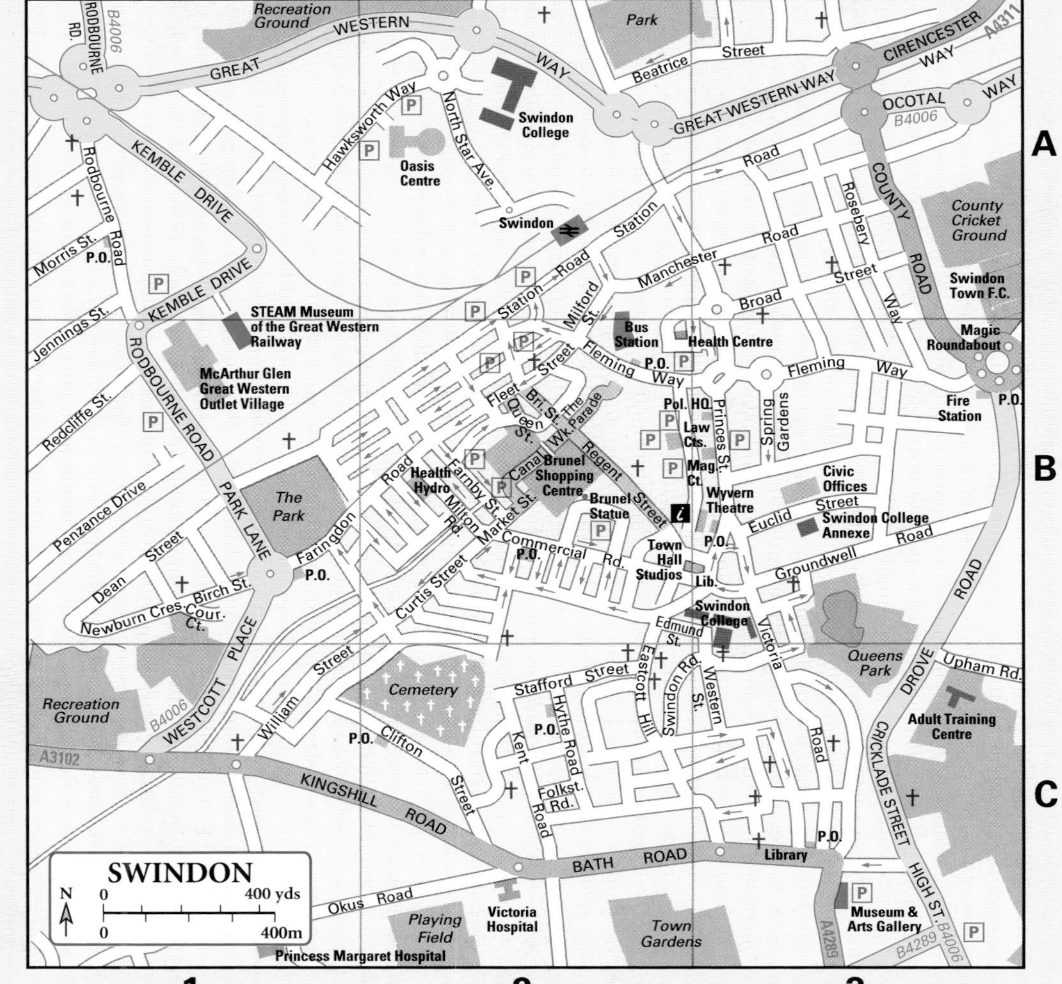

WEB-SITE	www.swindon.gov.uk

LOCAL RADIO	BBC WILTSHIRE SOUND 103.6 FM CLASSIC GOLD 1161 AM, GWR FM 97.2 FM

Easdon Tor
Manaton
Lustleigh
Hennock
Trusham
Canonteign Falls
Exeter
Haldon
A38
A380
Starcross
Mamhead
Grimspound
Hameldown Tor
Becky Falls
Trenchford Resr
Hamel Down
Bonehill Down
Hound Tor Medieval Village
Yarner Wood
A382
Bovey Tracey
House of Marbles & Teign Valley Glass
Devon Guild of Craftsmen
B3344
Chudleigh
Ugbrooke
Chudleigh Knighton
Ashcombe
Dawlish Water
Langdon House
A379
Ideford
Luton
Little Haldon
Haytor Vale
Brimley
Widecombe in the Moor
B3387
Heathfield
Cardew Design
Ilsington
Coldeast
Preston
Stover
B3193
B3192
Holcombe
Dunstone
Rippon Tor
Liverton
Sandygate
DARTMOOR
Horridge
Sigford
Trago Mills
Teigngrace
Kingsteignton
Bishopsteignton
A381
Teignmouth
Grand Pier
Ponsworthy
Buckland in the Moor
Bickington
Highweek
Hedgehog Hospital and Farm
Shaldon
Combeinteignhead
Caton
A383
Netherton
NEWTON ABBOT
Stokeinteignhead
NATIONAL
Rew
Combe Cross
Bradley Manor
West Ogwell
East Ogwell
Wolborough
Milber
Haccombe
Lower Gabwell
Higher Gabwell
Babbacombe Bay
Ashburton
River Dart
Holne
PARK
Abbey
Woodland
Denbury
Abbotskerswell
Coffinswell
Maidencombe
Buckfast
Forder Green
Daccombe
Barton
Kingskerswell
Torbryan
Ipplepen
North Whilborough
Landscove
Buckfastleigh
A3022
Broadhempston
Woolston Green
Compton
Edginswell
Babbacombe Model Village
St Marychurch
Shiphay
Buckfast Butterfly & Dartmoor Otter Sanctuary
B3380
Dean
Riverford Bridge
South Devon Rly
Staverton
Red Post
Cockington Court
Torre Abbey
Babbacombe
Kent's Cavern
TORQUAY
Dean Prior
A384
Dartington
Littlehempston
Marldon
Cockington
Dartington Crystal & Cider Press Centre
Shinner's Bridge
Berry Pomeroy
Rattery
Cott
A385
Motor Museum
Blagdon
Paignton
Pier
Tigley
Totnes
Collaton St Mary
Tor Bay
Belsford
Bowden
Lincombe
Harberton
Sharpham House
Zoo
Goodrington
Avonwick
Stoke Gabriel
Diptford
Ashprington
Bow
Berry Head
North Huish
Harbertonford
Tuckenhay
Cornworthy
Galmpton
Bickham Bridge
Washbourne
East Cornworthy
Dittisham
Churston Ferrers
Brixham
St Mary's Bay
Sharkham Point
Higher Brixham
Paignton & Dartmouth Steam Railway
Hillhead
Gara Bridge
A3122
Allaleigh
Capton
Downton
Halwell
Moreleigh
Woodhuish
Hemborough Post
Topsham Bridge
Woodlands Leisure Park
Dartmouth
Boohay
Scabbacombe Head
B3205
B3196
Coleton Fishacre (NT)
Blackawton
Kingswear
Millcombe
East Allington
Ashford
Loddiswell
Woodleigh
Dartmouth Pottery
Mew Stone
River Dart (Dart Pleasure Craft)
Bowden
Aveton Gifford
Coombe
Stoke Fleming
Avon
Cole's Cross
Venn
Goveton
Merrifield
Strete
Churchstow
Buckland-tout-Saints
Slapton
Start Bay
Slapton Ley
Slapton Sands
Cookworthy
Kingsbridge
Sherford
Upton
West Alvington
Stokenham
Frogmore
South Milton
West Charleton
East Charleton
Chillington
Torcross

Area Code 01803

Torbay

TORQUAY

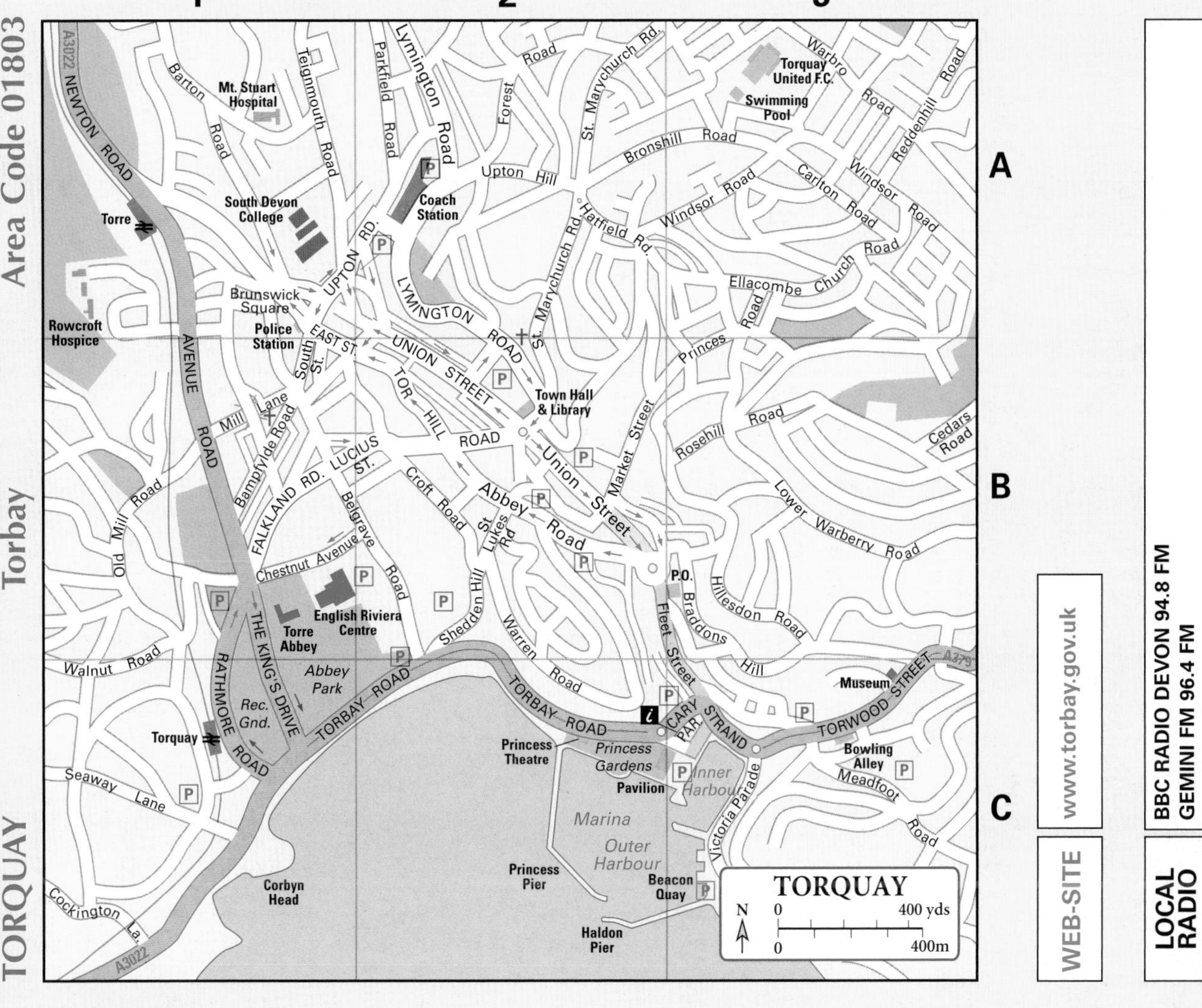

WEB-SITE

www.torbay.gov.uk

LOCAL RADIO

BBC RADIO DEVON 94.8 FM
GEMINI FM 96.4 FM

INDEX TO STREET NAMES

Abbey Road	B2	East Street	A1	Newton Road	A1	Teignmouth Road	A1
Avenue Road	B1	Ellacombe Church Road	A3	Old Mill Road	B1	The King's Drive	B1
Bampfylde Road	B1			Parkfield Road	A2	Torbay Road	C1
Barton Road	A1	Falkland Road	B1	Prince's Road	B3	Tor Hill Road	B2
Belgrave Road	B1	Fleet Street	B2	Rathmore Road	C1	Torwood Street	C3
Braddons Hill	B3	Forest Road	A2	Reddenhill Road	A3	Union Street	B2
Bronshill Road	A2	Hatfield Road	A2	Rosehill Road	B3	Upton Hill	A2
Brunswick Square	B1	Hillesdon Road	B3	St. Lukes Road	B2	Upton Road	A1
Carlton Road	A3	Lower Warberry Road	B3	St. Marychurch Road	B2	Victoria Parade	C3
Cary Parade	C3	Lucius Street	B1	Seaway Lane	C1	Walnut Road	C1
Cedars Road	B3	Lymington Road	A2	Shedden Hill	B2	Warbro Road	A3
Chestnut Avenue	B1	Market Street	B2	Shiphay Lane	A1	Warren Road	B2
Cockington Lane	C1	Meadfoot Road	C3	South Street	B1	Westhill Road	A2
Croft Road	B2	Mill Lane	B1	Strand	C3	Windsor Road	A3

TOURIST INFORMATION ☎ 01803 297428
VAUGHAN PARADE,
TORQUAY, TQ2 5JG

HOSPITAL A & E ☎ 01803 614567
TORBAY HOSPITAL, NEWTON ROAD,
TORQUAY, TQ2 7AA

COUNCIL OFFICE ☎ 01803 201201
TOWN HALL, CASTLE CIRCUS,
TORQUAY, TQ1 3DR

Torquay *Torbay* Population: 59,587. Town, 18m/30km S of Exeter. Chief town and resort of Torbay English Riviera district, with harbour and several beaches. Noted for mild climate. Torre Abbey with 15c gatehouse, is a converted monastery housing a collecion of furniture and glassware. Torquay Museum has display on crimewriter Agatha Christie born in Torquay. Kent's Cavern showcaves are an important prehistoric site. Babbacombe Model village 2m/3km N.

HEMEL HEMPSTEAD
ST ALBANS
WATFORD
Hatfield
Potters Bar
BARNET
Borehamwood
Radlett
Bushey
Abbots Langley
St Stephens
HARROW
South Oxhey
Rickmansworth
Chorleywood
AMERSHAM
CHESHAM
Berkhamsted
Beaconsfield
UXBRIDGE
HILLINGDON
BRENT
Wembley
CAMDEN
HARINGEY
Burnham
MAIDENHEAD
Kings Langley
Bovingdon
Chipperfield
Sarratt
Chenies
Latimer
Flaunden
Bucks Hill
Croxley Green
Northwood
Harefield
Denham
Gerrards Cross
Chalfont St Peter
Chalfont St Giles
Seer Green
Jordans
Little Chalfont
Coleshill
Penn
Holtspur
Wooburn
Stoke Poges
Farnham Royal
Farnham Common
Hedgerley
Fulmer
Iver Heath
Cowley
Ruislip
Ickenham
Eastcote
Pinner
Hatch End
Stanmore
Edgware
Elstree
Shenley
London Colney
Colney Heath
South Mimms
Arkley
Totteridge
Mill Hill
Hendon
Finchley
Golders Green
Hampstead
Kingsbury
Harrow Weald
Wealdstone
Sudbury
Greenford
Northolt
Perivale
Willesden
Harlesden
Paddington
Marylebone
Southgate
Cockfosters
New Barnet
East Barnet
Monken Hadley
Hadley Wood
Northaw
Cuffley
Brookmans Park
Welham Green
Bricket Wood
Chiswell Green
Potters Crouch
Bedmond
Leverstock Green
Apsley
Felden
Boxmoor
Bourne End
Northchurch
Whelpley Hill
Ashley Green
Botley
Lye Green
Chartridge
Bellingdon
Cholesbury
Buckland Common
St Leonards
Lee Clump
Ballinger Common
South Heath
Hyde Heath
Little Missenden
Little Kingshill
Winchmore Hill
Knotty Green
Forty Green
Hedsor
Dropmore
Taplow
Hitcham
Heronsgate
Maple Cross
West Hyde
Batchworth Heath
Moor Park
Eastbury
Merry Hill
Bushey Heath
Aldenham
Letchmore Heath
Shenleybury
Frogmore
Park Street
Colney Street
Smug Oak
Wrotham Park
Ridge
Enfield Chase
Trent Park
Grand Union Canal
M25
M1
M10
M40
A1(M)

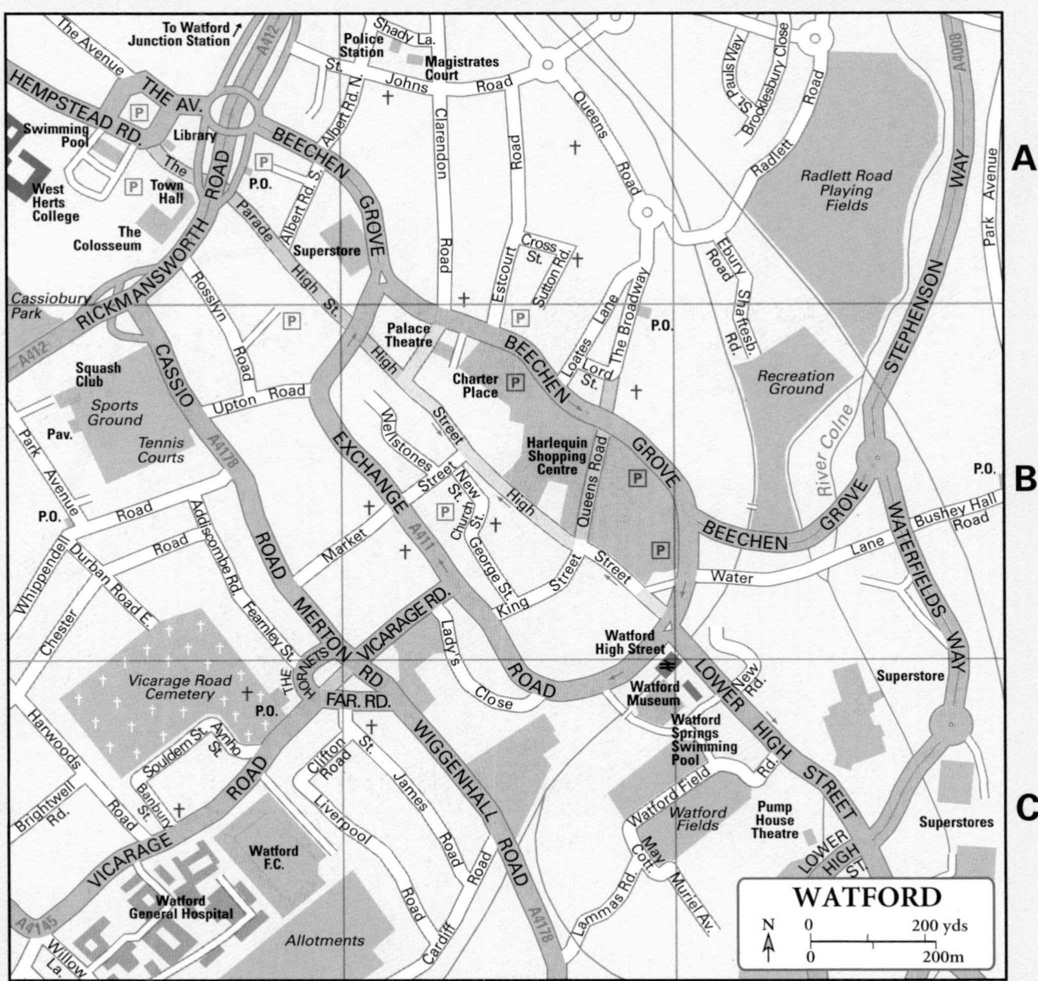

INDEX TO STREET NAMES

Street	Grid
Addiscombe Road	B1
Albert Road North	A1
Albert Road South	A1
Aynho Street	C1
Banbury Street	C1
Beechen Grove	A1/B3
Brightwell Road	C1
Brocklesbury Close	A3
Bushey Hall Road	B3
Cardiff Road	C2
Cassio Road	B1
Chester Road	B1
Church Street	B2
Clarendon Road	A2
Clifton Road	C1
Cross Street	A2
Durban Road East	B1
Ebury Road	A3
Estcourt Road	A2
Exchange Road	B1
Farraline Road	C1
Fearnley Street	B1
George Street	B2
Harwoods Road	C1
Hempsted Road	A1
High Street	A1/B2
King Street	B2
Lady's Close	B2
Lammas Road	C2
Liverpool Road	C1
Loates Lane	B2
Lord Street	B2
Lower High Street	C3
Market Street	B1
May Cottages	C2
Merton Road	B1
Muriel Avenue	C2
New Road	C3
New Street	B2
Park Avenue	A3
Park Avenue	B1
Queens Road	A2/B2
Radlett Road	A3
Rickmansworth Road	B1
Rosslyn Road	A1
Shaftesbury Road	A3
Souldern Street	C1
St. James Road	C2
St. Johns Road	A1
St. Pauls Way	A3
Stephenson Way	B3
Sutton Road	A2
The Avenue	A1
The Broadway	B2
The Hornets	C1
The Parade	A1
Upton Road	B1
Vicarage Road	C1/B2
Water Lane	B3
Waterfields Way	B3
Watford Field Road	C2
Wellstones	B2
Whippendell Road	B1
Wiggenhall Road	C2
Willow Lane	C1

TOURIST INFORMATION ☎ 01727 864511
TOWN HALL, MARKET PLACE,
ST ALBANS, AL3 5DJ

HOSPITAL A & E ☎ 01923 244366
WATFORD GENERAL HOSPITAL, VICARAGE ROAD,
WATFORD, WD1 8HB

COUNCIL OFFICE ☎ 01923 226400
WATFORD COUNCIL, TOWN HALL,
WATFORD, WD17 3EX

Watford *Herts.* Population: 113,080. Old market town on River Colne, 16m/26km NW of London. Printing and brewing developed as the main industries; now the industrial base is more diverse. Shopping and leisure centre with modern sculptures in redevolped central area. Parish church of Saint Mary's has 16c chapel. Local history museum housed in Georgian house. Edwardian Palace Theatre originally opened as a music hall in 1908.

WEB-SITE	www.watford.gov.uk

LOCAL RADIO	BBC THREE COUNTIES RADIO 103.8 FM, 1161 AM MERCURY 96.6 FM

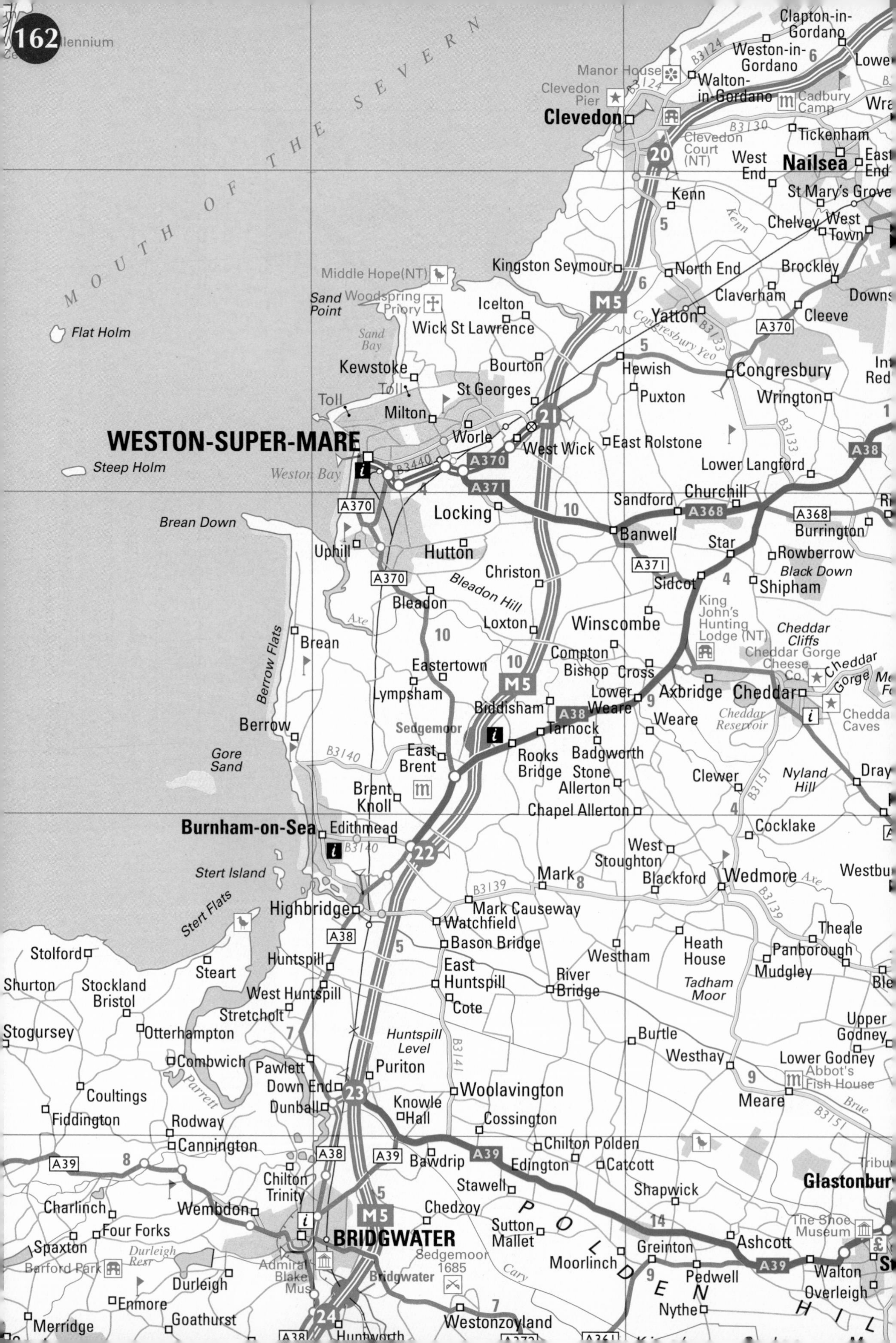
Millennium
MOUTH OF THE SEVERN
Clapton-in-Gordano
Weston-in-Gordano
Lower
Manor House
Walton-in-Gordano
B3124
Cadbury Camp
Clevedon Pier
Clevedon
Wra
B3130
Tickenham
Clevedon Court (NT)
20
West End
Nailsea
East End
Kenn
St Mary's Grove
Kenn
Chelvey
West Town
Kingston Seymour
North End
Brockley
Middle Hope(NT)
Sand Point
Woodspring Priory
Icelton
M5
Claverham
Downs
Yatton
Cleeve
Flat Holm
Sand Bay
Wick St Lawrence
Congresbury Yeo
B3133
A370
Kewstoke
Bourton
Hewish
Congresbury
Toll
St Georges
Puxton
Wrington
Milton
21
Worle
West Wick
East Rolstone
WESTON-SUPER-MARE
B3440
A370
Lower Langford
A38
Steep Holm
Weston Bay
A371
Churchill
A370
Locking
Sandford
A368
A368
Brean Down
Banwell
Burrington
Uphill
Hutton
Star
Rowberrow
A371
Black Down
Christon
A370
Bleadon Hill
Sidcot
Shipham
Bleadon
King John's Hunting Lodge (NT)
Axe
Loxton
Winscombe
Cheddar Cliffs
Berrow Flats
Brean
Compton Bishop
Cheddar Gorge Cheese Co.
Eastertown
Cross
Cheddar Gorge
M5
Lower Weare
Axbridge
Cheddar
Lympsham
Biddisham
A38
Cheddar Reservoir
Cheddar Caves
Berrow
Sedgemoor
Tarnock
Weare
East Brent
Rooks Bridge
Badgworth
Gore Sand
B3140
Stone Allerton
Clewer
Nyland Hill
Dray
Brent Knoll
B3151
Chapel Allerton
Burnham-on-Sea
Edithmead
Cocklake
B3140
22
West Stoughton
Westbu
Stert Island
Mark
Blackford
Wedmore
Axe
B3139
B3139
Stert Flats
Highbridge
Mark Causeway
Watchfield
Theale
A38
Bason Bridge
Heath House
Panborough
Stolford
Westham
Huntspill
East Huntspill
Mudgley
Steart
River Bridge
Shurton
Stockland Bristol
Tadham Moor
West Huntspill
Cote
Stretcholt
Upper Godney
Stogursey
Otterhampton
Huntspill Level
Burtle
B3141
Westhay
Lower Godney
Combwich
Pawlett
Abbot's Fish House
Puriton
Parrett
Down End
Meare
Coultings
23
Woolavington
Brue
Knowle Hall
Dunball
B3151
Fiddington
Cossington
Rodway
Chilton Polden
Cannington
A38
A39
Bawdrip
A39
Edington
Catcott
A39
Chilton Trinity
Stawell
Shapwick
Glastonbur
Charlinch
Wembdon
Chedzoy
M5
POLDEN HILLS
Four Forks
Sutton Mallet
The Shoe Museum
Spaxton
Durleigh Resr
BRIDGWATER
Ashcott
Barford Park
Sedgemoor 1685
Moorlinch
Greinton
A39
Walton
Admiral Blake Mus
Bridgwater
Pedwell
Durleigh
Cary
Overleigh
Enmore
Nythe
Merridge
Goathurst
24
Westonzoyland
A38
Huntworth

WESTON-SUPER-MARE North Somerset Area Code 01934

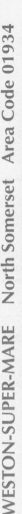

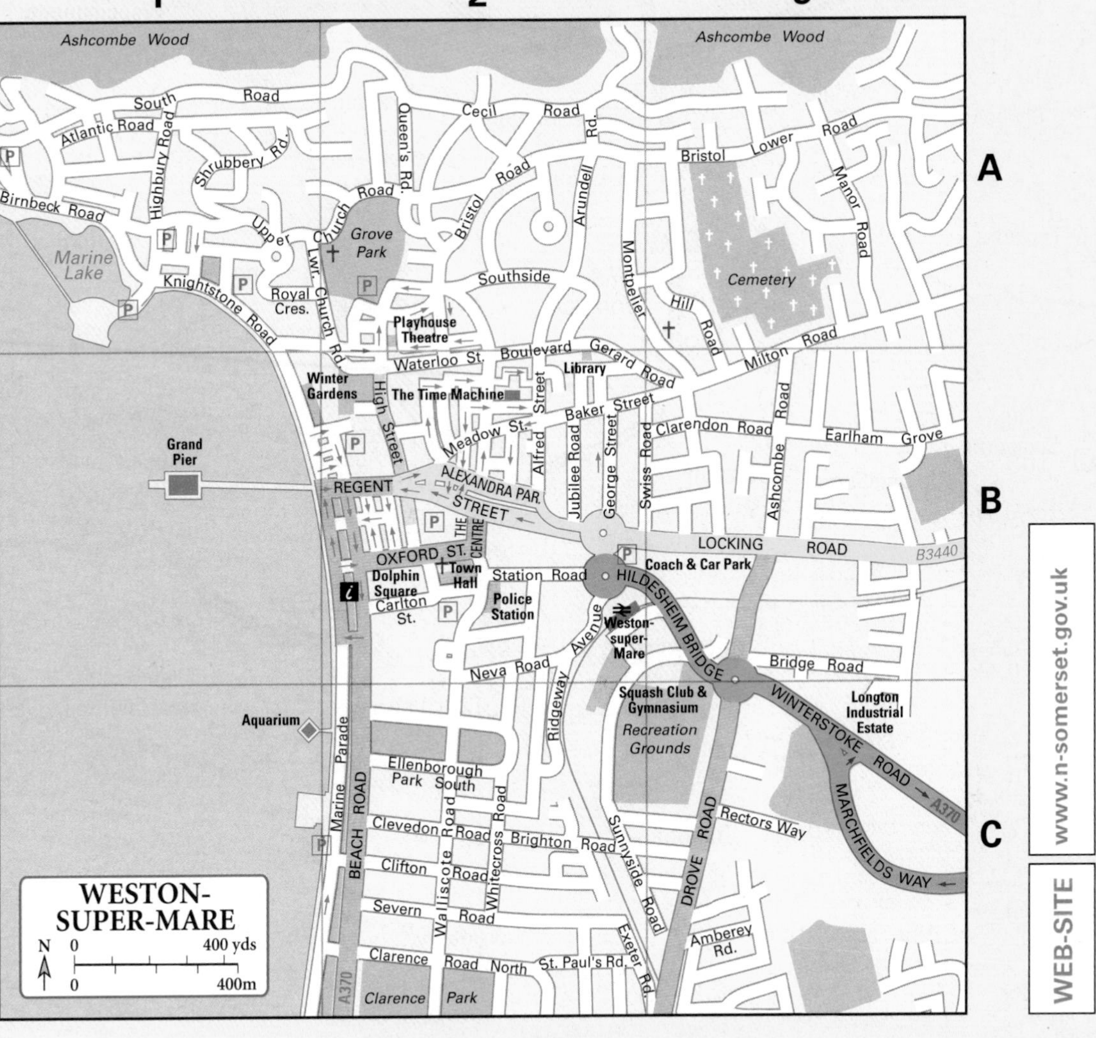

WEB-SITE

www.n-somerset.gov.uk

LOCAL RADIO

BBC SOMERSET SOUND 94.9, 104.6 FM
STAR 107.7 FM

INDEX TO STREET NAMES

Street	Grid
Alexandra Parade	B2
Alfred Street	B2
Amberey Road	C3
Arundell Road	A2
Ashcombe Road	B3
Atlantic Road	A1
Baker Street	B2
Beach Road	C2
Birnbeck Road	A1
Bridge Road	B3
Brighton Road	C2
Bristol Lower Road	A3
Bristol Road	A2
Carlton Street	B2
Cecil Road	A2
Clarence Road North	C2
Clarendon Road	B3
Clevedon Road	C2
Clifton Road	C2
Drove Road	C3
Earlham Grove	B3
Ellenborough Park South	C2
Exeter Road	C2
George Street	B2
Gerard Road	A2
High Street	B2
Highbury Road	A1
Hildesheim Bridge	B2
Hill Road	A3
Jubilee Road	B2
Knightstone Road	A1
Locking Road	B3
Lower Church Road	A1
Manor Road	A3
Marchfields Way	C3
Marine Parade	C2
Meadow Street	B2
Milton Road	B3
Montpelier	A2
Neva Road	B2
Oxford Street	B2
Queen's Road	A2
Rectors Way	C3
Regent Street	B2
Ridgeway Avenue	C2
Royal Crescent	A1
St. Paul's Road	C2
Severn Road	C2
Shrubbery Road	A1
South Road	A1
Southside	A2
Station Road	B2
Sunnyside Road	C2
Swiss Road	B3
The Centre	B2
Upper Church Road	A1
Walliscote Road	C2
Waterloo Street Boulevard	B2
Whitecross Road	C2
Winterstoke Road	C3

TOURIST INFORMATION ☎ 01934 888800
BEACH LAWNS,
WESTON-SUPER-MARE, BS23 1AT

HOSPITAL A & E ☎ 01934 636363
WESTON GENERAL HOSPITAL, GRANGE ROAD,
UPHILL, WESTON-SUPER-MARE, BS23 3NT

COUNCIL OFFICE ☎ 01934 888888
NORTH SOMERSET COUNCIL, TOWN HALL,
WESTON-SUPER-MARE, BS23 1UJ

Weston-super-Mare *N.Som.* Population: 69,372. Town and popular resort on the Bristol Channel, 18m/28km SW of Bristol, situated on Weston Bay and first developed in the 19c. Over 1m/2km of sands with traditional beach donkeys; promenade, marine lake, miniature steam railway and Winter Gardens. Amusement park located on the central Grand Pier, built in 1904. The Aquarium houses ocean and coastal waters display tanks. Local history and heritage museums give an insight into the town as a Victorian seaside resort. Annual motorbike beach race, Enduro, is held in October. International Helicopter Museum at Locking 2m/3km E.

Upper Clatford
Longparish
Middleton
Forton
Barton Stacey Camp
Barton Stacey
Goodworth Clatford
Wherwell
Newton Stacey
Bullington
Fullerton
Chilbolton
Sutton Scotney
Egypt
Hunton
West Stratton
Micheldever Sta.
Popham
Woodmancott
Preston Candover
Micheldever Forest
Chilton Candover
East Stratton
Micheldever
Wonston
Stoke Charity
Brown Candover
Micheldever Wood
Totford
Northington
Longstock
Leckford
Stockbridge
South Wonston
Crawley Down
Crawley
Winchester
The Grange
Kings Worthy
Old Alresford
Bighton
Alresford
Little Somborne
Up Somborne
Littleton
Itchen Abbas
Martyr Worthy
Itchen Stoke
Avington Park
New Alresford
Headbourne Worthy
Ashley
Easton
Avington
Ovington
King's Somborne
Sparsholt
Tichborne
Brook
Farley Down
Pitt Down
Farley Mount
WINCHESTER
Intech 2000
Cheriton 1644
Mottisfont Abbey Gardens (NT)
Pitt
Cath.
Chilcomb
Cheriton
New Cheriton
Hinton Ampner
Michelmersh
Standon
Oliver's Battery
Longwood Warren
Beauworth
Kilmeston
Braishfield
Hursley
Compton
Twyford
Morestead
Timsbury
Sir Harold Hillier Gdns
Shawford
Stanbridge Earls
Abbottswood
Ampfield
Otterbourne
Owslebury
Romsey Abbey
Romsey
Colden Common
Hensting
Marwell Zoo
Fisher's Pond
Exton
North Baddesley
Chandler's Ford
Upham
Corhampton Down
Corhampton
Chilworth
Crowdhill
Toothill
Bishopstoke
Lower Upham
Dean
Lee
EASTLEIGH
Fair Oak
Droxford
Upton
Rownhams
North Stoneham
Newtown
Rownhams
Nursling
Bassett
Southampton International
Horton Heath
Wintershill
Bishop's Waltham
Palace
Testwood
Itchen Valley
Durley
Swanmore
Swaythling
Hillpound
Totton
Shirley
Portswood
Long Common
Waltham Chase
Shirrell Heath
Soberton Heath
Millbrook
West End
Freemantle
Northam
Bitterne
Curdridge
Eling
Shedfield
Hounsdown
Thornhill
Botley
SOUTHAMPTON
Hedge End
Newtown
Colbury
Itchen
Manor Farm
Curbridge
Ashurst
Pooksgreen
Sholing
Lyndhurst Rd. Sta.
Burridge
Wickham
Hundred Acres
Marchwood
Woolston
Old Netley
Bursledon
Netley Abbey
Swanwick
North Boarhunt
Forest Museum
Dibden
Lower Swanwick
Park Gate
Whiteley
Boarhunt
Beaulieu
Hound
Netley Abbey
Hamble Sta.
Sarisbury
Funtley
Titchfield Abbey
Hythe
Royal Victoria
Wallington
Beaulieu Rd. Sta.
Beaulieu Heath
Dibden Purlieu
Hamble-le-Rice
Locks Heath
Warsash
FAREHAM
Hardley
Titchfield
Portchester
MEON VALLEY
A303
A34
M3
A30
A272
A3057
A33
A31
A3090
A27
A335
M27
A35
A36
M271
A326
A3024
A3025
A334
A3051
A32
B3420
B3048
B3049
B3046
B3047
B3404
B3335
B3043
B3037
B3055
B3035
B3354
B3177
B2177
B3056
B3054
B3334
B3342
Roman Road
Harewood Forest
Worthy Down

Area Code 01962

Hampshire

WINCHESTER

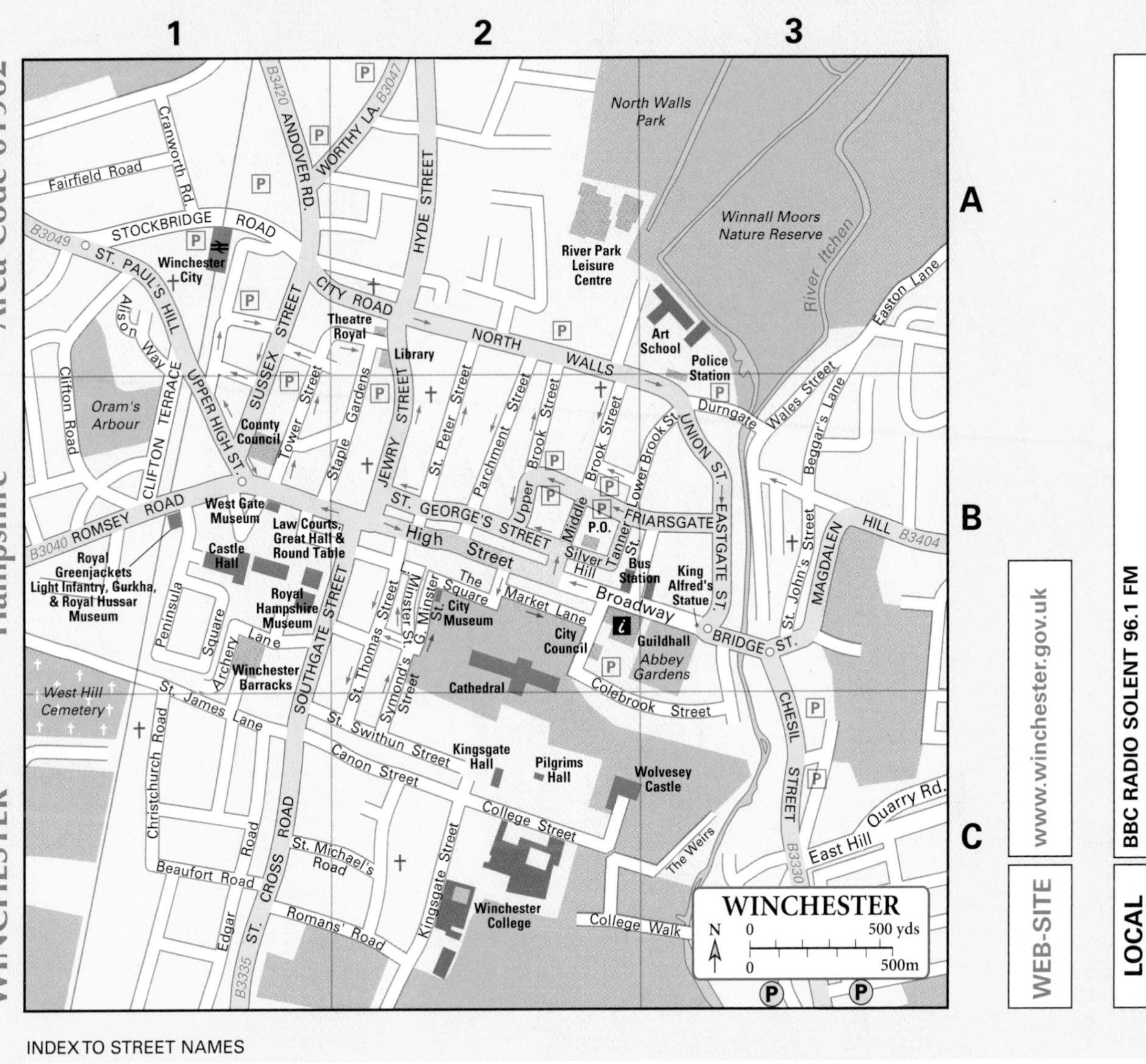

WEB-SITE www.winchester.gov.uk

LOCAL RADIO BBC RADIO SOLENT 96.1 FM OCEAN FM 96.7 FM, WIN 107.2 FM

INDEX TO STREET NAMES

TOURIST INFORMATION ☎ 01962 840500
GUILDHALL, THE BROADWAY, WINCHESTER
HAMPSHIRE, SO23 9LJ

HOSPITAL A & E ☎ 01962 863535
ROYAL HAMPSHIRE COUNTY HOSPITAL,
ROMSEY ROAD, WINCHESTER, SO22 5DG

COUNCIL OFFICE ☎ 01962 840222
CITY OFFICES, COLEBROOK STREET,
WINCHESTER, SO23 9LJ

Winchester *Hants.* Population: 36,121. City, county town on River Itchen on site of Roman town of Venta Belgarum, 12m/19km N of Southampton. Ancient capital of Wessex and of Anglo-Saxon England. 11c cathedral, longest in Europe with carved Norman font and England's oldest complete choir-stalls. Winchester College, boys' public school founded 1382. 13c Great Hall is only remaining part of Winchester Castle. Westgate Museum is in 12c gatehouse in medieval city wall, once a debtors' prison. 12c hospital of St. Cross. City Mill (National Trust), built over river in 18c. To S across river, St. Catherine's Hill, Iron Age fort. Extensive ruins of medieval Wolvesey Castle, also known as Old Bishop's Palace (English Heritage), 1m/2km SE.

Marlow
Wooburn
Bourne End
Hedsor
Dropmore
Cookham
Cookham Dean
Cookham Rise
Bisham
Hurley
Medmenham
Hurley Bottom
Burchett's Green
Pinkneys Green
Furze Platt
Cockpole Green
Warren Row
Knowl Hill
Littlewick Green
Woodlands Park
White Waltham
Wargrave
Kiln Green
Hare Hatch
Waltham St Lawrence
Ruscombe
Twyford
Whistley Green
Shurlock Row
Hurst
Binfield
Wokingham
Eastheath
Easthampstead
Crowthorne
Sandhurst
Yateley
CAMBERLEY
Bagshot
Lightwater
Windlesham
Chobham
West End
Burrowhill
Surrey Hill
Look Out Discovery Park
BRACKNELL
Popeswood
Newell Green
Warfield
Winkfield
Winkfield Row
Burleigh
North Ascot
Ascot
South Ascot
Sunninghill
Sunningdale
Cheapside
Virginia Water
Longcross
Chobham Common
Hawthorn Hill
Maiden's Green
Cranbourne
Woodside
Windsor Forest
Windsor Great Park
Savill
Englefield Green
Cooper's Hill
Egham
Legoland
MAIDENHEAD
Taplow
Hitcham
Burnham
Bray Wick
Bray
Dorney
Dorney Court
Boveney
Eton Wick
Eton
Holyport
Fifield
Oakley Green
Touchen-End
Paley Street
Stud Green
WINDSOR
Spital
Clewer Village
Old Windsor
Datchet
SLOUGH
Salt Hill
Upton
Langley
Farnham Royal
Farnham Common
Stoke Poges
Hedgerley
Burnham Beeches
Cliveden (NT)
Fulmer
George Green
Gerrards Cross
Denham Green
Denham
UXBRIDGE
Iver Heath
Iver
Richings Park
Colnbrook
Poyle
Horton
Wraysbury
Stanwell Moor
Hythe End
STAINES
Thorpe
Thorpe Park
Laleham
Littleton
Chertsey
Lyne
Ottershaw
Addlestone
Row Town
Woodham
New Haw
Byfleet
Weybridge
WALTON-ON-THAMES
Shepperton
Upper Halliford
Sunbury
Ashford
Stanwell
London Heathrow
Harmondsworth
Sipson
Longford
Yiewsley
Thorney
West Drayton
Cowley
HILLINGDON
Yeading
Hayes
Ickenham
Ruislip
Eastcote
Northolt
Greenford
Perivale
Southall
EALING
Hanwell
Acton
Norwood Green
Heston
Osterley
Cranford
Hatton
East Bedfont
Feltham
HOUNSLOW
Isleworth
Twickenham
Hanworth
Teddington
Ham
KINGSTON UPON THAMES
West Molesey
East Molesey
Hampton
Hampton Court Palace
Surbiton
Thames Ditton
Long Ditton
Weston Green
Tolworth
Hook
Chessington
ESHER
Claygate
Hersham
West End
Whiteley Village
Malden Rushett
Brentford
Kew
BRENT
Wembley
Sudbury
Harrow on the Hill
Greenhill
M4
M40
M25
M3
A404(M)
A329(M)
A30
A4
A3

WINDSOR — Windsor & Maidenhead — Area Code 01753

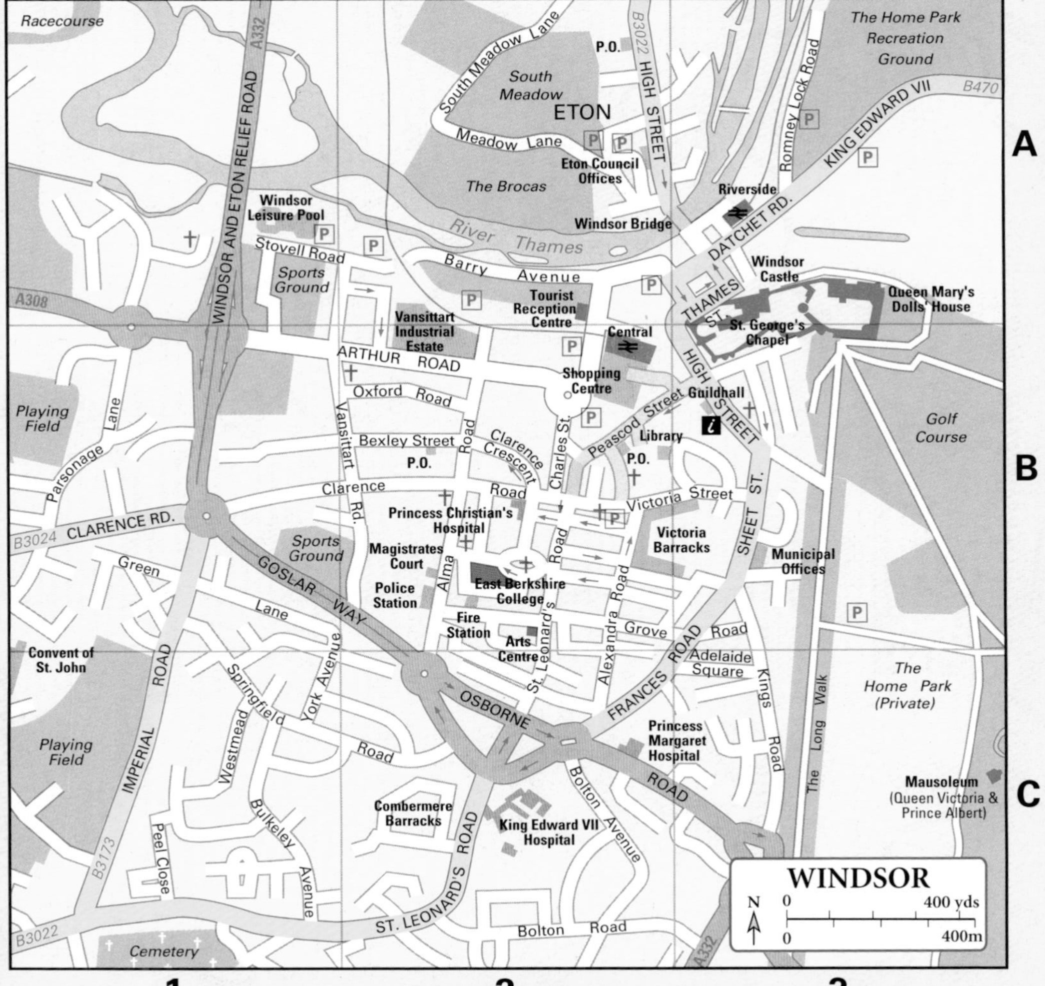

INDEX TO STREET NAMES

TOURIST INFORMATION ☎ 01753 743900
24 HIGH STREET,
WINDSOR, SL4 1LH

HOSPITAL A & E ☎ 01753 633000
WEXHAM PARK HOSPITAL, WEXHAM STREET,
SLOUGH, SL2 4HL

COUNCIL OFFICE ☎ 01753 810525
COUNCIL OFFICES, YORK HOUSE, SHEET STREET,
WINDSOR, SL4 1DD

Windsor *W. & M.* Population: 26,369. Town, attractive market town on S bank of River Thames, 2m/3km S of Slough and 21m/34km W of London. Castle is royal residence. Great Park to S of town is open to public; Home Park bordering river is private. St. George's Chapel is impressive. Many Georgian houses, and guildhall designed by Sir Christopher Wren.

WEB-SITE	www.rbwm.gov.uk

LOCAL RADIO	BBC RADIO BERKSHIRE 95.4 FM STAR FM 106.6 FM

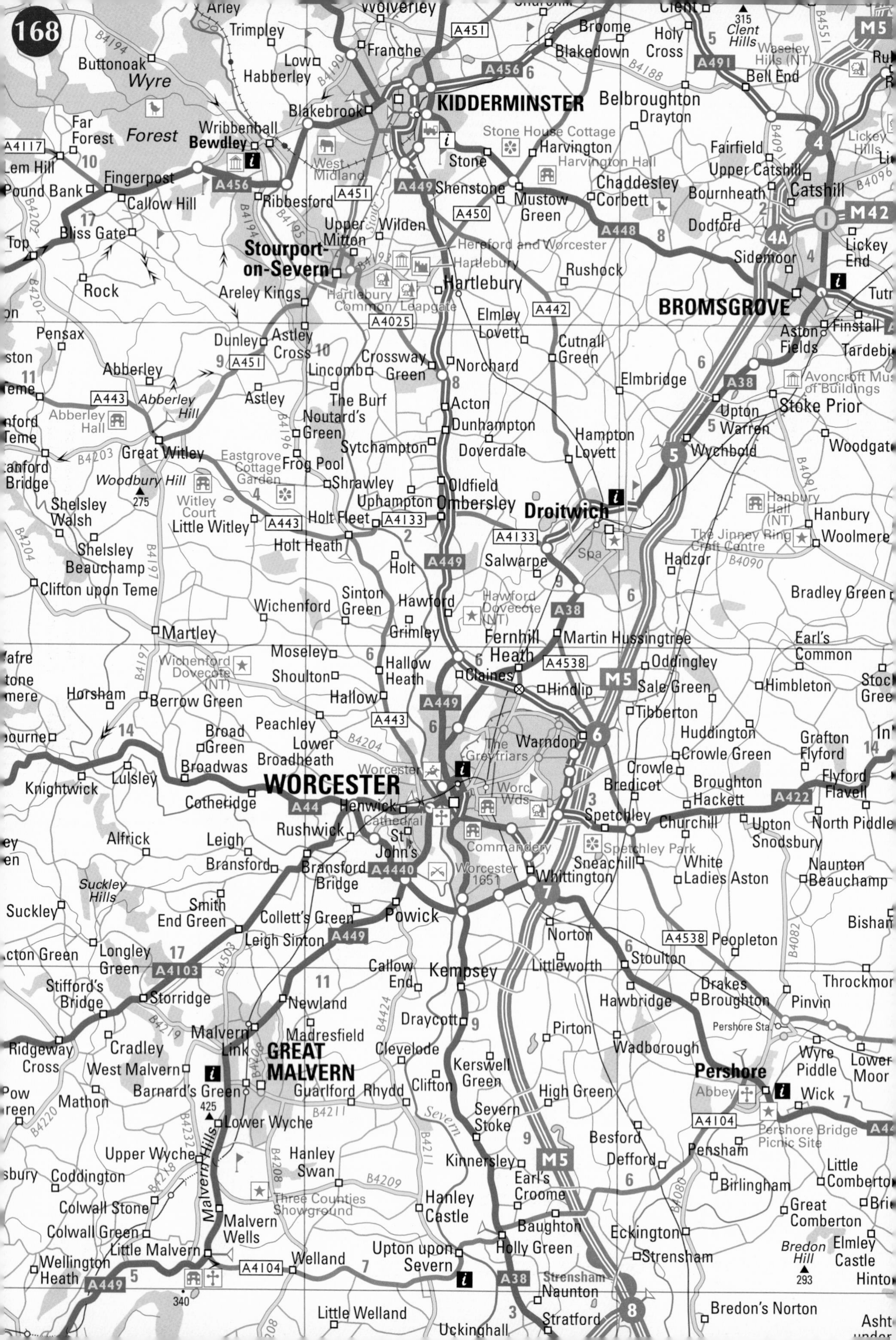

Arley
Trimpley
Wolverley
Franche
Broome
Clent
Holy Cross
315 Clent Hills
Waseley Hills (NT)
Buttonoak
Wyre Forest
Low
Habberley
Blakedown
KIDDERMINSTER
Bell End
Belbroughton
Drayton
Blakebrook
Far Forest
Wribbenhall
Bewdley
West Midland
Stone House Cottage
Harvington
Harvington Hall
Stone
Fairfield
Lickey Hills
Upper Catshill
Catshill
Lem Hill
Pound Bank
Fingerpost
Callow Hill
Ribbesford
Shenstone
Mustow Green
Chaddesley Corbett
Bournheath
Dodford
Lickey End
Bliss Gate
Top
Rock
Upper Mitton
Wilden
Stourport-on-Severn
Areley Kings
Hereford and Worcester
Hartlebury
Hartlebury Common
Leapgate
Rushock
Sidemoor
BROMSGROVE
Tutnall
Pensax
Dunley
Astley Cross
Elmley Lovett
Cutnall Green
Aston Fields
Finstall
Tardebigge
Abberley
Abberley Hill
Abberley Hall
Astley
Lincomb
Crossway Green
Norchard
Elmbridge
The Burf
Noutard's Green
Acton
Dunhampton
Upton Warren
Stoke Prior
Avoncroft Museum of Buildings
Great Witley
Eastgrove Cottage Garden
Frog Pool
Sytchampton
Doverdale
Hampton Lovett
Wychbold
Woodgate
Woodbury Hill
275
Shrawley
Oldfield
Hanbury Hall (NT)
Shelsley Walsh
Witley Court
Little Witley
Uphampton
Ombersley
Droitwich
Hanbury
Holt Fleet
Holt Heath
Salwarpe
The Jinney Ring Craft Centre
Woolmere
Spa
Hadzor
Shelsley Beauchamp
Holt
Clifton upon Teme
Wichenford
Sinton Green
Hawford
Hawford Dovecote (NT)
Bradley Green
Martley
Grimley
Fernhill Heath
Martin Hussingtree
Earl's Common
Wichenford Dovecote (NT)
Moseley
Shoulton
Hallow Heath
Claines
Oddingley
Horsham
Berrow Green
Hallow
Hindlip
Sale Green
Himbleton
Tibberton
Peachley
Huddington
Grafton Flyford
Broad Green
Lower Broadheath
Warndon
The Greyfriars
Crowle Green
Knightwick
Lulsley
Broadwas
Worcester
Crowle
Flyford Flavell
WORCESTER
Bredicot
Broughton Hackett
Cotheridge
Henwick
Worc. Wds
Spetchley
Churchill
Upton Snodsbury
North Piddle
Rushwick
Cathedral
St John's
Commandery
Spetchley Park
Alfrick
Leigh
Bransford
Bransford Bridge
Worcester 1651
Sneachill
Whittington
White Ladies Aston
Naunton Beauchamp
Suckley Hills
Suckley
Smith End Green
Collett's Green
Powick
Norton
Leigh Sinton
Peopleton
Longley Green
Callow End
Kempsey
Littleworth
Stoulton
Stifford's Bridge
Storridge
Newland
Hawbridge
Drakes Broughton
Pinvin
Throckmorton
Malvern Link
Madresfield
Draycott
Pirton
Pershore Sta.
Cradley
Ridgeway Cross
West Malvern
GREAT MALVERN
Clevelode
Kerswell Green
Wadborough
Wyre Piddle
Lower Moor
Pershore
Abbey
Wick
Mathon
Barnard's Green
Guarlford
Rhydd
Clifton
High Green
Severn
425
Lower Wyche
Severn Stoke
Pershore Bridge Picnic Site
Upper Wyche
Hanley Swan
Kinnersley
Besford
Defford
Pensham
Little Comberton
Malvern Hills
Coddington
Earl's Croome
Birlingham
Three Counties Showground
Colwall Stone
Hanley Castle
Great Comberton
Malvern Wells
Colwall Green
Baughton
Eckington
Little Malvern
Upton upon Severn
Holly Green
Strensham
Elmley Castle
Wellington Heath
Welland
Bredon Hill
293
340
Naunton
Little Welland
Bredon's Norton
Stratford
Uckinghall
M5
M42
A451
A456
A491
A449
A450
A448
A442
A4025
A443
A4133
A38
A4538
A44
A4440
A4103
A422
A4104

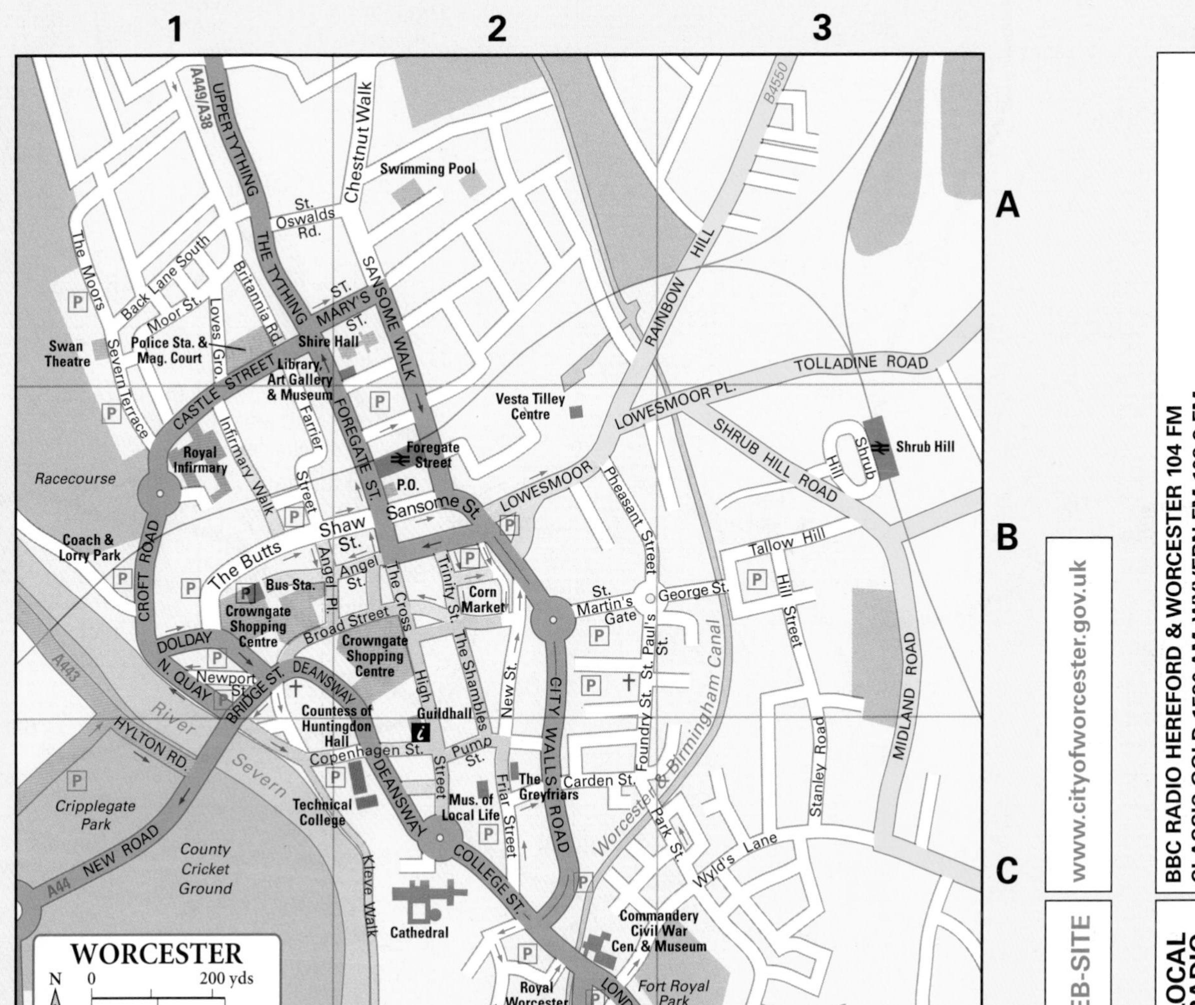

WEB-SITE www.cityofworcester.gov.uk

LOCAL RADIO BBC RADIO HEREFORD & WORCESTER 104 FM CLASSIC GOLD 1530 AM, WYVERN FM 102.8 FM

INDEX TO STREET NAMES

Angel Place	B1	Croft Road	B1	London Road	C2	Rainbow Hill	A2	Stanley Road	C3
Angel Street	B2	Deansway	B1	Loves Grove	A1	St. Martin's Gate	B2	Tallow Hill	B3
Back Lane South	A1	Dolday	B1	Lowesmoor	B2	St. Mary's Street	A1	The Butts	B1
Bath Road	C2	Farrier Street	B1	Lowesmoor Place	B2	St. Oswalds Road	A1	The Cross	B2
Bridge Street	B1	Foregate Street	B2	Midland Road	C3	St. Paul's Street	B2	The Moors	A1
Britannia Road	A1	Foundry Street	C2	Moor Street	A1	Sansome Street	B2	The Shambles	B2
Broad Street	B1	Friar Street	C2	Newport Street	B1	Sansome Walk	A2	The Tything	A1
Carden Street	C2	George Street	B3	New Road	C1	Severn Street	C2	Tolladine Road	A3
Castle Street	B1	High Street	B2	New Street	B2	Severn Terrace	A1	Trinity Street	B2
Chestnut Walk	A2	Hill Street	B3	North Quay	B1	Shaw Street	B1	Upper Tything	A1
City Walls Road	B2	Hylton Road	B1	Park Street	C3	Shrub Hill	B3	Wyld's Lane	C3
College Street	C2	Infirmary Walk	B1	Pheasant Street	B2	Shrub Hill Road	B3		
Copenhagen Street	C1	Kleve Walk	C2	Pump Street	C2	Sidbury	C2		

TOURIST INFORMATION ☎ 01905 726311
THE GUILDHALL, HIGH STREET,
WORCESTER, WR1 2EY

HOSPITAL A & E ☎ 01905 763333
WORCESTER ROYAL INFIRMARY, RONKSWOOD HOSPITAL, NEWTOWN ROAD, WR5 1HN

COUNCIL OFFICE ☎ 01905 723471
THE GUILDHALL, HIGH STREET,
WORCESTER, WR1 2EY

Worcester *Worcs.* Population: 82,661. City, on River Severn, 24m/38km SW of Birmingham. Shopping, cultural, sports and industrial centre; industries include porcelain and sauces and condiments. 18c Guildhall. Cathedral mainly Early English includes England's largest Norman crypt, 13c choir and Lady Chapel and tomb of King John. Three Choirs Festival held here every third year. Civil War Centre at the Commandery, headquarters for Charles II during Battle of Worcester. Factory tours and museum at Royal Worcester Porcelain. Elgar's Birthplace, home of composer Sir Edward Elgar, in Broadheath, 3m/5km W.

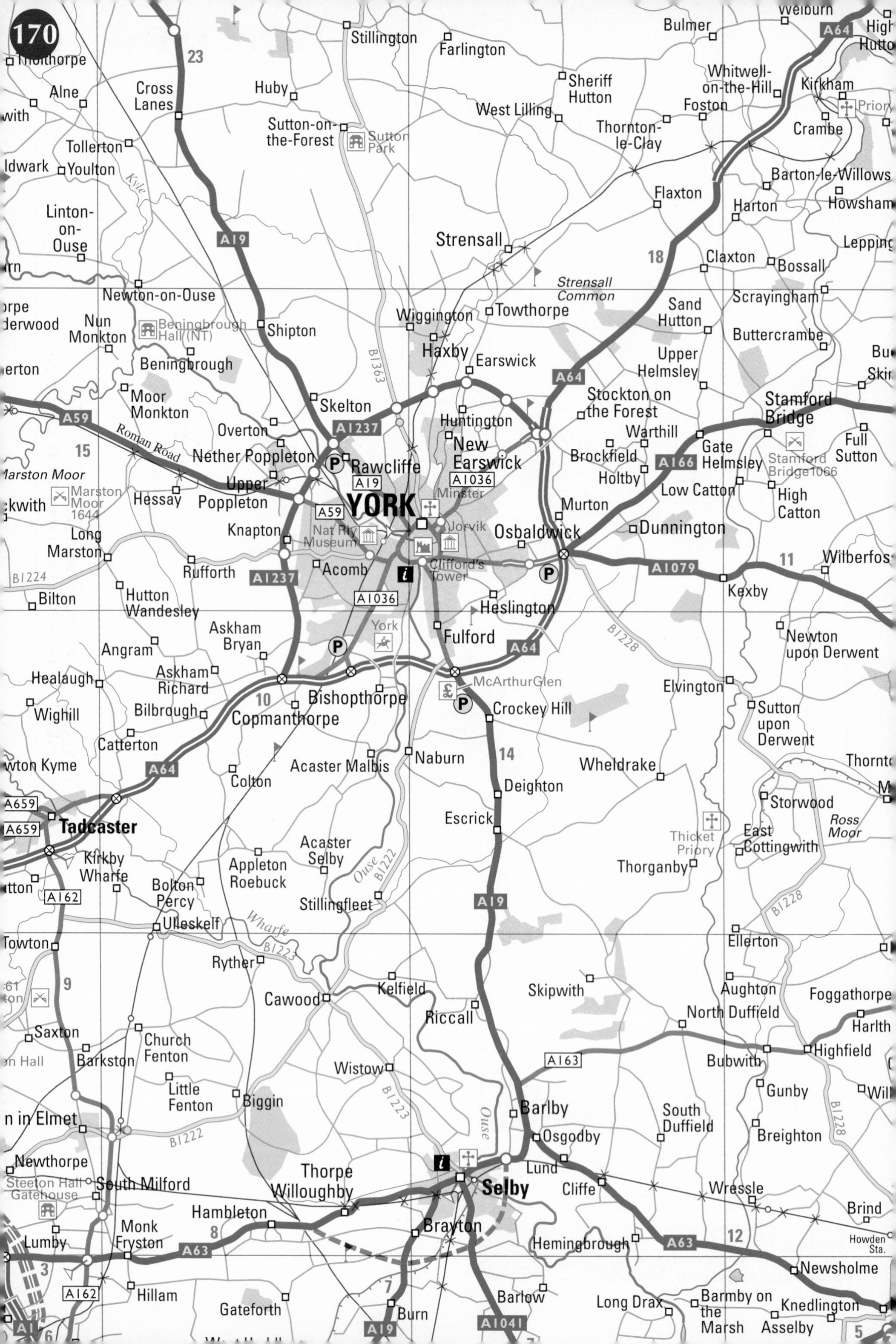

Tholthorpe
Stillington
Farlington
Bulmer
Welburn
A64
High Hutton
23
Alne
Cross Lanes
Huby
Sheriff Hutton
Whitwell-on-the-Hill
Kirkham
Priory
Foston
West Lilling
Crambe
Sutton-on-the-Forest
Sutton Park
Thornton-le-Clay
Tollerton
Youlton
Kyle
Barton-le-Willows
Flaxton
Harton
Howsham
Linton-on-Ouse
A19
Strensall
18
Claxton
Bossall
Leppington
Strensall Common
Newton-on-Ouse
Sand Hutton
Scrayingham
Nun Monkton
Beningbrough Hall (NT)
Shipton
Wiggington
Towthorpe
Buttercrambe
Beningbrough
Haxby
Earswick
Upper Helmsley
B1363
A64
Moor Monkton
Skelton
Stockton on the Forest
Stamford Bridge
A59
Roman Road
A1237
Huntington
Warthill
15
Overton
Nether Poppleton
New Earswick
Gate Helmsley
Full Sutton
Marston Moor
Rawcliffe
Brockfield
A166
Stamford Bridge 1066
Marston Moor 1644
Upper Poppleton
A19
Holtby
A1036
Low Catton
Hessay
Minster
High Catton
A59
YORK
Murton
Long Marston
Knapton
Nat Rly Museum
Jorvik
Osbaldwick
Dunnington
Acomb
Clifford's Tower
A1079
11
Wilberfoss
B1224
Rufforth
A1237
Kexby
Bilton
Hutton Wandesley
A1036
Heslington
B1228
Askham Bryan
York
Fulford
Newton upon Derwent
Angram
A64
Healaugh
Askham Richard
McArthurGlen
Elvington
10
Bishopthorpe
Crockey Hill
Wighill
Bilbrough
Copmanthorpe
Sutton upon Derwent
Catterton
Naburn
14
Newton Kyme
Acaster Malbis
Wheldrake
Thornton
A64
Colton
Deighton
A659
Storwood
A659
Tadcaster
Escrick
Ross Moor
Thicket Priory
East Cottingwith
Acaster Selby
Kirkby Wharfe
Appleton Roebuck
Ouse
B1222
Thorganby
Bolton Percy
Stillingfleet
A162
A19
B1228
Ulleskelf
Wharfe
Ellerton
Towton
B1223
Ryther
9
Kelfield
Skipwith
Aughton
Foggathorpe
Cawood
North Duffield
Riccall
Saxton
Harlthorpe
Church Fenton
Highfield
Barkston
A163
Bubwith
Wistow
Gunby
Little Fenton
Biggin
B1223
Ouse
Barlby
South Duffield
B1228
Sherburn in Elmet
Osgodby
Breighton
B1222
Newthorpe
Thorpe Willoughby
Lund
Steeton Hall Gatehouse
South Milford
Selby
Cliffe
Wressle
Hambleton
Brind
Monk Fryston
Brayton
8
Lumby
A63
Hemingbrough
A63
12
Howden Sta.
3
Newsholme
A162
Hillam
7
Barlow
Long Drax
Barmby on the Marsh
Knedlington
Gateforth
Burn
Asselby
A1
6
A19
A1041
5

Area Code 01904

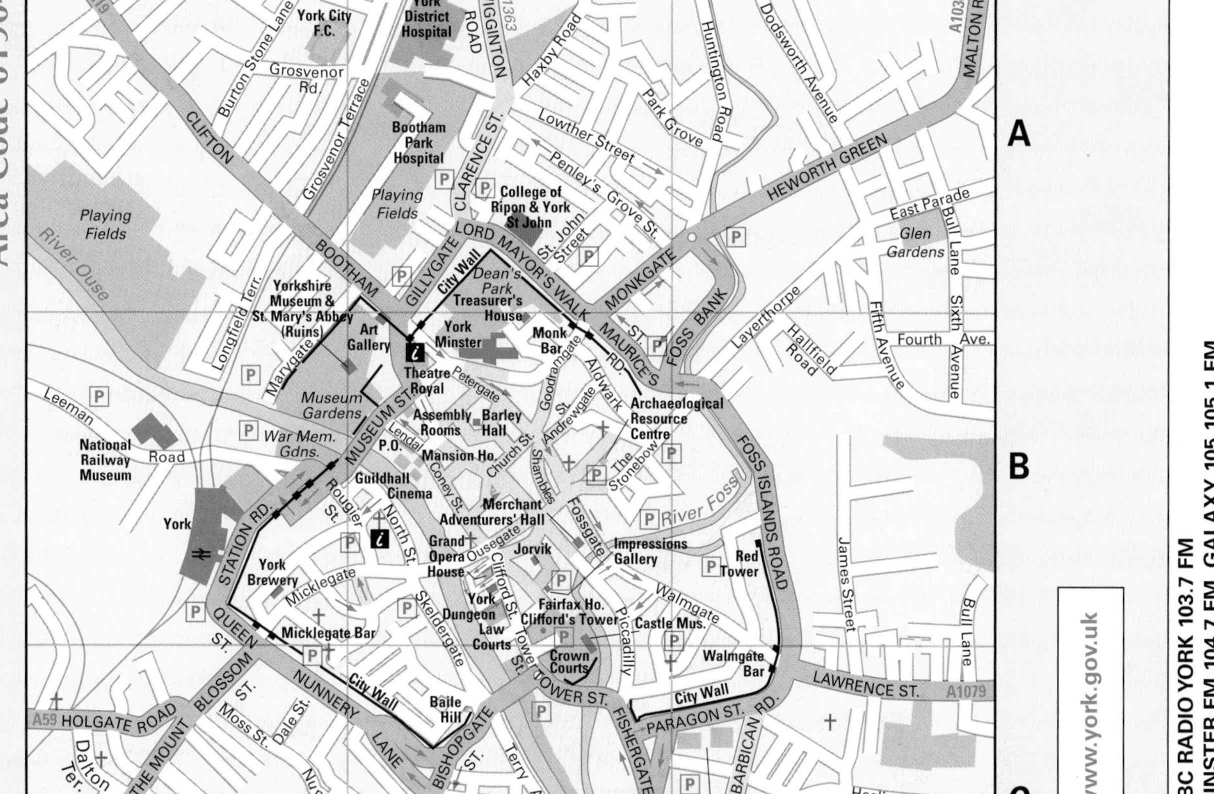

YORK

WEB-SITE

www.york.gov.uk

LOCAL RADIO

BBC RADIO YORK 103.7 FM
MINSTER FM 104.7 FM, GALAXY 105 105.1 FM

INDEX TO STREET NAMES

Albermarle Road	C1	Dalton Terrace	C1	Heworth Green	A3	Moss Street	C1	St. John Street	A2
Aldwark	B2	Dodsworth Avenue	A3	Holgate Road	C1	Mount Vale	C1	St. Maurice's Road	B2
Barbican Road	C3	East Parade	A3	Huntington Road	A3	Museum Street	B2	Scarcroft Hill	C1
Bishopthorpe Road	C2	Fifth Avenue	A3	James Street	B2	North Street	B2	Scarcroft Road	C1
Bishopgate Street	C2	Fishergate	C2	Lawrence Street	C3	Nunnery Lane	C1	Shambles	B2
Blossom Street	C1	Foss Bank	B3	Layerthorpe	B3	Nunthorpe Road	C1	Sixth Avenue	A3
Bootham	A1	Fossgate	B2	Leeman Road	B1	Ousegate	B2	Skeldergate	B2
Bull Lane	A3/B3	Foss Islands Road	B3	Lendal	B2	Paragon Street	C2	Southlands Road	C1
Burton Stone Lane	A1	Fourth Avenue	B3	Longfield Terrace	B1	Park Grove	A2	Station Road	B1
Cemetery Road	C3	Gillygate	A2	Lord Mayor's Walk	A2	Penley's Grove Street	A2	Terry Avenue	C2
Church Street	B2	Goodramgate	B2	Lowther Street	A2	Petergate	B2	The Mount	C1
Clarence Street	A2	Grosvenor Road	A1	Malton Road	A3	Piccadilly	B2	The Stonebow	B2
Clifford Street	B2	Grosvenor Terrace	A1	Marygate	B1	Queen Street	B1	Tower Street	B2
Clifton	A1	Hallfield Road	B3	Maurices Road	B2	Rougier Street	B1	Walmgate	B2
Coney Street	B2	Haxby Road	A2	Micklegate	B1	St. Andrewgate	B2	Wigginton Road	A2
Dale Street	C1	Heslington Road	C3	Monkgate	A2				

TOURIST INFORMATION ☎ 01904 554488
TIC TRAVEL OFFICE, 20 GEORGE HUDSON ST., YORK, YO1 6WR

HOSPITAL A & E ☎ 01904 631313
YORK DISTRICT HOSPITAL, WIGGINTON ROAD, YORK, YO31 8HE

COUNCIL OFFICE ☎ 01904 613161
THE GUILDHALL, YORK, YO1 9QN

York Population: 124,609. City, ancient city and archiepiscopal see on River Ouse, 22m/36km NE of Leeds. On site of Roman Eboracum. Constantine the Great proclaimed Roman Emperor in York in AD 306; only emperor to be enthroned in Britain. City fell to Danes in AD 867 and became known as Jorvik. Medieval wall largely intact, other fortifications including Clifford's Tower (English Heritage). York Minster has largest Medieval stained glass window in country. Previously a wool trading, craft and railway centre. Home to National Railway Museum. Jorvik Viking Centre in Coppergate. Merchant Adventurers' Hall in Fossgate is finest remaining guildhall in Europe. University of York at Heslington. Racecourse at Knavesmire.

Hemel Hempstead & Aylesbury
Luton, Luton Airport & the North
Hatfield, Stevenage & Welwyn Garden City
Bovingdon
Kings Langley
Abbots Langley
St Albans
London Colney
Colney Heath
Potters Bar
South Mimms Services
Chesham
Aylesbury
Amersham
Shenley
Radlett
Watford
Croxley Green
Borehamwood
High Wycombe
Chorleywood
Bushey
Barnet
London Gateway Services
Penn
Chalfont St. Giles
Rickmansworth
Stanmore
Edgware
Maple Cross
Beaconsfield
Northwood
Finchley
Chalfont St. Peter
Harefield
Hendon
Oxford & Birmingham
Gerrards Cross
Ruislip
Denham
Harrow
Wembley
Hampstead Heath
Burnham Beeches
Stoke Poges
Uxbridge
Hillingdon
Northolt
Hampstead
Willesden
Burnham
Slough
Cowley
Greenford
Ealing
Paddington
Maidenhead
Hayes
Southall
Acton
W. Drayton
Heston Services
Hammersmith
Reading, Swindon & South Wales
Eton
Datchet
Kew Bridge
Chiswick
Chelsea
Windsor
London Heathrow
Hounslow
Richmond upon Thames
Wandsworth
Stanwell
Twickenham
Richmond Park
Thames
Feltham
Wimbledon Common
Wimbledon
Egham
Staines
Ashford
Sunbury
Bushy Park
Kingston upon Thames
Merton
Ascot
Sunninghill
Sunningdale
Shepperton
Walton on Thames
Mole
Surbiton
Morden
Chertsey
Tolworth
Carshalton
Chobham Common
Weybridge
Esher
Windlesham
Addlestone
Sutton
Chobham
Woodham
Ewell
Basingstoke, Southampton & South-West
West End
Byfleet
Oxshott
Epsom
Bagshot Heath
Cobham
Banstead
Knaphill
Woking
Ashtead
Wey
Leatherhead
Kingswood
Send Marsh
Fetcham
West Horsley
East Horsley
Great Bookham
Guildford
Reigate
Box Hill
Ranmore Common
Dorking
Redhill
Portsmouth
Worthing
M25
M1
M10
M40
M4
M3
A1(M)

Ware & Hertford
Harlow, Stansted Airport & Cambridge
Cuffley
Cheshunt
Waltham Abbey
Epping
North Weald Bassett
M25
M11
A10
A414
B156
25
26
6
27
0 2 4 miles
0 2 4 6 kms
Epping Forest
Theydon Bois
Roding
A121
A1168
A113
A128
Doddinghurst
Ingatestone
Chelmsford, Ipswich & Harwich
A12
altham Cross
ENFIELD
Loughton
Abridge
5
BILLERICAY
A1023
uthgate
Chingford
Edmonton
WALTHAM FOREST
CHIGWELL
BRENTWOOD
28
HAVERING
Wood-ford
4
A406
A1112
REDBRIDGE
Tottenham
A503
A1400
A127
Basildon & Southend
Romford
Walthamstow
Laindon
Stoke Newington
Leyton
Hornchurch
29
Hackney
Wanstead
Upminster
A128
Ilford
Becontree
B186
A11
A406
ington
Bethnal Green
Stratford
East Ham
BARKING
Dagenham
Rainham
Poplar
A13
30
South Ockendon
City
London City
Thames
A2016
A1306
Southend
West-inster
Docklands
A102
Woolwich
Thamesmead
Purfleet
THURROCK SERVICES
Chadwell St. Mary
Greenwich
A205
31
West Thurrock
GRAYS
A126
A1089
Tilbury
A202
Camberwell
A207
A282
Lewisham
A20
A2
A208
Dartford
1A
1B
A226
Northfleet
GRAVESEND
Brixton
BEXLEY
Sidcup
Swanscombe
Rochester, Dover & Margate
A2018
Wilmington
Chislehurst
A223
Streatham
A21
2
Darenth
Hextable
Swanley
A212
Beckenham
A222
Istead Rise
South Darenth
BROMLEY
A224
3/1
Hartley
A227
A232
Orpington
West Wickham
Meopham
CROYDON
Farnborough
Eynsford
M20
New Ash Green
A235
A2022
New Addington
West Kingsdown
Maidstone & Folkestone
Biggin Hill
A233
NORTH DOWNS
A225
Otford
Kemsing
Warlingham
Coulsdon
A22
M26
2A
Caterham
CLACKET LANE SERVICES
10
A25
Sevenoaks
Borough Green
Westerham
B2042
A21
B2026
Oxted
Godstone
7/8
M23
Crawley, Gatwick Airport & Brighton
East Grinstead & Eastbourne
Tonbridge & Hastings
2 Full junction
2 Restricted junction

BLOOMSBURY
THE BRITISH MUSEUM
SOHO
STRAND
ST. JAMES'S
ST. JAMES'S PARK
WESTMINSTER
W1
WC2
SW1
OXFORD CIRCUS
PICCADILLY CIR.
TOTTENHAM COURT RD
CENTREPOINT
GOODGE ST
HOLBORN
COVENT GARDEN
LEICESTER SQ.
CHARING CROSS
EMBANKMENT
GREEN PARK
ST. JAMES'S PARK
NATIONAL GALLERY
TRAFALGAR
ROYAL OPERA HOUSE
ROYAL ACAD. OF ARTS
MIDDLESEX HOSP
UNI OF WESTMINSTER
BIRKBECK COLL
ROYAL MAIL
PALLADIUM
HAMLEYS
LIBERTY
FORTNUM & MASON
MARLBOROUGH HOUSE
LANCASTER HOUSE
WELLINGTON BARRACKS
HOME OFFICE
GUARDS MUS
Guards Memorial
Duck Island
Bandstand
Closed to Traffic on Sundays
OLD ADMIRALTY BUILDINGS
PARLIAMENTARY COUNSEL OFFICE
MINISTRY OF DEFENCE
ARMY HQ
CABINET OFFICE
FOREIGN & COMMONWEALTH OFFICE
CABINET WAR ROOMS
H.M. TREASURY
DEPT OF HEALTH & DWP
PORTCULLIS HO
WESTMINSTER
Westminster Pier
HOUSES OF PARLIAMENT
St. Stephen's Tower (Big Ben)
WESTMINSTER ABBEY
LONDON EYE
County Hall
London Aquarium
ST. THOMAS' HOSP
Cleopatra's Needle
Charing Cross Pier
HUNGERFORD BRI
WESTMINSTER BRI
OXFORD ST
NEW OXFORD ST
HIGH HOLBORN
KINGSWAY
SHAFTESBURY AV
CHARING CROSS RD
REGENT ST
HAYMARKET
PICCADILLY
PALL MALL
THE MALL
BIRDCAGE WALK
HORSE GUARDS RD
WHITEHALL
VICTORIA EMBANKMENT
PARLIAMENT ST
NORTHUMBERLAND AV
GT GEORGE ST
BRIDGE ST
BUCKINGHAM GATE
A B C D E F G
1 2 3 4 5 6 7 8 9

BARBICAN
FARRINGDON
CHANCERY LANE
HOLBORN
HOLBORN VIADUCT
CHARTERHOUSE ST
NEWGATE ST
ST. PAUL'S
ST. PAUL'S CATHEDRAL
BARTHOLOMEW'S HOSPITAL
CENTRAL CRIMINAL COURT (Old Bailey)
ROYAL COURTS OF JUSTICE
FLEET STREET
STRAND
CHEAPSIDE
MANSION HOUSE
CANNON STREET
QUEEN VICTORIA ST
LONDON WALL
GRAY'S INN GARDENS
EC1
EC2
EC4
SE1
TEMPLE
VICTORIA EMBANKMENT
BLACKFRIARS
CITY THAMESLINK
RIVER THAMES
MILLENNIUM BRIDGE
BLACKFRIARS BRI
SOUTHWARK BRI
WESTMINSTER
LAMBETH
SOUTHWARK
KING'S REACH
H.M.S. PRESIDENT
SHAKESPEARE'S GLOBE THEATRE
TATE MODERN
BANKSIDE GALLERY
OXO TWR WHARF
ROYAL NATIONAL THEATRE
IBM
The London Television Centre
NAT FILM THEA
HAYWARD GALLERY
IMAX
STAMFORD STREET
UPPER GROUND
SOUTHWARK STREET
BLACKFRIARS ROAD
WATERLOO ROAD
WATERLOO
WATERLOO INTERNATIONAL
WATERLOO EAST
THE YOUNG VIC
THE OLD VIC
THE CUT
UNION ST
SOUTHWARK BRIDGE ROAD
BOROUGH HIGH ST
MARSHALSEA RD
THE BOROUGH
BOROUGH
LAMBETH NORTH
WESTMINSTER BR RD
ST. GEORGE'S CATH (RC)
PEABODY ESTATE
PEABODY SQUARE
NELSON SQUARE
SCALE: 1 : 10,000 6.3 inches to 1 mile / 10 cm to 1km
1/4mile
0
0.25
0.50 km

Index to London street names

Abbreviations

All	Alley	Co	County	Ex	Exchange	Hts	Heights	Pas	Passage	Sta	Station
Allot	Allotments	Coll	College	Exhib	Exhibition	Ind	Industrial	Pav	Pavilion	Sts	Streets
Amb	Ambulance	Comm	Community	FB	Footbridge	Int	International	Pk	Park	Sub	Subway
App	Approach	Conv	Convent	FC	Football Club	Junct	Junction	Pl	Place	Swim	Swimming
Arc	Arcade	Cor	Corner	Fld	Field	La	Lane	Pol	Police	TA	Territorial Army
Av	Avenue	Coron	Coroners	Flds	Fields	Las	Lanes	Prec	Precinct	TH	Town Hall
Bdy	Broadway	Cors	Corners	Fm	Farm	Lib	Library	Prim	Primary	Tenn	Tennis
Bk	Bank	Cotts	Cottages	Gall	Gallery	Lo	Lodge	Prom	Promenade	Ter	Terrace
Bldgs	Buildings	Cov	Covered	Gar	Garage	Lwr	Lower	Pt	Point	Thea	Theatre
Boul	Boulevard	Crem	Crematorium	Gdn	Garden	Mag	Magistrates	Quad	Quadrant	Trd	Trading
Bowl	Bowling	Cres	Crescent	Gdns	Gardens	Mans	Mansions	RC	Roman Catholic	Twr	Tower
Br	Bridge	Ct	Court	Govt	Government	Mem	Memorial	Rd	Road	Twrs	Towers
C of E	Church of England	Cts	Courts	Gra	Grange	Mkt	Market	Rds	Roads	Uni	University
Cath	Cathedral	Ctyd	Courtyard	Grd	Ground	Mkts	Markets	Rec	Recreation	Vil	Villas
Cem	Cemetery	Dep	Depot	Grds	Grounds	Ms	Mews	Res	Reservoir	Vil	Villa
Cen	Central, Centre	Dev	Development	Grn	Green	Mt	Mount	Ri	Rise	Vw	View
Cft	Croft	Dr	Drive	Grns	Greens	Mus	Museum	S	South	W	West
Cfts	Crofts	Dws	Dwellings	Gro	Grove	N	North	Sch	School	Wd	Wood
Ch	Church	E	East	Gros	Groves	NT	National Trust	Sec	Secondary	Wds	Woods
Chyd	Churchyard	Ed	Education	Gt	Great	Nat	National	Shop	Shopping	Wf	Wharf
Cin	Cinema	Elec	Electricity	Ho	House	PH	Public House	Sq	Square	Wk	Walk
Circ	Circus	Embk	Embankment	Hos	Houses	PO	Post Office	St.	Saint	Wks	Works
Cl	Close	Est	Estate	Hosp	Hospital	Par	Parade	St	Street	Yd	Yard

Adam & Eve Ct, W1 **174** B2
Adam St, WC2 **174** F5
Addington St, SE1 **175** H9
Addle Hill, EC4 **175** M4
Addle St, EC2 **175** P1
Adelaide St, WC2 **174** E5
Adeline Pl, WC1 **174** D1
Adelphi Ter, WC2 **174** F5
Agar St, WC2 **174** E5
Air St, W1 **174** B5
Alaska St, SE1 **175** J7
Albany, W1 **174** A5
Albany Ctyd, W1 **174** B5
Albion Way, EC1 **175** N1
Aldermanbury, EC2 **175** P2
Aldermanbury Sq, EC2 **175** P1
Aldersgate St, EC1 **175** N2
Aldwych, WC2 **174** G4
Ambassador's Ct, SW1 **174** B7
Amen Cor, EC4 **175** M3
Amen Ct, EC4 **175** M2
America St, SE1 **175** N7
Andrew Borde St, WC2 **174** D2
Andrewes Ho, EC2 **175** P1
Andrews Crosse, WC2 **175** J3
Angel Ct, SW1 **174** B7
Angel St, EC1 **175** N2
Apothecary St, EC4 **175** L3
Apple Tree Yd, SW1 **174** B6
Aquinas St, SE1 **175** K7
Archer St, W1 **174** C4
Arches, The, WC2 **174** F6
Argent St, SE1 **175** M8
Argyll St, W1 **174** A3
Arlington St, SW1 **174** A6
Arne St, WC2 **174** F3
Arundel Gt Ct, WC2 **175** H4
Arundel St, WC2 **175** H4
Ashentree Ct, EC4 **175** K3
Ave Maria La, EC4 **175** M3
Avon Pl, SE1 **175** P9
Ayres St, SE1 **175** P8

B

Babmaes St, SW1 **174** B5
Bainbridge St, WC1 **174** D2
Banbury Ct, WC2 **174** E4
Bank End, SE1 **175** P6
Bankside, SE1 **175** N5
Barge Ho St, SE1 **175** K6
Barley Mow Pas, EC1 **175** M1
Barnard's Inn, EC1 **175** K2
Barons Pl, SE1 **175** K9
Barter St, WC1 **174** F1
Bartholomew Cl, EC1 **175** N1
Bartholomew Pl, EC1 **175** N1
Bartlett Ct, EC4 **175** K2
Bartletts Pas, EC4 **175** K2
Bateman's Bldgs, W1 **174** C3
Bateman St, W1 **174** C3
Bayley St, WC1 **174** C1
Baylis Rd, SE1 **175** J9
Beak St, W1 **174** B4
Bear All, EC4 **175** L2
Bear Gdns, SE1 **175** N6
Bear La, SE1 **175** M6
Bear St, WC2 **174** D4
Beauchamp St, EC1 **175** J1
Bedford Av, WC1 **174** D1
Bedfordbury, WC2 **174** E4
Bedford Ct, WC2 **174** E5
Bedford Sq, WC1 **174** D1
Bedford St, WC2 **174** E4
Bell Wf La, EC4 **175** P4
Bell Yd, WC2 **175** J2
Belvedere Bldgs, SE1 **175** M9
Belvedere Pl, SE1 **175** M9
Belvedere Rd, SE1 **175** H8
Bennet's Hill, EC4 **175** M4
Bennett St, SW1 **174** A6
Berners Ms, W1 **174** B1
Berners Pl, W1 **174** B2
Berners St, W1 **174** B1
Berwick St, W1 **174** C3
Betterton St, WC2 **174** E3
Birdcage Wk, SW1 **174** B9
Bishop's Ct, EC4 **175** L2
Bishop's Ct, WC2 **175** J2
Bittern St, SE1 **175** N9
Blackfriars Br, EC4 **175** L4
Blackfriars Br, SE1 **175** L4
Black Friars Ct, EC4 **175** L4
Black Friars La, EC4 **175** L4
Blackfriars Pas, EC4 **175** L4
Blackfriars Rd, SE1 **175** L9
Bleeding Heart Yd, EC1 **175** K1
Bloomsbury Ct, WC1 **174** F1
Bloomsbury Sq, WC1 **174** F1
Bloomsbury St, WC1 **174** D1
Bloomsbury Way, WC1 **174** E2
Blore Ct, W1 **174** C3
Blue Ball Yd, SW1 **174** A7
Bolt Ct, EC4 **175** K3
Book Ms, WC2 **174** D3
Booth's Pl, W1 **174** B1
Borough High St, SE1 **175** N9
Borough Sq, SE1 **175** N9
Boundary Row, SE1 **175** L8
Bourchier St, W1 **174** C4
Bourlet Cl, W1 **174** A1
Bouverie St, EC4 **175** K3
Bow Chyd, EC4 **175** P3
Bow La, EC4 **175** P3
Bow St, WC2 **174** F3
Boyce St, SE1 **175** H7
Boyfield St, SE1 **175** M9
Boyle St, W1 **174** A4
Brad St, SE1 **175** K7
Bread St, EC4 **175** P3
Bream's Bldgs, EC4 **175** J2
Brewers Hall Gdns, EC2 **175** P1
Brewer St, W1 **174** B4
Brick Ct, EC4 **175** J3
Bride Ct, EC4 **175** L3
Bride La, EC4 **175** L3
Bridewell Pl, EC4 **175** L3
Bridge St, SW1 **174** E9
Bridle La, W1 **174** B4
Brinton Wk, SE1 **175** L7
Broad Ct, WC2 **174** F3
Broad Sanctuary, SW1 **174** D9
Broadwall, SE1 **175** K6
Broadwick St, W1 **174** B4
Broken Wf, EC4 **175** N4
Brooke St, EC1 **175** J1
Brownlow St, WC1 **175** H1
Brydges Pl, WC2 **174** E5
Buckingham Arc, WC2 **174** F5
Buckingham Gate, SW1 **174** A9
Buckingham St, WC2 **174** F5
Buckley St, SE1 **175** J7
Bucknall St, WC2 **174** D2
Bull Inn Ct, WC2 **174** F5
Bull Wf La, EC4 **175** P4
Burgon St, EC4 **175** M3
Burleigh St, WC2 **174** G4
Burlington Arc, W1 **174** A5
Burlington Gdns, W1 **174** A5
Burrell St, SE1 **175** L6
Burrows Ms, SE1 **175** L8
Bury Pl, WC1 **174** E1
Bury St, SW1 **174** A6
Bywell Pl, W1 **174** A1

C

Caleb St, SE1 **175** N8
Cambridge Circ, WC2 **174** D3
Candover St, W1 **174** A1
Cannon St, EC4 **175** N3
Canon Row, SW1 **174** E9
Canvey St, SE1 **175** M6
Carey La, EC2 **175** N2
Carey St, WC2 **175** H3
Carlisle St, W1 **174** C3
Carlton Gdns, SW1 **174** C7
Carlton Ho Ter, SW1 **174** C7
Carlton St, SW1 **174** C5
Carmelite St, EC4 **175** K4
Carnaby St, W1 **174** A3
Carteret St, SW1 **174** C9
Carter La, EC4 **175** M3
Carting La, WC2 **174** F5
Castle Baynard St, EC4 **175** M4
Castle Yd, SE1 **175** M6
Cathedral Pl, EC4 **175** N2
Catherine St, WC2 **174** G4
Catherine Wheel Yd, SW1 **174** A7
Catton St, WC1 **174** G1
Cecil Ct, WC2 **174** D5
Central Mkts, EC1 **175** M1
Centre at the Circ, W1 **174** B5
Centrepoint, WC1 **174** D2
Chancel St, SE1 **175** L6
Chancery La, WC2 **175** J2
Chandos Pl, WC2 **174** E5
Chaplin Cl, SE1 **175** K8
Chapone Pl, W1 **174** C3
Chapter Ho Ct, EC4 **175** N3
Charing Cross, SW1 **174** E6
Charing Cross Rd, WC2 **174** D2
Charles II St, SW1 **174** C6
Charlotte Pl, W1 **174** B1
Charlotte St, W1 **174** B1
Charterhouse St, EC1 **175** K1
Cheapside, EC2 **175** P3
Cheshire Ct, EC4 **175** K3
Chicheley St, SE1 **175** H8
Chichester Rents, WC2 **175** J2
Ching Ct, WC2 **174** E3
Christ Ch Pas, EC1 **175** M2
Church Entry, EC4 **175** M3
Church Pl, SW1 **174** B5
Clare Mkt, WC2 **174** G3
Clement's Inn, WC2 **175** H3
Clement's Inn Pas, WC2 **175** H3
Clennam St, SE1 **175** P8
Cleveland Pl, SW1 **174** B6
Cleveland Row, SW1 **174** A7
Clifford's Inn Pas, EC4 **175** J3
Clifford St, W1 **174** A5
Clink St, SE1 **175** P6
Cloak La, EC4 **175** P4
Cloth Ct, EC1 **175** M1
Cloth Fair, EC1 **175** M1
Cock La, EC1 **175** L1
Cockpit Steps, SW1 **174** D9
Cockspur Ct, SW1 **174** D6
Cockspur St, SW1 **174** D6
Coin St, SE1 **175** J6
Cole St, SE1 **175** P9
College Hill, EC4 **175** P4
College St, EC4 **175** P4
Collinson St, SE1 **175** N9
Collinson Wk, SE1 **175** N9
Colombo St, SE1 **175** L7
Colville Pl, W1 **174** B1
Concert Hall App, SE1 **175** H7
Conduit Ct, WC2 **174** E4
Cons St, SE1 **175** K8
Cooper Cl, SE1 **175** K9
Copperfield St, SE1 **175** M8
Coptic St, WC1 **174** E1
Coral St, SE1 **175** K9
Cork St, W1 **174** A5
Cork St Ms, W1 **174** A5
Corner Ho St, WC2 **174** E6
Cornwall Rd, SE1 **175** J6
Covent Gdn, WC2 **174** F4
Coventry St, W1 **174** C5
Craigs Ct, SW1 **174** E6
Cranbourn All, WC2 **174** D4
Cranbourn St, WC2 **174** D4
Crane Ct, EC4 **175** K3
Craven Pas, WC2 **174** E6
Craven St, WC2 **174** E6
Creed La, EC4 **175** M3
Cross Keys Sq, EC1 **175** N1
Crown Ct, EC2 **175** P3
Crown Ct, WC2 **174** F3
Crown Office Row, EC4 **175** J4
Crown Pas, SW1 **174** B7
Cubitts Yd, WC2 **174** F4
Cursitor St, EC4 **175** J2
Cut, The, SE1 **175** K8

D

Dane St, WC1 **174** G1
Dansey Pl, W1 **174** C4
D'Arblay St, W1 **174** B3
Dartmouth St, SW1 **174** C9
Davidge St, SE1 **175** L9
Deans Ct, EC4 **175** M3
Dean St, W1 **174** C2
Denman St, W1 **174** C5
Denmark Pl, WC2 **174** D2
Denmark St, WC2 **174** D3
Derby Gate, SW1 **174** E8
Devereux Ct, WC2 **175** J3
Diadem Ct, W1 **174** C3
Disney Pl, SE1 **175** P8
Disney St, SE1 **175** P8
Distaff La, EC4 **175** N4
Dodson St, SE1 **175** K9

Dolben St, SE1 175 L7
Dolby Ct, EC4 175 P4
Doon St, SE1 175 J7
Dorset Bldgs, EC4 175 L3
Dorset Ri, EC4 175 L3
Dover Yd, W1 174 A6
Downing St, SW1 174 E8
Doyce St, SE1 175 N8
Drake St, WC1 174 G1
Drury La, WC2 174 F3
Dryden St, WC2 174 F3
Duchy St, SE1 175 K6
Duck La, W1 174 C3
Dufour's Pl, W1 174 B3
Duke of York St, SW1 174 B6
Duke St, SW1 174 B6
Duncannon St, WC2 174 E5
Dunns Pas, WC1 174 F2
Durham Ho St, WC2 174 F5
Dyer's Bldgs, EC1 175 J1
Dyott St, WC1 174 E2

E

Eagle Pl, SW1 174 B5
Eagle St, WC1 174 G1
Earlham St, WC2 174 D3
Earnshaw St, WC2 174 D2
Eastcastle St, W1 174 A2
East Harding St, EC4 175 K2
East Poultry Av, EC1 175 L1
Elm Ct, EC4 175 J4
Ely Ct, EC1 175 K1
Ely Pl, EC1 175 K1
Embankment Pl, WC2 174 F6
Emerson St, SE1 175 N6
Endell St, WC2 174 E2
Essex Ct, EC4 175 J3
Essex St, WC2 175 J4
Evelyn Yd, W1 174 C2
Ewer St, SE1 175 N7
Excel Ct, WC2 174 D5
Exchange Ct, WC2 174 F5
Exeter St, WC2 174 F4
Exton St, SE1 175 J7

F

Falconberg Ct, W1 174 D2
Falconberg Ms, W1 174 C2
Falcon Cl, SE1 175 M6
Falcon Ct, EC4 175 J3
Fareham St, W1 174 C2
Farnham Pl, SE1 175 M7
Farringdon St, EC4 175 L2
Fetter La, EC4 175 K3
Field Ct, WC1 175 H1
Finck St, SE1 175 H9
Fisher St, WC1 174 F1
Flaxman Ct, W1 174 C3
Fleet St, EC4 175 J3
Flitcroft St, WC2 174 D2
Floral St, WC2 174 E4
Foley St, W1 174 A1
Fore St, EC2 175 P1
Forum Magnum Sq, SE1 174 G8
Foster La, EC2 175 N2
Foubert's Pl, W1 174 A3
Fountain Ct, EC4 175 J4
Frazier St, SE1 175 J9
Friar St, EC4 175 M3
Friary Ct, SW1 174 B7
Friday St, EC4 175 N3
Frith St, W1 174 C3
Fulwood Pl, WC1 175 H1
Furnival St, EC4 175 J2

G

Gabriel's Wf, SE1 175 J6
Galen Pl, WC1 174 F1
Gambia St, SE1 175 M7
Ganton St, W1 174 A4
Garden Ct, EC4 175 J4
Gardners La, EC4 175 N4
Garlick Hill, EC4 175 P4
Garrick St, WC2 174 E4
Gate St, WC2 174 G2
George Ct, WC2 174 F5
Gerrard Pl, W1 174 D4
Gerrard St, W1 174 C4
Gerridge St, SE1 175 K9
Gilbert Pl, WC1 174 E1
Giltspur St, EC1 175 M2
Glasshill St, SE1 175 M8
Glasshouse St, W1 174 B5
Godliman St, EC4 175 N3
Golden Sq, W1 174 B4
Goldsmith St, EC2 175 P2
Goodge Pl, W1 174 B1
Goodge St, W1 174 B1
Goodwins Ct, WC2 174 E4
Goslett Yd, WC2 174 D3
Gough Sq, EC4 175 K2
Gower Ms, WC1 174 C1
Granby Pl, SE1 175 J9
Grange Ct, WC2 175 H3
Grape St, WC2 174 E2
Gray's Inn Pl, WC1 175 H1
Gray St, SE1 175 K9
Great Chapel St, W1 174 C2
Great Dover St, SE1 175 P9
Great George St, SW1 174 D9
Great Guildford St, SE1 175 N6
Great Marlborough St, W1 174 A3
Great New St, EC4 175 K2
Great Pulteney St, W1 174 B4
Great Queen St, WC2 174 F3
Great Russell St, WC1 174 D2
Great St. Thomas Apostle, EC4 175 P4
Great Scotland Yd, SW1 174 E7
Great Suffolk St, SE1 175 M7
Great Titchfield St, W1 174 A2
Great Trinity La, EC4 175 P4
Great Turnstile, WC1 175 H1
Great Windmill St, W1 174 C4
Greek Ct, W1 174 D3
Greek St, W1 174 D3
Greek Yd, WC2 174 E4
Green Arbour Ct, EC1 175 L2
Greenham Cl, SE1 175 J9
Green's Ct, W1 174 C4
Greet St, SE1 175 K7
Gresham St, EC2 175 N2
Gresse St, W1 174 C1
Greville St, EC1 175 K1
Greyfriars Pas, EC1 175 M2
Greystoke Pl, EC4 175 J2
Grindal St, SE1 175 J9
Groveland Ct, EC4 175 P3
Gunpowder Sq, EC4 175 K2
Gutter La, EC2 175 P2

H

Half Moon Ct, EC1 175 N1
Ham Yd, W1 174 C4
Hand Ct, WC1 175 H1
Hanover Pl, WC2 174 F3
Hanway Pl, W1 174 C2
Hanway St, W1 174 C2
Hare Ct, EC4 175 J3
Hare Pl, EC4 175 K3
Harp All, EC4 175 L2
Hatfields, SE1 175 K6
Haymarket, SW1 174 C5
Haymarket Arc, SW1 174 C5
Heddon St, W1 174 A4
Henrietta St, WC2 174 F4
High Holborn, WC1 174 F2
High Timber St, EC4 175 N4
Hills Pl, W1 174 A3
Hind Ct, EC4 175 K3
Holborn, EC1 175 J1
Holborn Circ, EC1 175 K1
Holborn Pl, WC1 174 G1
Holborn Viaduct, EC1 175 K1
Holland St, SE1 175 M6
Hollen St, W1 174 C2
Holmes Ter, SE1 175 J8
Honey La, EC2 175 P3
Hood Ct, EC4 175 K3
Hop Gdns, WC2 174 E5
Hopkins St, W1 174 B3
Hopton Gdns, SE1 175 M6
Hopton St, SE1 175 M6
Horse & Dolphin Yd, W1 174 D4
Horse Guards Av, SW1 174 E7
Horse Guards Rd, SW1 174 D7
Horsemongers Ms, SE1 175 P9
Horse Ride, SW1 174 C7
Hosier La, EC1 175 L1
Houghton St, WC2 175 H3
Huggin Ct, EC4 175 P4
Huggin Hill, EC4 175 P4
Hulme Pl, SE1 175 P9
Hungerford Br, SE1 174 F6
Hungerford Br, WC2 174 F6
Hungerford La, WC2 174 E6
Hunt's Ct, WC2 174 D5
Hutton St, EC4 175 K3

I

India Pl, WC2 174 G4
Ingestre Pl, W1 174 B3
Inigo Pl, WC2 174 E4
Inner Temple La, EC4 175 J3
Invicta Plaza, SE1 175 L6
Ireland Yd, EC4 175 M3
Irving St, WC2 174 D4
Isabella St, SE1 175 L7
Ivybridge La, WC2 174 F5

J

James St, WC2 174 F4
Jermyn St, SW1 174 A6
Joan St, SE1 175 L7
Johanna St, SE1 175 J9
John Adam St, WC2 174 F5
John Carpenter St, EC4 175 L4

K

Kean St, WC2 174 G3
Keeley St, WC2 174 G3
Kemble St, WC2 174 G3
Kemp's Ct, W1 174 B3
Kennet Wf La, EC4 175 P4
Keppel Row, SE1 175 N7
King Charles St, SW1 174 D8
King Edward St, EC1 175 N2
Kinghorn St, EC1 175 N1
King James St, SE1 175 M9
Kingly Ct, W1 174 A4
Kingly St, W1 174 A3
Kings Bench St, SE1 175 M8
Kings Bench Wk, EC4 175 K3
Kingscote St, EC4 175 L4
Kings Pl, SE1 175 N9
King's Reach Twr, SE1 175 K6
King St, EC2 175 P3
King St, SW1 174 B7
King St, WC2 174 E4
Kingsway, WC2 174 G2
Kirkman Pl, W1 174 C1
Knightrider Ct, EC4 175 N4

L

Lambeth Hill, EC4 175 N4
Lancaster Pl, WC2 174 G4
Lancaster St, SE1 175 M9
Langley Ct, WC2 174 E4
Langley St, WC2 174 E3
Lant St, SE1 175 N8
Launcelot St, SE1 175 J9
Lavington St, SE1 175 M7
Lawrence La, EC2 175 P3
Laytons Bldgs, SE1 175 P8
Leake St, SE1 175 H8
Leather La, EC1 175 K1
Leicester Ct, WC2 174 D4
Leicester Pl, WC2 174 D4
Leicester Sq, WC2 174 D5
Leicester St, WC2 174 D4
Leigh Hunt St, SE1 175 N8
Lewisham St, SW1 174 D9
Lexington St, W1 174 B3
Library St, SE1 175 L9
Limeburner La, EC4 175 L3
Lincoln's Inn, WC2 175 H2
Lincoln's Inn Flds, WC2 174 G2
Lisle St, WC2 174 D4
Litchfield St, WC2 174 D4
Little Argyll St, W1 174 A3
Little Britain, EC1 175 N2
Little Dorrit Ct, SE1 175 P8
Little Essex St, WC2 175 J4
Little George St, SW1 174 E9
Little Marlborough St, W1 174 A3
Little Newport St, WC2 174 D4
Little New St, EC4 175 K2
Little Portland St, W1 174 A2
Little Russell St, WC1 174 E1
Little St. James's St, SW1 174 A7
Little Sanctuary, SW1 174 D9
Little Titchfield St, W1 174 A1
Little Trinity La, EC4 175 P4
Little Turnstile, WC1 174 G2
Livonia St, W1 174 B3
Loman St, SE1 175 M8
Lombard La, EC4 175 K3
London Shop Pavilion, W1 174 C5
London Silver Vaults, WC2 175 J1
London Wall, EC2 175 P1
Long Acre, WC2 174 E4
Long's Ct, WC2 174 C4
Love La, EC2 175 P2
Lower James St, W1 174 B4
Lower John St, W1 174 B4
Lower Marsh, SE1 175 J9
Lowndes Ct, W1 174 A3
Ludgate Bdy, EC4 175 L3
Ludgate Circ, EC4 175 L3
Ludgate Hill, EC4 175 L3
Ludgate Sq, EC4 175 M3
Lumley Ct, WC2 174 F5

M

Macclesfield St, W1 174 D4
McCoid Way, SE1 175 N9
Macklin St, WC2 174 F2
Magpie All, EC4 175 K3
Maiden La, SE1 175 P6
Maiden La, WC2 174 F5
Maidstone Bldgs, SE1 175 P7
Mall, The, SW1 174 B8
Maltravers St, WC2 175 H4
Manette St, W1 174 D3
Margaret Ct, W1 174 A2
Marigold All, SE1 175 L5
Market Ct, W1 174 A2
Market Pl, W1 174 A2
Marlborough Ct, W1 174 A3
Marlborough Rd, SW1 174 B7
Marshall St, W1 174 B3
Marshalsea Rd, SE1 175 P8
Martlett Ct, WC2 174 F3
Marylebone Pas, W1 174 B2
Mason's Yd, SW1 174 B6
Matthew Parker St, SW1 174 D9
Matthews Yd, WC2 174 E3
Mays Ct, WC2 174 E5
Meard St, W1 174 C3
Melbourne Pl, WC2 175 H4
Mepham St, SE1 175 H7
Mercer St, WC2 174 E3
Meymott St, SE1 175 L7
Middlesex Pas, EC1 175 M1
Middle Temple, EC4 175 J4
Middle Temple La, EC4 175 J3
Middleton Pl, W1 174 A1
Milcote St, SE1 175 L9
Milford La, WC2 175 H4
Milk St, EC2 175 P3
Miller Wk, SE1 175 K7
Milroy Wk, SE1 175 L6
Mint St, SE1 175 N8
Mitre Ct, EC2 175 P2
Mitre Ct, EC4 175 K3
Mitre Rd, SE1 175 K8
Monkwell Sq, EC2 175 P1
Monmouth St, WC2 174 E3
Montague St, EC1 175 N1
Montreal Pl, WC2 174 G4
Moor St, W1 174 D3
Mortimer St, W1 174 A1
Morwell St, WC1 174 D1
Mumford Ct, EC2 175 P2
Murphy St, SE1 175 J9
Museum St, WC1 174 E1

N

Nassau St, W1 174 A1
Neal St, WC2 174 E3
Neal's Yd, WC2 174 E3
Nelson Sq, SE1 175 L8
New Br St, EC4 175 L3
Newburgh St, W1 174 A3
New Burlington Ms, W1 174 A4
New Burlington Pl, W1 174 A4
New Burlington St, W1 174 A4
Newbury St, EC1 175 N1
Newcastle Cl, EC4 175 L2
New Change, EC4 175 N3
New Compton St, WC2 174 D3
New Ct, EC4 175 J4
New Fetter La, EC4 175 K2
Newgate St, EC1 175 M2
New Globe Wk, SE1 175 N6
New Inn Pas, WC2 175 H3
Newman Pas, W1 174 B1
Newman's Row, WC2 175 H1
Newman St, W1 174 B1
Newman Yd, W1 174 C2
New Oxford St, WC1 174 D2
Newport Ct, WC2 174 D4
Newport Pl, WC2 174 D4
New Row, WC2 174 E4
New Sq, WC2 175 H2
New St Sq, EC4 175 K2
Newton St, WC2 174 F2
New Turnstile, WC1 174 G1
Nicholson St, SE1 175 L7
Noble St, EC2 175 N2
Noel St, W1 174 B3
Norris St, SW1 174 C5
Northumberland Av, WC2 174 E6

Northumberland St, WC2 **174** E6
Norwich St, EC4 **175** J2
Nottingham Ct, WC2 **174** E3

O

Oat La, EC2 **175** N2
Odhams Wk, WC2 **174** E3
Old Bailey, EC4 **175** M3
Old Bond St, W1 **174** A5
Old Brewers Yd, WC2 **174** E3
Old Bldgs, WC2 **175** J2
Old Burlington St, W1 **174** A4
Old Compton St, W1 **174** C4
Old Fish St Hill, EC4 **175** N4
Old Fleet La, EC4 **175** L2
Old Queen St, SW1 **174** D9
Old Seacoal La, EC4 **175** L2
Old Sq, WC2 **175** H2
O'Meara St, SE1 **175** P7
Orange St, WC2 **174** C5
Orange Yd, W1 **174** D3
Ormond Yd, SW1 **174** B6
Oxendon St, SW1 **174** C5
Oxford Circ Av, W1 **174** A3
Oxo Twr Wf, SE1 **175** K5

P

Pageantmaster Ct, EC4 **175** L3
Pall Mall, SW1 **174** B7
Pall Mall E, SW1 **174** D6
Palmer St, SW1 **174** C9
Pancras La, EC4 **175** P3
Panton St, SW1 **174** C5
Panyer All, EC4 **175** N2
Paris Gdn, SE1 **175** L6
Parker Ms, WC2 **174** F2
Parker St, WC2 **174** F2
Park Pl, SW1 **174** A7
Park St, SE1 **175** N6
Parliament Sq, SW1 **174** E9
Parliament St, SW1 **174** E9
Paternoster Row, EC4 **175** N3
Paternoster Sq, EC4 **175** M2
Paul's Wk, EC4 **175** M4
Peabody Est, SE1 **175** K7
Peabody Sq, SE1 **175** L9
Peabody Trust, SE1 **175** N7
Pear Pl, SE1 **175** J8
Pemberton Row, EC4 **175** K2
Pepper St, SE1 **175** N8
Percy Ms, W1 **174** C1
Percy Pas, W1 **174** B1
Percy St, W1 **174** C1
Perkins Sq, SE1 **175** P6
Perrys Pl, W1 **174** C2
Peters Hill, EC4 **175** N4
Peter St, W1 **174** B4
Phoenix St, WC2 **174** D3
Piccadilly Arc, SW1 **174** A6
Piccadilly Circ, W1 **174** C5
Piccadilly Pl, W1 **174** B5
Pickering Pl, SW1 **174** B7
Pickwick St, SE1 **175** N9
Pilgrim St, EC4 **175** L3
Playhouse Yd, EC4 **175** L3
Pleydell Ct, EC4 **175** K3
Pleydell St, EC4 **175** K3
Plough Pl, EC4 **175** K2
Plumtree Ct, EC4 **175** K2
Pocock St, SE1 **175** L8
Poland St, W1 **174** B3
Pontypool Pl, SE1 **175** L8
Poppins Ct, EC4 **175** L3
Porter St, SE1 **175** P6
Portland Ms, W1 **174** B3
Portsmouth St, WC2 **174** G3
Portugal St, WC2 **174** G3
Priest Ct, EC2 **175** N2
Primrose Hill, EC4 **175** K3
Prince's Arc, SW1 **174** B6
Princes Pl, SW1 **174** B6
Printers Inn Ct, EC4 **175** J2
Printer St, EC4 **175** K2
Procter St, WC1 **174** G1
Prudent Pas, EC2 **175** P2
Puddle Dock, EC4 **175** M4
Pump Ct, EC4 **175** J3

Q

Quadrant Arc, W1 **174** B5
Quality Ct, WC2 **175** J2
Queen Anne's Gate, SW1 **174** C9
Queenhithe, EC4 **175** P4
Queen St, EC4 **175** P4
Queen St Pl, EC4 **175** P5
Queen's Wk, SE1 **174** G7
Queen's Wk, SW1 **174** A7
Queen Victoria St, EC4 **175** M4
Quilp St, SE1 **175** N8

R

Ramillies Pl, W1 **174** A3
Ramillies St, W1 **174** A3
Rathbone Pl, W1 **174** C2
Rathbone St, W1 **174** B1
Redcross Way, SE1 **175** P8
Red Lion Ct, EC4 **175** K2
Red Lion Sq, WC1 **174** G1
Regent Pl, W1 **174** B4
Regent St, SW1 **174** C5
Remnant St, WC2 **174** G2
Rennie St, SE1 **175** L6
Richmond Bldgs, W1 **174** C3
Richmond Ms, W1 **174** C3
Richmond Ter, SW1 **174** E8
Riding Ho St, W1 **174** A1
Risborough St, SE1 **175** M8
Rising Sun Ct, EC1 **175** M1
Robert St, WC2 **174** F5
Rolls Bldgs, EC4 **175** J2
Rolls Pas, EC4 **175** J2
Romilly St, W1 **174** C4
Rose All, SE1 **175** P6
Rose & Crown Ct, EC2 **175** N2
Rose & Crown Yd, SW1 **174** B6
Rose St, WC2 **174** E4
Rotherham Wk, SE1 **175** L7
Roupell St, SE1 **175** K7
Royal Arc, W1 **174** A5
Royal Opera Arc, SW1 **174** C6
Royalty Ms, W1 **174** C3
Rupert Ct, W1 **174** C4
Rupert St, W1 **174** C4
Rushworth St, SE1 **175** M8
Russell Ct, SW1 **174** B7
Russell St, WC2 **174** F4
Russia Ct, EC2 **175** P2
Russia Row, EC2 **175** P3
Ryder Ct, SW1 **174** B6
Ryder St, SW1 **174** B6
Ryder Yd, SW1 **174** B6

S

Sackville St, W1 **174** B5
St. Albans St, SW1 **174** C5
St. Alphage Gdns, EC2 **175** P1
St. Andrew's Hill, EC4 **175** M4
St. Andrew St, EC4 **175** K1
St. Anne's Ct, W1 **174** C3
St. Bride's Pas, EC4 **175** L3
St. Bride St, EC4 **175** L2
St. Clement's La, WC2 **175** H3
St. Georges Ct, EC4 **175** L2
St. Giles High St, WC2 **174** D2
St. Giles Pas, WC2 **174** D3
St. James's Mkt, SW1 **174** C5
St. James's Palace, SW1 **174** B8
St. James's Pk, SW1 **174** C8
St. James's Pl, SW1 **174** A7
St. James's Sq, SW1 **174** B6
St. James's St, SW1 **174** A6
St. Margaret's Ct, SE1 **175** P7
St. Margaret's St, SW1 **174** E9
St. Martin's La, WC2 **174** E4
St. Martin's-le-Grand, EC1 **175** N2
St. Martin's Ms, WC2 **174** E5
St. Martin's Pl, WC2 **174** E5
St. Martin's St, WC2 **174** D5
St. Paul's Chyd, EC4 **175** M3
Salisbury Ct, EC4 **175** L3
Salisbury Sq, EC4 **175** K3
Sanctuary, The, SW1 **174** D9
Sanctuary St, SE1 **175** P9
Sandell St, SE1 **175** J8
Sandland St, WC1 **175** H1
Sardinia St, WC2 **174** G3
Savile Row, W1 **174** A4
Savoy Bldgs, WC2 **174** G5
Savoy Ct, WC2 **174** F5
Savoy Hill, WC2 **174** G5
Savoy Pl, WC2 **174** F5
Savoy Row, WC2 **174** G4
Savoy St, WC2 **174** G4
Savoy Way, WC2 **174** G5
Sawyer St, SE1 **175** N8
Scoresby St, SE1 **175** L7
Scotland Pl, SW1 **174** E6
Scovell Cres, SE1 **175** N9
Scovell Rd, SE1 **175** N9
Secker St, SE1 **175** J7
Serjeants Inn, EC4 **175** K3
Serle St, WC2 **175** H2
Sermon La, EC4 **175** N3
Shaftesbury Av, W1 **174** C4
Shaftesbury Av, WC2 **174** C4
Shavers Pl, SW1 **174** C5
Sheffield St, WC2 **174** G3
Shelton St, WC2 **174** E3
Sheraton St, W1 **174** C3
Sherwood St, W1 **174** B4
Shoe La, EC4 **175** K2
Shorts Gdns, WC2 **174** E3
Short St, SE1 **175** K8
Sicilian Av, WC1 **174** F1
Silex St, SE1 **175** M9
Silver Pl, W1 **174** B4
Silvester St, SE1 **175** P9
Skinners La, EC4 **175** P4
Slingsby Pl, WC2 **174** E4
Smart's Pl, WC2 **174** F2
Smithfield St, EC1 **175** L1
Smith's Ct, W1 **174** B4
Snow Hill, EC1 **175** L1
Snow Hill Ct, EC1 **175** M2
Soho Sq, W1 **174** C2
Soho St, W1 **174** C2
Southampton Bldgs, WC2 **175** J2
Southampton Pl, WC1 **174** F1
Southampton St, WC2 **174** F4
South Cres, WC1 **174** C1
South Sq, WC1 **175** J1
Southwark Br, EC4 **175** P6
Southwark Br, SE1 **175** P6
Southwark Gro, SE1 **175** N7
Southwark St, SE1 **175** M6
Spring Gdns, SW1 **174** D6
Spur Rd, SE1 **175** J8
Spur Rd, SW1 **174** A9
Stable Yd, SW1 **174** A8
Stable Yd Rd, SW1 **174** A7
Stacey St, WC2 **174** D3
Stafford St, W1 **174** A6
Staining La, EC2 **175** P2
Stamford St, SE1 **175** J7
Staple Inn, WC1 **175** J1
Staple Inn Bldgs, WC1 **175** J1
Star Yd, WC2 **175** J2
Station App, SE1 **175** H9
Stedham Pl, WC1 **174** E2
Stephen Ms, W1 **174** C1
Stephen St, W1 **174** C1
Stew La, EC4 **175** N4
Stone Bldgs, WC2 **175** H1
Stonecutter St, EC4 **175** L2
Stones End St, SE1 **175** N9
Store St, WC1 **174** C1
Storey's Gate, SW1 **174** D9
Strand, WC2 **174** E5
Strand La, WC2 **175** H4
Streatham St, WC1 **174** D2
Stukeley St, WC2 **174** F2
Sturge St, SE1 **175** N8
Sudrey St, SE1 **175** N9
Suffolk Pl, SW1 **174** D6
Suffolk St, SW1 **174** D6
Sumner St, SE1 **175** M6
Surrey Row, SE1 **175** L8
Surrey St, WC2 **175** H4
Sutton Row, W1 **174** D2
Swallow St, W1 **174** B5
Swiss Ct, W1 **174** D5

T

Tallis St, EC4 **175** K4
Tanswell Est, SE1 **175** K9
Tanswell St, SE1 **175** J9
Tavistock St, WC2 **174** F4
Temple Av, EC4 **175** K4
Temple La, EC4 **175** K3
Temple Pl, WC2 **175** H4
Tenison Ct, W1 **174** A4
Tenison Way, SE1 **175** J7
Thames Path, SE1 **175** K5
Thavies Inn, EC1 **175** K2
Theed St, SE1 **175** J7
Thrale St, SE1 **175** P7
Three Barrels Wk, EC4 **175** P4
Three Cups Yd, WC1 **175** H1
Took's Ct, EC4 **175** J2
Tothill St, SW1 **174** C9
Tottenham St, W1 **174** B1
Toulmin St, SE1 **175** N9
Tower Ct, WC2 **174** E3
Tower Royal, EC4 **175** P4
Tower St, WC2 **174** D3
Trafalgar Sq, SW1 **174** D6
Trafalgar Sq, WC2 **174** D6
Treveris St, SE1 **175** L7
Trig La, EC4 **175** N4
Trinity St, SE1 **175** P9
Trio Pl, SE1 **175** P9
Trump St, EC2 **175** P3
Trundle St, SE1 **175** N8
Tudor Pl, W1 **174** C2
Tudor St, EC4 **175** K4
Turnagain La, EC4 **175** L2
Tweezer's All, WC2 **175** J4
Twyford Pl, WC2 **174** G2
Tyler's Ct, W1 **174** C3

U

Ufford St, SE1 **175** K8
Union St, SE1 **175** M7
Upper Grd, SE1 **175** J6
Upper James St, W1 **174** B4
Upper John St, W1 **174** B4
Upper St. Martin's La, WC2 **174** E4
Upper Thames St, EC4 **175** M4

V

Valentine Pl, SE1 **175** L8
Valentine Row, SE1 **175** L9
Vernon Pl, WC1 **174** F1
Victoria Embk, EC4 **174** G5
Victoria Embk, SW1 **174** F8
Victoria Embk, WC2 **174** G5
Vigo St, W1 **174** A5
Villiers St, WC2 **174** E5
Vine St, W1 **174** B5
Vine Yd, SE1 **175** P8

W

Waithman St, EC4 **175** L3
Walkers Ct, W1 **174** C4
Wallis All, SE1 **175** P8
Wallside, EC2 **175** P1
Wardens Gro, SE1 **175** N7
Wardour Ms, W1 **174** B3
Wardour St, W1 **174** C4
Wardrobe Pl, EC4 **175** M4
Wardrobe Ter, EC4 **175** M4
Warwick Ct, WC1 **175** H1
Warwick Ho St, SW1 **174** D6
Warwick La, EC4 **175** M3
Warwick Pas, EC4 **175** M2
Warwick Sq, EC4 **175** M2
Warwick St, W1 **174** B4
Watergate, EC4 **175** L4
Watergate Wk, WC2 **174** F6
Waterhouse Sq, EC1 **175** J1
Waterloo Br, SE1 **174** G5
Waterloo Br, WC2 **174** G5
Waterloo Pl, SW1 **174** C6
Waterloo Rd, SE1 **175** J8
Water St, WC2 **175** H4
Watling Ct, EC4 **175** P3
Watling St, EC4 **175** N3
Waxwell Ter, SE1 **175** H9
Webber St, SE1 **175** K8
Wedgwood Ms, W1 **174** D3
Well Ct, EC4 **175** P3
Weller St, SE1 **175** N8
Wellington St, WC2 **174** F4
Wells Ms, W1 **174** B1
Wells St, W1 **174** A1
West Cen St, WC1 **174** E2
West Harding St, EC4 **175** K2
Westminster Br, SE1 **174** F9
Westminster Br, SW1 **174** F9
Westminster Br Rd, SE1 **175** H9
West Poultry Av, EC1 **175** L1
West Smithfield, EC1 **175** L1
West St, WC2 **174** D3
Whetstone Pk, WC2 **174** G2
Whichcote St, SE1 **175** J7
Whitcomb St, WC2 **174** D5
Whitefriars St, EC4 **175** K3
Whitehall, SW1 **174** E6
Whitehall Ct, SW1 **174** E7
Whitehall Gdns, SW1 **174** E7
Whitehall Pl, SW1 **174** E7
White Lion Hill, EC4 **175** M4
Whitfield St, W1 **174** C1
Whittlesey St, SE1 **175** J7
Wild Ct, WC2 **174** G2
Wild St, WC2 **174** F3
William IV St, WC2 **174** E5
Willoughby St, WC1 **174** E1
Windmill St, W1 **174** C1
Windmill Wk, SE1 **175** K7
Wine Office Ct, EC4 **175** K2
Winnett St, W1 **174** C4
Winsley St, W1 **174** A2
Wood St, EC2 **175** P3
Wootton St, SE1 **175** K8

Y

York Bldgs, WC2 **174** F5
York Pl, WC2 **174** F5
York Rd, SE1 **175** H8
Yorkshire Grey Yd, WC1 **174** G1

Z

Zoar St, SE1 **175** N6

Abbreviations

Aber.	Aberdeenshire	Flints.	Flintshire	Norf.	Norfolk	Som.	Somerset
Arg. & B.	Argyll & Bute	Glos.	Gloucestershire	Northants.	Northamptonshire	Staffs.	Staffordshire
B'burn.	Blackburn with Darwen	Gt.Man.	Greater Manchester	Northumb.	Northumberland	Stir.	Stirling
		Hants.	Hampshire	Notts.	Nottinghamshire	Suff.	Suffolk
Beds.	Bedfordshire	Here.	Herefordshire	Ork.	Orkney	Surr.	Surrey
Bucks.	Buckinghamshire	Herts.	Hertfordshire	Oxon.	Oxfordshire	T. & W.	Tyne & Wear
Cambs.	Cambridgeshire	High.	Highland	P. & K.	Perth & Kinross	Tel. & W.	Telford & Wrekin
Cere.	Ceredigion	I.o.M.	Isle of Man	Pembs.	Pembrokeshire	V. of Glam.	Vale of Glamorgan
Ches.	Cheshire	I.o.W.	Isle of Wight	Peter.	Peterborough	W'ham	Wokingham
Cornw.	Cornwall	Lancs.	Lancashire	R.C.T.	Rhondda Cynon Taff	W.Isles	Western Isles (Na h-Eileanan an Iar)
Cumb.	Cumbria	Leics.	Leicestershire	S.Ayr.	South Ayrshire		
D. & G.	Dumfries & Galloway	Lincs.	Lincolnshire	S.Glos.	South Gloucestershire	W.Loth.	West Lothian
Derbys.	Derbyshire	Med.	Medway			W.Suss.	West Sussex
Dur.	Durham	Mersey.	Merseyside	S.Lan.	South Lanarkshire	W.Yorks.	West Yorkshire
E.Ayr.	East Ayrshire	Mon.	Monmouthshire	S.Yorks.	South Yorkshire	Wilts.	Wiltshire
E.Loth.	East Lothian	N.Lan.	North Lanarkshire	Sc.Bord.	Scottish Borders	Worcs.	Worcestershire
E.Riding	East Riding of Yorkshire	N.Lincs.	North Lincolnshire	Shet.	Shetland	Wrex.	Wrexham
		N.Yorks.	North Yorkshire	Shrop.	Shropshire		

Abbeytown **29** E2
Abbots Bromley **20** C3
Abbotsbury **8** A4
Aberaeron **12** B3
Aberaman **7** D1
Aberavon **6** C1
Abercanaid **7** E1
Aberchirder **43** D2
Abercynon **7** E1
Aberdare **7** D1
Aberdaron **18** A3
Aberdeen **43** F4
Aberdeen Airport **43** E4
Aberdour **34** B1
Aberdyfi **12** C1
Aberfeldy **38** B2
Aberffraw **18** A2
Aberfoyle **38** A4
Abergavenny **7** E1
Abergele **19** D1
Abergynolwyn **12** C1
Aberkenfig **7** D2
Aberlady **34** C1
Aberlemno **39** E2
Aberlour **42** C3
Abernethy **38** C4
Aberporth **12** A3
Abersoch **18** A3
Abersychan **7** E1
Abertillery **7** E1
Aberuthven **38** C4
Aberystwyth **12** C2
Abhainnsuidhe **47** D3
Abingdon **15** D4
Abington **34** A3
Aboyne **43** D4
Abram **25** D4
Accrington **25** E3
Achadh Mòr **47** E2
Achahoish **32** C1
Acharacle **36** C2
Achavanich **45** E2
Achfary **44** B2
Achiltibuie **44** A3
Achintee **41** D3
Achnacroish **37** D3
Achnasheen **41** E2
Achosnich **36** C2
Achriesgill **44** B2
Ackworth Moor Top **26** A3
Acle **23** F3
Acomb **30** B1
Adderbury **15** D2
Addingham **25** F2
Addlestone **10** A2
Adlington **25** D3
Adwick le Street **26** B3
Ainsdale **24** C3
Aintree **24** C4
Aird Asaig **47** D3
Aird of Sleat **40** B4
Airdrie **33** G2
Airidh a'Bhruaich **47** E2
Airth **34** A1
Airton **25** E1
Aith *Ork.* **48** C2
Aith *Shet.* **49** E3
Akeld **35** E3
Albrighton **20** A3
Alcester **14** C1
Aldbourne **14** C4
Aldbrough **27** D2
Aldeburgh **17** F2
Aldenham **16** A4
Alderbury **8** C2
Alderholt **8** C3
Alderley Edge **20** B1
Aldershot **9** F1
Aldingham **24** C1
Aldington **11** E3
Aldridge **20** B4
Alexandria **33** E1
Alford *Aber.* **43** D4
Alford *Lincs.* **22** B1
Alfreton **21** D1
Allanton **34** A2
Allendale Town **30** B2
Allenheads **30** B2
Allhallows **11** D1
Allnabad **44** C2
Alloa **38** B4
Allonby **29** E2
Alloway **33** E3
Almondsbury **14** A4
Alness **42** A2
Alnmouth **35** F4
Alnwick **35** F4
Alresford **17** D3
Alrewas **20** C3
Alsager **20** A1
Alston **30** A2
Altnafeadh **37** F2
Altnaharra **44** C2
Alton *Hants.* **9** F2
Alton *Staffs.* **20** C2
Altrincham **25** E4
Alva **38** B4
Alvechurch **14** B1
Alveley **20** A4
Alves **42** B2
Alveston **14** A4
Alvie **42** A4
Alyth **39** D2
Ambergate **21** D2
Amble **35** F4
Amblecote **20** B4
Ambleside **29** F4
Ambrosden **15** E3
Amersham **15** F3
Amesbury **8** C2
Amlwch **18** B1
Ammanford **6** C1
Ampthill **15** F2
Amulree **38** B3
Ancaster **21** F2
Ancroft **35** E2
Ancrum **35** D3
Andover **9** D1
Andreas **24** B2
Angle **12** A2
Angmering **10** A4
Anlaby **27** D3
Annan **29** E1
Annbank **33** E3
Annfield Plain **30** C2
Anstey **21** D3
Anstruther **39** E4
An Tairbeart **47** E3
An t-Ob **47** D4
Aoradh **32** A3
Appleby-in-Westmorland **30** A3
Appleby Magna **20** C3
Applecross **40** C3
Appledore *Devon* **6** B4
Appledore *Kent* **11** E3
Appleton Thorn **19** F1
Appley Bridge **25** D3
Arbirlot **39** E3
Arbroath **39** E3
Ardchiavaig **36** B4
Arden **33** E1
Ardentinny **33** E1
Ardeonaig **38** A3
Ardersier **42** A2
Ardfern **37** D4
Ardgay **44** C4
Ardleigh **17** D3
Ardlui **37** F4
Ardlussa **32** B1
Ardmair **44** A4
Ardminish **32** B2
Ardmolich **37** D1
Ardrishaig **32** C1
Ardrossan **33** E3
Ardtalnaig **38** A3
Ardtoe **36** C2
Ardvasar **40** C4
Arinagour **36** B2
Arisaig **36** C1
Armadale **34** A1
Armitage **20** C3
Armthorpe **26** B4
Arncliffe **25** E1
Arnisdale **40** C4
Arnol **47** E1
Arnold **21** E2
Arnprior **38** A4
Arrochar **37** F4
Arundel **10** A4
Ascot **9** F1
Asfordby **21** E3
Ash *Kent* **11** F2
Ash *Surr.* **9** F1
Ashbourne **20** C2
Ashburton **5** D2
Ashbury **14** C4
Ashby de la Zouch **21** D3
Ashchurch **14** B2
Ashcott **7** F3
Ashford *Kent* **11** E2
Ashford *Surr.* **10** A1
Ashington **31** D1
Ashkirk **34** C3
Ashley **16** C1
Ashton **19** F2
Ashton-in-Makerfield **25** D4
Ashton-under-Lyne **25** E4
Ashurst *Hants.* **9** D3
Ashurst *Kent* **10** C3
Ashwick **8** A1
Askern **26** B3
Aspatria **29** E2
Aston Clinton **15** F3
Aston on Trent **21** D2
Astwood Bank **14** B1
Atherington **6** C4
Atherstone **20** C4
Atherton **25** D4
Attadale **41** D3
Attleborough **23** D4
Attlebridge **23** E3
Auchallater **38** C1
Auchenblae **39** E1
Auchenbreck **32** D1
Auchencairn **29** D2
Auchencrow **35** E2
Auchindrain **37** E4
Auchinleck **33** F3
Auchmull **39** E1
Auchnagatt **43** F3
Aucholzie **39** D1
Auchterarder **38** B4
Auchtermuchty **39** D4
Auchtertool **34** B1
Audlem **20** A2
Audley **20** A2
Aughton *Lancs.* **24** C4
Aughton *S.Yorks.* **26** A4
Auldearn **42** B2
Aultbea **41** D1
Aultguish Inn **41** E2
Aveley **10** C1
Aviemore **42** B4
Avoch **42** A2
Avonbridge **34** A1
Avonmouth **7** F2
Awre **14** A3
Awsworth **21** D2
Axminster **5** F1
Aycliffe **31** D3
Aylesbury **15** E3
Aylesford **11** D2
Aylesham **11** F2
Aylsham **23** E3
Ayr **33** E3
Aysgarth **30** C4

B

Babworth **26** B4
Backaland **48** B2
Backwell **7** F2
Bacup **25** E3
Badcaul **44** A4
Badenscoth **43** E3
Badlipster **45** F2
Badsey **14** B2
Bagh a' Chaisteil (Castlebay) **46** A4
Bagillt **19** E1
Baglan **6** C1
Bagshot **9** F1
Baildon **25** F2
Baile Ailein **47** E2
Baile a'Mhanaich **46** A2
Baile Mhartainn **46** A1
Baile Mòr **36** B3
Bainbridge **30** B4
Bainton **26** C2
Bala **19** D3
Balbeggie **38** C3
Balblair **42** A2
Balcombe **10** B3
Balderton **21** E2
Baldock **16** A2
Baldslow **11** D4
Balemartine **36** A3

C

D

Dundrennan **29** D2
Dunecht **43** E4
Dunfermline **34** B1
Dunholme **21** F1
Dunkeld **38** C3
Dunkirk **11** E2
Dunlop **33** E2
Dunnet **45** E1
Dunning **38** C4
Dunoon **33** E1
Dunragit **28** A2
Duns **35** D2
Dunscore **29** D1
Dunstable **15** F3
Dunster **7** D3
Dunure **33** E4
Dunvant **6** C1
Dunvegan **40** A3
Durham **31** D2
Durness **44** B1
Durrington **8** C1
Dursley **14** A3
Dyce **43** E4
Dyke **42** B2
Dykehead **39** D2
Dymchurch **11** E3
Dymock **14** A2
Dyserth **19** D1

E

Eaglescliffe **31** D3
Eaglesfield **29** E1
Eaglesham **33** F2
Earby **25** E2
Eardisley **13** E3
Earith **16** B1
Earls Barton **15** F1
Earls Colne **17** D3
Earl Shilton **21** D4
Earlston **35** D3
Earl Stonham **17** E2
Earsairidh **46** A4
Easdale **37** D4
Easebourne **9** F2
Easington *Dur.* **31** D2
Easington *E.Riding* **27** E3
Easington Colliery **31** D2
Easingwold **26** B1
East Bergholt **17** D2
Eastbourne **10** C4
East Bridgford **21** E2
East Calder **34** B1
East Dereham **23** D3
Easter Lednathie **39** D2
Easter Quarff **49** E4
Eastfield **27** D1
Eastgate **30** B2
East Goscote **21** E3
East Grinstead **10** B3
East Hanney **15** D4
East Harling **23** D4
East Haven **39** E3
East Horsley **10** A2
East Huntspill **7** F3
East Keal **22** B1
East Kilbride **33** F2
East Leake **21** D3
Eastleigh **9** D3
East Linton **35** D1
East Malling **11** D2
East Markham **21** E1
East Midlands International Airport **21** D2
Eastoft **26** C3
Easton **8** A4
Easton-in-Gordano **7** F2
Easton on the Hill **21** F3
East Preston **10** A4
East Retford (Retford) **21** E1
Eastriggs **29** F1
Eastry **11** F2
East Wemyss **39** D4
East Wittering **9** F3
Eastwood **21** D2
Eaton Socon **16** A1
Ebbw Vale **7** E1
Ecclaw **35** D1
Ecclefechan **29** E1
Eccles **35** D2
Ecclesfield **26** A4
Eccleshall **20** B2
Eccleston **25** D3
Echt **43** E4
Eckford **35** D3
Eckington *Derbys.* **21** D1
Eckington *Worcs.* **14** B2
Edderton **42** A1
Eddleston **34** B2
Edenbridge **10** C2
Edenfield **25** E3
Edgworth **25** D3
Edinburgh **34** B1
Edinburgh Airport **34** B1
Edlingham **35** F4
Edmundbyers **30** C2
Edwinstowe **21** E1
Edzell **39** E2
Egglescliffe **31** D3
Egham **10** A1
Eglingham **35** F3
Eglwys Fach **12** C1
Eglwyswrw **12** A4
Egremont **29** E3
Egton **31** F4
Einacleit **47** D2
Elgin **42** C2
Elgol **40** B4
Elham **11** E2
Elie **39** E4
Eling **9** D3
Elland **25** F3
Ellesmere **19** E3
Ellesmere Port **19** F1
Ellingham **35** F3
Ellington **35** F4
Ellon **43** F3
Elloughton **26** C3
Elm **22** B4
Elmswell **17** D1
Elmton **21** D1
Elphin **44** B3
Elsdon **35** E4
Elsrickle **34** B2
Elstead **9** F2
Elstree **16** A4
Elswick **24** C2
Elton *Cambs.* **22** A4
Elton *Ches.* **19** F1
Elvanfoot **34** A3
Elvington **26** B2
Ely *Cambs.* **16** B1
Ely *Cardiff* **7** E2
Embleton **35** F3
Emsworth **9** F3
Enderby **21** D4
Endon **20** B2
Enstone **15** D2
Enterkinfoot **34** A4
Eoropaidh **47** F1
Epping **16** B4
Epsom **10** B2
Epworth **26** C4
Eriboll **44** B2
Eriswell **16** C1
Errogie **41** F4
Errol **39** D3
Esher **10** A2
Esh Winning **30** C2
Eskdalemuir **34** B4
Eston **31** E3
Eton **10** A1
Etteridge **38** A1
Ettington **14** C2
Ettrick **34** B4
Ettrickbridge **34** C3
Euxton **25** D3
Evanton **41** F2
Evercreech **8** A2
Evesham **14** B2
Ewell **10** B2
Ewhurst **10** A3
Exebridge **7** D4
Exeter **5** D1
Exminster **5** D1
Exmouth **5** E2
Eye *Peter.* **22** A4
Eye *Suff.* **17** E1
Eyemouth **35** E2
Eynsford **10** C2
Eynsham **15** D3

F

Failsworth **25** E4
Fairford **14** C3
Fairlie **33** E2
Fairlight **11** D4
Fair Oak **9** E3
Fakenham **23** D3
Falkirk **34** A1
Falkland **39** D4
Fallin **34** A1
Falmouth **3** F3
Falstone **30** A1
Fareham **9** E3
Faringdon **14** C4
Farington **25** D3
Farmborough **8** A1
Farnborough **9** F1
Farndon **21** E2
Farnham **9** F1
Farnham Royal **10** A1
Farnsfield **21** E1
Farnworth **25** D3
Farr **42** A3
Fauldhouse **34** A2
Faversham **11** E2
Fawley **9** D3
Fazeley **20** C4
Fearnhead **19** F1
Fearnmore **40** C2
Featherstone *Staffs.* **20** B3
Featherstone *W.Yorks.* **26** A3
Felindre **13** E2
Felixstowe **17** E2
Felling **31** D1
Felsted **16** C3
Felton **35** F4
Feltwell **22** C4
Feniton **5** E1
Fenstanton **16** A1
Fenwick *E.Ayr.* **33** F2
Fenwick *Northumb.* **35** F2
Feochaig **32** C4
Feolin Ferry **32** B1
Fern **39** E2
Ferndown **8** C3
Ferness **42** B3
Fernhill Heath **14** B1
Fernhurst **9** F2
Ferryden **39** E2
Ferryhill **31** D3
Feshiebridge **42** A4
Fettercairn **39** E1
Ffestiniog **18** C3
Ffostrasol **12** B3
Filey **27** D1
Fillongley **20** C4
Filton **14** A4
Fimber **26** C1
Finavon **39** E2
Finchampstead **9** F1
Finchingfield **16** C3
Findern **20** C2
Findhorn **42** B2
Findochty **43** D2
Findon **10** A4
Finedon **15** F1
Finningham **17** D1
Finningly **26** B4
Finnygaud **43** D2
Finstown **48** B3
Fintry **33** F1
Fionnphort **36** B3
Fishburn **31** D3
Fishguard **12** B1
Fishnish **36** C3
Fiunary **36** C2
Flackwell Heath **15** F4
Flamborough **27** D1
Fleet **9** F1
Fleetwood **24** C2
Flempton **16** C1
Flimby **29** E3
Flimwell **11** D3
Flint **19** E1
Flitwick **15** F2
Flodden **35** E3
Flookburgh **24** C1
Fochabers **42** C2
Folkestone **11** F3
Folkingham **21** F2
Folly Gate **4** C1
Ford *Arg. & B.* **37** D4
Ford *Northumb.* **35** E3
Fordham **16** C1
Fordingbridge **8** C3
Fordoun **39** F1
Fordyce **43** D2
Forest Row **10** C3
Forfar **39** D2
Forgandenny **38** C3
Forgie **42** C2
Formby **24** C3
Forres **42** B2
Forsbrook **20** B2
Forsinard **45** D2
Fort Augustus **41** E4
Forth **34** A2
Fortingall **38** B2
Fortrose **42** A2
Fortuneswell **8** A4
Fort William **37** E1
Fotherby **27** E4
Foulden **35** E2
Foulridge **25** E2
Four Elms **10** C2
Four Marks **9** E2
Four Oaks **11** D3
Fowey **4** A3
Fownhope **14** A2
Foxdale **24** A3
Foyers **41** F4
Framfield **10** C3
Framlingham **17** E1
Frampton Cotterell **14** A4
Frampton on Severn **14** A3
Frankley **20** B4
Fraserburgh **43** F2
Freckleton **24** C3
Fremington **6** B4
Freshwater **9** D4
Freshwater East **12** B2
Fressingfield **17** E1
Freswick **45** F1
Freuchie **39** D4
Fridaythorpe **26** C1
Frimley **9** F1
Frinton-on-Sea **17** E3
Friockheim **39** E2
Frithelstock Stone **6** B4
Frizington **29** E3
Frodsham **19** F1
Frogmore **9** F1
Frome **8** B1
Fulbourn **16** B2
Fulford *Staffs.* **20** B2
Fulford *York* **26** B2
Fulham **10** B1
Fulwood **25** D2
Funzie **49** F1
Furnace **37** E4
Fyfield **16** B3
Fyvie **43** E3

G

Gaer **13** E4
Gainford **30** C3
Gainsborough **26** C4
Gairloch **40** C1
Galashiels **34** C3
Galmisdale **36** C1
Galston **33** F3
Gamlingay **16** A2
Gardenstown **43** E2
Garderhouse **49** E3
Garelochhead **33** E1
Garforth **26** A2
Gargrave **25** E2
Garlieston **28** C2
Garsdale Head **30** B4
Garstang **24** C2
Garth **13** D3
Garthmyl **13** E1
Gartocharn **33** F1
Garvald **35** D1
Garvamore **38** A1
Garvard **32** A1
Garve **41** F2
Gatehouse of Fleet **28** C2
Gateshead **31** D2
Gatley **25** E4
Gatwick (London) Airport **10** B3
Gawthrop **30** A4
Gayton **22** C3
Gearraidh na h-Aibhne **47** E2
Geddington **21** F4
Gedney **22** B3
Gelligaer **7** E1
Georgeham **6** B3
Gerrards Cross **10** A1
Giffnock **33** F2
Gifford **34** C1
Gilberdyke **26** C3
Gillamoor **31** E4
Gillingham *Dorset* **8** B2
Gillingham *Med.* **11** D2
Gilling West **30** C4
Gilmerton **38** B3
Gilsland **30** A1
Gilston **34** C2
Gilwern **7** E1
Girlsta **49** E3
Girvan **33** E4
Gisburn **25** E2
Glamis **39** D2
Glanaman **6** C1
Glanton **35** E3
Glasbury **13** E4
Glasgow **33** F2
Glasgow Airport **33** F2
Glassford **33** G2
Glastonbury **7** F3
Glemsford **16** C2
Glenbarr **32** C3
Glenbeg **36** C2
Glenborrodale **36** C2

M

N

O

Great Britain distance chart

DISTANCE IN KILOMETRES

	ABERDEEN	ABERYSTWYTH	AYR	BIRMINGHAM	BRADFORD	BRISTOL	CAMBRIDGE	CARDIFF	CARLISLE	COVENTRY	DERBY	DONCASTER	DOVER	EDINBURGH	EXETER	FISHGUARD	FORT WILLIAM	GLASGOW	GLOUCESTER	HARWICH	HOLYHEAD	HULL	INVERNESS	KENDAL	LEEDS	LEICESTER	LINCOLN	LIVERPOOL	MANCHESTER	NEWCASTLE UPON TYNE	NORWICH	NOTTINGHAM	OXFORD	PENZANCE	PERTH	PLYMOUTH	PORTSMOUTH	SALISBURY	SHEFFIELD	SHREWSBURY	SOUTHAMPTON	SOUTHEND-ON-SEA	STOKE-ON-TRENT	STRANRAER	THURSO	WORCESTER	YORK	LONDON
ABERDEEN		689	288	652	525	779	772	787	348	678	631	554	943	208	896	776	253	235	723	869	679	566	169	420	531	660	624	531	533	377	789	628	779	1069	135	977	904	866	584	628	872	858	592	370	365	689	509	816
ABERYSTWYTH	428		492	179	285	217	319	187	341	211	224	278	476	489	335	87	681	494	164	444	175	366	761	269	293	235	306	158	228	447	417	248	238	507	554	407	340	274	251	121	307	396	174	507	958	153	335	340
AYR	179	306		455	328	583	571	591	151	481	435	385	734	127	700	579	227	53	526	682	483	402	333	224	335	470	449	335	336	238	613	436	554	872	153	772	681	634	388	423	668	666	388	82	529	484	340	621
BIRMINGHAM	405	111	283		182	138	161	161	304	32	66	153	285	452	256	267	64	457	82	265	232	209	787	232	175	68	142	142	125	331	249	84	98	428	517	328	225	179	122	69	201	232	68	470	903	45	206	171
BRADFORD	326	177	204	113		309	249	333	177	190	117	55	426	323	439	372	517	330	253	354	254	106	578	100	15	162	119	100	56	156	283	122	270	599	389	499	397	352	61	164	377	351	114	343	774	217	51	312
BRISTOL	484	135	362	86	192		235	72	431	148	204	288	338	579	117	248	771	584	56	311	368	348	832	359	314	185	264	261	253	470	328	222	108	290	644	190	146	82	261	167	117	259	195	597	1028	100	346	196
CAMBRIDGE	480	198	355	100	155	146		286	425	129	146	179	185	549	340	404	752	565	193	105	383	201	826	348	228	101	134	270	240	381	93	127	127	497	637	425	200	225	179	232	211	101	191	591	1022	166	256	85
CARDIFF	489	116	367	100	207	45	178		439	185	227	314	351	587	190	175	779	592	93	364	343	370	840	367	336	222	301	261	275	491	380	245	161	362	652	262	217	150	286	167	185	299	220	605	1036	116	367	237
CARLISLE	216	212	94	189	110	268	264	273		330	283	233	582	148	549	428	340	153	375	531	331	251	401	72	183	319	298	183	185	90	460	285	402	721	212	621	529	483	237	272	517	515	237	166	597	333	187	470
COVENTRY	421	131	299	20	118	92	80	115	205		72	151	253	497	265	304	669	483	92	233	262	183	731	257	187	37	116	174	151	330	219	77	76	438	542	338	203	162	134	100	179	200	93	496	927	66	204	138
DERBY	392	139	270	41	73	127	91	141	176	45		87	309	431	322	311	623	436	150	251	248	146	684	211	109	45	82	129	90	264	217	24	148	494	496	394	272	235	56	103	251	240	56	449	880	116	140	187
DONCASTER	344	173	239	95	34	179	111	195	145	94	54		364	346	417	365	573	286	237	303	267	74	607	161	50	106	64	130	80	179	228	72	217	578	418	478	344	314	27	158	320	280	105	399	803	203	53	262
DOVER	586	296	456	177	265	210	115	218	362	157	192	226		718	396	581	932	745	312	188	533	386	996	517	420	264	319	426	404	566	262	306	209	554	808	460	201	256	365	352	220	116	346	748	1192	296	441	114
EDINBURGH	129	304	79	281	201	360	341	365	92	309	268	215	446		697	576	225	69	523	661	480	357	261	220	330	476	415	331	333	167	579	418	570	869	72	769	697	658	383	420	665	650	385	200	457	481	301	608
EXETER	557	208	435	159	273	73	211	118	341	165	200	259	246	433		365	888	702	174	399	486	449	949	476	431	303	381	378	370	587	430	340	212	158	761	69	203	140	378	285	171	344	312	715	1146	217	463	282
FISHGUARD	482	54	360	166	231	154	251	109	266	189	193	227	361	358	227		768	581	269	537	262	423	829	356	383	322	393	254	315	534	504	335	335	537	640	438	394	330	338	208	365	475	261	594	1025	238	422	430
FORT WILLIAM	157	423	141	400	321	479	467	484	211	416	387	356	579	140	552	477		187	715	871	671	591	108	412	523	658	637	523	525	415	801	624	742	1061	171	961	869	822	576	612	856	855	576	309	285	673	526	810
GLASGOW	146	307	33	284	205	363	351	368	95	300	271	240	463	43	436	361	116		528	684	484	404	280	225	336	471	451	336	338	228	615	438	555	874	100	774	882	636	389	425	669	668	389	135	476	486	340	623
GLOUCESTER	449	102	327	51	157	35	120	58	233	57	93	147	194	325	108	167	444	328		277	282	275	776	303	257	129	208	212	196	414	286	171	74	346	587	246	171	106	211	119	143	232	138	541	972	43	290	175
HARWICH	540	276	424	165	220	193	65	226	330	145	156	188	117	411	248	334	541	425	172		497	306	922	462	352	206	238	368	341	486	129	232	203	557	734	468	253	259	293	333	264	97	288	697	1118	290	361	117
HOLYHEAD	422	109	300	144	158	229	238	213	206	163	154	166	331	298	302	163	417	301	175	309		346	732	259	262	274	299	148	198	397	465	272	325	658	544	528	457	389	191	162	425	463	191	497	929	238	306	402
HULL	352	209	250	130	66	216	125	230	156	114	91	46	240	222	279	263	367	251	171	190	215		620	200	88	146	68	198	148	190	232	132	257	637	431	537	385	346	105	216	360	303	162	417	816	277	64	278
INVERNESS	105	473	207	439	359	517	513	522	249	454	425	377	619	162	590	515	67	174	482	573	455	385		473	584	713	677	584	586	430	842	681	832	1122	188	1030	958	919	637	681	925	911	645	415	196	742	562	869
KENDAL	261	167	139	144	62	223	216	228	45	160	131	100	321	137	296	221	256	140	188	287	161	124	294		111	246	225	111	121	138	383	220	330	649	285	549	457	410	161	200	444	451	164	238	669	261	142	406
LEEDS	330	182	208	109	9	195	142	209	114	116	68	31	261	205	268	238	325	209	160	219	163	55	363	69		154	114	114	64	154	278	114	265	603	396	504	393	354	53	172	360	343	116	349	780	212	37	304
LEICESTER	410	146	292	42	101	115	63	138	198	23	28	66	164	296	188	200	409	293	80	128	170	91	443	153	96		79	162	135	291	182	40	111	475	525	375	238	200	101	114	214	195	82	484	909	103	159	150
LINCOLN	388	190	279	88	74	164	83	187	185	72	51	40	198	258	237	244	396	280	129	148	186	42	421	140	71	49		195	151	248	164	58	190	554	489	454	317	278	74	185	303	235	134	463	874	174	122	211
LIVERPOOL	330	98	208	88	62	162	168	162	114	108	80	81	265	206	235	158	325	209	132	229	92	123	363	69	71	101	121		50	249	346	148	249	550	396	451	383	320	110	93	341	357	80	349	780	171	150	325
MANCHESTER	331	142	209	78	35	157	149	171	115	94	56	50	251	207	230	196	326	210	122	212	123	92	364	75	40	84	94	31		219	307	100	227	542	397	443	351	311	61	108	331	330	58	351	782	161	108	303
NEWCASTLE UPON TYNE	234	278	148	206	97	292	237	305	56	205	164	111	352	104	365	332	258	142	257	302	247	118	267	86	96	181	154	155	136		412	251	402	760	241	660	529	491	208	307	505	483	270	256	626	380	125	441
NORWICH	490	259	381	155	176	204	58	236	286	136	135	142	163	360	267	313	498	382	178	80	289	144	523	238	173	113	102	215	191	256		193	220	587	653	515	296	319	235	296	304	164	274	626	1038	259	286	171
NOTTINGHAM	390	154	271	52	76	138	79	152	177	48	15	45	190	260	211	208	388	272	106	144	169	82	423	137	71	25	36	92	62	156	120		157	512	492	417	278	240	61	127	254	228	80	451	877	122	125	192
OXFORD	484	148	344	61	168	67	79	100	250	47	92	135	130	354	132	208	461	345	46	126	202	160	517	205	165	69	118	155	141	250	137	94		397	644	298	127	97	209	162	103	156	169	568	1028	87	277	95
PENZANCE	664	315	542	266	372	180	309	225	448	272	307	359	344	540	98	334	659	543	215	346	409	396	697	403	375	295	344	342	337	472	365	318	247		933	125	360	298	576	443	328	502	484	887	1318	375	636	439
PERTH	84	344	95	321	242	400	396	405	132	337	308	260	502	45	473	398	106	62	365	456	338	268	117	177	246	326	304	246	247	150	406	306	400	580		842	769	731	449	492	737	723	457	235	385	554	373	681
PLYMOUTH	607	253	480	204	310	118	264	163	386	210	245	297	286	478	43	272	597	481	153	291	328	334	640	341	313	233	282	280	275	410	320	259	185	78	523		272	209	451	354	240	414	385	787	1226	286	536	351
PORTSMOUTH	562	211	423	140	247	91	124	135	329	126	169	214	125	433	126	245	540	424	106	157	284	239	595	284	244	148	197	238	218	329	184	173	79	224	478	169		64	336	290	32	191	293	695	1154	214	397	124
SALISBURY	538	170	394	111	219	51	140	93	300	101	146	195	159	409	87	205	511	395	66	161	242	215	571	255	220	124	173	199	193	305	198	149	60	185	454	130	40		306	225	35	204	246	649	1115	150	373	142
SHEFFIELD	363	156	241	76	38	162	111	178	147	83	35	17	227	238	235	210	358	242	131	182	149	65	396	100	33	63	46	69	38	129	146	38	130	358	279	280	209	190		130	307	290	77	402	834	171	84	253
SHREWSBURY	390	75	263	43	102	104	144	104	169	62	64	98	219	261	177	129	380	264	74	207	101	134	423	124	107	71	115	58	67	203	184	79	101	275	306	220	180	140	81		262	301	53	438	877	76	214	240
SOUTHAMPTON	542	191	415	125	234	73	131	115	321	111	156	199	137	413	106	227	532	416	89	164	264	224	575	276	224	133	188	212	206	314	189	158	64	204	458	149	20	22	191	163		200	280	682	1122	171	380	130
SOUTHEND-ON-SEA	533	246	414	144	218	161	63	186	320	124	149	174	72	404	214	295	531	415	144	60	288	188	566	280	213	121	146	222	205	300	102	142	97	312	449	257	119	127	180	187	124		274	681	1107	220	357	63
STOKE-ON-TRENT	368	108	241	42	71	121	119	137	147	58	35	65	215	239	194	162	358	242	86	179	119	101	401	102	72	51	83	50	36	168	170	50	105	301	284	239	182	153	48	33	174	170		402	842	97	161	245
STRANRAER	230	315	51	292	213	371	367	376	103	308	279	248	465	124	444	369	192	84	336	433	309	259	258	148	217	301	288	217	218	159	389	280	353	551	146	489	432	403	250	272	424	423	250		612	499	352	636
THURSO	227	595	329	561	481	639	635	644	371	576	547	499	741	284	712	637	177	296	604	695	577	507	122	416	485	565	543	485	486	389	645	545	639	819	239	762	717	693	518	545	697	688	523	380		938	758	1072
WORCESTER	428	95	301	28	135	62	103	72	207	41	72	126	184	299	135	148	418	302	27	180	148	172	461	162	132	64	108	106	100	236	161	76	54	233	344	178	133	93	106	47	106	137	60	310	583		256	171
YORK	316	208	211	128	32	215	159	228	116	127	87	33	274	187	288	262	327	211	180	224	190	40	349	88	23	99	76	93	67	78	178	78	172	395	232	333	247	232	52	133	236	222	100	219	471	159		315
LONDON	507	211	386	106	194	122	53	147	292	86	116	163	71	378	175	267	503	387	109	73	250	173	540	252	189	93	131	202	188	274	106	119	59	273	423	218	77	88	157	149	81	39	152	395	662	106	196	

DISTANCE IN MILES